A CONVENT GALLERY

Courtesy of the Dominican Nuns, Corpus Christi Monastery, Hunts Point, New York City

RELIGIOUS ORDERS OF WOMEN

in the

UNITED STATES

CATHOLIC

ACCOUNTS OF THEIR ORIGIN, WORKS AND MOST IMPORTANT INSTITUTIONS

Interwoven with histories of many famous foundresses

By

ELINOR TONG DEHEY

With an introduction by the
RIGHT REVEREND JOSEPH SCHREMBS, D.D.,
BISHOP OF CLEVELAND

REVISED EDITION

𝕹𝖎𝖍𝖎𝖑 𝕺𝖇𝖘𝖙𝖆𝖙

JOSEPH J. MULLEN, S.T.D.

Censor Librorum

𝕴𝖒𝖕𝖗𝖎𝖒𝖆𝖙𝖚𝖗

JOSEPH SCHREMBS, D.D.

Bishop of Cleveland

Cleveland, Ohio,
Feb. 2, 1930

W.B.CONKEY
COMPANY
PRINTERS   BINDERS
HAMMOND, INDIANA

As *Enfant de Marie* I dedicate
This little volume of historic lore,
Of sweetest, noblest, purest lives a store—
To Mary, truly the immaculate
Mother of God, and unto Heaven's Gate,
Our faithful guide, our pleader strong before
The Throne of Grace, forever as of yore
The Queen of Saints, incomparably great.

With her I link my earthly mother dear,
Best loved companion of my girlhood days,
Whose ever watchful care, from year to year,
Hath guided me through all life's devious ways.
May this small tribute of my love's full growth
Not vex my mothers twain, but please them both!

ISBN: 978-0-9769118-8-3

St Athanasius Press
133 Slazing Rd
Potosi, WI 53820 USA
melwaller@gmail.com
www.stathanasiuspress.com

Specializing in reprinting Catholic Classics

FOREWORD

*A*S, for more than two hundred years, religious orders of women in the United States have participated in well-organized and decisive activities in this country, it is fitting that this twentieth century, already noted as an age of specialization and organization, should be marked by a historical account of their development and achievements.

In pioneer days, when the zealous missionaries in north, south, east and west, traveled wide territories in their evangelical work, it was to religious communities, in their native European countries, that they appealed for aid in the great work to be done in the New World, and often with the financial assistance of the Society for the Propagation of the Faith, or sponsored by the generous aid of the wealthy, France, Belgium, Ireland, Germany and other European nations magnanimously sent valiant women who braved the seas and the hardships of travel, and came to our land, not only to pray for our needs, but to teach our children, to shelter the orphan, the destitute and the aged, to nurse the sick and to minister to the dying.

Providentially, not designedly, the first two religious congregations of women established in the United States represented the two distinct forms of religious life, the active and the contemplative, as exemplified in the Ursulines, followers of St. Angela Merici, and the Carmelites, followers of St. Teresa.

Meeting the exigencies of the times, the country early developed its own first religious communities, through the fervor of Alice Lalor in Washington, Mrs. Seton in Baltimore, and the zeal of the spirited women in Kentucky's Loretto and Nazareth, who combined in new congregations the duties of the active with those of the contemplative life.

In this day of open statistics, and exposition of the workings of great institutions and corporations, it is but fair appreciation of the various two hundred organized religious communities in the United States—in which more than one hundred thousand women, their personal identity voluntarily effaced, labor in the interests of their orders—that we know their individual histories, though necessarily briefly in this compact volume, their distinctive work, and the many centers from which they labor.

Prior to the publication, in 1913, of an edition of the original volume of which this work is a revision, there was no book treating in practical form solely of religious orders of women in the United

States, and their activities. In the preparation of the revision of this work renewed efforts have been made for completeness, and it is a matter of great satisfaction that histories of practically all the communities in the United States have been obtained, to make the work entire. The courteous and splendid co-operation of nearly all the orders—appealed to in a detailed nation-wide correspondence—has made this compilation what it is for presentation today.

That the possible utility of the book, for greater popular knowledge of the work of the nuns of the United States, may be realized, and that it may prove helpful to the Catholic young woman who aspires to the religious life—that she may be especially informed, and directed to the particular religious community and work for which her aptitudes fit her, is the most earnest wish of the author of this volume, and must stand as her eulogy of "The Sisters."

ELINOR T. DEHEY.
E. de M.

CONTENTS

ALPHABETICAL LIST OF ORDERS

ILLUSTRATIONS

PORTRAITS

VIEWS

INTRODUCTION

ℛELIGIOUS ORDERS OF WOMEN IN THE UNITED STATES is a comprehensive account of the origin, the growth, the development and the present day activities of the religious communities of women in the United States of America.

Archbishop Spalding once said that—"The greatest religious fact in the United States today is the Catholic School System, maintained without any aid except from the people who love it."

The life-giving soul of this wonderful system of education is, of course, the noble band of some seventy-five thousand religious teachers, who, in gladsome obedience to the Master's call, have left the world, have renounced all earthly ambition, and have consecrated themselves to the great work of Christian education.

To get a correct idea, however, of the enormous work of our Catholic sisterhoods in the United States of America, we must add to the seventy-five thousand teaching sisters the tens of thousands more who devote themselves to the many and varied works of Christian charity, or who have consecrated themselves to the great work of Catholic missions, or finally, who have buried themselves in their convents to live lives of holiest contemplation and atonement and reparation.

Many are the tributes that have been paid our Catholic sisterhoods, even by those not of our Faith. Let me here select just one.

Captain Jack Crawford was a famous army scout. He passed through the Civil War and this is how he speaks of the "Sisters of the Battlefields": "On all God's green and beautiful earth there are no purer, no nobler, no more kind hearted and self-sacrificing women than those who wear the sombre garb of Catholic sisters. During the war I had many opportunities for observing their noble and heroic work, not only in the camp and hospital, but on the death-swept field of battle. Right in the fiery front of dreadful war, where bullets hissed in maddening glee, and shot and shell flew madly by with demoniac shrieks, where dead and mangled forms lay with pale, blood-flecked faces, yet wearing the scowl of battle, I have seen the black-robed sisters moving over the field; their solicitous faces wet with tears of sympathy, administering to the wants of the wounded and whispering words of comfort into the ears soon to be deafened by the cold implacable hand of death. Now kneeling on the blood-bespattered sod to moisten with water the bloodless lips on which the icy kiss of the death angel has left its pale imprint; now breathing words of hope of an immortality beyond the grave into the ear of some mangled hero, whose last shots in our glorious cause had been fired but a moment before; now holding the crucifix to receive the last kiss from somebody's darling boy, from whose breast the life blood was splashing, and who had offered his life as a willing sacrifice on the altar of his country; now with tender touch and tear dimmed eye binding gaping wounds, from which most women must have shrunk in horror; now scraping together a pillow of forest leaves, upon which some pain-racked head might rest until the spirit took its flight to other realms—brave, fearless of danger, trusting implicitly in the Master, whose overshadowing eye was noting their every moment; standing as shielding, prayerful angels between the dying soldiers and the horrors of death. Their only recompense the sweet, soul-soothing consciousness that they were doing their duty; their only hope of reward that peace and eternal happiness which awaited them beyond the star-emblazoned battlements above. Oh! my friends, it was a noble work.

"How many a veteran of the war who wore the blue or the gray can yet recall the soothing touch of a sister's hand as he lay upon the pain-tossed couch of a hospital! Can we ever forget their sympathetic eyes, their low, soft-spoken words of encouragement and cheer when the result of the struggle between life and death yet hung in the balance? Oh! how often have I followed the form of that good Sister Valencia with my sunken eyes as she moved away from my cot to the cot of another sufferer, and I have breathed from the most sacred depths of my faintly beating heart the fervent prayer: 'God bless her! God bless her!'"

Mrs. Dehey has given us a most valuable book, encyclopedic in its nature. She presents the life story of each one of the many religious communities of women doing valiant service for God and humanity in our country. It contains a fund of information difficult to find elsewhere. It will prove invaluable for our libraries as a book of reference and will do much good in the Catholic home. God grant it may point the way to a solid religious vocation to many of our young people who are looking for guidance on the vital question of a life's decision.

+Joseph Schrembs
Bishop of Cleveland

FEAST OF THE CHAIR OF ST. PETER,
February the 22nd, 1930.
Cleveland, Ohio.

PREFATORY NOTE

In the following sketches, arranged in the chronological order of the inauguration of the activities of religious communities of women in the United States, equal opportunity was given for the supplying of historical material, portraits, and views of Motherhouses, Provincial houses and novitiates, without incurring any obligation. The fact that some congregations in the country are unfortunately without pictures of their venerated foundresses explains the absence of some of the few such portraits missing from this presentation.

Statements of the approximate number in communities in a formative stage, with varying memberships under a hundred, are usually omitted in the summaries.

In the title of this work the word "orders" is used broadly, to refer to not only religious orders, properly so called, but also recognized religious communities. In the text of the book the word is also sometimes used in the same popular sense.

THE URSULINES*

*A*LTHOUGH from the earliest ages of the Church women consecrated themselves to various forms of the religious life, individually or in communities of virgins, it was not until 1535, and the foundation of the Ursuline Order by St. Angela Merici, that they united the practice of the evangelical counsels to the work of the education of youth.

Angela Merici, of a highly respected and truly Christian family of Italy, was born on March 21, 1474, at Desenzano, a small town of Lombardy, at the foot of the Alps, on the shore of beautiful Lake Garda. Without serious sorrow in the Merici home until the angel of death entered it in her fifteenth year, and summoned first her father and then a cherished sister, Angela "advanced in wisdom, and age, and grace with God and men."

While still poignantly suffering in her grief over the loss of her sister, who had been her counselor, Angela, raising her eyes in prayer for her beheld, not Italy's blue sky, but Heaven, which opened before her. There she saw the Queen of Heaven, surrounded by angels and a multitude of lovely maidens, recognizing among them the familiar form of her sister, radiantly beautiful and happy, who bade her persevere in the path she was treading, and assured her that happiness, too, would be hers.

In a few short years Angela was alone, bereft by death of all her dear ones, and, latest, of a beloved companion and guide. In answer to her fervent prayer, then, to know and do the Divine Will, God again vouchsafed her an apparition, miraculously indicating His special designs in her regard. Kneeling with her eyes fixed on Heaven, she was suddenly enveloped in a brilliant light. A luminous ladder appeared, extending from earth up beyond the clouds, and a procession of beautiful maidens ascended and descended it, accompanied by a guard of angels singing enchanting celestial songs. Among the maidens Angela descried her lamented friend, who revealed to her the significance of the vision: that before her death she was to found in Brescia a society such as she beheld.

After this manifestation, the future was clear to Angela, though some years elapsed before she could definitely form such a society, composed of virgins, who, like guardian angels, are commissioned to lead souls up the ladder of virtue to God, their ultimate end.

Choosing as their patroness St. Ursula, the virgin martyr of

*From the annals of the Ursulines.

Cologne, who had been the protectress of the faith and purity of youth, Angela and the young women who assisted her gathered about them the young girls of Desenzano, and later of Brescia, and taught them the elements of Christianity. The Company of St. Ursula, they were called, even while they were living individually, in their own homes, and only meeting at intervals for conferences and united devotions, aside from their group meetings or classes for children.

Europe at this time had been roused by the discovery of America, by the contentions between its countries, and by the almost uninterrupted civil and religious dissensions of the early part of the sixteenth century. Angela, as a pilgrim, returning from a trip to the Holy Land, visited Rome during the jubilee year of 1525, and while there received the blessing of the Sovereign Pontiff, Pope Clement VII, before she returned to Brescia, where she had previously established her residence.

On the feast of St. Catherine of Alexandria, November 25, 1535, the Company of St. Ursula was canonically inaugurated. St. Angela —whose holiness and humility were notable—and her twelve companions, in an impressive ceremony in the Church of St. Afra in Brescia, bound themselves to observe the Rules of the Society. Five years later, after having given her followers—and they were then many—Constitutions and counsels, the holy foundress died. She was raised to the altars of the Church by Pope Pius VII in 1807.

Four years after the death of St. Angela, the Sovereign Pontiff, Pope Paul III, in a bull of approval, confirmed her foundation under the title which she had given to it, and the Rule of St. Augustine was adopted. The work of teaching was from the first recognized as the distinct object of the Order.

The following years witnessed the expansion of the Ursulines, not only throughout Italy, but into Germany and France, while early in the history of the Order several distinct congregations, each numbering many convents, were formed.

Toward the close of the sixteenth century, St. Charles Borromeo, Cardinal Archbishop of Milan, invited the Company of St. Ursula to his diocese. Believing that they could do more efficient work by living together, and following out the privilege of their bull, the cardinal obtained for those in the Congregation under his jurisdiction, the status of a monastic order with enclosure. At this time a definite religious garb was assumed.

In 1609, the Ursulines, who had first been established in France in 1592, came to Paris from Provence. Aided by Madame Acarie and

Madame Ste. Beuve, who wished to devote their wealth to the education of girls, they laid the foundation of what was to become the
famous Ursuline Convent, *Faubourg Saint-Jacques*—the source of

Courtesy of the Cleveland Ursulines

ST. ANGELA MERICI (1474-1540)
Foundress of the Ursuline Order
*(From a painting in the Ursuline Convent, Blackrock, Ireland, from an
original in Brescia)*

numerous other Ursuline schools for girls—and were granted the
privilege, in harmony with the original bull of St. Angela, of solemn
vows, with papal cloister, grilles, and the dignity of a religious order.
This was the beginning of the Usuline Congregation of Paris—

soon a large religious unit, and outstanding among the French Ursulines, who were to take an important part in the later colonizing
activities of the Order.

As other congregations of the Order developed in Europe, the
followers of St. Angela who preferred still to abide by her original
plan of a charitable company were called "congregated" Ursulines,
and distinguished from the "religious" Ursulines, who observed
enclosure and took solemn vows.

Before the lapse of a century after the canonical establishment
of the Order, in an Ursuline Convent in Tours, France, the *Jesuit
Relations,* which the Canadian missionaries began to publish in 1632,
came into the hands of Mother Mary of the Incarnation, and fanned
to flame her conviction that she was to labor for the salvation of
souls in that country, the land of her dreams, where the Church was
in its infancy.

She and her chosen companions, coming from separate Ursuline
congregations in Europe, soon set sail for Canada, and in August
of 1639 these followers of St. Angela Merici began teaching the
little Indian girls of Quebec, as well as the French girls of the missions.

NEW ORLEANS, LOUISIANA*
1727

To the son of one of the French pioneers in Canada do we owe
the coming of the first Ursulines—and the first nuns—to the United
States, from France to New Orleans, Louisiana, in the year 1727.
Governor Bienville, born in Montreal in 1680, who had been
appointed governor of Louisiana, in 1718 chose for the headquarters
of the province a deserted Indian village which he named New
Orleans, in honor of the Duc d'Orleans.

In 1726, with commissions from the governor, and in the interests
of his missions, there left New Orleans for France the Rev. Nicholas
Ignatius de Beaubois, who is generally regarded as the founder of
the Jesuit missions in Louisiana, of which he was at that time
Superior. He was also vicar general of the diocese, which included
in its territory not only Canada, but the Mississippi Valley, to which
the discoveries and explorations of the French missionaries had given
France a claim.

Mindful of a commission from the governor to secure some sisters

*From data and material supplied by the Ursuline Nuns, 2705 State
Street, New Orleans, La., and from *The Catholic Church in Colonial Days,
The Life and Times of Archbishop Carroll,* and *The History of the Catholic
Church in the United States,* by John Gilmary Shea.

for the settlement in Louisiana, Father de Beaubois visited the Ursulines in their convent in Rouen, and won for the American mission
Sister Mary Augustine Tranchepain and two other sisters. Recruits
from convents in other cities of France brought the number of volunteers to nine. Sailing from the port of l'Orient on February 23, 1727,
the little colony of French nuns, after a voyage beset with perils and
hardships, reached the mouth of the Mississippi River on the 23rd
of July. The difficult trip up the river could not be begun until a
week later, and then in two parties—having separated at Belize—
they arrived in New Orleans, by piroque and by skallop, on August
6th and 7th.

As August 7, 1727, inaugurated the history of the Ursulines in
the United States, the second centennial of their coming to the shores
of the Mississippi has been auspiciously celebrated, not only in the
great city of New Orleans, but throughout the country, where the
Ursulines—now many in number—worthily carry on, in their convent
homes and great educational institutions, the work for which their
Order was founded, "the formation and instruction of young girls."

For nearly one hundred years, in New Orleans, through varied
periods of ecclesiastical as well as civil upheavals, marked by history-
making events for Church and country, the Ursulines responded to
the needs of the times, in proportion to their number—increased by
additional nuns from France, and by candidates of their own training
—and engaged in hospital and orphanage work, and many charities,
together with the founding of the educational institutions which are
today among the prominent ones of the country.

Some time after the transfer of Louisiana to the commissioners
of the United States, in 1803, by the French Republic, the Ursulines
found their number so diminished, by the withdrawal to Havana—
for continued Spanish protection—of many of the sisters, that
remaining in New Orleans there were but six choir nuns and two
lay sisters.

One of the six, Mother St. Andre Madier, wrote to a relative
in France of the trials and vicissitudes of the community, owing to
the turbulent times. The relative to whom the letter was addressed
was Frances Agatha Gensoul, an Ursuline Nun who had returned
to her own home when the French Revolution forced the religious
from their convents. Mother St. Michel Gensoul, as she was known
in religion, had, in 1802, opened a boarding school in Montpellier,
and was carrying out, as well as circumstances permitted, the aim
of the Ursuline Order, to which she still clung in spirit with all the
force of a God-given vocation. Bishop Fournier, of the diocese of

Montpellier, knowing of her work, and of the many aspirants to the religious life who were with her, planned to establish anew, in his episcopal city, an Ursuline foundation of which Mother St. Michel should be Superior.

On reading the letter, and realizing the struggles of the little group of nuns in New Orleans, who were keeping up a boarding school, a day school and orphanage, and a regular course of instruction to negro slaves, Mother St. Michel experienced an ardent longing to go to the little community, crushed beneath the weight of apostolic burdens, in the far-away land beyond the seas.

Seeking counsel of Bishop Fournier, she was admonished to secure the authorization of the Sovereign Pontiff, before his episcopal sanction of her project for going to New Orleans. Access to Pope Pius VII, in person or by communication, was at that time almost impossible, owing to the political situation in Europe. However, Mother St. Michel wrote a letter, explaining her motives for her appeal, and humbly avowing her willingness to abide by the decision of the apostolic tribunal.

For three months, Mother St. Michel had not even the opportunity of sending the letter. Then, before a statue of the Blessed Virgin, she felt impelled to pray, "O Most Holy Virgin Mary, if you obtain for me a prompt and favorable answer to this letter, I make the promise to have you honored at New Orleans under the title of Our Lady of Prompt Succor!"

The suppliant's prayer was heard. A means of sending the letter was found, and to its entreaty the Holy Father swiftly responded, bestowing on the project, its leader, and the faithful followers who wished to accompany her, his apostolic benediction and approval.

The answer, then, was unquestionably prompt and favorable. The bishop of Montpellier, discerning the hand of God, assisted in the plans for early departure, and asked to be permitted to bless the statue which Mother St. Michel had at once ordered sculptured, that she might bring it to New Orleans—a beautiful and imposing image of the Holy Mother of God, holding in her arms the Divine Child, with the globe of the earth in His hand.

On December 31, 1810, Mother St. Michel, with the statue of Our Lady of Prompt Succor—in token of the promised devotion—and a band of brave women, reached New Orleans from France. At once the cherished statue was installed in the convent chapel, and the devotion to the Mother of God, under the new title of Our Lady of Prompt Succor, was then established in a convent shrine which has become a pilgrims' mecca in the historic creole city.

When the rumblings of battle reached the Ursulines of New Orleans—knowing how pitifully inadequate were the American troops, who, under Andrew Jackson, were facing the overwhelming forces of the British on the plains of Chalmette, on January 8, 1815— they fervently invoked Our Lady of Prompt Succor. The consequent remarkable victory—the anniversary of which has been made memorable as the feast of Our Lady, under this title—was readily attributed to supernatural aid, and when the war was over the general did not neglect to thank the nuns for their prayers, and when, some years later, the great warrior visited the cloisters of the old convent on

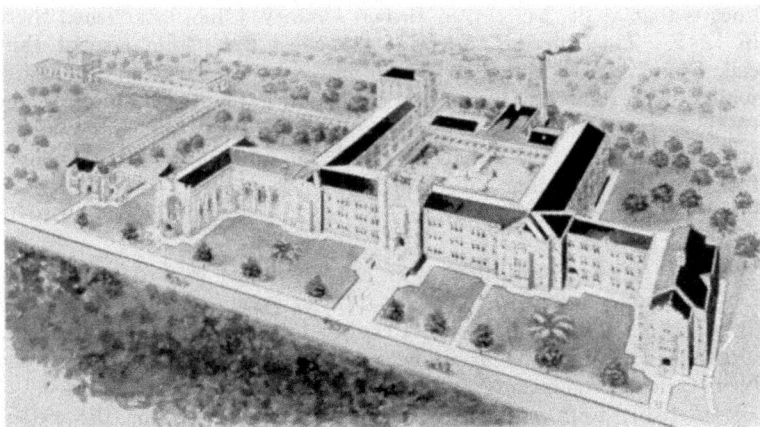

URSULINE CONVENT, NEW ORLEANS, LOUISIANA

Chartres Street, the first conventual structure in this country, it was the only time a president of the United States ever stood within its sacred precincts.

Those historic years past, with the advent into the vast apostolic field of other religious orders of women, doing various specific work, the Ursulines in New Orleans and its vicinity relinquished, in time, the hospital and other charitable work undertaken temporarily, as needed, and have since devoted themselves faithfully to the education of girls.

The modern and well equipped buildings of the Ursuline College and Academy, at their convent at 2705 State Street, in the archiepiscopal city, manifest the progressiveness of the Ursulines in the more than two hundred years of their labors there, the second centennial of which the alumnæ association of the institution commemorated by the erection at the convent of a beautiful church, as a shrine and place of pilgrimage in honor of Our Lady of Prompt Succor.

As members of the Roman Union of Ursulines, the Ursulines in New Orleans are affiliated with the Motherhouse in Rome, and are in the provincialate territory of the southern province.

ST. MARTIN, OHIO*
1845

The second oldest existing United States foundation of the Ursulines is that at St. Martin, in Brown County, Ohio, established there in 1845. Through the efforts of the Most Rev. John Baptist Purcell, D.D., who as bishop of Cincinnati, visited France in 1839, and while there took the initial steps to secure Ursuline Nuns of the Congregation of Paris for his diocese, this foundation was made— and memorable in the annals of the community is that to this institution of his founding the eminent prelate repaired in later years, his death occurring there on July 4, 1883, after a long and eventful episcopacy.

Prior to the establishment of the Ursulines in Brown County, Ohio, and subsequent to the foundation in New Orleans, other Ursulines had come to the United States, in addition to those from various Ursuline congregations in France and Canada who augmented the New Orleans community during its first century in the country.

In 1812, four years after the establishment of the diocese of New York, and during his term as its administrator, the Very Rev. Anthony Kohlmann, S. J., having founded the New York Literary Association for the educational benefit of the young men of New York, interested himself in a similar work for young ladies. Through Father Betagh, a famous Irish Jesuit, Father Kohlmann applied to the Ursuline Nuns of the Blackrock Convent, in Cork, for nuns to carry on this work, and on April 7, 1812, Mother Mary Anne Fagan, accompanied by Sister Frances de Chantal Walsh and Sister Mary Paul Baldwin, arrived in New York, and soon afterward opened a metropolitan academy. In the spring of 1815, in the midst of diocesan changes, the Ursulines, having received no novices, closed their convent and academy in New York, and returned to Ireland.

Marking another event in the chronology of the Ursuline foundations in the United States, was the establishment near Boston of a

---

*From data and material supplied by the Ursulines of Brown County, St. Martin, Brown County, Ohio, and from *The History of the Catholic Church in the United States,* by John Gilmary Shea.

small community of the Order. Two religious aspirants had come from Limerick, Ireland, and under the direction of the Right Rev. John Cheverus, first bishop of Boston, made their novitiate with the Ursulines at Three Rivers, Canada. Two others from Ireland, and two candidates from Boston were soon received at the convent, and completed this foundation community, in Boston. On St. Ursula's day, 1820, with Bishop Cheverus presiding, the two nuns who had made their novitiate with the nuns in Canada made their solemn vows during an impressive ceremony in the Cathedral.

Engaging at once in educational work in an academy which they opened, the sisters of this community, a little more than six years after their establishment, removed to Mount Benedict, at Charlestown, west of the famous Bunker Hill, and in the vicinity of Boston. The Right Rev. Benedict Joseph Fenwick, who had succeeded Bishop Cheverus in the see of Boston, gave his personal attention to the selection of this suitable and desirable new location for the Ursulines. The annals of United States history contain no more harrowing incidents than those of the trials suffered by the nuns of this community in the ensuing decade of years, and record, in 1834, the total destruction of the Mount Benedict Convent, followed by the final dispersion of the Boston community to convents in Canada or to those of the nuns' native countries.

Contemporaneous with the dissolution of the Ursuline community in Boston was the establishment in the United States of another colony of Ursulines from Ireland. Through the initiative of the Right Rev. John England, D.D., first bishop of Charleston, arrangements were made for the coming of the Ursuline community which was received in the episcopal city of Charleston, South Carolina, in 1834, where the nuns participated in educational work in the diocese until their removal to Covington, Kentucky, in 1847.

In this interval during which the Ursuline Nuns were in Bishop England's diocese, another Ursuline community, composed of nuns from the convent of Boulogne-sur-Mer, and from Beaulieu, France, eleven in number, arrived in New York on June 3, 1845. Continuing their trip, under the personal direction of the Ohio mission priest, a native of France, the Rev. J. P. Machebeuf—later first bishop of Denver—whom Bishop Purcell had delegated to accompany them from France, these first Ursulines to come to Ohio were soon established in community life in a substantial brick building, erected for a theological seminary near Fayetteville, in Brown County, and under the direct jurisdiction of the bishop of Cincinnati.

Mother Julia Chatfield, in religion Mother Julia of the Assumption, served as first Superior of the community, which, engaging at once in educational work, established at St. Martin's Ursuline Convent the academy for young ladies, which has ever maintained, in the more than four-score years of its existence, the high standard of excellence set by the daughters of St. Angela Merici in their specific work of the education of girls.

The Ursuline Academy of Our Lady of Victory, at Oak Street and Reading Road, in Cincinnati, in connection with which a school for small boys is conducted, is an outstanding institution conducted by nuns of this community. The Brown County Ursulines have also to their credit the Ursuline foundations established in Columbia, South Carolina, and Santa Rosa, California, as well at that at St. Ursula Convent, on East McMillan Street, in Cincinnati.

Under the superiorship of Mother M. Mechtilde Jones, the community at St. Martin, Brown County, Ohio, continuing the grade and academic educational work of the Order, is also progressively meeting a need of the day in developing and conducting rural religion schools and correspondence courses in religion.

> *Motherhouse and Novitiate,* Ursuline Convent, St. Martin, Ohio.
> (Archdiocese of Cincinnati.)

TEXAS*

1847

Though the Texas region was in the throes of the Mexican War, the Ursulines in New Orleans bravely responded to a call for sisters there, and in January of 1847 six nuns from New Orleans opened an Ursuline Convent in Galveston.

Under the auspices of the Right Rev. John M. Odin, D.D., Vicar Apostolic of Texas, and first bishop of Galveston, the nuns at once opened an academy at their convent in Galveston. Sixty pupils were soon enrolled at the new institution, the educational facilities of which were notably appreciated in the city, where it was the forerunner of St. Ursula's Academy and the Academy of the Sacred Heart, later established and conducted by the community.

Meeting the current exigencies, like the nuns of the mother foundation in New Orleans—who, though consecrated to educational work manned hospitals and orphanages, and performed other works of mercy—the Ursulines in Galveston lent aid during successive

---

*From data and material supplied by the Ursuline Nuns, Texarkana, Texas, and from *The History of the Catholic Church in the United States,* by John Gilmary Shea, and *The Catholic Church in the United States of America* (Vol. II) (The Catholic Editing Company, New York).

chaotic disturbances. They rendered service during the yellow fever epidemic; gave their convent and academy for hospital use during the Civil War—when they ministered to the sick and wounded of North and South, irrespective of creed or color—and, again during the floods which devastated Galveston in 1875, 1900 and 1915, their convent served as a refuge for hundreds.

In 1874, Ursulines of the community in Galveston opened an academy in Dallas, Texas, where the nuns are also in charge of the Cathedral and St. Patrick's schools. Upon the establishment of the Roman Union of Ursulines, in 1900, Dallas was chosen as the head-quarters for the Southern Province of the United States. It continues the site of the novitiate for the province, while the Ursuline Convent in Texarkana, Texas—also in the diocese of Dallas, and under the ecclesiastical jurisdiction of the Right Rev. Joseph P. Lynch, D.D.—is the seat of the provincialate, with Mother Mary Lucy residing there as Provincial Prioress.

ST. LOUIS, MISSOURI*

1848

In the year 1846, the Right Rev. Peter Richard Kenrick, then bishop of St. Louis, commissioned the vicar general of the diocese, the Very Rev. Joseph Melcher, to visit Europe and interest priests, ecclesiastical students and teaching sisterhoods in the needs of the diocese.

Providentially meeting a Redemptorist brother, in the course of his European travels, Father Melcher told him of his errand. The brother in turn confided to the traveler that his sister, an Ursuline Nun, Superior of a convent at Oedenburg, a town about thirty-seven miles from Vienna, was most desirous of carrying the standard of St. Angela and St. Ursula to the American missions. The zealous vicar general then urged that he be at once conducted to the Oeden-burg convent.

Mother Magdalen Stehlin proved a true apostle of education and promised herself for the distant mission.

On March 13, 1848, Mother Magdalen and two companion sisters left for Bremen to sail from there for the United States. One of their many stops during the journey to Bremen was made at the Ursuline Convent of Landshut, Bavaria, where the voyagers received many useful and valuable gifts; in addition a zealous postulant was

*From data and material supplied by the Ursuline Nuns, Ursuline Academy, Kirkwood, Mo.

granted permission to accompany them, and join in the labors of the little community.

June 22, 1848, the Austrian nuns boarded a sailing vessel—*The Andalusia*—at Bremen, and were soon on the North Sea. A terrific contrary wind, followed by rain and snow, plunged the voyagers into the throes of sea sickness. For three weeks *The Andalusia* was tossed along the coasts of Ireland and Scotland, often in imminent peril, but after sixty long, weary, anxious days and nights, the dangers of the deep were past, and they were in Baltimore harbor, reaching there on the 21st of August—the feast of St. Jane Frances de Chantal.

Upon their arrival in Baltimore, the Ursuline Nuns were hospitably received by the Ven. John Nepomucene Neumann, C.SS.R., at that time vice provincial of the Redemptorists in America. He conducted them to the Sisters of Notre Dame, whose guests they remained during their stay in Baltimore, while awaiting the arrival of Archbishop Kenrick of St. Louis—the archbishopric having been established the previous year.

On August 28th, the nuns from Austria left Baltimore on the last lap of their long journey which terminated on September 5th, when they arrived in St. Louis. There they were welcomed by their friend, the vicar general, Father Melcher, who conducted them to the Visitation Convent, where they remained as guests of the Visitandines until they were established in their own convent home, on 5th Street near the old French market.

AN URSULINE NUN, KIRKWOOD, MISSOURI

With the opening of a convent school, on November 2, 1848, by the four zealous missionary nuns, the work of St. Angela was begun in Missouri, and the first Ursuline foundation, under the jurisdiction of the archbishop of St. Louis was then made.

Early in the following year the community was augmented by four choir nuns and two lay sisters from the convent in Landshut, where the Ursuline Superior had not forgotten a promise to give it further aid. Interesting among the belongings considered as baggage, which arrived soon after the coming of the sisters from Landshut, were, in addition to clothing, a monstrance, a relic of the True Cross, bedding, materials for needle-work, and an excellent piano.

In November of 1850 the community removed to a newly-erected convent and school building on South 12th Street. Here, with the growth of the day and boarding school, as well as the community, and with the need of increased facilities, and for the efficient development of an educational curriculum, new buildings were erected and old ones remodeled or added to, until 1914, when removal of convent, day school, and boarding school for aspirants to the religious life, was made to a beautifully wooded twenty-eight acre tract of land, with a fine old Colonial mansion erected on it, which had been secured by the community.

Located at Kirkwood, on a main bus route, but twelve miles from the St. Louis Union Station, St. Angela Park, as the campus of this institution is named, with its picturesque lake, stately oaks, shady maples and neverfading evergreens, is a worthy setting for the splendid group of buildings erected by the Ursulines of St. Louis, who have now, for more than eighty years, devoted themselves continuously to teaching.

In addition to the academy conducted at the Motherhouse—from which have been sent Ursuline foundation communities to New York, Illinois, Kansas and Montana—members of this community are in charge of many parochial schools throughout the archdiocese, and in Arcadia—ninety miles south of St. Louis, in the Arcadia Valley, in the heart of the Ozark Mountains—conduct Arcadia College and Ursuline Academy. The academy, established by the community in 1877, and now affiliated with the Missouri University, is maintained as a boarding school, while the collegiate courses of the college, a former Methodist institution, are being planned by the community, which has so faithfully labored in the archdiocese of St. Louis—to which it confines its work—continuing under the jurisdiction of the archbishop, the Most Rev. John J. Glennon, D.D.

Motherhouse and Novitiate, Ursuline Convent, Kirkwood, Missouri. (Archdiocese of St. Louis.)

CLEVELAND, OHIO*

1850

Little more than five years after his ordination to the priesthood, by Cardinal Latour d'Auvergne, the Rev. Louis Amadeus Rappe was, in 1834, appointed chaplain at the Ursuline Convent of

*From data and material supplied by the Ursuline Nuns, Ursuline Convent, East 55th Street, and Ursuline College, 2234 Overlook Road, Cleveland, Ohio, and from *The Church in Northern Ohio and in the Diocese of Cleveland,* by the Rev. George F. Houck.

Boulogne-sur-Mer, France. During the years in which he continued to serve in that capacity, the young French priest read with interest the Annals of the Propagation of the Faith, and was filled with an intense desire to devote his life to the American missions. Meeting the Right Rev. John Baptist Purcell, D.D., who as bishop of Cincinnati visited Europe in 1839 in the interests of that diocese, Father Rappe zealously offered to go with him on his return to America.

A few years later, when Bishop Purcell petitioned the Holy See for a division of his vast diocese, then comprising the state of Ohio, the diocese of Cleveland was established in 1847, and Father Rappe, the zealous "missionary of the Maumee," was chosen its first bishop.

Early realizing the educational needs of the new diocese, and impressed with the advantages afforded by the co-operation of religious communities in the establishment and maintenance of schools, Bishop Rappe visited Europe, where he secured not only several priests and seminarians, but, from the Ursulines of Boulogne-sur-Mer, a colony of Ursuline Nuns, who with Mother Mary of the Annunciation as Superior opened an academy in Cleveland in the autumn of 1850.

The residence of Judge Cowles, on Euclid Avenue, was purchased for the nuns, and served as convent and academy during the epic years which followed for the Ursulines in Cleveland. Maintaining the high standards of this historic and first educational religious Order, and dispensed from the observance of the cloister, they early engaged in the conducting of parochial schools, as opened in the episcopal city with the establishment of its many parishes, in the years which followed.

Four years after their arrival in Cleveland, Bishop Rappe urged the Ursulines for a division of their number, that religious teachers might be permanently provided in the Maumee region, the scene of his pioneer missionary activities. Accordingly the Cleveland Ursulines made their first extension, and a foundation in Toledo followed. The community later established a foundation in Youngstown, and participated, indirectly, in the establishment of that in Montana, by the Ursulines from Toledo. A prosperous mission established at Tiffin, Ohio, in 1863, automatically came under the jurisdiction of the ordinary of the diocese of Toledo, upon its later erection.

In 1871, by a special act of legislature, the Ursulines in Cleveland were empowered "to confer on the recommendation of the Faculty such degrees and honors as are conferred by Colleges and Universities of the United States." The work of collegiate higher education then inaugurated by the community was continued with undiminished success for more than twenty-five years.

During this time the Ursuline Academy of St. Mary, a boarding school for girls, was opened in the splendid and well-equipped building which had been erected at Villa Angela, as was designated the tract of land along the shores of Lake Erie, with its present attractive frontage on Lake Shore Boulevard, in northeast Cleveland. St. Joseph's Seminary, a boarding school for boys under twelve years of age, was also established, and is located at Villa Angela.

URSULINE CONVENT, CLEVELAND, OHIO

Owing to the pressing need for teachers for these institutions, as well as for the rapidly growing parochial schools, the privileges of the college charter granted to the community were permitted to lapse.

Following a period of inactivity in collegiate work, the need of a Cleveland institution for the higher education of Catholic young women became apparent, and in 1922, with the authorization of the Right Rev. Joseph Schrembs, D.D., Bishop of Cleveland, the Ursuline College, fully accredited, was again opened to students, and through the courtesy of the bishop, temporarily located in Cathedral Latin Hall, on Euclid Avenue, in the heart of Cleveland's educational activities.

Upon the sale of this diocesan property to Western Reserve University, two spacious residences, adjoining each other on Overlook Road, in an attractive section of the city, were purchased by the community in 1927, and the college, which is affiliated with the Catholic University of America, was transferred to the new and advantageous location.

In 1893, the headquarters of the community were transferred to the new and well-arranged building erected on East 55th Street for a Motherhouse and novitiate, with ample provision for the academy which has been continuously maintained in connection with the convent.

With the rapid growth of the city, and the corresponding expansion of its business sections, which now surround the Motherhouse site, plans are being made by the community for a modern and commodious group of buildings to be erected on the recently purchased fifty-acre tract of land on Fairmount Boulevard, in the Shaker Heights district of the city.

While belonging to the Ursuline Congregation of Paris, the Cleveland Ursuline community, of approximately three hundred members, is distinctly diocesan, limiting its activities to the see, and subject to its ordinary, now being under the ecclesiastical jurisdiction of the Right Rev. Joseph Schrembs, D.D., as bishop of Cleveland.

Motherhouse and Novitiate, Ursuline Convent, East 55th Street and Scovill Avenue, Cleveland, Ohio.   (Diocese of Cleveland.)

TOLEDO, OHIO*

1854

On December 12, 1854, complying with a request of their bishop, the Right Rev. Amadeus Rappe, D.D., five sisters of the Ursuline community in Cleveland were sent to Toledo, Ohio—fourteen years after the founding of the city—to engage in school work there, in the vicinity of his first American missionary labors.   Mother des Seraphims, who had come to Cleveland from the Ursuline Convent at Boulogne-sur-Mer, France, served as first Superior.

Hardships and privations, the lot of pioneer religious, were not wanting in the early experiences of these educators in northwestern Ohio, but the cultural value of St. Ursula's Academy, which they established, was soon appreciated by the people of the city, who, regardless of creed, became its patrons.

Carrying out the purpose of the Order, the instruction of young girls in piety and knowledge, the Ursulines in Toledo, since 1854, have made steady progress, as evidenced by their college, academy and school for young boys, and in the parochial school work in the city developed under their direction.

In 1905 a new academy for boarders and day students—St. Ursula's, was opened on Collingwood and Parkwood Avenues, in

*From data and material supplied by the Ursuline Nuns, Toledo, Ohio.

Toledo, where the attractive group of buildings—each especially designed for the purpose for which it is used—is of fourteenth and fifteenth century Belgian and Norman architecture.

In 1910, in a division of the diocese of Cleveland, the diocese of Toledo—including in its territory Tiffin, where the Ursulines were prospering—was established, and Toledo selected as the episcopal site. The Right Rev. Joseph Schrembs, D.D., served as first bishop of the new see.

Upon Bishop Schrembs' appointment to the diocese of Cleveland, in 1921, he was succeeded in the diocese of Toledo by the Right

URSULINE CONVENT OF THE SACRED HEART, TOLEDO, OHIO

Rev. Samuel A. Stritch, D.D. After a survey of his new diocese Bishop Stritch at once took steps for an institution for the higher education of young women, by the establishment, in September, 1922, of Mary Manse College.

Mary Manse, conducted by the Ursulines in Toledo, is the woman's college of St. John's University, and its founder, Bishop Stritch, is the chairman of the board of directors of the institution.

It was from the Ursuline Convent in Toledo that in 1884, in response to a call from the Right Rev. Richard Gilmour, D.D., for a community for the Indian missions in Montana, that Mother Amadeus, a valued and efficient member of the Ursulines in Toledo, and a small band of companion sisters, left their home in Ohio and bravely planted the banner of St. Angela and the work of Christian education in the far west.

Meeting present-day needs, the Ursulines of Toledo recently secured a four hundred acre tract, Ladyglen-on-the-Maumee, with an extensive river frontage. Here—marking the Diamond Jubilee of

4

the community in 1929—Nazareth Hall, a boarding and day grade school for boys was opened in September, 1928, and a new Mother-house and novitiate are later to be located.

Confining its activities to the diocese of Toledo, and under the present ecclesiastical jurisdiction of its ordinary, Bishop Stritch, the community, of approximately two hundred and thirty members, is engaged actively in the work of the Ursuline Order and maintains its standards in the many institutions of which its members are in charge.

> *Motherhouse and Novitiate,* Ursuline Convent of the Sacred Heart, 2413 Collingwood Avenue, Toledo, Ohio. (Diocese of Toledo.)

NEW YORK CITY*

1855

The first Ursuline foundation made in New York, subsequent to that of the Ursulines from the Blackrock Convent in Cork, Ireland—in New York City, from 1812 to 1815—was in 1855.

In that year Mother Magdalen Stehlin, Superior of the pioneer Austrian colony which had established the Ursuline foundation in St. Louis, Missouri, less than ten years before, voluntarily served again as a pioneering Superior, and with a group of sisters from the Ursuline Convent in that city responded to a call for an Ursuline foundation at East Morrissania, in the environs of New York.

Transfers of the headquarters of the community, necessitated by the growth of the city, were made twice since 1855, prior to its present location, at Mt. St. Ursula, at Beford Park, 200th Street and Marion Avenue, New York City. In addition to their educational work at Mt. St. Ursula, sisters of the community are in charge of several academies and parochial schools in the archdiocese, and have established an Ursuline academy in Wilmington, Delaware.

Mt. St. Ursula is also the present site of the Provincial house of the Ursuline Nuns of the Canonical Roman Union, of the Province of the Northeast of the United States.

LOUISVILLE, KENTUCKY†

1858

Prior to his elevation to the archbishopric of Baltimore, during the term of the Right Rev. John Spalding, D.D., as bishop of the

---

*From the annals of the Ursuline community of St. Louis, Kirkwood, Missouri, and from the Official Catholic Directory, 1929.

†From data and material supplied by the Ursuline Nuns, Sacred Heart College, Louisville, Ky.

diocese of Bardstown and Louisville—fittingly because of his ardent advocacy of the Christian education of youth—activities of religious orders of women in Kentucky were notably developed.

With the whole-hearted approval of Bishop Spalding, the Rev. Leander Streber, O.F.M., pastor of St. Martin's Church in Louisville, Kentucky, made a voyage to Europe to procure teachers for his school. The efforts of the zealous Franciscan met with success in Bavaria, where, at the Ursuline Convent in Straubing, he was granted

URSULINE CONVENT OF THE IMMACULATE CONCEPTION,
LOUISVILLE, KENTUCKY

a small community of nuns, who, with Mother Mary de Sales Reit-meier as Superior, made in Louisville, in 1858, the first permanent Ursuline foundation in Kentucky.

The Ursuline Society and Academy of Education was then founded in Louisville, and that same year a novitiate was opened at the convent home which was established under the Rule of the Ursulines as approved by Rome, and under the jurisdiction of the bishop of the diocese.

As churches multiplied in the city of Louisville, and demands for teachers increased, so this community grew in its members, as it multiplied its schools, established its academies and, at the request of the ordinary of the diocese, presided over orphanages.

In addition to sending a colony of nuns in 1874 to the Green

River Hills of western Kentucky, where the mission then established has since become an independent foundation, the Ursulines of Louis-ville have extended their labors beyond Kentucky and conduct schools and orphanages in Omaha, Nebraska; Evansville, Indiana; Columbus, Ohio; Cumberland, Maryland; Morgantown, West Virginia, and other cities and towns of these states, as well as in Pennsylvania.

Prominent among the community's educational institutions in Louisville are the Ursuline Academy of the Immaculate Conception, at 806 East Chestnut Street, the Academy of the Sacred Heart, Crescent Hill, 3107 Lexington Road, and the Sacred Heart Junior College and Normal School, at 3111 Lexington Road, the last named institution not having been open to lay students until September 11, 1922. Up to this date it had been a training school exclusively for the postulants and novices of the community.

During the World War, the sisters of this community, meeting the needs of the times, were active in caring for the soldiers suffering from the influenza epidemic in the Alleghany Hospital at Cumber-land, Maryland, in many cases at that time nursing in private homes.

Under the present ecclesiastical jurisdiction of the Right Rev. John A. Floersh, D.D., Bishop of Louisville, and the superiorship of Mother Mary Theodore Guethoff, and her Council, composed of Sister M. Chrysostom Luecker, Sister M. Winefride Zink, Sister M. Michelle Leininger, and Sister M. Marcella Schrimph, the community of fully four hundred members is engaged chiefly in educational work in the archdiocese of Baltimore and the dioceses of Altoona, Colum-bus, Grand Island, Indianapolis, Louisville, Omaha and Wheeling.

Motherhouse and Novitiate, Ursuline Convent of the Immaculate Conception, 3115 Lexington Road, Louisville, Kentucky. (Diocese of Louisville.)

COLUMBIA, SOUTH CAROLINA*

1858

One of the first acts of the Right Rev. Patrick Neeson Lynch, D.D., as bishop of Charleston, following his consecration on March 14, 1858, was the re-establishment of an Ursuline foundation in the diocese. Upon his request to the Ursulines of Brown County, Ohio, nuns were sent to Columbia, South Carolina, where, securing an advantageous site in the center of the city, they at once opened an academy.

*From data and material supplied by the Ursuline Nuns, Ursuline Acad-emy, 1501 Assembly Street, Columbia, S. C., and from *The History of the Catholic Church in the United States,* by John Gilmary Shea.

Mother M. Baptista Lynch, the bishop's sister, one of the community from Ohio, was appointed Superior of the new foundation which was then established. In addition to candidates who early applied for admission to the Order, the community was augmented by the arrival of six Ursulines from Covington, Kentucky, members of the community which in 1847 had removed to Kentucky from Charleston, and whom Bishop Lynch had invited to return to the diocese as members of the new community.

The importance of their academy as an educational institution was soon recognized and the nuns won as their patrons many from distant places in the south. During the war, which commenced soon after the establishment of this convent school, many women, without distinction of creed or class, took refuge within its walls, attracted as much through the hope of protection as the desire for an education.

The convent, however, commonly regarded as a sanctuary immune to the outrages of war, became a prey to the flames which destroyed Columbia, February 17, 1865. Remaining in temporary quarters for some months following this disaster, the Ursulines removed to their new home at Valle Crucis—now Heathwood—about two miles from the city, where they again conducted their academy. At this location they remained for a little more than twenty years.

Transfer of the convent and academy was made, in 1887, to the Preston mansion on Blanding Street, however finding the structure not adapted to its purpose, the community acquired its present site, adjacent to St. Peter's Church, and the parochial school which the sisters conduct. In 1891 the community, whose present Superior is Mother M. Michel Spann, took possession of the newly erected building, which provides, in addition to the day and boarding school maintained for grade and academic pupils, convent headquarters for the Ursulines in the diocese of Charleston.

> *Motherhouse and Novitiate,* Ursuline Convent, Assembly and Hampton Streets, Columbia, South Carolina. (Diocese of Charleston.)

ALTON, ILLINOIS*

1859

Desirous that in his episcopal city there should be a foundation of the Ursulines to carry on their special work of educating young girls, the Right Rev. Damian Juncker, D.D., first bishop of Alton,

*From data and material supplied by the Ursuline Sisters, Ursuline Convent of the Holy Family, 845 Danforth Street, Alton, Ill.

appealed to the Ursuline Sisters in St. Louis to send a community to Alton for this purpose.

In response to the bishop's solicitation, seven Ursulines, with Mother M. Josephine Bruiding as Superior, were chosen from the St. Louis community. Arriving in Alton on March 22, 1859, they at once established their convent in a house already prepared for them, and on April 1st a school for girls was opened with an enroll-ment of about sixty.

Four years later Mother Josephine, accompanied by Mother Mary, visited Europe, and while there was successful in securing funds for the completion of the convent building erected on Fourth Street and dedicated on December 26, 1873.

URSULINE CONVENT OF THE HOLY FAMILY, ALTON, ILLINOIS

In 1880, at the request of the Right Rev. P. J. Baltes, D.D., suc-cessor to Bishop Juncker, the Ursulines of foundations which the sisters in Alton had made at Litchfield and Decatur, both in Illinois, united with the Ursulines of Alton to form a Diocesan Union, of which Mother Teresa Gillespie was elected first Superior.

Among the many schools established by the community in the diocese was that of St. Peter and Paul's parish in Springfield, Illinois, to which city the see was transferred in 1923.

In November, 1900, in compliance with the wishes of the Sov-ereign Pontiff, Pope Leo XIII, the Superior of the Ursulines of Alton attended the Chapter held in Rome, and the sisters were among the first Ursuline communities in the United States to become members of the Roman Union of Ursulines then formed. In July, 1911, a sub-novitiate for the northern part of the Southern Province was opened at Alton, and Mother Bernard was appointed Novice Mistress.

A new epoch in the annals of the community was inaugurated on July 26, 1926, when for the first time the Holy Sacrifice of the Mass was celebrated in a newly-erected convent on Danforth Street, where the community had purchased a tract of twenty-eight acres.

Following the razing of the Fourth Street Convent, a new Central High School was erected on the site, and on the completion of the building it was cermoniously blessed, August 31, 1927, by the Right Rev. James A. Griffin, D.D., Bishop of Springfield in Illinois.

Serving as Superior and Assistant Superior of the Ursuline community at the Convent of the Holy Family, in Alton, now are Mother M. Gertrude Froelich and Mother M. Aloysia Beall, and, as Novice Mistress and Sub-Mistress, Mother M. Bernard Walter and Mother M. Gertrude.

ST. JOSEPH, KENTUCKY*

1874

The Ursuline community of Mt. St. Joseph Ursuline Motherhouse at St. Joseph, Kentucky, owes its foundation to the Rev. Paul Joseph Volk, who in 1874 applied to the Right Rev. William George McCloskey, D.D., Bishop of Louisville, for sisters to open a boarding school in Daviess County in the vicinity of St. Alphonsus Church, of which he was the pastor.

Bishop McCloskey referred the zealous pastor's petition to the Ursuline Nuns in his episcopal city, who at once arranged for the departure of five of their number to the western county. On August 14, 1874, the sisters arrived at their destination where, on the feast of Our Lady's Assumption, they began the plans and preparations for their convent home and the school they were soon to open.

In 1880, the efforts of the community had resulted in the establishment of an academy which was incorporated that year by an act of the Kentucky state legislature, being empowered to grant the usual degrees conferred by other academies, colleges and universities.

With the increase in the enrollment of students at the Daviess County school, the community in Louisville sent additional teachers as needed. In 1895, under the auspices of Bishop McCloskey, a novitiate was established at Mt. St. Joseph, and five candidates were received, upon its opening. In 1912, the Ursulines of Mt. St. Joseph

*From data and material supplied by the Ursuline Nuns, Mt. St. Joseph, St. Joseph, Ky.

became an autonomous community, and Mother M. Aloysius Willett was chosen first Superior.

Throughout the years of her long administration, Mother Aloysius displayed in her direction of the affairs of the rapidly-growing community, unusual business acumen and sagacity, and with a keen-sighted vision of hidden possibilities she encouraged her spiritual daughters to assume the difficulties and responsibilities which were to be theirs, in their mission life in the schools which the community opened not only in Kentucky but in other distant as well as nearby states.

In response to an appeal for religious to conduct the rural schools of the diocese of Louisville, the Ursulines of Daviess County have generously sent sisters who have labored zealously to overcome the many handicaps which confront them in this field, where methods must be adopted to suit the prevailing conditions. In their desire to efficiently carry on this work, the rural school teachers of the community have tried out many theories. In their adaptation of what is known as the Dalton Plan the sisters have been particularly successful, and a superior degree of talent and ability has been frequently developed in the pupils of these schools by the sisters, anxiously endeavoring to retain the interest of the students and to guide them through the higher branches of study.

MOTHER M. ALOYSIUS WILLETT

In June, 1923, the Daviess County Ursulines inaugurated their work in another sphere of usefulness when they began to conduct summer schools in religion in several of the rural school districts, the assigned teachers usually spending two weeks at each of these schools, where they prepare the children for the reception of the sacraments, and give general catechetical instructions.

Progressively developing the educational advantages offered in the academy conducted at Mt. St. Joseph, a junior college curriculum was added to it in 1925. Located as they are, fifteen miles from Owensboro, and three miles from the Green River, on the Owens-boro-Henderson-Calhoun highway, the academy and junior college are now within easy access by motor and by bus. More than five hundred acres of land comprise the grounds of Mt. St. Joseph, which includes the convent, novitiate and school buildings, the campus of

MT. ST. JOSEPH URSULINE CONVENT, ST. JOSEPH, KENTUCKY

which contains pine avenues and terraced grounds beautified by shrubbery and flowers, in addition to the ancient grove of maples for which Mt. St. Joseph is beloved as *Maple Mount* by the many loyal pupils of the Kentucky Ursulines of Daviess County.

The community, of approximately three hundred sisters, now under the superiorship of Mother M. Agnes O'Flynn, confining its labors to educational work, in addition to its activities in the diocese of Louisville has extended its work to the archdioceses of St. Louis and Santa Fé, and the dioceses of Indianapolis, Lincoln and Omaha.

Motherhouse and Novitiate, Mt. St. Joseph's Ursuline Convent, St. Joseph, Kentucky. (Diocese of Louisville.)

YOUNGSTOWN, OHIO*

1874

Anxious to secure religious training for the youth of St. Columba's parish in Youngstown, the congregation of which had been organized nearly fifty years before, the pastor, the Rev. Patrick H. Brown, long solicited the Right Rev. Richard Gilmour, D.D., Bishop of Cleveland, for Ursuline Nuns from Cleveland. In 1874 his request was granted, and with Mother Mary Theresa as Superior, a com-

URSULINE CONVENT, YOUNGSTOWN, OHIO

munity of seven nuns was sent to Youngstown. A residence next to the school had been made ready for a convent home for these pioneers of Catholic education in Mahoning Valley, who in September of the year of their coming began the desired parochial school work at St. Columba's.

To supply the need for teachers in St. Joseph's School, and for additional ones at St. Columba's, Bishop Gilmour requested the Ursulines in Toledo, at that time under his episcopal jurisdiction, for an augmenting community for Youngstown, and in July, 1878, Mother Lawrence and seven nuns arrived from Toledo. Shortly afterward, Mother Lawrence was appointed Superior of the Ursulines in Youngstown, and continued in that position until 1903.

*From data and material supplied by the Ursuline Nuns, Youngstown, Ohio, and from *The Church in Northern Ohio and in the Diocese of Cleveland*, by the Rev. George F. Houck.

he first religious profession in the Youngstown community took
: in July, 1881, and annually since then the Ursulines there have
ved many candidates, both from the vicinity and others from
who have chosen to devote their lives to the cause of Catholic
ation in the northern Ohio diocese.

n addition to the academy, which was incorporated in 1882 as
Jrsuline Academy of the Holy Name of Jesus, the Ursuline High
ol, recently erected in Youngstown, is most prominent among
educational institutions of the community, which is under the
nt superiorship of Mother Mary Vincent, and subject to the
siastical jurisdiction of the Right Rev. Joseph Schrembs, D.D.,
p of Cleveland.

FRONTENAC, MINNESOTA*
1877

ominent among Ursuline communities of the northwest is that
illa Maria Academy at Frontenac, Minnesota.   Upon the invi-
n of the Most Rev. Thomas
race, D.D., then bishop of
'aul, Ursuline Sisters of the
nunity in Alton, Illinois,
ed in Minnesota in August
ie year 1877 and at once
lished a foundation of the
:r at Lake City, now in the
se of Winona.

Jnder the efficient superior-
of Mother Liguori Curran
ew community inaugurated
Jucational activities in the
with the opening of Naza-
School—now maintained as
reth School for Boys—
after its arrival at Lake
on August 25th.

1 1891, General Israel Gar-
a distinguished veteran of
Civil War, and the founder
ie town of Frontenac, pre-

MOTHER LIGUORI CURRAN

'rom data and material supplied by the Ursuline Sisters, Villa Maria
:my, Frontenac, Minn.

sented to Mother Liguori a more than one-hundred-acre tract of land
—of historical interest—near his Minnesota estate at Frontenac, five
miles north of Lake City.   There on a high point overlooking Lake
Pepin, and on the site of old Fort Beuharnais, Villa Maria Academy
was erected and was dedicated as a school for girls on September 8th,
1891.   On this occasion the Most Rev. John Ireland, D.D., Archbishop of St. Paul, gave the address of the day, and eloquently dwelt

VILLA MARIA URSULINE CONVENT, FRONTENAC, MINNESOTA

on the history of the northwest and the importance of the site of
Villa Maria, now the loved Alma Mater of loyal Ursuline alumnæ of
St. Paul, Minneapolis, and many other cities and towns of the north-
west.

Upon the academy and convent grounds of Villa Maria, at
Frontenac, in the archdiocese of St. Paul, stands St. Michael's Chapel,
which perpetuates in its name and by its site the little log church
wherein was celebrated the first holy sacrifice of the mass in the upper
Mississippi Valley, in 1727—co-incidentally the year of the coming
of the Ursulines to New Orleans from France.

In 1906 the Ursulines of Villa Maria Academy—now under the
superiorship and assistant superiorship of Mother Roberta and Mother

Agnes Dunne, and active in the archdiocese of St. Paul and the diocese of Winona—affiliated with the Ursulines of the Canonical Roman Union, and are in the Province of the Northeast of the United States, the novitiate for which is located at Hiddenbrook, Beacon, New York.

NEW ROCHELLE, NEW YORK*

1881

With zealous ambition for the further extension of the Order, the Ursulines missioned from East Morrissania, New York, forming the community of the Ursuline Convent of St. Teresa, on Henry Street, in New York City, petitioned for ecclesiastical recognition as a separate community, and were granted autonomy in 1881.

Mother Seraphine Leonard served as first Superior of the new community, whose work was rapidly developed, as evidenced by its successful opening of academies and schools in the archdiocese of New York. In these institutions, under the religious direction of the Ursulines, the highest educational standards are maintained, fully conforming to the requirements of the New York Board of Education.

In 1891, Leland Castle, a historic and picturesque landmark of Westchester County, was opened by the community as a "finishing school." Thirteen years later, in newly erected and suitable buildings, and three adjoining residences which were purchased for the purpose, the College of St. Angela—now the well-known College of New Rochelle—was opened as the Castle School in 1904, and was the first Catholic college for women in the state of New York. The curriculum of the College of New Rochelle was approved by the

MOTHER M. IRENE GILL

*From data and material supplied by the Ursuline Nuns, Ursuline Convent of St. Teresa, New Rochelle, N. Y.

State Department of Education and the City Board of Education of New York, and granted the same privileges as the secular colleges of the United States.

Scarcely a year has passed since the establishment of the College of New Rochelle without an addition to property, buildings and equipment. Among the more than twenty buildings on the institution's

URSULINE CONVENT OF ST. TERESA, NEW ROCHELLE, NEW YORK

expansive campus, the chapel, Tudor-Gothic in design, has been widely noted architecturally since its opening in 1923.

Since the establishment of the Roman Union of Ursulines, in 1900, the community of the Ursuline Convent of St. Teresa has been zealously interested in it. The Convent of St. Teresa, now at New Rochelle, was recognized in 1925 as the headquarters for the provincialate of the Roman Union known as the Province of the North of the United States, of which Ursuline Academy of the Sacred Heart, at Middletown, New York—one of the foremost of the prominent educational institutions of the community—was for a time the Provincial house and novitiate.

Mother Irene Gill, past Provincial Prioress, continues as Superior of the community at New Rochelle.

GREAT FALLS, MONTANA*

1884

Closely associated with Catholic missionary and educational work among the Indian tribes in the west are the Ursulines of the community which established its headquarters in Montana in January of 1884.

During the crucial period which followed the border wars in Wyoming, the Right Rev. John B. Brondel, as vicar apostolic—before his appointment to the newly-established see of Helena—appealed to the bishops of eastern dioceses for priests for his missions and for sisters to teach in schools for the Indians.

The appeal of Bishop Brondel, in his zeal for the Indians, reached the attention of the bishop of Cleveland, the Right Rev. Richard Gilmour, D.D., who a few years previously had granted a leave of absence to one of his priests, the Rev. Edward J. Lindesmith—resident pastor in Leetonia, Ohio—that he might accept a chaplaincy in the United States Army, and who was then assigned to Fort Keogh, Montana.

Bishop Gilmour referred Bishop Brondel's petition to the Ursulines in Toledo, and from those volunteering for the Montana missions six nuns were chosen to form a community of which Sister Amadeus was appointed Superior.

Sarah Theresa Dunne of Akron, Ohio, in religion Mother Mary Amadeus, had been sent to the boarding school of the Ursuline Convent in Cleveland, Ohio. Following her graduation she entered the Ursuline novitiate at Toledo, where she became a most active and efficient member of the community and served as its Superior for a number of years. Providence gratified a long cherished desire of Mother Amadeus' to go on missionary work, when she was chosen to go from her convent home in Ohio to the Indian missions in the west.

Upon the arrival of the Ursulines in Montana, on a bleak day early in January, 1884, Bishop Brondel and Father Lindesmith met them at Miles City, where they were soon established in a small house

*From data and material supplied by the Ursuline Nuns, Mt. St. Angela, Great Falls, Montana, and from *The Church in Northern Ohio,* by the Rev. George F. Houck, and the Official Catholic Directory, 1929.

allotted them, and where they opened the first school of this new community of Ursulines—the Ursulines of Montana.

Early in April of the same year, Mother Amadeus, accompanied by two of the nuns, took a four-days' journey in a mule-drawn conveyance to St. Labre's Mission on the Tongue River, which had been

Mt. St. Angela Ursuline Convent, Great Falls, Montana

established among the Cheyenne Indians the year before by a Jesuit missionary.

Learning the language and habits of the tribe, winning their friendship by her sympathy and her comprehension of them, Mother Amadeus soon extended her influences beyond the Cheyennes, and with her community opened schools for other tribes and established a community novitiate at St. Peter's Mission. Among other mission activities was the opening of a school for the Crow Indians in 1887, near the old Custer battlefield.

The monuments of the work of this community among the Indians, and of the enduring zeal and wisdom of Mother Amadeus are the many Ursuline institutions in Montana, prominent among which are the Indian Industrial Boarding School for Northern Cheyennes, at St. Labre's Mission, near Ashland; an Indian boarding school for girls, at Holy Family Mission at the Blackfeet Reservation; Villa Ursula Academy, a day and boarding school for girls, and St. Joseph's school for small boys, at St. Ignatius Mission.

The Holy Family and St. Ignatius Mission institutions, as well as an academy conducted by the Ursulines at Anaconda, Montana, being located in the diocese of Helena, are maintained under the jurisdiction of the Right Rev. George J. Finnigan, C.S.C., D.D., as bishop of that diocese.

In 1900, Mother Amadeus, representing the Ursulines in Montana, attended the Chapter held in Rome when, at the instance of the Sovereign Pontiff, Pope Leo XIII, the Roman Union of the Ursulines was formed. Following this, Mother Amadeus was elected Provincial Superior for the Province of the Northwest of the United States, the Provincial house of which is now maintained at the Ursuline Convent at Villa Ursula, St. Ignatius' Mission, Montana, at that time having been established at Mt. St. Angela Convent at Great Falls.

The first Ursuline mission in Alaska was made in 1905, at Akulurak, in the Yukon Delta, under the direction of Mother Amadeus, who two years later accompanied additional nuns to the mission, bravely enduring with them hardships of sickness, storms, and the intense winter cold.

At Mt. St. Angela, in Great Falls, which city was chosen as the episcopal site of the new diocese established in Montana in 1904, of which the Right Rev. Mathias C. Lenihan, D.D., was long bishop, the Ursulines maintain their Motherhouse for the Ursulines of Eastern Montana, and there also is Mt. St. Angela Academy, a boarding and day high school and normal school, one of the most successful institutions of the Ursulines in the state.

WATERVILLE, MAINE*

1888

Through the close relations ever maintained between the Ursulines in the United States and those in Canada—descendants of the ancient foundation made at Quebec by Ven. Mother Mary of the Incarnation

*From *The Catholic Church in the United States of America* (Vol II) (The Catholic Editing Co., New York) and from the Official Catholic Directory, 1929.

—Ursuline foundations in the United States have more than once benefited by their timely helpfulness.

To the Ursuline Motherhouse in the episcopal city of Three Rivers, in the Province of Quebec, is due the Ursuline foundation which was made at Waterville, Maine, in the spring of 1888. The sisters at once began teaching in the parochial school there, and the erection of Mt. Merici Academy and the establishment of a novitiate followed in a few years.

In addition to teaching in Mt. Merici Academy and in the parochial schools of St. Francis de Sales and Notre Dame in Waterville, the community has extended its educational work to many cities and towns in Maine, Fairfield being the site of its first outside mission. At schools in Lewiston and Springvale, under the care of the community, the enrollment of pupils in each is about eight hundred.

Ranking as an independent Ursuline community in the United States, this group of nearly one hundred and fifty sisters, active in the diocese of Portland, is under the ecclesiastical jurisdiction of the Right Rev. John G. Murray, D.D., as bishop of Portland.

Motherhouse and Novitiate, Mt. Merici Convent, Western Avenue, Waterville, Maine. (Diocese of Portland.)

YORK, NEBRASKA*
1890

URSULINES OF YORK, NEBRASKA

Representing a community of Ursulines who, with Mother Clare as Superior, suffered exile from Durm, Germany, during the period of the *Kulturkampf,* the Ursuline Convent of Nazareth, York, Nebraska, was founded in the year 1890.

Prior to the establishment of this foundation, the community from Germany had settled in Peoria, Illinois, and from this city the transfer

*From data and material from the Ursuline Convent of Nazareth, York, Neb.

was made to York, where, in connection with the convent, the community has established and conducts St. Ursula's Academy and Merici College.

In the year 1900 the Ursulines from York extended their labors to the diocese of Omaha, when they took charge of a parochial school in Huntington, Nebraska. Since then three parochial schools in the episcopal city of Omaha have also been placed in charge of the

URSULINE CONVENT OF NAZARETH, YORK, NEBRASKA

community, of which Mother Xavier is now Superior, and which continues to maintain its Motherhouse at York, in the diocese of Lincoln, where it also conducts parochial schools at Dwight, Orleans and Lawrence. Since affiliation with the Roman Union of Ursulines, in 1907, the novitiate for the community has been that of the Province of the Northeast of the United States, located at Beacon, New York.

ST. IGNACE, MICHIGAN*

1897

In the year 1897 the Ursulines of *The Pines,* Chatham, Ontario, responded to an appeal from the Right Rev. John Vertin, D.D., Bishop of Marquette, and established an Ursuline foundation in his diocese at St. Ignace, Michigan.

*From data and material supplied by the Ursuline Nuns, Academy of Our Lady of the Straits, St. Ignace, Mich.

In this historic city where Father Marquette landed in 1671, and where his remains were interred less than five years later, the requested foundation was made. Mother Angela, who for twenty-five years had filled the office of General Directress of Chatham College, was appointed Superior of the Canadian community in St. Ignace.

The sisters entered immediately upon their duties, their first work in the United States being the preparation of a class of seventy boys and girls for their first Holy Communion.

A permanent Motherhouse was erected on diocesan property generously presented to them, on a bluff overlooking Lake Huron, the Island and the Straits of Mackinac and the surrounding country, the natural beauty of the place being enhanced by hills and groves

URSULINE ACADEMY OF OUR LADY OF THE STRAITS, ST. IGNACE, MICHIGAN

of spruce and cedar interspersed with beech and maple. On January 2, 1898, the new convent was solemnly blessed and dedicated to the Blessed Virgin Mary under the title of Our Lady of the Straits.

In the Academy of Our Lady of the Straits, later established, and in its parochial school work, the community—now under the superiorate of Mother M. Gertrude—confining its labors to the diocese of Marquette, under the ecclesiastical jurisdiction of the Right Rev. Paul Joseph Nussbaum, C.P., D.D., zealously continues in the footsteps of its beloved foundress and first Ursuline teacher, St. Angela Merici.

Motherhouse and Novitiate, Ursuline Convent of Our Lady of the Straits, Church Street, St. Ignace, Michigan. (Diocese of Marquette.)

CINCINNATI, OHIO*

1910

Among the many Ursuline communities in Ohio is that in the archiepiscopal city of Cincinnati, whose foundation was made by a colony of nuns from Brown County, the site of the first Ursuline foundation in the state.

Establishing an academy for young ladies—day and boarding students—and a boarding school for small boys, in connection with their Motherhouse, St. Ursula Convent, on East McMillan Street, in the Walnut Hills section of Cincinnati, the sisters engaged also in the conducting of parochial schools in the city.

Under the auspices of the Most Rev. Henry Moeller, D.D., Archbishop of Cincinnati, the community was canonically established as a Motherhouse and novitiate, by a grant received from the Sacred Congregation of Religious, in Rome, on November 6, 1910.

MOTHER FIDELIS COLEMAN

Mother M. Fidelis Coleman served as first Superior of the com-

ST. URSULA CONVENT, CINCINNATI, OHIO

*From data and material supplied by the Ursuline Nuns, St. Ursula Academy, Cincinnati, Ohio.

munity, which beginning with twenty members, now includes about sixty, who are engaged chiefly in educational work at St. Ursula Academy, and in the schools of St. Francis de Sales', St. Monica's and Holy Name Churches, all in Cincinnati. Under the present ecclesiastical jurisdiction of the Most Rev. John T. McNicholas, O.P., D.D., the community confines its activities to the archdiocese of Cincinnati.

Motherhouse and Novitiate, St. Ursula Convent, 1339 East McMillan Street, Cincinnati, Ohio. (Archdiocese of Cincinnati.)

KENMARE, NORTH DAKOTA*

1910

In 1910, soon after the establishment of the diocese of Bismarck in North Dakota, the Rev. F. Junker, pastor of the mission church at

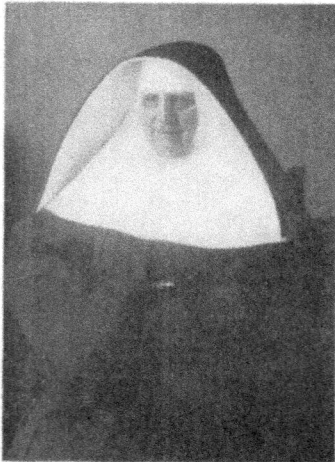

MOTHER GONZAGA

St. Anthony's, with the permission of the Right Rev. Vincent Wehrle, O.S.B., D.D., bishop of the new diocese, petitioned the Ursulines of the Congregation of Calvarienberg, with their Motherhouse at Ahr-weiler, Germany, for sisters to open a school at St. Anthony's.

Granting Father Junker's peti-tion, sisters, with Mother Leonie Rodgers as Superior, were then sent from Germany and upon arriving at their destination at once took charge of a school at St. Anthony's, and shortly afterward, on the re-quest of Bishop Wehrle, opened a parochial school at Strasburg in the adjoining county, in the southern part of the state. Two years later, an academy and boarding school was established at Kenmare, in northwestern North Dakota.

Retaining the affiliation of the community in the United States with the General Motherhouse of the Congregation of Calvarienberg —whose revised Constitutions were given papal approbation in 1909—a central house and novitiate of the Congregation for this

*From data and material supplied by the Ursuline Nuns, Ursuline Convent of St. Agnes, Kenmare, N. D.

country has been established at the academy at Kenmare. Mother Veronica Schmitt is Superior of the community, which has recently extended its labors to include the diocese of St. Cloud as well as the diocese of Bismarck.

> *U. S. Motherhouse and Novitiate,* Ursuline Convent of St. Agnes, Kenmare, North Dakota. (Diocese of Bismarck.)

CALDWELL, OHIO*

1915

Continuing the generosity of the Ursuline Nuns in their European convents, from which have been sent to the United States so many zealous apostles to labor for the Christian education of youth, there came to the diocese of Columbus, in the year 1915, nine sisters from the Ursuline Monastery at Erfurt, Germany, which had been founded in 1667.

The bishop of the diocese, the Right Rev. James J. Hartley, D.D., designated Noble County as a fertile field in his episcopal territory for the initial headquarters of the members of the new community, who upon their first election in the United States chose Sister M. Salesia, of their number, for Superior.

Until 1922, when removal in the county was made to the newly erected

MOTHER M. SALESIA

convent at Caldwell, the sisters made their home in the nearby small town of Fulda, where they taught in the Catholic district school and gave religious instruction by summer courses in the surrounding neighborhood. In the meantime they were given charge of the parochial school at Burkhart and assigned to St. Ladislas School in Columbus—their first mission in the episcopal city.

An apostolic Brief of the Holy See, issued in 1925, approved the autonomy of the community and confirmed the canonical erection of its novitiate. The community has in addition been incorporated according to the laws of the state of Ohio, and confines its activities to the diocese of Columbus.

> *Motherhouse and Novitiate,* St. Ursula's Convent, 615 Ross Street, Caldwell, Ohio. (Diocese of Columbus.)

*From data and material supplied by the Ursuline Nuns, St. Ursula's Convent, Caldwell, Ohio.

THE ROMAN UNION OF URSULINES*

An event of the highest importance in the annals of the Order of St. Ursula took place in Rome, in November of the year 1900. As the Sovereign Pontiff, Pope Leo XIII, favored a union of the Ursulines with headquarters at Rome, a General Chapter of the Order was then convened there, and Mother M. St. Julian, of the Ursulines of Blois, was elected the first Prioress General of the Ursuline Nuns of the Roman Union.

On July 17, 1903, Pope Leo XIII signed the Decree of the Roman Union and gave papal approbation of its Constitution.

With the Generalate established at 22 Via Nomentana, Rome, 27, the affiliated Ursuline houses in the different countries are divided into provinces under the government of Provincials. The provincial government of the provinces of the Roman Union is composed of a Provincial Prioress and two Councilors, assisted by a Provincial Secretary and Procurator.

Each of the provinces has its own novitiate, to which the communities send their postulants to receive the habit and pass the two years of formation preceding their temporary profession. The vow of stability does not prevent communities from rendering service to each other by the loan of subjects, under certain conditions whereby their mutual interests are safeguarded.

The Prioress General is provided with a category of Ursulines who place themselves at her disposal for foreign mission work or to assist the communities in need of religious teachers.

The Roman Union of Ursulines, formed as it is of communities in many different lands, while meeting with, in the affiliated houses, certain customs and usages due to the climate or the special needs of the district, does away with nothing individual that can be maintained, having at heart only the fostering of uniformity and unity in the vital rules, the religious spirit, and in the proper understanding of Christian education.

Representatives of many Ursuline communities in the United States were present in Rome and participated in the inauguration of the Roman Union of Ursulines. Other Ursuline communities, in the United States as elsewhere, have since joined the groups of affiliated ones, while some still continue as independent or diocesan communities.

*From material supplied by the Ursuline Nuns of the Roman Union, New Rochelle College, New Rochelle, N. Y., and data from the Official Catholic Directory, 1929.

PROVINCES IN THE UNITED STATES OF THE URSULINE NUNS
OF THE CANONICAL ROMAN UNION:

Province of the Northeast of the United States for affiliated Ursuline communities in the archdioceses of Baltimore, New York, San Francisco and St. Paul, and in the dioceses of Charleston, Great Falls, Lincoln, Monterey-Fresno, Ogdensburg, Omaha, Trenton, Wilmington and Winona.

Provincial house, Mt. St. Ursula, 200th Street and Marion Avenue, Bedford Park, New York City, New York. (Archdiocese of New York.)

Provincial Novitiate, Ursuline Novitiate, Hiddenbrook, Beacon, New York. (Archdiocese of New York.)

Province of the Northwest of the United States for affiliated Ursuline communities in the dioceses of Boise, Helena and Seattle and in the vicariate apostolic of Alaska.

Provincial house, Villa Ursula, St. Ignatius Mission, St. Ignatius, Montana. (Diocese of Helena.)

Provincial Novitiate, Ursuline Convent, Mukilteo, Washington. (Diocese of Seattle.)

Province of the South of the United States for affiliated Ursuline communities in the archdioceses of Chicago, New Orleans and San Antonio and in the dioceses of Dallas, Galveston, Little Rock and Springfield in Illinois.

Provincial house, Ursuline Convent, St. Joseph Street, Dallas, Texas. (Diocese of Dallas.)

Provincial Novitiate, Ursuline Convent, Texarkana, Texas. (Diocese of Dallas.)

CHRONOLOGICAL TABLE

EXISTENT URSULINE FOUNDATIONS IN THE UNITED STATES*

In this table no distinction is made between communities affiliated with the Roman Union of Ursulines and independent communities.

1727—New Orleans, Louisiana.
1845—St. Martin, Brown County, Ohio.
1847—Galveston, Texas.
1848—St. Louis, Missouri (Kirkwood, Mo.).

1850—Cleveland, Ohio.
1854—Toledo, Ohio.
1855—East Morrissania, N. Y. (Bedford Park, New York City, N. Y.).
1858—Louisville, Kentucky.

*Owing to the lack of available statistics it has been impossible to make this list entirely complete.

1858—Columbia, South Carolina.
1859—Alton, Illinois.
1863—Tiffin, Ohio.
1870—Pittsburgh, Pennsylvania.
1874—Dallas, Texas.
1874—St. Joseph, Kentucky.
1874—Youngstown, Ohio.
1877—Frontenac, Minnesota.
1881—New York City (New Rochelle, N. Y.).

1884—Miles City, Montana (Great Falls).
1888—Waterville, Maine.
1890—York, Nebraska.
1895—Paola, Kansas.
1897—St. Ignace, Michigan.
1898—Malone, New York.
1910—Cincinnati, Ohio.
1910—Kenmare, North Dakota.
1915—Caldwell, Ohio.

SUMMARY

The Company of St. Ursula—The Ursulines.
Founded in Italy in 1535.
Papal Approbation of Rules in 1612 by Pope Paul V.
Established in the United States in 1727.*
Habit: The habit is of black serge, made in tunic form and fastened with a cincture. A white linen bandeau and guimpe and a black veil are worn. The Ursulines of Paris adopted a black habit with a long trailing church mantle, and the leather cincture of St. Augustine, looping up the habit in the classroom in peasant fashion, showing a skirt and sleeves of gray undyed woolen serge.
Approximate number in communities in the United States, 3000.
Active chiefly in educational work, in the archdioceses of Baltimore, Chicago, Cincinnati, New Orleans, New York, St. Louis, St. Paul, San Antonio, San Francisco and Santa Fé, and in the dioceses of Altoona, Bismarck, Boise, Charleston, Cleveland, Columbus, Corpus Christi, Dallas, Galveston, Grand Island, Great Falls, Helena, Indianapolis, Lincoln, Little Rock, Louisville, Marquette, Monterey-Fresno, Ogdensburg, Omaha, Pittsburgh, Portland, St. Cloud, Seattle, Springfield in Illinois, Toledo, Trenton, Wheeling, Wilmington and Winona, and in the vicariate apostolic of Alaska.

*Louisiana, although a French possession at the time, was the site of the first foundation of the Ursulines in what is now the United States.

CARMELITE NUNS*

1790

*W*ITH the growing need for active laborers becoming evident throughout the new republic, in the ecclesiastical stress of pioneer days, the Carmelite Nuns—bound by strict enclosure and devoted exclusively to an interior life of retirement, prayer and penance in the cloister—were, nevertheless, providentially established in the United States as early as 1790, to pray for the American missions, and, by contemplation, to second Church activities, and invoke blessings on souls, the country, and the rising enterprises of active religious orders.

Carmelite Nuns, a branch of the ancient and ascetic Carmelite Order, of patriarchial origin, came into being at about the middle of the fifteenth century, when several communities of Beguines, a society of devout women, petitioned Blessed John Soreth, General of the Carmelite Friars, for affiliation with the Order. In 1452, therefore, they were given the Rule and Constitutions of the friars, to which were added some special regulations for the nuns.

The prestige of the Carmelite Nuns grew rapidly. The Duchess of Brittany, Blessed Frances d'Amboise, joined one of the convents, which she herself had founded. Before the end of the century there were convents in France, Italy and Spain, where especially, the mode of life of the nuns was greatly admired, and where, from a thoroughly Catholic and cultured Spanish household, there was destined to enter the Carmelite Order its heroic reformer and glory, St. Teresa.

Born at Avila, Old Castile, in 1515, St. Teresa was in her fourteenth year when her mother died, and she was sent, for her education, to the Augustinian Nuns, in her native town. Owing to illness, she left at the end of eighteen months, and for some years remained with her saintly father, and occasionally with other relatives, notably an uncle, who made her acquainted with the "Letters of St. Jerome," the study of which made her resolve to become a religious, not so much through sensible attraction to such a life, as through a desire of choosing the surest course.

In November, 1535, notwithstanding her father's objections, she entered the Carmelite Convent of the Incarnation, at Avila, where the community numbered one hundred and forty. Obtaining her father's consent, soon afterward, St. Teresa was given the habit.

*From data and material supplied by the Carmelite Nuns, Baltimore, Md., and from authentic historical facts.

During years of suffering, following a protracted serious illness after her profession, she began the practice of mental prayer, and God visited her with interior manifestations and counsels.

ST. TERESA OF JESUS (1515-1582)
Foundress of the Order of Discalced Carmelites

Learning that the primitive Rule of the Order aimed at the contemplative life, and enjoined certain austerities which had since been mitigated or dispensed with, St. Teresa resolved upon the establishment of a convent in Avila, based upon the observance of the ancient rigor of the Rule, and in 1562, after many difficulties, she thus became the founder of the reformed or Discalced Carmelites.

Nor did her zeal stop here, but, with the permission and approval of John Baptist Rubeo, then General of the Carmelite Order, extended itself to the foundation of other convents, as well as to a reformation of the friars, in which also, aided by the counsel and labors of St. Peter of Alcantara and St. John of the Cross, who joined the new Order, she was completely successful.

St. Teresa died in 1582. She was beatified in 1614, and canonized in 1622, under Pope Gregory XV. October 15th was then declared the date of her feast.

At the time of her death St. Teresa had assisted in the foundation of seventeen reformed convents for women and fifteen for men, and the Order of Discalced Carmelites, of her institution—surmounting persecution, and rapidly extended to all the Catholic countries of Europe—was, in 1593, by Pope Clement VIII, declared independent of the jurisdiction of the unreformed Order, and given a general of its own.

In 1619, Lady Mary Lovell, daughter of Lord Roper, founded

MOTHER CLARE JOSEPH DICKINSON

a Carmelite Convent in Antwerp, Belgium. Venerable Mother Ann of St. Bartholomew, who governed this community, and its first Prioresses, were imbued with the true spirit of the Order from its fountain source. The profession book of this monastery records some of the noblest names of England—Herbert, Somersett, Vaughn, and, for generations, a Howard. Later on, Brent, Pye and Matthews, old Maryland names, were added to the list, for these intrepid Americans crossed the ocean to enter Carmel, and through them the monastery of Antwerp became the parent house of the Discalced Carmelites in the United States.

In 1790, the Rev. John Carroll, D.D.—brother of Charles Carroll of Carrollton, the "signer," who for five years had been Superior of the American clergy—then numbering about thirty priests, in a territory comprising the entire United States—was appointed bishop of

Baltimore. His first act in his new capacity was to invite the Carmelites to his vast diocese "to pray for the American missions."

Mother Clare Joseph Dickinson, from Antwerp, and Mother Bernardina Matthews, Superior of the house at Hoogstraeten, and her nieces, Sister Aloysia Matthews and Sister Eleonora Matthews, accordingly braved an ocean voyage of three months, and untold privations, and on the feast of St. Teresa, 1790, the first Carmelite

CARMELITE MONASTERY, BALTIMORE, MARYLAND

Convent in the United States was dedicated. The convent was on the Brooke estate, about four miles from Port Tobacco, Charles County, Maryland.

In 1830 it was decided to remove the convent to a more convenient site; ground was therefore secured on Aisquith Street, in Baltimore, and a building was at once erected, the cornerstone being laid by the Most Rev. James Whitfield, D.D., Archbishop of Baltimore. To this location the community removed in 1831. In 1872 another change was found necessary, and removal was made to the present convent in Baltimore, on Caroline and Biddle Streets— the United States mother foundation of the Carmelites, the first religious community of women established within the limits of the thirteen original colonies.

In 1863 nuns from the Baltimore Carmel founded the monastery in St. Louis, which, in 1877, sent forth an offshoot to New Orleans, where a convent was established.

During the great Catholic Congress held in Baltimore in 1889, the Boston delegates learned of the esteem in which the Carmelites were held in that city, by both clergy and laity, and that blessings enjoyed by its citizens were attrib- uted to their prayers and holy lives. Devout Catholics in Boston then desired a Carmelite Convent for their city, and the wish was given episcopal approval. In 1890, the centennial year of the Carmelites in America, on August 28th, five nuns, appointed by His Eminence, James Cardinal Gibbons, from the Baltimore Carmel, established a foundation at Roxbury, Boston. Here the community has been en- abled to build a monastery adapted to its needs, with a chapel adequate for the numbers who gather, as at every Carmel, with their petitions and alms, or to participate in public devotions.

ST. THÉRÈSE OF THE CHILD JESUS
(1873-1897)
Carmelite of Lisieux, France

From these foundations many other Carmelite Convents have since been established in the United States, each an independent institution, and functioning as a Motherhouse and novitiate.

It is the spirit of the century to decry contemplative orders, because the spirit of the century is the spirit of activity. The con- templative Carmelite life, therefore, the antithesis of this general standard, and remarkable even among cloistered orders for its unqualified austere character, is seldom comprehended, and the ques- tion, "What is a Carmelite, and what does she do?" is asked.

The Carmelite Nun undertakes an expiatory life of penance in atonement for sin. She is called to an apostolic life of supplication for the salvation of souls, and especially for the needs of the Church, interceding for the temporal and spiritual aid of all who seek her prayers, for health and relief of soul and body, and for conversion of

heart and perseverance in well-doing. To make her prayers more efficacious, she purifies her soul by penances and perpetual abstinence, by almost continual fasting, by wearing coarse woolen, and by many other exercises of constant mortification.

The time of the Carmelite, after the recitation of the Divine Office and devotions, is employed in manual labor and needle-work to aid in the support of the community, including the chaining of rosaries and the making of vestments and scapulars, and articles for the Church.

The life of a Carmelite, then, is dedicated to prayer and contemplation, as voluntarily as that of an active religious is devoted to educational, charitable or missionary work, and is as actually, though perhaps less obviously, beneficial.

In an age of materialism and unbelief, as if to reveal to an inquiring and skeptical world the glory of the hidden life of the Carmelite, and establishing the closest of links with the Order of the illustrious St. Teresa of Avila, and modern times, St. Thérèse of Lisieux, the "Little Flower of Jesus," has appeared almost miraculously.

Canonized in 1925, less than thirty years after her death, due to her promised "shower of roses," in the form of numerous miracles, which testified to her sanctity, and owing to the extraordinary universal veneration she was receiving, although she had lived in a humble Carmel, and died at the age of twenty-four, Little Thérèse, whom thousands know and honor, has stirred the world. With her striking piety, and captivating "little way" of love and spiritual childhood, this young nun has won her way to and uplifted millions of hearts, satisfying modern spirtual needs and inclinations, while typifying the ideal follower of St. Teresa of Avila, and the spirit of the true Carmelite.

SUMMARY

The Carmelite Nuns (Discalced Carmelites).
Founded in Spain in 1562.
Established in the United States in 1790.
Habit: The habit is brown, with a black veil, white guimpe and white chapel cloak. The brown scapular of Our Lady of Mt. Carmel is worn.
Approximate number in communities in United States, 350.
Engaged in contemplative life in the following Carmels in the United States, each with its own novitiate:

Carmelite Monastery, Caroline and Biddle Streets, Baltimore, Maryland. (Archdiocese of Baltimore.)
Carmelite Monastery, 61 Mt. Pleasant Avenue, Roxbury, Boston, Massachusetts. (Archdiocese of Boston.)

Monastery of St. Joseph and St. Teresa, 1236 North Rampart Street, New Orleans, Louisiana. (Archdiocese of New Orleans.)

Carmelite Convent, 300 Gun Hill Road, Bronx, New York, New York. (Archdiocese of New York.)

Carmelite Convent, 66th Avenue and York Road, Oak Lane, Philadelphia, Pennsylvania. (Archdiocese of Philadelphia.)

Carmelite Monastery of St. Louis, Clayton, Missouri. (Archdiocese of St. Louis.)

Carmelite Monastery of the Infant Jesus, 1000 Lincoln Street, Santa Clara, California. (Archdiocese of San Francisco.)

St. Teresa's Carmelite Convent, 1138 Duane Street, Schenectady, New York. (Diocese of Albany.)

Carmelite Monastery, 5519 6th Avenue, Altoona, Pennsylvania. (Diocese of Altoona.)

Monastery of Our Lady of Mt. Carmel, 745 St. John's Place, Brooklyn, New York. (Diocese of Brooklyn.)

Carmelite Convent of St. Theresa of the Divine Child Jesus, 75 Carmel Road, Buffalo, New York. (Diocese of Buffalo.)

Carmel of the Holy Family, 11127 St. Clair Avenue, Cleveland, Ohio. (Diocese of Cleveland.)

Carmelite Monastery, 2003 Wichita Street, Dallas, Texas. (Diocese of Dallas.)

Regina Coeli Monastery, Bettendorf, Iowa. (Diocese of Davenport.)

Monastery of St. Thérèse of the Child Jesus, 1534 Webb Avenue, Detroit, Michigan. (Diocese of Detroit.)

Carmelite Monastery of Our Lady of Guadalupe, 1256 Walker Avenue, N. W., Grand Rapids, Michigan. (Diocese of Grand Rapids.)

Carmelite Monastery, 411 East 9th Street, New Albany, Indiana. (Diocese of Indianapolis.)

Carmelite Convent, 215 East Alhambra Road, Alhambra, California. (Diocese of Los Angeles and San Diego.)

Carmelite Monastery, 3803 Georgia Street, San Diego, California. (Diocese of Los Angeles and San Diego.)

Carmelite Monastery of Our Lady and St. Thérèse, Carmel-by-the-Sea, California. (Diocese of Monterey-Fresno.)

Monastery of the Most Blessed Virgin Mary of Mt. Carmel, 189 Madison Avenue, Morristown, New Jersey. (Diocese of Newark.)

Carmelite Monastery, Rochester, New York. (Diocese of Rochester.)

Carmelite Monastery, 1808 18th Street, Seattle, Washington. (Diocese of Seattle.)

Monastery of the Blessed Sacrament, 846 North 12th Street, Tucson, Arizona. (Diocese of Tucson.)

Monastery of St. Teresa and St. John of the Cross, Pleasant Valley, Wheeling, West Virginia. (Diocese of Wheeling.)

VISITATION NUNS*

THE Order of the Visitation was founded in Annecy, in Savoy, France, in the year 1610. Co-operating in the plans of her spiritual director and advisor, St. Francis de Sales, St. Jane Frances de Chantal—the widow of Baron de Chantal, twenty-eight years of age, and mother of four children—fulfilled the inspiration she had received for the founding of a religious congregation, by becoming the Superior and co-foundress of the Order of the Visitation.

The original plan of the holy founder was that of a Congregation in which only simple vows of religion should be pronounced, and visiting the sick should be the special work of the members, as implied by the name Visitation. With the canonical erection of the Institute, solemn vows and enclosure were stipulated in the rules which were drawn up, aiming especially to secure the benefit of the religious life for those who had neither the physical strength nor the attraction for the corporal austerities at the time general in religious orders.

St. Francis specified that widows as well as virgins were to be received into the Order, on condition that they were legitimately freed from the care of their children; the age limit was not to be stated, and the delicate in body but sound of mind were not to be refused participation in the religious life of the Visitandines.

With the observance of the cloister decreed, visitation of the sick was necessarily relinquished by the Sisters of the Visitation of Holy Mary. In their convent cloisters—in which either the purely contemplative life is observed, or the contemplative in combination with the active life, in behalf of the education and religious instruction of girls, in educational institutions at the convents—the Visitandines are not unmindful of the desire of their holy founder, St. Francis, for the preservation in a permanent institution of the spiritual method dear to him: to reach God chiefly through interior mortification, and to endeavor to do, in every action, only the Divine Will, with the greatest possible love.

Before the holy death of the saintly foundress, in 1641, in a convent which had been established in Moulins, convents had been opened in various dioceses of France, and before the end of the century their number had greatly increased. Renowned among them, and continuing so—now for more than two hundred years the annual mecca of thousands of pilgrims—is the Visitation Convent in the

*From the annals of the Visitandines.

50

little town of Paray-le-Monial in Autun, France, for to a humble nun of this community, St. Margaret Mary Alacoque, was revealed the

ST. JANE FRANCES DE CHANTAL (1572-1641)
Co-foundress of the Order of the Visitation

now world-wide devotion of reparation to and love of the Sacred Heart.

By the end of the eighteenth century, convents of the Visitation Order had been opened in various countries throughout Europe, each house becoming an independent institution, under the immediate juris-diction of the ordinary of the diocese. The communities, however, are very closely united by a bond of mutual charity, and aid and assist one another whenever possible. Circulars are sent from time to time to keep all acquainted with the events of each convent. In doubts regarding the observance of the rule, recourse is had to the house in Annecy, the *sainte-source,* which actually exercises no authority, but whose right to advise is recognized as that of an elder sister.

GEORGETOWN, DISTRICT OF COLUMBIA*

1799

The canonical establishment in the United States, in 1816, of the Visitation Nuns, whose history in this country is inseparably linked with historic Georgetown Visitation Convent in Washington, D. C., was antedated by the foundation, in 1799, of that institution, as a "Young Ladies' Academy," under the direction of three pious ladies.

Realizing that one of the foremost needs of the day was a convent school, the Rev. Leonard Neale, then President of Georgetown College, placed in charge of this academy Miss Alice Teresa Lalor,—who, planning to be a religious, had been under his spiritual direction in Philadelphia, and two pious widows, awaiting permission to make the vows of religion, and formal establishment as a religious community.

"From over the Arlington Hills and from down the Potomac as far as Mount Vernon came the daughters of Virginia. The old Manor houses of Prince George's and St. Mary's and of historical St. Inigoes sent fair young Maryland women to be educated at the hands of 'the sisters.' " Sisters and nuns the pious ladies were designated from the beginning, in this the first religious educational community in the original thirteen colonies, in the academy which they so successfully conducted, though under difficulties, and through years of privations and inconveniences bravely endured by pupils as well as nuns.

In 1807 Thomas Jefferson sent some pecan nuts from trees that grew at Monticello, to a Mr. Threlkeld, grandfather of one of the nuns, and, as related in the convent annals, Mr. Threlkeld presented Mr. Jefferson's gift to his grand-daughter, who planted the nuts— and the gathering of pecans from those trees is among happy incidents of the years long remembered by those claiming Georgetown Visitation Convent as their Alma Mater.

---

*From data and material supplied by the Visitation Nuns, Georgetown Visitation Convent, Washington, D. C., and from *The Life and Times of Archbishop Carroll* and *The History of the Catholic Church in the United States,* by John Gilmary Shea.

During the War of 1812, teachers and pupils watched from the garret windows of the Georgetown school the burning of Washington by the British.

In 1813, Bishop Neale, who had become co-adjutor bishop of Baltimore, though desirous that Miss Lalor and her companions should

GEORGETOWN VISITATION CONVENT, WASHINGTON, D. C.

be the nucleus of a United States foundation of the Visitation Order, a copy of whose Rule he had obtained, allowed them to take the simple vows of religion, while affiliation plans were pending.

In 1816, Bishop Neale, who succeeded that year to the arch-bishopric of Baltimore, was rewarded for his persevering efforts toward a Visitation affiliation for the community at the Georgetown Academy for Young Ladies, when he received from the Sovereign Pontiff, Pope Pius VII, the authority to establish canonically as a house of the Visitation Order—founded by the holy Doctor, St. Francis de Sales and by St. Jane Frances de Chantal—the community which had so patiently labored at Georgetown for the good of religion.

On December 28, 1816, Mother Teresa Lalor, Sister Frances McDermott and Sister Agnes Brent, before the mass which was celebrated by Archbishop Neale, were consequently admitted to the solemn profession of vows, with the indulgences and privileges of the Order of the Visitation of Holy Mary.

In January, 1817, the thirty others, who formed the community which had developed at the Georgetown Convent, were professed.

In the meantime, the regular choir service had been instituted, and the garb of the Visitandines adopted.

That the Visitation Nuns in this country might be imbued with the primitive spirit of the communities of the Order in the mother country, arrangements were made with the Annecy foundation for some nuns to spend a few years in America. Sister Mary Agatha Langlois of Nantes, Sister Mary Regis Mordant of Valence, and Sister Magdalen Augustine of Friburg, who arrived from Europe in 1829, found that their sisters in the United States had closely followed the rules and customs of the houses in Europe, and were edified by the spirit that pervaded the monastery of the Georgetown Academy, with its flourishing school of one hundred pupils, and its beautiful chapel, the first in the United States to be dedicated to the Sacred Heart.

At the graduation exercises of the year 1828, to which he was accompanied by his son and his wife, President John Quincy Adams distributed the school prizes and gave the address. Among those receiving awards were three daughters of Yturbide, at one time Emperor of Mexico, whose widow lived the life of a nun in the convent for a number of years, although she never took the vows. Before her death she presented her husband's cloth of gold coronation robe to the nuns, who converted it into a feast-day vestment.

Before the death of Mother Teresa Lalor, on September 9, 1846, Visitation foundations had been made from Georgetown in Mobile, Kaskaskia—later amalgamated with the foundation in St. Louis—Baltimore, St. Louis and Brooklyn.

During the Civil War the shadow of a country divided against itself fell upon Georgetown teachers and pupils alike. Through the influence of General Winfield Scott, the impending military use of the convent property, which contained the grave of his daughter Virginia who had entered the Order, was averted.

In the years since its establishment Georgetown Visitation Convent has recorded, in its academy roster, the names of hundreds, daughters of distinguished foreign as well as American citizens, while inscribed on its guest register are names of greatest distinction from amongst the hierarchy, and civic and social leaders.

In accordance with the Rule of the Visitandines, that each house function as an independent foundation under the immediate jurisdiction of the ordinary of the diocese in which it is established, the community of approximately fifty-five sisters of Georgetown Visitation Convent, of which Mother Jane Frances Leibell is the present Superior, is under the ecclesiastical jurisdiction of the Most Rev. Michael J. Curley, D.D., Archbishop of Baltimore.

Convent and Novitiate, Georgetown Visitation Convent, 1500 35th Street, N. W., Washington, District of Columbia. (Arch-diocese of Baltimore.)

MOBILE, ALABAMA*
1833

In 1833 the Right Rev. Michael Portier, D.D., first bishop of the newly erected see of Mobile, petitioned Mother Teresa Lalor at Georgetown Visitation Convent in Washington for a community for his episcopal city in Alabama.

In compliance with this request, the first foundation made by the Georgetown community was that year established in Mobile, where the Convent and Academy of the Visitation, on Spring Hill Avenue, are among the foremost Catholic institutions in the diocese, now under the episcopal jurisdiction of the Right Rev. Thomas J. Toolen, D.D.

Convent and Novitiate, Visitation Convent, Spring Hill Avenue, Mobile, Alabama. (Diocese of Mobile.)

BALTIMORE, MARYLAND†
1837

Following his elevation to the archbishopric of Baltimore in 1834, the Most Rev. Samuel Eccleston, D.D., made a personal visitation of the archdiocese, carefully studying its needs. His realization of the merit and value of Catholic education gave an impulse to its cause in the archdiocese, and under the auspices of Archbishop Eccleston, in November of the year 1837, ecclesiastically memorable in the province as the year of a Provincial Council, a colony of Visitation Nuns from the Georgetown Visitation Convent established a convent and academy on Mulberry Street, Baltimore. Mother Juliana Matthews was first Superior of the foundation.

Successfully continuing, as they have for nearly a century, in their educational work in the archdiocesan city, the Visitation Nuns there

---

*From the annals of the Visitation Nuns and from the Official Catholic Year Book, 1928 (P. J. Kenedy & Sons, N. Y.).

†From *The History of the Catholic Church in the United States* by John Gilmary Shea, and the Official Catholic Year Book, 1928.

conduct, in connection with the convent and novitiate, the academy known as the Baltimore Academy of the Visitation.

Convent and Novitiate, Convent of the Visitation, 604 Park Avenue, Baltimore, Maryland.   (Archdiocese of Baltimore.)

ST. LOUIS, MISSOURI*

1844

Under the superiorship of Mother Mary Agnes Brent, of the Georgetown Visitation Convent, a Visitation foundation was made in Kaskaskia, Illinois, in 1833, upon the request of the Right Rev. Joseph Rosati, C.M., Bishop of St. Louis and Vicar General of

VISITATION CONVENT, ST. LOUIS, MISSOURI

Bardstown, which diocese included the state of Illinois.   With the erection of the see of Chicago, in 1843, Kaskaskia was in its allotted territory, and the Visitandines automatically belonged to the new diocese.

The Right Rev. Peter R. Kenrick, D.D.—later first archbishop of St. Louis—having succeeded Bishop Rosati in the see of St. Louis, desirous that the Visitation Nuns should remain in the diocese, requested a foundation for his episcopal city.   This was made in May, 1844, by the community, from the newly created see of Chicago.

The following month, floods of the Mississippi washed away the

*From data and material supplied by the Visitation Nuns, Academy and Convent of the Visitation, 5448 Cabanne Avenue, St. Louis, Mo.

Illinois town of Kaskaskia. The furniture and personal belongings of the Visitandines were saved, and with them were carried in safety to St. Louis. Kaskaskia did not recover from the effects of the flood, and though encouraged to renew their Illinois foundation by establishing a convent in Chicago, the seat of the diocese, a decision was made, in 1846, to reunite the Illinois community with that established in St. Louis in 1844. Under Mother Mary Agnes Brent, this was accomplished, and for a time the community occupied the bishop's house, on Ninth Street, in St. Louis.

In 1858 the sisters removed to their newly erected building on Cass Avenue, where they remained until changes in the neighborhood necessitated a move farther west of the city center. In 1892, the present building on Cabanne Avenue, known as the Academy and Monastery of the Visitation of St. Louis, was completed, and the community and school were transferred to it.

Additions to this building have been made according to the needs of the community—of which Mother Raphael Kiley is present Superior—and the requirements for the boarding and day-pupils of the academy conducted there, as well as for the primary and intermediate departments.

Convent and Novitiate, Convent of the Visitation, 5448 Cabanne Avenue., St. Louis, Missouri. (Archdiocese of St. Louis.)

WHEELING, WEST VIRGINIA*
1848

In the spring of 1848, eight Visitation Sisters, under the superiorship of Mother Eleanora Walsh, arrived in Wheeling from the Visitation Convent in Baltimore, Maryland.

At that time Wheeling was included in the diocese of Richmond, with the Right Rev. Richard V. Whelan, D.D., occupying the episcopal see. With the erection of the diocese of Wheeling, two years later, Bishop Whelan was appointed its first bishop, and at once set himself to the task of providing facilities for the mental and moral training of the youth under his care. The initial step in that task was the establishment of Mt. de Chantal.

A residence on Eoff Street, on the site now occupied by St. Joseph's Academy, was the first abode of the Sisters of the Visitation in Wheeling, who began their educational work in the city with the conducting of the parochial school of the Cathedral. With the number of their pupils increasing, it was found necessary to rein-

*From data and material supplied by the Visitation Sisters, Mt. de Chantal Convent, Wheeling, W. Va.

force the teaching staff, and in 1856 the original community of eight sisters was augmented by the addition of three members sent to it from the Georgetown Convent.

Although Mt. de Chantal dates its foundation from 1848, it was not until the period of the Civil War that the first stone of the institution, as it is known today, was laid. In 1861, when the community and school had outgrown the limits of the Cathedral parish,

MT. DE CHANTAL VISITATION CONVENT, WHEELING, WEST VIRGINIA

the need for more commodious quarters led to the erection of the building on its present site. In 1865, the sisters moved into the completed part of the new building.

In the years following the Civil War, Mt. de Chantal, with its boarding school advantages, attracted many pupils from the southern states, at the same time gaining prestige in the north and east.

In 1923, under the episcopacy of the present incumbent, the Right Rev. John J. Swint, D.D., who the year previous had succeeded to the see of Wheeling, a formal celebration signalized the seventy-fifth anniversary of the foundation of Mt. de Chantal, where the Visitation Sisters, imbued with the spirit of their holy foundress, St. Jane Frances de Chantal, progressively maintain the high ideals of the Visitation Order.

    Convent and Novitiate, Mt. de Chantal Convent of the Visitation, Wheeling, West Virginia. (Diocese of Wheeling.)

PARKERSBURG, WEST VIRGINIA*

1864

Untiring in his labors in behalf of the religious education of the Catholic girls of his diocese, the Right Rev. Richard V. Whelan, D.D., in 1864, realizing the need of additional teachers, again had recourse to the Visitation Order for sisters.

To accede to this appeal, a community was formed of Visitation Sisters from the mother foundation in Georgetown, D. C., and from the foundation in Frederick, Maryland. Mother Appolonia Diggs was Superior of this newly-formed community, which in 1864 established the Visitation Convent in Parkersburg, West Virginia, south of the City of Wheeling, where the Visitation Sisters had for some time been zealously laboring in educational work.

In addition to the academy which was established, and consistent with the Rules of the Visitation Order, a novitiate was opened at the convent in Parkersburg, as each Visitation foundation automatically becomes a Motherhouse and maintains its own novitiate.

> *Convent and Novitiate,* De Sales Heights Convent of the Visitation, Murdock Avenue, Parkersburg, West Virginia. (Diocese of Wheeling.)

WILMINGTON, DELAWARE†

1868

Upon the invitation of the Right Rev. Mathias Loras, D.D., Bishop of Dubuque, Mother M. Mechtilde Pernaud, and some companion sisters from the Visitation Convent in Monthul, France, came to America in 1853 and established their Visitation community at Keokuk, Iowa. After some years of brave struggles and many handicaps, the community realized that the spiritual needs of a cloistered sisterhood could no longer be attended to in a town from which priestly assistance had to be withdrawn to supply other centers that were extending more rapidly.

Upon the erection of the diocese of Wilmington, in 1868, with the Right Rev. Thomas A. Becker as its first bishop, the community transferred to Delaware, and temporarily opened a small academy in the episcopal city, thus seconding the efforts of the bishop for the removal of prejudice and for the education of the laity.

---

*From data supplied by the Visitation Sisters, De Sales Heights, Parkersburg, W. Va.

†From data and material supplied by the Visitation Nuns, Visitation Monastery, Wilmington, Del.

In 1892, under the auspices of the Right Rev. A. A. Curtis, D.D., successor of Bishop Becker, the generosity of Miss Mary L. Abell— later known in the Order as Sister M. Joseph—enabled the sisters to build their present beautiful monastery in Wilmington, and embrace the original design of the holy founders, St. Francis de Sales and St. Jane Frances de Chantal, "to give God souls of prayer, entirely secluded from the world."

MONASTERY OF THE VISITATION, WILMINGTON, DELAWARE

The academy was closed in 1893, and the sisters, continuing the catechetical instruction of converts, and others needing special direc' tion, resumed the primitive observance of the rule, under the guidance of Mother M. Alexandrine de Butler, professed at the first monastery of the Order at Annecy, France, who became Superioress of the monastery in Wilmington, and remained there until her death, twenty-one years later.

Monastery and Novitiate, Visitation Monastery, 2002 Bayard Avenue, Wilmington, Delaware. (Diocese of Wilmington.)

DUBUQUE, IOWA*

1871

In August of 1871, in response to a request made in 1869, by the Most Rev. John Hennessy, D.D., then bishop of Dubuque, Mother Mary Agatha Russel, Superior of the Monastery of the Visitation

*From data and material supplied by the Visitation Sisters, De Sales Heights Visitation Academy, Dubuque, Iowa.

in St. Louis, sent a community of six Visitation Sisters to Dubuque, Iowa, where Bishop Hennessy was especially desirous of having a Visitation foundation and educational institution for girls.

On October 26th of the same year the new community, under the superiorship of Mother Mary Genevieve King, was installed in the convent and school prepared for it on Third Street, in the episcopal city.

For seven years the Visitation Sisters continued their school activities at this location, when the increasing number of pupils and the growth of the community necessitated a change to a locality better suited to the required expansion.

In the sixth and last year of her office as Superior, Mother Mary Juliana Anderson—successor of Mother Mary Genevieve—concluded the arrangements by which the community acquired possession of one of the finest sites in the city of Dubuque, and the property popularly known as "The General Jones' Old Home" on Julien Avenue and Alta Vista Street, became the Visitation Convent, De Sales Heights.

The Academy of the Visitation of Dubuque, connected with De Sales Heights Convent—where Mother Mary Catharine Gough has been Superior since 1924—was among the first of the Catholic educational institutions to be admitted into the North Central Association, and in its curriculum fully conforms to the requirements of the state of Iowa.

Other Visitation Sisters who have served as Superiors of this community, in what is now the archdiocese of Dubuque, have been Mothers Mary Xavier Conlin, Mary Stanislaus Fleming, Mary Aloysia Faherty, Mary Alphonsa Montague, Mary Bernardina McQuillan, Mary Antonia Ring and Mary Louise Genevieve O'Mara.

Convent and Novitiate, Visitation Convent, De Sales Heights, Dubuque, Iowa. (Archdiocese of Dubuque.)

GEORGETOWN, KENTUCKY*
1875

The Sisters of the Visitation now established at Cardome Academy in Georgetown, Kentucky, were founded as a community in the year 1875, at "Mt. Admirabilis," White Sulphur, Kentucky, by sisters from the Visitation foundation which had been made at Maysville, Kentucky in 1864, and later removed to Rock Island, Illinois.

*From data and material supplied by the Visitation Nuns, Cardome Academy, Georgetown, Ky.

The inevitable evolutions of time and circumstances decided the community at Mt. Admirabilis to transfer its establishment to a more central location. Consequently, under the auspices of the Right Rev. Camillus P. Maes, D.D., Bishop of Covington, the estate of Cardome was chosen and purchased by the community, as best meeting the indispensable requirements of space, good location and facility of access.

CARDOME VISITATION CONVENT, GEORGETOWN, KENTUCKY

This estate, on the Dixie Highway, now the site of the only Visitation foundation in Kentucky, has for more than a century held a distinctive place in the history of the state, and its traditions are closely associated with many of the most stirring episodes of the Revolution and the Civil War.

The house was built in 1821 by an officer of the war of 1812, who called it Acacia Grove. Later it became the property of a governor of the state, who changed its name to Cardome—*Cara Domus*, and by that apt and endearing title it has since been known, and remains, now, as Cardome Academy, a day and boarding school for girls.

More than once Lafayette, Webster, Clay, and other illustrious visitors honored the halls of Cardome, and to those fugitives whose homes and possessions had been engulfed in the upheaval and devastation of the south, it was an unfailing and generous refuge.

To the original mansion, the Visitation Nuns, on their removal to it in 1896, added spacious classrooms, study halls and dormitories. A few years later, a new convent building of imposing and consistent proportions was erected on the crest of an eminence overlooking an extensive panoramic view of the country, with picturesque Georgetown in the valley, about a mile distant, and the fertilizing waters of the Elkhorn encircling the grounds.

Convent and Novitiate, Visitation Convent, Cardome, Georgetown, Kentucky. (Diocese of Covington.)

TACOMA, WASHINGTON*

1891

The Visitation foundation in Tacoma, Washington, known as Visitation Villa, was established in the year 1891, with the transfer to that city of a community of Visitandines from Paris, Kentucky. The Paris foundation had been made in 1879 by sisters from the original Kentucky foundation in Maysville.

Prior to this change for the Kentucky community—negotiations for which had been occasioned, in Tacoma, by a resident there, the brother of Sister Mary Camillus Haniger of the Visitation community in Paris—the Rev. Peter Hylebos, with episcopal permission, acted on the brotherly suggestion, and appealed to the Right Rev. Camillus P. Maes, D.D., Bishop of Covington, asking for the Paris sisters, who were under his jurisdiction, for educational work in Tacoma.

Bishop Maes, remembering college days at Louvain with his friend, Father Hylebos, though reluctant to send the sisters where missionary pioneering conditions did not permit the spiritual benefit of frequentation of the sacraments and attendance at mass, gave his consent, but only after a promise from "Peter" that they should have at least Sunday mass.

On September 4, 1891, after an eventful and interesting transcontinental journey, the sisters arrived in Tacoma. Under Mother Mary Gonzaga Carreher as Superior, community life and school work was then begun in buildings vacated by Franciscan Sisters. In August,

*From data and material supplied by the Visitation Nuns, Visitation Convent and Academy, Visitation Villa, South Tacoma, Wash.

1923, the convent and school were transferred to South Tacoma, to the present desirable location—a villa, with more than two hundred acres of wooded land, offering every opportunity for expansion and advancement—which was purchased by the community.

The community, numbering approximately thirty sisters, with Mother Mary Clare Miller as Superior, according to the Rules of the Sisters of the Visitation of Holy Mary, is under the immediate jurisdiction of the ordinary of the diocese, the Right Rev. Edward J. O'Dea, D.D., Bishop of Seattle.

Convent and Novitiate, Visitation Convent, Visitation Villa, South Tacoma, Washington. (Diocese of Seattle.)

ROCK ISLAND, ILLINOIS*
1899

In August of the year 1899, Sisters of the Visitation of Holy Mary removed from the original foundation in Kentucky, which had been made at Maysville in 1865, to Rock Island, Illinois, in the diocese of Peoria, where the community—of which Mother Francis Borgia Nolan was Superior—was received by the Most Rev. John Lancaster Spalding, D.D., then bishop of that see.

Before many months had passed, it became evident that plans would have to be made for more spacious accommodations than those afforded by the Reynolds homestead, in which the Visitandines had opened a private school, and in 1900 Mother Francis Borgia and her co-laborers purchased the site now known as Villa de Chantal.

SISTER BENIGNA CONSOLATA
(1885-1916)
Visitation Nun of Como, Italy
Died a victim for peace

In Rock Island, on what is historically known as Ball's Bluff, looking down on the majestic Mississippi, and in view of its bridges, and the spires and domes of the city, and Davenport, across the river, the Sisters of the Visitation have built up a "home school for

*From data and material supplied by the Sisters of the Visitation, Villa de Chantal Academy, Rock Island, Ill.

girls" which ranks among the foremost Catholic academic institutions in the country.

In 1905, the first of many new building additions was begun at Villa de Chantal, to provide the rooms needed to relieve the crowded classroom conditions. Accredited by the Catholic University of America and the University of Illinois, and affiliated with the North Central Association, the study courses at the academy are kept conformable to college entrance requirements.

One of the outstanding achievements of the Visitandines at Villa de Chantal is the organization and development of an active alumnæ association, which was one of the first to espouse the cause of the formation of the International Federation of Catholic Alumnæ, and was represented at the organization convention in New York City in 1914.

The community of nearly fifty sisters is under the superiorship of Mother Mary Dolores Littig, and subject to the ecclesiastical jurisdiction of the ordinary of the diocese.

Convent and Novitiate, Visitation Convent, Villa de Chantal, 2000 Sixteenth Avenue, Rock Island, Illinois. (Diocese of Peoria.)

WYTHEVILLE, VIRGINIA*
1902

In the year 1867, complying with the desire of the Right Rev. Richard V. Whelan, D.D., the zealous and indefatigable bishop of the diocese of Wheeling, a community of Visitation Sisters, with Mother Borgia Tubman as Superior, was sent from the Visitation Convent of Mt. de Chantal, in Wheeling, to establish a foundation at Abingdon, Virginia, for the educational benefit of the daughters of the war-impoverished south.

In 1902, the sisters removed to Wytheville, Virginia, continuing in the diocese of Wheeling, then under the episcopate of the Right Rev. Patrick J. Donahue, D.D. The Academy of Villa Maria, chartered in 1877, was rechartered and established in the modern and well-equipped new building erected.

In 1920 the convent and this academy were totally destroyed by fire, and the present adequate institution, now under the superiorship of Mother M. Agnes Broughton, was at once planned, and its erection completed by 1922. As Villa Maria Academy is the only Catholic boarding school in its section of Virginia, the influence and

*From data and material supplied by the Visitation Sisters, Villa Maria Visitation Convent, Wytheville, Va.

7

consequences of the Catholic training imparted by the Visitation Sisters are widespread and beneficial.

The "Mountain City" in which Villa Maria Visitation Convent and Academy are located, two thousand three hundred feet above sea

Villa Maria Visitation Convent, Wytheville, Virginia

level, bounded as it is by encircling mountains, fully merits its epithet, the "Switzerland of America."

> *Convent and Novitiate,* Villa Maria Visitation Convent, Wytheville, Virginia. (Diocese of Wheeling.)

SPRINGFIELD, MISSOURI*

1906

That the southern part of Missouri might have a foundation of the Visitation Sisters, who would open a needed day school in Springfield, the Right Rev. John J. Hogan, D.D., first bishop of Kansas City, which includes in its territory that section of Missouri, invited the Visitandines of a foundation which had been established in St. Louis in 1887, from the original foundation in that city, to transfer to his diocese.

In 1906, under the superiority of Mother Jane Francis Fletcher, the transfer was made, and soon after their arrival in Springfield,

*From data supplied by the Sisters of the Visitation, St. de Chantal Academy of the Visitation, Elfindale, Springfield, Mo.

the academy known as St. de Chantal Academy of the Visitation, Elfindale, was opened by the sisters.

Convent and Novitiate, St. de Chantal Academy of the Visitation, Elfindale, Springfield, Missouri. (Diocese of Kansas City.)

PHILADELPHIA, PENNSYLVANIA*

1926

Philadelphia, the "city of brotherly love," through His Eminence, Dennis Cardinal Dougherty, proved worthy of that designation in October of 1926, when, with their courageous leader and Superior, Mother Margaret Mary Semple, forty Visitation Nuns, driven from their convent in Mexico, were received into the archdiocese of Philadelphia and cordially welcomed to the archiepiscopal city.

Nearly thirty years before the year of their exile, the Visitation foundation known as *La Visitation de Coyoacan, destrito Federal, Mexico,* had been made by a community of sisters from the Visitation Convent of Mobile, Alabama, at the request of three devout and wealthy persons, members of the Escudero family, distinguished at the court of Maximilian and Carlotta. The original foundress and co-foundress of the community, who in turn had preceded Mother Margaret Semple as Superior, were Mother Mary Stanislaus Campbell and Mother Mary Philomena Connelly, of the Visitandines in Mobile.

Not far distant from the home of Hernando Cortez, the conqueror, is the Coyoacan home from which the community has been expelled. There the sisters were living as in a free country, faithfully observing the Visitandine Rule, and moulding the characters of hundreds of the most prominent young women and girls in Mexico, who today, as "Visitation girls," are shedding lustre on their name, and on the spirit of St. Francis de Sales and St. Jane de Chantal.

Under the superiorship of Mother Louise Mitjans, this most recent of Visitation foundations established in the United States is temporarily located in three small houses—the property of the archdiocese. However, the community, here silently laboring over canvas and brush, or plying the needle in work far-famed for its exquisiteness, while praying for sorrowing Mexico, anticipates a home of its own, commensurate with the successful civil and ecclesiastical institutions of the city—a Visitation Villa of Christ the King, permanently established in the city of Philadelphia.

Convent, 225-227-229 North Camac Street, Philadelphia, Pennsylvania. (Archdiocese of Philadelphia.)

*From data and material supplied by the Visitation Nuns, Philadelphia, Pa.

CHRONOLOGICAL TABLE

Visitation foundations in the United States, subsequent to the canonical establishment of the Order at Georgetown Convent, founded in 1799:

1833—Mobile, Alabama.
1833—Kaskaskia, Illinois. (Transferred to St. Louis, Mo., in 1846.)
1837—Baltimore, Maryland.
1844—St. Louis, Missouri.
1846—Frederick, Maryland.
1848—Wheeling, West Virginia.
1850—Washington, District of Columbia. (Transferred to Bethesda, Md.)
1852—Catonsville, Maryland.
1852—Keokuk, Iowa. (Transferred to Wilmington, Del., in 1868.)*
1855—Brooklyn, New York.
1864—Parkersburg, West Virginia.
1864—Long Island, New York. (Transferred to Riverdale-on-Hudson, New York City.)*

1865—Maysville, Kentucky. (Transferred to Rock Island, Ill., in 1899.)
1866—Richmond, Virginia.
1867—Abingdon, Virginia. (Transferred to Wytheville, Va., in 1902.)
1871—Dubuque, Iowa.
1873—St. Paul, Minnesota.
1875—White Sulphur, Kentucky. (Transferred to Georgetown, Ky., in 1906.)
1879—Paris, Kentucky. (Transferred to Tacoma, Wash., in 1891.)
1887—St. Louis, Missouri. (Transferred to Springfield, Mo., in 1906.)
1915—Toledo, Ohio.*
1926—Philadelphia, Pennsylvania.

SUMMARY

Sisters of the Visitation of Holy Mary (Visitation Nuns).
Founded in France in 1610.
Papal Approbation of Rules, June 27, 1626, by Pope Urban VIII.
Established in the United States in 1816.
Habit: The habit is black, with a black veil, black forehead band and white guimpe.
Approximate number in communities in United States, 850.
Engaged in educational work and the contemplative life in convents and monasteries, each with its own novitiate, in the archdioceses of Baltimore, Dubuque, New York, Philadelphia, St. Louis and St. Paul, and in the dioceses of Brooklyn, Covington, Kansas City, Mobile, Peoria, Richmond, Seattle, Toledo, Wheeling and Wilmington.

*Purely contemplative.

SISTERS OF CHARITY*

1809

THE history of the founding in the United States of the Sisters of Charity of St. Vincent de Paul is the history of one whose name is known and reverenced in north, south, east and west, one whose virtues and sanctity have commended her for the altars of the Church—Mother Seton.

Elizabeth Seton was born in New York City, on August 28, 1774. Her parents were Richard Bayley, of a prominent Protestant family, who by his genius and industry had risen to a high rank in the medical profession in New York City, and Catherine Charlton, daughter of a distinguished Episcopalian clergyman. Mrs. Bayley dying when Elizabeth was but three years of age, the child's education devolved upon her father, who neglected nothing that could enhance the attainments of his daughter, who early gave promise of rare qualities, both intellectual and moral.

At the age of twenty, Elizabeth was married in Trinity Church, in New York, to Mr. William Magee Seton, a prominent and prosperous merchant of noted Scotch lineage.

In 1803, the rapid decline of Mr. Seton's health necessitated a climatic change, and in October a voyage to Italy was undertaken by the invalid, accompanied by his wife and Anna, their eldest daughter, while the four younger children were confided to the care of Mr. Seton's relatives. In former years Mr. Seton had had business relations with the Messrs. Filicchi, of Leghorn, and he looked forward to a renewal of this old friendship while enjoying the genial clime of Italy. However, the tedious voyage proved too much for his fast-failing strength, and he died at Pisa, December 27, 1803.

The Filicchi family received the widow and her child with every mark of sincere sympathy and generosity. As a guest in their home at Leghorn, before she returned to the United States, Mrs. Seton, bearing her affliction in a truly Christian spirit, was deeply impressed by the beauty of the Catholic religion as exemplified by her hosts, and before she left for America she visited many Catholic churches and sacred shrines of Europe.

*From data and material supplied by the Daughters of Charity, St. Joseph's College, Emmitsburg, Md., and from *Elizabeth Seton*, by Agnes Sadlier; *Life of Mrs. Eliza A. Seton*, by Rev. Charles I. White, D.D.; *Life of the Ven. Louise de Marillac*, by Alice Lady Lovat; (Longmans, Green and Co., N. Y.) *Life and Times of Archbishop Carroll* and *The History of the Catholic Church in the United States*, by John Gilmary Shea.

Reunited to her children in New York, and finally having tri-
umphed in the severe ordeal through which she passed in search of
the true religion, Mrs. Seton was received into the Catholic Church

MOTHER ELIZABETH SETON (1774-1821)
Foundress of the Sisters of Charity

on March 14, 1805, though knowing that by that step she was for-
feiting for herself and her children, not only the friendship of relatives, but financial maintenance needed owing to the fact that Mr.
Seton's business affairs had developed most discouragingly.

Prayerfully considering her future, while bravely attempting a
private school as a means of support, she had the happiness of seeing

her children embrace the true faith. At this time, through Mr. Filicchi, a correspondence was opened with the Most Rev. John Carroll, D.D., Archbishop of Baltimore, and with the Rev. John Cheverus, soon afterward consecrated bishop of Boston.

That the earnest woman might no longer be subjected to the trials she suffered following her change of faith, it was suggested, for her spiritual and material well-being, that she remove to Baltimore, where in that city—the cradle of Catholicism in the United States—she could open a school and at the same time be near her sons who should attend St. Mary's Seminary, as was generously planned in their interest by the Rev. William Dubourg, its president, who had become deeply interested in Mrs. Seton.

Some time passed before this suggestion could be acted upon, but on June 9, 1808, Mrs. Seton and her children left New York for Baltimore, where they arrived seven days later, having made the voyage on a sailing packet. Father Dubourg's mother and sister in Baltimore united with him in welcoming Mrs. Seton to that city, and assisted her in the establishment of her home in a house on Paca Street, rented for her by Father Dubourg. In the fall she opened here a boarding school for young girls, and easily obtained all the pupils that the small house could accommodate.

Impelled since the first dawn of faith in her soul, to consecrate herself to a religious life, Mrs. Seton, adjusting herself according to rule in her new and peaceful environment, but awaited the permission of her spiritual director for a definite step toward that end.

Early in December there was directed to assist her in her school work, Cecilia O'Conway of Philadelphia, who, desirous of embracing the religious life, had learned of the devout woman similarly inclined. Other like aspirants were soon received at the little boarding school on Paca Street, and Archbishop Carroll consented that, as far as was then possible, a religious community should be formed. Mrs. Seton, from that time known as Mother Seton, was permitted to make simple vows, binding but for a year, and Father Dubourg was appointed the ecclesiastical superior of the community, which was as yet without a name or a definite form. On June 1, 1809, a uniform dress was adopted for the community, and was much the same as that worn by Mother Seton since the death of her husband.

Just prior to this time, Mr. Samuel Cooper, a devout convert studying at the seminary, expressed a desire to found a school for the instruction of poor children, with Mrs. Seton—whose holiness and earnestness was known to him—in charge of it. With this in view, property was bought in the vicinity of Emmitsburg, a village about forty miles northwest of Baltimore.

On July 30, 1809, Mother Seton and her companions removed to the small stone house, included with the purchase by Mr. Cooper, which then became the home of the "sisters from Baltimore," a community composed of Sisters Elizabeth Seton, Cecilia O'Conway, Maria Murphy, Maria Burke, Suzanne Clossy, Mary Anne Butler, Rose White, Catharine Mullen and Helen and Sara Thompson.

In the first quarter of the 17th century, there had been instituted at Châtillon, and various provincial towns of France, the Association of the Ladies of Charity. Founded by the humane St. Vincent de Paul, seventeen eventful years after his ordination to the priesthood, this Association was composed of charitable women who assisted their poorer neighbors, spiritually as well as corporally, especially in times of sickness. About the same time there was referred to his spiritual direction in Paris, Mademoiselle Le Gras, who in order to profit more fully by the guidance of *le bon Monsieur Vincent* gave up her residence in the then fashionable Marais for the Rue Saint Victor, which was in his parish.

Mademoiselle Le Gras, the widow of Antoine Le Gras, and the daughter of the de Marillacs—a family that for many years had counted distinguished members in the military and civil service of France—was born in Paris, August 12, 1591, and received a superior education under the direction of her father, who died when she was about sixteen years of age.

Urged by an attraction to the religious life, Louise de Marillac desired admittance to a cloister, but submitting her will to the wishes of her paternal uncle, she was married to Antoine Le Gras, whose family was intimately connected with the family of the de Marillacs.

Mademoiselle Le Gras, as she was then called, according to the custom of the times, divided her thoughts between the child which blessed their union, and the poor, to whom she was one day to become such a universal mother. Unusual for one in her position, Mademoiselle Le Gras defied human respect and the conventions of the day, and visited and ministered to the sick poor, her devotion and activity in their service growing in proportion to the knowledge she gained by experience, of their needs and sufferings. Not long after her marriage, and during a severe illness, she was visited by St. Francis de Sales, who was passing through Paris and who had heard of her great charity.

Upon the death of her husband, in her thirty-fourth year, Louise, resuming her maiden name, as was commonly done in France, devoted herself to prayer, the duties of her state in life, the service of the poor, and the cultivation of such talents as she possessed, for the glory of God and the good of her neighbor.

After her son entered college in 1628, Louise had more time to give to good works, under the direction of St. Vincent de Paul, thus co-operating with him in his charitable enterprises, and with the Association of the Ladies of Charity.

May 6, 1629, marked the beginning of the life work of Louise de Marillac, who was then commissioned by St. Vincent to examine the organization of the newly founded *Charités*, as he styled the various groups of the Association, and report their progress to him. Soon after her return to Paris she was elected superior, or president, of the Association in her own parish.

Continuing, from time to time, the visitation of the different Associations, and seeing that the proper persons were in office, and that the members were "persons of known virtue and piety, and

BLESSED LOUISE DE MARILLAC
(1591-1660)
Foundress of the Company of the Daughters of Charity

whose perseverance could be trusted," Louise added to her activities, when visiting the country and village districts, by catechizing the children and preparing them for the sacraments, and she never left a district without finding some one to take her place, or training a member of the *Charité* to undertake this duty.

In 1631, the plague broke out in France with sudden violence, and Louise, returning from a visit to the *Charité* at Beauvais, found Paris panic-stricken. Realizing the immediate need of abundant help in the service of the victims of the dread disease, she at once began the foundation of new *Charités,* whose members heroically labored among the afflicted.

Some time after this it was found expedient to form the single *Charités,* now so prosperously established, into a working organization of more definite form. To train the members to be efficient nurses, and at the same time to provide for exercises of piety, Monsieur Vincent approved of Louise's receiving into her home the young women who desired to assist the Ladies of Charity in their work, and he appointed her Superior of the Community which she founded on November 29, 1633.

On March 25, 1634, Mlle. Louise de Marillac was permitted to bind herself, by an irrevocable vow, to her work. On July 31, 1634, St. Vincent approved in writing the rule drawn up by Mademoiselle de Marillac, which served as a guide for herself and her companions until 1645, when St. Vincent drew up a statement of the rules and objects of the Institute.

From that time the Community increased rapidly, and multiplied its work, which included the care of the sick in hospitals, as well as in homes, the care of foundlings and the orphaned, and the conducting of schools for girls. Under the direction of the holy foundress, the education of poor children also became one of the principal duties of the Daughters of Charity, who, through a privilege granted Mademoiselle de Marillac by the Holy See, are under the ecclesiastical superiorship of the successor of St. Vincent, the Superior General of the Congregation of the Mission—founded by St. Vincent in 1625—whose members are known as Lazarists or Vincentians.

Contemplating a union with this French Institute, Mother Seton, with her community at Emmitsburg, petitioned that representatives of it be sent to establish the community there in uniformity with the rules and observances of this Company, founded by St. Vincent de Paul and Bd. Louise de Marillac nearly two centuries before.

To accomplish this, three Daughters of Charity were sent from Paris, and had reached Bordeaux on their journey when Napoleon forbade them to leave the empire. The Right Rev. Benedict Flaget, D.D., newly appointed bishop of Bardstown, then in Paris— before establishing his episcopal see in Kentucky—had been arranging for the voyage of the little band of sisters, and upon the frustration of these plans a copy of the Rules of the Institute was confided to his care, for conveyance to Emmitsburg.

After some modification for local use, these Rules of St. Vincent de Paul, thus obtained, were adopted in 1812 by Mother Seton and her twenty companions at Emmitsburg, who remained organized as a separate body of Sisters of Charity until 1850, when the long desired affiliation with the French Community took place. At this time the sisters at Emmitsburg exchanged the black cap of their habit for the cornette, worn without a veil, adopted by Mademoiselle de Marillac for the *Filles de la Charité* in 1639.

St. Joseph's, Emmitsburg, Maryland

Like St. Vincent, Mother Seton wished the Sisters of Charity "to honor Our Lord Jesus Christ as the source and model of all charity, by rendering to Him every temporal and spiritual service in their power, in the person of the poor, the sick, prisoners, the insane and others in distress," and in 1814, when a request came to her asking that Sisters of Charity of Emmitsburg be sent to Philadelphia to take charge of an orphanage, she readily complied, by choosing three sisters to go there with Sister Rose White, who was appointed Sister-Servant, the rule prescribing this appellation for the one in charge of a mission from the Motherhouse.

The success of the Philadelphia institution becoming known in New York City, the Right Rev. John Connolly, O.P., D.D., second bishop of New York, wrote Mother Seton in 1817 urging that her community take charge of the orphan asylum then being established in New York. With great care Mother Seton and her Council chose the sisters of the community who were to go on this mission to her native city, where she still had many relatives, and where, ten years before, she had suffered so intensely from the intolerance and harsh-ness not only of relatives but of friends.

Sister Rose White, of the Philadelphia mission, chosen to take charge of that in New York, with Sister Cecilia O'Conway and Sister Felicité Brady from the Motherhouse, chosen to assist her, arrived in New York on June 28, 1817, and at once assumed the care of the orphanage, making their first home in a small wooden building on Prince Street near the first site of New York's Cathedral.

Giving great joy to the ardent foundress-Superior, now suffering from what proved a mortal malady, was the erection, in 1820, of a free school for the poor children in the neighborhood of the convent at Emmitsburg. Such a school had been in operation at St. Joseph's—as the Emmitsburg convent was known—from the first, but the very limited accommodations which the available house afforded kept the community from fully carrying on the work. These children were the objects of Mother Seton's deepest interest and care, and she arranged that in addition to their instruction, they would receive every day a substantial meal.

On Thursday, January 4, 1821, occurred the saintly death of this great foundress, who had been encouraged in her work by such distinguished ecclesiastics of the times as Archbishop Carroll, and—before their consecration to the episcopacy—Bishops Cheverus, Dubourg, Dubois and Bruté.

Two years later, and under the superiorship of Mother Rose White, who had been recalled from New York to succeed Mother Seton, the Sisters of Charity of Emmitsburg entered upon another phase of their work by taking charge of the Baltimore Infirmary. Since then the demand for their ministrations has increased far beyond the ordinary care of the sick in hospitals, infirmaries and all modern institutions for the purpose, and through free clinics and dispensaries, and they now include in the scope of their work, which has been extended throughout the land, the care of the insane and of lepers.

The last-named work was inaugurated when in 1896 a contract was entered into by Mother Mariana, then Visitatrix of the Com-munity, and the State Board of Control of the Leper Home of Louisiana. According to this contract, the Sisters of Charity—

whose work was well known to the president of the Board, who had witnessed it in Charity Hospital in New Orleans—were given full charge of the Home. The contract further agreed to pay "the sum of one hundred dollars per annum to each Sister of Charity engaged in the work, for clothing or other incidental expenses."* In 1921, the Federal Government took over this Leper Home at Carville, Louisiana, and established it as the National Leprosarium of the United States, with the Sisters of Charity remaining in charge of it.

MARILLAC SEMINARY, NORMANDY, MISSOURI

Scarcely had the Community become well established in its work of caring for the sick in the Baltimore institution, and in the St. Louis Mullanphy Hospital, opened in St. Louis, Missouri, in 1828, when its members were called upon to nurse the plague-stricken in New York, Baltimore and Philadelphia during the Asiatic cholera epidemic of 1832, many of the sisters at this time falling martyrs to their charity.

The year 1829 marked further extension of the work of the sisters at Emmitsburg, when, in response to an appeal from the Right Rev. Edward Fenwick, O.P., D.D., first bishop of Cincinnati, a band of sisters was sent to that city, where they at once opened a school, in addition to taking charge of an orphan asylum. Augmenting the initial community, and for the expansion of its activities in Cincinnati, additional sisters were sent there from Emmitsburg in 1841 and 1845.

*From *The Sisters of Charity and Our Lepers*, by Elizabeth R. Shirley (National Catholic Welfare Conference Bulletin).

At the Motherhouse during these years of growth and extension of the work of the Community to academies, asylums and hospitals in many of the most important cities of the United States, necessary buildings were erected, and the development of the splendid institution which today constitutes St. Joseph's at Emmitsburg is indicative of the far-seeing plans of the Community, which, in seeking the best educational advantages for its members and its students, does so remembering the assiduousness of its venerated foundress in her efforts in behalf of the Christian education of youth, and especially of young girls.

Little more than two decades of years had passed, after the death of Mother Seton, when renewed negotiations toward affiliation, finally effected in 1850, with the French Institute of the Daughters of Charity began to take definite shape at Emmitsburg.

In view of this amalgamation, and knowing that the Rule of the French Institute would necessitate the relinquishment of their work in orphan asylums for boys, the Sisters of Charity in New York, desiring to continue as a Community without this distant affiliation, were erected into a separate body and established their Motherhouse in New York City.

Similarly, in 1852, the Sisters of Charity in Cincinnati concluded their consultations on the same subject, and were likewise recognized as a separate Community, with their Motherhouse in Cincinnati.

Following the affiliation with the French Community, St. Joseph's at Emmitsburg became the site of the United States Province of the Daughters of Charity, subject to the Motherhouse at 140 Rue du Bac, Paris, in the chapel of which is the shrine of the Virgin of the Miraculous Medal, commemorating the vision of it there in 1830. Upon the later establishment, in 1910, of a novitiate at St. Louis, St. Joseph's Convent at Emmitsburg became the Motherhouse and novitiate of the Eastern Province, and Marillac Seminary, Normandy, Missouri, the Motherhouse and novitiate of the Western Province. Each province has its own Visitatrix—at present Sister Paula Dunn in the Eastern Province, and Sister Eugenia Fealy in the Western Province—while the Congregation of the Daughters of Charity is subject to the Superior General of the Lazarists.

In the years which have followed their adoption of the historic cornette and garb planned by St. Vincent de Paul and Bd. Louise de Marillac, the Daughters of Charity in the United States have participated in every emergency in the country. Through cholera, yellow fever, small-pox and influenza epidemics the "Cornette Sister of Charity" assisted the afflicted, giving spiritual as well as corporal courage. On the battlefields and in hospitals throughout the Civil, Spanish-American and World Wars, hundreds of sisters of the Community ministered to the wounded and the sick, as the records of the country show.

Just as the Community has kept apace with the needs of the day, in its hospitals, sanitariums, orphanages, infant asylums, day nurseries, and industrial and settlement schools, throughout the country—also extending its hospital work from the United States into China—the curriculum of its many educational establishments has been maintained to conform to the highest standards.

St. Joseph's, at Emmitsburg Motherhouse, chartered as an academic institution in 1816, was, by an amended act of the Maryland legislature, in 1902 empowered to conduct courses of higher education for women, and to confer degrees, and St. Joseph's College, situated in a valley of the Blue Ridge Mountains, in the heart of historic Frederick County, Maryland, stands today for those same noble ideals which the saintly Mother Seton inculcated upon the establishment of St. Joseph's more than a hundred years ago.

A "CORNETTE SISTER OF CHARITY"

SUMMARY

Company of Daughters of Charity (Sisters of Charity of St. Vincent de Paul). Founded in France in 1633.

Papal Approbation of Rules, July 8, 1668, by Pope Clement IX.

Habit: The habit is dark blue, with a large white collar. A white cornette is worn without a veil over a closely fitting white cap.

Approximate number in Community in United States, 2,000.

Active in educational, hospital, charitable and social service work, *Eastern Province* in the archdioceses of Baltimore, Boston and Philadelphia, and in the dioceses of Albany, Buffalo, Detroit, Grand Rapids, Hartford, Mobile, Portland, Raleigh, Richmond, Rochester, St. Augustine, Syracuse and Wilmington; *Central house and Novitiate,* St. Joseph's, Emmitsburg, Maryland (Archdiocese of Baltimore). *Western Province,* in the archdioceses of Chicago, Milwaukee, New Orleans, St. Louis and San Francisco, and in the dioceses of Dallas, Davenport, El Paso, Galveston, Indianapolis, Kansas City, Los Angeles and San Diego, Mobile, Monterey-Fresno, Nashville, Natchez, Peoria, St. Joseph, Salt Lake and Springfield in Illinois; *Central House and Novitiate,* Marillac Seminary, Normandy, Missouri (Archdiocese of St. Louis).

NEW YORK CITY*

1817

Hardly could Elizabeth Seton have foreseen, on the eve of her departure for Baltimore from New York, in 1808, that in less than ten years—in that city which trials and tribulations had almost compelled her to leave—she should direct the establishment of a small community of her sisters in religion, thereby beginning in New York what has proved a lasting memorial of her work, and a per-petuation, in the quiet garb of the Sisters of Charity of Mount St. Vincent, of her widow's costume, which, with but slight modification, was adopted for the uniform dress of the community of earnest women who early gathered with her in Baltimore, forming, in 1809, the nucleus of the Sisters of Charity in the United States.

Though Mother Seton had rendered her personal service to others through her devotion to the education of youth—especially needed in that period when the school system in the country had scarcely reached even a formative stage—it was with a consciousness of joy that in 1814 she accepted for her sisters the care of an orphanage in Philadelphia, thus taking the first step in expanding the work of the Community.

The success of the Philadelphia institution becoming known in New York, the Right Rev. John Connolly, O.P., D.D., second bishop of New York, wrote to Mother Seton asking her for sisters to conduct the orphan asylum the Catholic people wished to establish there.

The consequent arrival in New York City, on June 28, 1817, of three Sisters of Charity from St. Joseph's Convent at Emmitsburg, Maryland, marks the permanent inauguration of the activities of religious communities of women in New York. Sister Rose White and her two companion sisters, Cecilia O'Conway and Felicité Brady, chosen for this mission, established their residence on Prince Street, and at once opened New York's first Catholic orphan asylum, which was located on Mott Street, near what was then the site of St. Pat-rick's Cathedral.

Upon the death of the venerated foundress, at St. Joseph's, Emmitsburg, on January 4, 1821, in the forty-seventh year of her age, Sister Rose White, who had wisely guided the foundation work

---

*From data and material supplied by the Sisters of Charity, Mount St. Vin-cent-on-Hudson, New York City, and from *Elizabeth Seton*, by Agnes Sadlier; *A Famous Convent School*, by Marion J. Brunowe (The Meany Company, N. Y.), and *The History of the Catholic Church in the United States*, by John Gilmary Shea.

of the Sisters of Charity in New York, as also in Philadelphia, was chosen to succeed to the office of Superior.

Though an ardent worker in the cause of education, and active as a teacher in the first classrooms at St. Joseph's, Mother Seton did not survive to see the Community of her founding inaugurate that work in her native city. Early in the administration of the Right Rev. John Dubois, D.D.—founder of Mt. St. Mary's College, at Emmitsburg, and early friend and advisor of Mother Seton—who succeeded to the see of New York in 1826, the sisters took charge of St. Peter's School and opened two academies in the city, which were the first of the many thereafter under the direction of the Community.

When renewed negotiations were entered into at the Motherhouse at Emmitsburg, toward affiliation of the Community with the Company of Daughters of Charity in Paris, the Right Rev. John Hughes, D.D., then bishop of New York, before his appointment as its first archbishop, suggested that the Sisters of Charity in New York remain there as a separate Community, without obligation to a distant Motherhouse and conformance

MOTHER ELIZABETH BOYLE

with rules which would require their relinquishment of the care of orphan asylums for boys, already a prospering work of the sisters in the diocese.

The conferences which followed this suggestion of Bishop Hughes resulted in a circular announcement made by the Very Rev. Louis R. Deluol, ecclesiastical superior of all the Community, to the effect that those Sisters of Charity in New York who wished to continue their work in the diocese would be dispensed from their vow of obedience to the Superiors at Emmitsburg, while those wishing to adhere to the government of the Maryland Motherhouse would be recalled to it.

Acting under this dispensation, thirty-five out of the forty-five Sisters of Charity laboring in New York, chose to remain there. In December, 1846, Sister Elizabeth Boyle, who had previously suc-

8

ceeded Sister Rose White as Superior of the sisters, under Emmitsburg authority, at the orphan asylum on Mott Street, became the first
Superior of the new Community, which, retaining the rules and
garb adopted by Mother Seton, was organized as the Sisters of
Charity of St. Vincent de Paul.

Under the guidance of Bishop Hughes, the Community chose a
suitable site, known since Revolutionary days as McGowan's Pass,
on an eminence at One Hundred and Ninth Street and Fifth Avenue,
on which a Motherhouse, in combination with an academy for the
higher education of girls, was erected, soon being known as Mount
St. Vincent. On May 2, 1847, Bishop Hughes celebrated mass in
the new institution, and on September 13th of the same year, the
Academy of Mount St. Vincent was opened, with an enrollment of
forty students.

Three years after the establishment of the Community in New
York, Mount St. Vincent, under the government of Mother Elizabeth, sent four sisters to found a mission in Halifax, Nova Scotia, this
being later erected into a separate Community.

Also in 1849 St. Vincent's Hospital was opened under the direction of the Assistant Superior, Mother Angela Hughes, a sister of
Bishop Hughes. Until this time New York had but two hospitals,
and St. Vincent's—the first in the city under the care of sisters—
could not meet all the demands made upon it for the accommodation
of the sick, though adjacent property was soon rented to provide
a bed capacity of thirty, in the institution which today—ranking
among the foremost hospitals in New York City—has a bed capacity
of more than three hundred and fifty.

In the summer of 1850, the diocese of New York was created
an archbishopric, and Bishop Hughes was made its first archbishop.
As shown in the archdiocese during his administration, by the
increased number of parochial schools and academies, not only under
the care of the Sisters of Charity, but conducted by additional religious
communities invited to New York through European Motherhouses,
this eminent prelate—one of the most conspicious figures in the
history of the country—stressed the necessity of religious education,
and in his interest in its cause urged the faithful everywhere to erect
and maintain schools for the religious education of their children.

Under such forceful leadership, the Sisters of Charity, rapidly
increasing in number, multiplied their schools in the archiepiscopal
city, and in Albany and Brooklyn, as well as New Jersey, where, in
Newark, was later established the foundation of Sisters of Charity
in New Jersey.

In the New York annals of the Sisters of Charity of St. Vincent de Paul, the closing day of the year 1856 marked the purchase by the Community of the Fonthill Estate, owned by Edwin Forrest, a noted tragedian. The acquisition of this property, which consisted of fifty-five acres on the banks of the Hudson, fifteen miles from New York City Hall, was necessitated when the city plans for the development of Central Park included the rocky height of Mount

MT. ST. VINCENT-ON-HUDSON, NEW YORK CITY

St. Vincent, where for ten years the Community had maintained its Motherhouse and conducted a prospering academy. Mother M. Angela Hughes, elected Superior of the Community in 1855, personally transacted this purchase from Mr. Forrest, and formal possession of the property was taken on February 2, 1857, by placing in the grounds a statue of the Immaculate Queen of Heaven.

Though New York City was not the scene of actual hostilities during the Civil War, which paralyzed the country, it had its war victims, and numbered also mob victims. During this period the Sisters of Charity in New York, under the superiorship of Mother M. Jerome Ely, received the sick and wounded in the hospital wards of St. Vincent's, and indefatigably served in the temporary hospital into which their former convent home was converted.

Scarcely had the Community been relieved of this work in the country's need, when it was confronted with the necessity of providing a home for deserted children, the number of whom presented a problem to the authorities of the city. The New York Foundling Hospital, opened by the Sisters of Charity in 1869, was their solution of the problem, and is a monument to the memory of Sister M. Irene, whose years of labor brought about in it such gratifying results.

SISTER M. IRENE

Specializing in Pediatrics, under a most efficient staff, the sisters now conduct, in connection with the nurses' training school at this hospital, an affiliated school for Pediatrics, and a course in Pediatric Nursing.

Dating its incorporation as an academic institution from the period of the closing of the Civil War, Mount St. Vincent Academy was in due time affiliated with the University of the State of New York, under the Regents. In 1910 the College of Mount St. Vincent-on-Hudson was established, and provides a wide course of collegiate and pedagogical studies in its curriculum. In the course of the years, numerous buildings for convent, academy and college have been erected on the spacious grounds of Mount St. Vincent, where the influence of Mother Seton, whose ideas and scholastic methods entitle her to a high place among the advocates and promoters of higher education for girls, has ever been apparent.

In the more than one hundred years of their activity, the Sisters of Charity in New York have met every progressive need of the times, as their many and varied institutions attest, and today form one of the largest communities of women in the great archdiocese—now under the archiepiscopal jurisdiction of His Eminence, Patrick Cardinal Hayes, the "cardinal of charities," honored and beloved throughout the land, whose keen interest in the development of religious orders of women in the country must prove a motivating influence in the lives of those religiously inclined, as they read his admonishing words: "These are Christ's little ones; their souls must be protected; suffer them not to be separated from Him."

While the Mount St. Vincent Sisters of Charity, who have had a mission in the Bahama Islands since 1889, have established and maintain branch houses in many cities, they are chiefly identified with New York City, and with their chain of houses throughout its vast expanse—from its southern end, where, amid the rush of commerce, they labor in St. Peter's School, to its northernmost limit, where their Motherhouse—Mount St. Vincent—lifts high above the waters of the Hudson the statue of the benign saint whose name it bears.

SUMMARY

Sisters of Charity of St. Vincent de Paul (Mt. St. Vincent, New York).
  The Black Cap Sisters of Charity.
Established in 1817.
Habit: The habit is black, with a black silk cap, and a cape reaching to the waist. The collar and undersleeves are of white linen. A rosary of large beads is worn hanging from the belt.
Approximate number in Community, 1,500.
Active in educational, hospital and charitable work in the archdiocese of New York and in the dioceses of Albany, Brooklyn and Harrisburg.
Motherhouse and Novitiate, Mount St. Vincent-on-Hudson, New York, New York. (Archdiocese of New York.)

CINCINNATI, OHIO*

1829

The opening of the second decade of years of the existence of the Sisters of Charity, founded by Mother Seton in 1809, was marked by the death of this beloved and distinguished woman, who ranks today among the world's greatest foundresses of religious orders.

The closing days of the same decade were signalized by the extension of the activities of her daughters, into Ohio's fertile field for religious workers, with the arrival in Cincinnati, on Thursday, October 27, 1829, of a group of Sisters of Charity from their Mother-house in Emmitsburg, Maryland.

Historically, therefore, ranking first among the religious communities participating in the development of the Church in the state, Mother Seton's community at once opened an orphanage, and took charge of the Cathedral school. This was in accordance with the plans of the Right Rev. Edward Fenwick, O.P., D.D., upon whose

*From data and material supplied by the Sisters of Charity of Cincinnati, Mt. St. Joseph, Mt. St. Joseph, Ohio, and from *Life of Mrs. Eliza A. Seton* by Rev. Charles I. White, D.D., and *The History of the Catholic Church in the United States,* by John Gilmary Shea.

initiative Sister Mary Augustine Count, second successor to Mother Seton, as Superior at Emmitsburg, had accepted the Ohio mission.

Four years later, the rapid increase in the number of both orphans and pupils necessitated removal to a larger house obtained for the purpose. This was located on Sixth Street, and belonged to the bishop, the Right Rev. John Baptist Purcell, D.D., later first arch-bishop of Cincinnati, who had succeeded to the see upon the death of Bishop Fenwick, whose unre-mitting devotion to the afflicted during the cholera epidemic which swept his diocese in 1832, cost him his life.

MOTHER REGINA MATTINGLY
Third Superior of the Sisters of Charity
of Cincinnati

A further increase in the number of children who, bereft of their parents during this rav-aging epidemic, became the care of the Sisters of Charity, occa-sioned a transfer to a still more commodious building, St. Peter's Academy and Orphan Asylum, on Third and Plum Streets.

To supply an adequate num-ber of sisters to meet the de-mands made upon them in Cincinnati, two additional colo-nies were sent from the Mother-house at Emmitsburg—one in 1841 and another in 1845. Among these sisters was Sister Margaret Cecelia George, who was destined to become a notable figure among the Sisters of Charity in Cincinnati, and who, entering the Community at Emmitsburg in 1812, had been one of Mother Seton's companions and co-laborers, having served in various official positions in the Community, and like Mother Seton presided in the classrooms of the academy opened at St. Joseph's, the Motherhouse in Emmitsburg.

Scarcely had Sister Margaret George adjusted herself as Superior at St. Peter's in Cincinnati, when the Community at Emmitsburg entered upon a decisive plan affecting all its members, many of whom were active on missions in distant cities. This was the affiliation of the Sisters of Charity in the United States with the Daughters of

Charity in France, established by St. Vincent de Paul and Louise de Marillac, whose rule, modified for use in this country, had been adopted by Mother Seton and her companions, January 12, 1812.

During the progress of negotiations toward this step, which was finally taken at Emmitsburg, the realization that the acceptance of the rule followed by the Daughters of Charity would affect the work in many institutions being conducted by the Emmitsburg sisters led to definite action on the part of the archbishop of New York, and later the archbishop of Cincinnati.

As a result, in these respective archdioceses, the Sisters of Charity so electing were dispensed from their vows to the superiors at Emmits-burg, to form separate Communities—each independent, and with its own Motherhouse and novitiate.

On March 25, 1852, the Sisters of Charity in Cincinnati, electing to continue under the rules and wearing the garb adopted by Mother Seton, made their vows to Archbishop Purcell as their ecclesiastical superior. Mother Margaret George served as first Superior of the Community, whose novitiate was then opened at St. Peter's Academy, temporarily the Motherhouse.

Toward the close of 1852, Archbishop Purcell bought the *Hotel des Invalides* at Franklin Street and Broadway, in the archiepiscopal city, and at once placed it under the care of the sisters, changing the name to St. John's Hotel for Invalids. The following September, the sisters, at Sixth and Park Streets, opened St. Mary's Academy, as a boarding and day school.

Almost simultaneously, Mount St. Vincent Academy was opened on Mount Harrison, since known as Price Hill. This academy served as the Motherhouse of the sisters until 1857, when the property was exchanged for *The Cedars,* the home of Judge Alderson. A new Motherhouse, Mount St. Vincent, Cedar Grove, was then erected on this site by the Community, which in 1854 had been incorporated according to the laws of Ohio under the title *The Sisters of Charity of Cincinnati.*

Shortly after the establishment of the Motherhouse at Cedar Grove, Mother Seton's nephew, the Right Rev. James Roosevelt Bayley, D.D., bishop of the newly erected see of Newark, asked the Sisters of Charity of Cincinnati to receive five postulants for their novitiate, preliminary to the founding of a Community of Sisters of Charity for New Jersey. In compliance with the bishop's request, the little band of postulants was welcomed at Mount St. Vincent. At the end of ten months they returned to Newark, Mother Margaret George, Superior of the Cincinnati Community, having deemed them sufficiently well-equipped to do so, by reason of their ardent spirit and their devotion to the work before them.

The opening of the Civil War in 1861 brought the Sisters of Charity from their convent home at Cedar Grove to its battlefields.

MT. ST. JOSEPH-ON-THE-OHIO, MT. ST. JOSEPH, OHIO

In Camp Dennison, in Cumberland, in Nashville and in Gallipolis— wherever they were needed, were these black cap Sisters of Charity.

Under the leadership of Sister Anthony O'Connell, Superior of the hospital in Cincinnati, the sisters there cared for the soldiers, for whom beds were crowded into every available space. With this dauntless woman they ventured, without pause, onto the very fields of battle and scenes of bloodshed, as they cared for the sick and ministered to the dying throughout the period of the war.

Known as the Angel of the Battlefield, Sister Anthony, who had gone from Springfield, Massachusetts, to the Emmitsburg novitiate in 1835, was then missioned to Cincinnati, where she lived until 1897— dying at the age of eighty-three, having been one of the most active pioneer hospital workers in the state. The largest hospital of the Sisters of Charity of Cincinnati, the Good Samaritan Hospital in Cincinnati—immediate successor of St. John's Hotel for Invalids— was the outcome of Sister Anthony's labors and the esteem of the citizens for her, as expressed by their generosity which made possible the substantial foundation of the splendid, modernly equipped institution, which, with a six-hundred bed capacity, and an ever renowned staff, is monumental of the work of Mother Seton's daughters in Cincinnati.

Civil War days had scarcely passed when the Sisters of Charity of Cincinnati responded to a call from New Mexico, made by the Right Rev. J. B. Lamy, Bishop of Santa Fé. On August 21, 1865, four Sisters of Charity left Cincinnati to cross the great American desert, and open a hospital and orphan asylum in far away Santa Fé.

Five years later, the Community had not only extended its activities in New Mexico, but in addition to numerous schools in Ohio, had also established schools in Michigan and Colorado.

In 1870, four Pennsylvania postulants were received in Cincinnati for their novitiate, and upon the completion of it, five Sisters of Charity of Cincinnati accompanied the novices on their return to Altoona, Pennsylvania, the foundation home, then, of the Sisters of Charity of Mother Seton, whose Motherhouse is now at Greensburg, Pennsylvania. With ecclesiastical consent, two of the five sisters from Cincinnati, who were to have remained in Pennsylvania but for a limited time, were allowed to transfer permanently to the new sister Community, Mother Aloysia Lowe of Cincinnati becoming first Superior of the Greensburg foundation.

With the yearly increasing number of pupils and postulants at Cedar Grove, and the threatened encroachment of the city on the location, a new site for the Motherhouse was decided upon, and was followed by the purchase of the Biggs Farm, five miles farther from the city and situated on a hill overlooking the Ohio River.

On the feast of the Sacred Heart, in 1884, Mount St. Joseph Motherhouse and Chapel of the Immaculate Conception, erected on the new site, were dedicated. A year later found them totally destroyed by fire. However, by August 15, 1901, Mount St. Joseph-on-the-Ohio had become the Motherhouse and novitiate of the Sisters of Charity of Cincinnati, with the normal training school of the Community in connection with it, as well as Mount St. Joseph Academy—formerly Mount St. Vincent's—and the College of Mount St. Joseph.

The College of Mount St. Joseph-on-the-Ohio, accredited as a standard college by the Ohio State Department of Education, is affiliated with the Catholic Educational Association of Colleges and the Catholic University of America. Not only do the Sisters of Charity carry out standard college courses at Mount St. Joseph, but they have established, in co-operation with the Good Samaritan Hospital, a course leading to the Bachelor of Science degree and the Graduate Nurse diploma.

Since the inauguration of the work of the Community outside the archdiocese of Cincinnati, and the success of the institutions established, hospitals have been opened in Pueblo and Trinidad, Colorado, by the sisters, who also conduct the Glockner Sanatorium at Colorado Springs. The best that modern science has discovered or invented for the benefit of tuberculosis patients has been adopted by the sisters in this institution, and in a similar one, St. Joseph's Hospital, opened at Albuquerque, New Mexico, some years later.

SISTER MARY ALBAN KENNEDY
Youngest of the 1928 foreign mission band of the Sisters of Charity of Cincinnati

The conducting of such modern institutions as these in the west and southwest, together with the St. Joseph Hospital and Sanitarium at Mt. Clemens, Michigan—which with its mineral waters has brought relief to so many sufferers—constitutes a phase of work in which these daughters of Mother Seton have been most active, while at the same time they have multiplied the number of their charitable institutions, and developed their educational work, which has spread into many States of the Union.

In 1897 the Sisters of Charity from Mount St. Joseph opened a school for Italian children in Cincinnati, and began needed labor for the preservation of their faith and the faith of their parents. They thus undertook an enduring social work, and laid the foundation of the Santa Maria Institute—now for many years an important educa-tional, benevolent and social center for Italian Catholics of Cincinnati.

In charity toward the missions in foreign lands, the call for vol-unteers for China was responded to by many more than could be chosen to leave Mount St. Joseph-on-the-Ohio and go with the foreign mission band to Wuchang, China, in January, 1928.

The Sisters of Charity of Cincinnati wore the black habit and cap adopted by Mother Seton in 1809, until January 1, 1926, when a white cap covered with a black veil was reluctantly substituted in the habit, the change being necessitated by the impossibility of securing the material required for the former distinctive head-dress.

Under the present superiorship of Mother Irenaea Fahey, the sisters at Mount St. Joseph, in addition to their numerous other activities, have engaged, since 1917, in conducting the St. Rita School for the Deaf, at Lockland, Ohio, a suburb of Cincinnati. At this institution the Sisters of Charity are training as a religious community the little band of deaf mutes and their associates who are desirous of consecrating their lives to this special service in the Master's vineyard.

SUMMARY

Sisters of Charity of Cincinnati.
Established in 1829.
Habit: The habit is black, with a white cap and guimpe, and a black veil.
Approximate number in Community, 1,100.
Active in the United States in educational, hospital, charitable and social service work in the archdioceses of Chicago, Cincinnati and Santa Fé, and in the dioceses of Cleveland, Denver, Detroit, Grand Rapids, Nashville and Toledo.
Motherhouse and Novitiate, Mount St. Joseph-on-the-Ohio, Mt. St. Joseph, Ohio. (Archdiocese of Cincinnati.)

HALIFAX, NOVA SCOTIA*

1849

One of the first branch houses opened by the Sisters of Charity in New York under Mother Elizabeth Boyle, their first Superior, following their establishment as a foundation in 1846—after nearly thirty years of activity in the state—was that in Halifax, Nova Scotia, in 1849.

---

*From data and material supplied by the Sisters of Charity, Mount St. Vincent, Halifax, N. S., Canada.

The Canadian mission then established at St. Mary's by Mother Seton's daughters early attracted many candidates eager to join the community but deterred from doing so by the difficulty of traveling to New York for their novitiate.   Adding to the problematical situation was the fact that the constant growth of the works undertaken in Halifax required a larger community of sisters than could be supplied from the new Motherhouse in New York.

To provide the facilities of a home novitiate, with its consequently increased number of sisters available for the various local institutions, the Most Rev. William Walsh, Archbishop of Halifax, petitioned the archbishop of New York, the Most Rev. John Hughes, and the Superiors at Mount St. Vincent in New York, for the establishment of the sisters already in Canada, as an independent community.   The wishes of Archbishop Walsh in this regard met with gracious concurrence on the part of the New York authorities, while from the Sovereign Pontiff, Pope Pius IX, a papal blessing was bestowed upon the successful completion of the project, on December 8, 1855.

Having imbibed it from their first Superior, one who had received her early education at the hands of Mother Seton herself, the Sisters of Charity in Halifax were animated by the same spirit which characterized the pioneer Sisters of Charity in the United States in their educational activities and many works of charity.

Soon after 1830, the sisters from the Emmitsburg Motherhouse had inaugurated their mission work in Boston, with two hundred and fifty children enrolled in the school which the bishop, the Right Rev. Benedict J. Fenwick, placed under their care as the initial work of the Sisters of Charity in that diocese whose first bishop, the Right Rev. John Cheverus, had been one of Mother Seton's closest advisors and friends among the hierarchy.

In the years which followed the arrival of the Sisters of Charity in Boston and their educational and charitable activities in the city and its environs, the ever increasing demand for sisters to conduct the numerous schools and institutions being established, occasioned an invitation to the Sisters of Charity in Halifax to take charge of St. Patrick's parochial school in Roxbury, Massachusetts.

Soon after the introduction of the Community into the archdiocese, in 1887, for this mission in Roxbury, plans were made for the opening of the Academy of the Assumption, at Wellesley Hills, about thirteen miles from Boston.   Here a department is conducted for girls of five years and older, and in the high school the college-preparatory curriculum includes both classical and secretarial work. The sisters also conduct at Wellesley Hills, Massachusetts, St. Joseph's

Academy, an elementary school for boys, between the ages of five and fourteen.

Including the number of sisters of the Community active in these institutions, and in the numerous others now under their care in the archdiocese of New York as well as the archdiocese of Boston, and in the dioceses of Brooklyn and Seattle, where missions have been accepted, the Sisters of Charity in Halifax—whose Rules were given papal approbation in 1908 by Pope Pius X—are represented in the United States by nearly three hundred members, who go out to these missions from their Motherhouse—Mount St. Vincent-on-Bedford Basin, in Halifax, in connection with which a normal and general college is conducted.

Motherhouse and Novitiate, Mount St. Vincent, Halifax, Nova Scotia, Canada. (Archdiocese of Halifax.)

CONVENT STATION, NEW JERSEY*

1859

The New Jersey branch of the Sisters of Charity emanated directly from the Motherhouse in New York City, and its establishment in 1859 as a separate community was the result of the personal efforts of the Right Rev. James Roosevelt Bayley, D.D., first bishop of Newark, and later archbishop of Baltimore.

The entire state of New Jersey was included in the territory of the diocese of Newark at this time, and Bishop Bayley, at the time of his appointment to the see was secretary to the Most Rev. John Hughes, D.D., Archbishop of New York.

As nephew of Mother Seton, and like her a convert to the Church, Bishop Bayley was no stranger to the Sisters of Charity. As secretary to Archbishop Hughes, he was in close touch with the work of the New York Community, and appreciated its missions already established in New Jersey.

A spirit of religious intolerance, with its accompanying persecutions, which then pervaded the state, made the period a momentous one for the new bishop in the development of the diocese.

To provide, as in New York, for a Motherhouse in the diocese for the Sisters of Charity in New Jersey—with its consequent increased number of sisters available for the schools to be opened, Bishop Bayley at once took steps for such a foundation. With this in view,

*From data and material supplied by the Sisters of Charity of St. Elizabeth, Convent of St. Elizabeth, Convent Station, N. J., and from *The History of the Catholic Church in the United States,* by John Gilmary Shea.

he petitioned Mother M. Angela Hughes, Superior of the Sisters of Charity in New York, to permit the sisters of the Community already on missions in New Jersey—particularly Sister Mary Xavier Mehegan and Sister Mary Catherine Nevin, of the Newark and Paterson missions respectively—to remain there for five years with an option, at the end of that time, to return to New York or remain in Newark as the first members of the new Community.

MOTHER MARY XAVIER MEHEGAN

This request having been granted, when the time of trial expired Sister Mary Xavier Mehegan, who had been serving as Superior in Newark, and Sister Mary Catherine Nevin, elected to remain permanently to labor in the diocese, and to sever their ties with the New York Motherhouse.

Five candidates, who had signified their desire to be of the new Community, were sent to Cincinnati, Ohio, where Bishop Bayley had arranged that they should made their no-vitiate at Mount St. Vincent, Cedar Grove, then the Mother-house and novitiate of the Sis-ters of Charity of Cincinnati—established in the city from Emmitsburg in 1829, and later formed as a separate Commu-nity, retaining the rule and garb as adopted by Mother Seton and her companions at St. Joseph's, Emmitsburg, in 1812.

Imbibing the spirit and learning the letter of Mother Seton's Rule, the New Jersey novices assiduously adjusted themselves to community life, and after ten months, upon the recommendation of Mother Margaret George, the foundress-Superior of the Cincinnati Com-munity, they were recalled to Newark.

There on September 29, 1859, the five novices united with Mother Mary Xavier and Sister Mary Catherine and formed the New Jersey Community of the Sisters of Charity, now known as the Sisters of Charity of St. Elizabeth. Mother Mary Xavier was appointed Mother Superior of the Community, and Sister Mary Catherine,

Assistant Superior, and St. Mary's, the mission at Newark, was established as the temporary site of the Motherhouse, with a novitiate at once opened in connection with it.

The self-sacrificing spirit and religious zeal which had characterized the early years of Sister Mary Xavier and Sister Mary Catherine eminently fitted them for the laborious work which they then undertook, the splendid results of which, it may be said, are directly traceable to these two valiant women.

ST. ELIZABETH'S, CONVENT STATION, NEW JERSEY

Postulants soon came to the new Community, and within a year after the opening of the novitiate its cramped quarters were wholly inadequate.

About this time, Bishop Bayley, who had previously purchased the old Chegary mansion at Madison, New Jersey, and fitted it up as a diocesan seminary and college for young men, naming it Seton Hall after his venerable aunt, Mother Seton, found it necessary to seek a site for his seminaries nearer the cathedral city of Newark. The Chegary mansion was then offered to Mother Xavier as a Motherhouse for the young Community. The secluded shelter of the mansion, its opportunities for retirement and quiet, and the possibilities for future purchases of ground in the vicinity easily induced Mother Xavier to take advantage of the offer and to assume a burden of debt which at that time seemed almost hazardous. However, the purchase price of twenty-five thousand dollars was provided for, through the aid of benefactors and friends of the sisters.

On July 2, 1860, Mother Xavier and the sisters left the Newark house and proceeded to the new Motherhouse. Honoring both the saintly foundress, Mother Elizabeth Seton, and the feast of the establishment of the Community at Madison—the Visitation of Our Lady to St. Elizabeth—the new institution was named St. Elizabeth's.

As soon as possible it was arranged that a boarding school for young ladies should be opened at the Madison house, thus providing needful funds for carrying on the work of the sisters and supporting the rapidly growing novitiate. Pupils were soon forthcoming, and it was not long before St. Elizabeth's became the center of educational life and activity in New Jersey, while it continued to foster the work of religious zeal and piety through the devotion of the young sisters to their sacred calling.

From the one small mother foundation that marked the year 1860, succeeding years soon totalled mission houses throughout the state of New Jersey, and even beyond the state limits into Connecticut, Massachusetts and New York, the first out-state mission having been established in 1889, at St. Joseph's parish, in Boston.

In keeping with the special work of charity for which the Sisters of Charity of St. Vincent de Paul are everywhere adapted, yet not necessarily to the exclusion of educational activity, St. Joseph's Hospital, opened at Paterson in 1867—and noted today for its efficient work in the orthopedic field—early engaged the attention of Mother Mary Xavier. During many years that followed, other hospitals found in her a wise guide and helpful aid, while the care of the orphan and the foundling—dearest interests of St. Vincent de Paul— is not neglected by these Sisters of Charity of St. Elizabeth.

The excluding of the incurably sick from general hospitals as undesirable patients, or at least as patients who prevent, in a measure, the admission of the sick who could be permanently cured by hospital relief, impressed Mother Xavier with the necessity of a home for the destitute whose hope of cure was slight, yet who required care and attention. Accordingly, a desirable site at Ridgewood, New Jersey, was purchased, and the House of Divine Providence, as it was called, was formally opened in 1891. In this institution the preference is always given to the sick who have been pronounced incurable, and who find much relief in the pine groves which surround the Providence Home, and its recent addition, Mt. St. Andrew Villa.

The rapid growth of the new Motherhouse buildings toward the hilltop, and the purchase of lands near the railway, necessitated the establishment of a separate station on the convent grounds, which the Lackawanna Railroad opened midway between Madison and Morris-town, as *Convent Station*. The frequency of trains at this point makes the convent readily accessible from all nearby cities, and greatly adds to the advantages of the Academy and College of St. Elizabeth.

Keeping pace with the educational demands of the times, and realizing the necessity of providing Catholic young women with op-portunities for pursuing their higher courses of study where faith would not be endangered by false philosophy, Mother Mary Xavier opened a collegiate department of study, thus forming the nucleus of the Catholic college system, which has developed rapidly since the foundation of the College of St. Elizabeth in 1899, the first Catholic college for women in the United States.

With its status attested by its membership in and affiliation with secular as well as Catholic associations duly authorized to accredit and affiliate higher institutions of learning, St. Elizabeth's possesses a curriculum and a material equipment fully adapted to the require-ments of the best in modern education.

Serving under the direction of the Passionist Missionaries in the Prefecture Apostolic of Shenchow, the first band of Sisters of Charity from New Jersey left for China on September 22, 1924, thus inaugu-rating the participation of the Community in the foreign mission labor of the Church in the United States.

In every possible field of activity, in every sphere of charity and zeal, the Sisters of Charity in New Jersey have upheld the traditions of their predecessors in Maryland, in New York, in Cincinnati, and in Halifax, and imbued with the spirit of the saintly Vincent de Paul, they have borne into their work the zeal and self-sacrificing devotion to duty in its manifold forms that characterized the noble Madame Le Gras and the first Daughters of Charity.

SUMMARY

Sisters of Charity of St. Elizabeth. (New Jersey.)
Established in 1859.
Habit: The habit is of black flannel, with a flannel cape and serge apron. A black veil is worn over a white fluted double border cap.
Approximate number in Community, 1,525.
Active in the United States in educational, hospital and charitable work in the archdioceses of Boston and New York and in the dioceses of Hartford, Newark and Trenton.
Motherhouse and Novitiate, Convent of St. Elizabeth, Convent Station, New Jersey. (Diocese of Newark.)

PENNSYLVANIA*

1870

SETON HILL CONVENT, GREENSBURG, PENNSYLVANIA

The Community of Sisters of Charity specifically designated as Sisters of Charity of Mother Seton, whose Motherhouse is situated at Greensburg, Pennsylvania, in the diocese of Pittsburgh, owes its origin in Pennsylvania to the zeal of the Right Rev. John Tuigg, D.D., appointed bishop of Pittsburgh in 1876.

Among the earliest pastors in the diocese of Pittsburgh, Father Tuigg was appointed to the mission in Altoona, where, in the interests of religious educational work among the people of that region, he petitioned—through the Right Rev. M. Domenec, D.D., Bishop of Pittsburgh—that the Sisters of Charity of Cincinnati establish a foundation.

In view of the Community's favorable action in the matter, Father Tuigg sent four postulants to Cincinnati for their religious training, and their inclusion in the foundation Community.

The year 1870 saw the return to Altoona of these novices, who were accompanied from Cincinnati by five Sisters of Charity assigned from the Motherhouse, Mount St. Vincent, at Cedar Grove, for temporary mission work at the new foundation.

On the recall of the Sisters of Charity of Cincinnati to their Motherhouse, urgent appeals were made in Altoona for the permanent transfer to the new Community of Mother Aloysia Lowe, its acting Superior, and Sister Ann Regina Ennis, Mistress of Novices.

Urged by the bishop, the clergy and the Community, the two sisters, after prayerful deliberation, arranged with their Motherhouse for continuance with this youngest Community of Mother Seton's daughters.

At once engaged in school work in the parish schools of Altoona,

*From data and material supplied by the Sisters of Charity of Mother Seton, St. Joseph Motherhouse, Greensburg, Pa.

the little Community progressed as a foundation, receiving many fervent candidates who wished to join in the charitable enterprises of the sisters, who soon extended their labors beyond Altoona and to Pittsburgh.

By 1882, the increase in the number of sisters in the Community requiring larger accommodations than the Altoona house afforded, removal was made to Greensburg, and ample property which per-mitted the development of the ex-pansive institute which now in-cludes, at Seton Hill, St. Joseph's, the Motherhouse, novitiate and nor-mal training school of the Com-munity, St. Joseph's Academy, Seton Hill Conservatory and School of Art, and Seton Hill College for Women, which in 1918 was em-powered to confer degrees. Situ-ated near the Dixie Highway, and within an hour's railroad access of Pittsburgh, Seton Hill provides an advantageous location for the edu-cational facilities of its institutions, whose students come from many States of the Union.

A "SETON HILL SISTER"

Prominent among the establish-ments in Pittsburgh under the care of these Sisters of Charity of Mother Seton, are Pittsburgh Hospital, Roselia Foundling Asylum, and De Paul Institute for the Deaf. In these institutions the members of the Community carry on the diverse activities with which they occupy themselves together with their educational work, under the present superiorship of Mother Rose Genevieve Rodgers, and subject to the episcopal jurisdiction of the Right Rev. Hugh C. Boyle, D.D., as bishop of Pittsburgh.

SUMMARY

Sisters of Charity of Mother Seton. (Pennsylvania.)
Established in 1870.
Habit: The habit, adapted from the widow's dress and cap worn by Mother Seton, is black, with a cape to the waist line, and a black silk cap with a white lining.
Approximate number in Community, 550.
Active in educational, hospital and charitable work in the dioceses of Altoona and Pittsburgh.

Motherhouse and Novitiate, St. Joseph's Motherhouse, Greensburg, Pennsylvania. (Diocese of Pittsburgh.)

CHRONOLOGICAL TABLE

Foundations of the Sisters of Charity in the United States

1809—Emmitsburg, Maryland.
1817—New York City.
1829—Cincinnati, Ohio.

1849—Halifax, Nova Scotia.
1859—Convent Station, New Jersey.
1870—Greensburg, Pennsylvania.

GENERAL SUMMARY

Sisters of Charity.
Founded in the United States in 1809.
Habit: The habit worn is according to that adopted by the separate Communities.
Approximate number in Communities in United States, 9,000.
Active in the United States in educational, hospital, charitable and social service work in the archdioceses of Baltimore, Boston, Chicago, Cincinnati, Milwaukee, New Orleans, New York, Philadelphia, St. Louis, San Francisco and Santa Fé, and in the dioceses of Albany, Altoona, Brooklyn, Buffalo, Cleveland, Dallas, Davenport, Denver, Detroit, El Paso, Galveston, Grand Rapids, Harrisburg, Hartford, Indianapolis, Kansas City, Los Angeles and San Diego, Mobile, Monterey-Fresno, Nashville, Natchez, Newark, Peoria, Pittsburgh, Portland, Raleigh, Richmond, Rochester, St. Augustine, St. Joseph, Salt Lake, Seattle, Springfield in Illinois, Syracuse, Toledo, Trenton and Wilmington.

SISTERS OF LORETTO AT THE FOOT OF THE CROSS*

1812

*M*ORE than a century has passed since the establishment in the United States of the "first religious order founded in America, without foreign affiliation or connection." The Sisters of Loretto at the Foot of the Cross, the beloved "Lorettines," untiringly and unceasingly carry on, keeping pace with every modern demand and development, the educational work for which they were founded in the year 1812, in the State of Kentucky.

Under the direction of the Most Rev. John Carroll, D.D., then bishop of Baltimore, the Rev. Charles Nerinckx, an exiled Belgian priest, arrived in Kentucky in 1805, and actively and heroically at once shared in the labor of the saintly pioneer missionary, Father Badin.

Finding the missions wide apart and no schools established, the zealous priest was gratified when the estimable and cultured sister and guest of Bennet Rhodes, who had migrated to Kentucky with the Maryland colonists, requested that she be allowed to extend to others the daily instruction she gave her brother's children.

With the consent and help of Father Nerinckx and her brother, who was in full sympathy with her desire to make her life beneficial to the youth of the new country, thenceforth their home, Mary Rhodes opened a school in a little cabin where the children could come to her. She soon had a needed assistant in Christina Stuart, who, like herself, was desirous of engaging in this work.

When Miss Stuart took up her residence at Bennet Rhodes' hospitable home, the regard of the teachers for each other ripened into deep affection. They revealed to each other what had before been wisely hidden from the uncomprehending, and the higher thought that had led one on was now known to be the lodestar of the other. Thus drawn together by a spiritual kinship, they unconsciously advanced toward the hour decreed for them.

The social demands of the neighborhood soon distracted them in their interior progress, and interfered with their work in the school. Possessed of a desire for religious perfection, and realizing the need of quiet and seclusion in their pursuit, Mary Rhodes and her sister

*From data and material supplied by the Sisters of Loretto, Loretto Motherhouse, Nerinx, Ky., and from *Loretto Annals of the Century*, by Anna C. Minogue (America Press, New York).

co-laborer determined to take up their abode in a cabin adjoining the school. Family and friends thought the plan madness, but felt that the best cure for such folly was to allow it to run its course, and that within a short time the young women would return to their midst.

But the spirit of enterprise that so strongly filled the land, permeated these earnest souls, who now, bent upon planting Christian education on the frontier, accepted the condition of sacrifice gladly, and with sublime trust removed to their cabin-home.

Scarcely was this done when a third young lady, Nancy Havern, joined them in their labors and home.

No record shows which of the three intrepid ones suggested that step, the taking of which thousands of consecrated virgins were to bless as they followed in that glorious path, but the proposal of one found an echo in the hearts of the other two, and they turned to Father Nerinckx and zealously offered themselves, through him, to God and His Church, asking religious rule and spiritual guidance.

The diocese of Bardstown had been erected in 1808, and the Right Rev. Benedict Joseph Flaget was appointed its first bishop. To him, as his episcopal superior, Father Nerinckx went for advice and direction about the pious project. Bishop Flaget gave the undertaking his warmest approval. He knew that Christ would not fail His Church, and that in sparsely settled Kentucky as in the populous cities of the Old World He could raise up the much-needed religious orders.

On April 25, 1812, in the little log church of St. Charles, Hardin's Creek, Kentucky, in the presence of a large gathering of people from the surrounding country, Father Nerinckx officiated at the religious investiture of Mary Rhodes, Christina Stuart and Nancy Havern.

Soon after this, Ann Rhodes, Sally Havern and Nellie Morgan were received as postulants, and with their reception on June 29, 1812, Mother Ann Rhodes, elected by the members of the new Community, became the first Superior.

In 1812, the year of its foundation, the Society of Loretto was formally established as a self-governing body, with the rights and powers of such an organization. Father Nerinckx then gave the sisters their Rule, which in 1816 was commended by the Holy See, and their characteristic name, The Friends of Mary at the Foot of the Cross, was bestowed on them.

Mother Ann Rhodes' first act as Superior was the purchase of the land on which the cabins stood. For this she paid seventy-five dollars, the money being from the sale of her negro slave for whom she received two hundred dollars. Owning their own land was the first step toward the real home of the members of the Society. In the labor of erecting buildings, these gentle women of dignity and refine- ment participated actively, energetically and forcefully, with the determination so typical of the pioneer, that Loretto—Loretto of today—was bound to rise.

After the death of their first Superior, the sisters elected as her successor Sister Mary Rhodes, the actual foundress of the Society. For ten consecutive years Mother Mary presided over the Society,

LORETTO MOTHERHOUSE, NERINX, KENTUCKY

beholding almost with reverence its wonderful growth. The necessity of Christian education turned a lowly cabin into a schoolroom, and from that school Divine Providence brought forth Loretto.

Within two months after the Holy See's approval of the young Institute of four years, the Society opened its first mission, in Ken- tucky, naming this first actual foundation "Calvary."

In March, 1818, six Sisters of Loretto were sent to open the second mission away from the Motherhouse. At St. Barbara's Station, on Pottinger's Creek, in Kentucky, a school for girls was established on property donated to the sisters by Mr. James Dent. Father Nerinckx called the place Gethsemani, in memory of the Agony in the Garden. For thirty years this school was maintained by the sisters, until, when the erection of other schools made its continuance no longer necessary, it was sold to a colony of Trappist monks from

France, and the sisters, with eight boarding pupils, removed to Loretto Motherhouse, November 5, 1848.   Upon acquiring this property, the monks at once began there the United States establishment of their Order, and the institution, under the original title, flourishes as the noted Abbey of Gethsemani.

The Society of the Sisters of Loretto first extended beyond the confines of Kentucky when a school was opened in Perry County, Missouri, in May, 1823.   This foundation was made in response to the request of the Right Rev. Louis Dubourg, Bishop of Louisiana, residing at the episcopal seat, St. Louis.   The new school, Bethlehem —so called because of the poverty of the structure—was within ten years transferred and combined with a later school, that at Cape Girardeau.

Mission after mission was then established, more especially in the western dioceses of the country, where the "Lorettines" were the pioneer missionary sisters among the American Indians, as they were the "valiant women" pioneers of the great southwest, dotting the trails with schools.

Out of their generous response, in 1852, to the appeal of the Right Rev. J. B. Lamy, then newly appointed vicar apostolic of New Mexico, has sprung the great success of the Society in the west, proving Father Nerinckx' motto and admonition, "Do not forsake Providence and He will never forsake you."

In his interest for religious education for his people, Bishop Lamy, attending the Provincial Council held that year in Baltimore, sought sisters to undertake the work, and for this purpose visited Loretto. Realizing that the prospective volunteers should first know conditions in the distant vicariate, Bishop Lamy explained to the assembled community at Loretto the arduous nature of the work awaiting the future teachers.   Not without apprehension, yet not appalled, were the Lorettines, as was shown by the volunteers in response to the appeal, from among whom six were chosen to go to the Santa Fé mission.

Disheartening experiences were the lot of the brave band of sisters who met Bishop Lamy on June 27, 1852, in St. Louis, and with his party set out by the "traders' trail" for their destination.   Following from St. Louis to Independence by river, the trail led from Independence to Santa Fé, about nine hundred miles, by wagon.   Cholera menaced the passengers on the steamer, and during the river trip Mother Matilda Mills, the Superior of the little band of Lorettines, and a past assistant superior of the Society, was fatally stricken with the dread disease.   Two other sisters suffered serious attacks.

The caravan journey which was then made from Independence began with a storm of unabating fury. Adding to the dismaying experiences of the long and trying journey, the sisters found themselves surrounded by three or four hundred Indians, who, however, did not molest them.

On the afternoon of Sunday, September 26th, the caravan reached Santa Fé, accompanied from Arkansas by the vicar general, the Right Rev. J. P. Machebeuf, who had left his labors of nearly twenty years in Ohio to join his life-long friend Bishop Lamy, when he went to New Mexico.

Quickly adapting themselves to the new country, as they engaged in the work of religious education, the Lorettines forgot the hardships they had undergone, and their privations and sufferings since leaving their convent home in Kentucky.

To assist the sisters in Santa Fé in their evangelical work in the southwest, augmenting communities were from time to time sent from Loretto. In 1855 a novitiate was established at Santa Fé, and later at several branch houses, as the difficulties of travel made it impossible at that time to require all candidates to make their novitiate at the Motherhouse in Kentucky.

On February 19, 1858, a disastrous fire at Loretto swept away the material work of nearly fifty years, but the Lorettines, though overwhelmed, were not daunted. With faith in their work, and buoyed by the sympathy of neighbors, relatives and friends, as evidenced by their prompt generosity, Loretto was built anew and its interrupted Motherhouse work was resumed as soon as conditions permitted.

During the ensuing years, schools and academies of permanence were opened throughout Kentucky, Arkansas, Missouri, Colorado, Illinois, Alabama, Texas, Nebraska and other states—prominent among them being those in St. Louis, Denver and Montgomery— while to New Mexico had gone by caravan other bands of Lorettines, one especially, like the first, with its story of tragedy and hardship, but each with its record of stirring experiences, reward and blessings in the missions established.

Among the Sisters of Loretto who made the caravan journey to Santa Fé in 1875 was Sister Praxedes Carty, who, receiving the habit the previous year, had volunteered for the western missions, and who, twenty-one years later, was appointed Superior General at Loretto Motherhouse. In the party which the sisters accompanied was the Right Rev. J. B. Salpointe, D.D., then vicar apostolic of Arizona, and later successor to the archbishopric of Santa Fé. At this time Bishop

Salpointe was bringing the pallium from Rome for Bishop Lamy, who was that year made first archbishop of Santa Fé.

After three years spent at Santa Fé, Sister Praxedes made her first vows, following which she was successively appointed Superior at Bernalillo and Las Cruces, New Mexico, under the ecclesiastical jurisdiction of Archbishop Lamy. Mother Praxedes was later assigned to the superiorship at Florissant, Missouri, and was serving in the same capacity at Loretto Heights, Colorado, when in 1896 she was appointed Superior General at Loretto Motherhouse.

MOTHER PRAXEDES CARTY

In the interests of the Society Mother Praxedes, accompanied by Mother Wilfred LaMotte, one of her Councilors, visited Rome in December of 1903, and again in 1907. On the occasion of her second visit, when she was accompanied by Mother Evangelista Bindewald, also a Councilor, the Sovereign Pontiff, Pope Pius X, gave his final papal approbation of the Rules and Constitutions of the Sisters of Loretto at the Foot of the Cross, as his predecessors, Pope Pius VII and Pope Pius IX, had in turn given the varying degrees of approbation.

Ever mindful that the call that brought Loretto into existence was the necessity of Christian education, the Sisters of Loretto have devoted themselves to teaching, except when occasion has demanded other works of mercy. To prepare her sisters for their work, Loretto forms them to habits of solid study, close application, and constancy of purpose, the foundation for this course being laid in the thorough religious training given in the novitiate and in the Normal Training School which has been established at Loretto Motherhouse, wherein the sisters are fitted for their work of Christian education.

In 1916, four years after the celebration of the one hundredth anniversary of their founding, and the institution of that first school in the little log cabin, the Sisters of Loretto established, at Webster

Groves, Missouri, their first college for the higher education of women, Webster College, corporate college of St. Louis University, and affiliated with the Catholic University of America. In 1918, in the scenic Rocky Mountain region, near Denver, the Society established Loretto Heights College, in Loretto, Colorado. At both these institutions musical conservatories are conducted, operating under their special charters from Missouri and Colorado, respectively.

Another phase of educational work was written in the annals of Loretto, when on September 23, 1923, to assist the Fathers of the Chinese Mission Society of St. Columban, six Sisters of Loretto sailed from Seattle for Han Yang, Hupeh, China, (prefecture apostolic of Han Yang) where, in connection with their work, an embroidery school is now conducted.

As in 1833 the sisters had responded to the emergency, and, in the neighborhood of Loretto, which is located sixty miles from Louisville, nursed the victims of the cholera epidemic, so again in 1918, with influenza prevalent among the Kentucky miners, the services of the sisters were such as to be formally acknowledged by Brig. General Fred T. Austin, of the United States Army, in a letter to the Right Rev. D. O'Donoghue, D.D., Bishop of Louisville. At Mora, New Mexico, in 1918, the sisters also left their schools to nurse the stricken. During the World War the sisters nursed the soldiers in Camp Zachary Taylor, Louisville, Kentucky, and at the time of the influenza epidemic Sister Mary Jean Conner contracted the disease and gave her life in the cause of charity. A military funeral, with a requiem mass in Knights of Columbus Hall, in the camp, was accorded her, and her name was inscribed on the monument erected in her native town, Toronto, Ohio, in memory of those who made the supreme sacrifice.

In Loretto and its other schools the pupils combined in war-relief work by the purchase of Liberty Bonds, Thrift Stamps, and the knitting of needed garments, as well as by membership in the Junior Red Cross.

Through the National Catholic Welfare Council, organized during the World War, the Sisters of Loretto offered free scholarships. Two young ladies from France matriculated at Webster College, and one of them, after graduation, returned to her native country, where she carried off highest honors at the Sorbonne. Later she returned to her Alma Mater as a member of the faculty.

As a recent project the Loretto Society has offered to receive Chaldean girls, and give them religious training.

Since 1904 the Society of the Sisters of Loretto at the Foot of the Cross has been under the direct jurisdiction of the Holy See, being governed by a Superior General and her Council, who are elected by the General Chapter for a term of six years. The members of the General Council appoint the local Superiors.

Loretto Motherhouse is the seat of government for the Society, which at present is under the administration of Mother Mary Olivette Norton, Mother General, succeeding, in office, Mother Mary Clarasine Walsh; Mother Mary Edith Laughran, Mother Vicaress, succeeding Mother Mary Albertina Riordan; Mother Mary Bridget Fern, Second Assistant, succeeding Mother Mary Thomas Rodman; Mother Mary Assumpta McIntosh, Third Assistant; Mother Ann Marita Maley, Fourth Assistant and Secretary General, and Mother Genevieve Wheat, Treasurer General.

SUMMARY

Sisters of Loretto at the Foot of the Cross.

Founded in the United States in 1812.

Papal Approbation of Rules, Dec. 30, 1907, by Pope Pius X; revised to conform to the New Code of Canon Law, and ratified by the Sacred Congregation of Religious, July 29, 1920.

Habit: The habit is of serge, black in compassion for the sorrows of Mary at the foot of the Cross, and with a black veil lined with white.

Approximate number in Community, 950.

Active in the United States in educational work in the archdiocese of Chicago, St. Louis, San Francisco and Santa Fé, and in the dioceses of Belleville, Columbus, Denver, El Paso, Kansas City, Leavenworth, Lincoln, Los Angeles and San Diego, Louisville, Mobile, Oklahoma, Omaha, Rockford, St. Joseph and Tucson.

Motherhouse and Novitiate, Loretto Motherhouse, Nerinx, Kentucky. (Diocese of Louisville.)

SISTERS OF CHARITY OF NAZARETH*

1812

$\mathcal{S}$OON after taking up his residence at Bardstown as bishop of the see—erected in 1808, and comprising the states of Kentucky and Tennessee—the Right Rev. Benedict Joseph Flaget, D.D., co-operated with the Superior of his new seminary, the Rev. J. B. M. David, in his plans for the founding of a needed religious community of women.

Willing and anxious to be bound by the simple vows of poverty, chastity and obedience, and to devote themselves to works of mercy and the instruction of the young and the ignorant, Teresa Carrico and Elizabeth Wells presented themselves for admission into the proposed community. In January, Catherine Spalding joined them in the log house in Nelson County, where, under the direction of Father David, community life was inaugurated, with the exercises of the day according to rule.

A few months later there were six postulants at Nazareth, as the little log house was called. These sturdy women of strong faith and principle, ready to perform any duty pointed out to them, made rapid strides in the religious life under the careful training of the disciplinarian and zealous priest, Father David. In the month of June, 1813, following a retreat of seven days, the first election at Nazareth took place, and Catherine Spalding was chosen Superior, Harriet Gardiner, Assistant Mother and Elizabeth Wells, Procuratrix.

Mother Catherine Spalding, the first Superior of the Sisters of Charity of Nazareth, was born in Charles County, Maryland, in 1793. Her father and the father of the Most Rev. Martin J. Spalding, Archbishop of Baltimore, were cousins. Endowed with the dominant characteristics of courage—moral and physical—sagacity, prudence and executive ability, Mother Catherine, having served a second consecutive term as Superior, maintaining the provisional rule, steadfastly refused uninterrupted continuance in her office, in which capacity she served the Society—in the forty-five years of her religious life—through a period totalling twenty-five years.

Not for two years did the little Community begin its work of teaching. In the meantime, in their new home, the sisters were

*From data and material supplied by the Sisters of Charity of Nazareth, Nazareth, Ky., and from *The History of the Catholic Church in the United States*, by John Gilmary Shea, and *The Sisters of Charity of Nazareth, Kentucky*, by Anna Blanche McGill (The Encyclopedia Press, New York).

employed at the spinning-wheel and loom, with their needle-work, household tasks and their prescribed religious duties.

MOTHER CATHERINE SPALDING

Under the guidance of Sister Ellen O'Connell, an efficient teacher of recognized merit, who had come from Baltimore and joined the Community, a school for little girls was begun in 1814, and was of necessity a boarding school, as the distances were too great to permit day scholars.

In the little Community, soon after this, there was substituted for the provisional rule which the sisters had been following, the Rule of St. Vincent de Paul, with which both Bishop Flaget and Father

David had become familiar, through their acquaintance with Mother Seton and the Sisters of Charity of Emmitsburg, while in Maryland previous to their coming to Kentucky. Simultaneously with the adoption of a definite rule, the uniform garb such as is still worn, except that the cap was black instead of white, was assumed by the sisters, who themselves spun, wove and colored the materials needed to provide the first habits.

Four years after the commencement of their school work at Nazareth, sisters were sent to teach at Bethlehem Academy, opened at Bardstown upon the completion of the building of St. Joseph's Cathedral. Then was inaugurated the work through branch houses of the Sisters of Charity of Nazareth, who since have extended their labors into many States of the Union.

In 1822, the Community, numbering then twenty-five, moved to its present location, where a substantial building for convent and academy was erected two years later. With the growth of the Community, by the reception of the fervent candidates who applied for admission, and its continuance under the ecclesiastical superiorship of Bishop David—Father David having been consecrated bishop, and made co-adjutor of the bishop of Bardstown—several schools were opened in different counties in the state.

In 1829 the sisters received a papal Rescript conferring many privileges and blessings upon the Society, and that same year the Kentucky legislature granted Nazareth a charter, under the title *Nazareth Literary and Benevolent Institution.*

Inseparably linked with the pioneer institutions in Louisville is the name of Mother Catherine Spalding, who in 1831 founded the first Catholic school in the city—the well-known Presentation Academy. In 1832 and 1833, when the ravages of cholera were decimating the population of the city the school was closed, and the sisters devoted themselves entirely to the care of the sick. Children bereft of parents, victims of the plague, were cared for by Mother Catherine and the sisters, and the work then begun in their behalf is continued in Louisville's splendid establishments of St. Thomas' Orphanage for Boys and St. Vincent's for Girls, both under the care of the Sisters of Charity of Nazareth.

The next twenty years marked for Nazareth the death of its founders, Bishop Flaget and Bishop David, the death of the latter occurring at Nazareth that he loved so well, and to which he had retired. During these years the Society extended its missions beyond Kentucky and into Tennessee, where its first mission, though only temporary, was in Nashville.

Academies and mission houses were then opened in Covington, Newport, Lexington and Paducah, and before the decade of years had passed the Civil War had begun, and likewise a new era in the history of the Sisters of Charity of Nazareth. Mother Columba, Superior at the Academy at Nazareth, who as Margaret Carroll had entered the Community in 1825, was chosen its Superior in 1862, and valiantly guided it though the period of trial which followed. Many branch houses, being in or near the scenes of bloodshed, were converted into hospitals and infirmaries where the sisters,

NAZARETH MOTHERHOUSE, NAZARETH, KENTUCKY

veritable angels of the battlefield, ministered to the sick and wounded, whether Confederate or Union. Louisville, Paducah, Lexington, Owensboro and Bardstown were important Kentucky centers of the Civil War activities of the Sisters of Charity of Nazareth, and the names of those of the Community serving the victims of its battles form one of the long lists of sisters on the war records in Washington.

Upon recovery from the appalling disaster of the war, scarcely had the sisters returned to normalcy in the pursuit of their educational activities when they were again tried, and not found wanting.

Again, as during the cholera epidemic of 1832-33 and the Asiatic cholera in 1848, the sisters were among the nurses, and also among the victims, during the months of 1872, when small-pox was rampant in Kentucky. They took charge of St. John's Eruptive Hospital in Louisville, their work of mercy there through the pestilence being recorded by the mayor in the Municipal Reports of the year. When yellow fever swept the south, between 1870 and 1880, once more the sisters closed their classrooms and ministered to the plague-stricken, and martyr crowns were won by many who sacrificed their lives to care for those attacked by these dread diseases.

More than fifty years had passed—years of upheavals and trials, during which efficient Superiors in turn took their places at the helm of the Society, which yearly increased in members—when its work was extended beyond its southern environs into Maryland, where at Leonardtown, St. Mary's Academy was opened under the auspices of His Eminence, James Cardinal Gibbons, as archbishop of Baltimore. This expansion was followed shortly afterward by the establishment of branch houses in Massachusetts, Arkansas, Ohio, Mississippi and Virginia.

In addition to their educational work and the care of orphans and the aged, the Sisters of Charity of Nazareth, having engaged, according to need—since the first score years of their existence—in hospital work and the care of the sick, now conduct many of the most prominent hospitals in the country.

Ranking among the oldest of the permanent ones of their establishing is the St. Mary and St. Elizabeth Hospital, erected in Louisville, in 1873, by Mr. William Shakespeare Caldwell as a memorial to his deceased wife, Mary Elizabeth Breckinridge Caldwell, a graduate of Nazareth Academy. A modern fire-proof structure was in 1911 added to the main building, and later a training school for nurses was established, and this hospital, as well as the others of the Order, is maintained according to the highest standards of requirements.

Following the formal approbation of the Society by the Holy See in 1910, Mother Eutropia McMahon, then serving as Superior, was elected first Mother General under the newly approved Constitutions. Her death occurring soon after, Mother Rose Meagher was chosen to succeed her, and presided over the impressive ceremonies and program of the Centennial Celebration held at Nazareth in the autumn of 1912.

Sustaining the history of the Order, of meeting the needs of the day, the Sisters of Charity of Nazareth and their pupils generously shared in the war relief work of the country during the World War, as they pursued their labors in the various establishments of the Society.

To conform to the highest standards of excellence in the curriculum of their educational institutions, junior college courses were

10

added to those of the academy and school which have been continuously conducted at Nazareth Motherhouse since the opening of its first school in 1814. In 1920, Nazareth College, for the higher education of women, was founded in Louisville and, in addition to its affilia-tion with the Catholic University of America, ranks as one of the accredited colleges of the state.

Since the conferring of the papal approbation on the Society, placing it directly subject to the jurisdiction of the Holy See, with a Cardinal-Protector, the office of ecclesiastical superior, held origi-nally by Bishop David, has been given up, the government of the Society being vested in the Mother General and her assistants, who compose her Council.

SUMMARY

Sisters of Charity of Nazareth.

Founded in the United States in 1812.

Papal Approbation of Society, September 5, 1910, by Pope Pius X.

Habit: The habit is black, with a white cap and a small white collar.

Approximate number in Community, 1,100.

Active in educational, hospital and charitable work in the archdioceses of Baltimore and Boston and in the dioceses of Columbus, Covington, Little Rock, Louisville, Nashville, Natchez and Richmond.

Motherhouse and Novitiate, Nazareth Motherhouse, Nazareth, Kentucky. (Diocese of Louisville.)

RELIGIOUS OF THE SACRED HEART*

*P*ARALLEL with the history of the founding and the development of the Society of the Sacred Heart, established in France in the year 1800, is the history of the life and the spiritual development of its holy foundress, St. Madeleine Sophie, who was raised to the altars of the Church by His Holiness, Pope Pius XI, on May 24, 1925, the sixtieth anniversary of her saintly death.

In the little village of Joigny, in Burgundy, Madeleine Sophie Barat was born, December 12, 1779. From her earliest years she manifested exceptional gifts and qualities of heart and mind, and during France's Reign of Terror she was well schooled in sorrow and in the exercise of sympathy, when her beloved brother was imprisoned for two years and in imminent danger of the scaffold.

It was this brother, Father Louis Barat, under whose special tutelage St. Madeleine Sophie mastered lessons in Latin, Greek, Spanish, Italian, history and the sciences, surpassing his pupils at the seminary in reading the classics in the original.

Father Barat soon discerned that his sister had a marked vocation for the religious life. At the age of twenty, when she realized that she was to serve God in religion, she was at first impelled toward Carmel, not knowing that Providence intended her to combine, in a new institute, the contemplative with the active life.

Near the middle of the year 1800, Father Barat confided to his Superior, Father Joseph Varin, of the Fathers of the Faith, his concern for the vocation of his "little sister." Attracted by the description of St. Madeleine Sophie, Father Varin asked her age, ability and qualifications. The knowledge of a sister, who was as the same time the spiritual daughter and pupil of a man well qualified to adjudge virtue and talent, the classical education she had received, her religious vocation, and, above all, her youthfulness—ideal for spiritual direction and the moulding of the mind, all made a strong impression on Father Varin, and when Mademoiselle Barat was introduced to him his previsions were realized.

---

*From data and material supplied by the Religious of the Sacred Heart, of the Eastern Vicariate, and from the following referred bibliography: *St. Madeleine Sophie, a Sketch of Her Intimate Life* (Longmans, Green Co.); *Life of Ven. Mother Barat*, Fullerton; *Mother Philippine Duchesne*, by Marjory Erskine (Longmans, Green Co.); *Mary Aloysia Hardey*, by Mary Garvey, R.S.C.J. (Longmans, Green Co.); *The Society of the Sacred Heart*, by Janet Erskine Stuart (Roehampton Press).

From the saintly Léonor de Tournély, his predecessor, Superior
of the Fathers of the Faith, Father Varin had received a bequest
of a plan for a society of women, to be devoted to the Sacred

ST. MADELEINE SOPHIE BARAT (1779-1865)
Foundress of the Society of the Sacred Heart

Heart of Jesus and consecrated to the instruction of children, especially of the wealthy and influential classes. Father de Tournély had
been inspired with the project of this great work but the task of its
elaboration and achievement was committed to another.

Father Varin, in turn, confided in Father Barat, told him of the
bequest he had received and of his own plans for the founding of

such a society, as well as the presentiment he felt that his sister would be the foundation stone for the building of the Society of the Sacred Heart. When St. Madeleine Sophie learned from her brother of the hopes and designs of Father Varin, she hesitated, alarmed at the thought of her own incapacity. But there was little room for thought or doubt on the subject. The whole trend of her life had been to this end, and St. Madeleine Sophie received from Father Varin, who had become her director, such an assurance as to her vocation that she entered into his plans with generous self-devotion, and with that absolute reliance on God which was to become more and more the essence, as it were, of her spiritual life.

It was in the home of Madame Duval, in a quiet section of Paris, that the real foundation of the Society of the Sacred Heart was laid. Here St. Madeleine Sophie and the zealous souls who, under the direction of Father Varin, had joined her, now lived a community life. On November 21, 1800—the feast of the Presentation of the Blessed Virgin—they were allowed to make their vows of consecration to God. This feast, therefore, is kept by the Society as the date of its founding.

At Amiens, on October 15, 1801—the feast of St. Teresa—the first convent was established, and by the advice of Father Varin and with the consent of the community, Madeleine Sophie Barat was named Superior. A free school was then opened for the children of the poor, who attended it in large numbers. Nothing could have been more in accordance with the spirit of the new Institute than such a charitable undertaking. This work has been continued, and now flourishes whenever possible in connection with all the houses since established by the Society.

In 1804 a foundation was made in Grenoble. Intertwined with the history of the house established there is the history of the early religious life of a new member then received into the Society— Philippine Duchesne, who in 1818 carried the work of the Society beyond France, to the United States, where for thirty-five years she labored as a pioneer. By her steadfast faith, her perseverance through cold, hunger and illness, opposition, ingratitude and calumny—all hard to vizualize today—she merits well the reward which Mother Church conferred on her, when, on December 9, 1909, she was declared Venerable.

Rose Philippine Duchesne was born in Grenoble, France, on August 29, 1769. She was baptized about a week later on Our Lady's birthday, in the Church of St. Louis, France's Crusader King, and the patron of the far-distant mission to which she was destined to devote her life. In time, Philippine was sent to school at the Visitandine Convent of Ste. Marie d'en Haut. This house had been founded on the Hill of Chalmont, by St. Francis de Sales, who in 1618, at the request of the citizens of Grenoble, had sent for Mother Jane Frances de Chantal, to help him choose a suitable site for a foundation.

In the cloistered halls of Ste. Marie, Philippine absorbed the devotion to the Sacred Heart of Jesus, and even then cherished the desire to carry that devotion to the far-away land of the Indians, over whom her heart had thrilled with love and zeal, when she had heard a returned missionary tell of the great need for evangelization among them. In her maturing years her parents wished her to marry, but Philippine, feeling that as a Visitandine she was called to serve God, was received as a postulant at Ste. Marie d'en Haut.

The outbreak of the Revolution in France meant to Philippine the postponement of her religious profession. The Visitandines of Grenoble were ordered to give up their religious life or to abandon Ste. Marie. Their expulsion followed their signing a protest, and a declaration that they were religious until death.

VEN. PHILIPPINE DUCHESNE (1769-1852)

Before the closing of Ste. Marie d'en Haut was effected, Philippine had obeyed her parents' summons and returned to her home, where she continued, as best possible, the Rule and customs of the Order. In companionship with a friend doing likewise, she devoted herself to the poor, the sick and the imprisoned.

In the re-organization which followed the Revolution, the community failed to return to the convent on the Hill of Chalmont. Vainly the faithful Philippine waited, then purchased the deserted cloister herself, and with some devoted friends attempted its re-establishment. Meanwhile, from Father Varin, whom she had met, she learned of Mother Barat and of the Society of the Sacred Heart, and offered to them the ancient convent of Ste. Marie d'en Haut.

November, 1804, found Mother Barat in Grenoble, where she not only received from Philippine Duchesne the convent she loved, but as members, into her Institute, Philippine and her faithful friends.

In 1806 Mother Barat was elected Superior General of the Society, and for sixty-three years she bore the ever-increasing weight of the responsibilities of Superior. In 1815 was held the first Council of Superiors and the discussion of the Rule.

The Society of the Sacred Heart, whose interests are safe-guarded by a Cardinal-Protector at Rome, is governed by a Superior General who is elected for life, and by an assembly composed of Assistants General, who form her private council, and of the Vicar Superiors— corresponding to the Provincials in other orders. The Vicar Superiors are also local Superiors, governing one house themselves, and entrusted with the supervision of different groups of houses. According to the first plan there was to be only one novitiate, that all members might be trained in the same school, know each other personally, and, especially, be known by the Superior General. This ultimately became impossible and there have been established and are maintained central novitiates in various countries of Europe, and in South America, Canada and the United States. In addition to the usual three vows of religion, the Religious of the Sacred Heart take a vow of stability and a vow of consecration to the work of the education of youth. That membership in the educational Institute, and the obligations of a choir religious, might not exclude from the Society many willing to give their service and helpful co-operation, and in preference to the necessity of giving many dispensations from the obligation to teach, and to chant the Divine Office, there are in the Society both choir religious and lay sisters. The members of the Society retain their family names with the prefix of Mother or Sister, and all observe the prescribed enclosure.

At the Council, meeting in 1815, Ven. Philippine Duchesne was named Secretary General of the Society. Two years later it was Mother Duchesne who opened the door of the Motherhouse and ushered in, for a call on the Superior General, none other than the Right Rev. Louis Dubourg, Bishop of Louisiana.

During his visit, Bishop Dubourg told of his vast diocese in the United States, its needs—spiritual and temporal—and of his desire to have Religious of the Sacred Heart for his mission.   Mother Barat then, presenting Mother Duchesne, told the bishop of her longing for such work, and later promised to send a colony of nuns to his diocese.

CONVENT OF THE SACRED HEART, MARYVILLE, ST. LOUIS, MISSOURI

To her own dismay, the superiorship of the little band of religious, chosen to sail for the Louisiana mission, was laid on Philippine, but in the joy of the fulfillment of the desire of her heart and her vocation, the zealous religious humbly accepted the new responsibility.

Setting sail from France in mid-March of 1818, the travelers soon experienced the hardships of an ocean voyage of that period.   Toward the end of April the heat became intense; capricious winds drove the boat five times across the Tropic of Cancer.   Disorders and discomforts were disheartening.   In the wind and rain the sails were lowered, and the ship drifted aimlessly.   On May 29th Mother Duchesne and her companions reached New Orleans, and were there hospitably welcomed by Mother St. Michel Gensoul and her community at the Ursuline Convent on Chartres Street.

While awaiting directions from Bishop Dubourg, the Sacred Heart Nuns remained the guests of the Ursulines. Through a serious illness of Mother Duchesne and throughout their stay, Mother St. Michel continued her gracious kindness. At the Ursuline shrine of Our Lady of Prompt Succor, Mother Duchesne prayed for Divine Counsel. Plans were then made, in accordance with the wishes of the bishop, and the journey up the Mississippi to the scenes of their new mission was begun.

The small boat on which the journey was made was but the eleventh steamer to make the trip up the river, and the passengers were crowded together in a narrow space. The boat "glided between dark forest-walls of angular-limbed, moss-bearded cypresses, that seemed centuries old, while in the undergrowth palms grew as weeds and the Spanish grey moss swathed many a tree it had killed. The pilot shouted directions and warnings to the man at the engine as he avoided snags of water-logged forest trees, or floating islands formed of masses of logs, and safely shifted the boat across and across the river."

Many stops were made before they gained their destination— St. Louis. There, in the city founded in 1764, and named in honor of St. Louis, the patron saint of King Louis XV, Bishop Dubourg received and welcomed Mother Duchesne and her colony of French nuns on their arrival. They then learned that their first foundation would not be in the episcopal city of the diocese, but in St. Charles, at the time only a little smaller than St. Louis, and near the junction of the Missouri with the Mississippi.

On September 7, 1818, on the site chosen by the bishop of Louisiana, Ven. Philippine Duchesne established the first American foundation of the Society of the Sacred Heart. Then began that loyal service of Mother Duchesne in the country of her adoption. Her chosen work in behalf of the education of youth had many new phases in the varying experiences of pioneers. The gentle women of France hesitated not to milk the cows, to carry the water and make their fires, bravely meeting every emergency, with prayerful courage. From their persevering efforts grew the many convents and schools of the Society in the United States.

Difficulties and tribulations were their lot during the ensuing years. In 1821, soon after the opening of a convent in Florissant, a foundation was made, in a home given for the purpose, at Grand Coteau, a little hamlet near Opelousas, a settlement about one hundred and fifty miles northwest of New Orleans.

In 1826 the diocese of Louisiana was divided and the sees of St. Louis and New Orleans were erected. The Right Rev. Joseph Rosati, C.M., coadjutor of Bishop Dubourg, of Louisiana, was made bishop of St. Louis.

Bishop Rosati at once expressed the desire of having the Society of the Sacred Heart in St. Louis. Mother Duchesne, in 1827, there-fore, secured a large house located on the terraces above the Mis-sissippi and overlooking the city. The new foundation was blessed by the bishop, and the Religious of the Sacred Heart began their work of education in St. Louis.

In 1832 the Asiatic cholera came to North America. It swept the shores of the St. Lawrence and of the Great Lakes, then followed the course of the Mississippi south to the Gulf, with ever-increasing viru-lence. At New Orleans, the Right Rev. Leo R. de Neckère, C.M., D.D., successor of Bishop Dubourg, was among the vic-tims. Five Sacred Heart Nuns died of the plague, and others, especially in St. Louis, were seriously ill. With supernatural strength Mother Duchesne made herself all things to all.

MOTHER MARY ALOYSIA HARDEY

While the affairs of the Society had been progressing in the United States, St. Madeleine Sophie—ever in close touch with Mother Duchesne and her work, was extending the Society in Europe. Rules had been prepared and approved; Councils were held and the plan of the Institute thoroughly developed.

In 1834 the Council elected to the office of Secretary General, Mother Elizabeth Gallitzin. This remarkable woman, a princess, was a convert from the Russian schismatic church. At the age of nine-teen she followed her mother into the true fold, and ten years later she was received into the Society of the Sacred Heart. In 1839 Mother Gallitzin was elected Assistant General and named Visitatrix of the convents in the United States.

At this time there was as Superior at the convent which had been opened at St. Michael's, near New Orleans, Mother Aloysia Hardey. Born in Maryland, of loyal Catholic parents, December 8, 1809, Mary Hardey, when her family—in the tide of emigration that flowed steadily southward for some years after the Louisiana Purchase—journeyed to Louisiana and settled there, became one of the first pupils at Grand Coteau. Entering the Society as a young girl, she was trained, during the early years of her religious life, in the primitive spirit of the Society, and became imbued with the zeal and fervor of her heroic guides. Mother Hardey was endowed with an extraordinary fund of experience, and her natural and supernatural gifts were matured and strengthened by her successive appointments to office.

In 1840 the Right Rev. John Hughes—later first archbishop of New York—while administrator of the diocese of New York, visited Europe. In Paris, Bishop Hughes, in the interests of the educational development of his diocese, called upon the saintly Mother Barat, and received from her assurance of a foundation of the Society of the Sacred Heart in New York.

On May 6, 1841, during the visit to the United States of Mother Gallitzin, and under her guidance, Mother Hardey and a community of Religious of the Sacred Heart arrived in New York, and were soon established in their convent at the corner of Houston and Mulberry Streets. Having later purchased and removed to the Gibbs property at Astoria, and requiring soon afterward a more suitable location for necessary expansion, the Society acquired the Lorillard property at Manhattanville. In 1847 the activities of the Religious of the Sacred Heart in New York City were then transferred to the new institution, where they have continued their educational work, instilling into the lives of their pupils active principles of religion and right living.

Before Mother Gallitzin returned to France, she granted the petition of Ven. Mother Duchesne, and relieved her of her long borne responsibilities as Superior, further granting her, despite her advanced age, her life wish for missionary labor among the Indians.

When the great missionary of the Indians, Father De Smet, asked Mother Gallitzin for nuns for a settlement of the Pottawattomi Indians, at Sugar Creek, a four days' journey up the Missouri, the mission was at once accepted and Mother Duchesne was happily of the colony to carry the work of the Society to the red men.

Concluding her visitation, Mother Gallitzin resumed her duties at the Motherhouse in Paris. At her own request she was sent back for mission work in the United States, where, in the midst of an out-break of yellow fever in Louisiana, she nursed the sick with heroic devotedness, until, on December 8, 1843, she was herself a victim.

Ten years later, on November 17, 1852, Mother Philippine Duchesne—to the end a model of obedience, and love of poverty and humility—died a holy death in the convent at St. Charles, where as a pioneer religious she had made the first United States foundation of the Society.

Meanwhile, under the supervision of Mother Hardey, foundations of the Society were made in many states. Through the years of

CONVENT OF THE SACRED HEART, KENWOOD, ALBANY, NEW YORK

the Civil War, equally bound to the North and to the South, the Society, through Mother Hardey, sent—wherever suffering appealed—food, money, hospital supplies and provisions for the Holy Sacrifice of the mass. Twenty-five free schools were established in the United States and Canada by Mother Hardey, in connection with the numer-ous foundations made. In 1866 the novitiate for the country was established at Kenwood, in Albany, New York. This novitiate, which is continued there, is the only one maintained in the United States by the Society.

In 1871 Mother Hardey was appointed Assistant General, the office recalling her to the Motherhouse. Before her death, which occurred in Paris, June 17, 1886, Mother Hardey—whose strong soul and unflinching pioneer spirit exerted an important influence on the history of the Institute in the United States, had effectively consolidated all the houses under the General Motherhouse, in that unity of spirit and government which characterizes the Society of the Sacred Heart.

In all the institutions of the Society the same rules, customs and traditions are zealously cherished, by the pupils as well as by the religious. In 1832 the holy foundress established the Congregation of the Children of Mary, for the former pupils of the Sacred Heart, and today, wherever there is a Convent of the Sacred Heart, we find active this association of the "Children of Mary of the world,"

CONVENT OF THE SACRED HEART, SHERIDAN ROAD, CHICAGO, ILLINOIS

whose members welcome the meetings at their convent homes, the annual retreats and the continuance of the strong religious influence of their lives. In New York City, the Children of Mary of the three Sacred Heart Convents in the city, after a meeting at Manhattanville, were responsible for the inception of the Barat Settlement, the results of which show their constant interest, philanthropic service and helpful contacts. These daughters of Mother Barat—St. Madeleine Sophie—in the world but not of the world, are worthy representatives of one of the greatest yet humblest religious orders of women.

Foundations of the Society have been made throughout the world, including in extent the countries of the Orient, and the foreign missions. Educational standards, fulfilling the conditions and

requirements of the respective countries, are scrupulously me
maintained. In the United States, in the development of their
the Religious of the Sacred Heart, in addition to their nun
prominent convent schools—boarding, day and country—have
lished and conduct colleges for women, at Menlo Park, San
cisco, California; Maryville, in St. Louis, Missouri; Duchesne C
in Omaha, Nebraska; Manhattanville, in New York City; Clift
Cincinnati, Ohio, and maintain, at Grand Coteau, Louisian
Normal College of the Sacred Heart.

On May 24, 1925, with all the magnificence of papal cere
before a vast assemblage in which were included representati·
students, alumnæ and religious from every institution of the S
the canonization of the Blessed foundress took place in Rom
Madeleine Sophie Barat was proclaimed by His Holiness,
Pius XI, one of the saints of our holy Church, and May
established as the day of her feast.

During the one hundred and twenty-eight years of its exi
the Society has been under the administration of the Superior
erals, Mother Barat—St. Madeleine Sophie, and her succ
Mother Joséphine Goetz, Mother Adèle Lehon, Mother A
von Sartorius and Mother Mabel Digby, under whose superi
wise provision had to be made for two thousand five hundred rel
expelled from France by the government, though the Societ
previously undergone a like trial in Italy and Switzerland, a
Germany, at the time of the *Kulturkampf*. Mother Digby, a
as her successor, Mother Janet Erskine Stuart, in official caɪ
visited the convents of the Society in the United States.   Foll
the recent death of Mother Stuart's successor, Mother Marie d
Mother Manuela Vicente, a native of Spain, was, in the preseɪ
His Eminence, Cardinal Merry del Val, for some years Caɪ
Protector of the Society, elected on November 21, 1928, as Su
General of the Society of the Sacred Heart, whose General M
house is maintained in Italy, Via Nomentana, 118, Rome, 1:

SUMMARY

Religious of the Sacred Heart.
Founded in France in 1800.
Established in the United States in 1818.
Papal Approbation of Rules, December 22, 1826, by Pope Leo XII.
Habit: The habit, cape and transparent veil are plain black; the hea
    is close-fitting, with a fluted frill and a black bandeau. A silver
    bearing the emblem of the Society, and a French wedding ring are

chiefly in educational work, *Eastern Vicariate* in the archdioceses of
timore, Boston, New York and Philadelphia, and in the dioceses of
,any, Detroit, Hartford, Providence and Rochester; *Vicariate house,*
red Heart Convent, Kenwood, Albany, New York (Diocese of Albany);
ariate of St. Louis in the archdioceses of Cincinnati, New Orleans and
Louis, and in the diocese of Lafayette; *Vicariate house,* Sacred Heart
ivent, Meramec Street and Nebraska Avenue, St. Louis, Missouri
rchdiocese of St. Louis); *Vicariate of Chicago* in the archdioceses of
icago and San Francisco, and in the dioceses of Omaha, St. Joseph
. Seattle; *Vicariate house,* Sacred Heart Convent, 6250 Sheridan Road,
cago, Illinois (Archdiocese of Chicago); *United States Novitiate,*
red Heart Convent, Kenwood, Albany, New York (Diocese of
any).

SISTERS OF THE THIRD ORDER OF
ST. DOMINIC*

$\mathcal{A}$T the beginning of the thirteenth century, St. Dominic, born
in Calaroga, Spain, in 1170, began the active career in the
course of which took place the founding of the Dominican
Order, one of the outstanding events in the history of the Church.

Appalled by the conditions wrought in Southern France by dangerous enemies of the Church, especially the Albigenses, St. Dominic,
in his efforts to combat the evil, established at Prouille, in 1206, a
monastery where women were protected from the influence of the
heretics. This monastery with its rule provided by St. Dominic, was
the foundation of the Nuns of the Second Order of St. Dominic,
and preceded by a few years the formation of the Order of Preachers,
the principal part of the Order of St. Dominic—founded for the
uprooting of heresy and the defence of the faith, through the weapons
purity and penance, and still characterized by zeal and devotion to
the Church.

The Third Order of St. Dominic grew out of the institution known
as the Soldiery of Jesus Christ, which St. Dominic founded in his
lifetime. Some years after the death of St. Dominic, men and women
who were leading lives of penance in the world, influenced by the
teachings of the Dominicans, grouped themselves about their convents
and were called the Brothers and Sisters of the Penance of
St. Dominic.

To this Third Order belonged St. Catherine of Sienna, one of
the most remarkable characters in history, who became a Dominican
Tertiary in 1363, when but sixteen years of age. In 1586, one hundred and twenty-five years after the canonization of St. Catherine,
St. Rose of Lima was born, and early in her youth, imitating Sienna's
great saint, she too received the tertiary Dominican habit, and like
her model was vouchsafed signal favors by heaven.

From the first days of the existence of the Third Order of
St. Dominic, groups of its tertiaries have, with proper ecclesiastical
sanction, been formed into religious congregations, the members
living in communities and bound by the vows of poverty, chastity
and obedience, and devoting themselves to teaching, visiting the sick
and other charitable works. Like the Order of Preachers, and the
Nuns of the Second Order of St. Dominic, the members of these

*From the Catholic Encyclopedia and other authentic sources.

various congregations of the Third Order wear the white habit adopted by the Dominicans in the days of St. Dominic.

ST. CATHARINE, KENTUCKY*

1822

In true accord with the spirit of St. Dominic, and realizing that the full fruit of good to be hoped for as a result of their labors in the ministry could be effected only by securing culture for both mind and heart, the pioneer Dominican missionaries in the United States looked early to the Catholic education of the young.

Among these pioneer missionaries was not only the Rev. Edward Fenwick, D.D., a native of Maryland—who upon the completion of his studies at the Dominican College in Flanders, entered the Order of St. Dominic there, and later became the first bishop of Cincinnati—but also the Rev. Thomas Wilson, a learned and experienced priest, through whose zeal was founded in 1822 the first United States congregation of Dominican Tertiaries, or Sisters of St. Dominic.

Having previously established a school for boys at St. Rose, near Springfield, in Washington County, Kentucky, where Father Fenwick had purchased a farm in 1805, Father Wilson explained to the Catholic young women of Springfield the advantages of

MOTHER M. BERNARDINE

the religious life, the Rules and privileges of the Third Order of St. Dominic, and the great necessity of promoting religious education.

Answering the call to form the Dominican Community which Father Wilson wished to found, were Maria Sansbury, later known

---

*From data and material supplied by the Sisters of St. Dominic, St. Catherine of Sienna Convent, St. Catharine, Ky., and from *The History of the Catholic Church in the United States,* by John Gilmary Shea.

in religion as Sister Angela; Mary Carrico, Sister Margaret; Teresa Edelen, Sister Magdalen; Elizabeth Sansbury, Sister Beneven; Mary Ann Hill, Sister Ann; Rose Ann Sansbury, Sister Francis, and Mary Sansbury, Sister Catharine.

April 7, 1822, they entered upon their period of probation and chose as patron of the Community St. Mary Magdalen. On January 6, 1823, Sister Angela Sansbury was chosen first Superior of the little Community, and made her profession in St. Rose's Church

St. Catherine of Sienna Convent, St. Catharine, Kentucky

in Springfield, Kentucky. The newly appointed Prioress later received the profession of the six other sisters, and shortly afterward all began their life-work of instructing and training young girls. The Rev. Richard P. Miles, O.P., later first bishop of Nashville, was appointed first permanent director for the sisters, and instructed them in the duties of the religious life, the manner of reciting the office chorally, and the ceremonial of the Dominican Order.

Each sister received from her parents provisions for one year, but for future needs they tilled the soil, cut wood, spun flax and wool and wove cloth, besides instructing the pupils confided to their care. Ever mindful of the wish of St. Dominic—that his followers devote themselves to prayer, study and work, particularly the work of teaching, by which to aid in procuring the greater glory of God and the salvation of souls—the Community from its inception has been engaged, almost exclusively, in the education of youth.

In 1825 the sisters received the Sansbury estate, a small piece of property near Cartwright's Creek. A cabin of three rooms became the convent, to which was added a chapel, while a house nearby was converted into a home for the pupils. This was the beginning of the boarding school. By 1850 the sisters had succeeded in replacing the old buildings with a commodious church, convent and academy, built so as to form three sides of a square.

On December 19, 1839, the Congregation, as the *Literary Institution of St. Mary Magdalen,* was incorporated by an act of the General Assembly of the Commonwealth of Kentucky, but this name was changed, by Corporate Act of March 11, 1851, to the *Literary Society of St. Catherine of Sienna.*

As the Community grew in numbers and its patronage increased, larger buildings replaced the original ones, but these, on January 2, 1904, were totally destroyed by fire.

With undaunted faith and courage, however, the work of reconstruction was promptly begun, and in less than two years a new St. Catherine's had been erected. Beloved as was the old site, it was abandoned for a more healthful and accessible location. The new St. Catherine's graced one of the highest points in Washington County, and on this account is familiarly known to the pupils of the institution as *Sienna Heights,* while the old site is still affectionately termed *Sienna Vale.*

St. Catherine's Academy and Convent of today has a complete equipment embracing everything modern, even to its own electric plant.

As St. Dominic, from the very foundation of his Order, began to send his brethren in many directions, so the Dominican Sisters, not content with instructing the youth in Kentucky, soon sent members of their Community to other states. The first colony left St. Catherine's in 1830, and founded St. Mary's, in Perry County, Ohio. This foundation, like St. Catherine's, became a novitiate, from which members joined with the sisters from Kentucky in founding other Third Order Dominican communities in Tennessee, California, Texas and Wisconsin.

Each foundation was considered separate and diocesan, and several of the new establishments also sent out sisters to make other foundations. St. Agnes' Convent in Memphis, Tennessee, founded in 1850, lost so many members of its Community during the ravaging yellow fever epidemic that it could no longer supply sisters for the various parochial schools of the city or in the state.   In its need, the Community at St. Agnes' applied for affiliation with St. Catherine's, and was recognized as a mission house from that institution, that its academy work also might not suffer from lack of sisters.

While the work of the Dominican Community at St. Catherine's is mainly that of teaching, the sisters are free to undertake other works of charity.   Thus, in the course of the more than one hundred years of their existence, they have—as the times required—during pioneer days, throughout the siege of the Civil War, and through epidemics, assumed charge of orphanages and hospitals, relinquishing these, however, when there appeared in the field other religious who were by profession bound to such labors.

SUMMARY

Sisters of the Third Order of St. Dominic (St. Catherine of Sienna Convent). Established in the United States in 1822.
Approximate number in Community, 475.
Active chiefly in educational work in the archdioceses of Boston and Chicago, and in the dioceses of Brooklyn, Des Moines, Fort Wayne, Grand Island, Indianapolis, Lincoln, Louisville, Nashville, Omaha, Springfield in Illinois, and Wheeling.
Motherhouse and Novitiate, St. Catherine of Sienna Convent, St. Catharine, Kentucky.   (Diocese of Louisville.)

COLUMBUS, OHIO*

1830

When the zealous pioneer Dominican missionary, Father Edward Fenwick, reluctantly abandoned his missionary labors in 1822, and yielded to the command of the Sovereign Pontiff, accepting the episcopacy of the recently erected diocese of Cincinnati, comprising the entire state of Ohio, he had been for a time Superior of the house of his Order which he had established on the Dittoe farm near Somerset, in Perry County, Ohio.

Familiar as he was with the needs of the neighborhood, through his missionary activities while at Somerset, he at once appealed to the Community of Sisters of St. Dominic at St. Catherine's, near Springfield, Kentucky, to send sisters into Ohio to engage in religious education.   Founded nearly ten years before by the Rev. Thomas Wilson, of the pioneer Dominican missionary band, of which the

*From data and material supplied by the Dominican Sisters, St. Mary of the Springs, East Columbus, Ohio, and from *The History of the Catholic Church in the United States,* by John Gilmary Shea.

new bishop had been first Superior, the Community at St. Catherine's did not hesitate to comply with his request, and in mid-winter of 1830, Mother Emily Elder, Sister Beneven Sansbury, Sister Agnes Hurbin and Sister Catherine McCormick set forth from their convent home in Kentucky to brave the hardships incident to the establishment of a new foundation.

Arriving at Somerset, Ohio—their destination—they found a small brick house, together with an acre of land, assigned them, and an adjoining carpenter shop fitted up as a school. Conventual life was at once entered upon at the new foundation, which was named St. Mary's. A novitiate was immediately opened, the first novice being Sister Rose Lynch.

As Catholic education was from the outset the purpose of the Institute, no time was lost in opening a school, in which, on the 5th of April, 1830, forty pupils were enrolled. The establishment of a boarding school in connection with the day school had not entered into the original design of Bishop Fenwick, but while making his visitation of the diocese, finding the current of feeling in favor of such an academy, he saw the advisability of altering his plan.

MOTHER M. VINCENTIA

Accordingly, St. Mary's became a boarding school, and before the close of 1830 was legally incorporated under the title: *St. Mary's Female Literary Society.*

More commodious quarters having become necessary under the changed conditions, the sisters, with the approval of the bishop, and the generous help of friends, erected a new convent, a substantial brick structure of three stories, attic and basement. On April 23, 1833, Sister Angela Sansbury—the foundress-Superior of St. Catherine's—arrived at St. Mary's, where she remained, filling the office of Prioress until her death on November 30, 1839.

By 1850 the membership in the Community had so increased as

to permit participation in the establishment of a foundation in Mem-phis, Tennessee, and in the next five years sisters of the Community assisted foundations in Monterey, California; and Benton, Wisconsin; in addition to establishing an institution at Zanesville, Ohio. 1860 closed this era of foundations with the sending of a band of four sisters to Nashville, Tennessee, where St. Cecilia's Dominican Convent was founded.

In the early summer of 1866, fire broke out in the convent build-ing at Somerset and gained such headway that little could be done beyond saving the lives of pupils and sisters. Through the kindness

St. Mary of the Springs, East Columbus, Ohio

of the Dominican Fathers, who vacated their novitiate building for them, the sisters were at once provided with a home, where for the ensuing two years they conducted their school.

In this hour of trial for the Community other friends, too, came forward, chief among them Mr. Theodore Leonard of Columbus, Ohio, who not only offered the sisters any part of his land as a site for a new convent, but pledged his further assistance in building. The offer was gratefully accepted, and the present location in East Columbus—for many years designated as Shepard, Ohio—was selected. Its numerous gushing springs, which have long since dis-appeared, gave the Motherhouse its significant name, St. Mary of the Springs.

With the permission of the Right Rev. S. H. Rosecrans, D.D., then just installed as first bishop of Columbus, a convent and academy were erected, which the sisters took possession of on September 1, 1868. Mother Rose Lynch, who had held the office of Superior for some years, became the first Prioress of the new establishment.

In 1893, the Community was organized into a Congregation, and Mother Vincentia Erskine was elected Mother General. Under its new Constitutions, the Community received the official designation: *The American Congregation of Dominican Tertiaries of the Blessed Virgin Mary.*

While making definite provisions for the government of the Congregation in all its departments, the Constitutions exemplify that blending of the active with the contemplative life that has been the well-spring of Dominican power since the foundation of the Order, and one of the secrets of its adaptability to changing conditions.

Keeping in the foremost ranks of progress in all that pertains to general culture, the Community has steadily held in view the ideal of education set forth in its Constitutions—the training of souls for their immortal destiny. The educational work of St. Mary of the Springs, as it is today, with its college which was founded in 1924, combines the best features of women's colleges, breadth of training, and free development of individuality, with the higher requirements of the convent school in comprehension of the direction needful to prepare the young girl for the duties of the Christian woman.

Thoroughly imbued with this spirit of its Constitutions, the Congregation has carried its educational work beyond the convent, school and college at St. Mary of the Springs, to its later established St. Mary's Academy, in New Haven, Connecticut, and Albertus Magnus College, also founded there, in 1925, as well as many prominent academies and schools in other states.

SUMMARY

Sisters of the Third Order of St. Dominic (The American Congregation of Dominican Tertiaries of the Blessed Virgin Mary).
Established in 1830.
Papal Approbation of Rules in 1903.
Approximate number in Congregation, 450.
Active chiefly in educational work in the archdioceses of Chicago, Cincinnati and New York, and in the dioceses of Columbus, Detroit, Hartford and Pittsburgh.
Motherhouse and Novitiate, Convent of St. Mary of the Springs, East Columbus, Ohio. (Diocese of Columbus.)

SINSINAWA, WISCONSIN*
1846

Into Wisconsin, early in its history, there came in the missionary footsteps of Menard, Allouez, Hennepin, Marquette and other brave priests, one from Italy's sunny clime, who in the white robe of St. Dominic left the Ohio house of his Order, for the Indian missions along the shore of Lake Superior.

Soon after 1830, this zealous Dominican missionary, Samuel Mazzuchelli, began his labors among the various Indian tribes and ministered to the spiritual needs of the increasing number of settlers in the Wisconsin region, where he centered his work. Having established a college for boys, at Sinsinawa Mound, Father Mazzuchelli, in view of establishing a similar educational institution for girls, chose to conduct it four devout young women, whom he instructed in the methods of teaching, and—upon their desire of embracing the religious life—he guided according to the Dominican Rule, permitting them the habit of its tertiaries on August 4, 1846.

Sister Clara Conway was appointed Prioress of the little Community, which was composed of Sister Ignatia Fitzpatrick, Sister Josephine Cahill and Sister Ellen Conway. Four sisters from St. Catherine of Sienna Convent, near Springfield, Kentucky—the mother foundation in the United States of the Sisters of St. Dominic—came to Sinsinawa to assist in the Dominican training of the new Community. On August 15, 1849, the four novices made their religious profession.

St. Clara's Academy, which the sisters opened at Benton, Wisconsin, provided a convent home for the Community for many years. As St. Catherine's had sent assisting sisters to Sinsinawa, from Kentucky, the second Dominican foundation, that at Somerset, Ohio, also sent sisters—one of whom remained and later served for many years as Prioress—to continue the training in the religious life of this third United States foundation of Dominican Tertiaries. Father Mazzuchelli, at the same time, continued to instruct them in the various educational branches, in which he was a most proficient scholar.

Following the death of their Community founder, in 1864, the sisters at St. Clara's suffered a series of misfortunes in the loss by death also of tertiaries and of pupils. Triumphing through the trials of the period, transfer of the Motherhouse, St. Clara's, was made to

---

*From data and material supplied by the Dominican Sisters, St. Clara Convent, Sinsinawa, Wis., and from *The History of the Catholic Church in the United States,* by John Gilmary Shea.

Sinsinawa Mound, where the Community had purchased the site upon which Father Mazzuchelli had established the Dominican college for boys.

The growth of this first western Community of Dominican Sisters kept apace with the notable rapid increase in the population of Wisconsin, which, co-incident with its admission into the Union, received

ST. CLARA CONVENT, SINSINAWA, WISCONSIN

many German immigrants who fled Europe during the revolutionary disturbances of 1848.

In 1877, the Community at Sinsinawa and its missions was constituted by papal authority as the Dominican Congregation of the Most Holy Rosary.

While establishing mission schools, academies and high schools throughout the country, as indicated by the great number of archdioceses and dioceses in which its members are active, the Congregation, continuing its marked progressiveness in educational work, in 1904 established a college at the Motherhouse at Sinsinawa Mound, where St. Clara Academy—the first chartered private school for girls in the northwest*—is conducted as a standard high school for girls.

In 1922, during the administration of Mother Mary Samuel, who continues as Superior General of the Congregation, St. Clara College, Sinsinawa Mound, was transferred, as Rosary College, to River Forest, Illinois, an exclusive suburb of Chicago, ten miles from the heart of the city.

As a complement of Rosary College, the Sinsinawa Dominican Sisters in 1925 established at Fribourg, Switzerland, the *Institute des Hautes Études.*   Students of the junior class of Rosary College are permitted to make their entire junior year at *Villa des Fougères,* where the Institute is conducted, under members of the Rosary College faculty residing in Europe, assisted by professors from the Catholic University of Fribourg.   In addition to being the site of this Institute, *Villa des Fougères* has been established by the Sinsinawa Congregation as a center from which American young women may make tours of Europe under competent guidance and chaperonage.

SUMMARY

Sisters of the Third Order of St. Dominic (Congregation of the Most Holy Rosary).

Established in 1846.

Papal Approbation of Rules in 1888, by Pope Leo XIII.

Approximate number in Congregation, 1125.

Active chiefly in educational work in the archdioceses of Baltimore, Chicago, Dubuque, Milwaukee, New York and St. Paul, and in the dioceses of Denver, Des Moines, Green Bay, Helena, Kansas City, La Crosse, Omaha, Peoria, Rockford, Sioux City and Sioux Falls.

Motherhouse and Novitiate, St. Clara Convent, Sinsinawa, Wisconsin. (Diocese of La Crosse.)

SAN RAFAEL, CALIFORNIA†

1850

Inscribed among the names of the pioneer missionaries in the United States is that of the Spanish Dominican friar, Joseph Sadoc Alemany—first archbishop of San Francisco, who began his episcopal duties in California in 1850, as bishop of Monterey.

At the time of his appointment to the see in California, by the Sovereign Pontiff, Pope Pius IX, Bishop Alemany was in Europe

---

*From *The Catholic School System in the United States,* by the Rev. James A. Burns, C.S.C.   (Benziger Bros.)

†From data and material supplied by the Dominican Sisters, San Rafael, Calif.

where he had returned for a visit to his native land after an absence of many years. Following his consecration in Rome, and on his way to America, Bishop Alemany went to Paris where he made a personal appeal to the Dominican Nuns for a community for his see. The answer to his solicitation was that in the party which accompanied him from Europe was Mother Mary Goemaere, a Dominican Nun, and two tertiary postulants.

On the American lap of the trip to California, a stop was made at the Dominican Convent in Somerset, Ohio, where, in place of the postulants, who remained there, Mother Mary Goemaere was joined by two sisters of the Ohio Community, Sister Mary Francis Stafford and Sister Mary Aloysia O'Neil, who formed with her the first California Community of Sisters of the Third Order of St. Dominic.

Journeying by way of New York, Aspinwall and Panama— the trip from Aspinwall to Panama being made by mule-back—the little party reached San Francisco on December 6, 1850, and soon afterward the Dominican Sisters opened in Monterey the first convent school in California.

In the simple adobe house which became the Academy of St. Catherine of Sienna, these daughters of St. Dominic experienced many hardships during their early years in California, when their butter came from Ireland and their flour from Chile, the flour costing, in the famine year of 1852, eighty dollars a barrel.

Of these three ardent tertiary Dominicans, who then opened a novitiate in California, Mother Mary Goemaere, the foundress Superior, was a native of Belgium and of noble lineage, Sister Mary Stafford a native of England and Sister Mary Aloysia O'Neil, American born—a native of Virginia, and the adopted sister of the wife of General William Tecumseh Sherman. One of the first to enter the new novitiate was Donna Maria Concepcion Arguella, daughter of a governor, and whom the California poet, Bret Harte, made the subject of a notable poem.

In 1854, St. Catherine's Academy was removed from Monterey to Benicia, where it is maintained as a school for boys and girls. In 1862, St. Rose of Lima Academy was opened in San Francisco. Its building was destroyed by fire in 1893 and a new one, later erected, was one of the buildings which withstood the shocks of the San Francisco earthquake, and was used as a temporary city hall.

On November 25, 1868, sisters were sent from the Motherhouse in Monterey to San Rafael, in the vicinity of San Francisco, where, on the request of Bishop Alemany, they took charge of St. Vincent's

Orphan Asylum. The inauguration of the work of the Dominican Sisters in San Rafael at this time preceded the transfer there of the Motherhouse and novitiate and the founding there of the Dominican College of San Rafael, for the higher education of women. Successively a college preparatory high school and a junior college, the Dominican College of San Rafael, under the patronage of the Most Rev. Edward J. Hanna, D.D., Archbishop of San Francisco, conferred its first degrees in 1922.

SUMMARY

Sisters of the Third Order of St. Dominic (Congregation of the Most Holy Name of Jesus).
Established in 1850.
Approximate number in Congregation, 200.
Active chiefly in educational work in the archdiocese of San Francisco and in the dioceses of Los Angeles and San Diego, and Sacramento.
Motherhouse and Novitiate, Dominican Convent, Grand Avenue, San Rafael, California.   (Archdiocese of San Francisco.)

BROOKLYN, NEW YORK*
1853

Near the middle of the nineteenth century, in the ancient Dominican Convent of the Holy Cross, near Ratisbon, Bavaria, a plea was heard in behalf of the German Catholic children in the United States. Heeding it, four Dominican Sisters finally secured the permission of their superiors, and sailed for New York in July of the year 1853, that they might labor for the salvation of souls in that land to which so many of their compatriots had emigrated for peace and prosperity.

Tried by disappointments which delayed the inauguration of their activities, though not lessening their ardor, the Bavarian sisters were received into the diocese of Brooklyn, which had just been established, and on September 2, 1853, they took charge of the girls' classes in the Holy Trinity parochial school in Brooklyn.

The vicar general of the diocese, the Rev. Stephan Raffeiner, founder of the first German Catholic church in New York City, as pastor of Holy Trinity Church had provided this opening for the little community. In doing this Father Raffeiner laid in his parish the American foundation of the Dominican Congregation of the Holy Cross—destined, as time has proved, to be the mother foundation of various Dominican congregations now in the country, many

*From *The Catholic News of New York,* the Official Catholic Year Book, 1928, and *From Ratisbon Cloisters,* by Christine Sevier.

of which have in turn established other and widespread congregations of the Third Order of Dominicans, approximating in membership in the United States today about four thousand sisters, in the
Brooklyn and descendent congregations.

In addition to their extensive work in schools, hospitals and
orphanages in the archdiocese of New York as well as in their home
diocese of Brooklyn, the Dominican Sisters of this Congregation, now
approximately eight hundred in number, in 1910 responded to a
request of the Sovereign Pontiff, Pope Pius X, by taking charge of
schools in Porto Rico.

SUMMARY

Nuns of the Order of St. Dominic of the City of Brooklyn (Dominican
    Nuns of the Congregation of the Holy Cross).
Founded in Bavaria in 1232.
Established in the United States in 1853.
Approximate number in Community, 800.
Active in educational, hospital and charitable work in the archdiocese of
    New York and the diocese of Brooklyn.
Motherhouse, Holy Cross Convent, 157 Graham Avenue, Brooklyn, New
    York. (Diocese of Brooklyn.)
Novitiate, Amityville, Long Island, New York. (Diocese of Brooklyn.)

NEW YORK CITY*

1859

The histories of the Sisters of the Third Order of St. Dominic
in New York City begin with the establishment of the Dominican
Convent on Second Street in 1859, when a group of sisters was
sent from the Dominican Convent of the Holy Cross in Brooklyn
to engage in parochial school work in St. Nicholas' parish in the
archiepiscopal city.

Ten years later this branch house was constituted a foundation,
the community becoming the Congregation of the Holy Rosary, of
which Mother Augustine Reuhierl was appointed first Prioress.

The remarkable growth of the new Congregation soon permitted
of its acceptance of missions beyond New York. Extensions were
made into New Jersey, to Michigan and across the country to the
state of Washington—occasioning, for convenience in government,
provincialates which in time were established—and many of these
missions later became mother foundations.

*From *The Catholic News of New York*, the Official Catholic Year Book,
1928, and *From Ratisbon Cloisters*, by Christine Sevier.

At the Motherhouse and novitiate of the Congregation, located now, with Mount St. Mary's Academy, at Mount St. Mary-on-the-Hudson, Newburgh, New York, there was consecrated on May 19, 1928, by the Right Rev. John J. Dunn, D.D., V.G., Bishop Auxiliary of New York, the Chapel of the Holy Rosary. The architectural product of Emil G. Perrot, this chapel, the third unit in a group of buildings occupying a majestic position high above the Hudson River, is reputed one of the most beautiful in the country. Noteworthy among its precious treasures and works of art is one of the gifts of Bishop Dunn, an ebony and ivory crucifix surmounting the tabernacle, the Corpus of which—thirty inches in length—is said to be the largest carved ivory Corpus in existence.

The Dominican Sisters of this Congregation, numbering approximately four hundred, are now active in the archdioceses of Baltimore and New York and in the dioceses of Newark, Raleigh and Trenton.

Motherhouse and Novitiate, Mount St. Mary-on-the-Hudson, Newburgh, New York. (Archdiocese of New York.)

NEW ORLEANS, LOUISIANA*
1859

In 1859, not quite forty years after the Kentucky founding of the first United States Community of Third Order Dominicans—followed by the establishment of two other distinctly American Dominican Communities, and foundations from France and Bavaria—Ireland, already so generous in providing mercy workers and educators in this country, sent Dominican Sisters from Dublin to Louisiana. There in the ancient Catholic city of New Orleans they at once inaugurated their educational work, as planned by the Rev. Jeremiah Moynihan, the zealous pastor of the Church of St. John the Baptist, in the interests of his parochial school.

Under the superiorship of their first Superior, Sister M. John Flanagan, the Dominican Sisters opened, on Dryades Street, in 1862, St. Mary's Select School, chartered under the laws of the state of Louisiana.

Spanning the ensuing years of the Civil War period, and continuing St. Mary's School, the Community, finding the building could not meet the increasing requirements, secured the property on St. Charles Avenue now the site of the Motherhouse and novitiate, where Sister M. Pius McMullan is Prioress and Superior of

*From data supplied by the Dominican Sisters, New Orleans, La.

St. Mary's Dominican College and Diocesan Normal School, connected with the convent.

SUMMARY

Sisters of the Third Order of St. Dominic (Dominican Sisters, New Orleans).
Established in 1859.
Papal Approbation of Rules, July 24, 1928, by His Holiness, Pope Pius XI.
Approximate number in Community, 100.
Active chiefly in educational work in the archdiocese of New Orleans.
Motherhouse and Novitiate, St. Mary's Dominican College, 7214 St. Charles
Avenue, New Orleans, Louisiana. (Archdiocese of New Orleans.)

NASHVILLE, TENNESSEE*

1860

In the year of his accession to the see of Nashville, upon the
death of its first bishop, the Right Rev. Richard P. Miles, O.P., D.D.,
the Right Rev. James Whalan, D.D., who for a year had served as
coadjutor to Bishop Miles, having become familiar with the needs
as well as the activities in the diocese, purchased, with a view to its
adaptability for an academy for young ladies, Mount Vernon Garden,
a mansion home on a large acreage of ground on an elevation in
the northern part of the city of Nashville.

Bishop Whelan applied, then, to the Dominican Sisters at St.
Mary's, Somerset, Ohio, for a community of sisters to take charge
of the school he wished established. His request was granted, and
in the autumn of that year, 1860, four sisters sent to Nashville opened
Mount Vernon Garden as St. Cecilia's Academy.

Little more than a year had passed, filled with successful achievements for those in charge of the new institution for boarding and
day pupils, when its prosperous existence, but just begun, was checked
by the Civil War, with Tennessee one of the scenes of bloodshed and
havoc. However St. Cecilia's continued, though pupils as well as
teachers suffered during the years of the conflict between North
and South, and again through the epidemics of disease which swept
the entire country but especially ravaged Tennessee.

Trials for the Community were not wanting in the subsequent
years, but with the encouragement and the patient guidance of the
Right Rev. Patrick A. Feehan, who had become bishop of Nashville
late in the year 1865, financial difficulties were finally overcome and
the Community entered upon the career of steady development and
success in which it continues.

---

*From the annals of the Dominicans.

SUMMARY

Sisters of the Third Order of St. Dominic (Congregation of St. Cecilia).
Established in 1860.
Approximate number in Community, 120.
Active in educational and charitable work in the diocese of Nashville.
Motherhouse and Novitiate, St. Cecilia's Academy, Eighth Avenue, North,
and Clay Street, Nashville, Tennessee. (Diocese of Nashville.)

RACINE, WISCONSIN*

1862

As Prioress of that ancient Dominican Convent at Ratisbon, Bavaria, Mother Benedicta Bauer had heard the appeal of the Benedictine Abbot, the Right Rev. Boniface Wimmer, who, visiting his native land from the United States, had pleaded there for religious laborers for the fertile mission fields on the other side of the Atlantic.

Five years after the establishment in Brooklyn of the first band of Dominican Nuns who arrived in the United States from Ratisbon in 1853, in answer to this appeal, Mother Benedicta and three companions joined them to also labor in this country.

After some time spent with those of their Congregation at the Brooklyn foundation, impelled by the missionary spirit impregnating the pioneer sisters of the land, Mother Benedicta, accompanied by Sister Thomasina Ginker—one of her three companions from Ratisbon—set out to establish a foundation of the Order in the west.

Having been received into the diocese of Milwaukee by its bishop, the Right Rev. John Martin Henni, D.D., later first archbishop of the see, the zealous Dominican Sisters from Bavaria inaugurated their work in Wisconsin in 1861 when they established their convent home at Green Bay and took charge of St. Mary's parochial school. Joined by two candidates to their little Community, they also soon opened a private school.

Two other candidates had been admitted to the Community when, upon the advice of Bishop Henni, the foundation was transferred to Racine in 1862.

Trials and afflictions, more than once seemingly insurmountable, overwhelmed the Community, but the indomitable energy of Mother Benedicta overcame the many difficulties though she herself did not long survive the establishment in Wisconsin of this Dominican foundation, of now large membership, and wide diversity in its com-

*From data and material supplied by the Sisters of St. Dominic, Convent of St. Catherine of Sienna, Racine, Wis.

munity work, which is carried on in Michigan and Illinois as well as through Wisconsin.

In September of 1864 St. Catherine's Academy, a day and boarding school, was opened in Racine and was the forerunner of St. Catherine's High School which was formally opened in the city, Sep-

CONVENT OF ST. CATHERINE OF SIENNA, RACINE, WISCONSIN

tember 5, 1925, as a co-educational institution, a needed acquisition in the field of religious education in Racine, which had hitherto been without a provision for secondary education under Catholic auspices.

In the course of its establishment of many educational institutions, the Community in 1907 opened Holy Rosary Academy at Corliss, Wisconsin, not far distant from Racine. To this academy

12

the boarders from St. Catherine's were then transferred and Holy Rosary Academy remained a boarding school until 1922 when it was relinquished, upon the sale of the suburban property to the Franciscan Fathers, becoming St. Bonaventure's College at what is now known as Sturtevant, Wisconsin.

SUMMARY

Sisters of the Third Order of St. Dominic (Convent of St. Catherine of Sienna, Racine, Wisconsin).
Established in 1862.
Papal Approbation of Rules in 1905 by Pope Pius X.
Approximate number in Community, 430.
Active in educational and charitable work in the archdiocese of Milwaukee and the dioceses of Detroit, Green Bay, La Crosse, Peoria and Superior.
Motherhouse and Novitiate, Convent of St. Catherine of Sienna, 1209 Park Avenue, Racine, Wis. (Archdiocese of Milwaukee.)

CALDWELL, NEW JERSEY*
1872

Established in 1872 by the Dominican Sisters of the Second Street Convent in New York City as a mission community in charge of the parochial school of St. Boniface's Church in Jersey City, New Jersey, the sisters of the Congregation of St. Dominic, whose Motherhouse is at Caldwell, New Jersey, were, in 1882, erected as a new Congregation of which Mother Mary Catherine was elected first Superior.

Continuing the care of St. Boniface School, the Community is also in charge of many other parochial schools in Jersey City and other cities, as well as many academies of its establishing.

In addition to an academy which is conducted at the Motherhouse there is maintained at the same site the Villa of the Sacred Heart, a summer and winter rest house for ladies.

Having extended their educational labors to Ohio, the sisters established a novitiate in Akron, in the diocese of Cleveland, in the year 1924. In the late summer of 1929 the Dominican Sisters from Caldwell in the diocese of Cleveland were established as a new congregation.

With the increased growth in their Community the Sisters of St. Dominic at the Motherhouse in Caldwell—approximately three

*From *The Catholic Church in the United States of America* (The Catholic Editing Company, New York), current press reports, and the Official Catholic Directory, 1929.

hundred in number—have proportionately extended their activities, and are now engaged in educational work not only in the diocese of Newark but in the archdioceses of Baltimore and Boston and the dioceses of Toledo and Trenton.

Motherhouse and Novitiate, Dominican Convent, Caldwell, New Jersey. (Diocese of Newark.)

SPRINGFIELD, ILLINOIS*

1873

The Dominican Congregation of Our Lady of the Sacred Heart, whose Motherhouse and novitiate are located in Springfield, Illinois, was founded in 1873 by six Dominican Sisters who, upon the invita-

CONVENT OF OUR LADY OF THE SACRED HEART, SPRINGFIELD, ILLINOIS

tion of the Right Rev. P. J. Baltes, D.D., Bishop of Alton, were sent by Mother Regina, Prioress at St. Catherine's, near Springfield, Kentucky, to establish a foundation of the Order in Illinois.

The six sisters composing the Illinois foundation sent from the mother foundation in Kentucky were Sisters Osanna Rowell, Alberta Rumphff, Rachel Conway, Cecilia Carey, M. Agnes Maguire and Josephine Meagher—all of distinguished Dominican relationships and the last three notable for their services in the cause of suffering humanity on the battlefields of the Civil War, the history of which had just been written in the country's annals.

Under the superiorship of Mother Josephine Meagher the sisters arrived in Jacksonville, Illinois, their destination, on August 19, 1873. The Rev. P. J. Macken, pastor of the Church of Our Saviour, at

*From data and material supplied by the Sisters of St. Dominic, Convent of Our Lady of the Sacred Heart, Springfield, Ill.

whose instance, in the interest of the high school he had erected in Jacksonville, Bishop Baltes had invited the community to the diocese, received the Dominican Sisters and escorted them to the convent home hospitably prepared for them in the near vicinity of the school, where two weeks later the sisters took charge of the four hundred pupils enrolled.

Less than a year after their establishment in Jacksonville, the members of the Community participated in an event of historical interest in the country, the occasion being the dedication of the Lincoln Memorial Monument at Springfield, Illinois. President Grant had requested that the honor of unveiling the monument be conferred on some religious sisterhood as a token of gratitude for the faithful services of the nuns during the Civil War, and upon his suggestion, General Sherman, also one of the notables assembled in Springfield, sent to Jacksonville for sisters, who at once, with Bishop Baltes' permission, accepted the place assigned them on the program. Mother Josephine Meagher and Sister Rachel Conway, who had ministered to the wounded and dying on the battlefields under these great generals, shared honors on this day as they unveiled the statue of the martyr president.

May 3, of 1876, the centennial year, marked the first ceremony of reception into the Illinois Community—which, the year previous, had been established in a new home, dedicated to St. Rose of Lima— and, soon afterward, the election of a successor to the office of Prioress, as, according to the Rule, Mother Josephine was not eligible for re-election. At this time Sister Cecilia Carey was chosen Prioress.

In 1881 the Academy of St. Rose of Lima was opened by the sisters. Shortly after the incorporation of the Community in 1884, as the Convent of St. Rose of Lima, purchase was made of the property of former Governor Richard Yates, near the church and school, thus adding to the facilities of the academy in Jacksonville.

In September, 1890, the Community—which in the meantime had become active in many other missions established through the diocese— took charge of St. Mary's parochial school in Springfield. Following the advantageous disposal of the Motherhouse property at Jacksonville, and the erection of a suitable building in Springfield, in Dubois Valley, near the site of historic Camp Yates, the Community later transferred its headquarters to the new convent, which on June 28, 1893, was dedicated to Our Lady of the Sacred Heart.

Thirty years later, and in the year of the transfer of the episcopal see from Alton to Springfield, the convent, with its well established day and boarding school, the Academy of the Sacred Heart, was the scene of the Golden Jubilee celebrations held there marking the conclusion of the Dominican Sisters' first fifty years in Illinois.

SUMMARY

Sisters of the Third Order of St. Dominic (Congregation of Our Lady of the Sacred Heart).
Established in 1873.
Approximate number in Community, 300.
Active in educational work in the archdiocese of Chicago and in the dioceses of Belleville, Boise, Duluth, Peoria, Rockford and Springfield in Illinois.
Motherhouse and Novitiate, Convent of Our Lady of the Sacred Heart, West Washington Street and Lincoln Avenue, Springfield, Illinois. (Diocese of Springfield in Illinois.)

SPARKILL, NEW YORK*
1876

In the year 1876 there was founded in New York City by the Very Rev. J. A. Rochford, Provincial of the Dominicans, a community of Sisters of the Third Order of St. Dominic, for the special work of caring for friendless women and children.

Two Dominican Tertiaries, the Misses Alice and Lucy Thorpe, converts, and penitents of Father Rochford, formed—with Miss Alice Higgins—this community which on May 6, 1876, inaugurated its first ceremonies of religious life in the chapel of the house which had been fitted up for use as a convent, and which was called St. Joseph's Mission for Friendless Girls. The Dominican Provincial then appointed Alice Thorpe, as Mother Catherine M. Antoninus, Superior of the little community.

From this inception has developed the Dominican Congregation of Our Lady of the Rosary, whose Motherhouse and novitiate are at Sparkill, New York, where, on extensive grounds which had been secured, buildings have been erected not only for boys under the care of the sisters, but also for girls, as a means of keeping up relations between brothers and sisters of the same family.

In addition to, as well as in connection with, its many child-caring homes for orphans and destitute children, the Community now engages in school work, especially in New York City and its vicinity, though in its expansion it has extended the activities of its nearly three

---

*From *The History of the Catholic Church in the United States of America* (Vol. II) (The Catholic Editing Company, New York), and from the Official Catholic Year Book, 1928.

hundred and fifty members to this work beyond the archdiocese of New York to the archdiocese of St. Louis and the dioceses of Brooklyn, St. Joseph and Syracuse.

Motherhouse and Novitiate, Dominican Convent of Our Lady of the Rosary, Sparkill, New York. (Archdiocese of New York.)

MISSION SAN JOSÉ, CALIFORNIA*
1876

Inaugurating his episcopal work in California, the pioneer bishop, the Most Rev. Joseph Sadoc Alemany, D.D., of the Order of Preachers, had established Dominican Sisters in Monterey. In the years which followed, other religious communities took up their labors on the Pacific Coast, and though these were many in numbers, the fast-growing needs of the ever-increasing population of California required still others in the field for the religious education of its youth.

In 1876, the Dominican Sisters of the Congregation of the Holy Cross, in response to an appeal from the archbishop, sent from their Motherhouse in Brooklyn, New York, a small colony of sisters, who that year took charge of the parochial school of the Church of St. Boniface in San Francisco.

To augment the little community in California, the mother foun-dation in Brooklyn of the Dominican Congregation of the Holy Cross sent other sisters willing and eager to labor on this far mission. Dis-tance from the Motherhouse and the difficulties of travel, however, at length led to the establishment, in 1890, of the mission in California as an independent Dominican community.

Under the auspices of the Most Rev. Patrick Riordan, D.D., who had succeeded to the archdiocesan see, the Motherhouse, temporarily maintained as the Convent of the Immaculate Conception, in St. Boni-face's parish, was formally established at Mission San José, and diocesan buildings formerly used for seminary purposes became the Convent of the Holy Rosary, in 1906 constituting the Motherhouse and novitiate of the new Congregation. Connected with the Mother-house is St. Mary's Orphanage, where nearly two hundred girls are under the care of the Dominican Sisters of this Congregation, which is now in charge of missions not only in other sections of the state of California, but also in Oregon and Texas.

*From *The Catholic Church in the United States of America* (Vol. II) (The Catholic Editing Company, New York) and the Official Catholic Year Book, 1928.

SUMMARY

Sisters of the Third Order of St. Dominic (Congregation of the Queen of the Most Holy Rosary).

Established in 1890.

Approximate number in Community, 100.

Active in educational and charitable work in the archdioceses of Portland in Oregon, San Antonio and San Francisco, and in the diocese of Los Angeles and San Diego.

Motherhouse and Novitiate, Dominican Convent, Mission San José, California. (Archdiocese of San Francisco.)

GRAND RAPIDS, MICHIGAN*

1877

To the Dominican Sisters in New York City, of the first founda' tion made by the Dominican Sisters of the Congregation of the Holy Cross, in Brooklyn, Michigan owes its two foundations of congrega' tions of Sisters of the Third Order of St. Dominic.

Late in 1876 the Rev. George Ziegler, pastor of St. Francis parish in Traverse City, Michigan, appealed to the Dominican Sisters of the Second Street Convent in New York City for sisters to teach in his parish and in the surrounding missions. Mother M. Hyacinth, the Prioress, having known Father Ziegler from early years, soon arranged to comply with his request.

Mother M. Aquinata was chosen to conduct the little band of sisters to the middle-western state in the fall of 1877, those whom she accompanied being Sister M. Angela, Sister M. Camilla, Sister M. Martha and Sister M. Borromeo. After a trip made by land and water these pioneer Dominican Sisters in Michigan reached Traverse City, their destination, and the site of their first labors in behalf of the education of youth.

After a short stay with the sisters in their new home, Mother Aquinata returned to New York. Rejoining the community in Michigan, two years later, Mother Aquinata remained there perma' nently and untiringly labored in the development of the Commu' nity and the establishment of its many pioneer missions and institutions.

In May of the year 1882 the diocese of Detroit, the territory of which had until then included the entire state of Michigan, was divided by the Holy See, and the diocese of Grand Rapids, com'

---

*From data and material supplied by the Dominican Sisters, Sacred Heart Convent, Marywood, Grand Rapids, Mich., and from *The Catholic Church in the United States of America* (Vol. II) (The Catholic Editing Company, New York).

prising the northern peninsular section of the state, was established, with the Right Rev. Henry Joseph Richter, D.D., as its first bishop. One of the first episcopal functions over which Bishop Richter presided was the dedication of the newly built Dominican Convent in Traverse City. Two years later, in 1885, and until the formation of a province in the diocese of Detroit, this convent became the seat of the Michigan Provincialate of the New York Congregation, with its own novitiate, thus providing for the increased demands for teachers, which were far in excess of the number the New York Motherhouse could supply to Michigan.

In 1894 the Dominican Sisters in the diocese of Grand Rapids were formed into a separate Congregation, and those of the community desiring to retain their membership in the New York Community were given permission to do so. At the first General Chapter of the new Congregation, held at the convent in Grand Rapids in 1894, Mother M. Aquinata was unanimously elected Mother General.

Sacred Heart Academy was opened in Grand Rapids in 1900 and was the forerunner of the splendid academy located on the attractive and spacious grounds of Marywood, advantageously situated on the outskirts of the city.

Continuing their educational activities during the episcopacy of the Right Rev. Michael J. Gallagher, D.D., who, prior to his appointment to the bishopric of Detroit, succeeded Bishop Richter in the see of Grand Rapids, the Dominican Sisters rapidly expanded their work in the diocese in proportion to their growth in number, including in their activities the care of orphans and later opening homes for working girls.

In 1922, under the direction of Mother M. Benedicta, then Mother General of the Congregation, a junior college for girls was opened at Marywood. Normal courses have since been added to its curriculum of college studies, thus providing a state accredited Catholic institution for those preparing for the teaching profession. In connection with the Department of Art at Marywood College and Academy, Marywood serves as the center for summer normal courses conducted by the Art Publication Society of St. Louis.

With the approbation of the Right Rev. Joseph G. Pinten, D.D., as bishop of Grand Rapids, and under the superiorship of Mother M. Eveline, Mother General of the Congregation, the Sisters of St. Dominic have from their Motherhouse in Grand Rapids, recently made their first extension beyond their home diocese to educational work in the diocese of Green Bay.

SUMMARY

Sisters of the Third Order of St. Dominic (Grand Rapids, Mich.).
Established in 1877.
Approximate number in Community, 500.
Active in educational, charitable and social service work in the dioceses of
Grand Rapids and Green Bay.
Motherhouse and Novitiate, Convent of the Sacred Heart, Marywood, Grand
Rapids, Michigan. (Diocese of Grand Rapids.)

ADRIAN, MICHIGAN*

1878

Having established their first mission house in Michigan in 1877,
the Dominican Sisters of the Second Street Convent in New York

City sent a second small band of
sisters there the ensuing year,
and as the first mission was in
the northern section of the state
—at Traverse City—the second
was in the southern section, at
Adrian, where sisters at once
began their labors in educational
work in St. Mary's School, and
in the following year, 1879,
augmented by additional sisters
from New York, also opened
St. Joseph's School.

At this time plans were
made for the opening of a hospital at St. Joseph's, which,
however, developed into a home
for the aged, of which the sisters
were in charge for a number
of years.

Among the sisters from
New York forming the pioneer
Dominican community which

MOTHER M. CAMILLA

arrived in Traverse City in 1877 was Sister M. Camilla, destined
to become one of the foremost religious educators of the times, who
after participating in the initial work of the community in Traverse
City suffered a severe illness, following which she was recalled to

*From data and material supplied by the Sisters of St. Dominic, St.
Joseph's Convent, Adrian, Mich.

New York and later missioned to New Jersey where she was active in the affairs of the Dominican missions in Paterson and Greenville for a period of ten years, interrupted by a second mission in Michigan, where she was in charge of a school in Bay City for two years.

At the end of her eighth year in Greenville, New Jersey, Mother Camilla was sent to southern Michigan not only to take charge of the sisters' home for the aged at Adrian, but later to become first

ST. JOSEPH'S CONVENT, ADRIAN, MICHIGAN

Provincial Superior of the Province of St. Joseph upon its establishment in the diocese of Detroit by the Congregation in New York.

Following the establishment, in 1891, of the convent in Adrian as the seat of the new province of the Congregation, a novitiate was opened, and in April, 1893, the first reception took place when four postulants received the habit of the Sisters of St. Dominic.

In the work of the development of St. Joseph's Academy—a day and boarding school connected with what has in time become the Motherhouse, of the present Congregation in Adrian—Mother Camilla was encouraged and assisted by Dr. Charles O'Reilly, a priest of great intellectual attainments, who had been transferred from St. Patrick's parish in Detroit to St. Mary's in Adrian, and to whose efforts is due, in great part, the steady rapid growth of the student enrollment of the academy during its first years.

The almost phenomenal growth of the Community at Adrian permitted a wide expansion in the activities of the sisters, as missions were opened far beyond the confines of their home state and home diocese of Detroit, where, under the patronage of its present bishop, the Right Rev. Michael J. Gallagher, D.D., the Sisters of St. Dominic from Adrian conduct many parochial schools, in addition to maintaining St. Joseph's College and Academy at their Motherhouse.

SUMMARY

Sisters of the Third Order of St. Dominic (Adrian, Michigan). Established in 1878.

Approximate number in Community, 800.

Active in educational work in the archdioceses of Chicago and Santa Fé and in the dioceses of Cleveland, Des Moines, Detroit, Marquette, Rockford, St. Augustine and Toledo.

Motherhouse and Novitiate, St. Joseph's Convent, Adrian, Michigan. (Diocese of Detroit.)

GALVESTON, TEXAS*
1882

A few years before the death, in 1878, of the Right Rev. S. H. Rosecrans, D.D., Bishop of Columbus, Dominican Sisters from St. Mary's of the Springs in East Columbus had established in Columbus a day and boarding school which Bishop Rosecrans desired maintained in the episcopal city.

The year after the death of the bishop the community at the school transferred for a time to Somerset, Ohio, the original site of the Motherhouse. Upon the invitation of the Right Rev. Nicholas Gallagher, D.D., Bishop of Galveston, and with the permission of the Right Rev. John Waterson, who had succeeded to the see of Columbus, the sisters at Somerset removed to Galveston, Texas, in September of the year 1882, opening there on October 9th Sacred Heart Academy, a day and boarding school for girls.

A few years later the members of the Community took charge of the Cathedral School, and now also are, with the Ursuline Sisters, in charge of the Kirwin High School for Boys, which has more recently been established in the episcopal city.

In addition to their many missions in Galveston, Beaumont, Houston and other Texas cities, the sisters in 1906 opened St. Agnes' Academy in Houston, as a day and boarding school.

SUMMARY

Sisters of the Third Order of St. Dominic (Congregation of the Sacred Heart).

Approximate number in Community, 140.

Active in educational and charitable work in the dioceses of Galveston and Los Angeles and San Diego.

Motherhouse and Novitiate, Sacred Heart Convent, Almeda Road, Houston, Texas. (Diocese of Galveston.)

*From the annals of the Dominicans.

TACOMA, WASHINGTON*

1888

Honoring in their title St. Thomas Aquinas, the illustrious Dominican known as the Angelic Doctor of the Church, the Sisters of St. Dominic of the Dominican Congregation in New Jersey began their activities in the western missions upon their arrival at Pomeroy, Washington, in the fall of 1888.

After the establishment of their Motherhouse in Tacoma, in 1893, Aquinas Academy was soon opened, under the auspices of the Right Rev. Edward J. O'Dea, D.D., Bishop of Nesqually, as was then named the diocese which at that time comprised the entire state of Washington.

The year 1907 is doubly memorable for the Dominican Sisters of the Congregation of St. Thomas Aquinas as it marks for them the establishment at Tacoma of St. Edward's Hall, a boarding and day school for boys, the forerunner of the military academy for young boys now conducted by the Community at New St. Edward's Hall near the Motherhouse at Marymount. The other event of 1907 which stands out in the annals of the Community was the transfer at that time of the episcopal seat of the diocese of Nesqually from Vancouver to their nearer metropolis, Seattle, making possible not only for the Community but for the youth at St. Edward's a closer and more frequent contact with their beloved bishop.

SUMMARY

Sisters of the Third Order of St. Dominic (Congregation of St. Thomas Aquinas).
Established in 1888.
Approximate number in Community, 100.
Active in educational work in the diocese of Seattle.
Motherhouse and Novitiate, Marymount, Tacoma, Washington.   (Diocese of Seattle.)

FALL RIVER, MASSACHUSETTS†

1891

The Dominican Sisters of the Congregation of St. Catherine of Sienna, at Fall River, Massachusetts, were founded in 1891. Sisters

*From *The Catholic Church in the United States of America* (Vol. II) (The Catholic Editing Company, New York) and from the Catholic Encyclopedia and the Official Catholic Year Book, 1928.
†From the Official Catholic Directory, 1929.

of the Community, of approximately one hundred members, are engaged in parochial school work in the diocese of Ogdensburg as well as the diocese of Fall River. An academy is conducted by the sisters at their Motherhouse and novitiate in Fall River.

Motherhouse and Novitiate, Dominican Convent, Park Street, Fall River, Massachusetts. (Diocese of Fall River.)

GREAT BEND, KANSAS*

1902

Fulfilling the missionary desires of the Prioress of the Dominican Sisters of the Congregation of the Holy Cross, at their United States mother foundation in Brooklyn, New York, was her appointment, at the expiration of her term of office in 1901, as one of the community chosen to establish the Order in Kansas.

In 1887 the diocese of Leaven-worth, which included the entire state of Kansas, was divided into two additional sees, Concordia and Wichita. In the interests of the development of the new dioceses the respective bishops at once labored diligently. The Right Rev. John Hennessy, D.D., appointed to the diocese of Wichita on the death of the bishop-elect, immediately made plans for the introduction of the Dominican Sisters to the new dio-cese. Not until the summer of 1902, however, were these plans actualized, when Mother M. Anto-nina Fischer and six other Domini-can Sisters from Brooklyn arrived in Great Bend, Kansas, and at once began their community labors.

MOTHER M. SERAPHINE
15 years Prioress of the Domini-can Sisters, Great Bend, Kan.

With the opening of the schools in September the sisters opened a boarding school, and since then have actively participated in educa-tional work in the diocese of Wichita. Before the close of the

*From data and material supplied by the Sisters of St. Dominic, Immacu-late Conception Convent, Great Bend, Kan.

year 1906 the Community had met an evident need in Great Bend by the opening of a hospital, which as St. Rose's Hospital, with a bed capacity of more than one hundred, opened its modernly equipped and new built additions to the public in November of 1927, on the

IMMACULATE CONCEPTION CONVENT, GREAT BEND, KANSAS

occasion of the twenty-fifth anniversary of the establishment of the Dominican Sisters in Great Bend.

Under the episcopal jurisdiction of the Right Rev. Augustus J. Schwertner, D.D., Bishop of Wichita, the Sisters of St. Dominic with civic interest participate zealously in educational and charitable work in Great Bend, and also through the diocese.

SUMMARY

Sisters of the Third Order of St. Dominic (Great Bend, Kansas). Established in 1902.
Approximate number in Community, 150.
Active in educational and hospital work in the diocese of Wichita.
Motherhouse and Novitiate, Immaculate Conception Convent, 1715 Polk Street, Great Bend, Kansas.   (Diocese of Wichita.)

KENOSHA, WISCONSIN*

1911

The Congregation of St. Catherine of Sienna, Sisters of the Third Order of St. Dominic, whose Provincial house for the United States is in Kenosha, Wisconsin, was founded in Lisbon, Portugal, in 1855, by Lady Theresa Saldanha, daughter of the Count of Rio Maior, of Lisbon.

When Lady Theresa informed her confessor and spiritual director, the Very Rev. Father Russell, O.P., D.D., then Prior at Corpo

ST. CATHERINE OF SIENNA NOVITIATE, KENOSHA, WISCONSIN

Santo, the Dominican church in Lisbon, of her long cherished desire to consecrate her life to God, he told her that as the contemplative religious orders were suppressed in Portugal by the government in 1850, it was his project to establish the active Third Order of St. Dominic in Portugal.

Strongly opposed by her parents in her determination to pursue her religious vocation, Lady Theresa was instrumental in having a group of her friends, who also wished to give themselves to God's service, admitted to the Convent of the Dominican Nuns of the Second Order, at Drogheda, Ireland, where they were trained in the religious life. After some years, during which she financed the new Congregation, Lady Theresa was permitted to enter the novitiate, and upon the completion of her noviceship was, by dispensation and approval from Rome, at once appointed Mother General of the Community.

*From data and material supplied by the Dominican Sisters, Kenosha, Wis.

During the first half century of the existence of the Congregation, in the course of which it spread to many other countries of Europe, the Motherhouse was maintained in Lisbon.   When revolutionary disturbances and religious persecutions in Portugal, in 1910, forced a transfer of the Motherhouse, its present site, at Collegio del SS.mo. Rosario, Calle Zaniora, Salamanca, Spain, was secured.

At this time a band of the exiled sisters was sent to South America, where a Provincial house and novitiate were established at Brazil. The following year, 1911, a house was opened in La Panne, Belgium, and a small band of sisters was sent to North America, where they were received in the United States in the archdiocese of Milwaukee.

Soon after their arrival in the archdiocese, the Dominican Sisters from far-away Spain established their United States Provincial house at Kenosha, Wisconsin, and there the novitiate for the North American Province of the Congregation, of which His Eminence, Vincent Cardinal Vannutelli, is Cardinal Protector in Rome, was canonically erected in 1914.

In addition to engaging in parochial school and orphanage work the Community in the United States is in charge of St. Catherine's Memorial Hospital in Kenosha, and other hospitals in the dioceses in which its members have become active.

SUMMARY

Congregation of St. Catherine of Sienna (Sisters of the Third Order of St. Dominic).
Founded in Portugal in 1855.
Established in the United States in 1911.
Papal Approbation of Rule by Pope Pius IX.
Approximate number in Community in U. S., 200.
Active in educational, hospital and charitable work in the archdiocese of Milwaukee, and the dioceses of Baker City and Monterey-Fresno.
U. S. *Provincial house and Novitiate,* St. Catherine of Sienna Novitiate, Milwaukee Street, Kenosha, Wisconsin.   (Archdiocese of Milwaukee.)

AKRON, OHIO*

1929

Though laboring for some time in missions in the diocese, it was not until the fall of 1924 that the Sisters of St. Dominic from the Motherhouse in Caldwell, New Jersey, established a novitiate in Akron, Ohio, in the diocese of Cleveland.

*From data and material supplied by the Sisters of St. Dominic, Akron, Ohio, and from the *Catholic Universe-Bulletin,* Cleveland, Ohio.

MOTHER M. BEDA

To the zeal and the energy of the Right Rev. Joseph Schrembs, D.D., Bishop of Cleveland, in the interest of the schools in his diocese, and to provide a sufficient number of sisters to care for the large enrollment of pupils, as well as to teach in the many new parishes being established, is due the opening of the new novitiate.

On October 14th the bishop dedicated the property which had been purchased, the Marks estate of twenty-seven acres, with its splendid residence and connecting buildings of fifty rooms, and designated it Our Lady of the Elms Convent.

Marking a new epoch in the annals of the Sisters of St.

OUR LADY OF THE ELMS, AKRON, OHIO

Dominic in the diocese of Cleveland, was the establishment, on August 11, 1929, of the Convent of Our Lady of the Elms, in Akron, as the official Motherhouse and novitiate of the Sisters of St. Dominic of the diocese, as an independent community.

At the election which was then held the following were named officers of the new Congregation: Sister Mary Beda, Mother General; Sister Mary Clarissa, Vicaress; Sister Mary Jeannette, Sister Mary Clare and Sister Mary Bernadette, Councilors; Sister Mary Clare, Secretary General; and Sister Mary Pia, Bursar General.

SUMMARY

Sisters of St. Dominic (Akron, Ohio).
Established in 1929.
Approximate number in Community, 85.
Active in educational work in the diocese of Cleveland.
Motherhouse and Novitiate, Our Lady of the Elms, 1230 West Market Street, Akron, Ohio. (Diocese of Cleveland.)

ALBANY, NEW YORK*

The Dominican Sisters of the Congregation of St. Catherine de Ricci engage chiefly in maintaining rest and retreat houses for women, their institutions in the United States being located in the archdioceses of Cincinnati, New York and Philadelphia, and in the diocese of Albany. The Community numbers approximately a hundred and twenty members.

Motherhouse and Novitiate, 886 Madison Avenue, Albany, New York. (Diocese of Albany.)

BLAUVELT, NEW YORK*

The Sisters of St. Dominic of St. Dominic's Convent, Blauvelt, New York, with a membership of about three hundred, conduct parochial schools and engage in charitable work in the archdiocese of New York and the dioceses of Providence and St. Augustine.

Motherhouse, St. Dominic's Convent, Blauvelt, New York. (Archdiocese of New York.)
Novitiate, Convent of Our Lady of the Blessed Sacrament, Goshen, New York. (Archdiocese of New York.)

EVERETT, WASHINGTON*

The Dominican Sisters, Congregation of the Holy Cross, at

*From the Official Catholic Year Book, 1928, and the Official Catholic Directory, 1929.

Everett, Washington, numbering about a hundred members, are engaged in educational and hospital work in the diocese of Seattle.

> *Motherhouse and Novitiate,* Academy of St. Dominic, 2715 Everett Avenue, Everett, Washington. (Diocese of Seattle.)

DOMINICAN SISTERS OF THE PERPETUAL ROSARY*

1891

The Congregation of the Contemplative Third Order of St. Dominic, more generally known, from its nature, as the Congregation of the Dominican Sisters of the Perpetual Rosary, was established on May 20, 1880, at Calais, in the diocese of Arras, France.

In his apostolic zeal for the perpetuation of the work of the world-wide association of the Perpetual Rosary, the noted Dominican,

DOMINICAN MONASTERY, UNION CITY, NEW JERSEY

the Very Rev. Damien Marie Saintourens, of Paris, conceived the plan of the foundation of a religious community of women to form a guard of honor for the recitation of the rosary continually day and night before the Blessed Sacrament and an image of Our Lady of the Rosary.

The number of candidates for the new community then formed soon necessitated the opening of a second convent. France was in the turmoil of the Revolution, and for security Father Saintourens made this foundation at Bon Secours de Peruwelz, in Belgium. From

---

*From data and material supplied by the Dominican Sisters of the Perpetual Rosary, Union City, N. J.

there the work extended to Louvain, where it was under the personal direction of the Belgian Dominican Fathers.

At the desire of Father Saintourens, and through the joint sponsorship of the Most Rev. Michael Augustine Corrigan, D.D., Archbishop of New York, and the Right Rev. W. M. Wigger, D.D., Bishop of Newark, two Dominican Sisters of the Perpetual Rosary from the foundation at Bon Secours and two from that in Louvain came to the United States in December, 1891, and were received at West Hoboken, now known as Union City, New Jersey, in the diocese of Newark. The Dominican Nuns of the Second Order, from their monasteries at Newark and Hunts Point, New York, each sent welcoming help to the new community, which, with Mother Rose of St. Mary as Prioress, at once pursued its devotion of the Perpetual Rosary in the small house assigned as its temporary convent.

In the following year the community moved to property purchased from the Passionist Fathers, in Union City, and has since erected there the monastery wherein night and day, before the Blessed Sacrament, a guard of honor continues the uninterrupted recitation of the rosary in the cloister chapel of the community.

Other monasteries of the Dominican Sisters of the Perpetual Rosary have been established in the United States, each having its own novitiate, and being directed by a Prioress, while subject to diocesan and papal jurisdiction.

Aside from their predominantly contemplative life, the sisters are also consecrated to the active apostolic propagation of the devotion of the Perpetual Rosary among the laity, through affiliation with this Dominican confraternity.

SUMMARY

Dominican Sisters of the Perpetual Rosary.
Founded in France in 1880.
Established in the United States in 1891.
Habit: The Dominican habit, of white woolen serge, covered by a black woolen mantle, is worn.
Approximate number in communities in United States, 225.
Engaged in contemplative life, with the devotion of the Perpetual Rosary, in monasteries, each with its own novitiate, at the following locations:

    College Road, Catonsville, Maryland. (Archdiocese of Baltimore.)
    68th and Bennett Streets, Milwaukee, Wisconsin. (Archdiocese of Milwaukee.)
    335 Doat Street, Buffalo, New York. (Diocese of Buffalo.)
    Camp Hill, Pennsylvania, R.R. 1. (Diocese of Harrisburg.)
    La Crosse, Wisconsin, R.R. 3. (Diocese of La Crosse.)

14th and West Streets, Union City, New Jersey. (Diocese of Newark.)

1430 Riverdale Street, West Springfield, Massachusetts. (Diocese of Springfield.)

802 Court Street, Syracuse, New York. (Diocese of Syracuse.)

1500 Haddon Avenue, Camden, New Jersey. (Diocese of Trenton.)

SERVANTS OF RELIEF FOR INCURABLE CANCER*

1899

"I am trying to serve the poor as a servant. I wish to serve the cancerous poor because they are avoided more than any other class of sufferers; and I wish to go to them as a poor creature myself, though powerful to help through the open-handed gifts of public kindness, because it is by humility and sacrifice that we become worthy to feel the holy spirit of pity and to carry into the disorders of destitute sickness the cheerful love we have gathered from the Heavenly Kingdom for distribution."

These words of Mother M. Alphonsa Lathrop, foundress, and until her unexpected death on July 9, 1926, Superior General of the Dominican Congregation of St. Rose of Lima—the Servants of Relief for Incurable Cancer—memorably embody the special work to which, once she had taken it up, she devoted herself until summoned to give an account of her stewardship.

Of a long line of Puritan ancestors, Rose Hawthorne Lathrop, the daughter of Nathaniel Hawthorne, with her husband, George Parsons Lathrop, withdrew from the Unitarianism professed by her immediate family, and was received into the Catholic Church. Shortly afterward, and not long before the death of Mr. Lathrop, they both united in writing a last book, "The Story of Courage."

Conversing with her spiritual director, a Paulist Father in New York, Mrs. Lathrop on an occasion asked: "What can I do for God?" The priest had just come from the bedside of a cancer patient—a woman of refinement, left without money and without friends, who had become a city charge at Blackwell's Island. This and all the misery it meant he told his listener. "Oh," she exclaimed, "why do any of us sit idle when such suffering exists!" It was then that her resolve was made. Within a few weeks she had entered the Memorial Hospital (for cancer cases) at Central Park West and 106th Street, New York City, for training in the nursing of such patients.

*From data and material supplied by the Servants of Relief for Incurable Cancer, Hawthorne, N. Y.

In 1896, and in New York City, Mrs. Lathrop was ready to begin her life-work for God.   Her first patient—a worn-out old

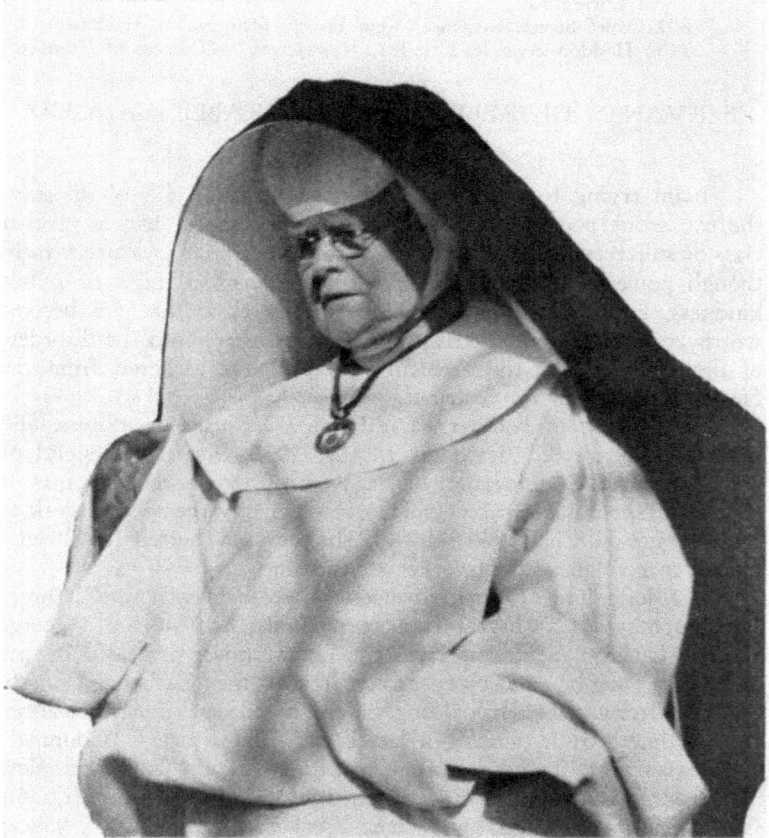

MOTHER M. ALPHONSA LATHROP (1851-1926)
Foundress of the Dominican Congregation of St. Rose of Lima
(Servants of Relief for Incurable Cancer)
Photographed in April, 1926, on the occasion of the conferring of a gold medal on Mother Alphonsa by the Rotary Club of New York City for service to humanity

woman deserted by her family—she not only nursed but took to rooms she rented on Scammel Street, and there she, Rose Hawthorne Lathrop, scrubbed the floors, cooked the meals, and did all for the care and relief of her poor suffering patient.   In the corner of one of the rooms she set up a little shrine. It was to the Dominican saint, St. Rose of Lima.

Other patients were commended to her, and to provide for them larger quarters being required, a frame house on Water Street, also on the lower East Side of the city, was secured, and transfer made to it. It was to this house that in mid-December of 1897 Miss Alice Huber, of Louisville, Kentucky, made her way, with a letter from the noted Passionist, the Rev. Father Fidelis Stone, introducing her to Mrs. Lathrop.

Mrs. Lathrop, "beautiful and youthful-looking, with a mass of rich auburn hair," and wearing a nurse's dress, she found ministering

ROSARY HILL HOME, HAWTHORNE, NEW YORK

to one of the cancer patients, while two others almost impatiently awaited her attentions. Before concluding her visit, Miss Huber was impelled to offer her assistance to Mrs. Lathrop an afternoon a week. The one afternoon of help in the dispensary soon became two, and in a few months she asked to share for all time in the work that was being carried on.

On May 1, 1899, for still larger accommodations than the tene-ment quarters on Water Street could afford, the patients were trans-ferred to a comfortable, old-fashioned house at 426 Cherry Street, which was at once named St. Rose's Free Home for Incurable Cancer.

Here then, in a little chapel which had been arranged, Mrs. Lathrop and Miss Huber, having long since consecrated their lives to God in their work, received the Dominican habit from the hands of the Rev. Clement M. Thuente, O.P., Mrs. Lathrop becoming in religion Mother Alphonsa, and Superior, and Miss Huber, Mother Rose, taking the name of the foundress as well as the patron of the new congregation.

Others having joined in the heroic work being carried on, and who likewise received the Dominican habit, the Cherry Street house soon became too small for community and patients, and on June 1, 1901, Rosary Hill Home, at Hawthorne, New York, was also opened.

There in Westchester County, far away from even the echo of the city's turmoil, yet near enough for easy access, is Mother Alphonsa's second institution. There the daughter of one of America's greatest authors, and the noble congenial wife of another, spent more than a score of years serving God in the afflicted poor. Often through the still watches of the night she rose to attend the sick and dying, the warm, firm clasp of her hand giving strength and confidence to the sufferer whose soul was passing to its Maker.

At Rosary Hill Home Mother Alphonsa planned and developed the work of the Congregation, which also continues to carry on its activities in New York City at St. Rose's Free Home for Incurable Cancer, this institution, with a bed capacity of ninety, and now located at 71 Jackson Street, ranking as a hospital for incurable cancer cases among the destitute poor of all religions, nationalities and colors.

To her first companion and associate worker, Mother Rose Huber, who has succeeded to the office of Superior General of the Congregation, is left the completion of the needed fire-proof buildings of Rosary Hill Home at Hawthorne, the erection of which Mother Alphonsa, after long years of waiting, had finally been able to inaugurate.

Assuming the responsibilities of her position, Mother Rose is also devoting herself to the task of financiering, by means of public appeals—the policy established by Mother Alphonsa, in place of modern drives—the completion of this lasting monument to the memory of one of America's noblest women, a woman of the world who, laying aside worldly habiliments for the sacred garb of a religious, won other fervent workers who will not let the work she founded die with her, but perpetuate it in the Dominican Congregation of St. Rose of Lima—the Servants of Relief for Incurable Cancer.

SUMMARY

Dominican Congregation of St. Rose of Lima (Servants of Relief for Incurable Cancer).

Founded in the United States in 1899.

Habit: The black and white Dominican habit is worn.

Approximate number in Community, 50.

Active in charitable work in the archdiocese of New York.

Motherhouse and Novitiate, Rosary Hill Home, Hawthorne, New York. (Archdiocese of New York.)

DOMINICAN SISTERS OF CHARITY OF THE PRESENTATION OF THE BLESSED VIRGIN*

1906

In Sainville, France, in 1684, through Marie Poussepin, the Dominican Sisters of Charity of the Presentation of the Blessed Virgin—familiarly known as Sisters of the Presentation, were founded, for the education of poor children, and the care of the sick and aged.

At the expressed wish of the Dominicans of the priory for French missions, in Fall River, Massachusetts, the Community was first established in the United States there, in February, 1906, with Mother Marguerite of the Sacred Heart as first Superior.

The Community in this country is subject to the jurisdiction of the Mother General at the Motherhouse in Grande-Breteche, Tours, France, while Mother Therese du Sauvreur serves as present United States Superior.

A DOMINICAN SISTER OF CHARITY OF THE PRESENTATION OF THE B.V.M.

SUMMARY

Dominican Sisters of Charity of the Presentation of the Blessed Virgin Mary (Sisters of the Presentation).

Founded in France in 1684.

Established in the United States in 1906.

Habit: The habit is of cream colored serge, with a pleated skirt, black serge apron with a bib, and white linen bands and cornette.

Active in educational and hospital work in the diocese of Fall River.

DOMINICAN SISTERS OF THE SICK POOR†

1910

The Community known as the Dominican Sisters of the Sick Poor was founded in New York City toward the close of the year 1879 by one who was long known there as Mother Mary Walsh,

*From data and material supplied by the Sisters of the Presentation, St. Ann's Hospital, Fall River, Mass.

†From data supplied by the Dominican Sisters of the Sick Poor, New York City, and from current news reports.

and who with a companion devoted herself to nursing the sick poor in their own homes. At times the two charitable women were joined by others equally zealous, but as often were left to continue in their work of mercy alone.

After several changes of residence in New York City, Mother Mary, who had entered the Third Order Secular of St. Dominic, with two associates became established in the vicinity of the Paulist Church. Materially assisted by an auxiliary which was formed in their behalf, they were enabled to continue the charitable work of nursing the sick poor.

Following their affiliation, in 1910, with the Third Order Regular of St. Dominic, and their adoption of the Dominican habit, a novitiate was opened at their convent home in New York, over which an efficient novice mistress from the Dominican Congregation at St. Mary of the Springs, in Columbus, Ohio, was placed for a time.

In addition to the labor of the Community in New York City, where it now maintains two convents, Columbus, Ohio, received a group of the sisters, who upon their arrival there found that a generous donor had provided them not only a furnished house, but supplies from which to draw for the possible needs of the sick poor, whom they were soon called on to attend. A little later, sisters from New York were sent to Denver, Detroit and Cincinnati for the same charitable work, and more recently another Ohio city, Springfield, welcomed a small community of these nurses of the sick poor. Here too they were met by public charity and co-operation, and in addition to the home and supplies provided them, a monetary allowance was early assured them from the Community Chest funds of the city.

Continuing in the footsteps of their great-hearted and humble foundress, the Dominican Sisters of the Sick Poor give their services without remuneration, and make no distinction as to race or creed. Besides caring for the sick, they look after the children, if there are any in the home, assist in the house, and in cases of extreme poverty provide bedding, fuel and other necessities. Their work affords them many opportunities of ministering not only to the physical but to the spiritual needs of the destitute, and frequently those who have long neglected their religious duties are brought back to the Church, and are encouraged to persevere, through the prayers and good works of the sisters.

SUMMARY

Dominican Sisters of the Sick Poor.
Founded in the United States in 1910.

Habit: The Dominican habit is worn.

Approximate number in Community, 75.

Active in charitable work in the archdioceses of Cincinnati and New York and in the dioceses of Columbus, Denver and Detroit.

Motherhouse and Novitiate, Convent of the Immaculate Conception, 140 West 61st Street, New York City. (Archdiocese of New York.)

DOMINICAN SISTERS OF PERPETUAL ADORATION AND THE PERPETUAL ROSARY*

1919

To pray and work through the devotion of the Perpetual Rosary, united to the Perpetual Adoration of the Blessed Sacrament, exposed on their chapel altar, the Dominican Sisters of the Perpetual Adora-

DOMINICAN CONVENT, SUMMIT, NEW JERSEY

tion and the Perpetual Rosary established a foundation for this twofold purpose at Rosary Shrine, Summit, New Jersey, in the year 1919. Mother Mary Imelda, of the Dominican Sisters of the Perpetual Rosary, in Union City, New Jersey, served as first Prioress of the new Community, and Mother Mary of Jesus was elected second Prioress, December 27, 1928.

Rosary Shrine, as the monastery chapel has become known, has

*From data and material supplied by the Dominican Sisters of Perpetual Adoration and the Perpetual Rosary, Summit, N. J.

been enriched with many indulgences and is noted throughout the country. To accommodate the number of pilgrims who in their visits there unite with these Dominican Sisters in Perpetual Adoration and the Perpetual Rosary, a church worthy of the purpose was dedicated, and the year 1926 marked its opening as a sanctuary devoted to the promotion of the holy rosary. Here, day and night, intercession is made through the Perpetual Rosary for the conversion of sinners, and especially in thanksgiving for the institution of the priesthood, in reparation for all sins which in any way are committed against this Divine benefit, and in petition for an increase in vocations to the priesthood, for the perseverance and sanctification of priests, and for the relief of the souls of priests detained in Purgatory.

In the interest of Rosary Shrine, *The Rosary Pilgrim* is issued quarterly by the sisters as the organ of the Rosary Pilgrimage League.

Compelling particular interest and devotion at Rosary Shrine in Summit, is a replica of the holy winding sheet of Our Lord, which is preserved at Turin, Italy. This replica was painted in 1624 and laid for a time upon the real winding sheet. When it was withdrawn it was found that the mark of the Wound in the Side had become damp on the original as though with blood, and this stained the copy, as may be plainly seen on it as it is exposed in the monastery chapel at Summit, where it is greatly venerated. This painting, the only copy of its kind known to be in existence in this country, was the treasure of the Dominican Nuns in Rome until after the World War, when, with civic and ecclesiastical permission, it was presented to the Summit shrine in appreciation of material assistance rendered by the members of the Community there to their sisters in religion in Italy, sorely afflicted in consequence of the war.

As in each foundation of the Dominican Sisters of the Perpetual Rosary, the cloistered contemplative life is observed by the sisters at Rosary Shrine, and the community is independent, maintaining its Motherhouse at the monastery in Summit.

SUMMARY

Dominican Sisters of Perpetual Adoration and the Perpetual Rosary.
Founded in the United States in 1919.
Habit: The Dominican habit—white, with a black cope—symbolizing purity and penance, is worn.
Approximate number in Community, 30.
Engaged in contemplative life in the diocese of Newark.
Convent and Novitiate, Rosary Shrine, 63 New England Street, Summit, New Jersey. (Diocese of Newark.)

FOREIGN MISSION SISTERS OF ST. DOMINIC*

1920

That one may be unwittingly the instrument of Providence is well demonstrated in the history and origin of the Foreign Mission Sisters of St. Dominic, founded at Maryknoll, near Ossining, New York, on February 14, 1920.

Such an agent was one in authority at Smith College, in Northampton, Massachusetts, who, with a suggestion to Miss Rogers, a Catholic teacher on the college staff, that she should do something for the religious interests of the Catholic students, laid the first stone in the foundation of the Congregation of the Foreign Mission Sisters of St. Dominic.

To "do something" Miss Rogers, familiar with visible Protestant missionary activities, organized a study group to learn about Catholic missions. For material from which to outline a program of study, she was referred by a resident pastor in Northampton to the office of the Society for the Propagation of the Faith in Boston. Here she found in the director, the Rev. James Anthony Walsh, one deeply interested in foreign missionary work—one filled with the missionary zeal of his French Sulpician professors, from whom he must have learned of the Sulpician foreign missionary labors in the United States, when crossing the seas from France to our ports was far more hazardous and trying than any trans-oceanic voyage of today from America to not a foreign mission, but foreign missions, in China, India, Africa or the Philippines.

When Father Walsh, whose zeal brought forth "The Field Afar" in 1907, united with the Rev. Thomas Frederick Price, for many years a missionary in the south, and founder of the Catholic magazine, "Truth," the Catholic Foreign Mission Society of America, established on June 29, 1911, with the blessing of the Sovereign Pontiff, Pope Pius X, was the result of the fusion of their efforts.

It is not to be wondered at that her study of the foreign mission situation, in the interest of the college student group, led Miss Rogers, with two companions, to offer their services to the organizers of the Catholic Foreign Mission Society. For the feast of the Epiphany, 1912, they were established in a little cottage at Hawthorne, in Westchester County, New York, not far distant from the first home of the new Society formed by Father Walsh and Father Price, from

---

*From data and material supplied by the Foreign Mission Sisters of St. Dominic, Maryknoll, N. Y.

which they removed to take possession of Maryknoll, near Ossining, New York.

In the fall of 1912, Miss Rogers and her two companions, together with three others who had joined them, moved from Hawthorne

MOTHER MARY JOSEPH ROGERS
Foundress and Superior of the Foreign Mission Sisters of St. Dominic
(Maryknoll Sisters)

to Maryknoll-on-Hudson, where one of the houses on the new property of the Catholic Foreign Mission Society had been assigned for their use. Naming the house in honor of St. Teresa—who while she labored in her native land, loved, prayed for and made sacrifices for pagan souls—the group of laywomen became known as the Teresians.

His Eminence, John Cardinal Farley, Archbishop of New York, becoming personally interested in the Teresians, whom he encouraged to adopt a uniform dress, gave them the great privilege of having the Blessed Sacrament reserved in their house, and advised them to place themselves under professed religious to be trained in the principles and the observance of the religious life.

In 1914, Mother M. Germaine, Superior General of the Sisters, Servants of the Immaculate Heart of Mary, of Scranton, Pennsyl-

MARYKNOLL CONVENT, OSSINING, NEW YORK

vania, with true apostolic charity responded to the request of Father Walsh that the Community undertake this training, and three sisters from the Motherhouse at Mt. St. Mary's, Sister M. Stanislaus as Superior and Novice Mistress, Sister M. Domitilla and Sister M. Gerard—later replaced by Sister M. Martha—were sent to St. Teresa's, where they remained for nearly two years, during which the Teresians followed the exercises of a novitiate.

Among the many members of the hierarchy and the clergy who visited Maryknoll was the zealous Dominican, the Rev. John T. Mc-Nicholas, later bishop of Duluth and present archbishop of Cincinnati. Largely through his counsel the Teresians were led to affiliate with one of the great religious orders of the Church, and share in its spiritual privileges, and on February 7, 1916, Father McNicholas enrolled the community of fourteen laywomen as Dominican Tertiaries.

Continuing his beneficent interest in the Teresians, Cardinal Farley approved a petition to Rome in June, 1916, asking their recognition as a religious body under the title "Dominican Tertiaries of the Foreign Missions." The following January, word was received from Rome, through Cardinal Farley, that the tertiaries were to consider themselves as a sodality of pious women, organized to aid the foreign missions.

In the fuller development of their work, Father McNicholas solicited the Sisters of St. Dominic at St. Clara Convent, Sinsinawa, Wisconsin, for sisters who should give the sodalists Dominican training. Responding to this request, Mother M. Samuel, Superior General of the Sinsinawa Congregation, sent Sister Mary Ruth, and later Sister Fidelia, to Maryknoll for this purpose.

Meanwhile Father Walsh, the Superior of Maryknoll, found the assistance of the sodality in household, clerical and literary work invaluable. Lack of accommodations, however, prevented the encouragement of many inquirers regarding the community, which nevertheless continued to grow.

In 1918, while awaiting Rome's answer as to their status, four of the Teresians were sent to Clarks Summit, Pennsylvania, where from Our Lady of the Missions Convent, which they then opened, they assisted in clerical and other work at Maryknoll Preparatory College which is established there.

On February 14, 1920, their patient waiting was rewarded when the approbation of the Maryknoll Sisters as a religious congregation was received from Rome, through His Eminence, Patrick Cardinal Hayes, who, upon the death of Cardinal Farley, had become archbishop of New York.

Upon their recognition by the Church as a religious community, the Foreign Mission Sisters of St. Dominic, Dominicans of the Third Order, were later incorporated under the laws of the state of New York. The Congregation, of which the foundress, as Mother Mary Joseph, is Superior General, is entirely separate and distinct, as a religious body and financially, from the Catholic Foreign Mission Society of America, although laboring with that organization for one end—the spread of the faith of Christ.

On September 8, 1921, the first Maryknoll Sisters left for their field afar, and began the practical foreign missionary work of the

Congregation in the Maryknoll section of South China. Today this, the only American community of sisters devoted exclusively to the work of foreign missions, numbers more than three hundred members, from states in the north, south, east and west, as well as from Hawaii, Canada, Europe, Australia, Japan, Korea and China. In their zeal for the salvation of pagans in the Orient, as well as for Asiatics in Christian countries, the sisters not only actually labor in the foreign missions, but also publish and mail books and do household work in its many phases. Some are engaged in school and catechetical work among the Japanese on the Pacific Coast; others labor in the Orient, where they conduct a school for girls, direct industrial works, and care for orphans, the blind, the aged and the sick. The sisters also conduct schools in the Hawaiian Islands, where more than fifty per cent of the children are Orientals.

In Manila the sisters conduct a normal school, a large hospital, and dormitories where they receive native girls attending secular institutions, giving them the spiritual

SISTER MARY DE PAUL COGAN
A Maryknoll Sister

and social safeguards needed in such a cosmopolitan center.

Vocations to the foreign mission work have been many, as evidenced by the already large number in the Community, whose activities are supported wholly by charity. Devoting themselves to the extension of the work for which they were founded, and the foundation and development of native sisterhoods in the foreign missions, the Maryknoll Sisters, as they are familiarly known, maintain their Motherhouse—as yet a temporary structure—at Maryknoll, and in Washington, D. C., have established a House of Studies at 105 Second Street, N.E., where the sisters reside while pursuing needed courses for their work.

As a source of income, the sisters conduct near Maryknoll a rest house for women. Guests at Bethany, in the beautiful Westchester Hills, enjoy the privileges of a house chapel and daily mass, and during Lent, as well as other periods through the year, week-end retreats for laywomen are conducted there.

14

SUMMARY

Foreign Mission Sisters of St. Dominic (Maryknoll Sisters).
Founded in the United States in 1920.
Habit: By a special privilege, the Maryknoll Sisters, although they follow
the Dominican Rule, wear a gray habit instead of the characteristic white
of the Dominicans.   The white scapular, however, is worn beneath one
of gray.   In the tropics and for hospital work, an all white habit is worn
indoors.
Approximate number in Community, 325.
Active in foreign missionary work and in missionary activities in the United
States in the archdioceses of Baltimore, New York and San Francisco,
and in the dioceses of Los Angeles and San Diego, Seattle and Scranton.
Motherhouse and Novitiate, Maryknoll, New York.   (Archdiocese of New
York.)

CHRONOLOGICAL TABLE*

*Foundations in the United States of Congregations of the Third Order
of St. Dominic*

1822—Springfield, Kentucky (St. Catharine, Kentucky).
1830—Columbus, Ohio.
1846—Sinsinawa, Wisconsin.
1850—San Rafael, California.
1853—Brooklyn, New York (Amity- ville, Long Island, N. Y.).
1859—New York City, New York (Newburgh, N. Y.).
1859—New Orleans, Louisiana.
1860—Nashville, Tennessee.
1862—Racine, Wisconsin.
1872—Caldwell, New Jersey.
1873—Springfield, Illinois.
1876—New York City (Sparkill, N. Y.).
1876—Mission San José, California.

1877—Grand Rapids, Michigan.
1878—Adrian, Michigan.
1882—Galveston, Texas.
1888—Tacoma, Washington.
1891—Fall River, Massachusetts.
1891—West Hoboken, New Jersey (Union City).
1899—New York City (Hawthorne, N. Y.).
1902—Great Bend, Kansas.
1906—Fall River, Massachusetts.
1910—New York City, New York.
1911—Kenosha, Wisconsin.
1919—Summit, New Jersey.
1920—Ossining, New York (Mary- knoll).
1929—Akron, Ohio.

GENERAL SUMMARY

Sisters of the Third Order of St. Dominic.
Established in the United States in 1822.
Papal Approbation of Rules, as given to various communities.
Habit: The Dominican habit, a cream white tunic and scapular, with a black
mantle, signifying purity and penance, is worn.   The veil is black.
Approximate number in communities in United States, 7,300.
Active in educational, hospital, charitable, social service and missionary work,
and engaged in the contemplative life, in the archdioceses of Baltimore,

*There are also Dominican communities, whose foundation dates were not
supplied, at Albany, N. Y., Blauvelt, N. Y., and Everett, Wash.

Boston, Chicago, Cincinnati, Dubuque, Milwaukee, New Orleans, New York, Philadelphia, Portland in Oregon, St. Louis, St. Paul, San Antonio, San Francisco and Santa Fé, and in the dioceses of Baker City, Belleville, Boise, Brooklyn, Buffalo, Cleveland, Columbus, Denver, Des Moines, Detroit, Duluth, Fall River, Fort Wayne, Galveston, Grand Island, Grand Rapids, Green Bay, Harrisburg, Hartford, Helena, Indianapolis, Kansas City, La Crosse, Los Angeles and San Diego, Louisville, Marquette, Monterey-Fresno, Nashville, Newark, Ogdensburg, Omaha, Peoria, Pittsburgh, Providence, Raleigh, Rockford, Sacramento, St. Augustine, St. Joseph, Scranton, Seattle, Sioux City, Springfield, Springfield in Illinois, Superior, Syracuse, Toledo, Trenton, Wheeling and Wichita.

OBLATE SISTERS OF PROVIDENCE*

1829

AMONG several unusual features which distinguish in its origin the Congregation of the Oblate Sisters of Providence, founded in Baltimore, Maryland, in the year 1829, is the fact that it stands alone on the records of the archdiocese of Baltimore as the only religious community of women founded there during the terms of the two successive archbishops, the Most Rev. Ambrose Marechal and the Most Rev. James Whitfield.

Early in the nineteenth century the large congregation which attended services held in the chapel of St. Mary's Seminary in Baltimore was composed chiefly of French, English, American and Negro people. For thirty-one years during that period the Rev. John Tessier, one of the Sulpician founders of the seminary, and in turn one of its presidents, devoted himself to giving catechetical instruction to and attending to the needs of the colored people of the congregation, many of whom had accompanied their old masters to Baltimore at the time of the insurrection of San Domingo.

Father Tessier was early associated in his chosen work among the colored people by one of his confrères at the seminary, the Rev. James H. Joubert de la Muraille, whose youth had been spent in San Domingo, and who, through the insurrection there, had suffered the tragic loss of his own family.

Desirous of making permanent provision in Baltimore for the education of colored girls, Father Joubert interested three zealous young women in the project of forming a religious community to carry on the work. On June 5, 1825, Archbishop Marechal approved the rule drawn up by Father Joubert for the community, in which Elizabeth Lange, Frances Balis and Miss Bogue, previously engaged in school work, had agreed to devote their lives to its furtherance.

Soon after his consecration for the archbishopric of Baltimore, in May, 1828, Archbishop Whitfield gave his approval to the then four members of the prospective sisterhood beginning a community life. In the house where they at once united for this purpose a boarding and day school was then opened, thus inaugurating the religious educational work of the Order.

*From data and material supplied by the Oblate Sisters of Providence, Baltimore, Md., and from *The History of the Catholic Church in the United States* by John Gilmary Shea, and *The Oblate Sisters' Centenary* by Cecilia A. Daniels in "Mission Fields at Home."

With the further approbation of Archbishop Whitfield, the little community—over which he placed Father Joubert as director, and of which Elizabeth Lange, as Sister Marie, had been appointed Superior —was permitted to make the vows of religion on July 2, 1829, and on that day was established as a religious society of colored women founded for the glory of God, the sanctification of its members and the Christian education of colored children. As Oblate Sisters of Providence, their origin dates from October 2, 1831, when the Holy See approved the rule of the Community and endowed its members with all the privileges and indulgences granted to the Oblates founded about the year 1425 by St. Frances of Rome.

Father Joubert continued to direct the affairs of the Congregation until his death in 1843. In the course of these years the sisters deviated, for the necessary time, from their work in behalf of the education of colored children to respond to a call for nurses during the cholera epidemic which swept Baltimore in 1832, one of their number being among the victims of the dread disease, following her faithful attendance on the stricken.

MOTHER MARY FRANCES FIELDERS
Former Superior of the Oblate Sisters of Providence

Mother Mary Elizabeth Lange, first Superior of the Congregation, reached the age of ninety-five, dying in February, 1882. She saw the Congregation through its many struggles and trials, and experienced with it for some time the deprivation of the aid and encouragement of a spiritual director, when, upon the death of Father Joubert, the Sulpician Fathers, occupied with their duties at the seminary, had no successor for his place.

After the Civil War the Congregation was encouraged to participate in the conducting of the many needed orphanages which were opened at that time. Today the Oblate Sisters of Providence, under Mother M. Consuella as Superior General, devote themselves chiefly, except when other need arises, to their work in schools, many being now under their charge not only in Maryland but also in Kansas, Missouri, South Carolina and Virginia, as well as in Cuba.

Honoring the sisters upon the occasion of the celebration of the centenary of their foundation, which was held in Baltimore in November, 1929, the pontifical high mass which opened the centennial festivities was celebrated by the Most Rev. Michael J. Curley, D.D., Archbishop of Baltimore, assisted by the Very Rev. John F. Fenlon, Provincial of the Sulpicians in the United States. The Rev. Peter V. Masterson, S.J., acted as deacon of honor, and Rev. Alonzo J. Olds, and the Rev. John La Farge, S.J., were deacon and subdeacon. The Right Rev. Msgr. M. F. Foley, present spiritual director of the Congregation, and many other distinguished clergy of Baltimore, Washington, Philadelphia and New York were present in the sanctuary, while representatives of the religious communities in the archdiocese and many hundreds of friends and benefactors of the sisters also attended this auspicious service. The sermon of the day was delivered by the noted historian, the Rev. Peter Guilday, Ph.D., of the Catholic University of America. Tracing the history of the Oblate Sisters of Providence from its beginning, in 1829, Dr. Guilday said in part: "They have come to this day with their record unblemished, and their courage unshaken. By the grace of God they have achieved remarkable progress for their race, and today they are one of Baltimore's proudest treasures. They have written by their lives of sacrifice and devotion all along these hundred years heroic pages in the history of Catholic education in the United States."

SUMMARY

Oblate Sisters of Providence.

Founded in the United States in 1829.

Habit: The habit, with a cape, is of heavy black serge, made in one piece, the skirt having wide plaits at the waistline, and a two-inch tuck above the hem. The veil is black. A lightweight black serge apron, made with plaits, is also worn. A fifteen-decade rosary is worn on the left side, hanging from a two-inch wide cincture, and a brass bound crucifix on a steel chain is worn on the breast.

Approximate number in Community, 175.

Active in educational and charitable work in the United States in the archdioceses of Baltimore and St. Louis and in the dioceses of Charleston, Leavenworth and Richmond.

Motherhouse and Novitiate, St. Frances' Convent, 501 East Chase Street, Baltimore, Maryland. (Archdiocese of Baltimore.)

SISTERS OF OUR LADY OF MERCY*

1829

HE Congregation of Our Lady of Mercy, which celebrated in the year 1929 the one hundredth anniversary of its founding, is a living work of one of the most remarkable men in the history of the Church in America. Through the realization of the value of the assistance of a religious community of women in the vast amount of educational and charitable work confronting him in the newly erected diocese of Charleston, of which he had been appointed bishop, the Right Rev. John England, D.D., gladly accepted the proffered services of three young ladies of Baltimore, natives, however, like himself, of Cork, Ireland.

The community Bishop England then planned was at once formed when the Misses Mary and Honora O'Gorman and Teresa Barry arrived from Baltimore in November, 1829, and accepted from the bishop the Rule of St. Vincent de Paul. On the 8th of December of the following year they made their vows of religion and adopted the name of Sisters of Our Lady of Mercy. Sister Mary Joseph O'Gorman was chosen first Superior of the new Community, which then began its labors in Charleston.

A little more than two years later, when the dread cholera epidemic reached Charleston, Bishop England—well pleased with the development and growth of the Community—was gratified when the sisters generously offered their services to the board of health, with the assurance of their willingness to serve in any required capacity. Before the siege was over, Julia Datty, a native of San Domingo, who had been received into the Order and was at the time Superior, became one of the cholera victims on October 3, 1836.

From this period on throughout the hundred years now just passed, the Sisters of Our Lady of Mercy have rallied to the country's every need in any way in which their merciful and charitable ministrations could be helpful. In the years which intervened between their founding and the disastrous and chaotic period of the Civil War, the sisters were zealously engaged in day and boarding school work and the care of orphans, and for a time maintained a school for free colored children, while also laboring at hospital work and the care of the sick almost continuously.

*From data supplied by the Sisters of Our Lady of Mercy, Charleston, S. C., and from *The History of the Catholic Church in the United States,* by John Gilmary Shea.

When the Civil War broke out, Charleston, a heated center of conflict, seething with feeling, suffered its resultant evils with the firing of the first gun.   In a fire which swept a portion of the city on December 11, 1861, the Cathedral, the bishop's house and the Convent of the Sisters of Our Lady of Mercy, with the orphan asylum and boys' school, were among the many buildings destroyed.   Little more than a year later the bombardment of Charleston began, and the sisters were forced to transfer the orphans under their care to Sumter, South Carolina, where a building had been generously placed at their disposal.

When the war was over the Community, having nursed the wounded and ministered to the dying and the dead throughout its entire period, returned to the calm of convent and classroom, and tenderly cared for the then greater number of orphans for whom they provided a home.

Continuing their educational work in academies and parochial schools in Charleston, Aiken and Sumter, the Sisters of Our Lady of Mercy also conduct at Charleston, in addition to the orphanage and a neighborhood house for district work among the poor, St. Francis Xavier Infirmary, with a training school for nurses.

On the occasion of the celebration, on December 8, 1929, of the Centenary of the founding of the Community, the celebrant of the pontifical mass in the Cathedral of St. John the Baptist, in Charleston, was the Right Rev. Michael E. Keyes, D.D., Bishop of Savannah— the diocese in which the sisters had early established a foundation, in addition to another in North Carolina.   The Right Rev. Emmet M. Walsh, D.D., Bishop of Charleston, delivered the sermon on this eventful occasion.   Following the solemn pontifical Benediction in the convent chapel, the first day of the three-day program closed with the unveiling of tablets to the memory of the Right Rev. John England and the co-foundresses of the Congregation of the Sisters of Our Lady of Mercy: Mother Mary Joseph O'Gorman, Mother Mary Martha O'Gorman and Mother Mary Teresa Barry.

SUMMARY

Sisters of Our Lady of Mercy.
Founded in the United States in 1829.
Approximate number in Community, 100.
Active in educational, hospital and charitable work in the diocese of
   Charleston.
Motherhouse and Novitiate, Convent of Our Lady of Mercy, Legare and
   Queen Streets, Charleston, South Carolina.   (Diocese of Charleston.)

SISTERS OF CHARITY OF THE BLESSED VIRGIN MARY*

1833

THE Congregation of the Sisters of Charity of the Blessed Virgin Mary was founded in Philadelphia, Pennsylvania, on November 1, 1833. Its establishment was the outgrowth of the generosity of five young women of Dublin, Ireland, who after uniting there to devote themselves to the cause of Christian education, eager for more complete self-sacrifice, and following the introduction of a national system of education, left their native land and the school which they had opened, to heed the command of Him who said: "Go forth out of thy country, and from thy kindred, and out of thy father's house, and come into the land which I shall show thee."

Miss Mary Francis Clarke and four companions, the Misses Margaret Mann, Rose O'Toole, Elizabeth Kelley and Catherine Byrne, reached Philadelphia from Liverpool on September 4, 1833, after a tempestuous voyage of fifty-one days. The bag into which had been placed the greater part of their money, had been confided to one of their number, who, in the excitement of reaching the American shore, had dropped it into the sea, and this mishap wrought unexpected discomfort and embarrassment to the heroic band of young women not yet vowed to the practice of holy poverty.

Upon the suggestion of one of his former parishioners, whom Miss Clarke and her companions had met upon their first visit to a church, on their arrival at their chosen destination, the Rev. Terence J. Donaghoe, newly appointed pastor of St. Michael's Church in Philadelphia, called upon the little group from Dublin, who, though wearing no special religious garb, were intent on following the religious life. Providentially for his own needs, and in the interest of the school he wished to open in his new parish, each wished to devote herself exclusively to the work of Christian education in the new land where pioneer educational laborers were so few.

With the approbation of the Right Rev. Francis Patrick Kenrick, D.D., then bishop of Philadelphia, Father Donaghoe drew up a rule of life for the five fervent women, and arranged for the establishment of a convent for them in his parish. Following their removal to it on November 1, 1833, they were immediately organized into a religious

*From data and material supplied by the Sisters of Charity of the B.V.M., Mt. Carmel, Dubuque, Iowa.

community, under the title of the Sisters of Charity of the Blessed Virgin Mary, with Sister Mary Francis Clarke as Superior, and Sister Mary Margaret Mann as Assistant Superior and Mistress of Novices.

Soon after its establishment, applications for admission to the Community began to be received. The new convent was used as a Motherhouse, novitiate and boarding school, and the sisters also conducted a day school. Thus the Community grew and prospered, and though the Right Rev. John Hughes, D.D., newly appointed bishop of New York, urged that the sisters establish a mission in New York City, it was the call of the west that was heard by his old-time friend, Father Donaghoe, and the Sisters of Charity of the Blessed Virgin Mary.

The zealous French missionary, Mathias Loras—one time schoolmate of the sainted Curé d'Ars, as bishop of Dubuque visited Philadelphia, and in the interest of his vast diocese asked that the sisters establish a mission in his episcopal city.

MOTHER MARY CECILIA DOHERTY

At that time the diocese of Dubuque comprised the entire territory of Wisconsin and the northern part of Illinois, embracing the area north of the Missouri River to Canada, and east of the Missouri to the Mississippi.

Assured of a band of sisters for his diocese, Bishop Loras proceeded to Baltimore and attended the Fifth Provincial Council, held there in May, 1843, after which he returned to Philadelphia and accompanied to Dubuque the five sisters chosen for this first mission of the Congregation of the Sisters of Charity of the Blessed Virgin Mary.

Journeying from Philadelphia to Pittsburgh by rail and canal, the travelers then went by steamboat down the Ohio River, stopping at Louisville. There, met by the bishop, the Right Rev. Benedict Flaget, they attended mass, celebrating the feast of Corpus Christi. Continuing on the Ohio to the Mississippi, they steamed up to Dubuque, where the ringing of the Angelus on the bell which Bishop Loras had procured in the east as a surprise for his people, and had with him on the boat, proclaimed their joyful arrival on June 23, 1843.

Soon after the establishment of the mission band of sisters in Dubuque, and their opening of St. Mary's Academy for boarders and day-pupils, Bishop Loras urged the transfer of the entire Community to Iowa, and the formal location of its Motherhouse and novitiate in Dubuque instead of Philadelphia. After serious consideration of this proposal, the bishop's request was granted, and the change was made.

Following the necessary readjustment in their new environment, Father Joseph Crétin—who had come from France in 1839 with Bishop Loras, when he visited his native land to secure mission priests for his new diocese—and who, in 1851, was consecrated first bishop of St. Paul, conducted a retreat for the newly established Community, and the following year, when visiting Rome, obtained from the Sovereign Pontiff, Pope Gregory XVI, a brief of special indulgences and blessings for the Sisters of Charity of the Blessed Virgin Mary.

Continuing under the direction of Father Donaghoe, whom Bishop Loras had appointed Vicar General of the diocese upon his transfer also from Philadelphia, the Community, increasing rapidly, soon outgrew the novitiate and convent facilities formerly provided. On a tract of land known as St. Joseph's Prairie new buildings suited for the convent needs were erected, as well as a building for a boarding school for young ladies, and here the daughters of many families prominent for their social and political influence were educated.

When the Community was prosperously established and flourishing at St. Joseph's Prairie a devastating fire interrupted the work of the pioneer sisters in their zealous efforts for the furtherance of Christian education, but with renewed zeal and fervor the institution was rebuilt, and St. Joseph's Academy was soon opened again to its pupils.

Events of importance and the innumerable changes wrought by time marked those years and the years which followed during the development of the Congregation. On June 28, 1885, at the petition of the entire Congregation, the Sovereign Pontiff, Pope Leo XIII, empowered the Right Rev. John Hennessy, D.D., then bishop of Dubuque, and second successor to Bishop Loras, to confirm for life in the office of Superior General the beloved foundress-Superior, Mother Mary Francis Clarke, who bore this honor during the two remaining years of her life—a life lived in perfect conformity to God's will, and during which she was the recipient of unusual spiritual favors. Her humble spirit concealed an extraordinary ability which became manifest only at the call of duty.

Since the death of Mother Clarke, the Superior Generals of the

Congregation have been Mother Mary Gertrude, Mother Mary Cecilia Doherty, Mother Mary Ascension, and Mother Mary Isabella Kane, who is at present in office.

A new epoch for the Congregation began in November, 1893, when the Motherhouse was removed to its present location at Mount Carmel in Dubuque, where the central novitiate is also maintained and where those received into the Congregation are trained for a life of service in the field of Christian education.

The Sisters of Charity of the Blessed Virgin Mary are a papal Institute, of which His Eminence, Cardinal Merry del Val was at the time of his death in 1930 Cardinal Protector. The Constitutions of the Institute provide for a central government, which is maintained at St. Joseph's Convent, Mount Carmel, Dubuque, Iowa, the administrative officers of the Congregation being the Superior General, assisted by four Councilors. These officials, together with the Secretary General and the Treasurer General, are elected for a term of six years. Provincial houses of the Congregation have been established in Davenport and Des Moines, Iowa; Chicago, Illinois; and Wichita, Kansas.

For the higher education of women, the Congregation opened in Dubuque in 1901 Mt. St. Joseph College, now, with its many architecturally harmonizing buildings, known as Clarke College, in memory of Mother Mary Francis Clarke, who faithfully guided the Community in its educational labors throughout years of trials and duress.

Long before the railroads had spanned the plains, the flat boats on the Mississippi brought young women from the south and the surrounding regions to the academy of Mt. St. Joseph. And during the stormy days of the Civil War the Sisters of Charity of the Blessed Virgin Mary taught and "kept bright home fires burning" for many whose fathers and brothers had answered their country's call, or whose native cities were so rent by civil strife that education at home was either unsafe or impossible.

In more recent years, when the United States entered the World War, the nearly one hundred schools of the Congregation, located in ten different states, became centers of instruction in the principles of our American democratic government, and the duty of citizens. Teachers and pupils responded with enthusiasm to the call for national patriotic service in emergency activities, and the Record of War Activities in the schools conducted by the Congregation—as compiled in response to an appeal of the National Catholic War Council through the Committee on Historical Records—presents accurately and concisely the material aspects of the World War activities carried on under the direction of the Sisters of Charity of the Blessed Virgin Mary.

In the hope of promoting, by Catholic teaching, the greater honor and glory of God and the salvation of souls, and in the true spirit of votive consecration, each member of the Congregation of the Sisters of Charity of the Blessed Virgin Mary makes the principles of educa-

ST. JOSEPH'S, MT. CARMEL, DUBUQUE, IOWA

tion the study and pursuit of her life. Strengthened and inspired she goes forth from her novitiate and normal training school to her mission to do her share of the world's work, to co-operate with all religious teachers, who have a common end and purpose to achieve— an end and purpose which are always the same—to take the children of men, and by means of a Christian education make them children of God and loyal citizens of the state.

SUMMARY

Sisters of Charity of the Blessed Virgin Mary.

Founded in the United States in 1833.

Papal Approbation of Rules in 1885 by Pope Leo XIII.

Habit: The habit is of black serge, with a serge cape and a linen collar. A black veil is worn over a white cap and hood.

Approximate number in Community, 1,650.

Active in educational work in the archdioceses of Chicago, Dubuque, Milwaukee, Portland in Oregon, St. Louis and San Francisco, and in the dioceses of Brooklyn, Cheyenne, Davenport, Denver, Des Moines, Helena, Kansas City, Lead, Lincoln, Los Angeles and San Diego, Omaha, Peoria, Rockford, Seattle, Sioux City and Wichita.

Motherhouse and Novitiate, St. Joseph's Convent, Mount Carmel, Dubuque, Iowa. (Archdiocese of Dubuque.)

THIRD ORDER CARMELITE SISTERS*

$\mathcal{S}$OON after its establishment in Europe from the east, in the thirteenth century, the penitential Order of Our Lady of Mount Carmel, even at that time known for its antiquity, admitted to participation in its apostolic works and privileges persons in the world. This, the Carmelite Third Order, was canonically instituted at an early date, under Blessed John Soreth as General of the Carmelite Order.

As in the other mendicant religious orders, groups of these secular tertiaries of the Carmelite Third Order in time formed religious communities, constituting the third order regular, united, in its labors, to the ideals of the First and Second Order of Carmelites—devoted to prayer and penance for the needs of the Church, the conversion of sinners and the salvation of souls.

The brown scapular—the livery of all Carmelites since its revelation by Our Lady to St. Simon Stock, on July 16, 1251—was early accepted as the insignia of, and has continued to mark, the tertiary members of this venerable Order, pre-eminently Mary's, and especially consecrated to her.

SISTERS OF OUR LADY OF MOUNT CARMEL†
1833

With the yellow fever—which had been lurking in the bayous and swamps of Louisiana—and cholera ravaging the city of New Orleans, and the imperative need for many willing workers to mercifully visit the sick and bury the dead, the Congregation of Our Lady of Mount Carmel—organized at Tours, France, little more than five years earlier—came to the stricken city in the United States, in October of that sorrowfully memorable year, 1833.

The Congregation, founded by Mlle. Pauline Marie Thérèse Bazire, for educational work in parochial, academic and normal Schools, had been invited by the Right Rev. Leo de Neckère, C.M., D.D., Bishop of New Orleans, to come to his distant diocese.

Tirelessly ministering to the plague-stricken, Bishop de Neckère was fatally overtaken by the fever and became its victim, a month

*From the Catholic Encyclopedia and Carmelite annals.
†From data and material supplied by the Sisters of Our Lady of Mount Carmel, Academy of Our Lady of Mount Carmel, Lakeview, New Orleans, La.

before the arrival in the United States of the community which, while he was visiting in France, he had personally urged to come.

MOTHER ST. PAUL BAZIRE
Foundress of the Congregation of Our Lady of Mount Carmel

Orphaned by the year's epidemic, many children were at once cared for by the sisters, under their Superior, Mother Marie Thérèse Chevrél, who guided the young Congregation in New Orleans until 1888—through the days of its youth, and until it was among the well-established religious communities in the country. A convent school had been opened in New Orleans almost simultaneously with the orphanage, and the Sisters of Our Lady of Mount Carmel had thus instituted in the United States the educational work for which the Congregation had been founded.

As the Congregation increased in numbers, academies and parochial schools were opened in New Orleans, Lafayette, Thibodaux,

MOUNT CARMEL CONVENT, NEW ORLEANS, LOUISIANA

New Iberia, Abbeville, Rayne, Carencro, St. John, Paincourtville and St. Charles, Louisiana; Vinita and Tulsa, Oklahoma; Bay St. Louis, Mississippi, and British Honduras, by the Superiors in charge of the Congregation. An academy and later a normal school were also opened at the Motherhouse.

In 1853, New Orleans was desolated by another epidemic of yellow fever, greatly exceeding that of 1833, in its severity and fatalities. The sisters left the school-rooms and again ministered to the afflicted. In 1878, the ravages of the dread disease were repeated, as was the generous work of the Congregation of Our Lady of Mount Carmel, and the various communities by that time established in Louisiana.

Between re-adjustment and the return to normalcy, following the havoc wrought by the visitation of disease, had come the Civil War, which left the south in dire distress. Throughout the period from 1861 to 1865, as the annals of history show, sisters of the Congregation of Our Lady of Mount Carmel were beside the suffering and the dying in hospitals, ministering to soul and body.

Orphans from the war, as in the days of the plague, filled anew the institution for the homeless little ones of Christ, bereft by the cruel scourge of war, of the father, in the rank and file, and the mother, broken down with care and sorrow.

As the centennial year of the establishment of the Congregation in the United States approaches, the splendid new buildings for Motherhouse, novitiate, academy and normal school, erected—under Mother Mary Clare Coady as Superior —on an expansive site overlooking Lake Pontchartrain, in the archiepiscopal city of fabulous New Orleans, have been opened, and provide for this Congregation—a hundred years faithful in the performance of duty—a home and an institution worthily signalizing its labors.

MOTHER MARY CLARE COADY

SUMMARY

Congregation of Our Lady of Mount Carmel.
Founded in France in 1825.
Established in the United States in 1833.
Habit: The veil—worn over a white cap—and habit are black. The brown scapular of Mount Carmel is worn under the habit.
Approximate number in Community, 135.
Active in educational and charitable work in the archdiocese of New Orleans and in the dioceses of Lafayette and Natchez.
Motherhouse and Novitiate, Mount Carmel Convent, Robert E. Lee Boulevard, Lakeview, New Orleans, Louisiana. (Archdiocese of New Orleans.)

CARMELITE SISTERS OF THE DIVINE HEART OF JESUS*

1912

The Carmelite Sisters of the Divine Heart of Jesus form a branch of the Carmelite Order, originating with the establishment of the

---

*From data and material supplied by the Carmelite Sisters, D.C.J., 168 Kavanaugh Avenue, Wauwatosa, Wis.

"St. Joseph Homes for Children." Founded in Berlin, Germany, July 2, 1891, by Mother Maria Teresa of St. Joseph, these Carmelites were soon known in the different countries of Europe for their works of mercy and charity.

In 1912 Mother Teresa and a companion came to the United States in the interests of their work. Disappointments and trying circumstances met them, but kindness and hospitality as well, for when the two sisters reached Milwaukee their efforts were crowned with success when His Grace, the Most Rev. Sebastian G. Messmer, D.D., agreed to the erection of a cloister of their Congregation in that city. On December 20, 1912, a St. Joseph's Home of St. Raphael was opened on South Pierce Street, in Milwaukee.

Within the year they were joined by eight sisters from the European Motherhouse, now located at Sittard, Holland.

With the growth of the Community, homes for the aged and for children have been established in connection with the home missions conducted in their convents.

MOTHER MARIA TERESA OF ST. JOSEPH
Foundress of the Carmelite Sisters of the Divine Heart of Jesus

In 1916 the sisters purchased an estate in Wauwatosa, Wisconsin, where a Motherhouse and novitiate have been established.

The special work of the sisters is conducted through their home missions and the St. Joseph Homes, the purpose of which is the care of legitimate children whose parents are sick or separated from each other, and those unprotected children who are threatened with neglect and ruin. The homes are not intended to serve the same purpose as orphanages or houses of correction.

These Carmelite Sisters have been among the first to realize that the "family system" has much to do with the preservation of health, and the making of a successful institution. The children at the St. Joseph Homes, therefore, live in single family groups, sixteen of about the same age, together with two sisters, forming a "family." These children eat together, and have their own dormitories and dwellings. In the event of any epidemic, through this system the disease is easily restricted to the respective family, and other inmates are shielded from infection.

This method of building and homes, adopted by the sisters in 1894, has been approved and acknowledged by all modern architectural and medical authorities.

SUMMARY

Carmelite Sisters of the Divine Heart of Jesus.
Founded in Germany in 1891.
Papal Approbation of Rules, January 7, 1915, by Pope Benedict XV.
Established in the United States in 1912.
Habit: The habit is the regular brown of the Carmelites, with a white choir
mantle.
Approximate number in Community in United States, 150.
Active in social service and charitable work in the archdioceses of Milwaukee,
St. Louis and San Antonio and in the dioceses of Corpus Christi, Detroit,
Fort Wayne and Los Angeles and San Diego.
United States Motherhouse and Novitiate, Convent of the Carmelite Sisters,
D.C.J., 168 Kavanaugh Avenue, Wauwatosa, Wisconsin. (Archdiocese
of Milwaukee.)

CARMELITE SISTERS OF ST. TERESA OF THE CHILD JESUS*

1928

Appreciating the fervor of three young women, Carmelite Tertiaries, who volunteered to do mission work in the diocese, the Right Rev. Theophile Meerschaert, D.D., first bishop of Oklahoma, gave them permission to open a school, and near the little town of Bentley, Oklahoma, in 1917, the missionary and charitable work now associated with the Carmelite Sisters of St. Teresa of the Child Jesus began.

Privations and the rigors which accompany almost all pioneer enterprises followed the self-imposed labors of the three. Although acting as religious teachers, and tentatively extending their work, and, —joined by others who aspired to their zealous apostolate, living as best possible a community life, it was not until December 27, 1928 that these Carmelite Sisters of St. Teresa of the Child Jesus, Third Order Carmelites, were canonically established.

*From data and material supplied by the Carmelite Sisters of St. Teresa of the Child Jesus, Carmel of the Little Flower, Oklahoma City, Okla.

Through the solicitude of the Right Rev. Francis C. Kelley, D.D., L.L.D., successor of Bishop Meerschaert, and present bishop of Oklahoma, and in accordance with the recommendation of the Very Rev. D. I. Lanslots, O.S.B., vicar in charge of religious orders of

CARMELITE SISTERS OF ST. TERESA OF THE CHILD JESUS

women in the diocese, official recognition of the Community, according to Canon Law, was obtained from the Holy See.

The Carmelite Sisters of St. Teresa of the Child Jesus are distinctively the only religious order bearing the title of and especially dedicated to the Little Flower. Clothed like her, their patroness, in the habit of Our Lady of Mt. Carmel, and observing the Rule of the Carmelite Order—modified and adapted to the active life of teaching in mission schools, catechetical work, and visitation of the sick, to which they are devoted—the sisters preserve the interior spirit of Carmel, and imitate the spiritual childhood of Little Therese.

In its union of the Carmelite contemplative mode of life with active labors, the Community—which continues under the superiorship of Mother Agnes Teresa, one of the original three mission workers—confines itself to the diocese of Oklahoma, and subject to the jurisdiction of the ordinary of that see, conducts various mission schools throughout the state.

Co-incident with taking charge of the parochial school for the Mexican children, in Oklahoma City, in the parish of Our Lady of Mt. Carmel, over which are priests of the Order of Discalced Carmelites, the Congregation of the Carmelite Sisters of St. Teresa of the Child Jesus established its Motherhouse in the episcopal city, and Mother Agnes Teresa gave her personal attention to this school, of now more than one hundred pupils, and its consequent Mexican welfare work.

SUMMARY

Carmelite Sisters of St. Teresa of the Child Jesus.
Established in the United States in 1928.
Habit: The brown Carmelite habit, similar to that of the Little Flower, is worn.
Active in educational and social service work in the diocese of Oklahoma.
Motherhouse and Novitiate, Carmel of the Little Flower, 520 West Wheeler Street, Oklahoma City, Okla. (Diocese of Oklahoma.)

CORPUS CHRISTI CARMELITES*

1929

The Community of sisters known as Corpus Christi Carmelites, canonically erected as such in the United States in the early summer of 1929, had its inception in Leicester, England, in the year 1908. At that time the Right Rev. R. Brindle, Bishop of Nottingham, gave Mary Ellerker and a small group of lay tertiaries permission to teach catechism, to instruct converts, to take charge of sodalities, to visit the sick and prisoners, to help the poor and endeavor to rescue the wayward.

Three of the little community in England, a little later, responded to a missionary call from across the ocean on the island of Trinidad, British West Indies, where, wearing their tertiary garb, they took charge of a hospice for aged colored women, aided in the hospital, in the government industrial school and in the homes of the poor.

It was Mary Ellerker, who as Mother Mary of the Blessed Sacrament, came then with a small group of companions to the United

---

*From data and material supplied by the Corpus Christi Carmelites, Corpus Christi Carmel, Middletown, N. Y.

States, to Duluth, Minnesota, in 1920, where they were encouraged in their earnest work and in the opening of Corpus Christi House as a protecting home for girls. In the rural districts of Duluth they early engaged in teaching in summer catechism schools, visiting the poor, and, when occasion required, attending the sessions of juvenile court in behalf of those needing their protecting interest.

MOTHER MARY OF THE BLESSED SACRAMENT AND TWO CORPUS CHRISTI CARMELITE NOVICES

A little later the Corpus Christi sisters, at the solicitation of the bishop of Oklahoma, as parish visitors took a census of his two largest cities. For more than three years this occupied the sisters assigned to the work, while others carried on social service and catechetical instruction, which for a time extended to the state of Oregon. There, in the vicinity of Portland, and under the supervision of the Rev. Edwin V. O'Hara, Director of the Rural Life Bureau of the Social Action Department of the National Catholic Welfare Council, they assisted in the establishment of a rural medical service and in the training of a group of zealous women as lay catechists.

At the time of the canonical erection of the Corpus Christi sisters as a Carmelite Community of the Third Order Regular, the community had recently taken charge of a home for the aged which was opened at Kearney, Nebraska, under the auspices of the Right Rev. James A. Duffy, D.D., Bishop of Grand Island.

The Motherhouse of the Corpus Christi Carmelites is located at Corpus Christi Convent, Port of Spain, Trinidad, British West Indies.

SUMMARY

Corpus Christi Carmelites.

Established in the United States in 1929.

Habit: A white tunic, brown scapular, white mantle, and a medal of the Blessed Sacrament are worn.

Active in catechetical and social service work in the United States in the archdiocese of New York and in the dioceses of Duluth and Grand Island.

United States Novitiate, Corpus Christi House, Duluth, Minnesota. (Diocese of Duluth.)

CHRONOLOGICAL TABLE

Foundations in the United States of Congregations of the Third Order of Mt. Carmel

1833—New Orleans, Louisiana.   1928—Oklahoma City, Oklahoma.
1912—Wauwatosa, Wisconsin.   1929—Duluth, Minnesota.

GENERAL SUMMARY

Sisters of the Third Order of Our Lady of Mt. Carmel.

Papal Approbation in 1668 by Pope Clement IX.

Established in the United States in 1833.

Habit: The brown Carmelite habit, with a white choir mantle is worn, or, under a different garb, the brown scapular of the Mt. Carmel is worn.

Approximate number in communities in United States, 350.

Active in educational, charitable and social service work in the archdioceses of Milwaukee, New Orleans, New York, St. Louis and San Antonio, and in the dioceses of Corpus Christi, Detroit, Duluth, Fort Wayne, Grand Island, Lafayette, Los Angeles and San Diego, Natchez and Oklahoma.

SISTERS OF ST. JOSEPH*

THE Congregation of the Sisters of St. Joseph was founded in 1650 at Le Puy, capital of ancient Velay, in France. Its origin was due to the zealous co-operation of an eminent and holy prelate, and a saintly Jesuit missionary, who sought to inaugurate a community of women without enclosure and with simple vows, thus executing the original plan of St. Francis de Sales. These two were Henry de Maupas du Tour, Bishop of Le Puy, and John Paul Médaille, of the Society of Jesus. Many of Father Médaille's missions were given in the diocese of Le Puy, where he met with a number of young women anxious to retire from the world and to devote themselves to the service of God. Appropriating the ideas of St. Francis, and desiring the formation of a community of women who "should unite exterior works of charity with the repose of contemplation," Father Médaille communicated to Bishop de Maupas his project of this religious institute, and received from him hearty approval of the plan.

Those eager for a life of retreat, and whose virtue and constancy had been tested, were then brought together at Le Puy to receive their spiritual training under the care of Bishop de Maupas, who, on the feast of St. Teresa, October 15, 1650, presided at their consecration ceremony, at its conclusion placing the Institute under the patronage of St. Joseph, and declaring that it should be known, thenceforth, as the Congregation of the Sisters of St. Joseph.

On March 10, 1651, less than a year after its foundation, Bishop de Maupas gave to the young Society and its Constitutions, as drawn up by Father Médaille, his episcopal approbation. At the same time he recommended the new Congregation to the bishops of the neighboring dioceses.

In the year 1666, that the Congregation might be given legal status, letters patent from the reigning king, Louis XIV, placed the seal of France on the official existence of the Institute. According to the Constitutions, each house, with its own officers and novitiate, was distinct and independent, and in each diocese the bishop was the superior. The Sisters of St. Joseph then spread throughout many

*From data and material supplied by the Sisters of St. Joseph of Carondelet, St. Joseph's Academy, St. Louis, Mo., and from referred bibliography: *Life of Rev. Mother St. John Fontbonne* by the Abbé Rivaux (Benziger Bros.), and supplied bibliography: *The Congregation of Saint Joseph of Carondelet*, by Sister Mary Lucida Savage, Ph.D., of the Sisters of St. Joseph of Carondelet, St. Louis, Mo. (B. Herder Book Co., St. Louis.)

dioceses of France besides those of Le Puy and Lyons, engaging, wherever they were established, in the work of education, the direction of orphanages and the care of the sick.

At the outbreak of the French Revolution, there was at Monistrol, a little town in Haute Loire, in the diocese of Le Puy, a community of Sisters of St. Joseph, under the direction of Mother St. John Fontbonne, who was born at Bas, in the department of Haute Loire, March 3, 1759. Jeanne, as she was called in baptism, was sent when still young, with an elder sister, Marguerite, to a convent of the Sisters of St. Joseph in Bas, where, under the careful training of her paternal aunts, she and her sister were educated. Both felt themselves drawn to the religious life, and on July 1, 1778, the two sisters, with their parents' consent, entered the newly founded novitiate of the Sisters of St. Joseph at Monistrol. Jeanne was called in religion Sister St. John, and Marguerite, Sister Teresa, and together they began the long career in the course of which they were to pass through many trials and to strengthen and console each other until separated by death. Their novitiate ended, they remained in Monistrol, and in October, 1785, Sister St. John was appointed Superior.

Six years later the community at Le Puy felt the effects of the Revolution. The venerable bishop of the diocese, refusing to take the civil oath required of the clergy, was forced into exile, and took up his residence in Switzerland.

Mother St. John, in the name of her community, likewise refused to comply with the civil regulations. After severe trials, threatened with violence, and deprived of help and protection, the intrepid Superior, fearing for the lives of the sisters, persuaded them to return to their families, there to await better times.

She, with Sister Teresa and a devoted companion, remained at the convent until they were forced to leave. They then sought refuge at the Fontbonne home in Bas, which had become a shelter for proscribed priests and religious. Here, in peasant dress, for two years Mother St. John and her two companions gathered together the children of the neighborhood, and instructed them in their religion. Discovered by their persecutors in the fall of 1793, they were taken to the prison of St. Didier, twelve miles from Bas. In 1794, after eleven months of confinement, deprived of the spiritual consolation of the sacraments, and of every physical comfort, daily in readiness for death, and not knowing when they might be summoned to the scaffold, they at length received word that their execution would take place the following day. They spent the night in final preparation for their approaching end; but when morning dawned, and the great doors of their dungeon swung open, they were called to meet not death, which they expected, but freedom and the friends they loved.

Courtesy of the Sisters of St. Joseph of Carondelet
MOTHER ST. JOHN FONTBONNE (1759-1843)

The Reign of Terror had been suddenly brought to a close by the fall of Robespierre. His death meant life and liberty for many, and Mother St. John and her two companions failed to win the crown of martyrdom which they so coveted, but which fell to the lot of many of their friends and several of their sisters in religion.

Again received into her paternal home, Mother St. John ardently desired to re-assemble her scattered community in their convent at Monistrol, but she found that this property had been sold by the government and could not be repurchased, as the laws dispersing the congregations still prevailed. For twelve years, then, these three fervent women devoted themselves to pious exercises, the instruction of the ignorant and the care of the poor and sick.

Throughout France in the next few years the Congregation slowly returned to its former activities, particularly its educational work. In the diocese of Lyons, at the wish of Cardinal Fesch, elevated to that see in 1802, the Sisters of St. Joseph, with Mother St. John as Superior, were re-established. Under the guidance of the Rev. Claude Cholleton, Vicar General of Lyons, and a returned exile of the Revolution, in whose charge Cardinal Fesch had placed the religious communities of the diocese, Mother St. John made the new foundation in his parish at St. Etienne. Arriving at St. Etienne on August 14, 1807, she found there a group of laborers already well trained in the spiritual life, for to her Father Cholleton entrusted a number of young women of his parish who were living as a community, and performing local works of mercy. On November 25, 1807, after a short illness, Father Cholleton died in Paris, having accompanied Cardinal Fesch to that city.

In 1808 another group of pious women entered the community, and a larger convent was acquired. Privations and difficulties awaited the sisters everywhere, but they resumed their work and carried it on with zeal. In less than three years Lyons had as many promising institutions in charge of the Sisters of St. Joseph, and new foundations had also been made in other parts of France. On April 10, 1812, the Congregation received the authorization of the State. By this time the need was felt of a general novitiate and a central Motherhouse under the direction of a Superior General. It was recognized everywhere that from unity and a centralized government there would result greater strength to resist such hostile forces as those to which the smaller communities had recently been subjected.

The united communities, with the approbation of the diocesan authorities, elected as their Superior General Mother St. John Fontbonne, "the strong-souled woman to whom the Community owed its regeneration." Lyons was designated as the place of the Motherhouse and novitiate, and Mother St. John was retained in office until her resignation in 1839. Her death occurred four years later. In 1822, Father Charles Cholleton, nephew of the former pastor of

St. Etienne, was named spiritual director of the Sisters of St. Joseph in the archdiocese of Lyons. The status of the Congregation was defined as diocesan, with the archbishop of Lyons as its spiritual head and first superior. Under him were the spiritual director, appointed from the vicars, and the Reverend Mother and her council, elected by the votes of the sisters of the diocese. As Le Puy was a separate diocese from that of Lyons, the communities there, on the advice of their episcopal superior, did not come under the jurisdiction of Mother St. John. Chambéry, in Savoy, and Bourg in the diocese of Belley, both owing their origin to Lyons, also became independent centers.

Belley, to which the sisters were sent from Lyons in 1819, was erected into a diocese in 1823, under Bishop Alexander Raymond Devie. The novitiate established there was afterward removed to Bourg, and, under the jurisdiction of the Holy See, the General Motherhouse of that Community was established at Bourg-en-Bresse, Ain, France. Other independent foundations were made in France by the Sisters of St. Joseph, and from these many others followed, but to the Motherhouse in Lyons, and the zeal of Mother St. John Fontbonne herself, does America owe the coming to her shores in 1836 of the Sisters of St. Joseph.

CARONDELET

1836

The first foundation of the Sisters of St. Joseph in the United States was made in the diocese of St. Louis.

In 1834, Father Cholleton, as an active member of the Society for the Propagation of the Faith, knowing the needs of the Right Rev. Joseph Rosati, C.M., bishop of that far-away diocese, broached to Mother St. John Fontbonne the question of sending some of her sisters to the missions in Missouri. At the same time there became interested in the project Madame de la Rochejaquelin, a devoted friend of Mother St. John and her Congregation.

Madame de la Rochejacquelin was the daughter of the Duchess de Duras of Ussé, in Touraine, and widow of the Prince of Talmont. She contributed generously to the Foreign Mission Society, and was interested in the instruction and conversion of the Indians. After reading the annals of the Propagation of the Faith, she communicated to Bishop Rosati her desire of aiding in the missionary work of the diocese of St. Louis, by assuming the expense of establishing there a community of the Sisters of St. Joseph. Bishop Rosati accepted the offer and especially requested Mother St. John to send, among the pioneer sisters, some who would be capable of instructing deaf-mutes.

From the many volunteers for the American mission, eight were selected: Sisters Febronie and Delphine, nieces of Mother St. John, the Superior General, Sister Marguerite Felicité Bouté, Sister Febronie Chapellon, Sister St. Protais Deboille, Sister Philomene Vilaine, Sister Celestine Pommerel and Julie Fournier, a postulant. The last two named were designated first to study the sign-language, and later to proceed to America. The six sisters, accompanied by Father James Fontbonne—brother of Sisters Febronie and Delphine, who had also volunteered for the foreign field, left Lyons for Havre, January 4, 1836. From there they embarked for their new mission. After weathering an almost disastrous storm, near the Gulf of Mexico, they reached the port of New Orleans on March 5th. After having been guests at the Ursuline Convent during their stay, they left the city on March 15th, traveling by steamer to St. Louis, where they were received by the Sisters of Charity, with whom they remained until after Easter.

Though Carondelet became the first permanent home of the Sisters of St. Joseph, their first mission in America was at Cahokia, Illinois. This town, across the river from St. Louis, was one of the early French villages in the Illinois country, and, after Kaskaskia, the oldest white settlement in the Mississippi Valley. Bishop Rosati selected as teachers for the school in Cahokia, Sisters Febronie Fontbonne, Febronie Chapellon and St. Protais. The remaining three, Sisters Felicité, Delphine and Philomene, were to remain in St. Louis until their house in Carondelet was ready.

On April 7th, the three sisters left St. Louis by boat for Cahokia, on the Illinois shore of the Mississippi. Bishop Rosati and the pastor met them and conducted them to the convent, located on a four-acre tract opposite the church. St. Joseph's Institute was the name given by the sisters to their convent and school, but the villagers dignified it by the name of "The Abbey." With the opening of school, a few days after their arrival, the Sisters of St. Joseph began their activities in the United States.

The other sisters in this pioneer band were then established in a simple abode in the village of Carondelet, near St. Louis, so named, in 1796, in honor of the last Spanish Governor-General of Louisiana, Baron de Carondelet. In September a school was opened and maintained through a winter of great severity and suffering. A year later, after a journey of hardships and delays, Sister Celestine Pommerel and Sister St. John Fournier arrived from France, and thus completed the original designate number of the community.   In 1839, Sister Delphine, having borne the responsibility of Superior, asked to be relieved of the office, and her term of three years having expired, she was succeeded by Mother Celestine Pommerel.   The year 1840 saw the erection of St. Joseph's Academy in St. Louis, and that year

ST. JOSEPH'S ACADEMY, ST. LOUIS, MISSOURI

registered the first of the hundreds of boarders, every loyal and true to this their Alma Mater.

In the interval between 1844 and 1847, when the archdiocese was created, the sisters from Carondelet assumed charge of their first institutions in St. Louis.   Two of these, St. Joseph's Orphan Asylum, and St. Vincent's parochial school, were permanent.   The third, a school for colored girls, established under the auspices of the Most Rev. Peter Richard Kenrick, D.D., successor of Bishop Rosati, and first archbishop of St. Louis, was giving promise of much success when civil obstacles led to its discontinuance, and Sunday-school classes alone were conducted for these pupils.

At the end of its first ten years in the United States, the Congregation had not yet extended its activities outside of the diocese of St. Louis, but it was steadily gaining in numbers, and receiving into the novitiate young American girls.

In 1847, by mutual agreement of the communities in Lyons and St. Louis, the latter became independent of the French Congregation.

During the next decade of years, foundations were made in the east and north, notably in Philadelphia, Pennsylvania; St. Paul, Minnesota; Wheeling, West Virginia, and in New York. Activities in Missouri increasing, Mother Celestine devoted her energies to the building up of the academy and novitiate in Carondelet. The academy was chartered in 1853. In 1856, following disastrous floods caused by the inundation of the Mississippi, the sisters were permanently withdrawn from the Cahokia mission. When the cholera swept St. Louis in 1849, and again in 1851, the sisters fearlessly gave themselves to the relief of the sick and dying, and among their own number were martyr-victims of the pestilence. With the passing of the plague and the need of sisters for the many and crowded orphanages, Mother Celestine appealed to the community in Lyons for recruits. Lyons could not spare subjects at the time, but aid came when sisters from a community at Moutiers responded, and reached St. Louis on December 21, 1854. Sister St. John Facemaz, of this band, was soon chosen a member of the council at the Mother-house, and in that capacity rendered great assistance to Mother Celestine.

Two more decades of years passed, and the Congregation in America, spreading beyond Missouri to other fields of labor, felt the need of a centralized government in the United States. With this in view, Mother Celestine contemplated a visit to all the convents of the Congregation which had been established in the United States and Canada, but her arduous labor of twenty years was ended. On June 7, 1857, Mother Celestine died, surrounded by her sorrowing community, at Carondelet.

The establishment of a Generalate was finally brought about by Mother St. John Facemaz, who succeded to the office of Superior General, and who prepared to carry to completion the plans for a central government for the Congregation. Her plans were interrupted by a fire which on January 21, 1858, destroyed all but the north wing of the Motherhouse. This first great disaster at Carondelet entailed heavy financial burdens and brought renewed trials to the sisters, but it gave new zest to the desire of all for a closer union of the communities, in view of the greater strength that would result therefrom.

Early in 1860, Mother St. John, acting on the advice of Archbishop Kenrick, invited representatives from each house of the Congregation to an assembly at Carondelet for the purpose of considering the proposed measure for a general government. Delegates came from each diocese in which the Sisters of St. Joseph were established, except Buffalo, Philadelphia and Brooklyn. Arch-bishop Kenrick submitted a plan which proposed a form of gov-ernment for the communities in the United States and Canada, similar to one which had recently gone into effect in the diocese of Lyons.

The measure was adopted practically as outlined, and in the elec-tion of officers which followed Mother St. John Facemaz was chosen as Superior General for a term of six years.

Mother St. John Facemaz served two terms as Superior General of the Congregation, during which time she led her Community safely through the trials and afflictions of the Civil War, when conditions required the recall of the sisters from missions in Mississippi, and the final relinquishment of all work in that state. Mother St. John throughout this trying period was actively engaged in making, by personal visitation, many new foundations, most of them permanent, and all with interesting histories.

In the election of 1872, Mother Agatha Guthrie was chosen to succeed Mother St. John as Superior General, and, known especially for her activities and charitable endeavors in behalf of the Indian missions, for thirty-two years she was retained in that office. In 1885, during her administration, the Convent of Our Lady of Good Counsel was built, in St. Louis, and established as a central house for the sisters of the Community teaching in the parochial schools of the city. The Superior of this house was appointed directress of schools, and placed in charge of the summer studies of the sisters. In 1894 this convent was the scene of the first teachers' institute in St Louis—participated in by sisters of various orders from the city and surrounding places.

During the yellow fever epidemics in the south, in the decade be-tween 1870 and 1880, Mother Agatha sent volunteer nurses into the stricken areas, and in the Spanish-American War of 1898 re-sponded generously to the call for nurses.

The last important work undertaken by Mother Agatha, before her death, January 16, 1904, was the erection of Holy Family Chapel at the Motherhouse, a noble effort and a monument to her own zeal for the beauty of God's house.

In the spring of 1905, an election, presided over by the Most Rev. John J. Glennon, D.D., Archbishop of St. Louis, was held at the Motherhouse, and resulted in the choice of Sister Agnes Gonzaga Ryan as Superior General.

Mother Agnes Gonzaga was particularly suited for the responsi-bilities of the twelve years during which she served the Congregation as Superior General. Prior to her election to this office, she had been a member of the council at the Motherhouse, and knew intimately the inner workings of the Community. The problems confronting the new Superior General were materially different from those of her predecessors in office, who had been called upon for the most part to inaugurate new movements and to be pioneers in many fields.

New conditions of progress in education and social service faced Mother Agnes Gonzaga, and she supervised the development of the grade school systems, the university affiliations of the high schools, and the establishment of colleges for the higher education of women.

Mother Agnes Gonzaga was succeeded in May, 1917, by Mother Mary Agnes Rossiter, as the fifth Superior General of the Congregation. During the last years of the administration of Mother Agnes Gonzaga her health had failed perceptibly, and on June 14, 1917, she died. Mother Mary Agnes Rossiter had proved a faithful co-operator in all the undertakings of the Congregation; with knowledge and understanding she performed the duties of her office as Assistant General, and as Superior General now competently directs

MOTHER AGNES GONZAGA RYAN

the welfare, spiritual and temporal, of a Congregation of nearly three thousand members.

While the Congregation is chiefly devoted to educational work, it has never relaxed in its care of the sick, the afflicted and the homeless, as is evidenced in the splendid hospitals, institutes for the deaf and dumb, and orphanages maintained by the sisters, in addition to their schools, academies and colleges, the latest of which, Fontbonne College—a corporate college of St. Louis University, immortalizes in its name the near-martyr and holy foundress of the Sisters of St. Joseph.

16

SISTERS OF ST. JOSEPH OF CARONDELET
PROVINCIALATE OF ST. PAUL

When in 1851 the Right Rev. Joseph Crétin, D.D., went to St. Paul as its first bishop, he sent at once to the Superior of the Congregation of Sisters of St. Joseph of Carondelet, for sisters for this diocese, which had been established the year before. Before he offered himself for the foreign mission field and accompanied Bishop Loras to America, Bishop Crétin had been closely associated with the work of the Sisters of St. Joseph in France, and he felt assured of the favorable reply which he received from the Superior General, Mother Celestine, in response to his request for sisters.

On the evening of October 28, 1851, Mother St. John Fournier, recently returned to Carondelet from Philadelphia, and three companions, left St. Louis by steamer for St. Paul. Ice was already forming on the Mississippi when the sisters made the trip, on which they had the good fortune to meet Father Lucien Galtier, who came aboard at Prarie du Chien on his way to one of the villages up the river. Father Galtier, the founder of the city of St. Paul, a remarkable man of distinct personality, familiar as he was with the trials and difficulties confronting these gentle missionaries in what was then the territory of Minnesota, told them the history and condition of the new region to which they were going, and encouraged them by his good wishes for their success.

The sisters arrived at their destination the night of November 2nd, and on November 10th opened a school for girls. Soon those living at a distance were accepted as boarders in the institution from which developed St. Joseph's Academy. The winter brought suffering and privation, which, however, did not lessen the zeal of these religious. In January, one of the sisters, assisted by a devout young French woman, was sent to instruct the Indian children among the Winnebagos in Long Prairie, and to prepare them for their First Communion. During the summer of 1852 Mother Celestine made her first visit to St. Paul. During this visit she arranged for a permanent mission among the Indians, and on her return to Carondelet sisters were sent especially for this work. The following year Mother St. John was recalled to Carondelet to return to Philadelphia, and was replaced in St. Paul by Mother Seraphine Coughlin. Shortly after the arrival of the latter, several young girls were received as postulants; the school increased in numbers and other schools were opened.

In 1853 Bishop Crétin began the erection of a hospital, but before its completion, cholera, which had wrought deadly havoc in the south, reached St. Paul and spread rapidly. An old log church was utilized as a hospital, and the sisters labored unweariedly as nurses. Rein-forcements of zealous workers came when the sisters intended for the new hospital arrived from Carondelet. In imminent need of the new building, bishop, priests and seminarians all lent aid to the workmen, and St. Joseph's Hospital, with a novitiate combined, was completed by the fall of 1854.

On the death of Bishop Crétin in 1857, the Right Rev. Thomas L. Grace, D.D., was appointed his successor. Bishop Grace's interest in the organization of Catholic schools was at once manifest, and schools were built or enlarged to meet the new demands.

With the establishment of the Generalate in St. Louis, in 1860, St. Joseph's Academy, in St. Paul, was made a Provincial house, and Mother Seraphine Coughlin was appointed first Provincial Superior of St. Paul. She made preparations for the erection of a new academy and novitiate, but because of ill health could not complete the work. Her death occurred on August 1, 1861. Among her successors was Mother Seraphine Ireland, who was appointed Pro-vincial Superior in 1868, and continued in that office for more than thirty years. To her zeal and efforts is due the great progress made in the provincialate during that time. Many missions were then established throughout the state of Minnesota, and in North and South Dakota, while the academy at the Provincial house, adapting itself to changing requirements, maintained through suc-ceeding years the splendid reputation which it had established early in its career.

With St. Joseph's Academy on the list of schools accredited by the State University, the Congregation soon prepared the way for the establishment of a college. In furtherance of its plan for greater expansion, property was secured between St. Paul and Minneapolis, for the erection of a college and academy. During the years that passed before the building plans could be acted upon and realized, the sisters made other necessary preparations for college direction, two of their number going to Europe for a study of the work of higher education, and while there making an exhaustive survey of the organ-ization and practical working of the *St. Anna Stift*, the Catholic Sisters' College of Münster, in Westphalia. In 1904, Derham Hall, the first building of the new college group, was erected, and the Col-lege of St. Catherine, St. Paul, Minnesota, has since become one of the recognized Catholic institutions in the country for the higher education of women.

SISTERS OF ST. JOSEPH OF CARONDELET
PROVINCIALATE OF TROY

The direct activities of the Sisters of St. Joseph of Carondelet in New York state began in 1858, with the opening by them of a school in Oswego, in the diocese of Albany, under the episcopacy of the Right Rev. John McCloskey, D.D., later the first American cardinal. In 1860 the second mission in eastern New York was established at Cohoes, followed by missions in Syracuse—Salina, as it was then called, Troy, and Albany. Shortly after the opening of the sisters' mission in Troy, that city was selected for the location of a novitiate,

ST. JOSEPH'S SEMINARY, TROY, NEW YORK

and later as the seat of the Eastern Provincialate. In 1861, prior to her election as Superior General of the Congregation, Mother Agatha Guthrie was appointed first Provincial Superior at Troy. The schools and institutions conducted by the Community in the various cities of the provincialate continued to advance in number and efficiency.

With the need of many sisters for the missions, the community outgrew the old convent, and a new novitiate was imperative. Mother Odelia Bogan, Provincial Superior at the time, feeling that the investment would be a wise one, purchased in 1908, from the archdiocese of New York, the ecclesiastical seminary in Troy, which had been vacated as such, on the opening of one at Dunwoodie, in 1896. On completion of repairs and remodeling, the new Provincial house was ceremoniously dedicated, and the name St. Joseph's Seminary retained. On December 11, 1912, His Eminence, John Cardinal Farley, Archbishop of New York, blessed anew the building consecrated to its holy purpose by one of his illustrious predecessors, Cardinal McCloskey, then bishop of Albany. The year 1920 marked the completion of the Community's splendid new building in the pine hills of Albany, the College of St. Rose of Lima, chartered and empowered by the Regents of the University of New York, to confer collegiate degrees.

SISTERS OF ST. JOSEPH OF CARONDELET
PROVINCIALATE OF LOS ANGELES

In 1870, seven Sisters of St. Joseph went from Carondelet to Arizona. The courageous band of volunteers set out on its long journey on April 20th, traveling by rail and sea, by horse and by foot, experiencing oppressive heat and intense cold, and delays occasioned by awaiting means of travel. At Arizona City, or Yuma, the sisters were met by the vicar general of Tucson, who was sent by the bishop, the Right Rev. J. B. Salpointe, D.D., Bishop of the diocese of Santa Fé, upon whose urgent and persistent invitations the mission was being made. With the fresh horses, provisions and other necessites provided by the vicar general, the traveling was facilitated. A week later, after passing through the valley of the Pima Indians, they were met by a detachment of United States cavalry, sent from the fort at Tucson to conduct them through a dangerous pass near Picacho Peak, in which a massacre by the Apaches had recently occurred. The sisters' long journey ended on May 26th.

The population of Tucson was largely Mexican, and almost entirely Catholic. Both the English and Spanish languages were used in the school opened by the sisters, which, as the bishop had anticipated, was soon filled to overflowing. It was patronized by Catholics and non-Catholics alike, as a boarding and day school, and such it remained until 1885.

Several bands of sisters had come from Carondelet in the meantime, the first of them arriving in 1874. Negotiations begun in the fall of 1873 for the opening of a school at the old Indian mission of San Xavier del Bac, under Government auspices, had called Bishop Salpointe to Washington. On his way he stopped in St. Louis, and visiting Carondelet, spoke to the Superior General, Mother Agatha Guthrie, of the advisability of having a larger number of sisters and more mission houses in the far west. To obviate the difficulty of providing sisters in sufficient numbers for the west, the question was considered of establishing a Provincial house and novitiate there. Bishop Salpointe advocated it as the most satisfactory means of keeping up the schools and other institutions needed in his diocese. Accordingly, with the permission of the Holy See, a Provincial Superior was appointed in 1876, in the person of Mother Irene Facemaz, and steps were at once taken for the opening of a provincialate novitiate.

In 1882, sisters from this provincialate opened their first mission in California, beginning their work in San Diego, where Father Junipero Serra had landed in 1769. The second mission was made, in the fall of 1883, in Oakland, on the invitation of the Rev. Bernard McNally, zealous pastor of St. Patrick's Church, in that city, and a prominent figure in the educational work of the archdiocese of San Francisco. In 1895, St. Joseph's Home for Deaf-mutes was opened by the sisters, in Oakland. An Ephpheta Society was organized and has since continued actively interested in the work of this institution.

On January 6, 1889, five sisters from Carondelet, accompanied by the Superior General, Mother Agatha, arrived at Los Angeles for the opening of St. Mary's Academy, in St. Vincent's parish, where, in November, 1903, the Provincial Superior, who had been residing in Tucson, took up her official residence, and where the novitiate, removed from Tucson, was established. Ecclesiastical approval of this had been given by the Right Rev. Thomas James Conaty, D.D., of the see of Monterey and Los Angeles, and also by the Most Rev. Diomede Falconio, Apostolic Delegate to the United States, then a guest in California.

In 1911, there was dedicated and opened in Los Angeles a new St. Mary's, built in Spanish Mission style of architecture, and located on rising ground eight miles from the ocean, commanding a fine view of the city, the Sierra Madre Range, and the slopes of the Palos Verdes. In 1925, Mt. St. Mary's College, fully satisfying modern requirements for the higher education of women, was formally opened.

SISTERS OF ST. JOSEPH OF CARONDELET
PROVINCIALATE OF AUGUSTA

On April 23, 1867, the Right Rev. Augustin Verot, D.D., Bishop of Savannah, and Vicar Apostolic of Florida, made the first foundation of the Sisters of St. Joseph in Savannah, Georgia. Mother Sidonia, Superior of the foundation established in St. Augustine the year before, by sisters from Le Puy, France, served as Superior of the new foundation, which remained under the control of Le Puy until 1871, when it was erected into a diocesan community, with Mother Josephine as Superior. The first work of the sisters in Savannah was the instruction and care of colored children; later the Barry Orphan Asylum, for the white orphan boys of the diocese, was placed in their charge.

In 1876, for more healthful location, this institution for boys was

*From data supplied by the Sisters of St. Joseph, Mt. St. Joseph, Augusta, Ga.

transferred to Washington, Georgia. In that year the novitiate was also removed to Washington, and an academy for young ladies was opened, which was one of the foremost schools of the south, until destroyed by fire in 1912. This disaster brought another change for the

MT. ST. JOSEPH ACADEMY, AUGUSTA, GEORGIA

sisters, and both novitiate and academy were transferred to Augusta, Georgia. On February 13, 1922, the Sisters of St. Joseph in the diocese of Savannah were affiliated with the Congregation of Sisters of St. Joseph of Carondelet, and with the approval of Pope Benedict XV were recognized as a distinct provincialate. Mother Rose Columba McGinnis and Sister St. John Hobbs were sent from Carondelet as the first Provincial Superior and Assistant Superior, respectively. The provincialate has a flourishing novitiate, and its schools rank with the best in the state.

SUMMARY

Sisters of St. Joseph of Carondelet.
Established in the United States in 1836.
Papal Approbation of Rules (Carondelet) in 1877, by Pope Pius IX.
Habit: The habit is of black serge, with a white linen guimpe, cornet and
     bandeau, and a black veil. A rosary is suspended from a woolen cincture,
     and a crucifix is worn on the breast.

Approximate number in Congregation, 2,800.

Active in educational, hospital and charitable work

Provincialate of St. Louis in the archdioceses of Chicago and St. Louis, and in the dioceses of Belleville, Denver, Green Bay, Indianapolis, Kansas City, Marquette, Mobile, Oklahoma, Peoria and St. Joseph; *Provincial house* Convent of Our Lady of Good Counsel, 1849 Cass Avenue, St. Louis, Missouri. (Archdiocese of St. Louis.)

Provincialate of St. Paul in the archdiocese of St. Paul, and in the dioceses of Fargo, St. Cloud, Sioux Falls and Winona; *Provincial house,* St. Joseph's Provincial house, Novitiate and Normal School, Fairview Avenue and Randolph Street, St. Paul, Minnesota.

Provincialate of Troy in the dioceses of Albany and Syracuse; *Provincial house and Novitiate,* St. Joseph's Seminary, Troy, New York. (Diocese of Albany.)

Provincialate of Los Angeles in the archdiocese of San Francisco, and in the dioceses of Boise, Los Angeles and San Diego, Monterey-Fresno, Spokane and Tucson; *Provincial house and Novitiate,* 3300 West Slauson Avenue, Los Angeles, California. (Diocese of Los Angeles and San Diego.)

Provincialate of Augusta in the diocese of Savannah; *Provincial house and Novitiate,* Mt. St. Joseph Provincial house, 2542 Belleview Street, Augusta, Georgia. (Diocese of Savannah.)

Motherhouse and Novitiate, St. Joseph's Academy, 6400 Minnesota Avenue, St. Louis, Missouri. (Archdiocese of St. Louis.)

PHILADELPHIA, PENNSYLVANIA*

1847

In 1847, the Right Rev. Francis Patrick Kenrick, D.D., then bishop of Philadelphia, visiting his brother, the Most Rev. Peter Richard Kenrick, D.D., first archbishop of St. Louis, heard from him of the success which was attending the labors of the Sisters of St. Joseph in the orphan asylum of that city. Going to their Mother-house in Carondelet, he asked Mother Celestine, the Superior General, for sisters to take charge of the boys' asylum in Philadelphia. Impossible as it seemed at first to comply with the request of the bishop, it was finally agreed that four sisters should be sent for the work, those chosen being Sisters Mary Magdalen Weber, Mary Joseph Clark and Mary Elizabeth Kinkeade, with Mother St. John Fournier as Superior.

Mother St. John Fournier had been one of the original band from Lyons, selected for the American mission in 1836, but, with Mother Celestine, had been detained for two years longer in France, studying the deaf-mute language.

*From data and material supplied by the Sisters of St. Joseph, Chestnut Hill, Philadelphia, and from referred bibliography: *Life of Rev. Mother St. John Fontbonne.* (Benziger Bros.).

Soon after their arrival in Philadelphia from St. Louis, on May 6, 1847, the Sisters of St. Joseph were given charge of St. John's Male Orphan Asylum, then on Chestnut Street. The forty boys in the home had previously been cared for by two secular ladies, one of whom, Miss Mary Meyer, became the first postulant of the community in Philadelphia.

Shortly after their establishment in Philadelphia, the sisters were called upon to take an important share in the parochial school work in the city, and were given charge of several parish schools, thus entering upon the educational work which was to be their chief interest in the ensuing years.

The early years of the Sisters of St. Joseph in Philadelphia were years when the Know-Nothing spirit, which but a short time previously had led

MOTHER ST. JOHN FOURNIER

to the Philadelphia riots, was still rampant. Wishing to render the sisters less conspicuous, and thereby spare them the observations of which they were the subject, as they went about their ministrations, Bishop Kenrick suggested that in addition to the ordinary habit of the Institute, there should be worn, when outside, a black bonnet and cloak, later superseded by a shawl. This appendage to the habit is still retained by many of the communities of Sisters of St. Joseph, although the occasion for its adoption has long since passed.

Upon a request made by the bishop of Toronto, to Bishop Kenrick, the Sisters of St. Joseph of Philadelphia established a foundation of the Congregation in Toronto, Canada, in 1851. Mother Delphine Fontbonne, at the time Superior of the community in Philadelphia, having replaced Mother St. John Fournier—who had been recalled to the Motherhouse, to open missions in St. Paul—was chosen foundress-Superior of the community for Canada.

At the instance of the Venerable John N. Neumann,

C.SS.R., who had become bishop of Philadelphia, Mother St. John was returned to Philadelphia in 1853, and three years later responded favorably to a request for a community of Sisters of St. Joseph for Brooklyn, New York.

MT. ST. JOSEPH, CHESTNUT HILL, PHILADELPHIA, PENNSYLVANIA

On April 25, 1858, "Monticello," at Chestnut Hill, long the residence of the Middleton family, passed into the hands of the Sisters of St. Joseph, becoming Mt. St. Joseph, the Motherhouse of the community in Philadelphia.

On October 4th, the first pupils were received at the academy then opened in connection with the convent at Mt. St. Joseph, and the educational history of the institution was begun. Extensions, improvements, and the acquisition of surrounding property marked the passing years, in the course of which the novitiate was also established at Mt. St. Joseph.

When, in 1862, the Civil War was desolating the land, Mother St. John Fournier, at the request of Surgeon-General Smith, sent sisters to take charge of Church Hospital of Harrisburg, and that improvised at Camp Curtin, outside the city, where they remained, ministering to the sick soldiers, until the camp was broken up. Later, sisters of the community were placed in charge of the floating hospitals which received the wounded from the battlefields of Virginia.

While continuing their work of education, and extending their labors to schools beyond Philadelphia, the sisters, in 1881, inaugurated the instruction of Catholic deaf-mutes, a work which they continue to carry on, at present, in the institution in Philadelphia which is in their charge and is known as the Archbishop Ryan Memorial for Deaf Mutes and Children Who Have Defective Speech.

In its Golden Jubilee year, 1908, collegiate courses were added to the educational curriculum of Mt. St. Joseph Academy, and Mt. St. Joseph College for the higher education of women, formally established on September 22, 1925, ranks among the foremost Catholic institutions in the United States.

SUMMARY

Sisters of St. Joseph of Philadelphia.
Established in 1847.
Papal Approbation of Rules (Philadelphia) in 1895, by Pope Leo XIII.
Approximate number in Community, 1,450.
Active in educational, charitable and social service work in the archdioceses
    of Baltimore and Philadelphia, and in the dioceses of Harrisburg, Newark
    and Trenton.
Motherhouse and Novitiate, Mt. St. Joseph, Chestnut Hill, Philadelphia, Pa.
    (Archdiocese of Philadelphia.)

WHEELING, WEST VIRGINIA*

1853

Early in the year 1853 the Right Rev. R. V. Whelan, D.D., first bishop of Wheeling, requested Mother Celestine, Superior General of the Sisters of St. Joseph of Carondelet, to send sisters to conduct a Catholic hospital in Wheeling, West Virginia.

Complying with the bishop's request, sisters were sent from Carondelet, among them Sister Agatha Guthrie, who later served many years as Superior General of the Carondelet Congregation.

On their arrival, the sisters were installed in the institution known as the Wheeling Hospital, which was used as a military hospital during the Civil War, when the sisters were enrolled in government service.

Mother Agnes Spencer was appointed first Superior in Wheeling, but the year after the establishment of the community, was recalled to Carondelet. The sisters successfully pursued their work in the diocese

---

*From data and material supplied by the Sisters of St. Joseph, St. Joseph's Convent, Wheeling, W. Va.

of Wheeling, and opened hospitals in Parkersburg, Clarksburg and Charleston, and schools and orphanages in those and other cities.

In October, 1860, the community in Wheeling became a diocesan Congregation, and has since confined its activities to the diocese of Wheeling, from which center the sisters participated in the Civil War relief work.

St. Joseph's Academy in Wheeling, accredited and well equipped, is among the most prominent of the educational institutions of the community.

SUMMARY

Sisters of St. Joseph—Wheeling.
Established in 1853.
Approximate number in Community, 160.
Active in educational, hospital and charitable work in the diocese of Wheeling.
Motherhouse and Novitiate, Villa St. Joseph Convent, Fairmont, West Virginia. (Diocese of Wheeling.)

BUFFALO, NEW YORK*
1854

In 1854, in response to the invitation of the Right Rev. John Timon, C.M., D.D., first bishop of Buffalo, a colony of Sisters of St. Joseph was sent from the mother foundation in St. Louis to the picturesquely situated little village of Canandaigua, New York, then included in the diocese of Buffalo.

Arriving at their destination on the 8th of December—that day forever glorious in the annals of the Church—the sisters placed the academy, which they at once opened, under the patronage of Mary Immaculate.

During the year, Mr. A. P. Le Couteulx, a generous benefactor of the Church in Buffalo, presented to Bishop Timon ground on which to erect an institute for the instruction of deaf-mutes.

Little more than two years later, with the Sisters of St. Joseph in charge—in three small houses purchased by the bishop, and moved to the site which had been donated for the purpose—Le Couteulx Institute was opened in Buffalo. Knowing that the Congregation of St. Joseph was, in several parts of France, engaged in work among the deaf-mutes, Bishop Timon applied to the Motherhouse in St. Louis for needed workers to assist the community already actively engaged in school work in the diocese. Three sisters who had studied the

*From data supplied by the Sisters of St. Joseph, Mt. St. Joseph Academy, Buffalo, N. Y., and from the *Life of Rev. Mother St. John Fontbonne*—Rivaux (Benziger Bros.).

methods employed in the Institution of Caen, France, in 1857, were accordingly sent to Buffalo, to inaugurate the work of the Institute— now noted not only as one of the most important establishments of the Buffalo community of Sisters of St. Joseph, but—as Le Couteulx St. Mary's Institution for the Improved Instruction of Deaf-Mutes— particularly outstanding among the philanthropies of the city.

With the community several times augmented in numbers by sisters from St. Louis, its headquarters had early been transferred from Canandaigua to Buffalo, where at Mt. St. Joseph Academy, the Motherhouse and novitiate have been established, and the community incorporated, under the title: Institute of the Sisters of St. Joseph of the Diocese of Buffalo.

SUMMARY

Sisters of St. Joseph—Buffalo.
Established in 1854.
Approximate number in Community, 470.
Active in educational, hospital and charitable work in the dioceses of Buffalo and Scranton.
Motherhouse and Novitiate, Mt. St. Joseph Convent, 2064 Main Street, Buffalo, New York. (Diocese of Buffalo.)

NEW ORLEANS, LOUISIANA*

1855

The advent to the United States from France, in 1855, of a com-munity of the Congregation of the Sisters of St. Joseph of Bourg, founded from Lyons, in the diocese of Belley, in 1819, was the result of a thoughtful gift of the Vicar General of Metz to a visiting priest from the far-away missions in Indiana.

Father Buteux, in the course of his travels in France, in the interest of the Indiana missions, had met the Very Rev. Msgr. Chalandon, then Vicar General of Metz. With apostolic zeal he told of his missions and his happiness in his labors, relating that owing to the distances between the Catholic settlements he was allowed to carry the Blessed Sacrament constantly with him. Deeply touched at this, the Vicar General inquired as to how the missionary carried the Eucharistic Host. Finding that a suitable receptacle had not been provided, and that a corporal was used instead of a pyx, he presented the ardent missionary gold with which to purchase a vessel for this sacred purpose.

*From data and material supplied by the Sisters of St. Joseph, St. Joseph's Academy, New Orleans, La.

Ten years later, as a parish priest in Bay St. Louis, Mississippi, in the diocese of Natchez, Father Buteux again visited France, and asked his former benefactor—who had become bishop of Belley—an alms of another kind. From him who had given gold to honor God

St. Joseph's Academy, New Orleans, Louisiana

hidden in the Eucharist, he asked for sisters who would gain and guard for God the souls of the children of that country, so destitute of religious aid. Again a benefactor, the bishop assented to the request, and arranged with Mother St. Claude, Superior of the Sisters of St. Joseph of Bourg, in the diocese of Belley, for sisters for this mission in the United States.

Mother Eulalia, as Superior for the American missions, and two companion sisters embarked at Havre, on November 19, 1854, and arrived at New Orleans on December 30th. From there they proceeded at once to the designated scene of their first labors in the United States, and on January 6, 1855, they were installed in a modest home in the parish of Father Buteux, at Bay St. Louis, in Mississippi.

The zest and evident spirit with which the Sisters of St. Joseph of Bourg accepted the difficulties of their first days in a strange country —attested in letters received at the Motherhouse—stimulated many vocations for the mission in America, and in the new field of labor there were also many applicants for admission to the community.

In 1863 a novitiate for the United States was established in New Orleans, and, in connection with the convent, which has become the Provincial house for the south, St. Joseph's Academy, a day and boarding school for girls, is maintained, and is one of the prominent educational institutions in the archiepiscopal city.

Extending their educational work to schools through the archdiocese of New Orleans, and continuing their labors in the diocese of Natchez, the sisters have also engaged in their community labors in the archdiocese of Cincinnati. In the city—in addition to a newly erected central novitiate—their activities have resulted in the opening, in 1925, of *The Fontbonne,* a club-house residence for girls and women, replacing the Sacred Heart Guild House as conducted there for many years by the community.

Substantial and attractive in appearance, and erected in the heart of the city, this spacious, modern institution, built under the efficient executive superiorship of Sister Mary Magdalen, is completely equipped for the convenience of the nearly two hundred and fifty women for whom it provides the protection and comfort of a home—with additional entertainment programs, lectures and retreats—in the hallowed atmosphere only to be found in the environment of a chapel, and a house presided over by religious.

In the northwest the labors of the Sisters of St. Joseph of Bourg began, when in August, 1903, the Rev. Father Barras, a French-Canadian priest, requested of the Motherhouse in France, sisters for his parish school at Argyle, Minnesota. The community has since established there Villa Rose Academy, a boarding and day school for girls.

In 1905 a second community of Sisters of St. Joseph of Bourg established a convent in Crookston, Minnesota, and opened an academy for day and boarding students. Soon after the erection, in 1910, of the diocese of Crookston, the convent there was established as a novitiate, and became the provincial residence of the Superior and Visitor of the houses in the northwest.

A convent of the Congregation was established in Superior, Wisconsin, in 1907, and from this center the community is engaged in school work in the French parish at Somerset, and is otherwise active in the diocese of Superior.

SUMMARY

Sisters of St. Joseph—Bourg.
Established in the United States in 1855.

Papal Approbation of Rules, July 27, 1919, by Pope Benedict XV.
Approximate number in Community in United States, 230.
Active in educational, charitable and social service work in the archdioceses
    of Cincinnati and New Orleans, and in the dioceses of Crookston, Natchez
    and Superior.
United States Provincial house and Novitiate for the South, St. Joseph's
    Academy, 2116 Ursuline Avenue, New Orleans, Louisiana. (Archdiocese
    of New Orleans.)
United States Provincial house and Novitiate for the Northwest, St. Joseph's
    Academy, Crookston, Minnesota. (Diocese of Crookston.)
Central Novitiate in United States, St. Joseph's Convent, 6532 Beechmont
    Avenue, Cincinnati, Ohio. (Archdiocese of Cincinnati.)

BROOKLYN, NEW YORK*
1856

In 1856, three years after the establishment of the diocese of
Brooklyn, its first bishop, the Right Rev. John Loughlin, D.D., appealed to Mother St. John Fournier, Superior of the Sisters of
St. Joseph in Philadelphia, asking her for a colony of sisters for the
diocese of Brooklyn.

On August 25, 1856, Bishop Loughlin was consequently gratified
to receive into the diocese the little community of Sisters of St. Joseph
sent from Philadelphia, who on September 8th opened, in Brooklyn,
St. Mary's Academy for Young Ladies, and a year later took charge
of their first parochial school, that of Sts. Peter and Paul's Church, and
thus inaugurated the educational work of their Order in that section
of the state of New York.

Applicants began to seek admission to the community, and the
facilities of the novitiate, which had been established at St. Mary's,
soon proved inadequate for the requirements. A desirable building
in Flushing, formerly used for college purposes, under Episcopalian
auspices, was then purchased by the community, and became the site
of the Motherhouse. The novitiate and academy were transferred to
the new location, where St. Joseph's Academy, for day and boarding
pupils, was opened in connection with the convent.

In 1868, St. John's Orphanage was given into the care of the
Sisters of St. Joseph—the first of their non-educational work in the
diocese, with the exception of their services in the cause of humanity
throughout the Civil War. In 1890 the sisters inaugurated their hospital work in the diocese of Brooklyn.

*From data and material supplied by the Sisters of St. Joseph, St. Joseph's
Convent, Brentwood, Long Island, N. Y.

Brentwood, Long Island, New York, in 1903 became the center of the activities of the community, with the transfer there of the Motherhouse, novitiate and academy, from Flushing. With the increased capacity for expansion permitted by the acquisition of a large acreage, strategically situated, modern buildings have been constructed to meet the requirements of the community, which has to

St. Joseph's Academy, Brentwood, Long Island, New York

its credit, in its annals, the foundations of the Sisters of St. Joseph in Vermont and Massachusetts, and in the diocese of Pittsburgh, in Pennsylvania, exclusive of its present membership of nearly one thousand religious. St. Joseph's Academy, of three hundred students, in addition to an academy for small boys, is included in the institution at Brentwood.

St. Joseph's College for Women, conducted by sisters of the community, was founded in 1916 by the Right Rev. Charles E. McDonnell, D.D., then bishop of Brooklyn. Fully cognizant of the grave dangers that threatened the faith of Catholic young girls who were attending the various day colleges of the metropolis, he requested Mother Mary Louis, of the Sisters of St. Joseph, as the Superior of the diocesan community, to provide an alternative in the establishment, in Brooklyn, of a Catholic day college for women.

Accordingly, a charter was obtained from the Regents of the State of New York, and on October 2, 1916, the college was opened, with full powers to confer degrees.

The number of students seeking admission to St. Joseph's College for Women, on Clinton Street, has so far exceeded its capacity that building expansion has already been necessitated more than once. The Right Rev. Thomas E. Molloy, D.D., Bishop of Brooklyn, is President of the college faculty, of which, prior to his consecration as bishop, he was a member, as professor of religion and philosophy.

17

SUMMARY

Sisters of St. Joseph—Brooklyn.
Established in 1856.
Approximate number in Community, 950.
Active in educational, hospital and charitable work in the diocese of Brooklyn.
Motherhouse and Novitiate, St. Joseph's Convent, Brentwood, Long Island,
    New York. (Diocese of Brooklyn.)

ERIE, PENNSYLVANIA*

1860

The activities of the Sisters of St. Joseph in the diocese of Erie, who are known as the Sisters of St. Joseph of Northwestern Pennsylvania, began in 1860, when, in response to the invitation of the Right Rev. J. M. Young, second bishop of Erie, Mother Agnes Spencer, of the Sisters of St. Joseph of Carondelet, and three companion sisters, took charge of St. Ann's Academy, at Corsica, Pennsylvania.

With the growth of the community it was found that Corsica was not well suited for the center of its development, and, with the

VILLA MARIA CONVENT, ERIE, PENNSYLVANIA

permission of the bishop, a transfer to Meadville, Pennsylvania, was decided upon. On May 8, 1864, Mother Agnes purchased property there, and at once began the erection of St. Joseph's Hospital, later known as Spencer Hospital. In Meadville the sisters also took charge of the orphans, and conducted two schools.

---

*From data and material supplied by the Sisters of St. Joseph, Villa Maria Convent, Erie, Pa.

During the episcopate of the Right Rev. Tobias Mullen, D.D., successor of Bishop Young, a commodious permanent orphanage, under the direction of the sisters, was built in Erie, and this was also made to serve as the Motherhouse and novitiate for the community.

In 1874 St. Vincent's Hospital was opened in Erie; here Mother Agnes spent the last years of her life, and died on March 22, 1882.

St. Mary's Home for the Aged was erected, and opened on September 8, 1884, and in 1923 the Eichenlaub Day Nursery was added to the active works of the community in Erie.

Through the generosity of the Rev. T. A. Casey, the erection of Villa Maria Academy, in Erie, was made possible, and this institution, where Villa Maria College has recently been established, was opened as a boarding and day school in 1892. In 1897 the Motherhouse was transferred to the new academy, thereby making the Convent of Villa Maria the center of the activities of the Sisters of St. Joseph of Northwestern Pennsylvania.

SUMMARY

Sisters of St. Joseph of Northwestern Pennsylvania.
Established in 1860.
Approximate number in Community, 360.
Active in educational, hospital and charitable work in the diocese of Erie.
Motherhouse and Novitiate, Villa Maria Convent, West 8th Street, Erie,
    Pennsylvania. (Diocese of Erie.)

ROCHESTER, NEW YORK*
1864

The early history of the Sisters of St. Joseph of the Diocese of Rochester antedates the actual establishment of the diocese, in the year 1868, as—in the fall of 1864—toward the close of the Civil War, the Right Rev. John Timon, C.M., D.D., Bishop of Buffalo, which then included in its territory the city of Rochester, New York, sent three sisters of the Buffalo community to Rochester, to open an asylum for soldiers' orphans.

Following the division of the diocese of Buffalo and the establish-ment of that of Rochester, of which the Right Rev. Bernard J. Mc-Quaid, D.D., was first bishop, the Sisters of St. Joseph in the diocese were established as a diocesan community, of which Mother Stanislaus Leary was appointed first Superior.

*From the *Life of Rev. Mother St. John Fontbonne,* by Rivaux, and from the Official Catholic Directory, 1929, and accumulated data.

In 1871, the sisters took possession of the spacious building which Bishop McQuaid had purchased for them, to serve as the Motherhouse and novitiate of the Sisters of St. Joseph of the Diocese of Rochester. At Nazareth, as the new convent was named, an academy, normal school and conservatory of music were soon opened.

The increased number of sisters in the community permitted, in 1908, an enlargement of the scope of its work, and St. Joseph's Hospital and training school for nurses was opened in Elmira, New York.

In 1924, under the auspices of the Right Rev. Thomas F. Hickey, D.D., Bishop of Rochester, Nazareth College of Rochester, for the higher education of women, was founded, and is conducted in the city by sisters from the community at Nazareth Motherhouse, now under the ecclesiastical jurisdiction of the Right Rev. John F. O'Hern, D.D., appointed bishop of Rochester, following Bishop Hickey's resignation of the responsibilities of that office.

SUMMARY

Sisters of St. Joseph of the Diocese of Rochester.
Established in 1864.
Approximate number in Community, 620.
Active in educational, hospital and charitable work in the dioceses of
    Rochester and Syracuse.
Motherhouse and Novitiate, Nazareth Motherhouse, Pittsford, Brighton Station, Rochester, New York. (Diocese of Rochester.)

ST. AUGUSTINE, FLORIDA*

1866

A few years after the erection of what is now the diocese of St. Augustine, into a vicariate apostolic, the Right Rev. Augustin Verot, D.D., its first bishop, appealed to the Sisters of St. Joseph at the mother foundation in Le Puy, France, for religious to teach in the diocese, to co-operate in instructing the negroes—just freed from slavery by the Civil War—and to visit the sick and poor in their own homes.

In response to this appeal a community composed of Mother Marie Sidonia Rascle, with companion Sisters of St. Joseph, arrived in St. Augustine from France, September 2, 1866, and began labor in Florida.

At once established in St. Augustine, and performing works, according to the needs of the diocese, having opportunity to practice

*From data supplied by the Sisters of St. Joseph, St. Joseph's Convent and Academy, St. Augustine, Fla.

well the corporal and spiritual works of mercy, especially throughout the yellow fever epidemics of 1877 and 1878, the community, in

ST. JOSEPH'S CONVENT, ST. AUGUSTINE, FLORIDA

1889, severed its connections with the Motherhouse in France, and became a diocesan Congregation.

The Congregation participated actively in war-relief work during the Spanish-American War, gave the use of its buildings in Fernandina and at Pablo Beach, to the Government, and rendered other services at that time.

The community is now under Mother Marie Louise, as present Superior, and subject to the jurisdiction of the Right Rev. Patrick Barry, D.D., Bishop of St. Augustine.

SUMMARY

Sisters of St. Joseph—St. Augustine, Florida.
Established in 1866.
Approximate number in Community, 150.
Active in educational and charitable work in the diocese of St. Augustine.
Motherhouse and Novitiate, St. Joseph's Convent, St. Augustine, Fla. (Diocese of St. Augustine.)

BADEN, PENNSYLVANIA*

1869

In 1869, three sisters of the community of the Sisters of St. Joseph of the diocese of Brooklyn were sent from the Motherhouse, then in Flushing, Long Island, to Ebensburg, Pennsylvania, to establish a novitiate in the diocese of Pittsburgh and to open a school for boys.

Carrying out this purpose, Mt. Gallitzin Seminary was established in memory of the Russian prince, the Rev. Demetrius Gallitzin, the pioneer priest of western Pennsylvania.

In 1901, the Motherhouse of the community was transferred to Baden, where as Mt. Gallitzin Academy, the preparatory school for boys is maintained. A preparatory school for girls who wish to enter the novitiate is connected with the Motherhouse.

In 1926, the community sent a band of volunteers to China, where, laboring with the Passionists in the prefecture apostolic of Shenchowfu, Hunan Province, they endured great hardships, with a fatality to one of their number during the tragic event of the spring of 1929, when three Passionist missionaries from the United States suffered the loss of their lives in the great field afar.

SUMMARY

Sisters of St. Joseph—Baden, Pennsylvania.
Established in 1869.
Approximate number in Community, 360.
Active in the United States in educational work in the dioceses of Altoona and Pittsburgh.
Motherhouse and Novitiate, Mt. Gallitzin Academy, Baden, Pa. (Diocese of Pittsburgh.)

CLEVELAND, OHIO†

1872

To continue the work of his episcopal predecessor, the Right Rev. Amadeus Rappe, D.D., first bishop of Cleveland, whose efforts were bent on the establishment in the new diocese of religious orders who should provide teachers for its Catholic youth, the Right Rev. Richard Gilmour, D.D., strove wisely and whole-heartedly for the same end,

*From data supplied by the Sisters of St. Joseph, Mt. Gallitzin Academy, Baden, Pa., and from *United States Sisters in Fields Afar* (The Catholic News, New York, May 11, 1929) by Sister Mary Just, of the Foreign Mission Sisters of St. Dominic, Maryknoll, N. Y.

†From data and material supplied by the Sisters of St. Joseph, St. Joseph's Academy, 3430 Rocky River Drive, Cleveland, Ohio.

and the year 1872—soon after his installation in the see—marks the advent to the diocese of Cleveland, through his initiative, of the Sisters of St. Joseph, as re-established in France, after the Revolution, by Mother St. John Fontbonne.

Mother George Bradley—Provincial Superior in St. Paul, Minnesota, of the Congregation of Sisters of St. Joseph of Carondelet, from 1865 to 1868, and two companion sisters, constituted the community which was founded in Painesville, Ohio, in the diocese of Cleveland, in August, 1872.

ST. JOSEPH'S CONVENT, WEST PARK, CLEVELAND, OHIO

Teaching in the parish school in Painesville was the first educational work of the new community. A novitiate was soon opened at the convent, and the first ceremony of investiture took place on March 19, 1873, with Bishop Gilmour officiating.

Desirous that the diocesan Sisters of St. Joseph should locate their Motherhouse, and eventually establish an academy, in the episcopal city, and confident that in Cleveland the sisters would soon be employed as teachers in the parish schools, Bishop Gilmour urged the transfer of their convent and novitiate to Cleveland.

For this purpose a building, formerly known as St. John's College, was rented, and in 1877 the community removed from Painesville and occupied the property, until three years later a site was purchased on Starkweather Avenue, where the community located until 1899.

Meanwhile, the community and its educational work had grown. The parochial school demands in Cleveland and throughout the diocese were more numerous than the supply of religious teachers could fill.

The sisters removed to a commodious building erected on a suburban site, a fifty-acre tract of land, purchased in 1898, near West Park, on the east bank of Rocky River.

On March 27, 1928, with impressive ceremonies, the Right Rev. Joseph Schrembs, D.D., Bishop of Cleveland, laid the corner-stone of a new and separate academy building for day and boarding pupils, at the Rocky River Drive location—where, since the construction, in 1905, of a first permanent building unit of the institution, the Motherhouse and academy of the Sisters of St. Joseph in the diocese had been jointly maintained.

Successors to Mother George, who held the office of Superior for twenty years, have been Mother Evangelista, Mother Teresa, Mother St. John and Mother Seraphine, the present incumbent, who, in the administration of the affairs of the community, under the ecclesiastical jurisdiction of Bishop Schrembs, as the ordinary of the diocese, is assisted by a Council composed of Mother Teresa, Mother St. John, Sister Ursula and Sister Berchmans.

SUMMARY

Sisters of St. Joseph—Cleveland.
Established in 1872.
Approximate number in Community, 265.
Active in educational work in the diocese of Cleveland.
Motherhouse and Novitiate, St. Joseph's Convent, 3430 Rocky River Drive, N. W., Cleveland, Ohio. (Diocese of Cleveland.)

RUTLAND, VERMONT*
1873

In 1873, in response to the request of the Right Rev. Louis De Goesbriand, D.D., Bishop of Burlington, a community of Sisters of St. Joseph was sent from the foundation of the Order in Brooklyn, New York, to Rutland, Vermont, where, under the superiorship of Mother M. Philip, the sisters engaged in educational work in parochial schools and in an academy which was opened in connection with the convent.

Building additions were made to the convent in 1876, and made possible the opening of a needed novitiate for the prospering community, which, being then diocesan, came under the direct jurisdiction of the ordinary of the diocese of Burlington.

*From data and material supplied by the Sisters of St. Joseph, Mt. St. Joseph Convent, Rutland, Vt.

The work of the community continues especially educational, through the number of parochial, graded, commercial and high schools of which the sisters are in charge.

In Bennington, Vermont, in addition to their school work, the sisters conduct a day nursery and in Rutland maintain the Loretto Home for Aged Women.

SUMMARY

Sisters of St. Joseph—Rutland, Vermont.
Established in 1873.
Approximate number in Community, 115.
Active in educational and charitable work in the diocese of Burlington.
Motherhouse and Novitiate, Mt. St. Joseph Convent, Rutland, Vermont.
  (Diocese of Burlington.)

BOSTON, MASSACHUSETTS*

1873

Two years before the diocese of Boston was made an archdiocesan see, the Most Rev. John Joseph Williams, D.D., its first archbishop, had requested of the community of Sisters of St. Joseph in Brooklyn sisters for the diocese of Boston, and upon the arrival of the new community, in 1873, the sisters had been placed in charge of St. Thomas' School, at Jamaica Plain.

The community rapidly increased in numbers, and in time many schools opened in Boston and its environs were placed under the direction of the Sisters of St. Joseph, whose work in the archdiocese has continued chiefly educational.

On September 22, 1927, with the opening of Regis College at Weston, Massachusetts, the community, pursuing its educational work, met the demand of the day for Catholic institutions for the higher education of women.

SUMMARY

Sisters of St. Joseph—Boston.
Established in 1873.
Approximate number in Community, 875.
Active in educational and charitable work in the archdiocese of Boston and
  the diocese of Los Angeles and San Diego.
Motherhouse, Mt. St. Joseph's Academy, 617 Cambridge Street, Brighton,
  Boston, Massachusetts.
Novitiate, Bethany House, Framingham, Massachusetts. (Archdiocese of
  Boston.)

*From the *Life of Rev. Mother St. John Fontbonne,* by Rivaux, and from the Official Catholic Year Book, 1928, and the Catholic Encyclopedia.

SPRINGFIELD, MASSACHUSETTS*

1880

The establishment of the community of Sisters of St. Joseph in Springfield, Massachusetts, in 1880, was due to the zeal of the Right Rev. Patrick T. O'Reilly, D.D., who applied to the Sisters of St. Joseph of the diocese of Brooklyn for a community to open a novitiate in the diocese of Springfield and to provide teachers in the Cathedral school.

With the growth of the community in the diocese, its work extended to other parishes in Springfield and to other cities and towns of the diocese.

Most recent in the development of the work of the community was the opening at Chicopee, Massachusetts, in September of 1928, under the auspices of the Right Rev. Thomas M. O'Leary, D.D., Bishop of Springfield, of a Catholic college for women. The new institution, Our Lady of the Elms College, the first completed unit of which is O'Leary Hall, has been erected in Chicopee on the site where for thirty years the Sisters of St. Joseph have conducted Our Lady of the Elms Academy and normal school.

SUMMARY

Sisters of St. Joseph—Springfield, Massachusetts.
Established in 1880.
Approximate number in Community, 500.
Active in educational work in the diocese of Springfield.
Motherhouse and Novitiate, 62 Elliot Street, Springfield, Massachusetts.
   (Diocese of Springfield.)

WATERTOWN, NEW YORK†

1880

From the community of Sisters of St. Joseph in Buffalo, New York, sisters were sent in 1880 to the diocese of Ogdensburg, where the bishop, the Right Rev. Edgar P. Wadhams, D.D., desired a Motherhouse established, at Watertown, to serve as a center for the sisters who should engage in parochial and mission school work in that section of the diocese in northern New York.

In addition to the numerous schools throughout the diocese, now under their charge, and their work at Immaculate Heart Academy

---

*From the *Life of Rev. Mother St. John Fontbonne,* by Rivaux, and from the Official Catholic Year Book, 1928, and current news.

†From data supplied by the Sisters of St. Joseph, Tipton, Ind., and Nazareth, Mich., and from the Official Catholic Year Book, 1928.

in Watertown, sisters from this community have established two of the prospering communities of the Congregation, that of Tipton, Indiana, which dates from 1888, and that of Nazareth, Michigan, founded one year later.

SUMMARY

Sisters of St. Joseph of the Diocese of Ogdensburg.
Established in 1880.
Approximate number in Community, 115.
Active chiefly in educational work in the diocese of Ogdensburg.
Motherhouse and Novitiate, Convent of the Sisters of St. Joseph, 362 West
  Main Street, Watertown, New York. (Diocese of Ogdensburg.)

CONCORDIA, KANSAS*
1884

When the Right Rev. Louis M. Fink, O.S.B., D.D., Bishop of Leavenworth, requested the Sisters of St. Joseph in Rochester, New York, to establish their community in his western diocese, Mother Mary Stanislaus Leary, who for fifteen years had been Superior of the Rochester community, wished to take charge personally of the far-away mission.

In 1884, with the consent of the Right Rev. Bernard J. McQuaid, D.D., Bishop of Rochester, Mother Stanislaus and three companion sisters left Rochester for Newton, Kansas, where they opened a school. Locating a year later in Concordia, as the center of their activities in what was then the diocese of Leavenworth, the sisters established a Motherhouse there.

Sister Mary Bernard Sheridan, of the Sisters of St. Joseph, Erie, Pennsylvania, volunteered her assistance at the new foundation, and arrived in time to take charge of a new mission opened in Abilene, Kansas. Mother Bernard later became the foundress-Superior of the Sisters of St. Joseph of Wichita.

Since the establishment of the diocese of Concordia in 1887, the community has been under the ecclesiastical jurisdiction of the ordinary of this diocese, now the Right Rev. Francis J. Tief, D.D.

With the large number of sisters in the community, missions have been opened in many dioceses, and the community has extended its work to include hospitals and charitable institutions. Prominent among its educational establishments is Marymount College and Academy, advantageously located in Salina, Kansas.

*From data supplied by the Sisters of St. Joseph, Marymount College, Salina, Kan., La Grange, Ill., and Wichita, Kan.

SUMMARY

Sisters of St. Joseph—Concordia, Kansas.
Established in 1884.
Approximate number in Community, 510.
Active in educational, hospital and charitable work in the archdiocese of
Chicago, and in the dioceses of Concordia, El Paso, Grand Island, Kansas
City, Leavenworth, Marquette and Rockford.
Motherhouse and Novitiate, Nazareth Convent, Concordia, Kansas. (Diocese
of Concordia.)

HARTFORD, CONNECTICUT*

1885

Following the post-revolutionary reconstruction, in France, of
the Sisters of St. Joseph, Mother St. John Fontbonne, in 1812, sent
a colony of sisters to Chambéry, in Savoy.

This foundation was later constituted a diocesan congregation,
but as years went on a stronger administration became necessary,
and the Rule was revised to meet the requirements of a Generalate,
under a Superior General. Papal approbation of this change was
granted in 1874, by a rescript of Pope Pius IX, and under the new
form, provinces were established, each with a novitiate.

To the convent in Chambéry, retained as the seat of the Motherhouse, the Congregation of the Propaganda, in Rome, sent, with its
favorable endorsement, a petition from a zealous woman in the United
States. For twenty years Miss Jane Sedgwick, of Stockbridge, Massachusetts, had vainly labored for the establishment of a Catholic school
in the Berkshires, and in efforts to bring this about, had spent a portion
of her fortune.

In response to this petition, referred to the Congregation of the
Sisters of St. Joseph in Chambéry, five sisters, under Mother Martha
of Jesus, were sent, in 1885, to the United States, and in the school
they opened in Lee, Massachusetts, in Berkshire County, began their
educational work in New England. Soon they extended their labors
to Northampton and other cities in Massachusetts, and into Connecticut.

In 1898, the Convent of Mary Immaculate, in Hartford, was
established as the seat of a United States Provincialate and novitiate
for the Congregation, of which Mother Josephine is Provincial
Superior, with Mother Angela as Assistant Provincial, residing at
the institution.

*From data supplied by the Sisters of St. Joseph, Convent of Mary Immacu-
late, Hartford, Conn.

SUMMARY

Sisters of St. Joseph—Chambéry.

Established in the United States in 1885.

Papal Approbation of Rules (Chambéry), by Pope Pius IX, in 1875.

Habit: The habit and veil are black, with a white coif and guimpe. After profession a crucifix is worn on the breast.

Approximate number in Community in United States, 320.

Active in educational, hospital and charitable work in the archdiocese of Baltimore and in the dioceses of Hartford and Springfield.

United States Provincial house and Novitiate, Convent of Mary Immaculate, 27 Park Road, Hartford, Connecticut. (Diocese of Hartford.)

WICHITA, KANSAS*

1888

In 1887, almost on the eve of a decree from Rome, re-apportioning the state of Kansas to constitute the dioceses of Concordia and Wichita —as well as the diocese of Leavenworth, which it had previously comprised, the Sisters of St. Joseph of Concordia opened a school in Abilene, Kansas.

By the specified change, the diocese of Leavenworth — although still containing Abilene, where the mission had been established—was temporarily deprived of an actual foundation of the Sisters of St. Joseph of Concordia, when ecclesiastically severed from the location of their Motherhouse.

Through an agreement, therefore, of the Right Rev. Louis M. Fink, O.S.B., D.D., who continued bishop of Leavenworth, and the Right Rev. Richard Scannell, D.D., consecrated bishop of the new see of

MOTHER M. BERNARD SHERIDAN

Concordia, the mission at Abilene—on March 25, 1888—was established as a foundation, by a community of Sisters of St. Joseph, under Mother M. Bernard Sheridan as Superior.

*From data and material supplied by the Sisters of St. Joseph, Mt. St. Mary's Convent, Wichita, Kan.

The sisters, headquartering at Abilene, had labored in the prairie country for nine years, with marked increase in their number, when—in view of a second division of his diocese—and the probable sever' ance from it of Abilene, Bishop Fink directed a transfer of the

MT. ST. MARY'S CONVENT, WICHITA, KANSAS

Motherhouse of the community to Parsons, in what he surmised would remain his diocese.

Parsons, however, was included in the diocese of Wichita, and these Sisters of St. Joseph, formerly of the see of Leavenworth, in 1897 thus became the Sisters of St. Joseph of Wichita.

Within three years the Right Rev. John J. Hennessy, D.D., transferred the Motherhouse to his episcopal city of Wichita, from which center the sisters at this time conduct eight hospitals and twenty-five schools. The community is now governed by Mother M. Aloysia Keleher as Superior, with Sister M. Prudentia Miller as Assistant, and Sister Baptista Casey as Mistress of Novices.

SUMMARY

Sisters of St. Joseph of Wichita.
Established in 1888.
Approximate number in Community, 300.
Active in educational and hospital work in the dioceses of Denver, Leavenworth, Oklahoma and Wichita.
Motherhouse and Novitiate, Mt. St. Mary's Convent, Wichita, Kansas. (Diocese of Wichita.)

TIPTON, INDIANA*

1888

In 1888, responding to a request from the Right Rev. Joseph Dwenger, C.PP.S., D.D., Bishop of Fort Wayne, for sisters to teach in parochial schools of the diocese, the Sisters of St. Joseph in Watertown, New York, to whom Bishop Dwenger had addressed himself, sent three sisters of their community, who arrived in Tipton, Indiana, on March 15th of that year.

Mother Gertrude Moffitt, as Superior, and two sisters accompanying her composed the first community of Sisters of St. Joseph in the state of Indiana, and in the small town chosen by the bishop for their headquarters, the sisters experienced the trials of the pioneer religious teachers,

MOTHER M. GERTRUDE MOFFITT

*From data and material supplied by the Sisters of St. Joseph, St. Joseph's Convent, Tipton, Ind.

but unfalteringly persevered in their labors in what was then almost a wilderness.

From the beginning, the little community from the New York foundation opened not only the academy at the Motherhouse, and schools in the vicinity, but a novitiate for the reception and training of the future workers in the diocese. Three years after the estab-

ST. JOSEPH CONVENT, TIPTON, INDIANA

lishment of the foundation in Tipton, Indiana had contributed a fair quota of the novices received, among whom was Miss Mary Elizabeth Donahue, of Kokomo, who, as Sister Xavier, became the co-worker of the foundress-Superior, and prior to the death of Mother Gertrude, in 1916, served for many years as Assistant Superior in the community.

Continuing her services with the community, of which she was second Superior, Mother Xavier pursued the designs and ideals of her predecessor, in her administration adhering chiefly to educational work for the community, as the purpose of its establishment, although in addition to their work in the schools, the sisters are in charge of the Good Samaritan Hospital, in Kokomo, Indiana, which was opened in 1909, inaugurating the hospital work of the community, now under the ecclesiastical jurisdiction of the Right Rev. John F. Noll, D.D., Bishop of Fort Wayne.

SUMMARY

Sisters of St. Joseph—Tipton, Indiana.
Established in 1888.
Approximate number in Community, 120.
Active in educational and hospital work in the dioceses of Baker City and
Fort Wayne.
Motherhouse and Novitiate, St. Joseph's Convent, Tipton, Indiana. (Diocese
of Fort Wayne.)

NAZARETH, MICHIGAN*

1889

To the zealous interest and energy of the Rev. Frank A. O'Brien, the beloved and loyal citizen-priest of Kalamazoo, Michigan, is due the establishment in the diocese of De-
troit, in 1889, of a diocesan foundation of the Sisters of St. Joseph.

Invited to the diocese by the Right Rev. John S. Foley, D.D., soon after his appointment to the Detroit episcopacy, a band of sisters from the community of Sis-
ters of St. Jo-
seph of the Diocese of Og-

NAZARETH CONVENT, NAZARETH, MICHIGAN

densburg was sent from the Motherhouse in Watertown, New York, to take charge of Borgess Hospital in Kalamazoo, and St. Francis' Home in Monroe, Michigan, both in the diocese of Detroit.

Mother Mary Margaret was Superior of the community which

*From data and material supplied by the Sisters of St. Joseph, Nazareth College, Nazareth, Mich.

13

began its hospital and charitable work in the diocese of Detroit in Kalamazoo, on July 6, 1889.

Applicants for admission to the community were not wanting, and necessitated the early opening of a diocesan novitiate in a cottage on the grounds of the hospital in Kalamazoo.

From this beginning, the Sisters of St. Joseph of the diocese of Detroit have developed the community and its well-located and modernly constructed Motherhouse buildings, where, in addition to the convent, Nazareth Academy, one of the prominent educational institutions of the community, has been established.

To meet the demands for the higher education of women, the sisters, in 1924, under the superiorship of Mother M. Marion, and the ecclesiastical auspices of the Right Rev. Michael J. Gallagher, D.D., Bishop of Detroit, opened at the Motherhouse, Nazareth College, for boarding and day students.

Barbour Hall—a branch of Nazareth Academy—a school for little boys, is also conducted in Kalamazoo by the community.

Among the charitable institutions in the care of the sisters of this community is St. Anthony's Home for Backward and Feebleminded Children, and a home for old people, both located in Comstock, Michigan.

A SISTER OF ST. JOSEPH, NAZARETH, MICHIGAN

SUMMARY

Sisters of St. Joseph of the Diocese of Detroit.
Established in 1889.
Approximate number in Community, 350.
Active in educational, hospital and charitable work in the diocese of Detroit.
Motherhouse and Novitiate, Nazareth Convent, Nazareth, Michigan. (Diocese of Detroit.)

LA GRANGE, ILLINOIS*

1900

In 1899, the Most Rev. Patrick A. Feehan, D.D., first archbishop of Chicago, invited Mother Stanislaus Leary, of the Concordia foun-

*From material supplied by the Sisters of St. Joseph, Convent of Our Lady of Bethlehem, La Grange, Ill.

dation of the Sisters of St. Joseph, to establish a school in the arch-diocese.

As in Concordia, Mother Stanislaus personally directed the making of the new foundation, in 1900. La Grange, a beautiful suburb of the great metropolis, was chosen for the site of the new institution, and plans were made for the erection of Nazareth Academy.

The sisters were scarcely established, when, on February 14, 1900, Mother Stanislaus died. This loss of their able executive and indefatigable foundress was keenly felt by the members of the sorrowing community of the new foundation.

To Sister Mary Alexine Gosselin, Mother Stanislaus had herself confided the responsibility of continuing this foundation. Young and inexperienced, Sister Alexine hesitated at the task, but Archbishop Feehan,

MOTHER M. ALEXINE

trusting the wisdom of Mother Stanislaus, vested her with authority as Superior, and commissioned her to carry on the work.

OUR LADY OF BETHLEHEM CONVENT, LA GRANGE, ILLINOIS

Nazareth Academy was completed, and Christmas Day, 1901, found the La Grange community established in this new home;

pupils were soon received in the now famous academy, of which Mother M. Patricia is Superior.

Parallel with the material progress of this community of religious workers, the intellectual progress of its members has kept apace, so that today a skilled body of teachers has been developed, capable of giving the best training in all the departments conducted in such an institution.

In addition to the academy for girls, Mother Alexine, yielding to the importune demands of many patrons, opened St. Joseph's Institute, a well-equipped boarding school for boys under fourteen years of age, and today this school is affectionately claimed, as the scene of happy boyhood days, by many prominent men of the country.

As in all convents of the Sisters of St. Joseph, the novitiate forms a large part of the institution of Nazareth, at La Grange, where the community is thoroughly cosmopolitan in its membership.

SUMMARY

Sisters of St. Joseph—La Grange, Illinois.
Established in 1900.
Papal Approbation of Rules, January, 1912, by Pope Pius X.
Approximate number in Community, 140.
Active in educational work in the archdiocese of Chicago.
Motherhouse and Novitiate, Convent of Our Lady of Bethlehem, Nazareth
    Park, La Grange, Illinois. (Archdiocese of Chicago.)

FALL RIVER, MASSACHUSETTS*
1902

In 1902, from the community of Sisters of St. Joseph, of the diocesan community at Le Puy, France, where in 1650 had been gathered together those who became the first Sisters of St. Joseph, of the thousands now active throughout the world, a group of sisters was sent to the United States—as before to Florida, in 1867—and in Fall River, Massachusetts, at once took charge of the school in the French parish of St. Roch.

Two other French parishes in the city, that of the Blessed Sacrament and that of St. John the Baptist, have since placed their schools under sisters of this community, which, retaining its affiliation with

*From the Catholic Encyclopedia and the Official Catholic Directory, 1929.

the Motherhouse in Le Puy, has been augmented, whenever necessary, by sisters sent from France.

To meet requests from candidates in the United States, for admission to the community, a novitiate has been established in connection with the convent in Fall River—now a Provincial house of the Le Puy community.

SUMMARY

Sisters of St. Joseph—Le Puy.
Established in the United States in 1902.
Approximate number in Community in United States, 30.
Active in educational work in the diocese of Fall River.
United States Provincial house and Novitiate, St. Teresa's Convent, 2501 South Main Street, Fall River, Massachusetts. (Diocese of Fall River.)

SOUTH BERWICK, MAINE*
1906

In 1906, from the General Motherhouse of the Congregation of the Sisters of St. Joseph de Lyon, in Lyons, France, a community was sent to the United States for educational work.

The activities of the community have been confined to the state of Maine, where the first foundation was made, in Jackman. To the convent and boarding school established in South Berwick, in 1909, a novitiate was added, to meet the demands in the United States of applicants for admission to the Community.

In 1926, continuing their labors in the southwestern part of the state, sisters of the community were placed in charge of Holy Family School in Lewiston.

From the convent in South Berwick, Maine, where Mother St. Radegonde is Superior, sisters of the community are on missions in Madura, South India, where the Congregation has schools and a hospital.

SUMMARY

Sisters of St. Joseph de Lyon.
Established in the United States in 1906.
Papal Approbation of Rules in 1909, by Pope Pius X.
Approximate number in Community in United States, 75.
Active in educational work in the diocese of Portland.
United States Novitiate, St. Joseph's Convent, South Berwick, Maine. (Diocese of Portland.)

*From data supplied by the Sisters of St. Joseph de Lyon, St. Joseph's Convent, South Berwick, Maine.

ORANGE, CALIFORNIA*

1912

Cognizant of the proficient work being done by the Sisters of St. Joseph in the archdiocese of Chicago, the Right Rev. Thomas Grace, D.D., second bishop of Sacramento, in 1912 solicited that community for a foundation for his California diocese.

The Most Rev. James Edward Quigley, D.D., Archbishop of Chicago, consented to a favorable response to this petition, and

SISTERS OF ST. JOSEPH OF ORANGE, CALIFORNIA

Mother Bernard Gosselin, an active executive in the Chicago community, was chosen to take up the work in the west.

Mother Gosselin and nine volunteer companions formed the nucleus of the new diocesan community which in 1912 began its activities in the northern part of California. Extending finally throughout the entire state, the community participated in educational and hospital work as diocesan needs required.

In 1921 the community was called upon by the Paulist Fathers to open a mission among the Chinese in San Francisco. The St. Mary's Catholic Chinese Mission then became a field for the exercise, at home, of a foreign missionary spirit, and more than three hundred Chinese were baptized at the mission during the first year of its existence.

Owing to the wide geographical range of the institutions in the sisters' charge, a decision was made to transfer the Motherhouse, from Eureka—the site of the community's first establishment—to a more central location at Orange, California.

On June 23, 1922, the Right Rev. John J. Cantwell, D.D., Bishop of Los Angeles and San Diego, officiated at the blessing and opening ceremonies of "Nazareth," the new Motherhouse and the center of activities of the Sisters of St. Joseph of Orange.

*From data and material supplied by the Sisters of St. Joseph, Orange, Calif.

Under Mother Bernard as Superior, well-equipped, modern boarding and day schools, academies and hospitals were established and
are conducted in north, south and central California by the community, among whose recent enterprises has been the opening of a
cosmopolitan school of more than five hundred pupils, at the old
mission of Our Lady of Angels, at the Plaza, in the city of Los
Angeles.

SUMMARY

Sisters of St. Joseph of Orange.
Established in 1912.
Approximate number in Community, 290.
Active in educational and hospital work in the archdiocese of San Francisco
   and in the dioceses of Los Angeles and San Diego, and Sacramento.
Motherhouse and Novitiate, Nazareth, 380 South Batavia Street, Orange,
   California. (Diocese of Los Angeles and San Diego.)

CHRONOLOGICAL TABLE

Foundations in the United States of the Sisters of St. Joseph

1836—Carondelet, St. Louis, Missouri.
1847—Philadelphia, Pennsylvania
   (Chestnut Hill).
1853—Wheeling, West Virginia.
1854—Buffalo, New York.
1855—New Orleans, Louisiana.
1856—Brooklyn, New York (Brentwood).
1860—Erie, Pennsylvania (Northwestern Pennsylvania).
1864—Rochester, New York (Nazareth).
1866—St. Augustine, Florida.
1867—Savannah, Georgia (Augusta).
1869—Baden, Pennsylvania (Pittsburgh, Pa.).

1872—Cleveland, Ohio.
1873—Rutland, Vermont.
1873—Boston, Massachusetts.
1880—Springfield, Massachusetts.
1880—Watertown, New York.
1884—Concordia, Kansas.
1885—Berkshire County, Massachusetts (Hartford, Conn.).
1888—Wichita, Kansas.
1888—Tipton, Indiana.
1889—Nazareth, Michigan (Detroit).
1900—La Grange, Illinois (Chicago).
1902—Fall River, Massachusetts.
1906—South Berwick, Maine.
1912—Eureka, California (Orange,
   Calif.).

GENERAL SUMMARY

Sisters of St. Joseph.
Founded in France in 1650.
Established in the United States in 1836.
Papal Approbation of Rules. (See individual communities.)
Habit: The habit and veil are black; the forehead band, cornette and guimpe
   are of white linen. A large rosary is suspended from a black woolen
   cincture at the waist, and a crucifix is worn on the breast.
Approximate number in communities in United States, 12,000.

Active in educational, hospital, charitable and social service work in the archdioceses of Baltimore, Boston, Chicago, Cincinnati, New Orleans, Philadelphia, St. Louis, St. Paul and San Francisco, and in the dioceses of Albany, Altoona, Belleville, Boise, Brooklyn, Buffalo, Burlington, Cleveland, Concordia, Crookston, Denver, Detroit, El Paso, Erie, Fall River, Fargo, Fort Wayne, Grand Island, Green Bay, Harrisburg, Hartford, Indianapolis, Kansas City, Leavenworth, Los Angeles and San Diego, Marquette, Mobile, Monterey-Fresno, Natchez, Newark, Ogdensburg, Oklahoma, Peoria, Pittsburgh, Portland, Rochester, Rockford, Sacramento, St. Augustine, St. Cloud, St. Joseph, Savannah, Scranton, Sioux Falls, Spokane, Springfield, Superior, Syracuse, Trenton, Tucson, Wheeling, Wichita and Winona.

SISTERS OF PROVIDENCE*

1840

*W*ITH the arrival in New York, on September 5, 1840, of a community of Sisters of Providence from their convent at Ruillé-sur-Loire, France, that country for the fifth time in the early history of the Church in the United States contributed members of her various religious orders of women for missionary and educational work in the New World.

As emissary of the Right Rev. Simon G. Bruté, Indiana's first bishop—whose diocese, that of Vincennes, established in 1834, comprised the territory of the state—the Rev. Celestine de la Hailandière had returned to France, his native country, to seek not only financial aid for the many needs of the new diocese, but missionaries, both men and women. The errands which had occasioned his journey had not been completed when Father de la Hailandière received word of the death of Bishop Bruté, on June 26, 1839, and of his own appointment as successor to the see. Before he left France, following his consecration in Paris less than two months later, Bishop Hailandière had been assured by the Sisters of Providence of sisters for what had become his own episcopal field.

The Sisters of Providence to whom Bishop Hailandière had appealed were founded in the diocese of Le Mans, France, in 1806, through the efforts of the Abbé François Jacques Dujarié of Ruillé-sur-Loire, to secure the assistance of young women who would devote themselves exclusively to the instruction of children and to the care of the sick in the desolation caused by the French Revolution.

In compliance with the desire of the earnest workers who banded together, and who called the home where they dwelt "Little Providence," l'Abbé Dujarié arranged for their training as religious by placing a first group of their number with the nuns at Beaugé. Nearly a year passed before Little Providence welcomed home its "sisters," to whom a religious costume had been given, the habit resembling that which they then adopted as Sisters of Providence.

Shortly after this period there was admitted to the Community Mademoiselle Joséphine Zoé du Roscoät, of a noble and ancient family of Brittany, who, completing her term of probation, according to

*From data and material supplied by the Sisters of Providence, St. Mary-of-the-Woods, Ind., and from *The Life of Mother Theodore Guérin* (Benziger Bros.) and Blanchard's *History of the Catholic Church in Indiana.*

conditions imposed by Abbé Dujarié, was the first of those in Little Providence to make public profession of her vows, as she was the first to be elected Superior and bear the title Mother. Mother du Roscoät has therefore always been looked upon as the foundress of the Sisters of Providence.

MOTHER THEODORE GUÉRIN (1798-1856)

Expanding with unprecedented rapidity, the Congregation became firmly established, and stimulated by the Superior General in her own efforts toward perfection, the young Community rose with her to heights of fervor, which while not lessening the sisters' sorrow,

found them better prepared to meet it, when Mother du Roscoät succumbed to typhoid fever in 1822.

Little more than a year after the death of Mother du Roscoät,
her successor, Mother Mary Lecor, welcomed to the Community
Mademoiselle Thérèse Guérin, destined, as Mother Theodore
Guérin, to rank among the noted foundresses of religious orders of
women in the United States.

Anne Thérèse Guérin, who was born at Étables, Côtes-du-Nord,
France, on October 2, 1798, was the eldest of two daughters of
Laurent Guérin and Isabelle Lefevre, whose families were avowed
Napoleonites on the one side and devoted royalists on the other.
Her early years being those closely following the period of the French
Revolution, when the havoc wrought by its fury was yet felt, making
the practice of religion difficult, and the means of securing education
arduous, Thérèse Guérin, growing in grace and wisdom, was well
fortified to meet the shock of her father's tragic death, to care for her
invalided mother through long years, and then to await that mother's
long withheld consent to the fulfillment of her own desire—to labor
as a religious for God and for souls.

Upon her admittance to the Congregation of the Sisters of Providence, Sister Theodore, as Mademoiselle Guérin became known in
religion, entered whole-heartedly into the practices of the religious
life. When only four months of her novitiate had passed she became
seriously ill. A violent remedy administered at this time permanently
impaired her digestive organs, so that she was never thereafter able
to take any solid food. While recovering from this illness, for the
benefit of her health by the change, Sister Theodore was transferred
for a time to Pruilly.

With her return to health, and to Ruillé-sur-Loire, so evident
was her progress in the highest paths of spirituality, and so marked
her natural endowments, that on the day of her profession she was
appointed Superior of the house in Rennes, one of the largest establishments of the Congregation. Here, and later at Soulaines, where
she was awarded medallion decorations by the French Academy for
personal qualifications and her efficient work in the schools, she
spent fifteen years.

When Bishop Hailandière's appeal for sisters for his distant mis-
sion reached Mother Mary Lecor, it was presented to the sisters.
Many at once volunteered, but the one chosen as best fitted to lead
the first foreign mission band from the Sisters of Providence in
France, and to undertake the foundation, was Mother Theodore
Guérin.

Filled with the spirit of a missioner, Mother Theodore responded to the invitation as a call from God, and with Sister St. Vincent Ferrer, Sister Basilide, Sister Olympiade, Sister Mary Xavier and Sister Mary Liguori, who shared her missionary spirit, said farewell to the Community at Ruillé-sur-Loire, on July 12, 1840, and after a visit to Le Mans, where they received the bishop's blessing, proceeded to Havre from whence they embarked for the United States, on July 16th, the feast of Our Lady of Mt. Carmel.

The sisters suffered much from sea-sickness during the voyage, but none so long or so severely as Mother Theodore. On September 5th, and in sight of the land of their adoption, they left the ship, descending by the rope ladder into the skiff which bore them on storm-tossed waves, and amid a downpour of rain, to the quarantine station. A little later a steamer took them to Brooklyn, where it was planned they would spend a few days before setting out on the long trip to be made by stage-coach and by boat on the Ohio River to Indiana. On the evening of October 22, 1840, they reached their journey's end.

The convent, a few miles distant from Terre Haute, which Bishop Hailandière had intended should be in readiness for the little band of French sisters, had not been completed, and they therefore made their first home near it in the midst of a forest, where a small frame farm-house was shared with them by a Catholic family.

A little hut nearby was the church and the domicile of the resident missionary, the Rev. Stanislaus Buteux, one of a group of Eudist Fathers who had come from Europe to establish a college at Vincennes.

With the postulants who were awaiting them, Mother Theodore and her companions inaugurated their community life, and while the postulants were initiated into the religious life by the sisters, the sisters diligently applied themselves, with the postulants as teachers, to the study of English.

Bishop Hailandière visited the new Community soon after its arrival, and through arrangements made by him the family sharing the house with the sisters was prevailed on to allow them its entire use. Thus was established St. Mary-of-the-Woods, the convent and Motherhouse of the Sisters of Providence in America.

While awaiting opportunities of exercising the principal object of their foundation, the instruction of youth, the sisters, occupying themselves more intimately with the work of personal sanctification, also became actively engaged in the improvement of their surroundings, while workmen completed the building for the academy which was dedicated on July 5, 1841, and which, the next day, registered four pupils.

St. Mary's Institute was begun on the same plan as the collegiate institutes of France. Higher education was its primary object. The.

Main Entrance
PROVIDENCE CONVENT, ST. MARY-OF-THE-WOODS, INDIANA

charter granted in 1846 by the Indiana legislature granted to St. Mary-of-the-Woods all the rights and privileges of chartered institutions, and empowered it to confer collegiate degrees whenever students were judged ready to receive them.

The Christmas of 1841 brought the sisters at St. Mary's a visit from the Rev. N.J. Perché, later archbishop of New Orleans. Father Perché, coming from Portland, Kentucky, brought two postulants to the Community. Remaining at St. Mary's for ten days, the zealous prelate gave a daily instruction to the sisters on the formation of the religious life.

The first of the many missions established by the Community was that undertaken at Jasper, Indiana, with the opening of a school there on March 19, 1842.

In the spring of 1843, Mother Theodore, accompanied by Sister Mary Cecilia, a novice, though not recovered from serious illnesses, returned to France in the interests of the Indiana foundation, where innumerable difficulties had arisen. Since their coming from Europe the sisters had been encouraged and aided continually by bishop, community and friends in France, and there was need of the visit to the Motherhouse for consultation and advice, and to appeal anew to the generous friends there in behalf of St. Mary-of-the-Woods.

MOTHER MARY CLEOPHAS FOLEY

Hurriedly recalled to the United States by perplexing circumstances which were developing in connection with the observance of the rules as brought over in 1840 from the Motherhouse in France, Mother Theodore and the pioneer Community were severely tried by conditions and events encountered in the fuller development of the foundation of the Sisters of Providence in the United States.

For upwards of sixteen years Mother Theodore guided the Community at St. Mary-of-the-Woods, infusing into the sisters, by the memorable conferences she gave them, and by the forceful example of her enduring virtues, her sublime faith in Divine Providence. To her far-seeing vision and motivating spirit is due the splendid structure of the Congregation, which has continued its progressive activities in the interests of religious education during the administrations of her successors as Superior General, Mother Mary Cecilia Bailly, Mother Anastasia Brown, Mother Mary Ephrem Glenn, Mother Euphrasie

Hinkle, Mother Mary Cleophas Foley, and Mother Mary Raphael Slattery, elected to office in 1926.

In these years since the death of Mother Theodore, their beloved foundress, who it is hoped will soon be raised to the altars of the Church, the Sisters of Providence have extended their educational activities far beyond Indiana—where schools and academies opened in early days are continued in Fort Wayne, Indianapolis, La Fayette, Madison, Terre Haute, Vincennes, Washington and other cities—to cities in California, Illinois, Maryland, Massachusetts and Oklahoma.

Prominent among the many institutions of the Congregation in the country is the academy opened in 1904 at Mount Marion, Washington, D. C., and which, known as Immaculata Seminary, recalls the celebration that year of the Golden Jubilee of the definition of the dogma of the Immaculate Conception. A more recent academic institution of the Order, likewise honoring in its name the Mother of God, is that opened in 1925 just northeast of Indianapolis, and which, as Ladywood, the mansion estate of Stoughton A. Fletcher, is now the site of an academy and school for girls.

To Mother Mary Cleophas Foley, who died on December 27, 1928, after a successful administration of thirty-six years as Superior General of the Congregation, is due the impetus given its prominent educational work, and the development at the Motherhouse site—the historic location of Indiana's oldest school for girls—of St. Mary-of-the-Woods College. No longer, however, is St. Mary-of-the-Woods a dense forest. Near Terre Haute, and a short ride from Indianapolis, on the cross-continent New York-St. Louis route, it is rather a city of itself, where harmonious and stately buildings stand well placed in the scenic landscape, with rolling lawns, asphalted paths and lake, and majestic trees which bespeak the near one hundred years of their peaceful growth.

As Mother Mary Lecor, appealed to for missionaries for America, in 1840, had sent to its distant shores Sisters of Providence from France, so Mother Mary Cleophas responded to the need for missionary sisters in China, and in 1920 sent to Kaifeng from St. Mary-of-the-Woods six Sisters of Providence, the first mission band of American sisters to leave this country for China. After eight years of labor there, civic disturbances necessitated a temporary interruption of their work, which however has been resumed, and is now carried on.

Mother Mary Raphael, who now serves at St. Mary-of-the-Woods as Superior General of the Congregation of the Sisters of Providence, is aided in the administration of the affairs of the Community of more than sixteen hundred, in place of the original six, by Sisters Mary Bernard, Berchmans, Gertrude Clare and Mary Ignatia as Assistants, Sister Francis Joseph, Supervisor of Schools, and Sister Geraldine, Secretary.

SUMMARY

Sisters of Providence.
Founded in France in 1806.
Established in the United States in 1840.
Papal Approbation of Rules, May 28, 1887, by Pope Leo XIII.
Habit: The habit is of black wool material. A black cape is also worn, and a starched white linen guimpe. A crucifix of white bone is suspended from the neck by a black silk cord, and a chaplet of large beads, with a crucifix and two medals attached, is worn at the side. A black veil is worn over a white muslin cap.
Approximate number in Community, 1,660.
Active in educational work in the United States in the archdioceses of Baltimore, Boston and Chicago and in the diocese of Fort Wayne, Indianapolis, Los Angeles and San Diego, Oklahoma, Peoria and Rockford.
Motherhouse and Novitiate, Providence Convent, St. Mary-of-the-Woods, Indiana. (Diocese of Indianapolis.)

SISTERS OF NOTRE DAME DE NAMUR*

THE Institute of the Sisters of Notre Dame de Namur, which was introduced into the United States in the year 1840, was founded at Amiens, France, in 1803.

The foundress of the Institute, Blessed Julie Billiart, who was declared Venerable on May 25, 1889, by the Sovereign Pontiff, Pope Leo XIII, and on May 13, 1906, pronounced Blessed by his pontifical successor, Pope Pius X, was born at Cuvilly, a village of Picardy, in the Department of Oise, France, on July 12, 1751.

Marie Rose Julie Billiart was one of seven children, and even in early childhood, when at the age of seven she knew the catechism by heart, she was remarkable for her piety and was frequently seen to withdraw herself from play with her young companions to pray in some secluded spot, with gravity and devotion far beyond her years.

When she was in her sixteenth year, financial reverses and other misfortunes befell her family, and Julie generously aided her parents to the best of her ability. Later a nervous shock—caused by an attempt against her father's life—so affected her that she became unable to walk, and was confined to her bed, a helpless cripple, for twenty-two years.

During the first years of this period, Julie spent several hours a day in prayerful contemplation, in making linens and laces for the altar, and in catechizing the children whom she gathered around her bed. In the pitiless strife of the French Revolution, this zeal and her reputation for sanctity drawing upon the cripple the hatred of the Revolutionists, who sought the death of "the devotee," she was taken to Compiègne, concealed in the bottom of a cart. During the three years of her subsequent stay there she was moved three times in order to save her life.

Julie's sufferings were intense, but she was less concerned over her bodily illness than over her utter lack of spiritual help. God, however, consoled His faithful servant with a heavenly vision. On the summit of Calvary she beheld our crucified Lord surrounded by a multitude of religious wearing a habit she had never seen. As Julie contemplated this wondrous spectacle, she distinctly heard a voice saying: "Behold the spiritual daughters whom I give to you in the Institute which will be marked by My Cross." So clear was

---

*From data and material supplied by the Sisters of Notre Dame de Namur, Cincinnati, Ohio, Belmont, Calif., and Waltham, Mass., and from Shea's *History of the Catholic Church in the United States*, and *Catholic Missions*, Official Organ of the Society for the Propagation of the Faith.

19

the vision, so deeply impressed on her memory the features of the religious, that in after years she said to postulants, "Yes, God wills

BLESSED JULIE BILLIART (1751-1816)
Foundress of the Institute of the Sisters of Notre
Dame de Namur

you in our Institute, for I saw you among ours at Compiègne." And when the time came for the choice of a religious dress for her sisters, without a moment's hesitation she gave detailed instructions as to its shape and material, saying: "So it was shown to me at Compiègne."

In 1794 Julie was removed to Amiens, where she took refuge with Countess Baudoin, and there met Marie Louise Françoise Blin de

Bourdon, Viscountess of Gézaincourt, later known as Mother St. Joseph, co-foundress and second Superior General of the Sisters of Notre Dame.

The viscountess was thirty-eight years old at the time of her meeting with Julie, and had spent her youth in piety and good works. A little company of friends gathered with her around Julie's couch, learning from her how to lead an interior life, while they devoted themselves generously to charitable works. Of the friends, however, only Françoise Blin de Bourdon remained, when in 1803, in obedience to Father Joseph Varin, who discerned saintly Julie Billiart's fitness for the work, despite her infirmity and helpless condition, the Institute of the Sisters of Notre Dame was formed.

On February 2, 1804, in the chapel of a little house in the Rue Neuve, Amiens, which Blessed Julie had rented and occupied since the previous August, the two foundresses and one postulant, made, or renewed, the vow of chastity, solemnly dedicated themselves to the Christian education of young girls, and further proposed to train religious teachers who should go wherever their services were solicited. A provisional rule for the Community, based upon that of St. Ignatius, drawn up by Blessed Julie and Father Varin, was so far-sighted that its essentials have never been changed.

Four months later, on the feast of the Sacred Heart, at the conclusion of a novena, Blessed Julie, who in unceasing suffering had been confined to her couch for twenty-two years, was miraculously cured, and thus enabled during the twelve years of life that remained to her, to labor actively for the glory of God, to travel about and transact business required for the establishment of houses of her Institute.

The first regular schools of the Sisters of Notre Dame were opened in France, in the diocese of Amiens, in August, 1806. The urgent need in the country at that time, of Christian education among all classes of society, led to the modification of the original plan of teaching only the poor, and to the opening of schools for the children of the rich as well.

On December 15, 1806, prior to the departure of a group of Sisters of Notre Dame to establish at St. Nicolas, near Ghent, Belgium, the first branch house of the Institute, the religious habit was assumed by the Congregation. The following year, the Institute was further extended by the establishment of a foundation at Namur, Belgium, with the co-foundress, Mother St. Joseph, as Superior.

Two years later, upon the invitation of the Right Rev. Pisani de la Gaude, Bishop of Namur, the convent at Namur became the

Motherhouse of the Institute.   When Belgium, in 1815, became the battlefield of the Napoleonic Wars, Blessed Julie happily saw her convents saved from injury, though several of them were in the paths of the armies.

Following the death of the holy foundress in January, 1816, Mother St. Joseph Blin de Bourdon was elected Superior General, and guided the Community during the most critical time of its exist-ence, through a period of persecution of religious orders, revolutions and national contentions.   Under her able government there was drawn up for the Institute the system of school management which it has followed ever since, with only such modifications of curricula and discipline as time, place and experience have rendered indis-pensable.

CINCINNATI, OHIO
1840

It was Mother Ignatius Goethals, third Superior General of the Congregation, whom the bishop of Cincinnati, the Right Rev. John B. Purcell, D.D., met, when during a visit in Europe in 1839, he called at the Motherhouse in Namur to see the Baroness de Coppens, then making a retreat at the convent.   Visiting the schools, noting the method of teaching, and the spirit of the Institute, Bishop Purcell asked for Sisters of Notre Dame de Namur for his diocese in the United States.

His request was granted the following year, when on the eve of the feast of All Saints, 1840, with Sister Louis de Gonzague as Superior, eight Sisters of Notre Dame arrived in Cincinnati, Ohio, from their European Motherhouse at Namur.

Becoming the guests of the Sisters of Charity in Cincinnati, the sisters from Namur, the first European community to come to Ohio, remained with them a little more than a fortnight, until they were established in a rented house on Sycamore Street, opposite what was then the Cathedral, where the Jesuit Church, St. Francis Xavier's, now stands.   Providentially, they were soon enabled to purchase the Spencer residence, not far distant from the Cathedral, to which they transferred a few days before their first Christmas in the United States.   In this house, which became in time but a fractional part of the large pile of buildings which composed historic Sixth Street Convent, the sisters, on January 18, 1841, opened simultaneously a boarding school and academy, and free school.

In 1843, when a second group of sisters arrived from Namur, the first extension outside of Cincinnati was made when sisters were sent to open a school in Toledo, Ohio, upon the request of the Rev. Amadeus Rappe, then pastor there, but soon after appointed first bishop of Cleveland, upon the division of the state of Ohio into a second diocese. After two years the Toledo mission was relinquished by the community.

Ill health necessitating the return to Europe of Mother Louis de Gonzague, Sister Louise, another of the original group of sisters, from Namur was appointed Superior, not only of the house in Cincinnati, but of all other houses of the Congregation founded, or to be founded, east of the Rocky Mountains.

NOTRE DAME CONVENT, GRANDIN ROAD, CINCINNATI, OHIO

A house was opened in Boston, Massachusetts, in 1848, and another in Dayton, Ohio, in 1849. Foundations in Lowell, Roxbury, Salem and Lawrence, Massachusetts; Columbus, Ohio, and Philadelphia, Pennsylvania, were also made, the Motherhouse at Namur giving generously of subjects and funds until the convents in America were able to supply their own needs.

In Cincinnati, which became an archiepiscopal see in 1850, the ever increasing number of pupils at the Sixth Street Convent, and the rapid encroachments of business sections, occasioned the removal of the boarding school to a more favorable location. In 1859 property suitable for this purpose was purchased near Reading, Ohio, about ten miles from the city, to which, as Mount Notre Dame, the boarding school was transferred in 1860.

In 1867, a second academy was opened in Cincinnati, and for the convenience of the pupils residing in the western section of the city this was located on West Court Street, where it was continued until 1927, when the convent was purchased as a central home for Sisters of the Blessed Sacrament for Indians and Colored People engaged in school work in the city, and who also now conduct at this convent site Madonna High School.

For more than forty years Sister Superior Louise governed the steadily growing Institute in America, where at her death, in 1886, she left in thirty convents more than eight hundred religious engaged in the work of Christian education. The first novice received in her administration, Sister Julia, having been her support and counselor for many years, succeeded her in office.

During the ensuing years, in addition to fifteen institutions established under Sister Julia, Cincinnati was made the seat of a United States provincialate of the Congregation, with its provincialate novitiate, and in answer to a general demand for increased facilities for the higher education of Catholic women, Trinity College was founded at Washington, D. C.

Dating from 1897, when a tract of thirty-three acres was purchased at Brookland, D. C., the seat of the Catholic University of America, and a charter was granted by the District of Columbia empowering the projected institution to confer degrees, far-famed Trinity College opened its courses on November 7, 1900, with twenty-two students in the freshman class. One of the recent splendid new buildings erected at the college site is that of the chapel which was dedicated on May 13, 1924, and which won for its architects, Messrs. Maginnis and Walsh of Boston, a gold medal from the Institute of American Architects.

Under the provincial superiorship of Sister Agnes Mary, suc-

SISTER SUPERIOR LOUISE

cessor of Sister Julia, a chapel had previously been built which was a particular source of interest and gratification to the Institute, as it was the first chapel in America dedicated to Blessed Julie Billiart. This chapel, a beautiful Gothic structure in stone, is at the site of Notre Dame Academy at Rose Valley, Pennsylvania, near Moyland, in the archdiocese of Philadelphia.

On August 22, 1929, a mission band of six sisters of the Congregation left the Cincinnati Provincialate for the prefecture apostolic of Wuchang, Hupeh, China, which is under the care of the Franciscan Fathers, also of Cincinnati.

Continuing in the United States, through three provincialates of the Institute, their filial relationship with their Motherhouse, located at Rue Emile Cuvelier, Namur, Belgium, the Sisters of Notre Dame, in what has been constituted the Provincialate of Cincinnati, maintain their Provincial Motherhouse at 111 Grandin Road, in Cincinnati, to which location the headquarters of the community were transferred in 1902, from the Sixth Street Convent, which is now maintained as a residence home for sisters of the community teaching in parochial schools in that section of the city. Other sisters engaged in like work go forth daily from the Motherhouse, where there is also conducted, in addition to an academy, the more recently established Summit Country Day School.

BELMONT, CALIFORNIA
1851

To the initiative of the noted Jesuit missionary of the North American Indians, Father Peter De Smet, is due the coming of the Sisters of Notre Dame to the Pacific Coast in 1844.

On a visit to Europe in 1843, to obtain recruits for the missions in the Rocky Mountain and Pacific Coast regions, Father De Smet, a native of Belgium, made a successful plea for help at the Motherhouse in Namur of the Sisters of Notre Dame. Remonstrances against the proposed apostolic mission were not wanting, but with magnanimous generosity the response was made, and of the volunteers Sisters Loyola, Mary Cornelia, Mary Catherine, Mary Aloysia, Norbertine and Mary Albine were chosen to form the mission band which early in December of 1843 accompanied Father De Smet and his party back to the scenes of his missionary labors.

On their way to Antwerp, from whence the brave band was to set sail, a stop was made in Brussels. At the convent there the sisters were joyfully surprised and privileged when the Papal Nuncio, the young Archbishop Joachim Vincent Pecci, destined to succeed to the Chair of Peter as Pope Leo XIII, came to the convent to give them his benediction and to present a memento to each sister.

During the long weary voyage of seven months, the sisters devoted themselves to the study of the English and the Indian languages, to spiritual exercises and domestic occupations. Among the last might

NOTRE DAME CONVENT, BELMONT, CALIFORNIA

be classed the providing of the milk to make the "black coffee" less distasteful to the sisters. Noting their heroic efforts to accustom themselves to this, Father De Smet had gone ashore at a little port before leaving the Netherlands and purchased a goat, the milking of which was left to the sisters, and which found them all novices. Later and in Oregon, the goat did service to the community, for it used its horns vigorously, and the Indians would regard it with fear and wonder.

The diary accounts of the trip, which was made entirely by water, contain records of storms and calms, of perils from floating icebergs and from fogs, and stories of vermin and of near wreckage, but with brave hearts the noble band of Belgian sisters, in August, 1844, entered upon their missionary labors in Oregon, and in October of that year opened its first Catholic school for girls.

Two years of history-making events in the missionary annals of the religious orders of women in the United States then elapsed before the Sisters of Notre Dame had any word from their Mother-house at Namur. By every chance steamer they hoped for some message, but not until November, 1846, were they gladdened by the longed-for news, when a packet of letters reached them from Sister

Louise and the Sisters of Notre Dame in Cincinnati, who had taken advantage of an opportunity to send mail by a mountain messenger.

The Rev. Francis N. Blanchet, who in 1835 had been sent by the archbishop of Quebec to minister to the Canadian settlers on the Pacific Coast, was made vicar general of Oregon in 1838, and in 1845 was consecrated its bishop. Upon the erection of the archiepiscopal see of Oregon City, the following year, Bishop Blanchet, at the time in Rome, was appointed its first archbishop. Returning to his see early in the ensuing year, he was accompanied by a colony of twenty-one persons, among whom were seven Sisters of Notre Dame de Namur, as a second missionary band from the Motherhouse.

Soon after the arrival of this second contingent of Sisters of Notre Dame for the Oregon missions during a stirring political period, schools were opened at Oregon City and at Willamette. Following the discovery of gold in California, Oregon's population suffered from the general exodus. The harvest season found few men for its work. The sisters labored to gather their scanty crops, and to care for the many sick children who succumbed when cholera spread in their midst. Finally they closed one of the mission schools and remained together at Oregon City, until realizing that the religious, social and economic conditions in Oregon made progress in the work of their Institute almost impossible, they withdrew from Oregon in 1853 and went to San José, California, where four Sisters of Notre Dame from the foundation in Cincinnati had established a mission two years previously.

With the increase in numbers upon the arrival of the sisters from Oregon, San José was established as a provincialate of the Sisters of Notre Dame de Namur and a novitiate was at once opened, under the auspices of the Most Rev. Joseph S. Alemany, O.P., D.D., archbishop of the new archiepiscopal see of San Francisco.

A school had been opened in San José the year of the arrival of the sisters from Cincinnati, augmented by two of the Oregon community who going to meet them, remained there. Sister Mary Cornelia, who for nearly forty years guided the Sisters of Notre Dame in the new provincialate in the United States, is looked upon as the foundress of the Institute in California.

Following a visit to the Motherhouse in Namur, in 1871, Sister Mary Cornelia was on her return accompanied by sisters from there and from the provincialate in Cincinnati. Less than five years later, the California community received into the province forty-two Sisters of Notre Dame, exiled from Guatemala.

After three score years and ten of growth and development in the far west of the Institute of the Sisters of Notre Dame de Namur— the alumnae of whose institutions have ever been foremost in pro- gressive activities not only of their schools but of the state—the site of the Provincial house and novitiate was transferred in 1923 from San José to Belmont, where the College of Notre Dame has been established. There at Belmont—so named by the owner of the vast estate, William Ralston, builder of San Francisco's famed Palace Hotel—from their beautiful convent home on the Half Moon Bay highway, the Sisters of Notre Dame go forth to their now numerous institutions on the Pacific Coast.

WALTHAM, MASSACHUSETTS

1889

The Sisters of Notre Dame who had come from their Motherhouse at Namur, Belgium, to the United States in 1840, early sent from Cincinnati, Ohio, their first mission, sisters to Boston and other Massachusetts cities, where they established a number of missions before they had been a decade of years in the country, and later extended their work to cities in the surrounding states. In 1877 a second novitiate of the Order was established for the east at Rox-

NOTRE DAME CONVENT, WALTHAM, MASSACHUSETTS

bury, Massachusetts, where it was continued until 1889, when it was transferred to Waltham, continuing in the archdiocese of Boston.

With the increasing expansion of the work of the Institute of the Sisters of Notre Dame in the east, Notre Dame Training School at Waltham became, in 1911, in addition to remaining the site of the novitiate for the east, the seat of a new United States provincialate of the Congregation.

In 1919, as an activity in the province, the Sisters of Notre Dame opened Emmanuel College at Boston, at the location of which they also conduct the Boston Academy of Notre Dame.

In 1924, participating in the now many foreign mission activities of the religious orders of women in the United States, the Waltham Province of the Sisters of Notre Dame established a high school for girls at Okayama, in the diocese of Hiroshima, Japan, five sisters of the community going there for this purpose.

The now large Community of the Sisters of Notre Dame de Namur, in the Eastern Provincialate in the United States as well as in the Provincialates of Cincinnati and California, devoted to the Christian education of girls, through grade, academic and collegiate work, proves by the perseverance of the sisters in their labors in this country through nearly one hundred years that they are the "great souls needed for the great work of the Institute," as said by their holy foundress, Blessed Julie Billiart, "souls of faith, able to sacrifice themselves; characters which know no difficulty where the glory of God is concerned."

SUMMARY

Sisters of Notre Dame de Namur.

Founded in France in 1803.

Established in the United States in 1840.

Papal Approbation of Rules, December 7, 1844, by Pope Gregory XVI; Revised in accordance with Canon Law; Approved November 27, 1921, by Pope Benedict XV.

Habit: The habit is of black serge, with long wide sleeves; the guimpe is of white linen. A black veil is worn over a close-fitting black bonnet.

Approximate number in Community in United States, 1,900.

Active in educational work, *Provincialate of Cincinnati,* in the archdioceses of Cincinnati and Chicago and the dioceses of Columbus and Peoria; *Provincial house and Novitiate,* Notre Dame Convent, 111 Grandin Road, East Walnut Hills, Cincinnati, Ohio. (Archdiocese of Cincinnati.) *Provincialate of Belmont,* in the archdiocese of San Francisco and in the dioceses of Los Angeles and San Diego, Monterey-Fresno and Sacramento; *Provincial house and Novitiate,* Convent of Notre Dame, Belmont, California. (Archdiocese of San Francisco.) *Provincialate of Waltham,* in the archdioceses of Baltimore, Boston and Philadelphia, and in the dioceses of Brooklyn, Providence and Springfield; *Provincial house and Novitiate,* Notre Dame Training School, 62 Newton Street, Waltham, Masachusetts. (Archdiocese of Boston.)

THE SISTERS OF THE HOLY FAMILY*

1842

HE Congregation of the Sisters of the Holy Family was founded in New Orleans, Louisiana, on November 21, 1842, by four zealous colored women in the interests of the education of youth and the care of the needy of their own race.

Under the direction of the Rev. Etienne Rousselon, Vicar General of what was then still the diocese of New Orleans, Josephine Charles and Harriet Delisle of New Orleans, Juliette Gaudin of Cuba, and Mlle. Alcot, a devout young French woman, united as a community, with Mother Harriet Delisle as first Superior, in teaching catechism and preparing children and adults for their first Holy Communion and the reception of the sacrament of Confirmation.

The first decade of years of the existence of the new Congregation was ecclesiastically historical in New Orleans. Churches were built and parishes organized, and in the course of the period the diocese was created an archdiocese by the Sovereign Pontiff, Pope Pius IX. The Right Rev. Anthony Blanc, who had not only been bishop of the diocese for fifteen years, but for a previous fifteen years an indefatigable missionary in the lower Mississippi region, was named first archbishop of the new see.

In his interest in behalf of the colored people of the archdiocese, Archbishop Blanc was particularly solicitous regarding the development and work of the Sisters of the Holy Family, whose community labors were soon needed in the orphanages which were opened following a devastating epidemic of yellow fever which broke out in New Orleans little more than ten years after the founding of the Congregation.

As the Community grew, and the times demanded, the Sisters of the Holy Family participated in educational and charitable work in New Orleans. Before the celebration of the fiftieth anniversary of their founding, their Motherhouse and novitiate, long and permanently established, had become a source of interest and gratification in the city, located as they were in a building once famous as the Orleans Ball Room, and with the convent chapel a memorial to the Crescent City's colored philanthropist, Thomy Lafon.

In the heart of old New Orleans, surrounded by the shops which

*From data and material supplied by The Sisters of the Holy Family, New Orleans, La., and from the Catholic Encyclopedia and the Official Catholic Year Book, 1928 (P. J. Kenedy & Sons, N. Y.).

lure the interested traveler, this historic convent of the Sisters of the Holy Family, now combined with a newer and larger building, yet serves as the Motherhouse and novitiate of the Congregation, in con-

MOTHER JULIETTE GAUDIN
Co-Foundress of The Sisters of the Holy Family

nection with which St. Mary's Academy, a school for colored girls, has been established.

In addition to their school work at St. Mary's Academy and in parochial schools for colored children not only in New Orleans, Baton Rouge and Donaldsonville, in Louisiana, but also in Galveston and San Antonio, Texas, and Apalachicola, Florida, the Sisters of the Holy Family, now under the superiorship of Mother M. Eusebia, are in charge of the Zimmer Memorial Orphanage, near Mobile, Alabama, and in New Orleans conduct the St. John Berchmans Asylum for

CONVENT OF THE HOLY FAMILY, NEW ORLEANS, LOUISIANA

Colored Girls, the Lafon Orphan Asylum for Colored Boys, and the Lafon Asylum of the Holy Family for Aged Colored Men and Women.

SUMMARY

The Sisters of the Holy Family.

Founded in the United States in 1842.

Habit: The habit is of black serge, with a cape and apron of the same material, and a tasseled cincture of white wool. The veil is black. A crucifix is worn on the chest, and, after six years of profession, a gold ring on the third finger of the left hand.

Approximate number in Community, 175.

Active in educational, charitable and social service work among colored people in the archdioceses of New Orleans and San Antonio and in the dioceses of Corpus Christi, Galveston and Mobile.

Motherhouse and Novitiate, Convent of the Holy Family, 717 Orleans Street, New Orleans, Louisiana. (Archdiocese of New Orleans.)

SISTERS OF THE HOLY CROSS*

1843

*A*MONG the many religious orders having their origin in France during the half century of religious renaissance which followed the Napoleonic period, was the Congregation of the Sisters of the Holy Cross, founded at Le Mans in 1841, by the Rev. Basil Anthony Moreau, professor of Divinity in St. Vincent's Seminary, and Canon of the Cathedral at Le Mans.

The four first candidates for the new Community—at first designated as the Congregation of the Seven Dolors—received the habit on September 29, 1841, in the Convent of the Good Shepherd at Le Mans. The four sisters then made their novitiate at this convent, where they learned the first lessons of the religious state, and laid deep the foundation on which they were to rear the structure of their spiritual life. Following this, they made their religious profession as Sisters of the Holy Cross, under the special patronage of Our Lady of the Seven Dolors.

In his direction of the new Congregation, Abbé Moreau left no means untried for the perfection of a foundation which he hoped would become an important factor in the work of Christian education. Placing before the sisters a plan of government he gave them also a summary of the obligations incumbent upon them in their double capacity of religious instructors of youth by both precept and example, and urged the cultivation of a truly apostolic spirit for the salvation of souls.

Realizing that every age has its special needs, the zealous founder —while inculcating the virtues of the hidden life, and exact observance of the vows of religion—so ordered the governing principles of the Congregation as to meet the demands of the times in presenting the best that an educational body could offer, without in any way allowing it to swerve from the way of the Holy Cross.

One of the earliest members of the Congregation of the Fathers of the Holy Cross was Edward Sorin of Ahuillé, near Laval, France. As a young student Edward Sorin had heard the appeal for aid made by the visiting bishop of Vincennes, the Right Rev. Simon Gabriel Bruté, a native of Rennes, France, and missionary to America, who had been appointed first bishop in Indiana.

*From data and material supplied by the Sisters of the Holy Cross, St. Mary's Convent, Notre Dame, Indiana, and from A *Story of Fifty Years* (The Ave Maria Press).

The burning words of the aged bishop in behalf of the needs of the scattered missions of his distant diocese were not forgotten, and when, in 1841, Bishop Bruté's successor, the Right Rev. Celestine de la Hailandière, applied to Abbé Moreau for volunteers for the Indiana missions, Father Sorin at once offered himself for the work and, with six members of the teaching community of the Congregation, left France, and arrived in New York on the eve of the feast of the Exaltation of the Holy Cross, September 13, 1841.

After a short time spent at a mission station near Vincennes, Indiana, Father Sorin and his companions were established at *Ste. Marie des Lacs,* on the banks of the St. Joseph River, where, dedicated as *Notre Dame du Lac,* the foundation was laid of the now world-famed University of Notre Dame.

Realizing the vast field of labor confronting them in the new mission, and appreciating the value of the co-operation of sisters in the work, Father Sorin appealed to Abbé Moreau for members of the new Congregation at Le Mans. Abbé Moreau's reply was the sending of Sister Mary of the Sacred Heart, Sister Mary of Calvary, Sister Mary of Bethlehem and Sister Mary of Nazareth, who left France on June 6, 1843, and soon after their arrival in the United States began their community labors, under the direction of Father Sorin.

Before long there was evident need of a permanent establishment for the sisters, as well as a novitiate for the reception and training of the candidates who presented themselves as willing and anxious to share the community life and work of these pioneer educators, in the vicinity of the historic Portage Prairie, which nearly two centuries before had been crossed by Marquette, and along the banks of the St. Joseph River, which had been discovered by La Salle in 1679.

Accordingly, on July 16, 1844, a novitiate for the sisters was established at Bertrand, a Michigan village, and one of the missions of the Fathers of the Holy Cross, not far distant from their headquarters at Notre Dame du Lac. On the ensuing September 8th Father Sorin conferred the habit on four postulants to the Community, the ceremony taking place in the village in the little log church which had been built by Father Theodore Badin during his missionary labors among the Pottawattomies.

The initial work of the sisters at Bertrand included the teaching of the children of the neighborhood and the care of several orphans. A little later sisters were sent to Pokagon, Michigan, where religious instruction was given to many Indians. A grant of five thousand francs by the Society for the Propagation of the Faith and a donation of seventy-five acres of land from the inhabitants of Bertrand made it possible to carry on the work of the sisters. Recruits for the community were sent from France, and later from Canada, and were able women of executive ability and strong religious spirit.

Mother Mary du Sauveur was appointed Superior in 1849, and soon after 1850—and the enrollment of fifty boarders in the academic course which had been established at the convent school in Bertrand— a prospectus of St. Mary's Academy was issued.   In this, in addition to such clauses as *Board and tuition, thirty-five dollars per session of five months,* and *Pockets must be inserted in all dresses of pupils,* directions for reaching the school were necessarily carefully given. Although the same institution, in a but slightly different location, is reached now by train from Chicago, or by motor route along the Lincoln Highway, in little more than two hours, at that time— before the completion of the Lake Shore and Michigan Southern Railroad, in 1851—a steamboat had to be taken across Lake Michigan to St. Joseph, and then travel was by stage to St. Mary's, whose asphalted entrance avenue today meets the Dixie Highway at its own imposing gateway.

In January, 1851, the state of Michigan recognized St. Mary's and granted it a charter.   The formation of a class for deaf-mutes necessitating the special training of teachers for the work, Sister Mary Angela Gillespie was sent to France to complete her novitiate and learn the science of their instruction.

Eliza Maria Gillespie, on her way from Lancaster, Ohio, to Chicago, where she was to enter a convent, visited Notre Dame for the purpose of saying goodby to her brother Neal, then preparing for the priesthood.   Of family affiliations with the Phelans, the Ewings, the Shermans and the Blaines, all distinguished not only in Ohio, but in the nation's capital, and most prominent in the annals of Notre Dame University and St. Mary's, Eliza Gillespie, at this time, while visiting the Sisters of the Holy Cross at Bertrand, relinquished her former plans and entered the novitiate there.   On the feast of the patronage of St. Joseph, 1853, she received the habit of the Congregation and the name of Sister Mary of St. Angela.

Upon the completion of her novitiate in France, and her return to St. Mary's, Sister Angela was soon afterward appointed directress of the academy, and from then until her death in 1887 Mother Angela continued in official position in the Congregation.

In 1855 St. Mary's Academy and the headquarters of the sisters were transferred from Bertrand, Michigan, to their present Indiana site on a picturesque bluff overlooking the St. Joseph River, two miles north of South Bend and just west of the University of Notre Dame.

Six years later the Civil War began, and on October 22, 1861, the sisters at St. Mary's responded to the call of Governor Morton of

MOTHER M. ANGELA GILLESPIE (1824-1887)

Indiana, who, at the instance of General Lew Wallace, asked for sisters to go and attend the sick, wounded and dying soldiers.

With Mother Angela in charge, the first band of sisters reached Cairo, Illinois, on October 24th; there they reported to General Grant and proceeded to Paducah, Kentucky, where they took charge of the

military hospital.   In November Mother Angela received a dispatch
from Washington, D.C., with orders to open a hospital in Mound
City.   Mound City, Memphis and Cairo were the general centers
of the war activities of the Sisters of the Holy Cross—though they
labored also in the military hospitals at Paducah and Louisville—and
under the efficient leadership of Mother Angela they continued their
ministrations throughout the period of the war.

An event of moment at Notre Dame, in May of 1865, and one in
which Mother Angela and the Sisters of the Holy Cross were directly
interested was the issuance of a journal in honor of the Blessed
Virgin, Mother of God, when Father Sorin founded, and himself
edited and published *The Ave Maria*.   Father Sorin was ably aided
in the work by Mother Angela, who continued her interest in it
when her brother, Father Neal Gillespie, returning the next year from
a three-year stay in Europe, took the editorship of the periodical, and
retained it until his death in 1874.   His successor, the Rev. Daniel E.
Hudson, for more than half a century inimitably carried on this work,
so inseparably ever the interest of the Sisters of the Holy Cross.

Severance from the Motherhouse in France, and the recognition
by Rome of the Sisters of the Holy Cross in the United States as a
distinct order, with St. Mary's as their headquarters, took place in
1869.   The Very Rev. Edward Sorin, Provincial Superior of the
Congregation of the Holy Cross since 1852, was then named
ecclesiastical superior of the Congregation of the Sisters of the Holy
Cross.

At the election of officers held at St. Mary's in August, 1869, the
following were chosen to compose the first Council of administration
under the new regime: Mother M. Angela, Mother Superior; Mother
M. Charles, First Assistant; Mother M. Eusebia, Second Assistant;
Mother Mary of the Ascension, Mistress of Novices; and Mother
M. Emily, Stewardess—all able women, and thoroughly imbued with
a deeply religious spirit.

Meanwhile, with the growth of the Community, missions were
undertaken not only in the nearby Indiana cities of South Bend,
Fort Wayne, Logansport, Elkhart, Anderson and others—some retained only temporarily, and others prosperously continuing—but in
Morris, Cairo, Jacksonville and Danville, Illinois, Philadelphia Pennsylvania, and Columbus, Ohio, where, in Mt. Carmel Hospital, the
Congregation maintains one of its many splendid institutions.

Among the earliest of its academic establishments were St.
Cecilia's and Holy Cross, in Washington, D. C., St. Mary's in
Alexandria, Virginia, and St. Catherine's Normal School in Baltimore.

St. Mary's Academy, in Austin, and in Marshall, Texas, St. Mary's at Davenport, Iowa, St. Mary-of-the-Wasatch, at Salt Lake City, and Sacred Heart Academy at Ogden, Utah—as well as many other schools and hospitals in cities from coast to coast, bespeak the activity of the Order in the years which have followed the coming of the sisters from Le Mans to the inland Indiana site. Under the auspices of the

ST. MARY'S, NOTRE DAME, INDIANA

Right Rev. John J. Mitty, D.D., Bishop of Salt Lake, a college for women has recently been established in connection with the Academy of St. Mary-of-the-Wasatch.

In 1898 another generation of Sisters of the Holy Cross responded to the country's need, serving in the hospitals of the south during the Spanish-American trouble. During this time Sister Brendan, directress of Mt. Carmel Hospital, in Columbus, Ohio, was in charge of two hospital trains which were sent south to bring the sick soldiers home, and was later sent to Porto Rico on a like errand.

Conditions in the educational world have brought about many changes in things pedagogical since the establishment of the Sisters of the Holy Cross at St. Mary's, and while adhering to the fundamental, time-tried principles of old methods, they quickly adopt the salient points of good in the new.

St. Mary's College conferred its first degree in 1898, and conforms to the highest educational requirements of the outstanding collegiate associations in which it holds membership. In September, 1926, the palatial new and Greater St. Mary's College, with its spacious convent grounds, was the hospitable scene of the Seventh Biennial Convention of the International Federation of Catholic Alumnae, and was the first convention of the kind held at one of the affiliated institutions whose loyal alumnae have been active participants in the affairs of the federation.

The foreign mission activities of the Sisters of the Holy Cross were inaugurated in 1853, when sisters from the Motherhouse at Le Mans, France, accompanied the first band of Holy Cross mis-sioners to Bengal, India. In 1889 a group of sisters from St. Mary's left for the far-away field, and July 22, 1927, marked the announce-ment by Mother M. Francis Clare, Mother General at St. Mary's of the Sisters of Holy Cross, of the appointment of four sisters, to go to India with the Fathers of the Holy Cross, forming the mission band of 1927.

MOTHER M. AUGUSTA
Mother General of the Sisters of the
Holy Cross from 1889 to 1895

Sisters Olga and Rose Ber-nard, of the Foreign Mission Convent, Brookland, Washing-ton, D. C., Sister Marie Estelle, of Holy Cross Academy in Washington, and Sister Rose Monica, of St. Pius' School in Baltimore, were chosen for this foreign mission apostolate of the Congregation, and their head-quarters were established at Holy Cross Convent, Catholic Mission, Toomiliah, Kaligaunj, Dacca, India.

To prepare its sisters for missionary work, the Congrega-tion sends its subjects to the Sis-ters' Convent at the Foreign Mission Seminary of Holy Cross, at Brookland, Washington, D. C., where Sister M. Patricia is Superior. The three-year course in missionology pursued there includes, in addition to a study of the Bengali language, lectures on Mission History and Mission Methods, and the study of Anthropology and Indian philosophy. Medical lectures, concluding with a clinic in the third year, are also given throughout the course. During this time in Washington, the sisters assist in the publication of *The Bengalese,* the official organ of Holy Cross foreign missions, issued monthly.

Among the most recent institutions of the Sisters of the Holy Cross—in their labors for the amelioration of human ills, through their many prominent hospitals—is one of the largest privately owned sanatoria in this country for the treatment of tuberculosis—Holy Cross Sanatorium—of which Sister M. Beniti is Superior, which was opened in 1923 in Mahoney Park, Deming, New Mexico, ideally in the health-giving climate of the southwest, and situated in a valley that irrigation has made fruitful.

Composing the present Council of administration of the Congregation, which continues to carry on its many and varied works, are Mother M. Francis Clare, Mother General; Mother M. Cecily, First Assistant and Superior at the Motherhouse; Mother M. Pauline, Second Assistant and President of the college; Mother M. Barbara, Secretary General, and Mother M. Bettina, Mistress of Novices.

With its numerous and well-equipped buildings, St. Mary's has become a distinct center in itself, the beloved home of the Sisters of the Holy Cross, and the mecca which each summer beckons them, in their turn, from their duties in schools, hospitals and orphanages, for the annual reunion and the yearly spiritual retreat and summer school studies, that each laborer in the Master's vineyard may be renewed in soul and body and mentally prepared for the best services in the interests of the Congregation.

SUMMARY

Sisters of the Holy Cross.

Founded in France in 1841.

Established in the United States in 1843.

Papal Approbation of Rules, May 12, 1896, by Pope Leo XIII.

Habit: The habit is of black serge, with flowing sleeves, a cape, tasseled blue cord, and a large rosary. A black veil is worn over a large fluted white cap with a white bandeau, and a silver heart—the insignia of profession—bearing the emblem of Our Lady of the Seven Dolors, is worn on a cord suspended from the neck, and looped under the stiffly starched white collar.

Approximate number in Community, 1,300.

Active in educational, hospital and charitable work in the archdioceses of Baltimore, Chicago, New York and San Francisco, and in the dioceses of Belleville, Boise, Columbus, Dallas, Davenport, Denver, El Paso, Fort Wayne, Galveston, Harrisburg, Lincoln, Los Angeles and San Diego, Monterey-Fresno, Peoria, Richmond, Rockford, Sacramento, Salt Lake and Springfield in Illinois.

Motherhouse and Novitiate, St. Mary's Convent, Notre Dame, Indiana. (Diocese of Fort Wayne.)

SISTERS OF OUR LADY OF CHARITY OF THE GOOD SHEPHERD OF ANGERS*

1843

O the wisdom and perseverance of Mother Mary of St. Euphrasia Pelletier—who died in the odor of sanctity in 1868, and was declared Venerable by Pope Leo XIII, December 11, 1897 does the world owe the splendid organization of the Congregation of Our Lady of Charity of the Good Shepherd, and to her personal activity is the United States indebted for the arrival of its first Good Shepherd Sisters, in the year 1843.

The founder of the Order of Our Lady of Charity was St. John Eudes, the ceremony of whose canonization took place on May 31, 1925, during the pontificate of His Holiness, Pope Pius XI.

Born in France in 1601, St. John Eudes was ordained to the priesthood in 1625. Following the preaching of a mission in Caen, France, in 1639, Father Eudes exerted himself to establish there a needed shelter for penitent fallen women. Experience soon proved the necessity and wisdom of the supervision of such a refuge by a religious order of women, consecrated to the work. No community existing for this purpose, Father Eudes obtained Visitation Nuns to aid him temporarily.

The house was to continue under the direction of the Religious of the Visitation until some sister of the new Institute—then approved and opened to candidates, was considered ready to undertake the office of Superior.

To the usual three vows of religion these Sisters of Our Lady of Charity of the Refuge added a fourth, binding themselves to labor for the conversion of fallen women and girls needing refuge from the temptations of the world. On the occasion of the first religious profession in the Community, January 2, 1666, Father Eudes, known as the earliest active propagator of the devotion to the Sacred Hearts of Jesus and Mary, dedicated to them the Order of Our Lady of Charity of the Refuge.

When the Revolution overwhelmed France the Order had seven houses, among which the first foundation, the community at Caen, survived the general dispersement of religious institutions. In the

---

*From data and material supplied by the Sisters of the Good Shepherd, Provincial Monastery of the Good Shepherd, Carthage, Ohio, and from Clarke's *Life of Reverend Mother Mary of St. Euphrasia Pelletier.* (Burns and Oates, London.)

re-establishment which followed the Revolution, the *Refuge* which had been established at Tours was restored, and here Rose Pelletier was received as a novice, October 20, 1814, later receiving the name Sister Mary of St. Euphrasia.

Because of her virtues and talents, Sister St. Euphrasia was early chosen Superior of the Community at Tours. While directing the foundation of a Refuge at Angers, in France, and later during her superiorate there, Mother St. Euphrasia labored to unify the then independent houses of the Institute through the establishment of a Generalate, or central Motherhouse and novitiate. In the accomplishment of this, delays, trials and difficulties were met and withstood by the able Superior, who was convinced of the wisdom of her project.

In 1835 a pontifical decree established the Generalate, with Angers as the Motherhouse of the Institute, and the Superior there as Superior General of all the houses that had been or might be founded from it. The distinctive name of the Congregation was therewith that of *Our Lady of Charity of the Good Shepherd,* and to this *of Angers* was added, for identification with the Motherhouse.

VEN. MOTHER MARY OF ST. EUPHRASIA PELLETIER
(1796-1868)
Foundress of the Congregation of Our Lady of Charity of the Good Shepherd

The geographical jurisdiction of the Superior General at Angers

was left unlimited. The only distinction in the habit of the sisters under the new name and ruling was that a blue cord replaced the former white girdle, and a silver heart, on which was engraved the figure of the Good Shepherd, was worn.

The Order of Our Lady of Charity of the Good Shepherd of Angers, during the superiorate of Mother St. Euphrasia at the Motherhouse in Angers, spread rapidly, and other houses were established in France, as well as in Italy, Germany, England, America, Ireland and Africa.

From the United States, soon after the transfer of his episcopal see from Bardstown to Louisville, Kentucky, in 1841, the Right Rev.

CONVENT OF THE GOOD SHEPHERD, LOUISVILLE, KENTUCKY

Benedict Joseph Flaget, D.D., Bishop of Louisville, wrote to Mother St. Euphrasia, renewing a request he had previously made for a colony of her sisters for his diocese. This request was timely. News of it was received with enthusiasm throughout the Community, and soon five Sisters of the Good Shepherd, each of a different nationality, were chosen to comprise the little band for the United States.

In Louisville, in a convent home on Eighth Street, the sisters, with Mother Marie des Ange Porcher as Superior, on September 8, 1843, began the labors which have since extended to the principal cities of the country.

To facilitate the executive work of the Institute in the United States, provincialates have been established, each with a central

Provincial house and novitiate, and all under a United States Visitor General, and subject to the jurisdiction of the Superior General at Angers.

In their six provincialates now in the United States, the sisters, cloistered, and under the Rule of St. Augustine, faithfully continue the work for which the Order was founded, co-operating with various branches and bureaus of the civil as well as the diocesan charities, in the cities of their activities.

Those given to the care of the Sisters of the Good Shepherd are placed in one of the departments uniformly established in their monasteries. The Preservation Class is composed of orphans and destitute girls, who have been rescued from surroundings that might prove harmful to their moral well-being. All the Preservation Children are given a solid education and taught industries that will enable them to earn a livelihood upon leaving the shelter of the school at the expiration of their eighteenth year.

The Penitent Class is an entirely separate department for wayward girls and unfortunate women, many of whom voluntarily seek the protection and care of the sisters, while others are sent to the monastery by their parents or guardians, or brought by officers of the law. The penitents are usually employed at machine and laundry work, and are given every opportunity of mental, moral and physical improvement.

Members of the Penitent Class who have given ample proof of their sincere conversion, and who desire to consecrate their services to the welfare of their wayward sisters, are invested with a simple black habit, and are called Consecrates. Without assuming the responsibility of vows, the Consecrates exercise a salutary influence in the class, and thus become a powerful factor in the work of the reformatory.

The crowning work of the Sisters of the Good Shepherd is the Magdalen Sisterhood. One of the first great achievements of Mother Euphrasia's administration, this Community was established for the especial benefit of those sincere penitents who desired to embrace the religious life, in a penitential spirit, but because of their past were prohibited admission into any congregation. The Magdalens occupy a separate building on the premises of the Sisters of the Good Shepherd, and are governed by a directress appointed by the Provincial Superior. They take the three vows of religion, live and dress according to the Rule of the Carmelites, and are under the jurisdiction of the bishop in whose diocese they reside. The Magdalen Sisters observe perpetual cloister, and recite the Office of the Blessed

Virgin.   They give about seven hours daily to spiritual exercises, and devote the remaining time to quiet employment.

Many who have not been members of the Penitent Class, but who are desirous of living a life of perfect seclusion, penance and prayer, also join this Sisterhood—the richest reward of the labors of the Sisters of the Good Shepherd, as it is the fruit of their zeal for souls.

SUMMARY

Sisters of Our Lady of Charity of the Good Shepherd of Angers.
Founded in France in 1835.
Established in the United States in 1843.
Habit: The habit, symbolizing purity, is white, with a white guimpe and bandeau and a black veil. A blue cord and a silver heart, representing the images of the Good Shepherd and the Blessed Virgin, are worn.
Approximate number in Community in United States, 1,500.
Active in social service work of reclamation and preservation of girls in monasteries; *Provincialate of Baltimore* in the archdiocese of Baltimore; *Provincial house and Novitiate,* Monastery of the Good Shepherd, Mount and Hollins Streets, Baltimore, Maryland.   (Archdiocese of Baltimore.) *Provincialate of Carthage* in the archdiocese of Cincinnati and in the dioceses of Cleveland, Columbus, Covington, Detroit, Grand Rapids, Indianapolis, Louisville and Toledo; *Provincial House and Novitiate,* Our Lady of the Woods, Monastery of the Good Shepherd, Carthage, Ohio (Archdiocese of Cincinnati); *Provincialate of New York* in the arch-diocese of Boston and New York and in the diocese of Albany, Brooklyn, Hartford, Newark, Providence and Springfield; *Provincial house and Novitiate,* Monastery of the Good Shepherd, Mt. Florence, Peekskill, New York (Archdiocese of New York); *Provincialate of Philadelphia* in the archdiocese of Philadelphia and the diocese of Scranton; *Provincial house and Novitiate,* Monastery of the Good Shepherd, Chew and Penn Streets, Germantown, Philadelphia, Pennsylvania (Archdiocese of Phila-delphia); *Provincialate of St. Louis* in the archdioceses of Chicago, Mil-waukee, New Orleans and St. Louis, and in the dioceses of Galveston, Kansas City, Los Angeles and San Diego, Nashville, Peoria and Sioux City; *Provincial house and Novitiate,* Monastery of the Good Shepherd, 3801 Gravois Avenue, St. Louis Missouri (Archdiocese of St. Louis); *Provincialate of St. Paul* in the archdioceses of Dubuque, Portland in Oregon, and St. Paul, and in the dioceses of Denver, Omaha, Seattle and Spokane; *Provincial house and Novitiate,* Monastery of the Good Shepherd, Milton and Blair Streets, St. Paul, Minnesota (Archdiocese of St. Paul).

SISTERS OF MERCY*

*P*ARAMOUNT in the history of the founding and development of the Institute of Our Lady of Mercy is the immortalization, in it, from its beginning and throughout its continuance, of the personality and spirit of the holy foundress, Catherine McAuley—at heart and in act, from her early youth, a Sister of Mercy in embryo, and a Sister of Mercy in fact, by vow and papal approbation of her work, before the closing of her earthly career.

Catherine McAuley was born September 29, 1787, in Stormanstown House, County Dublin, Ireland. From her father, and through him, she learned her first lessons in faith and charity. The sorrow of his death, and later of the death of her mother, came to Catherine by her eleventh year. Changes and domestic experiences, unsual in number and of serious moment, were hers in early youth.

Upon the death of her foster father, Catherine, in mature years, received from him wealth—unrestricted, because he knew her nobility of soul and her ability to make a right use of her fortune. At one time, having noted the disposition of her allowance for her charities —one thousand pounds a year—Mr. Callaghan, her foster father, inquired what she intended to do when he died. The answer was, "I will take a small house and care for a few poor women, whom I shall instruct and teach to work." The works of the Sisters of Mercy proclaim that Catherine McAuley was true to her holy ambitions.

When she found herself in the possession of temporal wealth, she planned to use it for God's glory, in the service of the poor, whose needs she knew so well. Eager to help save children to the faith, to reclaim the wayward and the erring, prayerfully she sought advice in Dublin, offering her life and wealth for whatever good work was needed. A home for working girls and for orphans was suggested, and Catherine at once took steps for the erection of a building for this purpose.

In 1824 the heiress bought property on Baggot Street in Dublin, and in that year the corner stone of Mercy Home was laid. Catherine, from the beginning dedicating her work to God, planned a home for poor girls, specifying her desire for large class-rooms and

*To the Sisters of Mercy in Pittsburgh, Chicago, New York City, Cincinnati and Grand Rapids, special credit is due for material used in this introduction and in the sketches of the various communities of the Congregation, as well as for the use of *Leaves from the Annals of the Sisters of Mercy*, by Mother Mary Austin Carroll (Vol. III and Vol. IV).

dormitories, a room for a chapel, and some smaller rooms for helpers. Her architects built a convent.

On September 24, 1827, the feast of Our Lady of Mercy, the building, which was placed under her special protection, was auspiciously opened.

While the house on Baggot Street was under construction, Catherine lived with her married sister, while much of her time was spent in teaching sewing in the parochial schools. Plainly garbed and gentle mannered, she visited the poor and the sick, even then leading the life of a true Sister of Mercy. In June, 1828, she took up her residence at the Baggot Street house, with two of her friends, who as workers were already residing there. Before long the number of inmates was seventy, and there were twelve teachers and helpers, among whom was Miss Frances Warde.

In a short time the home was crowded with orphans who were housed there and well provided for. Schools for the poor were opened, and working girls received instruction at night. Before the close of the year the ladies at Mercy House were, as a charitable body, given permission to visit the city hospitals, and the sick, wherever found. It was then that Miss McAuley and her co-workers began to make plans for their own hospitals.

On Christmas, 1828, mass was celebrated for the first time in the chapel room of the Baggot Street home. A Christmas dinner was given the inmates and the poor, and Daniel O'Connell—ever a personal friend of Mother McAuley, and loyal to her Institute—whose daughters were among the volunteer teachers assisting in the school, ate with the poor, and presided on this occasion.

The following year the chapel was dedicated. The Institute was almost automatically developing into a community, when the question as to its religious or secular character arose.

The Most Rev. Daniel Murray, Archbishop of Dublin, who, as the Rev. Dr. Murray, had been Miss McAuley's earliest friend and first religious advisor, visited the Institute, and recognized, before the noble foundress did, that a religious congregation had developed there. In her humility, Miss McAuley offered the Institute to the archbishop, asking only permission to continue in her labors among the poor. Archbishop Murray, however, as coadjutor of Dublin, had felt the need of sisters to devote themselves to outside charitable work, and planned the Congregation of the Sisters of Charity in Ireland. Under his direction, Mary Aikenhead—who, like Catherine McAuley, was born in Dublin in 1787, was sent to England, at the age of twenty-five, to the ancient convent at Micklegate Bar, York, where she received the religious training which fitted her to be the foundress of that Congregation in Dublin.

MOTHER M. CATHERINE MCAULEY (1787-1841)
Foundress of the Order of Mercy

Seeing for himself Catherine McAuley's work, the archbishop saw God's hand, and left the future of the Institute to the choice of the workers in the Mercy House. And they chose to be a religious congregation, with religious garb, and bound by the vows of religion.

Upon this decision, the archbishop, after examining the rules of various orders, advised Miss McAuley, and two of her first assistants, to make their religious novitiate in the Presentation Convent, established by Nano Nagle. Like other famous foundresses, then, the foundress of the Congregation of the Sisters of Mercy began her religious life late in life.

To prepare herself for the work planned by the archbishop of Dublin, Miss McAuley left all at Baggot Street in charge of her faithful co-laborers, and with the two chosen to accompany her, entered the Presentation Convent at George's Hill, Dublin, as a postulant, ready and willing to be trained in the principles of religious life. In time, the three aspirants were given the religious habit, and on December 12, 1831, they made their vows, with Archbishop Murray officiating at the ceremony.

The three sisters returned at once to Mercy Home, and the archbishop appointed Sister Catherine McAuley the Mother Superior of the Order, vesting her with the right of all foundresses to govern during her life-time. Thus Mother McAuley began the great work in which today, nearly a hundred years later, her spirit continues to live in the many communities which the Sisters of Mercy have established throughout the world.

Mary Frances Warde, in religion Sister M. Francis Xavier Warde, was the first to pronounce the vows of religion in the Baggot Street Convent. She and three others consecrated themselves to God on January 24, 1833, and this date marks the first religious profession in the Order of Mercy. When Mother McAuley began to write the rules for the Congregation she had only to formulate what she and the first members of the Institute were already faithfully observing in their community life. When the rule was presented in Rome, for papal approbation, this was so strong an endorsement of it that there was no delay in receiving the approval of the Holy See.

The distinctive feature of the Order is that its works are the works of mercy, and that it unites the active with the contemplative life. Mother McAuley labored, however, not without sorrows and troubles. Ecclesiastics, other orders, and even the public, had opposed for a time her work of going out among the poor, the sick and the abandoned, and of teaching. Only a few encouraged the new active order, but Mother McAuley by her personal influence, tact and exertion, broke down the barrier which had hitherto prevented sisters from engaging in such work.

Institutes, schools and hospitals having been established throughout Ireland, in 1839 a Convent of Mercy was opened in London. From this convent the Sisters of Mercy went, in 1854, to care for the soldiers in the Crimean War. The Greeks and Turks in Constantinople respected them, and Florence Nightingale worked with them.

Two years after the establishment of the first foundation in England, and soon after receiving for her Order the papal approbation of Pope Gregory XVI, Mother McAuley became seriously ill. Knowing her end was approaching, she said to her sisters: "My legacy to the Order is charity; if you preserve the peace and union which have never yet been violated amongst us you will feel, even in this world, a happiness which will surprise you, and which will be for you a foretaste of the bliss prepared for you in heaven. My only boast is that charity has never been broken amongst us." The holy death of Mother McAuley occurred at the Baggot Street Convent, on November 11, 1841.

The perfect harmony and accord among the hundreds of communities of Mercy, carrying on her work, bespeak the value of that legacy of charity which the saintly foundress left to the Sisters of Mercy of the Order of her founding.

PITTSBURGH, PENNSYLVANIA*

1843

Two years after the death of the foundress of the Order of Mercy, there took place in Rome, on August 15, 1843, the consecration of the bishop for the newly erected see of Pittsburgh, in the United States, the Right Rev. Michael O'Connor. The Rev. Michael O'Connor had been a pastor in County Cork, Ireland, knowing the Sisters of Mercy before beginning his activities in the United States, where, in 1841, he had become pastor of St. Paul's Church in Pittsburgh, then in the diocese of Philadelphia.

After his consecration in Rome, Bishop O'Connor proceeded to Ireland, where he graphically described to the Sisters of Mercy of the convent at Carlow, the work to be done and the need for religious co-laborers in his new diocese.

The young bishop's eloquent appeal was not in vain. He was granted a community of sisters, who with Mother Mary Xavier Warde as Superior, sailed for America and established in Pennsylvania, in the episcopal city of Pittsburgh, the first convent of the Order of Mercy in the United States, December 22, 1843.

Mother Mary Xavier Warde, like Mother M. de Pazzi Delany, who the year before had made in St. John's, in New Foundland,

*From data and material supplied by the Sisters of Mercy, Convent of Mercy, Mt. Mercy, Pittsburgh, Pa.

the first American foundation at the Order of Mercy, had been one of Mother McAuley's companion workers at Mercy Home on Baggot Street in Dublin, and had been one of the original community group to remain there during the time of Mother McAuley's novitiate at the Presentation Convent.

MOTHER M. FRANCIS XAVIER WARDE
(1810-1884)

In 1837 Mother Warde had been appointed Superior of the convent at Carlow, the first house of the Congregation outside of Dublin, and the first of other foundations made, under her supervision, before the acceptance of the mission in Pittsburgh. The enterprise, zeal and experience of Mother Warde therefore qualified her for the superiorship of the community of seven, chosen for the first Mercy foundation in the United States.

Leaving Carlow, the valiant seven proceeded first to Dublin. There was then—in 1843—but one railway in Ireland. It connected Dublin with its port, Kingstown. As scarcely any of the party had ever traveled by steam, this mode of conveyance was deemed perilous, and they proceeded to Kingstown in carriages, from there crossing to Liverpool. After delay while awaiting a favorable wind, the sisters sailed on November 10th for the United States.

On their arrival, a month later, in New York, where they were welcomed by the Most Rev. John Hughes, D.D., then bishop of the diocese, Mother Warde and her companions spent a few days as the guests of the Religious of the Sacred Heart. Proceeding to their destination, a stop was made in Philadelphia and a welcome given the community by the Right Rev. Francis Patrick Kenrick, later archbishop of Baltimore. During their stay there the sisters were the guests of the Sisters of Charity, at the orphanage in their charge.

On December 22, 1843, in Pittsburgh, the Sisters of Mercy took possession of their first convent home in the United States, a four-story brick structure on Penn Street, sufficiently spacious for their immediate needs.

Shortly after Christmas, the sisters began their active work in the new field by visiting the sick. With the opening of the year

St. Mary's Convent of Mercy, Mt. Mercy, Pittsburgh, Pennsylvania

1844, they at once took charge of the Cathedral Sunday-school, of more than five hundred girls. From this time on, instruction classes of adults and children were conducted at the convent.

For the immense fixed and floating Catholic population, there were, at this time, but the bishop and three priests. The Allegheny and Monongahela Rivers, on which Pittsburgh was built, and which united to form the Ohio, afforded decided facilities for water traveling; Catholics who came up the river would usually manage to go to confession before returning home, and before long they began to call at the convent to be instructed and prepared for the sacraments, and the sisters gladly gave them all possible help.

In September, 1844, the Sisters of Mercy opened in Pittsburgh their first school in the United States. In the spring of 1845 Bishop

O'Connor entered into an agreement with the community from Carlow, for the establishment of a boarding school for girls, on land
donated for that purpose to "The Sisters of Mercy of Allegheny
County," that being their corporate title. The generous benefactor
of Christian education, and early friend of the community, first among
the founders of St. Xavier's Academy, then erected, was Henry Kuhn,
a descendant of one of the pioneer Catholic families who, before 1790,
crossed the Allegheny Mountains and settled near Beatty, Pennsylvania.

Until a new and suitable building could be erected on the farm
of more than one hundred and eight acres given to them, the sisters
used the pastoral residence at St. Vincent's for the convent and the
academy which was maintained there from April, 1845, to May, 1847.
On May 14, 1847, the sisters of the Pittsburgh community moved
into the new building, the nucleus of the present St. Xavier's Academy, which ranks today among the foremost schools in the United
States, deeply loved and much visited—on the modern Lincoln Highway—by the many loyal alumnæ of St. Xavier's.

From the first, the members of the Pittsburgh community visited
the poor in institutions, and the imprisoned, carrying on the works
of mercy as planned for her followers by the saintly foundress of
the Congregation of the Sisters of Mercy, and as promulgated in
the United States by Mother Warde, her companion and sharer
in the foundation experiences at the Baggot Street Mercy Home in
Dublin.

Two years after the establishment of the foundation in Pittsburgh,
Mother Warde visited Ireland, and on her return was accompanied
by enthusiastic volunteers from the convents there. This increase
in the community, together with the reception of the first subjects
from the United States, necessitated a more commodious convent
home, and to the one secured for them by the bishop the sisters
removed, with their pupils, in 1846.

September of the year 1846 saw the establishment of the first
foundation to be made by the community from Pittsburgh. In fulfillment of a promise made by Mother Warde to the Right Rev.
William Quarter, D.D., Chicago's first bishop, this foundation was
made in his episcopal city, and Mother Warde accompanied the band
of six sisters whose services had been accepted for the new field, the
first of the many important foundations made by the Pittsburgh community of the Sisters of Mercy.

January 1, 1847, Mercy Hospital, the first hospital in western
Pennsylvania—now located at Pride and Locust Streets—with a bed

capacity of six hundred and sixty, and an active council of fifty-two sisters, was established by the Sisters of Mercy of this community. This was opened opportunely in time to meet the exigencies caused by the Mexican War, and the ship fever which became an epidemic in 1848.

At this period, expansion of their work was made by the sisters, beyond the confines of the episcopal city to missions established through the diocese. Perseveringly and successfully, through successive administrations, the community — now numbering approximately four hundred members, labored on, through epidemics and, during the long years of the Civil War, on battlefield or hospital ship, and in hospitals, as the historical records of the United States tell of their works.

Mother M. Sebastian Gillespie
Sixty-four years a Sister of Mercy. Several times Superior of the Sisters of Mercy in Pittsburgh

Motherhouse and Novitiate, St. Mary's Convent of Mercy, Mt. Mercy, 3333 Fifth Avenue, Pittsburgh, Pennsylvania. (Diocese of Pittsburgh.)

NEW YORK CITY*

1846

Toward the close of 1845, the Most Rev. John Hughes, D.D., bishop of what was then the diocese of New York, applied in person to the parent-house of the Institute of Mercy in Dublin, for sisters for his episcopal city.

It was impossible for the Superior, Mother Mary Cecilia Marmion, to accede to the bishop's request at the time. In the fourteen years of the existence of the Institute, the numerous foundations already

*From data and material supplied by the Sisters of Mercy of New York City, St. Catherine's Convent, 1075 Madison Avenue, New York City, and referred bibliography: *The Golden Milestone,* by Helen M. Sweeney (Benziger Brothers).

made had required the attentions of all the available executives fitted by temperament and constitution to carry on the work entailed in the establishment of new houses. However, appreciating the earnestness of Bishop Hughes' persistence in his appeal for a community of her nuns, Mother Cecilia told the bishop of the temporary Superior of their new convent in London, and of her ability, and consented to leave with this Superior, Mother M. Agnes O'Connor, the decision as to the undertaking of his proposed mission.

Bishop Hughes proceeded to London, where he found the presiding bishop, on whom he called in the interest of his cause, more disposed to take sisters than to give them. Appealed to in behalf of the New York diocese, Mother M. Agnes became enthusiastic over the prospect of the labors in the New World, and consented to make the Baggot Street Convent's first United States foundation.

As Mother M. Xavier Warde, and the band of seven valiant Sisters of Mercy, had sailed from Carlow, three years before, so Mother Agnes and another colony of seven intrepid Sisters of Mercy sailed from Liverpool, April 13, 1846.

MOTHER M. AGNES O'CONNOR

On their arrival in New York, on May 14th, the sisters were received by the Sisters of Charity, whose guests they were for the ensuing two weeks.

On June 18th, the feast of Corpus Christi, the Blessed Sacrament was placed in the chapel of their own new convent home, temporarily in Washington Place. The first work of the Sisters of Mercy of New York was the visiting of the sick poor, while the opening of a circulating library brought to the convent many young girls who soon availed themselves of the sisters' teaching and instruction. Upon the invitation of the Commissioners of Charity, the sisters visited the hospitals and prisons, glad to begin thus in New York one of the great works of the Order of Mercy.

The first candidate for admission to the New York community of the Sisters of Mercy was Josephine Seton, the youngest daughter of Mrs. Elizabeth Seton, foundress of the Sisters of Charity in the United States. Miss Seton, though blest with a religious vocation, felt no attraction to the Congregation established by her pious mother. From the time of her reception into the community, she devoted herself especially to the relief and instruction of the sick poor, and the inmates of hospitals and prisons. Until incapacitated by age, Mother Catherine Seton, for twenty-five years, while interested in all the works of the Institute, prepared for death every Catholic prisoner executed in New York.

In May, 1848, the community removed to the convent on Houston and Mulberry Streets, vacated by the Religious of the Sacred Heart on their removal to Astoria, and in the more commodious house the sisters were better able to further the work of their holy foundress, as they cared for the many destitute and friendless girls, driven from Ireland during the disastrous famine of 1847-1848. A House of Mercy was built adjoining the convent, and these girls, previously lodged in the convent, were transferred to the dormitories which were provided in the new building. Here workrooms were established where plain sewing and needlework of all kinds were taught to those who desired to become seamstresses. Everything was done at the new House of Mercy to fit the inmates for industrious lives, and lessons of religious instruction were zealously imparted by Mother Agnes and her co-laborers.

In the summer of 1862 the Sisters of Mercy of New York carried the work of their Institute to the scenes of the Civil War. At the request of the Secretary of War, the community sent sisters to take charge of the soldiers' hospital at Beaufort, North Carolina. The touching and beautiful incidents experienced by the Sisters of Mercy through the Crimean War repeated themselves during the days of the secession. The soldiers of the Civil War were young and old; educated and ignorant; American, Irish, Creole and German; but all alike to the nuns of the battlefield. When the war was ended the Sisters of Mercy were recalled to their convent home, where they spent many years in caring for the widows and orphans of the war victims.

During these years the New York community, besides establishing branch houses in the city, extended Mother McAuley's work into other dioceses in the country, in response to episcopal appeals for foundations, which were subsequently made in Brooklyn, New York, in 1855; in St. Louis, Missouri, in 1856; Albany, New York, in 1861; Worcester, Massachusetts, in 1864; and Eureka, California, in 1871.

September 24, 1886, found the community established in a new convent home in New York City, as the encroachments of commercial institutions and an advantageous offer from a publishing company had made it expedient to dispose of the property at Houston and Mulberry Streets. The new St. Catherine's Convent, to which the community then removed, was erected on Madison Avenue at East 81st Street, adjoining St. Joseph's Industrial School and the House of Mercy, established in 1869.

In 1894 an Institution of Mercy was opened at Tarrytown, in Westchester County, New York. This institution, with its present capacity of accommodating two hundred and twenty girls, is one of the outstanding works of the New York community, of now approximately one hundred and seventy-five members, which continues the work of the holy foundress, Mother McAuley, in a Vacation Home for Children and Convalescents—with a capacity of three hundred and fifty—in free and boarding homes for women, and in its many other charitable institutions, as well as in schools and academies in New York City.

> *Motherhouse*, St. Catherine's Convent, 1075 Madison Avenue, New York City, New York.
> *Novitiate*, Our Lady of Victory Convent, Tarrytown, New York. (Archdiocese of New York.)

CHICAGO, ILLINOIS*

1846

St. Xavier's

Among those in New York who welcomed the Sisters of Mercy on their arrival in the United States, in 1843, was the Rev. William Quarter, then pastor of St. Mary's Church in New York City, who a year later was appointed first bishop of the newly erected see of Chicago.

In September of 1846, Mother M. Xavier Warde, in response to Bishop Quarter's personal appeal for Sisters of Mercy for his diocese, established in Chicago a colony from the Pittsburgh community. Those in the community which arrived in Chicago with Mother Warde, after a perilous journey by stage and boat, were Sisters Mary Vincent McGirr, Mary Gertrude McGuire, Mary Eliza Corbitt,

*From data and material supplied by the Sisters of Mercy, St. Xavier's College and Academy, 4928 Cottage Grove Avenue, Chicago, Ill., and from supplied bibliography: *The Beginnings of the Works of the Sisters of Mercy in Chicago*, by Sister Mary Fidelis.

Mary Eva Schmidt, and Sister Mary Agatha O'Brien, who was appointed Superior.

The Sisters of Mercy then established the first permanent convent in Chicago and were the pioneers in all Catholic activities in Illinois, after 1846 laying the foundations of many of the charitable and educational institutions of Chicago. The sisters visited the sick in their homes, the prisoners in Chicago's first jail; they opened the first five parochial schools, the first night school for Catholic adults, the

ST. XAVIER'S CONVENT OF MERCY, CHICAGO, ILLINOIS

first convert class for adults, the first Catholic academy, the first working-girls' home, the first orphanage, the first Magdalen asylum, the first Catholic high school, the first Catholic training school for nurses and the first Catholic women's college. They nursed the sick in the first City Alms House and in the first County Hospital; they took over the care of Chicago's first hospital, the Illinois General Hospital, in the Lake House; they erected and maintained Chicago's first permanent hospital, the Mercy Hospital—which until 1866 was the only general hospital in the state of Illinois. They took charge of the cholera victims in 1849 and again in 1854, and rendered service through various other epidemics; they attended the sick in the United States Marine Hospital from 1850 to 1858.

In 1852 Mother Agatha purchased, with six hundred dollars, the property at 26th Street and Calumet Avenue, where Mercy

Hospital, with its great equipment and noted staff, and surrounded by its Nurses' Home, Guest House, and other modern annexes, now stands. Two years later, when the Asiatic cholera broke out in Chicago, Mother Agatha and four companion sisters were among the victims.

In 1861 Mother Frances Monholland, who served as Superior of the Sisters of Mercy in Chicago from 1858 to 1867, in fulfillment of a promise to care for the soldiers of the "Irish Brigade," organized by Col. James Mulligan, accompanied a band of the sisters from the Chicago community to Missouri, where, aside from Chicago, their efficient participation in relief work during the Civil War was centralized.

During the administration of Mother Scholastica Drum, 1867-1873, following the celebration, on September 24, 1871, of the Silver Jubilee of the Chicago community, property was purchased for a new academy, and an agreement had been made to sell the property on which St. Xavier's stood, when Chicago's historic fire of October 9, 1871, demolished all.

With fully a hundred thousand people rendered homeless by the fire, and the losses of the Sisters of Mercy severe, the future, after twenty-five years of labor, was dark and unpromising. Mercy Hospital—Providentially spared in the conflagration—became temporarily the Motherhouse, as well as a refuge for pupils, and many of the afflicted of Chicago. The United States Marine Hospital was burned and the marines were among those cared for at Mercy Hospital. Many generous donations were received after the fire. The great calamity evoked the charity of not only the entire country but the world, as was evidenced by the benevolence of the people in their contributions for the relief of the sufferers in the stricken city.

MOTHER M. GENEVIEVE GRANGER

Hard times and hardships then followed for the Sisters of Mercy in Chicago, when years of skillful management were required to place the community's financial affairs in order. To Mother Genevieve Granger, elected Superior in 1873, fell this task, and through a period of thirty-one years, with wisdom and ability, she guided the community, into which she received many new subjects.

Outstanding events of her administration were several foundations, and the openings of numerous schools, over which were placed competent members of the community.

Under the superiorship of Mother Xavier Flanagan, St. Xavier's Academy was granted a college charter from the state of Illinois, and in 1914 St. Xavier College was opened, and was the first Catholic college for women incorporated in Chicago.

Unique in the history of the religious orders of women in the United States is the work of Sister Mary Fidelis, of the Sisters of Mercy at St. Xavier's in Chicago, whose history of "Mother Catherine McAuley and the Beginnings of the Works of the Sisters of Mercy in Chicago" has been written and arranged with screen illustrations and lecture notes covering concisely and chronologically the chief events of this history, thus immortalizing this holy foundress and her works, especially those in Chicago.

Since the erection of the diocese, and their advent to it, upon the invitation of Chicago's first bishop, co-operating loyally with the hierarchy of the Church, as bishop succeeded bishop, and archbishop succeeded archbishop, until the present time, when the episcopal city has become the residence of His Eminence, George Cardinal Mundelein, the Sisters of Mercy have faithfully pursued their work of now more than seventy-five years, at present under Mother M. Cyril as Superior at St. Xavier's, and her Council, composed of Mother M. Evangelist, Assistant Superior; Mother M. Mercedes, Bursar; and Mother M. Evangeline, Mistress of Novices.

Motherhouse and Novitiate, St. Xavier's Convent of Mercy, 4928 Cottage Grove Avenue, Chicago, Illinois. (Archdiocese of Chicago.)

PROVIDENCE, RHODE ISLAND*
1851

At this period in the history of the Catholic Church in the United States, the diocese of Hartford, erected in 1843, embraced the states of Connecticut and Rhode Island. Providence was the seat of the

*From data supplied by the Sisters of Mercy, St. Xavier's Convent of Mercy, Providence, R. I., and from *Leaves from the Annals of the Sisters of Mercy* (Vol. III), and the following referred bibliography: *A History of the Institute in Rhode Island,* by Sister M. Catherine Morgan; *Seventy-Five Years in the Passing,* by Sister M. Josephine.

diocese of Hartford until 1872, when the diocese of Providence was established.   In 1850, the Right Rev. Bernard O'Reilly, D.D., who had just become bishop of Hartford, applied to the Sisters of Mercy in Pittsburgh for sisters to open schools in Providence.

Appreciating the critical religious situation in New England at this time, and knowing the bigotry and intolerance rampant, Bishop O'Reilly asked of the Pittsburgh community that an experienced and prudent religious be placed in charge of the new foundation.

Mother M. Xavier Warde, having just resigned the office of Superior of the community in Pittsburgh, was requested to direct the establishment of the Order in this region, where courageous leadership was especially necessary.

Accepting the responsibility, Mother Warde and her chosen companions left Pittsburgh, and reached their destination in 1851, on March 12th, a day on which is celebrated the translation of the relics of St. Francis Xavier, the patron of Mother Warde.   Traveling in secular garb, received quietly and without ostentation or ceremony, Mother Warde, with indispensable prudence and wisdom established the new convent home, and with her companions began the educational and charitable work of the Sisters of Mercy in Providence.

In 1857 the convent was removed to Broad Street property bought by the bishop.   At this time there was opened, adjoining the convent and under the direction of the sisters, the first orphanage established in New England, outside of Boston, under Catholic auspices.   As the community increased, an academy was opened, as well as free schools, in different parts of the city.

Through a period of torture and persecution almost unparalleled in the history of religious orders of women in the United States, Mother Warde bravely and unflinchingly, with intrepid spirit, remained at the helm, as the prayers of many holy souls, the gallantry of loyal defenders and staunch friends averted, in 1855, what would have been a disastrous event and an indelible blemish on the pages of the history of New England.   But the spirit of bigotry which so fiercely assailed them in the beginning has passed, and the blameless, useful and edifying lives of the religious have won the love and esteem of all denominations.

Proving that persecutions are blessings, the growth of the Providence community was so phenomenal as to permit not only the establishment of branch houses, but also of new foundations.   In addition to augmenting, in 1857, a community already active in Little Rock, Arkansas, sisters from the community in Providence established foundation units in Manchester, New Hampshire, in 1858; St. Augustine,

Florida, in 1859; Columbus, Georgia, in 1862; Nashville, Tennessee, in 1866, and St. George's, West Newfoundland, in 1893.

The Providence community, of now approximately three hundred and twenty members, is engaged in educational and charitable work

ST. XAVIER'S CONVENT, PROVIDENCE, RHODE ISLAND

in the diocese of Providence, and composing the present administra-tion of the community are Mother M. Matthew Doyle, Superior; Mother M. Hilda Miley, Assistant Superior; Mother M. Teresita Cor-rigan, Bursar, and Mother M. Austin Mallon, Novice Mistress.

> *Motherhouse*, St. Xavier's Convent of Mercy, 60 Broad Street, Providence, Rhode Island.
> *Novitiate*, Mt. St. Rita, Grants Mills, Cumberland, Rhode Island.
> (Diocese of Providence.)

LITTLE ROCK, ARKANSAS*

1851

To the zeal and perseverance of the Right Rev. Andrew Byrne, first bishop of Little Rock—the friend, student and co-laborer, in the south, of the beloved and noted Bishop England—the United States owes the community of Sisters of Mercy, which in 1850 left its con-vent home in Ireland to labor in the vast territory of the new diocese which had been erected in far-away Arkansas.

In the autumn of that year, Bishop Byrne visited Ireland, his native land, to procure sisters for his new diocese. Mother M. Vin-cent Whitty, at the parent-house of the Sisters of Mercy, had no

*From *Leaves from the Annals of the Sisters of Mercy.*

available sisters for a foundation at this time; however, in her realization of the bishop's needs, and his desire to have the Sisters of Mercy,
Mother M. Vincent referred him to the community at Naas, in
County Kildare, from which fewer foundations had then been made.
Anticipating the bishop's visit, Mother M. Vincent personally presented the cause for workers for the new mission, inspiring the
Kildare sisters with zeal and fervor for the work to be done, and
when Bishop Byrne himself pleaded his needs, volunteers were not
wanting who were willing to leave their own country and perform
their works of mercy in the new field, fertile for the laborers.

Sailing from Ireland on November 30, 1850, the Sisters of Mercy
of the little community, of which Mother M. Teresa O'Farrell had
been appointed Superior, did not await their designated mission field
before beginning their labors. On the boat—aboard which there were
three hundred emigrants—the sisters were soon giving religious
instruction to children and adults, and visiting and ministering to
the sick. Christmas day was fittingly celebrated during the voyage.
Bishop Byrne, who was on board, said the early masses and gave
Holy Communion to the many communicants. The singing of the
Christmas hymns by the sisters added to the memorable beauty of
the services.

After weathering storms, winds and calms, the boat entered the
Gulf of Mexico, and on January 23, 1851, reached New Orleans,
where the Sisters of Mercy from the convent at Naas were hospitably welcomed by the nuns of the historic Ursuline Convent of
that city.

On February 2nd the journey was resumed. After a four-day
trip up the sinuous Mississippi, the steamer reached the Little Rock
wharf, where the Sisters of Mercy were joyfully welcomed.

Preparations for the reception of the community had not been
completed, owing to the death of the vicar-general, in whose care the
bishop had left such arrangements. At once, therefore, Bishop Byrne
placed his own house at their disposal until a convent home was
ready for them. Without delay the community began active work
in the new field. The visitation of the sick and the instruction
of adults were the first duties of the sisters, and Sunday-school
classes for the children were begun, followed by the opening of
a school.

Throughout the hardships and struggles of pioneer days, the community perseveringly labored, and with success. The first extension
of the work of the sisters beyond the episcopal city was the opening,
in 1853, of a convent and school at Fort Smith, on the border of the

Indian Territory. Among the early pupils of the sisters there were three princesses, daughters of the chief of the Cherokee Nation, and three others, from the Choctaws.

In 1857, as few recruits had entered the Little Rock community, and those from Ireland rather than the United States, the community was augmented by sisters from the foundation in Providence, Rhode Island.

In June, 1862, at the mission which had been established at Helena—in what was, at that time, the richest county in Arkansas, in planters and plantations—occurred the death of the community's friend and counselor, Bishop Byrne. The war was the next disaster felt. A week after the bishop's death, thirty thousand soldiers of the Federal army encamped at Helena, and after the battle there on July 4th, the sisters had ample scope for their work of mercy among the poor sufferers in the hospital and refuge houses.

In Little Rock and Fort Smith the sisters labored among the afflicted and stricken of the war, endeavoring to alleviate the sufferings of Confederate and Federalist, all alike at the hands of the gentle Sister of Mercy.

The effects of the war were disastrous for the convents in Arkansas. In 1868 the work in Helena was relinquished, and the sisters were recalled to the convent in Little Rock.

With the growth of the community, the activities of the Sisters of Mercy of Little Rock extended to hospitals which they established, among the foremost of which is St. Joseph's Infirmary, opened at Hot Springs in 1888.

Confining its educational, hospital and charitable labors to the diocese of Little Rock, the community, of approximately three hundred sisters, is now under the ecclesiastical jurisdiction of its bishop, the Right Rev. John B. Morris, D.D.

Motherhouse and Novitiate, Mt. St. Mary's Convent, 4920 Prospect Avenue, Pulaski Heights, Little Rock, Arkansas. (Diocese of Little Rock.)

HARTFORD, CONNECTICUT*

1852

One year after the introduction of the Sisters of Mercy, from the Pittsburgh foundation, into the diocese of Hartford, by the Right Rev. Bernard O'Reilly, D.D., the Rev. John Brady, pastor of

*From data and material supplied by the Sisters of Mercy, St. Joseph's Convent of Mercy, Hartford, Conn.

St. Patrick's Church in the city of Hartford, arranged with Bishop O'Reilly for some Sisters of Mercy for Hartford from the newly established foundation in Providence.

At once, therefore, Mother M. Xavier Warde extended the work of the new community beyond the episcopal city, to Hartford. In September, 1852, with Sister M. Paula Lombard as Superior, four Sisters of Mercy opened a school in the temporary convent which they established on Allyn Street. The year 1855—during the pastorate of the Rev. James Hughes, and memorable in the annals of the Sisters

St. Joseph's Convent of Mercy, Hartford, Connecticut

of Mercy in Hartford because of the Know-Nothing movement, then prevalent—marked the opening of the first convent proper which was erected in Connecticut. To this, then, the sisters removed, and opened St. Catherine's, a boarding school and day academy.

At this time, to fill the demand for more teaching sisters in Connecticut and Rhode Island, then composing the diocese of Hartford, Mother M. Xavier Warde appealed to the Sisters of Mercy of the community in Cork, Ireland, of which her own sister, Mother M.

Josephine Warde, was Superior. One of the two sisters then sent to Providence was Sister M. Teresa Austin Carroll, a native of Clonmel, the gifted writer of the "Leaves from the Annals of the Sisters of Mercy," who, in her administrative and executive work in the United States, surpassed even Mother Warde in the number of schools she helped to establish in the east, south and west.

In 1872 the diocese of Hartford was divided and the diocese of Providence established. The Sisters of Mercy were allowed to choose the see of their subsequent residence. Mother Pauline Maher, who had formerly been one of the teachers in Hartford, was Superior of all the Sisters of Mercy in Rhode Island and Connecticut. Mother Pauline and her assistant, Mother Angela Fitzgerald, elected Hartford for their future labors, and established a Motherhouse at St. Catherine's Academy. The Right Rev. Francis P. MacFarland, D.D., transferred his episcopal residence from Providence to Hartford, where he at once proceeded with plans for the erection of a Cathedral and residence, and a Motherhouse for the Sisters of Mercy. The question was which building would go up first. The bishop's decision was firm and definite. "I will build a Motherhouse and school first, where young women may be trained to teach in the parochial schools of the diocese." At that time, in nearly all the large towns of the state, the parish schools were taught by seculars; since then, not only secular teachers, but hundreds of religious teachers, have been trained in the academy and novitiate of the historic building then erected by the zealous bishop.

In the spring of 1874 the new Motherhouse and academy, erected on Farmington Street, was completed, and the community and school accordingly transferred from the congested quarters at St. Catherine's to the spacious institution of St. Joseph's, from which now, under the superiorship of Mother M. Benedict Conroy, and the episcopal jurisdiction of the Right Rev. John Joseph Nilan, D.D., radiate the nearly eight hundred Sisters of Mercy active throughout the diocese, justifying Bishop MacFarland's noble and unselfish ambition of providing first the institution for the training of religious teachers, the need for which is shown by this great number of educational workers, successors of the intrepid first Superior, Mother M. Xavier Warde, and her companions.

Motherhouse, St. Joseph's Convent of Mercy, 160 Farmington Avenue, Hartford, Connecticut.

Novitiate, St. Augustine's Novitiate and Normal School, 481 Quaker Lane, South, West Hartford, Connecticut. (Diocese of Hartford.)

SAN FRANCISCO, CALIFORNIA*

1854

In the ecclesiastically historic year, 1854, the Most Rev. Joseph Sadoc Alemany, O.P., D.D., first archbishop of San Francisco, deputed the zealous San Francisco priest, the Rev. Hugh Gallagher, to visit Ireland and request of the Sisters of Mercy at Kinsale a community for his archdiocese.

Upon presentation of the archbishop's petition, from the volunteers who at once offered their services for the distant mission, Mother Mary Baptist Russell was chosen to be the Superior of the community of seven Kinsale Sisters of Mercy, who arrived in San Francisco on December 8, 1854.

The following year, though scarcely established, the sisters were plunged into more than the educational work in which they had already engaged. Cholera broke out, and throughout the siege there were none more assiduous in aiding the afflicted than the Sisters of Mercy, who labored night and day, ministering to bodies and souls, then, and again during the havoc wrought by earthquakes and by the smallpox.

MOTHER MARY BAPTIST RUSSELL

With the cessation of the cholera epidemic, the community returned to normalcy, and to its work in the schools, developing, as needed, on the Pacific Coast, the works of the Order of Mercy. In the public institutions, open to them at all times, the sisters were treated with marked courtesy by the officials, and welcomed by the prisoners at San Quen-

*From data and material supplied by the Sisters of Mercy, Convent of Our Lady of Mercy, Burlingame, Calif.

tin, on the San Francisco Bay, and by the inmates in the House of Refuge, industrial schools, and in the city and county hospitals.

With the growth of the community, and the inauguration of its many works, branch houses were established throughout the state, many of which later became independent foundations of the Order.

In 1921, the foundations of the Sisters of Mercy in the archdiocese of San Francisco, and in the California dioceses of Monterey-Fresno, Los Angeles and San Diego, and Tucson, in Arizona, amalgamated as the "United Houses," which now include the Mercy communities whose institutions are in the following California cities: Bakersfield, Burlingame, Del Mar, Fruitvale, Los Angeles, Modesto, Oakland, Oxnard, Redlands, Rio Vista, San Diego, San Francisco and Sausalito, and in Nogales, Phoenix and Prescott, Arizona.

CONVENT OF OUR LADY OF MERCY, BURLINGAME, CALIFORNIA

The new epoch in the community dates from July 10, 1923, when for the first time, in accordance with Canon Law, a General Chapter was held at St. Mary's Hospital, in San Francisco. Previous to this Chapter, every professed member of the community, on May 1, 1923, had received a copy of the Revised Constitutions for the Sisters of

Mercy of the "United Houses of the Dioceses of San Francisco, Monterey-Fresno, Los Angeles and San Diego, and Tucson," approved by His Holiness, Pope Pius XI, November 21, 1922.

With the Most Rev. Edward J. Hanna, D.D., Archbishop of San Francisco, presiding, the following were elected to office at this Chapter: Mother M. Bernard O'Brien, Mother General, Mother M. Gertrude Reid, Vicar General, Sister M. Rosarii Wood, Secretary General, Sister M. Paschal McGee, Procurator General, and Sister M. Pius Savage and Sister M. Emmanuel Spelman, Councilors.

On Feb. 25, 1924, the Motherhouse, from St. Mary's Hospital, in San Francisco, and the novitiate, from Fruitvale, were transferred to Burlingame, San Mateo County, California.

The approximately three hundred and thirty-five Sisters of Mercy of the "United Houses" of the dioceses of San Francisco, Monterey-Fresno, Los Angeles and San Diego, and Tucson, confine their activities—in carrying on the ideals and works of Mother McAuley—to these dioceses, through the present twenty-one branch houses, all under the jurisdiction of the Mother General and her Council, residing at the Motherhouse at Burlingame, California.

> *Motherhouse and Novitiate,* Convent of Our Lady of Mercy, Burlingame, California.   (Archdiocese of San Francisco.)

BALTIMORE, MARYLAND*
1855

In the year 1854, the Right Rev. Msgr. Edward McColgan, pastor of St. Peter's parish, in Baltimore, Maryland, applied to the Right Rev. Michael O'Connor, D.D., Bishop of Pittsburgh, for a colony of Sisters of Mercy.   Bishop O'Connor was finally able to gratify the zealous pastor with the promise of the needed sisters, from the community in Pittsburgh, for the Baltimore mission.

Composing the community of Sisters of Mercy who arrived in Baltimore in June, 1855, were Sister M. Neri Bowen, Sister M. Colette O'Connor and Sister M. Agnes Rigney, with Mother M. Catherine Wynne as Superior.   A residence near the parochial residence was fitted up as a convent, and presented to the new community by Mrs. Emily McTavish.

In September the Sisters of Mercy began their work of education in Baltimore, with the opening of an academy which at once attained success.   A parochial school, held in the basement of the church,

---

*From data and material supplied by the Sisters of Mercy, Mt. St. Agnes, Mt. Washington, Md.

was also conducted by the sisters, who labored on in the face of difficulties and many misunderstandings, during these pioneer days.

The first choir postulant to receive the habit in the Baltimore community was Sister M. Josephine Medcalf, of a highly respectable Baltimore family of Quakers or Friends, who had entered the community a month after its arrival in Baltimore. At about the same time, the God-child of the venerated Mother McAuley, Teresa Byrne—in religion, Sister M. Camillus, was transferred to the Baltimore community by Mother Warde, and assisted in the work of the new foundation.

By October, 1859, the community, though yet small, complied with the request of the Right Rev. William Elder, D.D., and sent sisters

MT. ST. AGNES, MT. WASHINGTON, MARYLAND

to establish a foundation in Vicksburg, Mississippi, in his diocese of Natchez.

Throughout the Civil War the Baltimore community served the Government, and ministered to the wounded and dying at the Douglas, the military hospital to which they were assigned when they offered their services to their country.

The "Sisters of Mercy in the City of Baltimore" early extended their labors beyond educational work in that city and parochial school work in Washington, D.C., to the establishment, in Baltimore, of Mercy Hospital, and Mercy Villa for convalescents. They also assumed care of the orphan boys at St. Vincent's, in Baltimore, and in Washington—fostering one of the original works of the Order—established and maintained St. Catherine's Home for Girls.

Mt. St. Agnes School, a junior and senior high school for girls, affiliated with the Catholic University of America, and accredited

"A" by the Maryland State Department of Education, established in 1867 with Mother de Chantal Digges as first Superior, is foremost among the educational institutions of the community, and with Mt. Washington Seminary for boys, aged six to thirteen, is located on the grounds, purchased in 1867, in the hills of Maryland, where the Baltimore community of approximately two hundred and twenty Sisters of Mercy, now under the superiorship of Mother M. Carmelita Hartman, maintains its Motherhouse and novitiate.

Motherhouse and Novitiate, Mt. St. Agnes, Mt. Washington, Maryland. (Archdiocese of Baltimore.)

BROOKLYN, NEW YORK*
1855

In 1855, nearly ten years after the arrival in New York City of seven Sisters of Mercy from the Motherhouse on Baggot Street, Dublin, Mother M. Agnes O'Connor, still serving as Superior of the Baggot Street Convent's first United States foundation, sent a community to Brooklyn, under the superiorship of Mother M. Vincent Haire, one of the intrepid seven from Dublin, to establish there the first foundation of the New York community.

The advent of the sisters to Brooklyn, which was two years after the establishment of the diocese, was in response to a request from the Right Rev. John Loughlin, D.D., first bishop of the see. The first Mercy Convent in Brooklyn was on Jay Street, near the Cathedral. On December 3, 1862, Mother Vincent and the community removed to the newly erected and commodious convent at the corner of Willoughby and Classon Avenues.

The Sisters of Mercy of Brooklyn, with the exception of three orphanages which are under their care, are engaged in educational work in the diocese, where, in addition to conducting a commercial school, other schools and a Juniorate, they also serve on the teaching faculty of the Bishop McDonnell Memorial High School.

In the spring of 1929, the community of approximately one hundred and fifty members, with Mother M. Dominic as Superior, and her Council, composed of Sisters M. Regina, M. Philip and M. Rosalie, removed to the recently completed new Motherhouse, novitiate and academy, at Syosset, Long Island, New York.

Motherhouse and Novitiate, Syosset, Long Island, New York. (Diocese of Brooklyn.)

*From data and material supplied by the Sisters of Mercy, St. Francis Convent of Mercy, 273 Willoughby Avenue, Brooklyn, N. Y.

ST. LOUIS, MISSOURI*
1856

In the summer of 1856, through the instrumentality of the Rev. A. Damen, S.J., pastor of St. Xavier's Church, in St. Louis, and upon the formal application of the archbishop, the Most Rev. Peter Richard Kenrick, D.D., who promised them his care and protection, Sisters of Mercy from St. Catherine's Convent in New York City were sent to establish a foundation of the Order in St. Louis, Missouri. The Rev. P. J. Ryan, later archbishop of Philadelphia, was deputed by the archbishop to act as escort during the trip.

Under the superiorship of Mother Mary de Pazzi Bentley, the new community at once began its work of visiting the sick in their homes, aiding the poor, and teaching. The opening of an industrial school

ST. JOSEPH'S CONVENT OF MERCY, WEBSTER GROVES, MISSOURI

and Mercy Home for the protection of young women was a memorable event of the community's early years in St. Louis.

In 1860, the community having outgrown its first convent home in St. Louis, on 20th and Morgan Streets, a commodious convent was built on property secured at 22nd and Morgan Streets. A day school was conducted in connection with the convent until 1871, when it was closed, and until the opening of St. John's Hospital, in 1890, the building was utilized as an infirmary for the destitute.

In 1912, St. John's Hospital was transferred to a new building, with a bed capacity of more than three hundred, on Euclid and Parkview, where the St. Louis community of the Sisters of Mercy

*From data and material supplied by the Sisters of Mercy, St. Joseph's Convent of Mercy, Webster Groves, Mo.

now carries on its efficient hospital work. The institution, with its well established training school for nurses, is connected with the St. Louis University. The building at 23rd and Locust Streets, vacated by the hospital in 1912, is used as a Mercy Home for girls.

The year 1919 saw the transfer of the headquarters of the community at 22nd and Morgan Streets, when on February 2nd, removal was made to the splendid new buildings erected at Webster Groves, Missouri, a suburb of St. Louis, where the sisters have established a home and school for girls.

In addition to its hospital and charitable work, the community, now under the superiorship of Mother M. Ignatius Greene, is engaged in educational work throughout the archdiocese of St. Louis and in the diocese of Springfield in Illinois.

Since its foundation in St. Louis in 1856, the community has sent out foundations to New Orleans, Louisville, Conejos and Denver, and made a branch foundation in Springfield, Missouri, where St. John's Hospital and Training School is foremost among its institutions.

At the time of the small-pox epidemic in Springfield, the Sisters of Mercy met the call—some of them spending eight and nine months in the pestilential area—and ministered to the afflicted throughout the siege of the disease.

Numbering approximately two hundred members, the community, now under the archiepiscopal jurisdiction of the Most Rev. John J. Glennon, D.D., Archbishop of St. Louis, is active in educational, hospital and charitable work in not only the archdiocese of St. Louis, but also in the dioceses of Kansas City and Springfield in Illinois.

Motherhouse and Novitiate, St. Joseph's Convent of Mercy, Webster Groves, Missouri. (Archdiocese of St. Louis.)

SACRAMENTO, CALIFORNIA*

1857

Sisters of Mercy from St. Mary's Hospital, in San Francisco, California, accompanied by Mother M. Baptist Russell, foundress of the Order on the Pacific Coast, came to Sacramento, California, on October 2, 1857.

On October 5th, the community, under Mother M. Gabriel Brown as Superior, opened the first sisters' school in Sacramento—so named

*From data and material supplied by the Sisters of Mercy, St. Joseph's Convent of Mercy, Sacramento, Calif.

in honor of the Blessed Sacrament—where, as St. Joseph's Academy, it has grown and prospered, and is one of the foremost Catholic institutions in the diocese. In 1875, the state of California granted the Sisters of Mercy a charter permitting them to teach high school subjects, and for many years St. Joseph's Academy has been accredited to the University of California. Well established commercial and music departments are conducted at the high school, where a grade school is also maintained.

In addition to their school work, the sisters visit the sick in their homes and minister to the poor. On Sundays they conduct catechism classes in the various parishes of the city and its suburbs.

In 1895 the sisters purchased and took charge of a small hospital known as the Ridge Home. When it became inadequate a larger building, known as Mater Misericordia Hospital, was erected. This was sold, with the land on which it stood, in 1925, when the new Mater Misericordia Hospital, in its present beautiful location, was opened by the sisters.

The Stanford Lathrop Memorial Home, opened May 16, 1900, donated to the Right Rev. Patrick Manague, D.D., for the diocese of Sacramento, and endowed for the care of homeless children, by Mrs. Leland Stanford, in memory of her only son Leland, who was born there, is in charge of the Sisters of Mercy.

On May 2, 1887, the community in Sacramento was established as an independent foundation of Sisters of Mercy, with its Mother-house and novitiate at St. Joseph's Convent, and with Mother M. Vincent Phelan serving as first Superior.

The present administration of the community—under the ecclesiastical jurisdiction of the Right Rev. Robert J. Armstrong, D.D., Bishop of Sacramento—is composed of Mother M. Aloysius Nolan, Superior, Sister M. Francis Sheridan, Assistant Superior, Sister M. de Sales Harris, Bursar, and Sister M. Agnes Leahy, Mistress of Novices.

Motherhouse and Novitiate, St. Joseph's Convent of Mercy, 9th and G Streets, Sacramento, California. (Diocese of Sacramento.)

ROCHESTER, NEW YORK*

1857

In 1857, ten years after the establishment of the diocese of Buffalo, the repeated efforts of its first bishop, the Right Rev. John Timon,

*From data and material supplied by the Sisters of Mercy, Mercy Convent, Rochester, N. Y.

C.M., D.D., for a foundation of Sisters of Mercy in his diocese, met at last with success, when he appealed to Mother Warde, in Providence, for a community for his diocese. Prior to this, Bishop Timon had directed his requests for sisters to the community in Pittsburgh.

Accompanied by Mother Warde herself, a community of six sisters, with Mother Mary Baptist Coleman as Superior, set out from Providence, and on June 9, 1857, established a long-awaited foundation of the Sisters of Mercy in Rochester, New York, then in the diocese of Buffalo.

The activities of the community began at once, and in time its educational and charitable work was extended to other cities in the state, including the episcopal city of Buffalo. Throughout the stress of the Civil War, the sisters did special work among the poor, visiting them in their homes and ministering to them.

Upon the division of the diocese of Buffalo and the erection of that of Rochester, in 1868, the Sisters of Mercy in Rochester, and their missions included in the counties composing the new diocese, passed under the jurisdiction of the bishop of Rochester.

With the opening of St. James' Mercy Hospital, at Hornell, New York, in 1890, the community engaged in its initial hospital work in the diocese. Among the recent activities of the sisters has been the opening of Our Lady of Mercy High School, on Clover Road, in the episcopal city.

Under the present superiorship of Mother Mary Liguori McHale, the community, of approximately one hundred and seventy-five members, loyally carries on its work, in the spirit of the noble religious whose personal attention was given to the foundation at its beginning.

> *Motherhouse and Novitiate*, 90 St. John's Park, Rochester, New York. (Diocese of Rochester.)

CINCINNATI, OHIO*

1858

Thoroughly cognizant of the object and works of the Sisters of Mercy, the Most Rev. John Baptist Purcell, D.D., first archbishop of Cincinnati, in 1856 had been for several years desirous of having a community of them in Cincinnati.

*From data and material supplied by the Sisters of Mercy, Convent of Mercy, Cincinnati, Ohio, and from *Leaves from the Annals of the Sisters of Mercy*. (Vol. IV.)

While in Ireland, during a visit to Europe in that year, Mrs. Sarah Peter of Cincinnati, distinguished for her great fervor and benevolence, called on the Sisters of Mercy at the Kinsale convent, of which Mother Frances Bridgman was the foundress and Superior. Doing so at the request of Archbishop Purcell, and in his name, she besought Mother Frances to send Sisters of Mercy to the Ohio city, and, as authorized by the archbishop, assured her of permanent protection, patronage and co-operation, should the foundation be accorded the archdiocese.

Not until the summer of 1858 was it possible for the Kinsale Superior to comply with this request, which she had assured Mrs. Peter would be given favorable consideration.

The Superior of the colonizing band, chosen from those volunteering for the new mission, was Mother Teresa Maher. Destined to become one of the pioneer American community foundresses, Teresa Maher was born in Carlow, Ireland, in 1824, of a family illustrious for the number of its zealous ecclesiastics and devoted religious. Entering the Mercy Convent in Kinsale, in County Cork, in 1845, and, in time, occupying various offices in the community, Mother Teresa possessed, in an eminent degree, the qualities necessary to inspire the love, faith and confidence of those in the little community chosen for the American mission.

With Mrs. Peter—who, during the two years after her call at the convent in Kinsdale, had remained in Europe, and in Germany arranged for a Cincinnati foundation of Mother Schervier's nursing sisters—the Sisters of Mercy left for their Ohio mission field.

Since the year 1858, August 24th has been celebrated annually as the date of the foundation of the Order of Mercy in the archdiocese of Cincinnati.

For two months after their arrival in Cincinnati, the sisters were guests in Mrs. Peter's home, a portion of which had been prepared as a convent for them. Devoting themselves almost at once to visiting the sick and instructing the ignorant, they did not engage in the work of teaching until their removal, in October, to a humble convent home and school in St. Thomas' parish.

On November 7th, the first Ohio reception of a Sister of Mercy took place with impressive ceremony in St. Thomas' Church, when Miss Agnes McCoy received the veil from the hands of Archbishop Purcell.

By 1861, the community, which had greatly increased, had transferred to a spacious convent on Fourth Street. In October of that year of the opening of the Civil War, the military authorities rented the convent home as an auxiliary hospital for sick and wounded soldiers. In February, 1862, the mayor of Cincinnati applied to the archbishop for sisters to nurse the sick and wounded in Ohio regiments. Mother Teresa herself headed the Sisters of Mercy who went immediately to the scenes of suffering, when the Union and Confederate armies met at Shiloh, and the battle of Pittsburgh Landing was fought.

Following its use as an army hospital, the Mercy Convent in Cincinnati became, in turn a House of Mercy, a night refuge, and a school for young boys. Then again came an appeal from the mayor of the city, and the house was utilized as a hospital for cholera patients during an epidemic, when day and night the sisters labored for the corporal and spiritual welfare of the plague-stricken. With a return to normalcy, the sisters resumed their school work and general works of mercy.

A week after the feast of St. Teresa, in 1877, though not advanced in years, Mother Teresa died after a short illness, and was succeeded by Mother M. Baptist Kane, who long had been her faithful companion and assistant in all her works.

In 1892, during the administration as Superior of Mother Mary de Sales Douglas, Mercy Hospital was established in Hamilton, Ohio, and is now maintained, with its training school for nurses, at 116 Dayton Street.

Upholding continuously the high standard of efficiency maintained by the Sisters of Mercy, the community, of now approximately one hundred and forty-five members, has ever been among the foremost in participation in educational and charitable activities in Cincinnati.

Today, the Cincinnati Sisters of Mercy, under the ecclesiastical jurisdiction of the Most Rev. John T. McNicholas, O.P., S.T.M., Archbishop of Cincinnati, and the superiorship of Mother Mary Bernardine, in addition to their many schools throughout the city, conduct at the Motherhouse a high school for girls, and, at Epworth Avenue and Werk Road, Westwood, Mother of Mercy Academy. Near the Motherhouse there is also maintained by the sisters Mt. Carmel Home for Working Girls and Women.

In this noteworthy divergence of its labors, the community carries on the work of the Sisters of Mercy as developed through the activity of the zealous foundress, Catherine McAuley.

Motherhouse and Novitiate, Convent of Mercy, 1409 Freeman Avenue, Cincinnati, Ohio. (Archdiocese of Cincinnati.)

MANCHESTER, NEW HAMPSHIRE*

1858

The foundation of the Sisters of Mercy in Manchester, New Hampshire, was made in 1858, four years after an outbreak of "Know-Nothingism" in the region included then in the newly erected see of Portland.

Through the zeal of the Rev. William McDonald, and upon the earnest solicitation of the Right Rev. David W. Bacon, D.D., first bishop of Portland, Mother M. Xavier Warde, the indefatigable United States foundress of the Sisters of Mercy, consented to head the foundation community for Manchester, from the convent in Providence.

Mother Warde had braved one mob persecution in Hartford, Connecticut, and she was undaunted by the prospect facing religious workers courageous enough to venture north to the untilled fields of the Lord.

On the feast of Our Lady of Mt. Carmel, July 16, 1858, with the blessing of their bishop, the Right Rev. F. P. MacFarland, D.D., Mother Warde and her companions left Providence and the diocese of Hartford for their future home in New Hampshire, then in the diocese of Portland.

Upon their arrival in Manchester they were met by Father McDonald, and to their joy and surprise they were asked to take possession of a convent home especially prepared for them.

The sisters were a subject of mingled curiosity and alarm to the "natives," who, however, when they saw them visiting the sick and poor, gradually became friendly. An academy was opened in September, 1858, and was well attended, while the free schools and evening schools which were established were crowded.

Little more than a month had passed, after the arrival of the sisters in Manchester, when two prospective converts, a Baptist and a Universalist, presented themselves at the convent seeking instruction in the Catholic faith. Later formally received into the Church, they were the first of hundreds who have since followed in their path.

With the notable progress of their work in Manchester, the sisters extended their labors to missions, and to the establishment of foundations, which, in sequence, were made in Philadelphia, Omaha,

---

*From data and material supplied by the Sisters of Mercy, Convent of Mercy, Manchester, N. H., and from *Leaves from the Annals of the Sisters of Mercy.* (Vol. IV.)

Bangor, Maine; Yreka, California; Jersey City, New Jersey; and St. Johnsbury, Vermont.

In 1873 Mother Warde sent Sisters of Mercy to take charge of the parochial schools in Portland, Maine, where sisters had been sent the year previous to care for the orphans.

On September 17th, in 1884, the year of the division of the diocese of Portland and the establishment of that of Manchester, Mother M. Xavier Warde—the "Great Mother," as the Indians of Maine styled her, died at the Mercy Convent in Manchester, at the age of seventy-four, after fifty-three years as a professed religious. The Right Rev. Denis M. Bradley, D.D., newly appointed bishop of the diocese, officiated at the funeral services of the courageous, fervent religious, efficient executive of the Sisters of Mercy, and a tireless leader among pioneer religious workers in the United States.

The Sisters of Mercy of the Manchester community have established and maintain, in that episcopal city, not only schools and orphanages, but also conduct Sacred Heart Hospital and Training School for Nurses, homes for the aged, and an infant asylum. In addition, the sisters conduct there St. Martha's Home for Working Girls, and St. Philomena's House, a residence home for business women.

The well known Catholic periodical, "The Magnificat," of which Sister M. Ignatia McDonald is editor, is published monthly by the Manchester community of the Sisters of Mercy. The magazine is issued from the press of the Magnificat Publishing House, in connection with the Magnificat Vocational School conducted by the sisters, and located at the site of the Motherhouse.

Under the ecclesiastical jurisdiction of the Right Rev. George Albert Guertin, D.D., present bishop of Manchester, the community, of nearly four hundred members, with Mother M. Evarista Dolan as Superior, is active in its educational, hospital and charitable work in the archdiocese of Boston, as well as in the diocese of Manchester, where the Motherhouse and novitiate are maintained.

Motherhouse and Novitiate, Mt. St. Mary's Convent, 435 Union Street, Manchester, New Hampshire. (Diocese of Manchester.)

BUFFALO, NEW YORK*

1858

The Sisters of Mercy, of a community which, the year before, upon the invitation of the Right Rev. John Timon, C.M., D.D., Bishop of Buffalo, had made a foundation in Rochester, New York—

*From the Official Catholic Directory, 1929, and from accumulated data.

then included in the diocese of Buffalo, extended their educational activities to schools in the diocese, by opening, in 1858, a mission house in the city of Buffalo, and one in Batavia, New York, in 1862.

Following the death of Bishop Timon in 1867, the diocese was divided, and in January, 1868, the diocese of Rochester was established. The Sisters of Mercy in Rochester were then recognized as a diocesan community, and those in Buffalo and in Batavia, to continue also as diocesan, united to form the community of Sisters of Mercy for the diocese of Buffalo.

In addition to Mt. Mercy Academy, at the Motherhouse, and the many parochial schools in the diocese in their charge, the sisters in 1904 opened Mercy Hospital in Buffalo, and, in 1917, St. Jerome's Mercy Hospital in Batavia.

In two homes for girls, also maintained by the sisters, in Buffalo, the ideals and plans of Mother McAuley, in her interest for such establishments, are carried out by this community, of approximately three hundred and fifty members.

Motherhouse and Novitiate, Convent of Our Lady of Mercy, 1475 Abbott Road, Buffalo, New York. (Diocese of Buffalo.)

OTTAWA, ILLINOIS*

1859

St. Joseph's Convent of Mercy, at Ottawa, Illinois, was founded August 20, 1859, from the Convent of Our Lady of Mercy in Chicago. To it was attached the Academy of St. Xavier, which was then opened.

Mother M. Frances Monholland accompanied the community to Ottawa, and upon its installation there, Sister Mary Xavier McGirr was appointed the local Superior. The community remained under the authority of the Motherhouse in Chicago until the establishment of the diocese of Peoria in 1877. Ottawa being in the territory included in that of the new diocese, the sisters who so desired were permitted to return to Chicago, while others, who then remained, formed the Ottawa foundation community of Sisters of Mercy in the diocese of Peoria.

The community is engaged chiefly in educational work in parochial schools throughout the diocese. In Ohio City, Illinois, the sisters have established and maintain Mercy Home for the Aged.

Motherhouse and Novitiate, St. Joseph's Convent, Ottawa, Illinois. (Diocese of Peoria.)

---

*From the annals of the Sisters of Mercy.

VICKSBURG, MISSISSIPPI*

1860

In 1860 the Right Rev. William Elder, D.D., then bishop of Natchez, later archbishop of Cincinnati, solicited Mother M. Catherine Wynne, Superior of the newly founded community of the Sisters of Mercy of the City of Baltimore, for sisters for his diocese.

Reluctantly, because of the small number in her own community, but generously—as a courtesy to the Most Rev. Francis Patrick Kenrick, D.D., Archbishop of Baltimore, who especially desired that Bishop Elder's request be granted—Mother Catherine consented to the southern foundation.

Sister M. de Sales Browne was chosen Superior of the new community, which consisted of Sisters M. Vincent Browne, M. Ignatius Sumner, M. Stephana and Miss Rosa Farmer, a postulant. The new

St. Francis Xavier's Convent of Mercy, Vicksburg, Mississippi

community left Baltimore on the morning of October 9th, and reached its destination, Vicksburg, Mississippi, on the evening of the 12th.

On October 15th, 1860, the feast of St. Teresa, the community was installed in its convent home. Here a school was at once opened, and successfully carried on until the height of the Civil War, and

*From data supplied by the Sisters of Mercy, Vicksburg, Miss., and from *Leaves from the Annals of the Sisters of Mercy.* (Vol. IV.)

the bombardment of Vicksburg, when it was utilized as a hospital, and the Sisters of Mercy acted as nurses. They tended the sick and wounded, successively at Mississippi Springs, Oxford, Jackson, and Shelby Springs. On their return to Vicksburg, at the beginning of the last year of the war, the convent, which had become the headquarters of General Slocum, was restored to them through Secretary of War Stanton, upon the request of his friend, Father Michael O'Connor, S.J., formerly bishop of Pittsburgh.

In 1870 the Sisters of Mercy in Vicksburg established a school at Pass Christian, on the Mississippi Sound, where eighty white children were soon enrolled. A separate school was established for colored children. Other missions were also opened through the diocese in that year, including a school for the Indians in the Indian Reservation.

During the yellow fever epidemic of 1878, the City Hospital was placed under the sisters' charge, and they were constantly occupied there and in the homes of the stricken, in their efforts to mitigate suffering. Among the victims of the fever were four of the community; others were attacked but recovered from the dreaded malady.

In the years which have elapsed since this period, in the history of the community, the sisters have devoted themselves to many works of mercy, but especially as religious teachers fill the need in the southern diocese, where their principal educational institution is St. Francis Xavier's Academy, in Vicksburg, connected with the Motherhouse.

The community, of approximately one hundred and ten sisters— most of whom are Mississippians—under the ecclesiastical jurisdiction of the Right Rev. Richard Oliver Gerow, D.D., is presided over by Mother M. Bernard McGuire, Superior, Sister M. Clementine Phelan, Assistant, Sister M. Camillus Fitzpatrick, Bursar, and Sister M. Clare O'Brien, Novice Mistress.

> *Motherhouse and Novitiate,* St. Francis Xavier's Convent of Mercy, Vicksburg, Mississippi. (Diocese of Natchez.)

PHILADELPHIA, PENNSYLVANIA*

1861

In 1861, the year following his appointment to what was then the diocese of Philadelphia, the Most Rev. James Frederic Wood, D.D.—

*From data supplied by the Sisters of Mercy, Merion, Pa., and from *Leaves from the Annals of the Sisters of Mercy.* (Vol. IV.)

elevated to the archbishopric in 1875, with the erection of the arch-diocese of Philadelphia—delegated the Very Rev. Father Carter, of Philadelphia, to visit Manchester and there confer with Mother Xavier Warde concerning a community of Sisters of Mercy for Philadelphia.

Courteously, Mother Warde accorded Bishop Wood's request favorable consideration.   Mother M. Patricia Waldron was appointed Superior of the group of sisters chosen from the Manchester community, who established a convent in Philadelphia in August, 1861. With the fall opening of school, the Sisters of Mercy formally began their labors in this new field.

Academies, parochial schools, homes for business women and girls, and Misericordia Hospital are the results of the years of the community in Philadelphia.   Commemorating the zealous endeavors of the foundress-Superior, is the Waldron Academy, a Junior School for Boys, conducted by the community at the Motherhouse, Mater Misericordiae Convent, in Merion, with which the Academy of the Mater Misericordiae is connected.

The activities of the community, of approximately two hundred members, are chiefly in Philadelphia, as implied by the title, "The Sisters of Mercy in the City of Philadelphia."

Motherhouse and Novitiate, Convent of Mater Misericordiae, Merion, Pennsylvania. (Archdiocese of Philadelphia.)

ALBANY, NEW YORK*
1861

During the episcopacy in the diocese of Albany of the Right Rev. John McCloskey, D.D., later the first American cardinal, the Rev. John Carry, pastor of St. John's Church in Rensselaer—then known as Greenbush, petitioned the Sisters of Mercy of the community with its Motherhouse at St. Catherine's Convent, New York City, for sisters to conduct the school of his parish.

In 1861, in response to this request, which had been approved by Bishop McCloskey, Mother M. Austin Horan—who had recently succeeded to the superiorship of the New York community, following the death of the foundress Superior, Mother M. Agnes O'Connor—sent a small community of sisters to Greenbush.   Mother Vincent Sweetman served as first Superior of the community, which then began its activities in the diocese of Albany, where it is now engaged in

*From data and material supplied by the Sisters of Mercy, Convent of Mercy, Rensselaer, N. Y.

hospital and charitable work, as well as the conducting of parochial schools and a boarding school for girls.

In September, 1926, the community, of one hundred and seventy-five members, of which Mother Mary Aloysia Carmody is Superior, sent forth its first foreign mission band, when from those volunteering for the new field, sisters were chosen to pursue the works of the Congregation of Mercy on the Island of St. Thomas, of the Virgin Islands, possessions of the United States since their purchase from Denmark in 1917.

On August 15, 1928, the community transferred its Motherhouse and novitiate to the newly erected convent in Albany, New York, which was dedicated with auspicious ceremony on November 17, 1928, by the Right Rev. Edmund F. Gibbons, D.D., Bishop of Albany, assisted by the Right Rev. Msgr. Joseph A. Delaney, Vicar General of the diocese, and the Right Rev. Msgr. Michael J. Looney.

SISTERS OF MERCY MISSION BAND OF
1926 TO THE VIRGIN ISLANDS

Motherhouse and Novitiate, Mercy Convent, New Scotland Avenue, Albany, New York. (Diocese of Albany.)

MACON, GEORGIA*

1862

While retaining his duties as vicar-apostolic of Florida, the Right Rev. Augustin Verot, D.D., was, in 1861, transferred to the see of Savannah, and desirous of having the Sisters of Mercy in the diocese, requested for Georgia a community from the foundation in St. Augustine—established there in 1859 by the Mercy community in Providence—to whom he, at that time bishop of St. Augustine, had applied for sisters.

---

*From the annals of the Sisters of Mercy.

Scarcely had sisters from Florida responded to Bishop Verot's request—and in 1862 opened their convent in Columbus, Georgia, in the diocese of Savannah—when the peninsular region of Florida felt the devastating effects of the Civil War. Finding damages beyond repair, the Sisters of Mercy remaining in Florida then removed from there entirely, establishing or augmenting communities of the Congregation in other states.

Continuing their labors in Georgia, the sisters, in 1871, opened a convent at Macon. In 1876, on the purchase there of property most desirably located, removal was made to it, and Mt. de Sales Academy and boarding school was opened. Soon afterward the Motherhouse and novitiate were added to the institution at Mt. de Sales, the community, however, continuing to maintain the convent and school in Columbus.

Motherhouse and Novitiate, Mt. de Sales Convent, Macon, Georgia. (Diocese of Savannah.)

OMAHA, NEBRASKA*
1864

The first western foundation of the Sisters of Mercy made under the direction of Mother Xavier Warde, was in 1864, when in response to the importuning of the Right Rev. James O'Gorman, D.D., of Omaha, six sisters of the community in Manchester, New Hampshire, were chosen, in the days of arduous travel, for that distant territory.

In the heat and dust of the western journey, begun on July 27th, the little community, under the superiorship of Mother M. Ignatius, made many stops, most important of which was that made in Indiana. There, in South Bend, the Very Rev. Edward E. Sorin, founder of the world-famed University of Notre Dame, extended the Sisters of Mercy most courteous attention, as did Mother M. Angela Gillespie, of the Sisters of the Holy Cross, at St. Mary's.

Continuing their trip, the sisters reached Chicago, where they spent six weeks, and then, under escort sent by Bishop O'Gorman, for protection through the region menaced by guerilla warfare, they were conducted to their destination, where they arrived by boat, after a voyage up the Missouri, from St. Joseph.

At once established in the convent prepared for them, the sisters

*From data supplied by the Sisters of Mercy, Convent of Mercy, Omaha, Neb., and from *Leaves from the Annals of the Sisters of Mercy* (Vol. IV.).

began their labors in Nebraska, and in turn, as and where needed, conducted schools, orphanages and hospitals.

After the death of Bishop O'Gorman, the Right Rev. James O'Connor, D.D., brother of the Right Rev. Michael O'Connor, D.D., —co-founder, with Mother Warde, of the Congregation of the Sisters of Mercy in the United States—became vicar-apostolic of Nebraska, and, like his predecessor, maintained his headquarters in Omaha, so continuing after the establishment of the diocese in 1885.

Under the direction of Bishop O'Connor, the activities of the sisters were intensified, and the College of St. Mary, recently merged with Creighton University, and their many institutions in Omaha and throughout the diocese, as well as in the dioceses of Grand Island and Lincoln, where missions are maintained, attest the progressiveness, zeal and fervor of the community, numbering approximately one hundred and thirty members, at present under the ecclesiastical jurisdiction of the Right Rev. Joseph F. Rummel, D.D., as bishop of Omaha, and the superiorship of Mother Leo Gallagher, and her Council composed of Mother M. Genevieve, Mother M. Bernard and Mother M. Isabelle.

Motherhouse and Novitiate, Convent of Mercy, 1424 Castellar Street, Omaha, Nebraska. (Diocese of Omaha.)

WORCESTER, MASSACHUSETTS*
1864

In response to a request, in 1864, from the Right Rev. John Bernard Fitzpatrick, Bishop of Boston, Mother M. Austin Horan, then Superior of St. Catherine's in New York City, sent a foundation community of Sisters of Mercy to Worcester, Massachusetts, at the time included in the territory comprising the diocese of Boston, before the establishment of that of Springfield.

The community, now under the ecclesiastical jurisdiction of the Right Rev. Thomas M. O'Leary, D.D., Bishop of Springfield, is devoted chiefly to parochial school work and the care of orphans in that diocese.

In connection with the orphanage for girls, maintained by the community in Worcester, St. Joseph's Home for Working Girls has been established.

Motherhouse and Novitiate, St. Gabriel's Convent of Mercy, 46 High Street, Worcester, Massachusetts. (Diocese of Springfield.)

*From the annals of the Sisters of Mercy.

PORTLAND, MAINE*

1865

The histories of the Sisters of Mercy in Portland, Maine, and in Manchester, New Hampshire, were identical for many years, as the territory of the two states, having been withdrawn from the diocese of Boston, constituted, until the later establishment of the diocese of Manchester, the diocese of Portland, as erected by the Holy See in 1853, with the Right Rev. David M. Bacon, D.D., its first bishop.

In behalf of the religious education of children throughout the diocese, Bishop Bacon had appealed to the Sisters of Mercy in Providence, Rhode Island, for a foundation to be established in Manchester, New Hampshire, where the Rev. William McDonald, who had zealously labored since 1848 as first resident pastor, was most desirous of their assistance.

Mother Warde, then in Providence, entered fully into the sentiments of the bishop and the pioneer pastor, arranged to be one of the community promised for the waiting field, and in her efficient capacity of leader and executive became Superior of the group of sisters composing the foundation colony, which arrived in Manchester in July, 1858.

The labors of the new community were for several years confined to Manchester and missions in its vicinity in New Hampshire.

In 1865, the Sisters of Mercy began their activities in Maine, with the opening not only of the first parochial school in Bangor, but also of St. Xavier's—its first academy—and the organization of a night school for adults.

The year 1873 marked the initial work of the community in Portland, the episcopal city of the diocese, when the sisters began to teach in the parochial schools, and opened St. Elizabeth's Academy, St. Elizabeth's Orphanage, and a night school.   In 1877 the sisters organized the classes in Kavanagh School, which had been erected near the Cathedral, through the generosity of the sister of Maine's Catholic governor, Edward Kavanagh.

The years of '78 and '79 carry in their annals the history of the beginning of the labors of the Sisters of Mercy among the Indians of Maine, when they were placed in charge of the Indian Reservation at Old Town, and the mission at Pleasant Point, on Passamaquoddy Bay, as well as at Dana's Point, on the Schoodic Lakes.

---

*From data and material supplied by the Sisters of Mercy, St. Joseph's Convent, Portland, Me., and from *Leaves from the Annals of the Sisters of Mercy.*

In 1881, complying with the request of the Right Rev. James A. Healy, D.D., who had succeeded to the bishopric of Portland, Mother Warde sent sisters to Deering—now a part of Portland and described as Deering District. The opening of St. Joseph's Home for Aged

ST. JOSEPH'S CONVENT, PORTLAND, MAINE

Women, and the establishment of St. Joseph's Academy followed the advent of the Sisters of Mercy to the district.

For the next decade of years, and through the episcopacy in Portland of His Eminence, William Cardinal O'Connell—consecrated bishop of Portland in 1901—the Sisters of Mercy devoted themselves to the opening of schools in various cities and missions in the diocese.

In 1908, under the jurisdiction of the Right Rev. Louis S. Walsh, D.D., appointed to the see of Portland in 1906, the dedication ceremony of the new Motherhouse took place. In 1909, the community transferred to the new convent, at which, in connection with St. Joseph's Academy, St. Joseph's College for Women, incorporated under the laws of the state of Maine, with full power to confer degrees, was opened in 1915.

With a membership of approximately two hundred and fifty, the Portland community of the Sisters of Mercy, now under the ecclesiastical jurisdiction of the Right Rev. John Gregory Murray, D.D.—appointed to the see of Portland in 1925—and the superiorship of

Mother Emmanuel Joseph Scanlan, systematically continues the works of Mother McAuley, inaugurated in the diocese of Portland by the indefatigable Mother M. Xavier Warde.

Motherhouse and Novitiate, St. Joseph's Convent, 605 Stevens Avenue, Portland, Maine. (Diocese of Portland.)

NASHVILLE, TENNESSEE*

1866

The Sisters of Mercy of the community whose Motherhouse is maintained at St. Bernard Convent, Nashville, Tennessee, are descended from the house in Carlow, Ireland, through St. Mary's Convent, Pittsburgh, and St. Xavier's Convent, Providence, Rhode Island.

In 1866, soon after his consecration as bishop of Nashville, the Right Rev. Patrick A. Feehan, D.D., wishing to have a community of sisters identified with the Cathedral parish, applied in person to the Sisters of Mercy at the Motherhouse in Providence, Rhode Island, for a colony of Sisters of Mercy.

With Mother Mary Clare McMahon as Superior, Sisters Mary Sebastian Thynne, Mary Dominica Coffee, Mary Isadore Dillon, Mary Joachim O'Connor and Mary Basilia Callaghan, a novice, were chosen from the volunteers in the Providence convent to make the foundation in the far-away southern diocese. In the fall of the same year, 1866, the little band of sisters arrived in Tennessee, and in the episcopal city of Nashville at once began their first community work in the south, in the cause of the education of youth.

MOTHER M. CLARE MCMAHON

On March 25, 1867, Sister Mary Basilia made her religious pro-

*From data and material supplied by the Sisters of Mercy, St. Bernard Academy, Nashville, Tenn., and from *The Golden Milestone.*

fession in the Cathedral. This was the first ceremony of the kind witnessed in the city, and the first such event of the new community. Two months later, Mother Mary Clare returned, temporarily, to the convent in Providence, and succeeded in securing nine postulants to augment the nucleus of the Tennessee community. On August 28th, the impressive ceremony of the conferring of the religious habit was held in the Cathedral at Nashville, and the nine new Sisters of Mercy soon afterward began their active participation in the life and works of the community.

In December, 1868, the residence of ex-Governor Brown, where Andrew Johnson lived in his youth, was purchased by Bishop Feehan as a home for the sisters, and there was opened there an academy for young ladies, from which many of the most talented and fairest women of the south have been graduated.

ST. BERNARD CONVENT, NASHVILLE, TENNESSEE

The first mission undertaking of the community was ventured in 1869, when sisters were sent to Memphis, Tennessee, to open St. Patrick's School, but owing to the scarcity of sisters, and the growing needs of Nashville, they were recalled in 1871.

In the summer of 1873 the cholera broke out; the Sisters of Mercy at once offered themselves as nurses, and for five weeks were out night and day attending the afflicted. The scenes the sisters witnessed were appalling—sometimes as many as three dead at a time, in one family, and others dying. Much courtesy was shown the sisters by the city officials, in appreciation of their work; carriages were placed at their disposal and supplies furnished for the needy sick whom they attended.

Ten years later, the community at St. Bernard's sent forth its first band of sisters for a new foundation. On the transfer of Bishop Feehan to Chicago, where he was appointed first archbishop, he requested of the foundation in Tennessee, a new colony of Sisters of Mercy for Chicago, and asked that his own sister, Mother Mary Catherine Feehan, might be of the group chosen.

On November 1, 1891, the Silver Jubilee of St. Bernard's was celebrated, with the bishop of the diocese, the Right Rev. Joseph Rademacher, D.D., pontificating—as, in another twenty-five years, did his successor, the Right Rev. Thomas S. Byrne, D.D., on the occasion of the "Golden Milestone" of the Sisters of Mercy in Nashville, Tennessee, who in 1905 had removed to a newly erected Motherhouse on Hillsboro Road. There, crowning one of the beautiful hills that encircle Nashville, its location is superb, not only for the convent, but for the academy connected with it, which in 1914 was affiliated with the Catholic University of America.

In the course of the years, the Tennessee community has extended its teaching activities in schools throughout the city of Nashville, and to parishes in Knoxville, Memphis, and other cities of the diocese.

MOTHER XAVIER YOUNG
Several times Superior of the Sisters of Mercy, Nashville, Tennessee

In 1928, with the approbation of the Right Rev. Alphonse J. Smith, D.D., Bishop of Nashville, the community proceeded with plans for the erection of St. Mary's Hospital at Knoxville, Tennessee. In their interest for the success of the project for the opening of the needed institution by the sisters, the citizens of Knoxville, both Catholics and Protestants, responded generously, and subscribed to the three hundred thousand dollar building fund, for the erection of the hospital on an advantageous site in Oak Hill, which was the gift of Mr. Dan DeWine, and his daughter, Mrs. L. W. Harris.

An event of recent importance to the community was the acquisition, through the inheritance of one of the sisters—whose desire it is that the property be used for community purposes—of the stately and expansive Valley View Farm, of eleven hundred acres, from the estate of her father, the late George W. Callahan of Nashville.

Motherhouse and Novitiate, St. Bernard Convent, Hillsboro Road, Nashville, Tennessee. (Diocese of Nashville.)

DAVENPORT, IOWA*

1867

Though two mission schools had previously been established in Iowa—in De Witt in 1867, and Independence in 1869, by Sisters of Mercy from Chicago, Iowa was without an actual foundation of the Order until 1869, when a Motherhouse and novitiate were established in Davenport, with Mother M. Borromeo Johnson serving as first Superior. Mother M. Borromeo was later succeeded as Superior by Mother M. Baptist Martin.

In 1881 the vast diocese of Dubuque, which then included the state of Iowa, was divided, and the diocese of Davenport was created. The next year, the Right Rev. John McMullen, D.D., former vicar-general in Chicago, was installed as first bishop of the new diocese. Upon Bishop McMullen's request to the Most Rev. John Hennessy, D.D., then bishop of Dubuque, Mother M. Frances Monholland—whom he had known in Chicago during her term as fifth Superior of the Mercy community there—was granted a transfer to Davenport from the mission in Independence, which she had successfully established in 1869, and which remained in the Dubuque diocese, later becoming a Motherhouse, which it continued until the community amalgamated with that in Dubuque.

Though protesting her age as excusing her from executive responsibility, Mother Frances displayed in the new diocese the same unflagging energy that had characterized her in every capacity, and in the annals of the Sisters of Mercy in the west, her name must ever be conspicuous among the revered of pioneer days.

To the zeal and industry of the early superiors, and their co-laborers in the community, is due Mercy Hospital and many of the institutions of the Sisters of Mercy in the diocese. The community, numbering approximately one hundred members, engaged in educational, hospital and charitable work, has extended its labors beyond

---

*From data and material supplied by the Sisters of Mercy, St. Joseph's Convent of Mercy, Davenport, Iowa, and from *Leaves from the Annals of the Sisters of Mercy.* (Vol. IV.)

the diocese of Davenport, and maintains missions and institutions also in the archdiocese of Dubuque and in the diocese of Sioux City.

Motherhouse and Novitiate, St. Joseph's Convent of Mercy, Davenport, Iowa.   (Diocese of Davenport.)

NEW ORLEANS, LOUISIANA*

1869

For some years efforts had been made to secure a foundation of the Sisters of Mercy for New Orleans, but fruitlessly, despite appeals to various communities, even in Ireland, the fear of yellow fever fatally attacking the un-acclimated, and the urgent need of sisters, equally as pressing in other localities, being one of the deterrents of a foundation in the Crescent City.

At last the Sisters of Mercy in St. Louis, after consultation with their ecclesiastical superior, the Most Rev. Peter Richard Kenrick, D.D., who had recently visited New Orleans, decided in favor of the southern foundation, and suitable sisters were chosen from the number volunteering for the new mission.

On March 19, 1869, a small band of Sisters of Mercy, with Mother M. Ignatius as Superior, left St. Louis on the "Mollie Able." The first stop scheduled on the sail down the Mississippi was at Cairo. As the steamer was to stay there all day, the sisters went ashore and visited the church, Loretto Convent, and the hospital conducted by the Sisters of the Holy Cross, where they had dinner. On their return to the steamer, Sister Augusta—who later became Superior General of her Order—accompanied them and solicitously remained with them until the Captain gave the order to start.

Memphis and Vicksburg were other stops; in the latter city the voyagers were received by the Sisters of Mercy there, and the day, Good Friday, was appropriately spent together. On Easter Sunday the "Mollie Able" reached New Orleans, and the ten-day river trip was ended.

The Sisters of Mercy were joyously welcomed, and escorted to the convent home prepared for them at the corner of Magazine and Jackson Avenues, and for several days were the recipients of courtesy calls of welcome from both laity and clergy, including the archbishop, the Most Rev. J. M. Odin, D.D., then in ill health, and the Redemp-

*From data supplied by the Sisters of Mercy, New Orleans, La., and from *Leaves from the Annals of the Sisters of Mercy* (Vol. III).

torist Fathers, who had been foremost in endeavors to obtain the foundation for the city.

Without delay the sisters began their labors in the new field. Visiting the sick and preparing them for the sacraments was the first work of mercy engaged in, but before they had been a month in Louisiana their work extended to schools, public institutions, and a House of Mercy, though the community numbered only six. In September their number was augmented by two sisters from New York and one from St. Louis, and later by two postulants from New York and candidates from the surrounding parishes.

Little more than a year had passed when the dreaded yellow fever claimed two of the community for its victims. The youngest of their number, Sister Benedicta Shields, was the first taken, and the second was Sister M. Xavier McDermott, whom the sisters had named "the saint of the band."

Before the lapse of a decade of years, and while the community had become actively engaged in teaching and works of mercy, the sisters were plunged into the horrors of the "epidemic of '78," and spent their days and nights among the stricken. Cavalcades of death turned the corners from all directions, and a pall lay over the Crescent City.

In the years that have followed, the Sisters of Mercy in New Orleans, continuing their labors, have established many branch houses and other foundations.

On request of the Jesuit Fathers, in January, 1883, a community was sent from New Orleans to British Honduras, and established there, in Belize, the first convent of the Order of Mercy in the tropics.

At the New Orleans Mercy Convent, Sister M. Teresa Austin Carroll, active in the establishment of many institutions, compiled the four volumes of *Leaves from the Annals of the Sisters of Mercy,* the invaluable and interesting history of the foundation of the Order up to the year 1895.

Notable among institutions in New Orleans is the Leonce Soniat Memorial Mercy Hospital and Training School for Nurses, established by the Sisters of Mercy and conducted by the community, of which the present officers are Mother M. Kilian, Superior; Mother M. Borgia, Assistant; Mother M. Benedicta, Bursar, and Mother M. Patricia, Mistress of Novices.

Motherhouse and Novitiate, Convent of Mercy, 1017 St. Andrew Street, New Orleans, Louisiana. (Archdiocese of New Orleans.)

HARRISBURG, PENNSYLVANIA*

1869

In 1869, the year following the establishment of the diocese of Harrisburg, the Sisters of Mercy in Chicago, then under the superior-ship of Mother M. Scholastica Drum, sent a community of sisters to found a house in the episcopal city of the new Pennsylvania diocese.

In addition to the Motherhouse in Harrisburg the sisters have established Mercy Home for Working Girls, and the Sylvan Heights Home, for orphan girls.

The Catholic High School, Cathedral School, and other schools in the city of Harrisburg are conducted by the Sisters of Mercy of this community, which numbers approximately one hundred and fifteen members, under the ecclesiastical jurisdiction of the Right Rev. Philip R. McDevitt, D.D., Bishop of Harrisburg.

> *Motherhouse and Novitiate,* St. Genevieve's Convent of Mercy, Fifth and Maclay Streets, Harrisburg, Pennsylvania. (Diocese of Harrisburg.)

LOUISVILLE, KENTUCKY†

1870

In the year 1870, Mother M. Ignatius Walker, Superior of the Sisters of Mercy in St. Louis, established a foundation of the Con-gregation in Louisville, Kentucky, where the new community at once engaged in parochial school work.

As the community increased in numbers, the sisters extended their labors to the opening of schools beyond Louisville, in various missions throughout the diocese.

In addition to their educational work, the Sisters of Mercy in Kentucky also conduct the Visitation Home for Working Girls, and the Sacred Heart Home, both in Louisville, where, in connection with the Motherhouse, the Academy of Our Lady of Mercy has been established.

> *Motherhouse and Novitiate,* St. Catherine's Convent, 1174 East Broadway, Louisville, Kentucky. (Diocese of Louisville.)

*From *Leaves from the Annals of the Sisters of Mercy* and from the Official Catholic Year Book, 1928.

†From data supplied by the Sisters of Mercy, St. Catherine's Convent, Louisville, Ky.

TITUSVILLE, PENNSYLVANIA*

1870

In 1870 the Right Rev. Tobias Mullen, D.D., Bishop of Erie, applied to the Sisters of Mercy of Pittsburgh for a foundation community for Titusville, Pennsylvania, in his diocese.

Complying with this request, Mother Evangelist Kinsella herself accompanied the seven sisters forming the community, who with Mother M. Nolasco Kratzer as Superior, reached Titusville on September 24th, the feast of Our Lady of Mercy.

MERCYHURST, GLENWOOD HILLS, ERIE, PENNSYLVANIA

During the fifty-nine years of its existence, the Titusville community has labored principally in the parochial schools of the diocese, where in addition to St. Titus' and St. Walburga's, and St. Joseph's Academy, in Titusville, many branch houses and institutions have been established and are maintained, among which are DuBois Hospital, DuBois, Pennsylvania, and Our Lady of Peace House, a home for business girls, in Erie, Pennsylvania.

In 1921 the community, with the consent of the Right Rev. John Mark Gannon, D.D., Bishop of Erie, arranged to transfer its headquarters from Titusville to Erie. A site of seventy-five acres was purchased in South Erie, on the highest point of Glenwood Hills, and on September 8, 1924, ground was broken for the modern and well-

*From data and material supplied by the Sisters of Mercy, Mercyhurst College, Glenwood Hills, Erie, Pa.

equipped building which was then erected, and on its completion in 1926 Mercyhurst College and Seminary, an outgrowth of St. Joseph's Academy in Titusville, was opened for the reception of resident and non-resident students.

The Titusville community of the Sisters of Mercy in the diocese of Erie, numbering approximately one hundred and seventy-five sisters, is under the superiorship, at present, of Mother M. Borgia.

Motherhouse, Mercyhurst, Glenwood Hills, Erie, Pennsylvania.
Novitiate, St. Joseph's Convent, 512 West Main Street, Titusville, Pennsylvania. (Diocese of Erie.)

JANESVILLE, WISCONSIN*

1870

Though for six years Sisters of Mercy had been teaching in a temporary school of St. Patrick's Church at Janesville, Wisconsin, it was not until 1870 that, under the superiorship of Mother M. Francis Jackson, the Motherhouse of the community was established there, in the Convent of Mercy which was built through the efforts of the Rev. James M. Doyle, pastor of St. Patrick's Church.

Prominent among the Sisters of Mercy who labored long and zealously in the community at Janesville was Sister Mary Joseph, a native of Ireland, who had come to America as a postulant, filled with the desire of doing foreign mission work. For more than fifty years Sister Mary Joseph participated in the activities of the community, which has devoted itself principally to the work of education, through the many parochial schools in the archdiocese of Milwaukee and in missions in the dioceses of La Crosse and Peoria.

In 1911, the community engaged in its first hospital work, with the opening, in Janesville, of Mercy Hospital, which, with its training school for nurses, ranks among the foremost prominent institutions of southern Wisconsin.

Mother M. Alphonsus is Superior of the Sisters of Mercy in Janesville, and is assisted in the administration of the affairs of the community by Mother M. Cecilia as Mother Assistant, Sister M. de Sales, as Bursar, and Sister M. Francis, as Mistress of Novices.

Motherhouse and Novitiate, St. Joseph's Convent of Mercy, 505 Holmes Street, Janesville, Wisconsin. (Archdiocese of Milwaukee.)

*From data and material supplied by the Sisters of Mercy, St. Joseph's Convent of Mercy, Janesville, Wis.

BURLINGTON, VERMONT*
1872

Co-operating with the Right Rev. Louis De Goesbriand, D.D., Bishop of Burlington, in his efforts to procure religious for educational and charitable work in his diocese—which included the entire state of Vermont—Mother M. Xavier Warde, in 1872, responded to an appeal for sisters to teach in the parochial school in the Vermont village of St. Johnsbury.

Mother Warde, Superior of the community of Sisters of Mercy in Manchester, had not forgotten an occasion in 1846, when, traveling from the east on her way to the Chicago Convent of Mercy, she became acquainted with Bishop De Goesbriand, then vicar-general of the diocese of Cleveland, who assisted her in many ways.

Two years after the sisters had begun their mission in St. Johnsbury, the bishop requested their transfer to Burlington, and placed them in charge of the Cathedral school there.

Forming the community which on September 10, 1874, began its labors in the episcopal city of Burlington, were Mother M. Stanislaus O'Malley, Superior, and Sisters M. Pauline Whalen, M. Ita Murphy and M. Joachim Higgins, a novice. The following year, Sisters M. Magdalen Yorke and M. Clare McManus, both novices, came from Manchester, and all, together, are looked upon as the pioneer members of the community of Sisters of Mercy of the diocese of Burlington.

MOTHER M. STANISLAUS O'MALLEY

The Burlington community's first ceremony of profession took place on Whitsunday, July 4, 1876, in the Cathedral of the Immaculate Conception, when Sister M. Clare McManus, Sister M. Magdalen Yorke and Sister M. Joachim Higgins made their perpetual vows

*From data and material supplied by the Sisters of Mercy, Mt. St. Mary, Burlington, Vt.

24

during the mass, at which Bishop De Goesbriand pontificated. Mother Warde came from Manchester for this occasion. On the following day the Burlington foundation, which, up to that time, had been a branch house from Manchester—then in the diocese of Portland— was formally separated from the Motherhouse there, and became an independent foundation, with the Motherhouse in Burlington, of which Mother Mary Stanislaus was canonically appointed first Superior. The novitiate was established in 1877.

In 1878, the sisters opened a boarding school in connection with the academic day school at their convent on St. Paul Street, in Bur, lington. As the boarding school enrollment grew, and the commu, nity increased, a new location was sought. In 1882 Mother Stanislaus

MT. ST. MARY CONVENT, BURLINGTON, VERMONT

purchased property which was later sold, for the opening of Clarke Street. Mother Stanislaus applied the money realized from this sale to the purchase of a thirty-acre tract on Mansfield Avenue—now, as Mt. St. Mary, the center of the activities of the community.

St. Michael's Convent, established at Montpelier, Vermont, in 1899, was the first mission house of the community; others followed, in Barre and at White River Junction.

In 1914 the sisters opened the Sancta Maria, a home for aged women, which in time gave place to St. Joseph's Villa, on Colchester Street in Burlington, where the community conducts a home for the aged and a home for working girls.

In 1925, under the auspices of the Right Rev. Joseph J. Rice, D.D., Bishop of Burlington, Trinity College of Burlington, Vermont, a college for women, was opened at Mt. St. Mary, in connection with Mt. St. Mary Academy and Boarding School.

The Sisters of Mercy of the diocese of Burlington, numbering in their community approximately one hundred and twenty members, are at present under the superiorship of Mother Mary Alphonsus.

Motherhouse and Novitiate, Mt. St. Mary, Mansfield Avenue, Burlington, Vermont. (Diocese of Burlington.)

GABRIELS, NEW YORK*
1872

In 1872, soon after the establishment in northern New York of the diocese of Ogdensburg, and his installation as first bishop, the Right Rev. Edgar P. Wadhams, D.D., former vicar general of Albany, interested himself in the educational needs of the new see, and invited to the diocese, among other religious communities, the Sisters of Mercy.

Upon the earnest solicitation of Bishop Wadhams, to the community at Rochester, Mother M. Baptist Coleman and three companion Sisters of Mercy, from there, opened a school at Malone, New York, and thus in that year began the activities of the Congregation of the Sisters of Mercy in the diocese of Ogdensburg, in the Adirondack Mountains.

The rigorous climate and unsettled conditions of the region were severe trials to the pioneer community, and ill-health necessitated the return to Rochester of Mother M. Baptist and her companions. Three postulants, at the instance of Bishop Wadhams, remained as teachers, while negotiations were pending for the coming of other sisters. Mother Mary Francis McGarr and Mother Mary Stanislaus Jerome, of the Mercy community in Buffalo, volunteered their aid to the bishop, and the community at Malone was re-established.

1878 was a year of heroic struggles for the little community, as it encountered financial disaster and innumerable discouragements, but a generous gift of one thousand dollars built a convent home for them on the banks of the St. Regis, and the three postulants to the community received the habit, Anne Kiernan becoming, in religion, Sister Mary of Perpetual Help, Anna Scanlon, Sister Mary of the

---

*From data and material supplied by the Sisters of Mercy, Sanatorium Gabriels, Gabriels, N. Y., and from *Forest Leaves,* a quarterly magazine published by the Sisters of Mercy, Gabriels, N. Y.

Sacred Heart, and Margaret McCue, Sister Mary of Mercy. From this time the now stabilized community increased in membership, and extended its labors to parochial schools in other parts of the diocese. Where it was impossible for the community to respond to the invitation to open schools, sisters were sent during the summer vacations to instruct the children of these parishes.

MOTHER M. STANISLAUS McGARR
Died April 14, 1906
Superior for many terms of the Sisters
of Mercy of the diocese of
Ogdensburg

In 1895, in addition to the school which the sisters had established at Watertown, the community, with the opening of a hospital, inaugurated the type of work for which it has become especially noted. This hospital —formerly known as St. Joachim's—was replaced in October, 1926, by Mercy Hospital, one of the best equipped hospitals in northern New York.

The year 1895 also marked another event of significance in the annals of the community. The Right Rev. Henry Gabriels, D.D., who had succeeded to the Adirondack diocese, suggested to Mother Mary of Perpetual Help the building of a sanatorium for tuberculosis patients. From that recommendation Sanatorium Gabriels evolved.

Through the generosity of Dr. Seward Webb and Mr. Paul Smith, one hundred acres of land were secured; to this six hundred acres were added from the state, and there, in the heart of the Adirondacks, on July 26, 1897, Sanatorium Gabriels was opened by the Sisters of Mercy of the diocese of Ogdensburg.

Built on an undulating plain, beginning with a broad park and rising gradually to a beautiful hill, "Sunrise Mount," eleven miles from Saranac Lake, and surrounded by the mountains, this institution—which, in 1900, was awarded a medal by the Paris Exposition, for the perfection of its many details of construction—is an immortal work of Mother McAuley's daughters, who thus apply and effi-

ciently exercise the works of the Order of Mercy in their care of
tuberculosis sufferers.

Conceived and adhered to through many years, by the indefatigable Mother Mary, the plan of the institution, which provides for
ten hospital buildings, an infirmary, an administrative building, a

MT. MERCY CONVENT-IN-THE-ADIRONDACKS, GABRIELS, N. Y.

chapel, and a resident physician's home, is now being developed
by Mother M. Patricia Craven, under whose able administration
as Superior the work of the sanatorium has made remarkable
progress.

In July, 1926, impressive ceremonies presided over by the Right
Rev. Joseph H. Conroy, D.D., Bishop of Ogdensburg, marked the
laying of the corner-stone of the first unit of the Knights of Columbus
buildings at Gabriels, in the Adirondacks—the New York State
Council, through its Hospital Association, having undertaken this
work in co-operation with the Sisters of Mercy in their labors in
behalf of the afflicted.

The community has further extended its hospital work in the
diocese by the opening of St. Mary's of the Lake Hospital, at Saranac
Lake, and Mercy General Hospital, at Tupper Lake.

With the activities of the community centering at Gabriels, the
Motherhouse, maintained originally at Malone, has been transferred to Gabriels, while the novitiate has been established in
Plattsburg, where the community is engaged in grade and high school
work.

In the community of the Sisters of Mercy of the diocese of
Ogdensburg—of now approximately one hundred and fifty sisters—
"Mother Mercy," who, as Sister Mary of Mercy McCue, was one

of the first three members, continues active in the affairs of the community of which she is the pioneer religious.

> *Motherhouse,* St. Margaret's Convent, Gabriels, New York.
> *Novitiate,* Loretto Novitiate of the Sisters of Mercy, Plattsburg, New York. (Diocese of Ogdensburg.)

NORTH PLAINFIELD, NEW JERSEY*

1873

Among the religious communities of women introduced into New Jersey early in the episcopacy of the Right Rev. Michael Augustine Corrigan, D.D., as bishop of Newark—before his elevation to the archbishopric of New York—was that of the Sisters of Mercy, established at Bordentown in 1873.

In compliance with a request for sisters, made by Bishop Corrigan to Mother Xavier Warde, of the Sisters of Mercy in Manchester, New Hampshire, a community of six sisters was sent to establish a foundation at Bordentown, New Jersey. Among those composing the new community was Mother Mary Raymund, who occupied successively all the positions of trust in the community, and was, at the time of her death, on November 21, 1928, Superior of St. Mary's Academy at the Motherhouse.

Prior to the establishment of the diocese of Trenton in 1881, the entire state of New Jersey was included in the territory of the diocese of Newark. In the diocesan division of the state, the New Jersey community of the Sisters of Mercy was in the locality which became part of the diocese of Trenton.

This community, of approximately three hundred members, under the present ecclesiastical jurisdiction of the Right Rev. John J. McMahon, D.D., Bishop of Trenton, maintains its Motherhouse at North Plainfield, New Jersey, transferred there from the original location at Bordentown.

Connected with the Motherhouse is St. Mary's Academy, a day and boarding school. Mt. St. Mary's College, established at the Motherhouse in 1908, for the higher education of women, has been transferred to Lakewood, New Jersey, to the more recently acquired property secured from the estate of George M. Gould, and is now known as Georgian Court College.

> *Motherhouse and Novitiate,* Mt. St. Mary's Convent, North Plainfield, New Jersey. (Diocese of Trenton.)

---

*From data supplied by the Sisters of Mercy, Mt. Mercy, North Plainfield, N. J., and from the Catholic News of New York.

GRAND RAPIDS, MICHIGAN*

1873

September 24, 1873, the feast of Our Lady of Mercy and the patronal feast of the Congregation of the Sisters of Mercy, witnessed the coming to Michigan, from the Mercy foundation in Brooklyn, New York, of a little band of five Sisters of Mercy, and today the community of which they were the nucleus numbers over three hundred members, actively engaged in carrying on the works of the Order of Mother McAuley's founding, in the diocese of Grand Rapids.

The first convent and Motherhouse of the Sisters of Mercy in Michigan was established at Grand Rapids, at the request of the Rev. P. J. McManus, pastor of St. Andrew's Church, with the permission and the approbation of the Right Rev. Caspar Henry Borgess, D.D., Bishop of Detroit, in which diocese Grand Rapids was then included.

With the opening of St. Andrew's School, a week after their arrival, the Sisters of Mercy engaged in their first educational labors in the new field. In connection with the school, they organized sodalities, established a circulating library, gave lessons in vocal and instrumental music, formed evening and Saturday classes for instruction in needle-work,

MT. MERCY CONVENT, GRAND RAPIDS, MICHIGAN

Irish-point lace and wax flower making. The sisters also visited the sick and poor daily, after school hours, and on Saturdays and Sundays.

On June 9, 1875, the first religious profession in the community took place, when Sister M. Agnes Boland, who had come from

*From data and material supplied by the Sisters of Mercy, Mt. Mercy, Grand Rapids, Mich.

Brooklyn with the original band of sisters, as a novice, pronounced her vows. On the same day two postulants received the white veil of novices.

In October, 1878, Mother M. Joseph Lynch, the foundress Superior of the community, with nine sisters, keenly alive to the needs, spiritual and temporal, of the workers in the lumber camps of Michigan, left Grand Rapids to establish a hospital in Big Rapids, in that district. Mother M. Joseph was eminently fitted to undertake this work, having nursed in the Crimean War and also in the cholera hospital.

In November, 1879, Mercy Hospital was opened in Big Rapids, the sisters, in the interval after their arrival there, during its construction, having engaged in school work. The Motherhouse was then transferred to Big Rapids, and for thirty-six years the Sisters of Mercy of the diocese of Detroit maintained their headquarters there.

On July 14, 1914, the Motherhouse and novitiate were permanently located at Mt. Mercy, a fifty-three-acre estate on Bridge Street, in Grand Rapids, which in 1882 had become the site of the see of the newly established diocese of Grand Rapids, with St. Andrew's Church, where the Sisters of Mercy had begun their parochial school work, as the Cathedral.

The first ceremony of profession and reception of novices and postulants at Mt. Mercy occurred on August 14th, following the installation of the community in the new Motherhouse. This initial ceremony was presided over by the venerable bishop, the Right Rev. Henry Joseph Richter, D.D., first bishop of the diocese, who for thirty-one years had guided and encouraged the community in all its zealous endeavors.

On July 1, 1917, with auspicious ceremony, the Right Rev. Michael James Gallagher, D.D., who, on the death of Bishop Richter, in 1916, had succeeded to the diocese of Grand Rapids, laid the corner-stone of the new fire-proof structure, the first unit of the new Motherhouse buildings at Mt. Mercy.

Since the opening of Mercy Hospital in Big Rapids, later relinquished owing to changing conditions and the transfer of the community to Grand Rapids, the Sisters of Mercy of the diocese of Grand Rapids have been most active in this work, as evidenced by the hospitals they have established and operate in Grand Rapids, Bay City, Cadillac, Grayling and Muskegon.

On Christmas Day, 1889, the gift of the deed for Mercy Hospital Sanitarium, in Manistee, the "Salt City," was presented the Sisters of Mercy by the wealthy lumberman, Mr. John Canfield, who had purchased the ground, on the crest of a hill, between Lake Michigan and Lake Manistee, and erected the building, and the Messrs. E. G. Filer and Sons, who had supplied the entire equipment for the institution. In 1901 the salt and mineral baths were added to the hospital, which with the passing of the saw mills and lumbering camps, was transformed into the sanitarium it is today, under the efficient management of the Sisters of Mercy.

The parent-house of the Sisters of Mercy in the Grand Rapids diocese has sent out three foundations, to Los Angeles, California, in 1888; Toledo, Ohio, in 1912; and Jackson, Michigan, in 1915, for the diocese of Detroit. The foundation established in 1896 in Portland, Oregon, may also be considered, although indirectly so, as a foundation of the Grand Rapids community.

In May, 1924, Mt. Mercy Academy, conducted by the community, now under the superiorship of Mother Mary Joseph Miller, was incorporated as Mt. Mercy College and Academy, and is one of the foremost of its educational institutions in the diocese of Grand Rapids.

Motherhouse and Novitiate, Mt. Mercy Convent, 1425 Bridge Street, Grand Rapids, Michigan. (Diocese of Grand Rapids.)

IOWA CITY, IOWA*
1873

Among the earliest institutions established in Iowa by the Sisters of Mercy of Davenport was Mercy Hospital, in Iowa City, in the year 1873.

The convent established at the hospital has since become a Mother-house for the community, which is recognized as an independent foundation, devoted to hospital work in the diocese of Davenport.

St. Joseph's Sanitarium, for the insane and weak minded, is also maintained in Iowa City by the community.

Motherhouse and Novitiate, St. Francis Xavier Convent, 505 Bloomington Street, Iowa City, Iowa. (Diocese of Davenport.)

DALLAS, PENNSYLVANIA†
1875

Through the interest of the Rev. Denis O'Hearn, pastor of St. Mary's parish in Wilkes-Barre, Pennsylvania, and in response

*From the annals of the Sisters of Mercy.
†From data supplied by the Sisters of Mercy, College Misericordia, Dallas, Pa., and from *Leaves from the Annals of the Sisters of Mercy* (Vol. IV).

to an application from the Right Rev. William O'Hara, D.D., Bishop of Scranton, a foundation community of Sisters of Mercy, sent from Mercy Convent in Pittsburgh, arrived in Wilkes-Barre on September 8, 1875.

Serving as Superior of the community which then began its labors in the diocese of Scranton was Mother Mary de Chantal Donnelly. On October 11th the sisters opened their first school in Wilkes-Barre with an attendance of five hundred children.

The first extension of the community was the opening of a convent in Towanda; the second of the many missions it now conducts in the diocese was at Plymouth, a mining town in the near vicinity of Wilkes-Barre.

In September, 1924, the center of the activities of the Wilkes-Barre community was transferred to Dallas, a suburb ten miles distant from Wilkes-Barre. College Misericordia, empowered by the state of Pennsylvania to confer degrees, was then opened at this new location, where in connection with the college Our Lady of Mercy High School is also conducted by the sisters.

The community, now numbering approximately two hundred and ninety members, under the ecclesiastical jurisdiction of the Right Rev. Thomas C. O'Reilly, D.D., Bishop of Scranton, and the superiorship of Mother M. Ricarda Caran, with Mother M. Catharine McGann as Assistant; Mother M. Mercedes McHale, Bursar; and Mother M. Cecilia Huston, Mistress of Novices, is active in educational, hospital and charitable work in not only the diocese of Scranton but also in the archdiocese of Philadelphia and the dioceses of Brooklyn, Harrisburg and Sioux City.

Motherhouse and Novitiate, Villa St. Teresa, Dallas, Pennsylvania. (Diocese of Scranton.)

MOBILE, ALABAMA*

1877

The foundation of the Sisters of Mercy in Mobile, Alabama, was made in 1877 by sisters from the Mercy Convent, New Orleans.

Prudently and from experience, having twice suffered disappointment in establishments he had considered permanent, the Right Rev. John Quinlan, D.D., Bishop of Mobile, insisted that sisters should visit the prospective field, before taking final steps for the foundation he desired.

*From *Leaves from the Annals of the Sisters of Mercy* (Vol. III).

In September, 1877, following a preliminary visit therefore by two sisters, in compliance with the bishop's wishes, seven sisters of Mercy began their labors in the diocese of Mobile, which comprises the state of Alabama and counties of northwestern Florida.

In August, 1884, following Bishop Quinlan's death in 1883, and under his successor, the Right Rev. Dominic Manucy, D.D., from the Mercy Convent in New Orleans another group of seven sisters was sent to the diocese of Mobile, where, now under the jurisdiction of the Right Rev. Thomas J. Toolen, D.D., the community is active in educational and charitable work.

> *Motherhouse and Novitiate, Convent of Mercy,* 853 St. Francis Street, Mobile, Alabama. (Diocese of Mobile.)

DUBUQUE, IOWA*
1879

Desirous of having a hospital conducted by the Sisters of Mercy in his episcopal city of Dubuque, the Most Rev. John Hennessy, D.D., then bishop of the diocese, solicited the community at the Motherhouse in Davenport for sisters for this purpose.

On January 13, 1879, Mother Mary Baptist Martin, accompanied by Sister M. Agatha Murphy and Sister M. Euphrasia Butler, arrived in Dubuque from Davenport. Completing the community necessary for the new mission were Sisters M. Angela Lawler, M. Gertrude Hardy and M. Veronica Buckley, who later joined them from Davenport.

A picturesque site at the top of Third Street Hill, commanding a splendid view for miles down the Mississippi, was chosen by Mother Baptist for the prospective hospital. Plans were made and work on the building was begun as soon as the season permitted.

During the period of waiting, the sisters cared for a few patients in their temporary habitation, and for some orphans who were to be transferred to an orphanage then under construction in the city.

St. Joseph's Mercy Hospital was ready for patients in the summer of 1880, and the pioneer community of Sisters of Mercy inaugurated, then, the first of its institutional work in what is now the archdiocese of Dubuque. A year later, Davenport was created a diocese, after which, with ecclesiastical authority so decreeing it, the community in Dubuque was recognized as an independent separate

*From data and material especially prepared by the Sisters of Mercy, Mt. St. Agnes, Dubuque, Iowa.

foundation from the Motherhouse in Davenport, and Mother Mary Agatha Murphy was appointed its first Superior.

The new community increased in members, and proportionately responded to calls in other localities in Iowa—after opening, in 1887, just outside the city limits of Dubuque, St. Joseph's Sanitarium, for patients suffering from curable mental ailments—establishing Mercy Hospital in Sioux City, in 1890, and Mercy Hospital in Clinton, in 1892.

MOTHER M. AGATHA MURPHY

Upon the death of Mother Mary Agatha in 1894, Mother Mary Agnes Hanley was chosen Mother Superior. For thirty years, thereafter, she held important offices in the community, and to her executive and administrative ability is due much of the progress of the Sisters of Mercy in Dubuque during those three decades of years, in the course of which a home for the aged was built in Dubuque, a training school for nurses was established at Mercy Hospital there, and hospitals were opened in Waverly, Webster City, Fort Dodge, Cresco and Mason City, Iowa, and in Ann Arbor and Dowagiac, Michigan. Mercy Hospital in Dubuque was also replaced by an entirely new structure, equipped with all modern facilities for increased efficiency in hospital work, and a new home, Mt. St. Agnes, overlooking two neighboring states across the historic Mississippi, was provided for the novitiate. During part of this time Mother Mary Pius Hogan was Mother Superior.

In 1921 Mother Mary Ursula Dunn was chosen fourth Mother Superior, and the work of administration and expansion was carried on zealously and successfully. In 1922 a nurses' home was erected; a convent Motherhouse connected with the hospital in Dubuque was built, and a hospital was opened in Detroit.

On March 16, 1922, for the better pursuance of the works of the Institute, the Holy See ratified the union of the community of the Sisters of Mercy of Independence, Iowa, established in 1869, with the community of Mercy of Dubuque.

Under the continued direction of Mother Mary Ursula, two hospitals were opened in Michigan in 1927, St. Joseph's in Pontiac,

MT. ST. AGNES, DUBUQUE, IOWA

and the Leila Y. Post Montgomery Hospital in Battle Creek. Six hundred and fifty thousand dollars was given to the Sisters of Mercy by Mrs. Leila Y. Post Montgomery for the purpose of building this hospital. She also gave twenty-five thousand dollars toward paying for the site. One hundred and fifty thousand dollars, left by Mr. Louis F. Weistein for a hospital, was used for a nurses' home.

The community, now numbering approximately two hundred members, with Mother Mary Daniel Gorman as Superior, is active chiefly in hospital labor, although also engaged in educational and benevolent work, in the dioceses of Davenport, Detroit and Sioux City, as well as the archdiocese of Dubuque.

Motherhouse, St. Joseph's Mercy Hospital, Dubuque, Iowa.

Novitiate, Mt. St. Agnes, Asbury Drive, Dubuque, Iowa. (Archdiocese of Dubuque.)

CRESSON, PENNSYLVANIA*

1879

The second branch house established beyond the city of Pitts-burgh by the Sisters of Mercy of Allegheny County, was at Loretto, in Cambria County, Pennsylvania, in 1848.

Mother Mary Catherine Wynne, who, as the daughter of Major Wynne of Pittsburgh, had been among the first Americans received into the community, was named local Superior of the new mission.

With the sisters sent with her, Mother Catherine labored untir-ingly among the mountain children of the little Catholic village which had been laid out in 1803 by the saintly missionary priest, Demetrius Gallitzin, the Russian prince and fervent convert. Eight years prior to the arrival of the Sisters of Mercy in the region, Loretto had mourned the death of this "Apostle of the Alle-ghenies, distinguished for faith, zeal and charity."

In 1853, in connection with the convent, the community opened Mt. Aloysius Academy, the buildings of which were completed in 1881.

In May, 1879, the Sisters of Mercy of Loretto were estab-lished as a separate community, under the authority of Mother M. de Sales Ihmsen and Mother M. Gertrude Cosgrove.

During the superiorship of Mother M. de Sales a site was purchased in Cresson for a new and more commodious academy building, which was opened in 1897, when "old Mt. Aloysius" was given up for a Children's Home.

MOTHER DE SALES IHMSEN

In 1901, Cambria County was one of the Pennsylvania counties included in the territory of the newly erected diocese of Altoona, and the community accordingly came under the ecclesiastical juris-

*From data and material supplied by the Sisters of Mercy, Mt. Aloysius Academy, Cresson, Pa.

diction of the ordinary of that diocese, at present the Right Rev. John Joseph McCort, D.D.

Besides Mt. Aloysius Academy for young ladies, the Cresson community, of approximately one hundred and fifty members, of which Mother M. Annunziata is now Superior, numbers among its missions Mercy Hospital in Johnstown, Pennsylvania, as well as schools there and in other cities of the dioceses of Altoona and Pittsburgh.

> *Motherhouse and Novitiate,* Convent of Mercy of Mt. Aloysius Academy, Cresson, Pennsylvania. (Diocese of Altoona.)

CEDAR RAPIDS, IOWA*
1879

In the year 1879 the community of Sisters of Mercy in Davenport, Iowa, established a branch house in Cedar Rapids, then, with Daven-

MT. MERCY CONVENT OF THE SACRED HEART, CEDAR RAPIDS, IOWA

port, included in the diocese of Dubuque, and under the jurisdiction of the Right Rev. John Hennessy, D.D., later first archbishop of Dubuque.

The community, of one hundred and eighty-five members, is engaged principally in educational and hospital work in the arch-diocese of Dubuque, and in the dioceses of Davenport, Helena and

*From material supplied by the Sisters of Mercy, Cedar Rapids, Iowa, and from the Official Catholic Year Book, 1928.

Sioux City. Connected with the Motherhouse is Mt. Mercy Junior College and Academy, a day and boarding school for girls.

> *Motherhouse and Novitiate,* Mt. Mercy Convent of the Sacred Heart, Elmhurst Drive, Cedar Rapids, Iowa. (Archdiocese of Dubuque.)

DENVER, COLORADO*

1882

Throughout the years of his life as a missionary priest, appointed vicar general of the diocese of Santa Fé in 1860, under the jurisdiction of the Right Rev. J. B. Lamy, and later for many years vicar apostolic of Colorado and Utah, before his appointment in 1887 as bishop of Denver, the Right Rev. Joseph P. Machebeuf, D.D., laboring in the interests of the Church in the region under his jurisdiction, made many efforts to secure the co-operation of religious communities, then successfully and helpfully establishing foundations through the western section of the United States.

In 1864 the Sisters of Loretto—who, from their distant Kentucky Motherhouse, had sent a band of brave Lorettines in 1852 to the vast southwest, where Bishop Lamy labored in the stupendous task of not only the evangelization but the civilization of the unlearned of the plains—heard the call of Bishop Machebeuf, and the annals of St. Mary's Academy, established that year in Denver, must tell of many hardships and struggles endured by that pioneer band in Colorado.

In 1873 the Sisters of Charity of Leavenworth heard the appeal from Colorado's apostolic missionary, and Denver's St. Joseph's Hospital was their heroic answer.

The year 1882 marks the beginnings of the works of the community of the Sisters of Mercy in Colorado, in what was formally recognized, five years later, as the diocese of Denver.

Through the friendship of the Right Rev. Patrick J. Ryan, D.D., then coadjutor bishop of St. Louis, later archbishop of Philadelphia, the work of the Congregation was extended to the vicariate. Bishop Ryan, with characteristic eloquence, had, in an address delivered to the Sisters of Mercy at the Mercy Convent in St. Louis, effectively presented a petition for sisters to aid the western mission.

The Sisters of Mercy in St. Louis heard the call, and volunteers at once formed a community which was offered to Bishop Machebeuf in Denver. Those who composed the new community were Sister Mary Michael Cummings, Sister M. Baptist Meyers, Sister M.

*From data and material supplied by the Sisters of Mercy, Mercy Hospital, Denver, Colo.

Ignatius de Hatre, Sister M. Euphrasia Hanker, and Miss Margaret Coleman, a postulant, in religion, Sister Mary Claver.

MOTHER M. BAPTIST MEYERS

On the feast of the Purification, 1882, Bishop Machebeuf sent the Superior of the St. Louis community full instructions for the sisters' journey, and a draft for the traveling expenses of the four professed sisters and postulant who arrived in Denver February 11, 1882. Soon after their arrival Bishop Machebeuf canonically appointed Mother Mary Baptist Meyers first Superior of the community of Sisters of Mercy in the vicariate apostolic of Denver.

For a time the Sisters of Mercy located in Conejos, where they were in charge of the County Hospital. On April 29th, they removed to Durango, where they at once engaged in the works of the Order, as they visited the poor and sick, organized Sunday-schools and soon opened St. Columba's parochial school and erected a spacious building for a convent, academy and boarding school.

A small building had been erected for the care of the sick, and such hospital service as could be provided was bestowed by the community, whose subsistence in the remote region depended largely on contributions collected at the mines, where the generous miners and their families looked for the visits of the sisters and their messages of God and religion.

In 1884 Bishop Machebeuf, who in the interval had officiated for the community at a double ceremony of profession and reception, assisted in the selection of the site for a new Mercy Hospital, which was erected, and with additions made as needed, has been continued, and is today the only general hospital in the San Juan Basin. Its school of nursing is an affiliated branch of Mercy Hospital in Denver.

A second school was opened in Durango in 1903. The Sisters of Mercy teach gratuitously in this school of the Sacred Heart Church, which is in charge of the Theatine Fathers, who are devoting their missionary labors to the Spanish-Americans and the Indians in the great Smelter district.

A recent development in the educational work of the sisters in Durango was in 1928, when a new modern school building and sisters' residence, replacing the old convent at St. Columba's, was blessed and auspiciously opened by the Right Rev. J. Henry Tihen, D.D., Bishop of Denver. In addition to these schools, and those in Denver conducted by the community, the sisters are also engaged in school work in San Luis and in Greeley.

In June, 1889, the metropolis of Denver was chosen for the future center of operations for the Sisters of Mercy in the diocese of Denver, and the Motherhouse of the community was transferred there from Durango. St. Catherine's Home for Working Girls was also established, and the Sisters of Mercy formed the teaching corps of St. Joseph's parochial school opened in September of that year, in Denver.

MERCY HOSPITAL, DENVER, COLORADO

In 1899 Mother Mary Baptist planned Mercy Hospital, the construction of which, in Denver, was nearly completed at the time of her death on August 29, 1901.

On November 21st, the new institution, at Sixteenth Avenue and Milwaukee Street, was formally opened, with impressive ceremonies presided over by the Right Rev. Nicholas C. Matz, D.D., then bishop of Denver. In 1910 a building was completed for a nurses' home in connection with the hospital. During the influenza epidemic of 1918, the entire capacity of Mercy Hospital was devoted to the service of the afflicted, and from 1919 to 1923, until the Fitzsimons Government Hospital could make full provision for the ex-service patients, the United States Public Health Service arranged with the sisters for hospitalization in Mercy Hospital, particularly for operative cases.

A Cardinal Protector was nominated for the Sisters of Mercy in Colorado, in 1915, in the person of Cardinal Diomede Falconio, who was succeeded to this appointment, upon his death in 1917, by Cardinal Donatus Sbarretti. In a Rescript of the Sacred Congregation, dated August 24, 1915, special faculties were granted to the bishop of Denver for the canonical erection of a new novitiate for the Sisters of Mercy. This house was established for the spiritual training and education of candidates for the religious life, and for the works of mercy engaged in by the community.

The community of the Sisters of Mercy in the diocese of Denver, numbering approximately one hundred members, is under the present superiorship of Mother Mary Evangelist Meyers, and her Council composed of Mothers Mary Philomene Fitzgerald, Mary Peter Foule and Mary Angela Dinan. Previous to the election to the office of Superior of Mother Mary Evangelist Meyers, in 1928, the successors to that office, following the death of the foundress Superior, Mother Mary Baptist Meyers, on August 29, 1901, had been Mother Mary Xavier Meyers, Mother Mary Alacoque Houle, Mother Mary Regis Regan, and Mother Mary Ignatius Orr.

> *Motherhouse,* Mercy Hospital Convent, 16th Avenue and Milwaukee Street, Denver, Colorado.
> *Novitiate,* Novitiate of Our Lady of Mercy, 1661 Milwaukee Street, Denver, Colorado. (Diocese of Denver.)

CHICAGO, ILLINOIS*

St. Patrick's

1883

On June 3, 1883, a second Motherhouse of the Sisters of Mercy was established in Chicago, when the community at St. Bernard Convent, in Nashville, Tennessee, sent its first foundation band to that metropolis.

---

*From the annals of the Sisters of Mercy in Chicago, Ill., and Nashville, Tenn.

Three years prior to this, Chicago's archbishopric had been cre-ated, and the Right Rev. Patrick A. Feehan of Nashville appointed its first archbishop.

Soon realizing the need of additional sisters in Chicago, Arch-bishop Feehan applied to the diocese of Nashville for a new founda-tion of Sisters of Mercy, and requested that among the sisters chosen for the new community would be his sister, Mother Mary Catherine Feehan, then serving as Superior of the community at St. Bernard's, in Nashville.

To accede to the request of the archbishop of Chicago, Mother Mary Catherine's resignation as Superior was accepted, and at a special election meeting, held at St. Bernard's, she was relieved of her duties in Nashville and appointed Superior of the foundation community which arrived in Chicago on June 3, 1883.

The new community, designated the West Side Community of the Sisters of Mercy—now numbering more than one hundred and fifty members—began its labors in St. Malachy's parish, and grew rapidly, extending its scope as needed, to the various works of mercy of the Order, and establishing many noted schools, the most recent being St. Catherine's High School, on North Central Avenue, erected in Chicago in 1925, and dedicated with impressive ceremony by His Eminence, George Cardinal Mundelein.

Motherhouse and Novitiate, St. Patrick's Academy, 2303 Park Avenue, Chicago, Illinois. (Archdiocese of Chicago.)

DEVILS LAKE, NORTH DAKOTA*

1883

In 1883, under the superiorship of Mother M. Genevieve Sheri-dan, a colonizing band of Sisters of Mercy from the Convent of Mercy in Omaha, Nebraska, established a foundation of the Con-gregation at Belcourt, North Dakota. At this time the entire state of North Dakota was included in the ecclesiastical territory of the diocese of St. Paul.

The community at once engaged in works of mercy and opened mission and parochial schools in the vicinity of Belcourt. After the establishment in 1889 of the diocese of Fargo, known originally as the diocese of Jamestown, the community, in 1903, under the juris-diction of the Right Rev. John Shanley, D.D., first bishop of the diocese, established at Devils Lake, Mercy Hospital.

*From data and material supplied by the Sisters of Mercy, Devils Lake, N. D.

In the winter of 1908, following a disastrous fire which destroyed the Motherhouse convent at Belcourt, Mother M. Genevieve and her Council, with the approbation of Bishop Shanley, transferred the

MERCY HOSPITAL AND CONVENT, DEVILS LAKE, NORTH DAKOTA

Motherhouse and novitiate to St. Mary's Academy which was at once built at Devils Lake.

In 1920 the hospital work of the community was extended to the diocese of Bismarck, where under the auspices of the Right Rev. Vincent Wehrle, O.S.B., D.D., Mercy Hospital was opened at Williston. In 1928, continuing their hospital labors in the diocese of Fargo, under the jurisdiction of the Right Rev. James O'Reilly, D.D., present incumbent of the see, the sisters opened Mercy Hospital at Valley City, North Dakota.

Those forming the present administrative Council of the community are Mother M. Michael Kelleher, Superior; Mother Catherine Doherty, Assistant Superior; Mother Patricia O'Gorman, Bursar, and Mother Cecilia Gallant, Mistress of Novices.

Motherhouse and Novitiate, Convent of St. Mary of the Lake, Seventh Street, Devils Lake, North Dakota. (Diocese of Fargo.)

OKLAHOMA CITY, OKLAHOMA*
1884

In the year 1884 the Right Rev. Isadore Robot, O.S.B., first prefect apostolic of the vicariate apostolic of Indian territory, appealed to the Right Rev. John Lancaster Spalding, D.D., Bishop of Peoria, for Sisters of Mercy who should establish their works in his vast field.

At that time Sisters of Mercy from Chicago were in the diocese

*From data and material supplied by the Sisters of Mercy, Mt. St. Mary's, Capitol Hill, Oklahoma City, Okla.

of Peoria, having established a branch house in Ottawa, Illinois, in 1859, which, with the erection of the diocese of Peoria in 1877, became the Motherhouse for the Sisters of Mercy in the new see. In addition to the Ottawa community, there were also in the diocese Sisters of Mercy from the community in Florida, who had become established at Lacon, Illinois, upon relinquishing, after the Civil War, the foundation which had been established at St. Augustine, also in 1859.

To the community at Lacon Bishop Spalding referred the request of the zealous Benedictine bishop. Soon afterward, five Sisters of Mercy, who were chosen from those volunteering for the proposed mission in the Indian territory, left their Peoria diocesan home, and when within seventy miles of their destination were met by the prefect

MT. ST. MARY'S CONVENT, OKLAHOMA CITY, OKLAHOMA

apostolic and an escort of Indians, who accompanied them over the trail to Sacred Heart Mission, in Oklahoma.

Experiencing, in the days which followed, their first thrills of missionary life, journeying in the "covered wagon," then known as the prairie schooner, and having forded the treacherous Canadian River, the little community of Sisters of Mercy arrived at Sacred

Heart Mission on July 12, 1884, and established the foundation of the Congregation of the Sisters of Mercy in the territory which was included in the diocese of Oklahoma, on its erection in 1905.

With the opening of a school in September, the Sisters of Mercy began their activities in the new field, where they kept apace with the development and prosperity of the region. St. Mary's, an industrial school opened by them at Sacred Heart Mission, received compensation from the Government from 1888 to 1900. On the withdrawal of Government aid, the Bureau of Catholic Indian Missions assumed responsibility for the maintenance of the Indian children at the school. At the same time, Mother Katharine Drexel inaugurated her contribution to the support of the school, and has continued this in behalf of the Indian children attending it, in excess of the quota allowed by the Mission Bureau.

In 1904 the Motherhouse and novitiate, which had been established at the mission, were transferred to Oklahoma City, where a spacious and well-equipped structure had been erected, and where, in connection with the convent, Mt. St. Mary's College and Academy has been opened as a day and boarding school, with the academic and collegiate courses taught by efficient sisters of the community.

In addition to these institutions, and their parochial, grade and high schools, and charitable work in the diocese of Oklahoma, the sisters have also established and maintain St. Agnes' Boarding and Industrial School for Indian Girls and small boys, at Ardmore, Oklahoma.

The community—whose present Superior, Mother M. Aloysius Lonergan, was, with her assistant, Mother M. Catherine Troy, a member of the pioneer missionary band—numbering approximately one hundred and ten sisters, confines its activities to the diocese of Oklahoma, now under the ecclesiastical jurisdiction of the Right Rev. Francis C. Kelley, D.D.

Motherhouse and Novitiate, Mt. St. Mary's Convent, Capitol Hill, Oklahoma City, Oklahoma. (Diocese of Oklahoma.)

MILWAUKEE, WISCONSIN*

1885

The community of the Sisters of Mercy of Milwaukee was founded indirectly from the Chicago foundation. Mother Mary Francis Jackson, who made her profession in the Chicago community of the Sisters of Mercy, was transferred to Davenport, from which

*From material supplied by the Sisters of Mercy, Convent of Our Lady of Mercy, Milwaukee, Wis.

community she made a Mercy foundation in Sterling, Illinois, in 1869. The following year, this foundation was transferred to Janes-ville, Wisconsin.

In 1885, upon the suggestion of the Most Rev. Michael Heiss, D.D., Archbishop of Milwaukee, sisters from the convent in Janes-ville established a house at Fond du Lac. Mother M. Aloysius served

CONVENT OF OUR LADY OF MERCY, MILWAUKEE, WISCONSIN

as Superior of this community, whose activities were principally in educational and charitable work in Milwaukee. Foremost among its institutions are two homes for working girls, St. Clara's and St. Catherine's, modern and imposing institutions.

In 1894, during the archiepiscopacy in Milwaukee of the Most Rev. F. X. Katzer, D.D., and the superiorship of Mother M. Evan-gelist Holcomb, the headquarters of the community were transferred from Fond du Lac to Milwaukee, where the sisters are now under the ecclesiastical jurisdiction of the Most Rev. Sebastian Messmer, D.D., with Mother M. Bernardine Clancy as Superior, and Sister M. Evangelist Holcomb, Assistant, Sister M. Xavier Massey, Bursar, and Sister M. Augustine Shelton, Mistress of Novices, constituting the Council.

> *Motherhouse and Novitiate,* Convent of Our Lady of Mercy, 666 24th Avenue, Milwaukee, Wisconsin. (Archdiocese of Mil-waukee.)

COUNCIL BLUFFS, IOWA*
1887

Ireland had sent another band of Sisters of Mercy and the Kinsale convent was again generous to the United States, and to Iowa, for the Rev. Bernard McMenamy, at the time pastor of St. Francis' Church, in Council Bluffs, solicited the community from Kinsale, temporarily with the Sisters of Mercy in Minnesota, to establish a foundation in Council Bluffs.

Accordingly, Mother M. Vincent McDermott and Mother M. Magdalene Bennett came to the city in 1887, and were welcomed to the diocese by the Right Rev. Henry Cosgrove, D.D., Bishop of Davenport, who had fully approved Father McMenamy's plan.

Soon after their arrival, the ground and building were purchased for St. Bernard's Convent, where the sisters at once opened a hospital, and thus began the works of the Order of Mercy in Council Bluffs, then in the diocese of Davenport.

As needed, additions were made to the convent and hospital building, until, with the erection of Mercy Hospital, the convent remained as St. Bernard's Sanitarium. St. Mary's Home, a residence home for working girls, and Our Lady of Victory Preparatory High School were early institutions established by the community, steadily increasing in number.

In 1906, St. Catherine's Hall for working girls, with a capacity of one hundred, was erected in Des Moines, and St. Joseph's Mercy Hospital, in Centerville, was opened in 1910.

In 1911 the diocese of Des Moines was erected, with Council Bluffs included in its territory, and under the jurisdiction of the Right Rev. Austin Dowling, D.D., appointed first bishop of the new see, the Sisters of Mercy progressively and successfully continued their labors. In 1919 Bishop Dowling was appointed to the archbishopric of St. Paul, and under the present incumbent, the Right Rev. Thomas W. Drumm, D.D., the Sisters of Mercy have made rapid expansion, extending their work in the diocese of Des Moines, and to the diocese of Davenport, establishing thoroughly modern hospitals, homes, and catechetical classes, and, with the growth of the community, which now numbers one hundred members, undertaking more educational work.

Motherhouse, St. Bernard's Convent, Council Bluffs, Iowa.
Novitiate, Mt. Loretto Place, Council Bluffs, Iowa. (Diocese of Des Moines.)

*From data and material supplied by the Sisters of Mercy, St. Bernard's Convent, Council Bluffs, Iowa.

FORT SCOTT, KANSAS*

1887

Upon the request of the Right Rev. Louis M. Fink, O.S.B., D.D., Bishop of Leavenworth, arrangements were made by the Sisters of Mercy of Grand Rapids, Michigan, for a foundation in Fort Scott, Kansas.

In 1887, before the execution of plans for the departure of sisters from the community in Michigan, the see of Leavenworth was divided, and that of Wichita, which was established, included in its territory Fort Scott.

MERCY HOSPITAL, FORT SCOTT, KANSAS

In November of that year, Sisters of Mercy, under the superiorship of Mother Mary Teresa Dolan, were received at Fort Scott, and welcomed to the diocese by Bishop Fink, who continued as ecclesiastical administrator in the territory, in the interval, owing to the death of the Right Rev. James O'Reilly, D.D., who had been appointed to the new see but never occupied it.

The Sisters of Mercy in the diocese of Wichita, with Mother Mary Francis de Sales as present Superior, and now under the episcopal jurisdiction of the Right Rev. Augustus Schwertner, D.D.,

*From data and material supplied by the Sisters of Mercy, Fort Scott, Kan.

devote themselves to the instruction of youth in parochial schools, and to hospital work in the diocese.

Motherhouse and Novitiate, Mercy Convent, Fort Scott, Kansas. (Diocese of Wichita.)

KANSAS CITY, MISSOURI*

1887

In 1887, during the episcopacy of the Right Rev. John Joseph Hogan, D.D., first bishop of the diocese of Kansas City, the Sisters of Mercy in Louisville, Kentucky, sent a foundation colony of sisters to Missouri, where, in the episcopal city of Kansas City, they engaged in educational, hospital and charitable works.

St. Agnes Academy, a high school for girls, is one of the foremost of the educational institutions conducted by the community, now under the jurisdiction of the Right Rev. Thomas F. Lillis, D.D., Bishop of Kansas City.

Motherhouse and Novitiate, Convent of Mercy, Hardesty and Scarritt Avenues, Kansas City, Missouri. (Diocese of Kansas City.)

SAVANNAH, GEORGIA†

1892

In the year 1845 there had been established in Savannah, then included in the diocese of Charleston, a community of the Sisters of Our Lady of Mercy, as founded in Charleston by the Right Rev. John England, D.D. Mother Vincent Mahoney served as first Superior of the community from Charleston, when the sisters were given charge of a school and orphanage in Savannah.

Soon after the erection of the diocese of Savannah, in 1850, the sisters, on the request of the Right Rev. Francis X. Gartland, who had been appointed its bishop, extended their activities in Georgia by opening St. Mary's Academy, in Augusta, and some time later, Immaculate Conception Convent, in Atlanta.

In 1891, following a deliberation on the question of the affiliation of the community with the Congregation of Mother McAuley's founding, the matter was submitted to Rome, and to the parent-house in Ireland, by the Right Rev. Thomas A. Becker, D.D., Bishop of Savannah.

---

*From data supplied by the Sisters of Mercy, Kansas City, Mo.

†From data supplied by the Sisters of Mercy, Convent of St. Vincent de Paul, Savannah, Ga., and from *Leaves from the Annals of the Sisters of Mercy* (Vol. IV).

In March, 1892, the Savannah community of Sisters of Our Lady of Mercy was formally affiliated with the Order of Mercy, and adopted its habit, customs and rule, continuing, without interruption, its educational, hospital and charitable work in the diocese, where the sisters, under the ecclesiastical jurisdiction of the Right Rev. Michael J. Keyes, D.D., as Bishop of Savannah, are now under the superior-ship of Mother M. Clare, at the Motherhouse, located on the site of the first foundation in Savannah.

Motherhouse and Novitiate, Convent of St. Vincent de Paul, 207 E. Liberty Street, Savannah, Georgia. (Diocese of Savannah.)

LAREDO, TEXAS*
1894

The community of Sisters of Mercy active in educational and hospital work in the diocese of Corpus Christi was established in 1894 in Laredo, Texas, having been transferred there from the town of Refugio. Mother M. Clare O'Connell served as first Superior at Laredo, then included in the diocese of San Antonio, before the erection of that of Corpus Christi, in 1912.

Serving as present officers of the community, of nearly one hun-dred members, under the ecclesiastical jurisdiction of the Right Rev. Emmanuel B. Ledvina, D.D., Bishop of Corpus Christi, are Mother M. Baptist Molloy, Superior, Mother M. Clare O'Connell, Assistant Superior, Mother M. Anthony McRae, Bursar, and Mother M. Xavier McGlennon, Mistress of Novices.

Motherhouse and Novitiate, Mercy Hospital, Jarvis Plaza, Laredo, Texas. (Diocese of Corpus Christi.)

STANTON, TEXAS†
1894

In 1894, accompanied by a few sisters from the community of Sisters of Mercy in San Francisco, California, Mother M. Berchmans Kast arrived in Stanton, Texas, and established there a foundation of the Congregation of the Sisters of Mercy.

In addition to the Academy of Our Lady of Mercy, which was opened in connection with the Motherhouse, a school for boys under twelve years of age was established. A number of mission and

*From data supplied by the Sisters of Mercy, Mercy Hospital, Laredo, Tex.
†From data and material supplied by the Sisters of Mercy, Academy of Our Lady of Mercy, Stanton, Tex, and from *Our Sunday Visitor,* Huntington, Ind.

parochial schools in the region are also under sisters of this community, laboriously pioneering in this fertile field.

In 1926 the diocese of Amarillo was erected, and the Right Rev. Rudolph A. Gerken, D.D., was appointed its first bishop. Martin County, of which Stanton is the county seat, was included in the Texas territory comprising the new diocese.

With the impetus given by the efforts of Bishop Gerken, the community of Sisters of Mercy in Stanton, under his episcopal jurisdiction, has increased in number, and proportionately extended the

CONVENT OF OUR LADY OF MERCY, STANTON, TEXAS

scope of its activities, the latest of which is the opening of the recently established hospital at Slaton, Texas.

With the lack of a sufficient number of sisters, and the urgent need for religious workers in the vast area of this Texas diocese of more than seventy counties, in which four-fifths of the faithful are Mexicans driven from their native land by persecution, Bishop Gerken, imbued with zeal, issued, in 1928, through the medium of the columns of "Our Sunday Visitor," a nation-wide call for "Mercy Workers."

Offering material compensation to volunteer workers, for their services, one year at a time, and placing the work of these lay missionaries under the immediate care of the Sisters of Mercy, the plan inaugurated by the bishop of Amarillo in behalf of the needs of the diocese has already proved practical.

To co-operate with Bishop Gerken and the Sisters of Mercy, the National Council of Catholic Women sent from the National Catholic

School of Social Service, in Washington, D.C., an experienced social service worker, in the person of Miss Martina Pleace, who has been of great assistance, not only in directing, but in actively developing the plans for the recently opened Catholic Community Center in Amarillo, as well as in organizing, with the Sisters of Mercy, for the work of teaching school, catechizing, visiting homes, caring for the sick, and general assistance of the priest of the missions, to which the "Mercy Workers" devote themselves.

The community of Sisters of Mercy in the diocese of Amarillo is under the present superiorship of Mother M. Columba Salmon.

Motherhouse and Novitiate, Mercy Convent of the Academy of Our Lady of Mercy, Stanton, Texas.   (Diocese of Amarillo.)

PORTLAND, OREGON*
1896

In 1895, the Most Rev. William H. Gross, C.SS.R., D.D., desirous of having a community of Sisters of Mercy in the archdiocese of Oregon City—now known as the archdiocese of Portland in Oregon, requested Mother Mary Joseph Lynch to establish a foundation in the archiepiscopal city of Portland.

Mother Mary Joseph, formerly of the community of Kinsale, Ireland, and one of the volunteer band of the Sisters of Mercy who nursed the sick and wounded soldiers of the Crimean War, had come to the United States at its close, and for a time was with the community of Sisters of Mercy in Brooklyn, and later in Rochester, New York.

Inspired with missionary zeal, Mother Mary Joseph had volun-teered for the foundation in Grand Rapids, Michigan, where she served as first Superior, and in 1895 was temporarily in Morris, Minnesota, where the sisters had established an Indian school, as well as a parochial school.

At the request of Archbishop Gross, Mother M. Agnes Boland and six sisters of the Michigan foundation in Minnesota were sent to Portland, Oregon, in 1896.   They began there, then, the works of the Congregation of Mercy, by opening schools, establishing hospitals and homes for girls, and eventually other charitable institutions.

Later Mother Mary Lynch was prevailed upon to relinquish the foundation in Minnesota, and unite her labors, and those of that foundation, with the community in Portland, now under the ecclesi-

*From the annals of the Sisters of Mercy, Grand Rapids, Mich., and the Official Catholic Directory, 1929.

astical jurisdiction of the Most. Rev. Edward D. Howard, D.D., Archbishop of Portland in Oregon.

> *Motherhouse and Novitiate,* Mercy Convent of Mt. St. Joseph, E. 30th and Stark Streets, Portland Oregon. (Archdiocese of Portland in Oregon.)

FALL RIVER, MASSACHUSETTS*

1905

Though the Sisters of Mercy had labored in the city of Fall River, Massachusetts, since 1874, when the Providence community opened a convent and school there it was not until July 26, 1905, that the sisters there were recognized as an independent community.

The establishment of the foundation followed the creation of the diocese of Fall River in 1904, and the separation from the diocese of Providence of the southeastern portion of Massachusetts, including in it the city of Fall River, which was then chosen as the new episcopal site.

Co-operating in the work of the first bishop, the Right Rev. William Stang, D.D., the Sisters of Mercy remained in Fall River and established their convent there as the Motherhouse for the Congregation in the diocese.

The community, of approximately one hundred and seventy-five members, confines its activities to the diocese of Fall River.

> *Motherhouse and Novitiate,* Mt. St. Mary's Convent, 755 Second Street, Fall River, Massachusetts. (Diocese of Fall River.)

AURORA, ILLINOIS†

1910

With Mother Mary Magdalene Bennett as Superior, in December, 1910, six Sisters of Mercy from Council Bluffs, Iowa, came to Aurora, Illinois, to establish the Order of Mercy in the diocese of Rockford.

The sisters, two months after their arrival in Aurora, bought the Ryburn property, situated on the corner of West Park Avenue and North Lake Street. They opened St. Joseph Hospital, and received their first patient March 16, 1911. A month later the adjacent building, at 185 North Lake Street, was bought for a home for the aged. A year later, a home for working women and girls was established at the corner of Galena Boulevard and Chestnut Street.

---

*From data supplied by the Sisters of Mercy, Fall River, Mass., and from *Leaves from the Annals of the Sisters of Mercy* (Vol. III).

†From data and material supplied by the Sisters of Mercy, St. Joseph Hospital, Aurora, Ill.

Late in 1912, a one hundred and sixty acre tract of land, two miles north of the city, on the present Lincoln Highway and overlooking the Fox River, was secured as the site for Mercyville Sanitarium, with a bed capacity of one hundred and fifty, which the sisters maintain for the treatment and care of nervous and mental patients.

In addition to these institutions, Sisters of Mercy of this community conduct schools at Sycamore, Dundee and Elgin, Illinois, and St. Mary's Hospital in DeKalb, Illinois, all in the diocese of Rockford.

Motherhouse and Novitiate, St. Joseph Hospital, Aurora, Illinois (Diocese of Rockford.)

POCATELLO, IDAHO*

1910

The community of the Sisters of Mercy in Idaho was established on September 12, 1910, in Salt Lake City, Utah. Mother Mary

St. Anthony's Mercy Hospital, Pocatello, Idaho

Vincent, who for twenty-five years had been an active member of the community of Sisters of Mercy in Macon, Georgia, was foundress and

*From data and material supplied by the Sisters of Mercy, Pocatello, Idaho.

first Superior of the new community. Before Mother Mary Vincent's death, September 9, 1916, the community numbered twenty-three members.

Carrying out the plans of the foundress-Superior, the first Convent of Mercy of the community was opened in Pocatello, Idaho, on September 24, 1916, the sisters, in the interim, at the request of the Right Rev. Lawrence Scanlan, D.D., of Salt Lake City, having been temporarily in charge of a hospital.

On January 29, 1918, St. Anthony's Mercy Hospital, with a training school for nurses, was opened at the Motherhouse in Pocatello. The following year the novitiate was opened in connection with the hospital, where, consistent with the modern structure of the institution, every facility is available for the rapidly increasing western community.

On November 4, 1919, took place the formal opening of the newly erected Mercy Hospital in Nampa, located in the western part of Idaho. The new building replaced tents and cottages occupied by patients and sisters for the preceding two and a half years. In 1922, a training school for nurses was annexed to this hospital.

Mother M. Laurence is present Superior of the Sisters of Mercy in Idaho, to which state the community confines its activity, under the ecclesiastical jurisdiction of the Right Rev. Edward J. Kelly, D.D., Bishop of Boise.

    Motherhouse and Novitiate, St. Anthony's Mercy Hospital, Pocatello, Idaho. (Diocese of Boise.)

FREMONT, OHIO*
1912

The Right Rev. Joseph Schrembs, D.D., having been appointed, in 1911, bishop of the newly erected diocese of Toledo, viewed the various needs of the Church in that part of Ohio included in the new diocese, and at once realized the imperative necessity for more Catholic hospitals and religious teachers.

Further realizing the advantages of having a community of Sisters of Mercy in the diocese, Bishop Schrembs applied to his former bishop, the Right Rev. Henry Joseph Richter, D.D., Bishop of Grand Rapids, for Sisters of Mercy from the Michigan foundation there to take charge of a new hospital in Tiffin, Ohio.

Acceding to the request of Bishop Schrembs, a community of

---

*From data supplied by the Sisters of Mercy, Fremont, Ohio, and the annals of the Sisters of Mercy, Mt. Mercy, Grand Rapids, Mich.

sisters was sent to the diocese of Toledo, and in April, 1912, Sister M. Bernardine McMullen, as Superior, with Sister M. de Chantal

CONVENT OF OUR LADY OF THE PINES, FREMONT, OHIO

Lyons and Sister M. Anthony McMullen, opened in Tiffin the first Convent of Mercy in that diocese.

Under the guidance and supervision of Bishop Schrembs, this community grew rapidly. Mercy Hospital, in Tiffin, was built and dedicated in 1913. In 1920, Mercy Hospital was opened in Toledo, and later St. Rita's Hospital was established in Lima, Ohio.

Keeping pace with their work in the hospitals, the Sisters of Mercy became active in school work in the diocese. The community, now numbering fully one hundred members, and under Mother M. Helena as Superior, Mother Magdalen, Assistant, Mother Joan, Bursar, and Mother Margaret Mary, Mistress of Novices, confines its activities to the diocese of Toledo.

Motherhouse and Novitiate, Convent of Our Lady of the Pines, Fremont, Ohio. (Diocese of Toledo.)

JACKSON, MICHIGAN*

1915

The Congregation of the Sisters of Mercy, with its many communities throughout various dioceses of the Church in the United States, was, for an interval, without a community centered in the diocese of Detroit. The diocese, as it was in 1873, had been accorded a foundation colony of Sisters of Mercy from Brooklyn, New York, but in

*From data and material supplied by the Sisters of Mercy, Jackson, Mich., and from the annals of the Sisters of Mercy of Grand Rapids, Mt. Mercy, Grand Rapids, Mich.

1882 Grand Rapids, Michigan, where the Detroit community had established its Motherhouse and novitiate, became the episcopal seat of another Michigan diocese, and the Sisters of Mercy belonged to the new see.

To the efforts of the Rev. E. M. Cullinane, pastor of St. Mary's Church in Jackson, Michigan, is due the re-establishment of the Sisters of Mercy in the diocese of Detroit.

On January 6, 1915, with the approbation of the Right Rev. John S. Foley, D.D., Bishop of Detroit, and the consent of their

MERCY HOSPITAL, JACKSON, MICHIGAN

ecclesiastical superior, the Right Rev. Henry J. Richter, D.D., the Sisters of Mercy of Grand Rapids, then under the superiorship of Mother M. Joseph Miller, sent a foundation colony to Jackson for the purpose of establishing a hospital. Those comprising the new community, of which Mother M. Assisium Hynes was named Superior, were Sisters M. Stanislaus Poulin, M. Pius Broderick and M. Gonzalva Baumann.

Pending the erection of a new hospital building on the Governor Blair property, which had been secured for them, the sisters made temporary hospital use of the White Cross Sanitarium, which was transferred to the new community and opened as Mercy Hospital, February 5, 1915.

On December 17, 1918, the new Mercy Hospital and Sacred Heart Chapel, modern fire-proof structures, erected on the Blair site, were dedicated by the Right Rev. Michael J. Gallagher, D.D., Bishop of Detroit, and ecclesiastical superior of the community, whose Motherhouse and novitiate are maintained at the hospital convent.

On April 3, 1924, in Lansing, the capital city of Michigan, Bishop Gallagher ceremoniously presided at the dedicatory service of St. Lawrence Hospital, opened as a branch house of the Sisters of Mercy of the diocese of Detroit.

Motherhouse and Novitiate, Mercy Hospital Convent, 124 Lansing Avenue, Jackson, Michigan.   (Diocese of Detroit.)

SISTERS OF MERCY OF THE UNION IN THE UNITED STATES*

1929

Convoked by the Apostolic Delegate to the United States, the Most Rev. P. Fumasoni-Biondi, at the command of the Sacred Congregation of Religious, there was held at Cincinnati, Ohio, during the last week of August, 1929, the first General Chapter of the Sisters of Mercy in the United States.   Through the courtesy of the Most Rev. John T. McNicholas, O.P., D.D., Archbishop of Cincinnati, the meetings of the Chapter were held at Mount St. Mary's Seminary, Norwood, Cincinnati.

Each of the communities of the Sisters of Mercy which had signified a desire to enter a Generalate† was represented at the General Chapter by its Mother Superior and two delegates elected by the sisters.

Following the formal opening of the General Chapter on Monday, August 26th, with the celebration of the mass by the Apostolic Delegate, the election of a Mother General and other administrative officers took place.   Mother M. Carmelita Hartman, of Mount Washington, Baltimore, was elected Superior General, and Mother M. Bernardine Purcell, of Cincinnati, Assistant Superior General, while Mother Acquin Gallagher, of Omaha; Mother M. De Neri McConologhue, of New York, and Mother M. Dominica McGowan, of Mobile, were elected Counselors.   Sister M. Gregory Finnegan, of Chicago, South Side, was elected Secretary General and Sister M. Thomasina O'Hara, of Mount Washington, Baltimore, Procuratrix General.

*From press reports by the N.C.W.C. News Service.
†For verification of Motherhouse and novitiate locations of the Sisters of Mercy in the United States since the establishment of the Generalate, see Supplement.

CHRONOLOGICAL TABLE*

*Foundations in the United States of the Congregation of the
Sisters of Mercy*

1843—Pittsburgh, Pennsylvania.
1846—New York City.
1846—Chicago, Illinois.
1851—Providence, Rhode Island.
1851—Little Rock, Arkansas.
1852—Hartford, Connecticut.
1854—San Francisco, California.
1855—Baltimore, Maryland.
1855—Brooklyn, New York.
1856—St. Louis, Missouri.
1857—Sacramento, California.
1857—Rochester, New York.
1858—Cincinnati, Ohio.
1858—Manchester, New Hampshire.
1858—Buffalo, New York.
1859—Ottawa, Illinois.
1860—Vicksburg, Mississippi.
1861—Philadelphia, Pennsylvania
(Merion).
1861—Rensselaer, New York (Albany).
1862—Columbus, Georgia (Macon).
1864—Omaha, Nebraska.
1864—Worcester, Massachusetts.
1865—Bangor, Maine (Portland).
1866—Nashville, Tennessee.
1867—DeWitt, Iowa (Davenport).
1869—New Orleans, Louisiana.
1869—Harrisburg, Pennsylvania.
1870—Louisville, Kentucky.
1870—Titusville, Pennsylvania
(Erie).
1870—Janesville, Wisconsin.
1872—St. Johnsbury, Vermont (Burlington).

1872—Malone, New York (Gabriels).
1873—Bordentown, New Jersey
(North Plainfield).
1873—Grand Rapids, Michigan.
1873—Iowa City, Iowa.
1875—Wilkes-Barre, Pennsylvania
(Dallas).
1877—Mobile, Alabama.
1879—Dubuque, Iowa.
1879—Cresson, Pennsylvania.
1879—Cedar Rapids, Iowa.
1880—New Mexico.
1882—Denver, Colorado.
1883—Chicago, Illinois (West Side).
1883—Devils Lake, North Dakota.
1884—Sacred Heart, Oklahoma
(Oklahoma City).
1885—Milwaukee, Wisconsin.
1887—Council Bluffs, Iowa.
1887—Grass Valley, California.
1887—Fort Scott, Kansas.
1887—Kansas City, Missouri.
1888—Los Angeles, California.
1890—San Diego, California.
1892—Savannah, Georgia.
1894—Laredo, Texas.
1894—Stanton, Texas
1896—Portland, Oregon.
1905—Fall River, Massachusetts.
1910—Aurora, Illinois.
1910—Salt Lake City (Pocatello,
Idaho).
1912—Tiffin, Ohio (Fremont).
1915—Jackson, Michigan (Detroit).

SUMMARY

Sisters of Mercy.
Founded in Ireland in 1831.
Papal Approbation of Rules, May 3, 1835, by Pope Gregory XVI.
Established in the United States in 1843.
Habit: The full-length habit is of black wool, plaited at the waist, with inner
sleeves fitting close to the arm, and wide outer sleeves. The cincture is of

*There is also a community of the Sisters of Mercy, whose foundation
date was not supplied, at Belmont, N. C.

black leather.ʾ A rosary of large black beads hangs from the cincture at the right side. After profession, a veil of light, black woolen material is worn, and a silver ring engraved with a pious motto.

Approximate number in communities in United States, 10,000.

Active in educational and hospital work, and the Works of Mercy, in the archdioceses of Baltimore, Boston, Chicago, Cincinnati, Dubuque, Milwaukee, New Orleans, New York, Philadelphia, Portland in Oregon, St. Louis, San Francisco and Santa Fé, and in the dioceses of Albany, Altoona, Amarillo, Bismarck, Boise, Brooklyn, Buffalo, Burlington, Corpus Christi, Davenport, Denver, Des Moines, Detroit, Erie, Fall River, Grand Island, Grand Rapids, Harrisburg, Hartford, Helena, Kansas City, Lincoln, Little Rock, Los Angeles and San Diego, Louisville, Manchester, Mobile, Monterey-Fresno, Nashville, Natchez, Ogdensburg, Oklahoma, Omaha, Peoria, Pittsburgh, Portland, Providence, Rochester, Rockford, Sacramento, Savannah, Scranton, Sioux City, Springfield in Illinois, Springfield, Trenton, Toledo, Tucson and Wichita, and Belmont Abbey.

SISTERS OF THE PRECIOUS BLOOD*

OHIO

1844

⟨⟩ HE Congregation of the Sisters of the Precious Blood, which inaugurated its work in the United States in 1844, was founded at Graubunden, Switzerland, in 1833, by Maria Anna Brunner, a devout widow.

In that year Mrs. Brunner and her son, the Rev. Francis de Sales Brunner, made a pilgrimage to Rome, visiting many holy shrines and churches. Deeply impressed with the veneration and adoration of the Most Precious Blood, practiced in the Eternal City, especially by the Missionary Society of the Precious Blood, founded by Blessed Caspar del Bufalo, Maria Anna Brunner, filled with an ardent desire of seeing this devotion introduced and propagated in her native country, conceived the idea of forming there a little group of pious women who should unite with her for this purpose.

Her saintly son assisted her in carrying out her project, and that year prepared for her use the old Castle Loewenberg, Ct. Graubunden, in Switzerland. The following year the bishop of Chur sanctioned the devotion which Mother Maria Anna Brunner and her associ-

MOTHER MARIA ANNA BRUNNER
Foundress in 1833 of the Sisters of the Precious Blood

ates were already successfully practicing, and gave his episcopal approbation of the rule of life which Father Brunner had written for the new Congregation, and which he modeled on the Rule of St. Benedict.

Soon after the death of his pious mother in 1836, Father Brunner returned to Rome and became a member of the Congregation of the

*From data and material supplied by the Sisters of the Precious Blood, Salem Heights, Dayton, Ohio.

Most Precious Blood.   Less than ten years later he was appointed Superior of a community of priests missioned to the United States in 1843, where, upon the invitation of the Most Rev. John B. Purcell, D.D., then bishop of Cincinnati—including in its diocesan territory the entire state of Ohio—the see of a new province of the Order was then established at St. Alphonse, near Norwalk.

Answering Father Brunner's appeal for sisters to teach in the school which his community was establishing in its new missionary district, Sister Clara, successor of the foundress-Superior, Mother Maria Anna Brunner, came to Ohio with a small community and

CONVENT OF OUR LADY OF THE PRECIOUS BLOOD, SALEM HEIGHTS, DAYTON, OHIO

established a foundation at New Riegel, Seneca County, Ohio, where on Christmas Eve, 1844, the sisters, six in number, began their nightly vigils before the Blessed Sacrament.

On September 24, 1846, the community removed to its new Motherhouse built in Mercer County, Ohio.   Maria Stein, as the convent was named, then served as the Motherhouse and novitiate of the sisters until it became inadequate for their needs,

In 1850, upon the sale of Castle Loewenberg in Switzerland, the entire Community transferred to America.   Thus augmented in number, the sisters in time established convents in many Ohio localities, and in the course of the years extended their work to Tennessee, Missouri, Arizona and Indiana.   Prominent among the institutions of the Congregation in Indiana, other than those devoted to educational work, is the Kneipp Sanitarium at Rome City, opened in 1901, and which fifteen hundred or more patients visit annually.

In founding the convents of their Order, the Sisters of the Precious Blood do so first, for the adoration of the Precious Blood in the Most Holy Sacrament of the altar by uninterrupted prayer in order to obtain from God vocations for the priesthood, especially for the missionary career, that thus the Precious Blood of Our Redeemer may be rendered fruitful to souls; secondly, for the education of youth, and the care of orphans and poor, homeless or destitute girls.

Consistent with their prayers in behalf of vocations, the Sisters of the Precious Blood, from their Ohio Motherhouse, now engage also in domestic work at the seminary in Carthagena, Ohio, and at St. Joseph's College, Rensselaer, Indiana, where the students are candidates for the priesthood, as well as at Mt. St. Mary and St. Gregory Seminaries of the Cincinnati archdiocese. In Cincinnati they are also in charge of the domestic departments of the archbishop's residence, the Fenwick Club and St. Theresa's Home for the Aged. In Washington, D. C., they carry on this department of the Sisters' College. Among the most recent developments of the extension of their activities has been the opening of convents and boarding schools at Phoenix, Arizona, and at the ancient San Luis Rey Mission, in California.

After the headquarters of the Community had been maintained for more than three-quarters of a century at Maria Stein, removal of the Motherhouse and novitiate was made on September 8, 1923, to the newly erected buildings of the Convent of Our Lady of the Precious Blood, at Salem Heights, Dayton, Ohio.

MOTHER M. AGREDA
Superior General of the Sisters of the Precious Blood

On May 12, 1925, the sisters were granted the privilege of conducting their adoration before the Blessed Sacrament perpetually exposed in the convent chapel, the shrine of a wealth of precious relics, and the source of signal favors to those in pressing need.

SUMMARY

Sisters of the Precious Blood.
Founded in Switzerland in 1833.

Established in the United States in 1844.

Habit: The habit, as worn at present, with the cape and guimpe, is of black serge, with a white linen collar. A black veil is worn over a white linen cap. A nickel crucifix is suspended from the neck on a red cord, and a cincture, also red, in honor of the Precious Blood, is worn. After pro-fession a gold ring is worn.

Approximate number in Community, 715.

Active in educational, hospital and charitable work in the archdiocese of Cincinnati and in the dioceses of Cleveland, Fort Wayne, Kansas City, Los Angeles and San Diego, Monterey-Fresno, St. Joseph, Toledo and Tucson.

Motherhouse and Novitiate, Convent of Our Lady of the Precious Blood, Salem Heights, Dayton, Ohio. (Archdiocese of Cincinnati.)

SISTERS OF THE MOST PRECIOUS BLOOD*

O'FALLON, MISSOURI

1870

The Congregation of the Sisters of the Most Precious Blood, whose Motherhouse is located at O'Fallon, Missouri, was introduced into the United States in 1870.

The Old World history of the founding of this Congregation begins in the year 1845, when a pious young woman of Baden, Germany, visiting a place of pilgrimage on the summit of Steinerberg, Canton Schwyz, Switzerland, was inspired to found a convent, where, far from the turmoil of the world, devout souls might devote themselves to the adoration of the Most Blessed Sacrament, and consecrate their lives wholly to the service of God in prayer and contemplation.

Returning to her own home, Mother Ursula—as she was later known—told her confessor of her great desire. After some time spent in prayerful consideration of her proposed plan, one in which he knew other penitents of his would welcome the opportunity to co-operate, the spiritual director, convinced of the sincerity of each, assisted in the establishment of the community whose members became known as Sisters of the Most Precious Blood, as they had previously been enrolled in the Archconfraternity of the Most Precious Blood, and revered its founder, Blessed Caspar del Bufalo, as theirs.

Before long, companions having joined them in their convent home which had been established near the shrine of St. Anne in Steiner-berg, they were asked to take charge of a school in Seelisberg, Canton Uri, and this request, because of their number, they did not refuse. A little later, on September 8, 1847, a second convent of the pros-

*From data and material supplied by the Sisters of the Most Precious Blood, O'Fallon, Mo.

pering Community was opened, and this at Au, at the foot of Stein-erberg, became another home wherein the Perpetual Adoration of the Blessed Sacrament was carried on.

However, soon feeling the effects of a hostile government, the sisters made plans to remove to Alsace. On their way there they stopped at Ottmarsheim, a vil-lage near the Rhine, where visiting the church, they were met by the pastor, who on learn-ing of their plans prevailed on them to remain there. Having been given suitable accommo-dations upon their consent, the sisters were soon joined there by the remainder of the Com-munity from Au.

Another decade of years passed, and there called on the Community at Ottmarsheim the Rev. Herman Kessler, a devout and zealous priest of Gurtweil, a Catholic village, picturesquely situated in the Grand-Duchy of Baden. Father Kessler's call was for the purpose of securing a community of the sisters to take charge of a school for the care and instruction of destitute children. Assenting to this re-

MOTHER M. WILHELMINE
Elected Superior General in 1920 of the Sisters of the Most Precious Blood, O'Fallon, Missouri

quest, sisters from the Ottmarsheim convent then went to Gurtweil, where they at once took charge of twelve children, previously in the care of two pious women, one of whom soon joined the Community.

The active life then engaged in by those of the Ottmarsheim community at Gurtweil being contrary to the exclusively contempla-tive, austere life the Ottmarsheim community was endeavoring to return to, in accordance with the original object of its founding, the Congregation of the Missionaries of the Precious Blood at Rome was appealed to for advice as to further procedure. In the fall of 1860 the sisters in each locality were consequently given their indi-vidual choice in the matter. Those preferring the contemplative religious life then formed anew the community at Ottmarsheim, while the others, remaining at Gurtweil, became a new congregation, taking the rule of the Sisters of the Congregation of the Most Precious Blood, at Rome, which had been founded in 1834, by Ven. Maria de Mattias, under the personal direction of Blessed Caspar del Bufalo.

In 1867, a third decade of years opening for the Sisters of the Congregation of the Most Precious Blood in Germany brought as caller at the convent in Gurtweil the Right Rev. Damian Juncker, D.D., Bishop of Alton, in the United States, who asked sisters in the interests of the schools of his diocese. At the time the bishop's request could not be granted, and upon his death, the following year, the project was no longer considered by the Community. However, when a year later a letter was received from a pastor at Belle Prairie, Illinois, in that diocese, pleading for sisters to take charge of his school, there was no hesitancy in accepting the opportunity of establishing a new mission.

Already Bismarck's inexorable militant policy against the Church and affecting religious communities, had been inaugurated, and the Superiors of the Congregation availed themselves of the timely opportunity to secure the peaceful pursuit of their labors in the rural quiet of southern Illinois.

From the volunteers for the new mission nine sisters were chosen, and of their number Sister Albertine Bogg was appointed Superior of the community, which after a voyage of but twelve days reached the land of its new field of labor on February 16, 1870. Completing their journey by traveling from New York to Cincinnati by railroad, then going by the Ohio River to Shawneetown, the sisters, hospitably welcomed, awaited conveyances to take them to their destination. Upon the arrival at Belle Prairie of the messenger from Shawneetown, apprising the people of the presence of the sisters there, farmers went with their wagons to bring the sisters through the wilderness to the convent home prepared for them, which they reached on February 28th. The next day the community provided the Church music and singing at a wedding in the parish where they then began their activities in the New World.

Suffering the difficulties and hardships, the lot of the pioneer religious communities of women in the United States, the sisters, often without the consolation of frequenting the sacraments, owing to the scattered missions of the pastor, were for a time left in a state of indecision as to their status in the diocese.

Following a return visit to Gurtweil regarding this, made by Sister Albertine, she was accompanied back to the United States by Mother M. Augustine Volk, Superior of the Congregation, the comfort of whose visit was needed by the community, distressed by the mandate of the Right Rev. Peter J. Baltes, D.D., Bishop of Alton, that no sisters of the Congregation in the diocese should return to Europe without his consent.   In view of this ultimatum from Bishop Baltes, headquarters of the community, which had been greatly aug-mented by the other sisters from Gurtweil, were not established in the

ST. MARY'S INSTITUTE, O'FALLON, MISSOURI

United States until 1873.   In that year, following the reception of the sisters into the archdiocese of St. Louis, where, under the auspices of the vicar general, the Very Rev. Henry Muehlsiepen, they had been placed in charge of various schools, the convent of the sisters at St. Agatha's parochial school in St. Louis became the mecca for the entire Community from Gurtweil, where its missions had all been closed.

Pending the erection, at a location which had been secured for the purpose at O'Fallon, Missouri, thirty-six miles from St. Louis, of a suitable building for the Motherhouse and novitiate to which transfer was made on its completion in 1875, twenty novices from Germany and America followed their novitiate exercises at Belle Prairie, where they were directed by Mother Clementine Zerr as Novice Mistress.

Upon the later transfer of the novices to the new Motherhouse, Mother Clementine Zerr, with some of the professed sisters on a mission at Ruma, Illinois, together with a small number of the novices, having decided to accede to the conditions specified by Bishop Baltes for a community in the diocese, remained there.

In the more than fifty years now passed since the establishment of the Congregation of the Sisters of the Most Precious Blood at the Motherhouse in O'Fallon, its members, long noted for their Church embroidery work, an art learned at Gurtweil, have extended their educational activities to many institutions in the archdiocese, and through Missouri into Nebraska, as well as to many of their original and to new missions in Illinois. Prominent among its educational institutions is St. Elizabeth's Academy, a boarding and day school in St. Louis, which dates its existence from 1882.

Following the Rule of Ven. Maria de Mattias, modified to fit their needs, the sisters of the Congregation of Gurtweil, and later of O'Fallon, were affiliated as a community with the Congregation in Rome only from 1865 to 1872. Upon the revision of its Rule and Constitutions, according to requirements, following the promulgation of the new Code of Canon Law, the Congregation at O'Fallon, Missouri, whose Cardinal Protector is His Eminence, Cardinal Thomas Pius Boggiani, O.P., Archbishop of Genoa, was given recognition among the religious congregations of the Church.

SUMMARY

Sisters of the Most Precious Blood.
Founded in Germany in 1857.
Established in the United States in 1870.
Papal Approbation of Rules in 1918 by Pope Benedict XV.
Habit: The habit and cape are black, with a white collar; the veil is black. The cincture is red in honor of the Precious Blood, and a gold heart, with drops of blood engraved on it, and containing relics, is worn around the neck on a gold chain.
Approximate number in Community, 350.
Active in educational work in the archdiocese of St. Louis and in the dioceses of Lincoln, Omaha, Springfield in Illinois and St. Joseph.
Motherhouse and Novitiate, St. Mary's Institute, O'Fallon, Missouri. (Archdiocese of St. Louis.)

SISTERS ADORERS OF THE MOST PRECIOUS BLOOD*

RUMA, ILLINOIS

1876

The Community of Sisters of the Precious Blood, properly designated because of its affiliation with the Motherhouse in Rome, as

*From data and material supplied by the Sisters Adorers of the Most Precious Blood, Ruma, Ill.

Sisters Adorers of the Most Precious Blood, was established in the United States at Ruma, Illinois, in 1876.

At the time of the transfer to St. Louis of the larger number of the Community of sisters which since 1870 had been several times increased by additions from Gurt-weil, Mother Clementine Zerr, elected Novice Mistress of the Gurt-weil Community in 1865, had remained at Belle Prairie, Illinois, in charge of the novices and pending the establishment of a Motherhouse and novitiate in the country.

VEN. MARIA DE MATTIAS
(1805-1866)
Foundress of the Congregation of the Sisters of the Most Precious Blood

Acceding to the request of the Right Rev. Peter J. Baltes, D.D., Bishop of Alton, for the establish-ment of a Motherhouse in the diocese, Mother Clementine re-maining became first Superior of the Community of which the sis-ters on mission in Ruma, together with some of the novices, formed a part.

Upon the establishment of the diocese of Belleville, in 1887, Randolph County, Illinois, in which is located Ruma, where the con-

PRECIOUS BLOOD INSTITUTE, RED BUD, RUMA, ILLINOIS

vent, novitiate and teacher training school of the Community have been established, was included in the district of the new diocese, of which the Right Rev. Henry Althoff, D.D., is now bishop.

Affiliated since with the Congregation of the Most Precious Blood, founded in 1834, by Ven. Maria de Mattias, the Motherhouse at Ruma, Illinois, has become a United States Provincial house of the Congregation, whose Motherhouse is maintained in Rome.

SUMMARY

Sisters Adorers of the Most Precious Blood (Ruma, Illinois).
Founded in Italy in 1834.
Established in the United States in 1876.
Papal Approbation of Rules in 1897 by Pope Leo XIII.
Habit: The habit is of black serge, with a cape of the same material, closed in front with seven black buttons. The head-dress consists of a white frill with a black veil. A small white collar is also worn. A gold heart mounted by a small cross is suspended around the neck on a gilded chain, and, signifying the Precious Blood, a red cincture and sash with seven tassels at each end are worn.
Approximate number in Community, 490.
Active in educational, hospital, charitable and social service work in the archdiocese of St. Louis and in the dioceses of Belleville, Concordia, El Paso, Lincoln, Oklahoma, St. Joseph, Springfield in Illinois and Wichita.
United States Provincial house and Novitiate, Precious Blood Institute, Red Bud, Ruma, Illinois. (Diocese of Belleville.)

COLUMBIA, PENNSYLVANIA*

1906

The Community of the Sisters Adorers of the Most Precious Blood, whose United States Motherhouse is at St. Joseph's Convent, Gethsemane, at Columbia, Pennsylvania, began its activities in this country in 1906.

Obeying a commission from Mother Catharina Pavoni, Superior General of the Sisters of the Congregation of the Most Precious Blood, in Rome, where they were founded in 1834 by Ven. Maria de Mattias under the direction of Blessed Caspar del Bufalo, Mother Paulina Schneeberger, after twenty-nine years of labor in Banjaluka, Bosnia, part of what is now known as Jugoslavia, came to this country to establish a provincialate of the Congregation.

With the fifteen sisters who accompanied her, Mother Paulina was received by the Right Rev. James Ryan, D.D., Bishop of Alton, into his diocese—now the diocese of Springfield in Illinois—and there

---

*From data and material supplied by the Sisters Adorers of the Most Precious Blood, Columbia, Pa.

the sisters began teaching in parochial schools. On December 16, 1908, a Provincial Motherhouse and novitiate were established at Nazareth Home, a home for the aged which had been opened by the sisters.

Under the continued superiorship of Mother Paulina, the Provincial Motherhouse and novitiate were maintained at Alton until

ST. JOSEPH'S CONVENT, GETHSEMANE, COLUMBIA, PENNSYLVANIA

1924, when owing to their proximity to the Motherhouse at Ruma, Illinois, also become a Provincial Motherhouse of the Congregation, ecclesiastical authorities in Rome sanctioned the transfer of the more recent foundation to the eastern section of the country.

Having been received into the diocese of Harrisburg by its bishop, the Right Rev. Philip R. McDevitt, D.D., the Community purchased a desirable site at Columbia, Pennsylvania, and the Motherhouse was transferred there on April 1, 1925, following the disposal of the property at Alton.

Since their arrival at Columbia the sisters have established at the Provincial Motherhouse there not only the novitiate and a training school for teachers but St. Ann's Home, a home for the aged.

SUMMARY,

Sisters Adorers of the Most Precious Blood (Columbia, Pennsylvania).
Founded in Italy in 1834.
Established in the United States in 1906.
Papal Approbation of Rules in 1897 by Pope Leo XIII.
Habit: See description on page 384.
Approximate number in Community, 100.
Active in educational and charitable work in the archdioceses of Chicago, New York and St. Louis and in the dioceses of Altoona, Fort Wayne, Harrisburg and Pittsburgh.
United States Provincial house and Novitiate, St. Joseph's Convent, Gethsemane, Columbia, Pennsylvania. (Diocese of Harrisburg.)

SISTERS, SERVANTS OF THE IMMACULATE HEART OF MARY*

1845

*O*F American foundation, and with its earliest community history the history of pioneer missionary struggles in the country, the Congregation of the Sisters, Servants of the Immaculate Heart of Mary, dating from 1845, was nevertheless linked, in its origin, with the Old World.

Louis Florent Gillet, the founder of the Congregation, was born at Antwerp, Belgium, on January 12, 1813, and was educated at the College of Liege and at Louvain. A Redemptorist priest at the age of twenty-five, Father Gillet, a relative of St. John Berchmans, was four years later appointed to the missions of the Order in America.

At the Redemptorist foundation in Baltimore the Right Rev. Peter Paul Lefevre, D.D., Bishop of Detroit, appealed to the young priest in behalf of the spiritual needs of the French Canadians in his diocese, and Father Gillet, anxious to labor among the French, was placed in charge of this new Redemptorist mission.

Foreseeing that if his work in Michigan was to endure it must be built on the sure foundation of Christian education, Father Gillet soon took steps for the establishment of a religious community for Catholic teaching.

Four zealous young women, Teresa Maxis and Ann Schaaf, of Baltimore, Teresa Renauld of Grosse Pointe, and Madame Josette Godfroy Smith, whose brother was then mayor of Monroe, Michigan, volunteered for the proposed foundation, and on November 10, 1845, at Monroe, where the Redemptorists were stationed, met and formed the nucleus of the now large Congregation of the Sisters, Servants of the Immaculate Heart of Mary. Their first convent home was a little log cabin on the banks of the Raisin River, not far distant from where ivy-covered St. Mary's Convent now stands.

Teresa Maxis and Ann Schaaf received the habit privately in the sacristy of St. Mary's Church, Sunday, November 30th, 1845, each retaining her baptismal name. Father Gillet placed the Rule in Sister Teresa's hand as she was the elder of the two, naming her

*From data and material supplied by the Srs., Servants of the I.H.M., Monroe, Mich., and from *A Retrospect* (Benziger Bros.) and *A Jubilee Souvenir, 1845-1920.*

the Superior. He deferred the reception of Teresa Renauld a week, when on the feast of the Immaculate Conception it took place pub-licly in the church, and she received the name of Sister M. Celestine.

MOTHER M. TERESA

As Madame Godfroy Smith could not then enter, her reception was held the following May, when the vicar general, the Very Rev. P. Kindekins, presided, giving her the name of Sister M. Alphonsine.

With the approval of Bishop Lefevre, the sisters early adopted the Rule which Father Gillet had prepared, based on the Rule of St. Alphonsus. Father Gillet himself directed the spiritual affairs of the community, training its members as religious teachers, and fostering in them the spirit of charity, humility and simplicity which St. Alphonsus had bequeathed the Redemptorist Order of his founding.

Confident that it was by the inspiration of the Holy Ghost that he had established an organization of religious women, Father Gillet labored with prudence, zeal and energy to carry the work to com-pletion.. He placed the members under the patronage of the Immacu-late Conception, naming them "Sisters of Providence," a title which they retained until the 8th of December, 1847, when, at the request of his successor, the Rev. E. Smulders, C.SS.R., and with episcopal approbation, the title was changed to that which the Congregation bears today, "Sisters, Servants of the Immaculate Heart of Mary."

On January 15, 1846, the first parochial school in the diocese, outside the city of Detroit, was opened and conducted by the sisters. When the school was beginning its fourth successful term, in 1847, Father Gillet was recalled to Baltimore. For two years, subsequently, he gave missions in Ohio, but in 1850 he withdrew from the Redemp-torist Order and returned to Europe. Later, drawn to retirement from the world, and a contemplative life, he entered the Cistercian Order.

A period of upbuilding and progress began for the Community of fourteen professed sisters and four novices, under the Rev. Edward Joos, later Monsignor, who was appointed director of the Congre-gation in August, 1857—following an interval during which, as the Redemptorists had been recalled to Baltimore, the sisters were often without the solace of the sacraments.

For forty-four years Father Joos devoted himself to the cause of Catholic education, and in his devotedness and foresight for the growing Community, which he wished to provide with an adequate course of instruction, he translated from the French a Psychology of Pedagogy, and for two score years he gave each week an hour's con-ference upon this subject to the assembled sisters.

During these and the following years, in addition to the develop-ment at Monroe of the convent and novitiate, St. Mary College and and Academy, a normal training school, and the Hall of the Divine Child—a boarding school for little boys—the Congregation extended its educational activities beyond its natal state. In Pennsylvania, in 1858, where their missions preceded the establishment of independent Motherhouses, and later in Illinois and Ohio, the Sisters, Servants of the Immaculate Heart of Mary, in proportion to their number, took charge of parochial, grade and high schools.

Upon the invitation of the Right Rev. Michael J. Gallagher, D.D., Bishop of Detroit, St. Mary College, established at Monroe in 1905, was transferred to the Michigan metropolis, where, as Marygrove

ST. MARY'S CONVENT, MONROE, MICHIGAN

College, advantageously situated on Palmer Boulevard, in the northwest section of Detroit, it was opened in September, 1927, and formally dedicated on November 10th, as a Founder's Day event.

In its new location Marygrove College, in charge of the Sisters, Servants of the Immaculate Heart of Mary, who have proved their ability to inculcate sound religious principles, strengthen the moral fibre, and cultivate the graces of the heart and soul, offers its students—numbering, in 1929, more than five hundred, in addition to those in late hour classes for teachers and other adults—every modern

ST. MARY'S NOVITIATE, MONROE, MICHIGAN

educational facility, while standing for active Catholicity and Catholic action.

A disastrous event in the history of the Congregation occurred on June 3, 1929, when fire razed St. Mary's Academy, erected in 1905 at the Motherhouse seat in Monroe. Two hundred and fifty of the pupils, in the building at the time, thoroughly drilled in fire practice, with forty sisters and fifty rescue workers who were endangered, escaped unharmed.

Recently concluding negotiations with ecclesiastical and civil authorities, both in this country and in Europe, Mother M. Domitilla, Superior General of the Congregation, secured for the Sisters, Servants of the Immaculate Heart of Mary, the object of their hope when the remains of the body of their venerated founder were removed from the Cistercian cemetery in Savoy and brought to Monroe, where, in the new mortuary chapel built for them in the Community cemetery, they were reverently interred on August 2,

1929. So has Father Gillet, known in the Cistercian Order as Dom Marie Celestin, come back to honor the scene of his early labors.

SUMMARY

Sisters, Servants of the Immaculate Heart of Mary (Monroe, Michigan).
Founded in the United States in 1845.
Papal Approbation of Rules, July 26, 1920, by Pope Benedict XV.
Habit: The habit and scapular are of blue serge, with a white guimpe and a black girdle, with which a rosary is worn. The veil is black. A crucifix is worn on the chest. A gold ring is also worn.
Approximate number in Community, 810.
Active in educational work in the archdioceses of Chicago and Milwaukee, and the dioceses of Cleveland and Detroit.
Motherhouse and Novitiate, St. Mary's Convent, Monroe, Michigan. (Diocese of Detroit.)

IMMACULATA, PENNSYLVANIA*

1858

In his zeal for the education of youth in his diocese, the holy Redemptorist bishop of Philadelphia, Ven. John Nepomucene Neumann, heartily concurred in the plans of the Rev. John Vincent O'Reilly, a fervent young priest, who, naming the little village in Susquehanna County in northeastern Pennsylvania in which he established his headquarters, St. Joseph's, requested, in 1858, episcopal permission for the introduction there of the Sisters, Servants of the Immaculate Heart of Mary.

Assured by Bishop Neumann of a welcome in what was then the diocese of Philadelphia, and with the approbation of their episcopal superior, Bishop Lefevre of Detroit, Mother Teresa and her little Community at Monroe, Michigan, rejoiced at the opportunity of once more co-operating with the Redemptorists.

Sister M. Magdalen was appointed Superior of the group chosen to go to St. Joseph's—Sister M. Gerard, Sister M. Agnes and Sister M. Clara. Mother M. Teresa, accompanied by Sister M. Aloysius, had preceded them to this their first distant mission, and on the occasion of Bishop Neumann's visit of welcome to the sisters was promised his personal attention to the completion of the rule of the community.

St. Joseph's Academy of the Immaculate Heart of Mary, in Susquehanna County, Pennsylvania, chartered by the State Legislature

---

*From *The Sisters of the I.H.M.,* by a member of the Scranton Community (P. J. Kenedy & Sons, New York), and from the Official Catholic Year Book, 1928.

in 1861, soon became an educational center for which additional sisters were sent, as needed, from Monroe. Many young women anxious to consecrate themselves to the religious life were received at St. Joseph's, where a novitiate was opened, owing to the distance from the Motherhouse at Monroe. With Bishop Neumann presiding, a first ceremony of reception and profession was held in the convent chapel on July 24, 1859.

At this time also a second mission in Pennsylvania was undertaken. At the request of Bishop Neumann, Mother Teresa, who, following the appointment of her successor as Mother Superior at St. Mary's, had become local Superior at St. Joseph's, established this new mission at Reading, sisters for it being chosen from those already in the diocese, and Mother M. Magdalen being named Superior.

Soon after the establishment of the Reading convent, three postulants were received, and other presenting themselves for admission, a novitiate was also opened. In a short time the sisters opened a boarding school in connection with the day school; here the enrollment of early boarders listed students not only from Pennsylvania, but from New York and other states as well.

In 1864 the novitiate at St. Joseph's was closed and transferred to that at Reading, the convent there being constituted then the Motherhouse and novitiate for all the Sisters, Servants of the Immaculate Heart of Mary in Pennsylvania, as it had been decreed by episcopal decision and the consent of the sisters that the community in the diocese of Philadelphia would be a separate foundation, having its own Motherhouse, while retaining friendliest relations and union in spirit with the Michigan mother foundation at St. Mary's in Monroe.

Between 1860 and 1871 many new missions were opened in Pennsylvania, prominent among them the school established in September, 1864, at Pittston, where Sister Mary Cephas and the first band of sisters arriving were agreeably surprised to find awaiting them the convent completely furnished, even to the luxury of a piano.

With the erection of the diocese of Scranton in 1868, the Right Rev. William O'Hara, who was vicar general of the Philadelphia diocese, appointed its first bishop, early formulated plans for providing religious teachers for the see, and in 1871 the Sisters, Servants of the Immaculate Heart of Mary in that diocese became a diocesan foundation.

The following year, under Mother Mary Gonzaga as Superior

General of the Philadelphia diocesan Community, the sisters acquired the property of Wyer's Military Academy, formerly a young ladies' seminary, at West Chester, Pennsylvania, which upon the completion of necessary improvements was established as Villa Maria, the Mother-house and novitiate for the Community in the archdiocese of Philadelphia, the diocese becoming an archiepiscopal see in 1875.

To this new and more advantageous location the academy and boarding school were transferred from Reading, forming the foundation of the well known educational institutions of the Community, outstanding among which is Immaculata College, for the higher education of women, founded in 1920, and located, with Villa Maria Academy, at Immaculata Pennsylvania, on a beautiful site on the highest point of land between Philadelphia and Harrisburg.

Continuing to maintain the novitiate at West Chester, the Community also conducts there St. Agnes' High School, and in addition St. Aloysius Academy, a boarding school for boys under twelve years of age, which was opened in 1894.

With the increased growth in numbers of the Philadelphia Congregation of the Sisters, Servants of the Immaculate Heart of Mary, its work was extended not only beyond the limits of the archdiocese in the state, and to Virginia, but also, more recently, to distant South America, to the city of Lima, Peru.

SUMMARY

Sisters, Servants of the Immaculate Heart of Mary. (Archdiocese of Philadelphia.)
Established in 1858.
Habit: See General Summary (page 398).
Approximate number in Community, 1,200.
Active in the United States in educational and social service work in the archdiocese of Philadelphia and the dioceses of Harrisburg and Richmond.
Novitiate, Villa Maria, West Chester, Pennsylvania. (Archdiocese of Philadelphia.)

SCRANTON, PENNSYLVANIA*

1864

Upon the erection in 1868 of a new diocese in the northeastern part of Pennsylvania, with Scranton as the episcopal city, the Right Rev. William O'Hara, D.D., vicar general of the diocese of Philadelphia, was appointed its first ordinary. At this time the only reli-

---

*From data and material supplied by the Sisters, Servants of the Immaculate Heart of Mary, Scranton, Pa., and from *The Sisters of the I.H.M.*, by a member of the Scranton Community.

gious in the district of the new see were Sisters, Servants of the Immaclulate Heart of Mary, from the Motherhouse in Reading, who were in charge of Laurel Hill Academy, St. John's at Susquehanna and St. John's at Pittston.

In full accord with the Church regarding the necessity of Christian education, Bishop O'Hara at once made plans for the establishment of a system of parochial schools. Foreseeing the necessity of providing a sufficient number of sisters to teach in these schools, he asked the sisters already in the diocese to remain as a foundation. Twelve of the fifteen sisters thereupon chose to stay, while three elected to return to the Motherhouse at Reading.

Upon this decision at the end of their retreat, in August, 1871, and approval of it by the Right Rev. James F. Wood, D.D., Bishop of Philadelphia, Mother M. Joseph, then local Superior at St. John's, in Pittston, was appointed first Superior of the new foundation, and Laurel Hill Academy was chosen as temporary Motherhouse and novitiate. On the opening of the novitiate, September 8, 1871, six candidates were at once received as postulants. Mother M. Aloysius, who as Miss Mary Ann Walker, of Rochester, New York, had entered the Community at the mother foundation in Monroe, in 1853, became first Novice Mistress of the Scranton Community.

When Mr. John Clarke of Susquehanna learned that Bishop O'Hara desired to open a convent in Scranton, he at once placed within the bishop's means a site he possessed not far distant from the Cathedral, which became the first location of the sisters' convent in Scranton. On July 2, 1872, the new convent was blessed as St. Cecilia's Academy. Upon the opening of St. Cecilia's the Mother-house and novitiate were transferred to it, and maintained there until removal to their present location.

The academy opened at St. Cecilia's became a center of educa-tional activity in the diocese, and its academy roster contains the names of those whose families were then and are yet, through their children and their children's children, foremost in every progressive step in the furtherance of Catholicism and the upholding of Catholic education.

The years which followed for the Sisters of the Immaculate Heart of Mary in the diocese of Scranton were years of splendid growth and development. To fill a diocesan need the Community in 1875, deviating from the hitherto exclusively educational work of the Congregation, took charge of St. Patrick's Orphanage in Scranton, and while continuing in charge of that institution the sisters also now maintain the St. Joseph's Children's Hospital. Day schools and boarding schools, grade and high, of highest accredited standards, now under the direction of the Community throughout the diocese, are the result of the labors of the early years there, as prosperous institutions also established in near and distant states are the result of the expansion and extension of its work, in proportion to its great increase in numbers.

With the need of larger quarters that St. Cecilia's could afford, the novitiate was in time transferred to St. Rose's Academy, opened as a boarding school in Carbondale, Pennsylvania, where it was continued until 1902, when the resident students and novices at St. Rose's, and the resident students at St. Cecilia's, removed to Mount St. Mary's in Scranton, the new site of the Motherhouse.

Mt. St. Mary of the Immaculate Conception, Scranton, Pa.

The first public entertainment given at Mount St. Mary's was the patronal feast day celebration of the Right Rev. Michael J. Hoban, D.D., who had succeeded to the see of Scranton upon the death of Bishop O'Hara. For three decades of years, Mount St. Mary's enjoyed the patronage and friendship of Bishop Hoban, who showed himself ever solicitous for the advancement of the Community, and who encouraged the students in their work by his gracious and frequent tutelage. Once a week, for several years, he held classes in Sacred Scriptures for the novices and sisters at the Motherhouse.

Various agencies calling into action different charities, made demands on the Community, the scope of whose rule permitted their undertaking the new needed labors. In addition to the orphanage and children's hospital work the sisters, in 1911, inaugurated new missionary activities when they responded to a call to take charge of the instruction of the children of St. Cecilia's parish in Wyoming, in the heart of northeastern Pennsylvania's industrial and coal region.

Prior to this time, Mount St. Mary's had become the center for the establishment of several religious communities, founded there for work not only among the many immigrants in the diocese, but extending far beyond it to settlements and parishes in other archdioceses and dioceses. These communities instituted at Mount St. Mary's, and with their first members trained in its novitiate, now rank among the well established congregations in the United States, and worthily reflect the religious spirit and thoroughness of their foundations.

Marywood College, the crowning work of the Sisters of the Immaculate Heart of Mary in Scranton, was chartered in May, 1917, and empowered, by the University Council of the State of Pennsylvania, to confer degrees. Although, with the establishment of this first Catholic college for women in the state, the educational system of the sisters had attained an unusual distinction, they immediately began the work of college expansion to authorize their granting higher degrees. Extension courses and lectures have been opened to religious and lay teachers, and, at the request of the State Department, summer schools have been provided, enabling teachers to meet new scholastic requirements. At the close of the ninth year of the existence of Marywood College, more than a thousand teachers had taken qualifying courses there, in addition to the larger enrollment of students seeking the opportunity it offered for higher education.

Besides the participation of the Congregation in war work during the period of the World War, and in nursing during the later epidemic, a party of French girls was received and educated at Marywood College, at the request of the French government and the National Catholic War Council.

Soon after the election as Superior of Mother M. Casimir, who continues in that office, assisted in the administration of the affairs of the Community by Sister M. Pius as Assistant; Sister M. Borgia, Bursar, and Sister M. Berchmans, Mistress of Novices, the development of a new phase of social service work was begun when the management of the *Casa Regina* in Altoona, Pennsylvania, was undertaken by the Scranton sisters. This work was the outcome of a movement inaugurated by the Rev. Edward F. Garesché, S.J., founder, and at the time editor of "The Queen's Work," and a devoted promoter of the interests of Our Lady and the sodalities established in her honor.   The project of sodality homes, each to be known as a *Casa Regina,* where self-supporting girls might find their needs satisfied within the limits of their earnings, was part of this movement.   The *Casa Regina* at Altoona was formally opened on December 3, 1919, with the sisters from Mount St. Mary's Mother-house in charge.   There they watch carefully over the temporal and spiritual needs of the girls under their care, and while providing them a home conduct classes and give educational assistance to those desiring it.

Following the successful opening of the *Casa Regina* at Altoona, Bishop Hoban urged Mother Casimir to place sisters in charge of St. Joseph's Shelter and a day nursery in Scranton, formerly con-ducted by the ladies of St. Joseph's Society.   The bishop's request was at once complied with, and sisters of the Community continue work in these institutions, providing a haven for the homeless or friendless woman, and during hours when mothers must labor, capably care for the little ones confidingly entrusted to them daily.

Taking up the modern social service movement, which has secured scientific support in colleges and universities throughout the country, where social service departments have been organized and equipped for the development of research and service from the college stand-point, the Sisters, Servants of the Immaculate Heart of Mary opened such an extension course in connection with the department of soci-ology at Marywood College in 1920.

When the Right Rev. Thomas C. O'Reilly, D.D., Vicar General of the see of Cleveland, succeeded as bishop of Scranton in 1928, he found there, where he had had only two episcopal predecessors, remarkable developments and achievements, and, in the heart of this "most cosmopolitan diocese in the United States," the Sisters, Servants of the Immaculate Heart of Mary, already qualified to co-operate in any undertaking in which religious might assist.

SUMMARY

Sisters, Servants of the Immaculate Heart of Mary.   (Diocese of Scranton.) Established in 1864.
Habit: See General Summary (page 398).
Approximate number in Community, 720.
Active in educational and charitable work in the archdioceses of Baltimore, New York and Portland in Oregon, and in the dioceses of Altoona, Boise, Brooklyn, Harrisburg, Providence, Raleigh, Scranton and Syracuse.
Motherhouse and Novitiate, Mt. St. Mary of the Immaculate Conception, Marywood, Scranton, Pennsylvania.   (Diocese of Scranton.)

GENERAL SUMMARY

Sisters, Servants of the Immaculate Heart of Mary.

Founded in the United States in 1845.

Papal Approbation of Rules, July 26, 1920, by Pope Benedict XV.

Habit: The habit worn by each community differs but slightly from that worn at the mother foundation. (See page 391.)

Approximate number in Congregation, 2,730.

Active chiefly in educational work in the archdioceses of Baltimore, Chicago, Milwaukee, New York, Philadelphia, and Portland in Oregon, and in the dioceses of Altoona, Boise, Brooklyn, Cleveland, Detroit, Harrisburg, Pittsburgh, Providence, Richmond, Raleigh, Scranton and Syracuse.

SCHOOL SISTERS OF NOTRE DAME*

1847

THE Congregation of the School Sisters of Notre Dame is, as its name indicates, a teaching order, and is devoted to the Christian education of youth, from kindergarten to college. The Congregation is a transformation of the French *Congrégation de Notre Dame,* founded in France in 1597 by St. Peter Fourier, an Augustianian canon, remarkable for his learning, zeal for souls, and such kindness of heart that he was surnamed *le bon père de Mattaincourt.*

Realizing the neglected condition of the education of the young women in his own parish at Mattaincourt, in Lorraine, the good father of Mattaincourt was inspired to found a congregation of women for the Christian education of girls. He soon recognized in a few pious virgins the suitable subjects for the accomplishment of this important project, and Miss Alice LeClerc, whose gifts of mind and heart the holy founder fully discerned, was joined by four courageous young women ready to devote themselves to the new work.

Peter Fourier had directed the five pioneers of the Congregation to present themselves during the midnight mass of Christmas, 1597. They appeared garbed and veiled in plain black, as a sign of their renunciation of the world. However simple this initial act of the foundation of the Congregation was, it was, nevertheless, indescribably solemn and impressive. The saint gave Holy Communion to the five virgins now consecrating themselves to God, before giving It to any of the faithful. At the crib of the Divine Infant, therefore, the Order that was destined to lead thousands of children to the knowledge and love of the Divine Friend of children, had its birth.

Under the care of a great saint and a holy Superior the Community grew in numbers and spread over France, and toward the close of the seventeenth century also over Germany. During the French Revolution, however, all its ninety convents in France were suppressed, and soon afterward those in Germany fell a prey to the so-called secularization.

The convent school of the Congregation of Notre Dame in Ratisbon, Germany, was among those secularized and closed. However, to a former pupil of this suppressed school—Caroline Gerhardinger—

---

*From data and material supplied by the School Sisters of Notre Dame, Convent of Notre Dame, Milwaukee, Wis.

is due the link between the French *Congrégation de Notre Dame* and the new Congregation then formed, known as the School Sisters of Notre Dame.

Caroline Gerhardinger, as Mother Mary Teresa of Jesus, became first Superior General of the Congregation, whose first convent was established in Neunburg vorm Wald, Bavaria, and was dedicated October 24, 1833.

Ratisbon's saintly bishop, George Michael Wittmann, and his pious friend, the priest, Francis Sebastian Job, chaplain at the imperial court of Austria, and confessor of the empress, agreed that the Rules and Constitutions of St. Peter Fourier should be the fundamental guide of the new Congregation, but with such modifications as to allow the sisters to teach in the schools of smaller towns and rural parishes, in school-houses belonging to the parishes and not to their convents. Thus the sisters were enabled to meet the school needs in a greater measure than in the former Congregation.

With the rapid growth and the increasing extension of the new Community, the mother institution at Neunburg soon proved too small. In 1841, at the request of King Louis I of Bavaria, the Motherhouse was established at Munich, at first in *The Au*—The Meadow. This again proving too small, the former convent of the Poor Clares, dating from 1284, was purchased and restored. Archbishop Lothaire Anselm of Munich, who contributed twelve thousand gulden toward defraying the cost of the cloister and its improvements, blessed the Motherhouse and its oratories October 16, 1843, five hundred and fifty-nine years after the first dedication of the convent.

At the instance of the Redemptorist Fathers, who had begun their missionary work in America in 1832, and who saw the necessity of parochial schools in their new field, a gentleman was sent to Bavaria by the Right Rev. Michael O'Connor, D.D., first bishop of Pittsburgh, to obtain School Sisters of Notre Dame for a German Catholic colony which, as St. Mary's, had been established in Elk County, Pennsylvania. The archbishop of Munich, to whom the zealous emissary appealed, advised Mother Teresa to accept the proposed mission, which she accordingly did.

Among those volunteering for this mission, Mother Teresa selected Sisters M. Barbara Weinzierl, M. Magdalen Steiner, M. Seraphina von Pronath, and M. Caroline Friess. Mother Teresa herself conducted them to their new field of labor, taking with her a traveling companion, Sister M. Emmanuela Breitenbach, who was to accompany her on her return trip to Europe. On June 18, 1847, they left Munich for Bremen, where they boarded the American steamer

Washington, and after a prosperous voyage landed in New York on the feast of St. Ignatius, July 31, 1847.

MOTHER M. CAROLINE FRIESS

After a rest of a few days, during which they were received by the Bavarian Consul, the sisters set out for their destination, St. Mary's, Elk County, Pennsylvania. On this trip one of their number, Sister Emmanuela, succumbed to the heat, and died at Harrisburg, Pennsylvania.

On the feast of the Assumption, August 15, 1847, after a long and tedious journey through the forests of Pennsylvania, the four pioneer School Sisters of Notre Dame, with their Mother General,

28

reached St. Mary's, where they were welcomed by the Redemptorist Fathers and the colonists.

That St. Mary's was not the place for a permanent location of her Community, least of all for a Motherhouse, was at once evident to Mother Teresa, who then began to look for a more suitable site. With the assistance of Ven. John Neumann, at the time Provincial of the Redemptorists, later bishop of Philadelphia, she secured for a convent the Redemptorists' novitiate house, near St. James' Church, Aisquith Street, Baltimore.

During the first days of October, Mother Teresa and two sisters took possession of this new home, and on October 8, 1847, St. James' School, with an enrollment of seventy-five girls, was given in charge of Sister Magdalen. On October 21st, St. Michael's School was opened, under Mother Teresa, and on November 3rd, St. Alphonsus' School was entrusted to the sisters, and Sister Caroline was placed in charge of it.

At the outset the Community was blessed with the entrance of postulants. On March 25, 1848, also, eleven other sisters arrived from the Motherhouse in Munich. These at once rendered their services in the schools, becoming devoted co-laborers in the founding of the Congregation in America.

When the success of the sisters' work in Baltimore became known, invitations to extend it to various parts of the country were received. Mother Teresa, therefore, resolved to make a personal inspection of the places already offered them, and of other likely locations, and chose for her companion on this tour Sister Caroline. They set out for Pittsburgh, where arrangements were made with Bishop O'Connor for the opening of a school. Detroit, Buffalo, Rochester and Philadelphia were then visited. Upon the invitation of its first bishop, the Right Rev. John Martin Henni, D.D., they also visited Milwaukee. Before their arrival, however, the bishop had left for Europe, in consequence of which no definite arrangements for the establishment of a house there could then be made.

Returning to Baltimore, Mother Teresa made her plans for her home journey to Europe. She appointed the senior sister, Mother M. Seraphina, Superior of the American Community, but the management of the already existing schools and the foundation of future ones she placed in the hands of Sister Caroline. In July, 1848, Mother Teresa left for Europe, and never re-visited America.

Particularly anxious to secure the School Sisters of Notre Dame for his new diocese, erected in 1844, and to have them establish their American Motherhouse in his episcopal city, Bishop Henni, while in

Europe, visited Munich, and expressed his desires in this regard to Archbishop Reisach—later cardinal, and Cardinal Protector of the Congregation—and with the approval of King Louis I, the generous

CONVENT OF NOTRE DAME, MILWAUKEE, WISCONSIN

patron of the Congregation, and on the return of Mother Teresa, the matter was quickly decided in the bishop's favor.

On October 10, 1850, Sister Caroline was named Vicar General of the Congregation, and directed to establish in the episcopal city of Milwaukee the American Motherhouse of the School Sisters of Notre Dame.

On December 15, 1850, Mother Caroline arrived in Milwaukee, accompanied by three sisters and one candidate to the Community. With money donated by King Louis I, Bishop Henni had bought for the sisters a house at the southwest corner of Knapp and Milwaukee Streets. Though small, it had four chimneys, and was therefore generally known as "the house with the four chimneys."

Mother Caroline, imbued with zeal and energy, began at once to furnish the little convent, and on Christmas Day the bishop cele-brated mass in the little chapel into which one of the rooms had been converted. The Congregation of the School Sisters of Notre Dame thus began its career of faithful and efficient work in the cause of Christian education. From the smallest of beginnings, in both the east and west, it has grown into one of the foremost teaching orders in the United States.

In January, 1851, Mother Caroline opened the first parish school of the Order in the west, at St. Mary's Church, of which the Rev. Dr. Salzmann was the rector. Soon after this, in accordance with the wish of the bishop for a select day school, an addition was built to the convent on Milwaukee Street, and a boarding school, St. Mary's Institute, was opened.

On July 31, 1876, the Congregation in the United States, on account of its rapid growth and wide extensions, was divided into two provinces, the Western Province, retaining its Motherhouse at Milwaukee, and the Eastern Province, with its Provincial Mother-house at Baltimore.

EASTERN PROVINCIALATE

Having been the site of the first American Motherhouse of the School Sisters of Notre Dame, from 1847 until its establishment in Milwaukee in 1850, Baltimore was the logical site for the seat of the Eastern Province upon its erection.

The Institute of Notre Dame, and academy for boarders and day pupils, located on Aisquith Street and Ashland Avenue, is con-nected with the Motherhouse and novitiate which are maintained

INSTITUTE OF NOTRE DAME, BALTIMORE, MARYLAND

there. In 1873 the academy known as Notre Dame of Maryland was established in the suburbs of Baltimore, upon the purchase by the Congregation of a most desirable and spacious estate. The year 1896 marks for the Eastern Provincialate the founding of the College of Notre Dame of Maryland, which, affiliated from the first with the

Catholic University of America, and accredited by outstanding educational associations and departments, is today one of the prominent
institutions of the country for the higher education of women. Affiliated with the college is Notre Dame of Maryland High School and
Preparatory School for Girls.

In addition to their educational work in Baltimore and its vicinity,
the School Sisters of Notre Dame of the Eastern Province conduct,
among their many institutions, orphanages for the care of children,
thus continuing one of the first works of the Congregation upon its
founding.

For the benefit of the nearly sixteen hundred School Sisters of
Notre Dame in the Eastern Province of the Congregation in the
United States, Villa Marie, at Notchcliff, Maryland, is maintained
as a country home.

SOUTHERN PROVINCIALATE

On March 19, 1895, the Western Province of the School Sisters
of Notre Dame was divided, and the Southern Province formed,
with its Motherhouse and novitiate in one of the suburbs of St. Louis,
on the banks of the Mississippi, hence appropriately named *Sancta
Maria in Ripa*. Here a junior college is conducted, and from this
southern center the sisters labor in many charitable and educational
institutions.

SANCTA MARIA IN RIPA, ST. LOUIS, MISSOURI

Notable among the institutional work carried on in this provincialate of the Congregation is that of the Institute for Deaf Mutes
at Chinchuba, near Manville, Louisiana, in the archdiocese of New
Orleans. Particularly memorable in connection with the work of
the School Sisters of Notre Dame at this institution is the fact that

it was one of the last activities undertaken by Mother Caroline, whose achievements in the number of institutions of the Congregation she established in the United States place her among the most inde, fatigable of the foundresses in the history of the Church in this country.

NORTHWESTERN PROVINCIALATE

The fall of 1912 saw the establishment of a fourth United States province of the Congregation, when, following the formation in 1910 of northwestern missions, a Provincial Motherhouse erected at Man, kato, Minnesota, was blessed and dedicated to Our Lady of Good Counsel.

CONVENT OF OUR LADY OF GOOD COUNSEL, MANKATO, MINNESOTA

Upon the selection of Mankato, in the diocese of Winona, for the location of the seat of the Northwestern Provincialate of the Congregation, a distinguished Protestant gentleman presented the Congregation a gift of fifteen acres of fine park land for the erection of an academy—the Academy of Our Lady of Good Counsel— while the Catholic citizens of Mankato purchased forty-four acres adjoining the park land and donated them for the site of the Mother, house and novitiate for the Northwestern Province.

WESTERN PROVINCIALATE

While serving as the seat of the Western Province, the Mother-house in Milwaukee ranks also as the principal Motherhouse in America of the School Sisters of Notre Dame, and is the residence of not only the Provincial Superior but of the Commissary General—Mother M. Stanislaus Kostka being the present incumbent of that office, to which she was elected in 1917. Prior to becoming first assistant to the Commissary General, Mother Marianne—upon whose death she succeeded to that office—Mother Stanislaus served as Mistress of Novices at the Provincial Motherhouse in St. Louis, her native city. In August, 1927, Mother Stanislaus was one of twenty-six members of the Congregation who celebrated at the Motherhouse in Milwaukee the Golden Jubilee of their religious profession, while at the same time six sisters celebrated the sixtieth.

The Congregation of the School Sisters of Notre Dame is under the government of the Mother General at Munich, Bavaria, who, with her four assistants, heads the Generalate. The government of the Congregation in the United States is in the hands of the Commissary General and her assistants, and at the head of each province there is a Provincialate Superior and her assistants. For the election of the Mother General and for the General Chapter, a deputation of sisters from the United States is sent to Munich, this deputation being composed of the Commissary General and the Mother Provincial, *ex officio,* and one companion of each Mother Provincial, elected by the respective province. In addition to this General Chapter, a General Congregation convenes at stated intervals in the principal Motherhouse at Milwaukee, and at specific periods the sisters engaged in educational work meet for summer schools and teachers' institutes held at appointed houses of the Order.

Owing to the growth of the number of missions in Ontario Province, Canada, where the School Sisters of Notre Dame have labored since 1871, and the inconvenience of having all who entered there go to Milwaukee for their novitiate, it was deemed expedient to form a Canadian province of the Congregation. In 1925, there-fore, a site for a Provincial Motherhouse was secured at Watertown, Ontario, in the diocese of Hamilton. On February 14, 1927, the sisters, candidates and boarders, until that time in Kitchener, trans-ferred to the new buildings erected on this site. Besides the schools in the Province of Ontario, the sisters have two schools in Sas-katchewan, opened in 1926 and 1927 respectively.

In August, 1915, at the invitation of the Redemptorist Fathers, eleven School Sisters of Notre Dame sailed from New York to become the pioneer missionaries of the Congregation in Porto Rico, where they are now in charge of four schools.

The most recent work of the Congregation in the United States was the transfer, in August, 1929, of St. Mary's College, Prairie du Chien, Wisconsin, to Milwaukee. Under the name of Mount Mary College, the new school is located on a beautiful site in the north-western part of the city, and its opening attendance of about one hundred and fifty boarders and day pupils augurs well for the coming years. St. Mary's College at Prairie du Chien has been super-seded by St. Mary's Academy, a boarding and day school for girls.

SUMMARY

School Sisters of Notre Dame.
Founded in France in 1597.
Established in the United States in 1847.
Papal Approbation of Rules, June 6, 1859, by Pope Pius IX.
Habit:- The habit is black, with white wimple. A black veil lined with white is worn.
Approximate number in Community in United States, 5,100.
Active in educational and charitable work in the archdioceses of Baltimore, Boston, Chicago, Dubuque, Milwaukee, New Orleans, New York, Phila-delphia, St. Louis, St. Paul, and in the dioceses of Albany, Altoona, Belleville, Brooklyn, Buffalo, Dallas, Davenport, Detroit, Fort Wayne, Grand Rapids, Green Bay, Hartford, Kansas City, La Crosse, Lincoln, Little Rock, Marquette, Natchez, Newark, Peoria, Pittsburgh, Providence, Rochester, Rockford, San Antonio, Sioux Falls, Spokane, Springfield in Illinois, Superior, Toledo, Trenton and Winona.
Motherhouse and Novitiate for the Eastern Provincialate, Institute of Notre Dame, Aisquith Street and Ashland Avenue, Baltimore, Maryland. (Arch-diocese of Baltimore.)
Motherhouse and Novitiate for the Southern Provincialate, Sancta Maria in Ripa, Ripa Avenue, South St. Louis, Missouri. (Archdiocese of St. Louis.)
Motherhouse and Novitiate for the Northwestern Provincialate, Convent of Our Lady of Good Counsel, Mankato, Minnesota. (Diocese of Winona.)
Principal Motherhouse in America, and Motherhouse and Novitiate for the Western Provinicialate, Notre Dame Convent, 676 Milwaukee Street, Milwaukee, Wisconsin. (Archdiocese of Milwaukee.)

THIRD ORDER FRANCISCAN SISTERS*

IN 1209 St. Francis of Assisi, who had renounced a life of wealth, and had espoused poverty and humiliation, striving to recall mankind to the profession and practice of Gospel principles, established the Order of Friars Minor.

A few years later, when St. Clare with a few companions embraced the life of penance St. Francis had instituted, the foundation of his Second Order, known as the Poor Clares, was laid.

Realizing that not all who caught the spirit of unworldliness, self-denial and brotherly love, which was the burden of his preaching, could enroll themselves in the Order of Friars Minor or of the Poor Clares, St. Francis then established a third fraternity for persons living in the world.

As members of this Third Order, founded in 1221, nobility and the learned, men and women of every station, gladly undertook the tertiary apostolate—lives of especial piety and rectitude, and active Christianity—rejoicing in a brotherhood with the humble saint of Assisi.

Throughout the centuries the followers of the tertiary rule of this third and largest branch of the great Franciscan or Seraphic Order have been innumerable.

Secular Franciscan Tertiaries, desirous of conventual life, in time have come to constitute various religious communities, following a special rule for members of the Third Order living in community, approved by Pope Leo X in 1521. This rule, however, is modified by the particular constitutions of each foundation.

Among these congregations, which make up the now widespread Third Order Regular of St. Francis, only the communities bound by solemn vows and subject to the Minister General of the Third Order are Regular in the strict canonical sense, although the term is popularly applied to others bound only by simple vows and not subject to the Minister General, because they follow the tertiary rule in the religious life.

These numerous congregations of Third Order Franciscan Sisters, wearing the typical Franciscan habit, or its characteristic white cord, and sharing, with secular tertiaries, in the aims and many spiritual privileges of the entire Franciscan Order, zealously labor in a wide range of activities within their scope as followers of the poor little man of God of Assisi.

*From Franciscan sources.

SISTERS OF THE THIRD ORDER OF ST. FRANCIS ASSISI*

(SISTERS OF PENANCE AND CHARITY)

1849

The history of the community which forms the Congregation of the Sisters of the Third Order of St. Francis Assisi, Sisters of Penance and Charity, as they are also known, begins in 1849. In that year six young women, Tertiaries of the Third Order Secular of St. Francis, from the old manufacturing town of Kaufbeuren, in the diocese of Augsburg, Germany, came to Milwaukee, Wisconsin, to found a community of the Third Order Regular of St. Francis.

Upon the advice of the Right Rev. John Martin Henri, D.D., then bishop of Milwaukee, the little band of ardent tertiaries estab-lished themselves at Nojoshing, now known as St. Francis, Wisconsin, where they purchased with their united means thirty-eight acres of land along the shores of Lake Michi-gan and made their temporary abode in the small house included in the purchase, while they labored with the workers in the building of a first convent home.

Three years later, the Rev. Michael Heiss, later bishop of La Crosse and archbishop of Milwau-kee, was appointed chaplain of the little community, whose original members were the Misses Ottilia Duerr, Crescentia Eberle, Maria Eisenschmied, Teresa Moser, Anna Ritter and Maria Saumweber. Father Heiss compiled for the community

A SISTER OF THE THIRD ORDER OF ST. FRANCIS OF ASSISI

a rule which was approved by Bishop Henni, and in which the special work of the sisterhood was defined as the education of Catholic youth in schools and orphanages, the care of the deaf and feeble-minded, and the performance of any other charities by which the members could best serve Holy Mother Church.

*From data and material supplied by the Sisters of St. Francis, St. Francis, Wis., and from the Official Catholic Year Book, 1928, and *Catholic Missions,* Official Organ of the Society for the Propagation of the Faith.

On June 16, 1853, the six members of the Community were admitted to the profession of the vows of religion. The following year, under their first Superior, Mother M. Aemiliana Duerr, they took charge of St. Aemilian's Orphan Asylum, and upon the founding in 1856 of St. Francis Seminary, at St. Francis, Wisconsin, by the distinguished Austrian scholar and cleric, Dr. Joseph Salzmann, the sisters, at the invitation of Father Heiss, its first rector, took charge of the household duties of the new institution. On the elevation of Father Heiss, their first guide and counselor, to the episcopal dignity, the sisters continued, under the rectorship of his successor, Dr. Salzmann, the founder of the seminary, their indefatigable labors there.

CONVENT OF ST. FRANCIS OF ASSISI, ST. FRANCIS, WISCONSIN

Although during the ensuing thirty years the Community passed through a series of trials and hardships, it experienced a remarkable growth in numbers. Throughout this period the sisters continued in charge of St. Aemilian's Orphanage at St. Francis and were conducting parochial schools. In 1885, carrying out one of the aims of the Congregation, the sisters accepted the charge of the deaf at St. John's Institute, also at St. Francis, Wisconsin.

The success of the Community through the next twelve years was secured through the valiant efforts of Mother M. Antonine Thren, during whose superiorate the Congregation became firmly established and many more schools were placed under its direction.

Upon the death of Mother M. Antonine in 1898, her sister, Mother Mary Thecla Thren, was elected to succeed her as Superior General of the Congregation, and during her administration the sisters entered upon new fields of endeavor. In 1904 St. Coletta's Institute for Backward Youth, the only Catholic school of its kind in the north-west, was founded at Jefferson, Wisconsin, and in that year the Community also began its work in academies by opening St. Mary's Academy at Milwaukee. Three years later, the sisters extended their academic educational work to Colorado, where they opened at Longmont St. Joseph's Academy.

Under Mother M. Celestine as present Superior General, and her Council at the Motherhouse, the Congregation, imbued with the zeal and dauntless spirit of its six devout foundresses, sent, in the summer of 1929, four of its members to China, to establish a Catholic high school at Hung Kja Lou, in the vicariate of Tsinanfu, Shantung.

SUMMARY

Sisters of the Third Order of St. Francis Assisi (Sisters of Penance and Charity.)
Founded in the United States in 1849.
Papal Approbation of Rules, March 2, 1924, by Pope Pius XI.
Habit: The habit is black, with a black veil, white coif and collar, and a white girdle with a rosary.
Approximate number in Community, 615.
Active in educational and charitable work in the United States in the arch-dioceses of Chicago and Milwaukee, and in the dioceses of Cleveland, Davenport, Denver, Green Bay, La Crosse, Peoria, Rockford, Sioux City, Sioux Falls and Superior.
Motherhouse and Novitiate, Convent of St. Francis Assisi, St. Francis, Wisconsin. (Archdiocese of Milwaukee.)

SISTERS OF THE THIRD ORDER OF ST. FRANCIS OF THE PERPETUAL ADORATION*

1849

The annals of the Franciscan Sisters of the Perpetual Adoration, at their Motherhouse in La Crosse, Wisconsin, show an unwonted, possibly unparalleled experience in the history of religious orders of women in the United States.

To the venerable Superior General of the Congregation, Mother M. Ludovica Keller, fell the favor of seeing the Community, of which she was Superior General, increase in numbers from less than a hundred—when on July 10, 1871, its Motherhouse was transferred from its site in the archdiocese of Milwaukee to one in the new diocese of La Crosse—to almost eight times that number, before her

*From data and material supplied by the Franciscan Sisters of the Perpetual Adoration, La Crosse, Wis., and from *Our Community* by a mem-ber of the Congregation.

death recently shortly after the celebration of her forty-fifth year as its Superior General.

Until the election of Mother M. Antonia Herb as Superior General in 1863, the Community, which had been founded in 1849 at what is now known as St. Francis, Wisconsin, had maintained its headquarters at St. Francis Seminary, where the sisters were then chiefly engaged.

Realizing the great need for religious teachers in the many schools to be opened, with the erection of parishes in the quickly populating centers of the country, and knowing the desires of many applicants to the Community, Mother Antonia soon took a drastic step toward the preparation of the Community for educational work.

Encouraged by the development of her plans to do this, and having finally secured the acquiescence of the bishop of Milwaukee, the Right Rev. John Martin Henni, D.D., to the project, Mother Antonia en-

MOTHER M. LUDOVICA KELLER

gaged a lay teacher of experience to take charge of a first normal school, this being conducted in the winter of 1863 and 1864.

In late September, 1864, the Community at St. Francis transferred to a new Motherhouse which was then founded at Jefferson, Wisconsin, as St. Coletta Convent. Here, under the direction of the chaplain, the Rev. Kilian Flasch, of St. Francis Seminary, later second bishop of La Crosse, and with the pedagogical help of the succeeding chaplain, the Rev. Francis X. Obermueller, the sisters continued their normal school studies and prepared themselves for the county examinations which teachers were required to pass before being awarded certificates.

Beginning their work in the little parish school, a two mile walk from St. Coletta Convent, the sisters early extended their activities in this new field, as evidenced by the large number of schools since established and now conducted by the Community.

The gradual increase of the Community had more than once necessitated the enlargement of the new convent which had been built at Jefferson, despite the realization of the unsuitability of the location for headquarters. The gift of property for the site of a Motherhouse at La Crosse, the episcopal city of Wisconsin's new diocese, erected in 1868, and of which the guide and counselor of the Community, the Rev. Michael Heiss, was consecrated first bishop, materially made possible the removal of the Motherhouse to this location, when Bishop Heiss had obtained for the Community the necessary permission for its transfer from the diocese of Milwaukee. By June of the year 1871, the main part of the building being completed, the Community took possession of the new Motherhouse, St. Rose de Viterbo Convent.

ST. ROSE CONVENT, LA CROSSE, WISCONSIN

Mother Antonia had then attained two of the objects she had in view for the Congregation, the establishment of its Motherhouse and the placing of the Community on a firm and enduring basis. A third wish in her heart for it had not yet been realized. This cherished desire, however, was attained in the winter of 1878, when the Community was granted the privilege of Perpetual Adoration of the Blessed Sacrament in the Motherhouse Chapel of Maria Angelorum— the original of the present spacious and beautiful chapel of the same name—which had been dedicated on July 2, 1874.

Upon the death of Mother M. Antonia, on January 26, 1882, after serving nineteen years as Mother General, Mother M. Ludovica

Keller and Mother Rose François—elected Mother General and Mother Assistant respectively—took up the direction of the work of the Congregation at the Motherhouse, normal school and parochial schools, as well as at an orphanage at Sparta, Wisconsin.

The first mission opened by Mother Ludovica was at Bad River Reservation at Odanah, in northern Wisconsin. This Indian Mission at Odanah, where fifteen sisters of the Community are now engaged in conducting St. Mary's Industrial School for Boys and Girls, was undertaken at the request of the Franciscan Fathers of the St. Louis Province, the Rev. Casimir Vogt, the zealous Franciscan missionary among the Indians of Wisconsin and Arizona, having made a special trip to La Crosse, in order to personally present a petition for sisters for this mission.

In 1883, the Community, which that year became incorporated, inaugurated its work in hospitals when, upon erection of St. Francis Hospital at La Crosse by the Congregation, the twenty-seven year old city was provided with its first hospital. Today this institution, with a maternity annex, contagious disease annex and training school for nurses—with nearly one hundred student nurses enrolled—indicates, together with the many other such hospitals since established by these Franciscan Sisters of the Perpetual Adoration, the permanency of their success in this work.

With more than two score years past since she accepted for her Community the care of the little school at Odanah, in the mission fields at home, Mother Ludovica's great heart did not refuse a more recent call to the mission fields afar. With her Congregation she bravely said God Speed to the six sisters who on September 6, 1928, left La Crosse for the west, where after visiting houses of their Community at Bozeman, Montana, and Spokane, Washington, they sailed from San Francisco for Wuchang, China, there to assist, by establishing a school, in the missionary labors of the Franciscan Fathers from the Province of Cincinnati.

Under the episcopal jurisdiction of the Right Rev. Alexander J. McGavick, D.D., present bishop of La Crosse, the Congregation—which in 1870 was affiliated with the Order of Minor Conventuals—in addition to its educational and charitable activities, keeps unbroken in the Chapel of Maria Angelorum at the Motherhouse the Perpetual Adoration begun more than fifty years ago.

SUMMARY

Sisters of the Third Order of St. Francis of the Perpetual Adoration. Founded in the United States in 1849.

Papal Approbation of Rules, Jan. 28, 1917, by Pope Benedict XV.

Habit: The habit and veil are black, with a white collar and rounded white neck-dress. A white girdle and rosary are worn.

Approximate number in Community, 800.

Active in educational, hospital and charitable work in the United States in the archdiocese of Dubuque and the dioceses of Boise, Davenport, Des Moines, Helena, La Crosse, Sioux City, Spokane and Superior.

Motherhouse and Novitiate, St. Rose Convent, La Crosse, Wisconsin. (Diocese of La Crosse.)

SISTERS OF THE THIRD ORDER REGULAR OF ST. FRANCIS*

OLDENBURG, INDIANA

1851

Through the zeal and energy of a pioneer pastor at Oldenburg, Indiana, the Rev. Francis Joseph Rudolf, the Congregation of the

CONVENT OF THE IMMACULATE CONCEPTION, OLDENBURG, INDIANA

Sisters of St. Francis, of the Convent of the Immaculate Conception, at Oldenburg, Indiana, was established on January 6, 1851.

*From data and material supplied by the Sisters of St. Francis, Oldenburg, Indiana, and from the Official Catholic Year Book, 1928.

Having realized the need of Catholic teachers and charitable workers, in his labor of saving souls, Father Rudolf appealed to the Rev. Ambrose Buchmaier, a Franciscan missionary of New York, to procure for his assistance Franciscan sisters.

Sisters of the Third Order of St. Francis from their Motherhouse in Vienna, Austria, responded to this call, and Mother Theresa Hackelmeier and a companion sister from Vienna left their convent home in Austria, and in 1851 began their labors in the United States, in the diocese of Indianapolis.

Youthful aspirants soon placed themselves under the amiable yet potent guidance of Mother Theresa; others followed, and the Oldenburg Community of Franciscan Sisters early extended its activities beyond the confines of Indiana, to other states near and far.

Oldenburg, in Franklin County, has been retained as the location of the Motherhouse of the Congregation, of which Mother M. Clarissa Dillhoff, having recently succeeded Mother M. Veneranda Huser, is the present Superior General. In connection with the Motherhouse the Institute of the Immaculate Conception is conducted by the Community.

On October 4, 1920, the feast of St. Francis, the Right Rev. Joseph Chartrand, D.D., Bishop of Indianapolis, officiated at the ceremony of the laying of the cornerstone of the Adoration Chapel of St. Clara, erected on the Motherhouse grounds at Oldenburg. Following its opening and consecration on May 4, 1922, Bishop Chartrand, on a visit to the Holy See in 1924, obtained for the Community the privilege of having the altar of this chapel privileged *in perpetuam,* and also obtained the granting of the indulgence of the Forty Hours' devotion for every visit to the chapel.

A SISTER OF THE THIRD ORDER REGULAR OF ST. FRANCIS, OLDENBURG, INDIANA

SUMMARY

Sisters of the Third Order Regular of St. Francis (Oldenburg, Indiana).
Established in the United States in 1851.
Papal Approbation of Rules, August 5, 1891, by Pope Leo XIII.
Habit: The habit is of black wool, with a white woolen girdle, a rosary, and a crucifix worn on the chest. The black veil is worn over a white headdress, and a gold band ring is worn.
Approximate number in Community, 770.

29

Active in educational and charitable work in the archdioceses of Cincinnati, St. Louis and Santa Fé, and in the dioceses of Amarillo, Covington, El Paso, Indianapolis, Kansas City and Peoria.

Motherhouse and Novitiate, Convent of the Immaculate Conception, Oldenburg, Indiana. (Diocese of Indianapolis.)

SISTERS OF ST. FRANCIS*

PHILADELPHIA, PENNSYLVANIA

1855

No more lasting monument exists today to the memory of Philadelphia's saintly Redemptorist bishop, Ven. John Nepomucene Neumann, than the Philadelphia foundation of Sisters of St. Francis.

Soon after his return from Rome, where he had gone late in the fall of 1854 to be present on December 8th at the solemn promulgation of the dogma of the Immaculate Conception of the Blessed Virgin Mary, Bishop Neumann, acting on the suggestion of the Sovereign Pontiff, Pope Pius IX, formed this community of Sisters of the Third Order of St. Francis.

On April 9, 1855, Bishop Neumann invested with the habit of the Order of St. Francis, three devout women, Marianne Bachmann, who became Mother Mary Francis, Barbara Boll, who became Sister Mary Margaret, and Anna Dorn, who became Sister Mary Bernardina. The Community then formed was delegated to visit and care for the sick, and to undertake other charitable work, as well as the instruction of youth.

A GLEN RIDDLE FRANCISCAN   In 1858 the Sisters of St. Francis opened their first school in Philadelphia, this being in St. Alphonsus' parish, where at the time of his appointment as bishop Ven. John Neumann was rector. The same year also marked the opening of their novitiate which was established at their convent in this parish.

As the Community increased in numbers, the sisters not only undertook teaching in various other parish schools in Philadelphia,

*From data and material supplied by the Sisters of St. Francis, Glen Riddle, Pa.

but were also soon nursing the sick during the smallpox epidemic which ravaged the city and the country in 1858, as again in 1871 and 1872, and in 1883.

CONVENT OF OUR LADY OF ANGELS, LA VERNA HEIGHTS,
GLEN RIDDLE, PENNSYLVANIA

In 1860 the Community opened St. Mary's Hospital in Philadelphia, and in addition had soon established several missions beyond the state of Pennsylvania. Shortly after the death of Mother Mary Francis in 1863, two of these missions in New York, one in Buffalo and one in Syracuse, were constituted foundations.

Upon the accession of the Most Rev. Patrick J. Ryan, D.D., to the archiepiscopal see of Philadelphia in 1884, the Sisters of St. Francis experienced a distinct change in their Community, hitherto composed for the most part of members who were German or of German extraction. From this time on, with the admission to the Community of candidates who in a short time formed a notably cosmopolitan Congregation, its number increased rapidly.

In 1896 the Motherhouse was transferred from Philadelphia to Glen Riddle, nearby, where the novitiate had been maintained since 1871. With the extension of the Congregation to cities in the south and in the far west, as well as to many other localities in the eastern states, provinces have been established, under the jurisdiction of the Motherhouse. The General Novitiate for the Congregation is continued at the Motherhouse at Glen Riddle, though one is now also maintained at St. Joseph Academy, Pendleton, Oregon, the seat of the Western Provincialate.

The year 1930, bringing the Diamond Jubilee anniversary of the Glen Riddle Franciscans, finds them one of the largest congregations of Franciscan Sisters in the United States, and engaged almost throughout the expanse of the land in conducting academies, grade and high schools, hospitals and training schools for nurses, schools for Indians and schools for negroes, orphanages, day nurseries, homes for the aged, and a home for working girls—practically every field of activity open to religious orders of women.

SUMMARY

Sisters of the Third Order of St. Francis (Philadelphia Foundation).
Founded in the United States in 1855.
Papal Approbation of Rules, July 7, 1907, by Pope Pius X.
Habit: The habit is of coarse black serge, with a black veil lined with white, a white linen cap, forehead band and collar. A crucifix is worn on the breast, and the white Franciscan cord is worn with a rosary suspended from it.
Approximate number in Community, 1275.
Active in educational, hospital, charitable, social service and missionary work in the archdioceses of Baltimore, Boston, Oregon City and Philadelphia, and in the dioceses of Altoona, Baker City, Cheyenne, Fall River, Harrisburg, Hartford, Oklahoma, Providence, Seattle, Spokane, Trenton and Wilmington.
Eastern Provincial house, St. Francis Convent, Philadelphia, Pa. Archdiocese of Philadelphia.)
Western Provincial house and Novitiate, St. Joseph Academy, Pendleton, Oregon. (Diocese of Baker City.)
Southern Provincial house, St. Anthony Convent, Gardenville, Baltimore, Md. (Archdiocese of Baltimore.)
General Motherhouse and Novitiate, Convent of Our Lady of Angels, La Verna Heights, Glen Riddle, Pa. (Archdiocese of Philadelphia.)

SISTERS OF THE POOR OF ST. FRANCIS*

1858

The Sisters of the Poor of St. Francis form a Congregation founded by the Venerable Mother Frances Schervier, at Aix la Chapelle, Germany, in the year 1845. The members observe the Rule of the Third Order of St. Francis—as given by Pope Leo X for tertiaries living in community—adapted to their special work, the care of the sick poor, both in homes and hospitals.

Frances Schervier, born at Aachen, Germany, January 3, 1919, was the child of John Henry Casper Schervier, proprietor of a needle manufactory and Associate Magistrate of the city, and Maria Louisa Migeon. While Frances was receiving a thorough education it was always her desire to serve the sick and the poor. She began her charities by giving them food and clothing, laboring for them, and visiting them in their homes and hospitals, and in 1840 she joined a charitable society in order to exercise this charity more ably.

In 1844 Frances, with four other young ladies, Catherine Daverkosen, Gertrude Frank, Joanna Bruchhans and Catherine Lassen, became members of the Third Order of St. Francis. The following year, with the approbation of their pastor, they went to live together, and Frances was chosen Superior of the little community, living a conventual life, and devoting its time to the practice of religious exercises and the visiting of the sick poor.

Late in 1848 a mild form of cholera broke out in Aachen, followed by an epidemic of small-pox, and an infirmary was opened by the sisters in an old Dominican building, the property of the city. The sisters were authorized by the city to take up their abode in the building, and their services as nurses were accepted. In 1850 they established a hospital for incurables in the old Dominican building, and home nursing and charity kitchens in different parishes were entrusted to them.

On August 12, 1851, Mother Frances and her twenty-three associates were invested with the habit of St. Francis, and continued their hospital and nursing work.

When the home of the Poor Clares, before their suppression in 1803, was offered for sale in the summer of 1852, Mother Frances purchased the spacious building for a convent—the first Motherhouse. The Congregation grew steadily and rapidly, and the year 1858 marked its extension to America.

---

*From data and material supplied by the Sisters of the Poor of St. Francis, St. Clara Convent, Hartwell, Cincinnati, Ohio.

Visiting in Europe, Mrs. Sarah Peter of Cincinnati, Ohio, a fervent convert, had received a commission from the Most Rev. John Baptist Purcell, D.D., Archbishop of Cincinnati, to procure for

MOTHER FRANCES SCHERVIER
Foundress in 1845 of the Sisters of the Poor of St. Francis

America German sisters for the destitute German poor, and Irish sisters for the Irish, in the episcopal city. While in Rome, in 1857, she submitted her hopes to Pope Pius IX, and was advised by him. Cardinal Von Geissel, Archbishop of Cologne, recommended for the proposed German community the Congregation of Mother Frances.

Mother Frances consented to found a house in Cincinnati, and

on August 24, 1858, the six sisters chosen by her set sail for America. Upon their arrival in Cincinnati, the Sisters of the Good Shepherd kindly gave them hospitality. Soon they were offered the gratuitous use of a vacated orphanage for their patients. The following year three more sisters arrived from Europe, and the community purchased several lots at the corner of Linn and Betts Streets—the present site of St. Mary's Hospital—and began the erection of a hospital. More sisters soon arrived from the Motherhouse, and in 1860 the sisters established St. Elizabeth's Hospital in Covington, Kentucky.

Chapel View
ST. CLARA CONVENT, HARTWELL, CINCINNATI, OHIO

In the spring of 1861, Mrs. Peter, reserving for herself the use of several rooms, wherein she lived a life of retirement until her death in 1877, gave her Cincinnati residence on Third and Lytle Streets to the Community for a novitiate and home for the Clarisses or recluses, a contemplative branch of the Congregation, for whose coming she had negotiated with Mother Frances. In October, 1861, three recluses came to America, and upon their arrival Perpetual Adoration of the Blessed Sacrament was inaugurated in the novitiate of the Convent of St. Clara.

With the opening of the Civil War members of the Community were placed in charge of a Marine Hospital in Cincinnati for a short time. Some of them nursed the wounded on the steamer "Superior," and large numbers of wounded soldiers and sailors were cared for in the general wards of the hospitals conducted by the sisters. During this time the venerable foundress visited America, and shared actively in the labors of the Community in the war-work immortalized in the United States by the erection, in 1924, in Washington, D. C., of the Monument to the Nuns of the Battlefield, through the efforts of the Ancient Order of Hibernians and the Ladies' Auxiliary of America.

It was during the Civil War period also that the Community opened St. Mary's Hospital in Hoboken, New Jersey, as well as St. Peter's in Brooklyn, New York, and St. Francis' in Columbus, Ohio.

In the decade of years following this time the Sisters of the Poor of St. Francis established St. Francis Hospital, Bronx, New York City, St. Michael's Hospital in Newark, New Jersey, and St. Mary's in Quincy, Illinois.

Since then, with the continued growth of the Community, other hospitals have been established and are conducted by the sisters in Kansas City, Kansas; Woodhaven, New York; a second one in Cincinnati and a second one in Columbus, while in Dayton, Ohio, St. Elizabeth's Hospital, which was established in 1878, has now become, with its bed capacity of more than five hundred, one of the largest institutions conducted by the Congregation in the United States.

In the interval, the increasing number of the Community exceeding the accommodations available at the convent on Third and Lytle Streets, the novitiate was removed in 1896 to its present site at Hartwell, Cincinnati, Ohio.

Here the United States Provincial Motherhouse of the Congregation is now located, with Sister M. Alacoque serving as Provincial Superior of the Community in the United States, which continues under the jurisdiction of the General Motherhouse at Aix la Chapelle, Germany.

SUMMARY

Sisters of the Poor of St. Francis.
Founded in Germany in 1845.
Established in the United States in 1858.
Papal Approbation of Rules, October 6, 1908, by Pope Pius X.

Habit: The habit is of brown cloth, cinctured with a gray linen cord with five knots, to which a rosary is attached. A brown scapular, white collar and head-dress and black veil are worn. After profession a red cross and the emblems of the passion are worn embroidered on the scapular.
Approximate number in Community in United States, 690.
Active chiefly in hospital work in the archdioceses of Cincinnati and New York, and in the dioceses of Brooklyn, Columbus, Covington, Leavenworth, Newark and Springfield in Illinois.
U. S. Provincial Motherhouse and Novitiate, St. Clara Convent, Hartwell, Cincinnati, Ohio. (Archdiocese of Cincinnati.)

SISTERS OF ST. FRANCIS*

ALLEGANY, NEW YORK

1859

The Congregation of the Sisters of St. Francis whose Motherhouse is maintained at Allegany, New York, near the postal station of St. Bonaventure's, was founded at Allegany in the year 1859.

The founding of the Congregation, whose initial community work was the conducting of a school, was due to the zeal of the Very Rev. Pamfilo da Magliano, Custos Provincial of the Friars Minor of the province which had been established in the vicinity of Allegany. Father Pamfilo and a group of Friars Minor had come to the United States from Italy but four years previously, and through the generosity of Mr. Nicholas Devereux of Utica, New York, had established themselves at Ellicottville, in the diocese of Buffalo, their monastery being later transferred to St. Bonaventure's, at Allegany.

St. Elizabeth's Academy, which now forms part of the Mother-house institutions of the Sisters of St. Francis at Allegany, ranks among the oldest convent academies in the diocese and today is but one of the many such schools conducted by this Community of five hundred members.

In addition to their work in academies and grade schools, hospitals, homes for the aged and boarding homes for girls, in cities in the archdioceses of Boston and New York and the dioceses of Buffalo, Hartford, Pittsburgh, Providence and Trenton, the sisters from Allegany are also engaged in school work at Jamaica, British West Indies.

Noteworthy in the history of the Congregation is its establishment of St. Joseph's Normal College for Teachers, located at Kingston, in the vicariate apostolic of Jamaica, under the episcopal jurisdiction of the Right Rev. Joseph N. Dinand, S. J., formerly president of

---

*From *The History of the Catholic Church in the United States* by John Gilmary Shea, and from current news and the Official Catholic Directory, 1929.

Holy Cross College, at Worcester, Massachusetts. The Sisters of St. Francis also conduct in the vicariate St. Joseph's Continuation School and the Academy of the Immaculate Conception, as well as a preparatory school for small boys, all at Kingston, and St. James' Academy at Montego Bay.

Motherhouse and Novitiate, St. Elizabeth's Convent, St. Bona-venture P. O., Allegany, N.Y. (Diocese of Buffalo.)

SISTERS OF THE THIRD FRANCISCAN ORDER*

MINOR CONVENTUALS

1860

Through the need of the Fathers Minor Conventuals in Utica and Syracuse, New York, for religious teachers in the parochial schools opened by them soon after their introduction into the country from Germany by the Ven. John Neumann, C.SS.R., Sisters of St. Francis were sent from Philadelphia to take charge of these schools.

The Right Rev. James F. Wood, D.D., succeeding to the see of Philadelphia early in 1860, following the death of its renowned and saintly bishop, the Right Rev. John N. Neumann, took the initial step in establishing the Franciscan sisters laboring outside the diocese as separate foundations.

This step therefore occasioned the establishment as a new founda-tion of the Sisters of St. Francis in Syracuse, which was effected in the month of November, 1860, with the approbation of the Right Rev. John McCloskey, D.D., then bishop of Albany, whose episcopal terri-tory then included Syracuse.

Under Mother M. Bernardine, its first Superior, the new Com-munity, whose convent in Syracuse became its Motherhouse, was affiliated with the Franciscan Minor Conventuals by the Right Rev. Louis Marangoni, Minister General of the Order.

From the earliest foundation of the Community the sisters labored zealously and successfully in parochial schools, hospitals and institu-tional homes.

Little more than two decades of years after its establishment the Community harkened to a call from the distant Hawaiian Islands, Bishop Herman, in charge of the Catholic Mission in Hawaii, having sent forth a request for sisters to nurse the lepers, then segregated by the Hawaiian government. Of the many volunteers offering

*From data and material supplied by the Sisters of the Third Franciscan Order, M.C., Syracuse, N. Y.

themselves for this first foreign mission of the Community, six sisters, with Mother Marianne as Superior, were chosen for the heroic band which reached its destination in November, 1883. Two months later

ST. ANTHONY CONVENT, SYRACUSE, NEW YORK

part of the group began the work of the mission at the Honolulu Hospital, where two hundred lepers were being harbored, and in another two months the remainder of the mission band were given charge of the Malulani Hospital, where those sick, but with non-contagious diseases, were cared for. Before the end of the following year, 1884, the sisters had opened a home at Honolulu for the education of girls, the non-leprous children of leper parents.

The Molokai mission proper being offered the sisters by the government in 1888, Mother Marianne accepted it, and with three sisters took charge of the Bishop Home at Kalaupala to care for the leper girls and women.

In 1893 the Motherhouse at Syracuse, New York, established St. Francis Novitiate at Honolulu for the reception and training of aspirants to missionary work in the Hawaiian Islands, for the benefit of those who wished to devote their lives to the suffering members of Christ at the leper settlement on the island of Molokai.

In 1900 the Sisters of St. Francis from Syracuse took charge of the parochial school at Hilo and in 1928 of the school at Lahaina, in the meantime having also opened a hospital of their own at Honolulu.

Upon the separation by the Holy See, in 1886, of Onondaga County—in which Syracuse is located—and other New York counties, from the diocese of Albany, to form a new diocese of which Syracuse was made the site of the see, the Congregation of the Sisters of St. Francic, O.M.C., with its Motherhouse in the episcopal city, accordingly became subject to the jurisdiction of the bishop of Syracuse, at present the Right Rev. Daniel J. Curley, D.D.

While now conducting schools, hospitals, and homes throughout the eastern and central section of the country, the Community has also maintained since 1869 St. Joseph's Hospital in Syracuse. There too, in addition to Loretto Rest, a diocesan home for the aged, which is in their charge, the sisters conduct in connection with the Motherhouse St. Anthony's Convent School.

A FRANCISCAN SISTER, O.M.C.

A recent departure in the activities of the Community, now under the superiority of Mother M. Margaret, has been the establishment in Rome, Italy, of Villa Marguerita, a novitiate and hospice for travelers, located conveniently near the Vatican City.

SUMMARY

Sisters of the Third Franciscan Order, Minor Conventuals.

Founded in the United States in 1860.

Papal Approbation of Rules, April 23, 1923, by Pope Pius XI.

Habit: The habit is of plaited black serge, with a black mantle, white collar and cord and a black rosary. A crucifix is worn on the breast. The head-dress consists of a white cornette and band, and a black veil over a shorter white one. A fine black veil is added on formal occasions.

Approximate number in Community, 300.

Active in educational, hospital and charitable work in the United States in the dioceses of Albany, Cleveland, Newark, Rochester, Syracuse, Toledo and Trenton.

Motherhouse, St. Anthony Convent, 1024 Court Street, Syracuse, New York.

Novitiate, 1108 Court Street, Syracuse, New York. (Diocese of Syracuse.)

SISTERS OF ST. FRANCIS*

BUFFALO, NEW YORK

1861

The Congregation of the Sisters of St. Francis whose Motherhouse is maintained at 337 Pine Street, Buffalo, New York, originated in 1861 as a mission community from the Sisters of St. Francis in Phila-delphia, Pennsylvania, founded there in 1855 by Ven. John Nepomucene Neumann, C.SS.R., Bishop of Philadelphia.

In the year 1863 the Sisters of St. Francis in Buffalo were estab-lished as a diocesan community.

With a present membership of nearly four hundred and fifty sisters, the Community is active in educational, hospital and charitable work in the dioceses of Buffalo and Scranton.

Motherhouse and Novitiate, Convent of Perpetual Adoration, 337 Pine Street, Buffalo, New York. (Diocese of Buffalo.)

SISTERS OF ST. FRANCIS OF MARY IMMACULATE†

1865

The Congregation of the Sisters of the Third Order of St. Francis of Mary Immaculate, at Joliet, Illinois, was established August 2, 1865, by Sister M. Alfred Moes, under the direction of the Very Rev. Pamfilo da Magliano, Custos Provincial of the Friars Minor of the Province of the Immaculate Conception at Allegany, New York, and with the approbation of the bishop of Chicago, the Right Rev. James Duggan, D.D.

Sister M. Alfred Moes and three other sisters, Sisters M. Bernard Peacard, M. Barbara Moes and M. Alberta Stockhof had been with the Sisters of the Holy Cross, at St. Mary's, Notre Dame, Indiana, during the years when the community there was adjusting its relations with the Motherhouse at Le Mans, France. Dispensed from their obligations toward the community, Sister Alfred and her companions in 1863 obtained affiliation with the Third Order of St. Francis, then with Sister Bernard, Sister Alfred became engaged in teaching at St. John the Baptist School at Joliet, Illinois.

In the summer of 1865, accompanied by the first postulant to the Community, Sister Alfred visited Allegany, New York, where, on

*From data supplied by the Sisters of St. Francis, 337 Pine St., Buffalo, N. Y., and from the Official Catholic Year Book, 1928.

†From data and material supplied by the Sisters of St. Francis of Mary Immaculate, Joliet, Ill.

the feast of the Portiuncula, the postulant was invested with the religious habit.   On the same day Father Pamfilo appointed Sister Alfred the first Superior of the new Congregation at Joliet. Following the call to Rome of its founder, in 1867, the newly-established Order was directed by his secretary, to whom he had referred the sisters, the Rev. Diomede Falconio, O.F.M., later cardinal, and Apostolic Delegate to the United States.

Mother Alfred presided over the Community as Superior until 1876, when her successor, Sister M. Alberta Stockhof, was elected. She was then appointed to extend the work of the sisters to the diocese of St. Paul, where the Congregation engaged for a time in educational work.

MOTHER MARY THOMASINE
Superior General of the Sisters of the
Third Order of St. Francis
of Mary Immaculate

St. Francis Academy, connected with the Motherhouse at Joliet, was organized as a boarding and day school about 1869, and was chartered as an educational institution under the laws of Illinois in 1874.   In 1904, with the consent of the archbishop of Chicago, the academy, with the exception of the art and music departments, was temporarily closed to extern pupils, and became St. Francis Normal School, for the preparations of teachers for the numerous schools entrusted to the Congregation.

In addition to their work in schools the sisters have established and maintain in Joliet the Guardian Angel Home—a home for neglected and destitute children. An industrial school for Indian girls, which was opened at Bayfield, Wisconsin, as also the Red Cliff Reservation School in Wisconsin, is presided over by sisters of the Congregation.

Though founded especially for the training and education of children and youth, with the responsiveness of true religious members of the Community took part in relief work during the yellow fever epidemic in Memphis, Tennessee, two of their number being among the victims of the disease. In 1918 the sisters were among the volunteer nurses during the influenza epidemic, closing their schools when

ST. FRANCIS CONVENT, JOLIET, ILLINOIS

they visited the sick in their own homes, and ministered to their needs.

In 1915, upon the completion of a modern and well-equipped building annex at the Motherhouse, St. Francis Academy was again opened for day and boarding students. This institution, which comprises the Motherhouse and novitiate, and which is now affiliated with Assisi Junior College, founded at the same site in 1925, is one of the most prominent and progressive in the archdiocese of Chicago, and for a radiating center for the Community, active now in many dioceses, the city of Joliet, about thirty-eight miles southwest of Chicago, is most advantageously located.

SUMMARY

Sisters of the Third Order of St. Francis of Mary Immaculate.
Founded in the United States in 1865.
Papal Approbation of Rules, Feb. 21, 1924, by Pope Pius XI.
Habit: The habit is of dark brown wool, with a scapular and a white woolen cord. The veil is black.
Approximate number in Community, 630.
Active chiefly in educational work in the archdioceses of Chicago and St. Louis and in the dioceses of Altoona, Cleveland, Columbus, Peoria, Rockford, Springfield in Illinois, Superior and Toledo.
Motherhouse and Novitiate, St. Francis Convent, Plainfield Avenue and Taylor Street, Joliet, Illinois. (Archdiocese of Chicago.)

FRANCISCAN MISSIONARY SISTERS OF THE SACRED HEART*

1865

The Congregation of the Franciscan Missionary Sisters of the Sacred Heart, or Gray Franciscan Sisters, as they are more familiarly described, was founded in Rome in 1858, by the Very Rev. Gregory delli Grotte de Castro, O.F.M., for definite co-operation in apostolic mission work, and the education and care of children. In carrying out the plans for such an Institute, Father Gregory was aided materially by the Duchess de Beauffremont, who contributed a large portion of her wealth to promote the interests of the new Community destined for the apostolic missions.

Though sanctioned and granted special favors and blessings by the Sovereign Pontiff, Pius IX, the Congregation suffered, as did other religious communities, during the period of civic unrest which then followed in Rome. At this time the munificence of the Duchess de Beauffremont enabled the sisters to secure, for their Motherhouse, an ancient monastery situated at Gemona, and formerly occupied by a community of Poor Clares.

In the year 1865, at the close of the Civil War in the United States, on the recommendation of the Franciscan Minister-General at Rome, the Franciscan Missionary Sisters were petitioned to extend their labors to this country, then endeavoring to regain normalcy, and much in need of laborers in its vast mission fields.

Filled with zeal for God's glory and the salvation of souls in America, which at that time was considered a foreign mission, the Missionary Sisters in Rome acceded to the petition, and on November 16, 1865, Mother Gertrude, with two companion sisters, sailed from Brest, France, and after a tedious and stormy voyage, reached New York on December 5th. On their arrival there, these Gray Franciscan Sisters were guests of the Sisters of Mercy until their own first convent home in the United States was ready for them.

On December 11th the three sisters and a postulant—representing four different nationalities, assumed charge of St. Francis School, with its cosmopolitan enrollment, which had been established by the Franciscan Fathers.

Scarcely had the community been established when applicants presented themselves for admission, regardless of the apparent

*From *Franciscan Missionary Sisters of the Sacred Heart*, by Maol-iosa, (P. J. Kenedy & Sons, N. Y.) and from data and material supplied by the Gray Franciscan Sisters, Mount St. Francis, Peekskill, N. Y.

austerity and the penitential poverty of the little community, followers of the "Poor little man of Assisi."

On June 29, 1867, in the Church of St. Francis Assisi, on West 31st Street, New York City, the habit of the Gray Franciscans was conferred on the band of candidates. With zealous regard for the welfare and progress of the recent adjunct to his extensive archdiocese, the Most Rev. John McCloskey—subsequently the first American cardinal—presided at the impressive ceremony, and set the seal of his approval on the labors to be perpetuated by the Franciscan Missionary Sisters of the Sacred Heart. Thus in America, as in Europe, the Franciscan Missionaries began their labors with the sanction of the Church's highest authority.

As the number in the community increased, the sisters extended their activities, catechetical work and the visitation of prisons, as well as teaching, engaging their attention.

MOTHER M. JOSEPH
U. S. Provincial Superior of the Franciscan Missionary Sisters of the Sacred Heart

As the Convent of St. Francis Assisi, on West 31st Street, in New York City, could no longer accommodate the rapidly growing community, a new location was sought, and on March 27, 1869, the "Townsend Homestead," an estate then consisting of suitable buildings and sixteen acres of ground at Peekskill, on the Hudson, was purchased by Mother M. Gertrude and the community. The property, now known as Mount St. Francis, was then incorporated, and became the Provincial house and novitiate of the Community in America, as filial relations with the General Motherhouse in Gemona, Italy, were continued, under the Cardinal-Protectorate, in Rome, of Gaetano Cardinal Bisleti.

Under Mother M. Bonaventure, successor in office of the indefatigable foundress-Superior, Mother M. Gertrude, the work of caring for dependent children was inaugurated in 1879, with the establishment of St. Joseph's Home, at Mount St. Francis.

30

The splendid well-equipped buildings which in time have been erected on adjacent land secured for the purpose are monuments of the labors of the Gray Franciscans, whose sagacity and foresight has resulted in this village, with its capacity for the care of the nearly one thousand children now in their charge.

To meet the exigencies of the day, when the labor of cutting bread for the many children to be served, required time almost unimaginable, the procuratrix, Sister Francesca, a Gray Franciscan in St. Joseph's Home, devised the plan by which a bread cutter at one operation might be made to cut a whole loaf into portions.

Ladycliff-on-the-Hudson, well described by its name, was secured by the Community on January 4, 1900. Formerly a world-famed hostelry, bearing on its registry such names as General Sherman and the Prince of Wales—afterward King Edward VII of England—and on an occasion in 1861 the meeting place of President Lincoln and General Scott, Cranston's, of the old days, became the site to which the Gray Franciscans transferred, from Mount St. Francis, the Academy of Our Lady of the Angels, which had been established there.

With its formal and ceremonious opening, on September 11th, the name Academy of Our Lady of the Angels gave place to that of Ladycliff Academy, now one of the most important institutions of the community.

In 1911 the Right Rev. Msgr. James W. Power, pastor of All Saints Church, one of the most important parishes of New York City, applied to Mount St. Francis for sisters to take charge of the work in the "Parish House," in which he planned to open commercial and sewing classes, and a kindergarten and day home for children of working mothers. The Provincial Superior, Mother M. Elizabeth, sent three sisters from the Peekskill Convent, who at once took up their residence at the "Mater Dei," at 12 West 129th Street. Here not only Hallowmas Business School, but also one of the model nurseries of New York City, have developed as a result of the efficient efforts of the sisters.

Among other institutions developed in New York City by the sisters, under Mother M. Joseph, Provincial Superior since 1914, is Assisium Institute, established with the approbation and under the patronage of His Eminence, Patrick Cardinal Hayes. This institution, which was opened on September 2, 1917, has the distinction of being the first school in New York City entirely devoted to training young girls for commercial or secretarial careers, under the guidance and personal instruction of religious teachers.

In 1923 a high school, with evening classes, was opened at the Institute, connected with which is also Assisium Casa Maria, the residence of the boarding pupils.

The first apostolic mission attended by the Franciscan Missionaries in the extension of their activities beyond the confines of the arch-

St. Joseph's Convent, Peekskill, New York

diocese of New York was in 1871, when they were welcomed to the diocese of Newark, and began the first of their missions in New Jersey, by taking charge of the parochial school connected with the parish conducted by the Passionists in what is now Union City.

In 1872 the community, having responded to a request for sisters to conduct a school in Philadelphia, began there strenuous work among the thousands of Italian nationality. To cope with the need, sisters were sent from the Motherhouse in Gemona, to augment the community sent from Mount St. Francis.

Pilgrimage visitors to the famous shrine of St. Rita, erected in Philadelphia by the Augustinian Fathers, see the Gray Franciscan Sisters of the nearby convent and school, as they light the hundreds of votive lamps throughout the noted church.

In 1918, when the influenza epidemic ravaged the city of Philadelphia, the Gray Franciscans were among the first to respond to the call for volunteers to care for the poor and afflicted. Of their own number were victims of the disease, willing workers in the cause of suffering humanity.

In addition to their other work in Philadelphia, and to provide a thorough business training for the girls of the city and elsewhere, the Community, in 1921, opened the Alvernia Business School, which the sisters now conduct.

During the fifty years and more, since the coming to the United States of the first little band of Gray Franciscans, the Motherhouse in Italy has not been unmindful of the activities of the large community, yet under the provincial superiorship of Mother M. Joseph, and in perfect accord with their far away Motherhouse, and visited at intervals by its representatives, the Franciscan Missionary Sisters in the United States progressively carry on the apostolic work for which they were founded.

SUMMARY

Franciscan Missionary Sisters of the Sacred Heart (Gray Franciscan Sisters.) Founded in Italy in 1858.
Papal Approbation of Rules in 1860, by Pope Pius IX.
Established in the United States in 1865.
Habit: The habit is gray, wide-sleeved and plainly made. A gray cloak and long scapular are worn, with white wimple, a black band and veil, and an extra veil for Holy Communion. The Franciscan Crown and the Immaculate Conception rosary are suspended from a woolen cord about the waist, and, as a distinctive mark of the missionary, a large crucifix is worn on the left side of the scapular.
Approximate number in Community in United States, 400.
Active in educational, charitable and social service work in the archdioceses of New York and Philadelphia, and in the diocese of Newark.
United States Provincial house and Novitiate, St. Joseph's Convent, Mt. St. Francis, Peekskill, New York. (Archdiocese of New York.)

SISTERS OF THE THIRD ORDER REGULAR OF ST. FRANCIS*

CLINTON, IOWA

1868

The Congregation of the Sisters of the Third Order of St. Francis of the Immaculate Conception of the Blessed Virgin Mary was founded at Mt. Olivet, Nelson County, Kentucky, in the year 1868 by the Right Rev. Peter J. Lavialle, D.D., Bishop of Louisville, and the Right Rev. Abbot Benedict, of Gethsemani, Kentucky.

It was the intention of the founders to establish a congregation of sisters who should engage in educational work, and especially conduct

---

*From data and material supplied by the Sisters of the 3rd Order Regular of St. Francis, Clinton, Iowa, and from the Official Catholic Year Book, 1928.

an industrial school and enable girls of moderate means to obtain a Catholic education.

For this purpose three young ladies, who were to form the nucleus of the new community, were sent to the Convent of the Sisters of St. Francis at Oldenburg, Indiana, where, after making their novitiate, they pronounced their vows on June 18, 1868. Returning to Mt. Olivet, one of the three, Mother M. Paula Beaven, was chosen first Mother Superior.

A boarding and industrial school then opened was continued until 1874, when, upon the advice of the Right Rev. William G. McCloskey, D.D., who had succeeded to the see of Louisville, the site of the Mother-house of the Community was transferred from Mt. Olivet to Shelbyville. Shelbyville, however, was found unsuited to the purpose, and the sisters met with scant success in the new location, where they continued their boarding school throughout a long period of struggles and trials, in spite of which the Community slowly but steadily increased.

A SISTER OF THE THIRD ORDER REGULAR OF ST. FRANCIS, CLINTON, IOWA

In 1890, through the efforts of the Jesuit Fathers, the sisters secured an opening in Iowa, where, under the jurisdiction of the Right Rev. John Hennessy, D.D., then bishop of Dubuque, they established their Motherhouse at Anamosa, Iowa. Three years later the diocese of Dubuque was made an archdiocese, and the same year marked another and a permanent change for the Sisters of St. Francis.

With episcopal permission the Community purchased property in Clinton, in the diocese of Davenport, where on October 4, 1893, they located their Motherhouse.

Prosperity attended the labors of the sisters in the boarding school which they at once opened, and which, the following year, it was found necessary to enlarge to provide for the increased attendance. Five years later the sisters purchased additional property, and new and commodious buildings were erected for Motherhouse, novitiate and academy, and later the junior college also conducted at the site.

Though engaged chiefly in the conducting of schools, not only in Iowa, but in Illinois, Nebraska and Missouri, the Congregation also

Main Entrance
MT. ST. CLARE CONVENT, CLINTON, IOWA

has charge of three hospitals, while at Clinton the sisters conduct Mt. Alverno Home for the Aged.

SUMMARY

Sisters of the 3rd Order of St. Francis of the Immaculate Conception of the B.V.M.
Founded in the United States in 1868.
Approximate number in Community, 270.

Active chiefly in educational and hospital work in the archdioceses of Chicago and Dubuque and the dioceses of Covington, Davenport, Des Moines, Lincoln, Omaha, Peoria, Rockford, St. Joseph and Sioux City.

Motherhouse and Novitiate, Mt. St. Clare Convent, Fairview Avenue, Clinton, Iowa. (Diocese of Davenport.)

SISTERS OF ST. FRANCIS*

PITTSBURGH, PENNSYLVANIA

1868

The genealogy of the Congregation of the Sisters of St. Francis at Millvale, Pennsylvania, proves the Community, founded there in 1868, of direct descent, through the community in Buffalo, from the mother foundation in Philadelphia, made in 1855 by the holy Redemptorist bishop, Ven. John Nepomucene Neumann.

The Community now has a membership of nearly three hundred and eighty sisters, engaged in conducting schools, hospitals, orphanages and homes for the aged in the dioceses of Altoona and Pittsburgh. St. Francis Hospital, established in Pittsburgh in 1865, in care of the sisters, ranks as one of the largest hospitals in the country conducted by religious orders of women.

Motherhouse and Novitiate, St. Francis Convent, Mt. Alvernia, Millvale Station, Pittsburgh, Pennsylvania. (Diocese of Pittsburgh.)

FRANCISCAN SISTERS OF CHRISTIAN CHARITY†

1869

In a small settlement from the midst of a colony of loyal Catholics, who had migrated from Baden, Germany, to far away Wisconsin, and established a settlement at St. Naziens, the Congregation of the Franciscan Sisters of Christian Charity arose.

Sickness among their number had caused a party of travelers from Ohio to stop at St. Naziens. Hospitably received and assisted, the sufferers recovered strength and made preparations to resume their trip. Three young women of the party, impressed with the peace and spirit of the little settlement, arranged to remain, and bade adieu to their traveling companions.

*From the annals of the Sisters of St. Francis, and the Official Catholic Year Book, 1928.

†From *Alverno, the Story of the Franciscan Sisters of Alverno, Wisconsin, 1866-1919,* by Sister M. Florence Kientz, M.A., of the Franciscan Sisters of Christian Charity, of Alverno (Catholic Education Press, Washington, D. C.), and data and material supplied by the Franciscan Sisters of Christian Charity, Manitowoc, Wis.

There was living at St. Naziens at this time Theresa Gramlich, a devout and charitable young woman, whom the pastor, the Rev. George Fessler, had asked to teach the children, during sessions which were held in the gallery of the little church.

Theresa soon made friends with the newcomers, Mary Graff, Josephine Thoeing and Rosa Wahl. She inspired them to assist her, and the spirit of their united labors seemed contagious, for soon Father Fessler's sister imitated her friends and added her talents and efforts to the splendid work being done by the four young women.

They then agreed to live together, that they might more conveniently assemble for mutual assistance in their school tasks. Their house was, in reality, the nursery of a community, and these earnest workers the nucleus of a future religious congregation.

Impelled to consecrate their work to the service of God, and perceiving the necessity of mental and spiritual training, the four teachers placed themselves under the direction of Mother Caroline, of the School Sisters of Notre Dame, in Milwaukee.

After a year there the four aspirants went to Manitowoc, to continue under the spiritual direction of Father Fessler, who had been transferred there.

Encouraged by Father Fessler, Miss Gramlich opened a private school in the parish, and in a short time the number of pupils reached seventy-five. The school was a repetition of the peaceful tenor of the life they had led in their former community home. Meanwhile their spiritual director, realizing their earnest longing to be enrolled as religious in the Church of the New World, was

MOTHER ODELIA WAHL

awaiting the approval of the archbishop of the diocese, as well as that of the Capuchin Provincial, the Very Rev. Francis Hass, to whom he had applied for permission to incorporate the little band into a religious society.

The Rule of St. Francis was selected and adopted as that most suitable for the guidance of these souls, who wished to unite to the duties involved in school management the spiritual life of religious.

The career of the new establishment began, then, at Manitowoc. Mother Odelia Wahl was chosen Superior, and she administered, for a long period, the affairs, temporal and spiritual, of the young Community.

In the spring of 1874 the building erected for a new Motherhouse was dedicated and occupied. The new convent was built on an attractive site, and came to be known as "Silver Lake Convent," from the beauty of the nearby lake. The circumstance of the changing

HOLY FAMILY CONVENT (Entrance), ALVERNO, MANITOWOC, WISCONSIN

of the name, a few years later, to "Alverno," gave great joy to the followers of the saint who had received the stigmata on Alverno's holy mountain. When a legal title was bestowed on the Community, it read, "Holy Family Convent of the Franciscan Sisters of Charity, Alverno, Wisconsin." The Community soon seemed assured a secure foothold among the sisterhoods of the west.

Experiencing the struggles and difficult lot of the pioneer religious congregations in the country, the Community, nevertheless, received many candidates, and proportionately opened needed mission schools.

The Congregation was augmented in number, before the end of the first decade of its existence, by the arrival from Germany of twenty-seven sisters, who, as a result of the *Kulturkampf,* sought refuge in America, and were amalgamated with the Community at Alverno.

The sisters, having extended their labors beyond the state of Wisconsin, added to their work of teaching, the direction of a home for the aged, and of hospitals.

During an administration of twenty years, 1891-1911, under Mother M. Alexia, a *scholasticate,* later affiliated with the Catholic University of America, was officially established and maintained at the Motherhouse. The Rules and Constitutions of the Order were revised, and on August 3, 1894, received the episcopal approval of the Most Rev. F. X. Katzer, D.D., Archbishop of Milwaukee.

Mother M. Generose Cahill, as Superior General of the Congregation, continues to carry out the work of her predecessors in that position, maintaining intimate association between every mission house and the Motherhouse at Alverno.

SUMMARY

Franciscan Sisters of Christian Charity.
Founded in the United States in 1869.
Approximate number in Community, 600.
Active in educational, hospital and charitable work in the archdioceses of Chicago and Milwaukee, and in the dioceses of Columbus, Grand Rapids, Green Bay, La Crosse, Marquette, Omaha, Superior and Wheeling.
Motherhouse and Novitiate, Holy Family Convent, Alverno, Manitowoc, Wis. (Diocese of Green Bay.)

SISTERS OF ST. FRANCIS*

TIFFIN, OHIO

1869

Through the benevolence of Mr. John Grieveldinger of Tiffin, Ohio, with whom resided, on his farm, his widowed daughter, Mrs. Elizabeth Schaefer, with her two daughters and a sister-in-law, Miss Mary Schaefer, all were enabled to carry out a mutual desire to devote their lives to the care of the poor and the orphaned.

Established in 1869 as a community of Sisters of the Third Order of St. Francis, and in time allowed to make their profession as

*From data supplied by the Sisters of St. Francis, Tiffin, Ohio.

religious, the number of members grew, as candidates asked to unite with them in their community life and good works.

In 1868 a building suitable for an orphanage was built on the farm and there the community began its first institutional work. Mrs. Schaefer, becoming Sister Francis, served as Superior until her death in 1893.

In addition to its work in connection with St. Francis Orphanage and Home for Aged Persons, conducted at the Motherhouse site in Tiffin, the Community, of now nearly a hundred and twenty sisters, engages in parochial school work in the diocese of Toledo.

A further activity of the Community is the conducting at Carey, Ohio, of the Pilgrims' House, for the benefit of those who in a spirit of devotion visit the more than fifty-year-old shrine of Our Lady of Consolation at Carey.

Motherhouse and Novitiate, St. Francis Convent, St. Francis Street and Melmore Avenue, Tiffin Ohio. (Diocese of Toledo.)

SISTERS OF ST. MARY*

ST. LOUIS, MISSOURI

1872

The history of the Congregation of the Sisters of St. Mary of the Third Order of St. Francis begins in the United States in the year 1872, when five Sisters of St. Francis of the Franciscan community founded in Pirmasenz, Bavaria, in 1855, were welcomed to the arch-diocese of St. Louis by the vicar general, the Very Rev. Henry Muehlsiepen, in the name of the archbishop, the Most Rev. Peter R. Kenrick, D.D.

Mother M. Odilia Berger, Superior of the little group of sisters from Bavaria, while working at a mission in Paris had been forced because of her German nationality to leave France at the beginning of the Franco-Prussian War. With Sister M. Magdalen as a companion, she went to Elberfeld, Germany, where both then engaged in nursing in one of the military hospitals and later, under direction of the pastor, and joined by three aspirants, established religious community life. Nursing of patients in their own homes was undertaken, and their services were eagerly sought.

Almost coincident with the close of the Franco-Prussian War was the beginning of the *Kulturkampf* in Germany, and the withdrawal

*From data and material supplied by the Sisters of St. Mary, St. Mary's Infirmary, St. Louis, Mo.

from the country of numerous religious communities, whose members sought new homes in strange lands rather than relinquish their sacred garb, and community life.

Through former patients who had emigrated at about this time to the United States, and to whom Mother Odilia had appealed regarding the advisability of a timely change for herself and the little Community, the sisters were assured of a welcome in St. Louis.

Accordingly five sisters, Sisters Magdalen Fuerst, Sister Elizabeth Becker, Sister Frances Reuter, Sister Marianna Herker, and a postulant, Margaret Schneider, with Mother Odilia as Superior, sailed from Hamburg on October 18, 1872, and arrived in St. Louis on the sixteenth of the following month.

The little group of Franciscan Sisters then became guests at the Ursuline Convent in St. Louis until they secured quarters in the upper story of a house opposite St. Mary's Church. Before the end of the ensuing year, through the zealous efforts of Mother Odilia, a Motherhouse, the first headquarters of the Sisters of St. Mary, as they were henceforth known, was built on a site directly south of the church, at the corner of Third and Gratiot Streets. On November 18, 1874, under the title of Sisters of St. Mary, the Community, which had already more than doubled in numbers, was incorporated under the laws of the state of Missouri.

Previous to this progressive and permanent step, the sisters had become actively engaged in the work in which they were destined to become one of the foremost communities in the country. Scarcely had they been established in St. Louis when they were devoting themselves heart and soul, both day and night, to the nursing of those stricken by smallpox in the epidemic which then began. With two aspirants to the Community joining with them in their merciful ministrations, rendered especially and almost exclusively to the poor, the sisters labored so assiduously that they came to be called the "Smallpox Sisters."

In 1876 the increase in their number permitted the sisters' engaging in the care of orphans and the conducting of a home for girls. St. Joseph's Home, then established, and conducted until it was relinquished in 1882, that the Community might devote itself exclusively to the work of nursing, was also the site of the Motherhouse, while the more centrally located convent on Third Street served as a residence for the sisters who went out nursing the sick in their own homes.

To provide for a greater number of sick than was possible by visiting them in their homes, and to do so more advantageously, plans were made for the erection of a hospital for which the sisters secured residence property in St. Louis on Fifteenth and Papin Streets.

Arranging the house, one part for patients and one part for the requisite number of sisters, a small but suitable room for a chapel

ST. MARY'S INFIRMARY, ST. LOUIS, MISSOURI

was also added, and on May 24, 1877, the institution was blessed by the vicar general. On June 1st the hospital, under the name St. Mary's Infirmary, was opened to patients.

Under the direction of Mother Odilia and the five original members of the Community, and the staff of prominent St. Louis physicians with whom they worked, the Sisters of St. Mary became efficient nurses. To take charge of the hospital drugs, one of their number, Sister M. Aloysia, was chosen to study pharmacy, and was the first of a number of the Community who have since successfully passed the State Board Examinations and received certificates as registered pharmacists.

In the summer of 1878, when the south was in the throes of a yellow fever epidemic, Mother Odilia and her sisters in religion heard the appeal for nurses, and were given ecclesiastical permission to respond to it.

The noble and self-sacrificing labors of the volunteers who then went to the stricken city of Memphis, Tennessee, five to become martyr victims of the pestilence, when priests, sisters and nurses died at their posts, have recently been recalled by United States Senator Joseph T. Robinson of Arkansas, through whose efforts Congress accorded an appropriate monument in Calvary Cemetery, Memphis, to the Catholic sisters who gave their lives in the cause of humanity during the yellow fever scourge in the city in 1878.

During these years of activity and permanency as a community, the Sisters of St. Mary, living according to the Rule of the Third Order of St. Francis, and Constitutions adapted to their secondary end, were not yet bound by the regular vows of religion. Upon receiving the approbation of the Holy See for the Community, seventeen of the oldest members, on the feast of the Seraphic St. Francis, October 4, 1880, handed their spiritual director, Father Muehlsiepen, the vicar general, their first vows in accordance with the Rule of the Tertiaries of St. Francis living in community, and with a particular clause relating to the Sisters of St. Mary.

Little more than a week later Mother Odilia succumbed to a serious illness, and died on October 17, the feast of her chosen patroness, St. Margaret Mary. Upon the request of the foundress-Superior, Sister M. Seraphia succeeded her in office.

In 1883, when smallpox again became prevalent in St. Louis, the Sisters of St. Mary, in response to a request from the municipal authorities, at once took charge of the nursing at the Quarantine Hospital. Here in the year between May, 1883, and May, 1884, they cared for between fourteen hundred and fifteen hundred patients, many of whom recovered. To provide for the spiritual consolation of the sisters during this period the authorities gratefully set aside a room for them as a chapel.

Soon after this the Community took charge for long periods of hospitals for the Missouri Pacific and the Missouri, Kansas and Texas Railroads.

In 1885 the sisters, who had nursed in St. Charles, Missouri, in the epidemic of 1873, returned there to make their first permanent hospital foundation beyond the archiepiscopal city. St. Joseph's Hospital at St. Charles was then followed in time by the establishment of hospitals now maintained in Jefferson City and Kansas City, Missouri; Baraboo and Madison, Wisconsin, and Blue Island, Illinois.

St. Mary's Hospital, St. Mary's Infirmary and Mt. St. Rose Sanatorium, established in St. Louis by the Community, are affiliated with

St. Louis University, and are known as the St. Louis University Hospital group, St. Mary's Infirmary being devoted entirely to charity, and having a large dispensary connected with it.

It was given to Mother M. Aloysia, successor in office in 1910 of Mother M. Seraphia, to lead the Community through the country's scourge of 1918, when the surgical wards of hospitals were closed to all but emergency cases, that as many as possible of those stricken with influenza might be given attention, and when the sisters, worn by long hours of continual strain at the post of duty, were themselves victims of the disease.

Upon the expiration of Mother Aloysia's term of office, Sister M. Concordia, who for fifteen years had been Mistress of Novices, was elected Superior General of the Congregation, and with Mother Aloysia as

MOTHER M. CONCORDIA

first Assistant; Sister M. Eulalia as Vicar Superior, and Sisters M. Liberata, M. Petronilla and M. Constantia as Assistants, at present carries on the ever progressive activity of the Community. In addition to the hospitals they have established, the sisters have recently opened at University City, Missouri, in the Clayton vicinity, St. Mary's Retreat House for Women, which is attended by the Jesuit Fathers from St. Louis University.

SUMMARY

Sisters of St. Mary of the Third Order of St. Francis.
Founded in the United States in 1872.
Papal Approbation of Rules, December 31, 1922, by Pope Pius XI.
Approximate number in Community, 410.
Active chiefly in hospital work in the archdioceses of Chicago, Milwaukee and St. Louis and the dioceses of Kansas City and La Crosse.
Motherhouse, St. Mary's Infirmary, 1536 Papin Street, St. Louis, Missouri.
Novitiate, St. Mary's Hospital, Clayton Road and Bellevue Avenue, St. Louis, Missouri. (Archdiocese of St. Louis.)

FELICIAN SISTERS, ORDER OF ST. FRANCIS*

1874

The Felician Sisters of the Order of St. Francis, the largest congregation of Franciscan Sisters in the United States, began their labors in this country in 1874.

From their Motherhouse in Cracow, Poland, sisters of the Congregation, which was founded at Warsaw in 1855, came to the diocese of Green Bay, where for a time they established their first United States Provincial headquarters at Polonia, near Stevens Point, Wisconsin.

In 1882, under the provincial superiorship of Mother Mary Monica, transfer of the convent was made from Polonia to Detroit, where Mother Mary de Sales now serves as Provincial Superior of the Community of nearly five hundred and fifty sisters, who are engaged in teaching in forty parochial schools, six of which are high schools. Two orphanages are also conducted by the Felician Sisters in the Provincialate of Detroit.

In the year 1900 Mother Mary Brunona was appointed first Provincial Superior of a new province of the Order, which was established at Buffalo, with the Provincial Convent located then at William and Kennedy Streets. Mother Mary Angelina now serves as Provincial Superior of this province, in which more than five hundred sisters are under her jurisdiction.

The year 1911 saw the establishment of a necessary third United States provincialate of the Felician Sisters, and Milwaukee, Wisconsin, was chosen for the seat of the provincialate, with Mother Mary Veronica as first Provincial Superior. However, in 1927 this Provincial Convent was transferred from Milwaukee to Chicago, Illinois, where now under the provincial superiorship of Mother Mary Seraphine, the large community of nearly six hundred and fifty sisters of the Congregation engages in educational and charitable work in the archdioceses and dioceses of the provincialate territory.

For the convenience of the many Felician Sisters of the Order of St. Francis engaged in educational and charitable work in the eastern section of the United States, a provincialate of the Order was established at Lodi, New Jersey, in 1913.

Mother Mary Benedicta was appointed first Provincial Superior at Lodi, which then became the house, instead of the convent at Buffalo, for members of the Order active in the district included in the new provincialate, where Mother Mary Angelica is now Provincial

*From data and material supplied by the Felician Sisters, O.S.F., in Detroit, Mich.; Buffalo, N. Y.; Chicago, Ill.; Lodi, N. J., and McKeesport, Pa.

Superior of the approximately seven hundred sisters who compose this largest of the United States communities of the Order.

Excepting the transfer of the Provincial Convent from Milwaukee to Chicago, the most recent establishment of the Felician Sisters of the Order of St. Francis was made in 1921, when a division of the community in the Provincialate of Detroit took place, and a new Provincial Convent was opened at McKeesport, Pennsylvania, in the diocese of Pittsburgh. Mother M. Pancratia served as first Provincial Superior of the community of more than two hundred members, of which Mother M. Leonissa is present Provincial Superior. The sisters are active in educational and charitable work in the archdioceses and dioceses of the new provincialate, which with the four others previously established in the United States is under the jurisdiction of the General Motherhouse, located at Batorego St. No. 16, Cracow, Poland, and which is the residence of the Mother General of the Order, at present Mother Mary Bonaventura.

SUMMARY

Felician Sisters of the Order of St. Francis.
Founded in Poland in 1855.
Established in the United States in 1874.
Habit: The habit and scapular are brown, with a black veil. A rosary of large wooden beads, having seven decades, of Franciscan origin, is suspended from the cincture of white hemp rope, and a wooden crucifix is worn on the breast. A silver lined steel ring is given at final profession.
Approximate number in communities in United States, 2,650.
Active in educational, charitable and social service work: *Provincialate of Detroit,* in the dioceses of Cleveland, Detroit, Fort Wayne, Grand Rapids and Toledo; *Provincial house and Novitiate,* Convent of the Felician Sisters, 4232 St. Aubin Avenue, Detroit, Michigan (Diocese of Detroit); *Provincialate of Buffalo,* in the dioceses of Altoona, Buffalo, Erie and Syracuse; *Provincial house and Novitiate,* Immaculate Heart of Mary Convent, 600 Doat Street, Buffalo, New York (Diocese of Buffalo); *Provincialate of Chicago,* in the archdioceses of Chicago, Milwaukee, and St. Paul, and in the dioceses of Grand Island, Green Bay, La Crosse, Leavenworth, Lincoln, Peoria, Rockford, St. Cloud and St. Joseph; *Provincial house and Novitiate,* Mother of Good Counsel Convent, 3800 Peterson Avenue, Rogers Park, Chicago, Illinois (Archdiocese of Chicago); *Provincialate of Newark,* in the archdioceses of Baltimore, Boston, New York and Philadelphia, and in the dioceses of Albany, Brooklyn, Burlington, Hartford, Manchester, Newark, Springfield, Trenton and Wilmington; *Provincial house and Novitiate,* Convent of the Felician Sisters, South Main Street, Lodi, New Jersey (Diocese of Newark); *Provincialate of Pittsburgh,* in the archdioceses of Cincinnati and Philadelphia and in the dioceses of Columbus, Erie, Harrisburg, Pittsburgh and Wheeling; *Provincial house and Novitiate,* Convent of Our Lady of the Sacred Heart, McKeesport, Pennsylvania (Diocese of Pittsburgh).

SCHOOL SISTERS OF ST. FRANCIS*

1874

The School Sisters of St. Francis of St. Joseph's Convent form a Congregation which was founded at Schwarzach, Baden, Germany, November 13, 1857. To provide a new community of sisters for the special care of orphans, the Rev. F. X. Lender effected the founda-

St. Joseph's Conve

tion of this Order of religious women, whose community life is conducted according to the Rule of St. Francis.

During the time of the Prussian May Laws the little community at Schwarzach was dissolved, and the orphanage, the special work of the sisters, was taken over by the government. The sisters were released from their vows and were free either to continue their work at the orphanage, without the religious garb and without vows, or to return to their homes. Those who refused to lay aside their religious garb were forced to leave the country.

Mother M. Alexia, who was then Superior at Schwarzach, Sister Alfons and Sister Clara sought refuge in America in 1873. On April 28, 1874, the sisters were received in the diocese of Milwaukee by the Right Rev. John Martin Henni, D.D., and their convent home was established at New Cassel, Wisconsin. The following year the archdiocese of Milwaukee was created, and Bishop Henni was raised

*From data and material supplied by the School Sisters of St. Francis, St. Joseph's Convent, Milwaukee, Wis.

to the archiepiscopal dignity on February 11, 1875. From that year the School Sisters of St. Francis, continuing under the superiorship of Mother M. Alexia, began their special work of teaching in the United States.

With a growth remarkable in the history of religious orders of women in the United States, the Congregation, in little more than fifty years, has increased from three hundred to more than

WAUKEE, WISCONSIN

fifteen houndred members, all under the jurisdiction of the General Motherhouse of the Congregation, which was established at Milwaukee.

Presiding as Superior General until her death on April 5, 1929, over the affairs of the now large Congregation was Mother M. Alfons, one of the three, who, animated by a religious fervor and exaltation of purpose which upheld the little band, made the long journey to a new home in a strange land. Assisting Mother M. Alfons in the executive work of the Congregation at the time of her death were Mother M. Stanislaus and Council Sisters, Sister M. Josepha, Sister M. Serafica and Sister M. Corona.

A Provincial house of the Congregation has been established at *Kloster der Franziskanerinnen,* Erlenbad, Germany.

In 1906 the Congregation sent sisters to the Caroline Islands, but recalled them to the United States during the World War.

Prominent among the many educational institutions conducted by the School Sisters of St. Francis, one of the largest congregations of Franciscan Sisters in the United States, are Alvernia High School and Alvernia Conservatory of Music and Expression, in Chicago, and Madonna High School in Aurora, Illinois.

MOTHER M. ALFONS

Other prominent institutions engaging the labors of the Congregation are the Sacred Heart Sanitarium and St. Mary's Hill Sanitarium in Milwaukee.

SUMMARY

School Sisters of St. Francis.
Founded in Germany in 1857.
Established in the United States in 1874.

Habit: The habit is black, with a scapular, a black veil lined with white, and a white cincture to which is attached a large rosary. A crucifix is worn on the breast.

Approximate number in Community, 1,600.

Active in educational and hospital work in the archdioceses of Chicago, Dubuque, Milwaukee, Portland in Oregon, St. Louis and St. Paul, and in the dioceses of Davenport, Denver, Des Moines, Detroit, Fort Wayne, Grand Island, Green Bay, Kansas City, La Crosse, Lincoln, Marquette, Omaha, Peoria, Pittsburgh, Rockford, Sioux City, Sioux Falls, Springfield in Illinois, Superior and Wichita.

Motherhouse and Novitiate, St. Joseph's Convent, Layton Boulevard and Greenfield Avenue, Milwaukee, Wisconsin. (Archdiocese of Milwaukee.)

SISTERS OF ST. FRANCIS OF PENANCE AND CHRISTIAN CHARITY*

1874

The Congregation of the Sisters of St. Francis of Penance and Christian Charity, a branch of the great Third Order of St. Francis, was founded at Heythuizen, Holland, in 1835.

Catherine Dahmen, whose organized charitable labors, with the co-operation of several other young women, were directly responsible for the establishment of this Community, was born November 19, 1787, at Laek, Holland.

France was in the iron grip of the Revolution, and the part of Holland in which the Dahmens lived was affected, during Catherine's pious girlhood, by the troubled times. Most of the convents had been closed and the religious dispersed, and, a desire she cherished for the cloister seeming impossible of attainment for the time being at least, Catherine became a Tertiary of St. Francis, and went to live with several other young girls at the little town of Maeseyk.

To this little group of pious women who devoted themselves to prayer, labor for poor churches, and works of mercy, the parish priest of Heythuizen, the Rev. Father van der Zandt, applied for someone to take charge there of the altar linen, and to teach the children their catechism. In response, Catherine Dahmen was sent to this little nearby village, destined to be the cradle of the flourishing congregation she was to found.

In the new work, furthered by her unassuming gentleness, Catherine was soon joined by others who wished to aid her, and to those munity she replied, in the words which became habitual to her, and who made light of her hopes for the formation of a religious com-

*From data and material supplied by the Sisters of St. Francis, Stella Niagara, N. Y.

which were later adopted as a becoming motto for her Congr(
"God will provide."

Her confidence was justified, for in 1835, with the consen[
bishop of Roermond, the Motherhouse of the new Congregat[
present *Klooster St. E*
at Heythuizen, was dedic
Father van der Zandt.

For the guidance of [
Community, the approve
stitutions of the Recollec[
of the Third Order, wit
modifications by Cather
religion Mother Magdal(
men, were adopted.

The Sisters of St.
of this Congregation da
activities in America fror
In that year, a number (
schools in Germany havi[
closed by the May La
forced in the country, :
M. Aloysia, the Superio
eral, accompanied by th
ters, came to the United
in advance of the others
Community, and in I
New York, at the reques[
Rev. Father Behrens, S
sumed charge of St. M

MOTHER M. VALESCA
Superior General in 1925 of the Fran-
ciscan Sisters of Penance and Christian
Charity, Stella Niagara, N. Y.

and St. Anne's parochial schools. In the meantime the Rig[
S. H. Rosecrans, D.D., Bishop of Columbus, had asked the si:
conduct St. Vincent's Orphanage in that city, and with the ar[
recruits from the Community in Europe this was entrusted t
charge.

In 1876, shortly after the sisters had begun their work in (
bus, they were offered a site for an academy in New Lexington
in the diocese. This was accepted and a building was at once
for the purpose, and opened as St. Aloysius' Academy, a b(
school which has attained the success merited for it by the
struggles in its interests in their pioneer days in the country.

From the first a novitiate had been established by the Com:
at Sacred Heart Academy, opened in Buffalo. To accommod:

Community in its increasing number, as well as to open a boarding school, an advantageous site picturesquely located on the banks of the Niagara, not far from Lewistown, New York, was secured. Upon the completion in 1909 of the first building then erected there, it was

SEMINARY OF OUR LADY OF THE SACRED HEART, STELLA NIAGARA, NEW YORK

dedicated to Our Lady of the Sacred Heart, and made the United States Provincial Motherhouse and Novitiate of the Congregation.

The academy then opened at the Motherhouse as the Seminary of Our Lady of the Sacred Heart is frequently described by its postoffice name, Stella Niagara.

During more than fifty years of activity in the country, the Community has developed its work in many schools, elementary and secondary, particularly in cities of the western states. Twenty Franciscan Sisters from Stella Niagara are engaged in the school for Indians at St. Francis Mission on the Pine Ridge Reservation of the Cheyenne Agency in South Dakota, while nineteen members of the Community, likewise, labor at Holy Rosary Mission on the same reservation and in the diocese of Lead.

In addition to the many educational institutions now under the direction of the Congregation in the United States, the sisters are also engaged in conducting hospitals, orphanages and homes for girls, and in the care of a day nursery, and in these varied activities "the spirit which animates them is that of their founder, St. Francis—the spirit of simple, humble self-surrender to the cause of Jesus Christ."

SUMMARY

Sisters of St. Francis of Penance and Christian Charity.
Founded in Holland in 1835.
Papal Approbation of Rules in 1869, by Pope Pius IX.
Established in the United States in 1874.
Habit: The habit is the regular brown of the Franciscans, with the white Franciscan cord.
Approximate number in Community in United States, 525.
Active in educational, hospital, charitable, social service and missionary work in the archdiocese of Portland in Oregon and in the dioceses of Bismarck, Buffalo, Columbus, Denver, Grand Island, Great Falls, Lead, Los Angeles and San Diego, Omaha, Sacramento, Seattle, Spokane, Trenton and Wheeling.
United States Motherhouse and Novitiate, Seminary of Our Lady of the Sacred Heart, Stella Niagara, New York. (Diocese of Buffalo.)

SISTERS OF THE THIRD ORDER OF ST. FRANCIS OF THE HOLY FAMILY*

1875

The Congregation of the Sisters of the Third Order of St. Francis of the Holy Family was founded at Herford, Westphalia, Germany, in the year 1864, by Mother Mary Xaveria Termehr, for the special work of the education of children in parochial schools and orphanages and for the nursing of the sick in their own homes.

The Community, which was established in the United States in the fall of 1875, at Iowa City, Iowa, had been compelled to leave its native field of labor because of the so-called "May Laws" passed by the new imperial government of Germany.

Before leaving Germany, Mother Mary Xaveria received for herself and her companions, eighteen professed sisters, seven novices and four postulants, a letter of recommendation to the Right Rev. John Hennessy, D.D., then bishop of Dubuque, later its first archbishop. The letter which Mother Mary Xaveria presented, and which secured for the Community a hearty welcome to the diocese in Iowa, was from the Right Rev. Conrad Martin, Bishop of Paderborn, who had written it while held captive at Wesel for defending the prerogatives of the Church.

---

*From data and material supplied by the Sisters of St. Francis of the Holy Family, Dubuque, Iowa.

On December 17, 1878, upon the request of Bishop Hennessy, the sisters transferred from Iowa City to Dubuque, where early in 1879 they took charge of St. Mary's Orphanage, established that year by the diocese, and which has continued the Community's charge throughout the past fifty years.

Simultaneously with the inauguration of their work at the orphanage, the sisters began their work of teaching in parochial schools in the country of their adoption, and today conduct more than fifty high schools and grade schools. Prominent among the academic institutions which they have established is the Academy of the Immaculate Conception, opened in Dubuque in 1907, and which is accredited to the State University of Iowa City, the State College of Agriculture and Mechanic Arts at Ames, and the State Teachers' College at Cedar Falls.

MOTHER M. DOMINICA WIENEKE

ST. FRANCIS' CONVENT, MT. ST. FRANCIS, DUBUQUE, IOWA

Prior to the opening of this academy the Community had in 1888 taken the initial step in a work which today is being rapidly developed by the religious orders of women in the United States. This was the opening by the Sisters of St. Francis in Dubuque of Mary of the Angels Home for Young Ladies, an institution offering a home and protection to employed young women in the city, and accommodating nearly a hundred residents.

In addition to its school and orphanage work, and this philan-thropy, the Congregation, of which Mother M. Dominica Wieneke is the present Superior, also engages in hospital work and the care of the aged.

SUMMARY

Sisters of the Third Order of St. Francis of the Holy Family.
Founded in Germany in 1864.
Established in the United States in 1875.
Papal Approbation of Rules, December 2, 1914, by Pope Benedict XV.
Habit: The habit and scapular are brown, with a black veil. A cincture of white wool is worn, with a seven-decade rosary, or the Franciscan Crown, suspended from it, and a crucifix is worn on the breast. A silver ring is received when perpetual vows are taken.
Approximate number in Community, 640.
Active in educational, hospital, charitable and social service work in the archdioceses of Chicago, Dubuque and Portland in Oregon, and in the dioceses of Davenport, Des Moines, Lead and Sioux City.
Motherhouse and Novitiate, St. Francis Convent, Mt. St. Francis, Dubuque, Iowa. (Archdiocese of Dubuque.)

HOSPITAL SISTERS OF ST. FRANCIS*

1875

Little more than fifty years ago sisters from a Community at St. Francis' Hospital, Münster, Germany, came to Springfield, Illinois, for the definite work of caring for the sick poor in homes and hos-pitals.

Sister Angelica, the Superior, and her little band of ardent workers accepted the hospitality of the Ursulines in Springfield, until they secured a home.

Beginning its labors in the United States with its members few in number, but fervent, and with little more than those receiving its ministrations, the Community has become one of the recognized insti-tutions in Springfield and throughout and beyond that diocese. In the early development of its members to the highest perfection of religious life, stress was so laid on the need for a spirit of social

*From data supplied by the Hospital Sisters of St. Francis, Springfield, Ill.

service, and for aptitude in the adoption of progressive methods, that today the reward of the perseverance of the Congregation and its service to the poor is evidenced in the success of the hospitals established and conducted by the sisters.

At St. John's Hospital in Springfield, a school of nursing for sisters and laity is maintained, and the standard training in the school has been recognized and accredited in Illinois and New York. At the Motherhouse adjoining the hospital Mother Afra, Provincial Superior, has, as Assistant Superiors, Sister Teresa, Registered Pharmacist, Sister Fridoluie, and Sister Magdalene, R.N., Ph.D.

Having extended its labors into many dioceses, and having participated according to the need, in World War relief work, and cyclone relief, the Community, in 1925 opened and has since conducted St. John's Hospital and Dispensary, at Tsinanfu, Shantung, China.

In the building expansion necessitated by the growth of the Order, a novitiate has been established near Riverton, Illinois, within the diocese of Springfield, the home-diocese of the Community. The General Motherhouse of the Congregation is in Münster, Germany.

SUMMARY

Hospital Sisters of St. Francis.
Founded in Germany.
Established in the United States in 1875.
Papal Approbation of Rules, September 27, 1901, by Pope Leo XIII.
Habit: The habit is black, with a circular guimpe and rather square headband. A white woolen cord, with three knots is worn.
Approximate number in Community in United States, 700.
Active in hospital and nursing work in the archdioceses of Milwaukee and St. Louis, and in the dioceses of Belleville, Green Bay, La Crosse, Peoria, Rockford and Springfield in Illinois.
United States Provincial House, St. John's Hospital, Springfield, Illinois. (Diocese of Springfield in Illinois.)
United States Novitiate, Riverton, Illinois. (Diocese of Springfield in Illinois.)

POOR SISTERS OF ST. FRANCIS SERAPH OF THE PERPETUAL ADORATION*

1875

The Congregation of the Poor Sisters of St. Francis Seraph of the Perpetual Adoration originated in Olpe, in the province of West-

*From data and material supplied by the Poor Sisters of St. Francis Seraph of the Perpetual Adoration, La Fayette, Ind.

phalia, Germany, when on September 29, 1859, Mary Teresa Bonzel and two companions were presented to the Right Rev. Conrad Martin, Bishop of Paderborn, and received his approval of their

MOTHER M. TERESA (1830-1905)
Foundress of the Congregation of the Poor Sisters of St. Francis Seraph of the Perpetual Adoration

united work of caring for poor and neglected children. Other devout and zealous young women joining with them, they extended their labors to the care of the sick and the education of youth.

On December 20, 1860, Bishop Martin gave the little community the religious habit of the Third Order Regular of St. Francis, and constituted it, by his episcopal authority, the Congregation of the Poor Franciscan Sisters of Perpetual Adoration, the sisters taking up—upon the completion of their convent chapel—in addition to their active work, the Perpetual Adoration of Our Lord in the Holy Eucharist, in hourly rotation, day and night.

On August 6, 1865, Mother M. Teresa was appointed Superior General of the Congregation, and as foundress continued in that position until her holy death, which occurred on February 6, 1905, at the Motherhouse at Olpe.

During four decades of years Mother Teresa saw her labors blessed in the growth of the Community and its works. She bravely led her sisters as they ministered to the wounded and dying on the battlefields of the Franco-Prussian War, and after receiving—by decree of Emperor Wilhelm—the country's decoration for their devoted services, Mother Teresa and her Community were not spared in the oppression following soon after, upon the issuance, at Bismarck's command, of the "May Laws."

With desolation and upheaval among the many religious orders of the country, Mother Teresa, strong and determined as to their rights, with her Community prayed and hoped, and as they prayed there visited the Motherhouse in Olpe, from America, the Right Rev. Joseph Dwenger, C.PP.S., D.D., of the diocese of Fort Wayne, who was returning to the United States after a visit in Rome.

Consulted regarding the establishment of a house in the United States, Bishop Dwenger told Mother Teresa of the wide field there awaiting sisters, and assured the Congregation of a welcome to his diocese.

The bishop's hospitable offer was accepted by Mother Teresa, and on November 26, 1875, six sisters, with Mother Mary Clara Thomas as Superior, left for America. They arrived in New York on December 12th, and on the 14th reached La Fayette, Indiana, the destination in the diocese planned for them by the bishop.

The citizens of La Fayette, without distinction of creed or nationality, and the clergy—Franciscans and seculars—came forward to welcome and aid the sisters, who at once opened a hospital in the temporary home provided for them. From Mr. Albert Wagner, whose family has been unceasing in its interest in and munificence to the Community, the sisters received a gift of land on which was erected St. Elizabeth's, their first hospital in the United States.

Mother Teresa visited the Community in this country three times, and participated in its extension and the erection of many of its well-equipped hospitals, schools and benevolent institutions.

Among the first institutions opened by the sisters in their expansion beyond the diocese of Fort Wayne was the St. Joseph Creighton Memorial Hospital in Omaha, Nebraska, which was established in 1880. At the instance of the Right Rev. James O'Connor, D.D., then vicar apostolic of Nebraska and later first bishop of the diocese

St. Francis Convent, La Fayette, Indiana

of Omaha, Mother Teresa's Community in La Fayette sent sisters to Omaha to nurse the sick. Through the generosity of the Hon. John A. Creighton, who was created a Papal Count by Pope Leo XIII, and his wife, this hospital was developed, and ranks as one of the oldest and foremost of those conducted by the Congregation.

On July 16, 1884, through the early efforts of the Franciscan Fathers, and upon the request of the Right Rev. Richard Gilmour, D.D., Bishop of Cleveland, sisters were sent to Cleveland to establish a hospital there. Sister Leonarda and a companion, Sister Alexia, were sent to the Ohio city for this work. Perseveringly and persistently they labored to accomplish that which was entrusted to them, and today St. Alexis Hospital in Cleveland, with its newly constructed (1927) Leonarda Memorial Hospital building—the first unit of a new group of hospital buildings—is a monument bespeaking Cleveland's appreciation of the labors of the courageous Mother

Leonarda and of the Congregation which provides the staff of efficient religious to carry on the work of the institution.

On the site of their first foundation in the United States, the Poor Sisters of St. Francis Seraph of the Perpetual Adoration have established on their spacious grounds a greater St. Elizabeth's Hospital and training school, while St. Francis' Convent has also been erected, and is the American Provincial house and Novitiate of the Congregation, and the residence of the present Provincial Superior, Mother Mary Bernarda Welles.

Under the administration of the Right Rev. John F. Noll, D.D., Bishop of Fort Wayne, and to meet a need of the city, the Congregation has recently established at the Motherhouse in La Fayette, in connection with the normal school, a high school, conducted according to the standards maintained in all its educational institutions.

With its growth, and development of many prominent hospitals, schools and institutions throughout the country, the Community in the United States remains affiliated with the General Motherhouse in Olpe, Germany, and faithfully carries on the work of the Congregation as planned by the saintly foundress who so long directed it, Mother Teresa.

SUMMARY

Poor Sisters of St. Francis Seraph of the Perpetual Adoration.
Founded in Germany in 1860.
Established in the United States in 1875.
Papal Approbation of Rule in 1899, by Pope Leo XIII.
Habit: The brown Franciscan habit and scapular and white cord are worn.
Approximate number in Community in United States, 1,000.
Active in educational, hospital and charitable work in the archdioceses of
    Chicago, New Orleans, St. Louis and Santa Fé, and in the dioceses of
    Cleveland, Denver, Fort Wayne, Grand Island, Indianapolis, Leavenworth,
    Lincoln, Louisville, Nashville and Omaha.
United States Provincial house and Novitiate, St. Francis Convent, Hartford
    Street, La Fayette, Indiana. (Diocese of Fort Wayne.)

FRANCISCAN SISTERS OF THE SACRED HEART*

1876

The Franciscan Sisters of the Sacred Heart, whose Motherhouse is maintained at Joliet, Illinois, in connection with St. Joseph's Hospital which they established in 1880, came to the United States from Germany in 1876.

---

*From *The Catholic Church in the United States of America* (Vol. II) (The Catholic Editing Company, N. Y.), and from the Official Catholic Year Book, 1928.

Received into the diocese of Fort Wayne by its bishop, the Right Rev. Joseph Dwenger, C.PP.S., D.D., the sisters were established in Avilla, Indiana. There they began their labors in this country by teaching in the parish school of the Church of the Assumption. In time, Joliet, Illinois—where members of the Community had gone to engage in nursing—was chosen for the site of the Motherhouse and novitiate, the sisters, however, continuing as a mission the parish school work at Avilla.

The now large Congregation of more than five hundred sisters, engages in educational, hospital and charitable work in the archdioceses of Chicago and San Francisco, and in the dioceses of Fort Wayne, Los Angeles and San Diego, Peoria, Springfield in Illinois, and Rockford.

Motherhouse and Novitiate, St. Joseph's Hospital, 426 North Broadway, Joliet, Illinois. (Archdiocese of Chicago.)

SISTERS OF ST. FRANCIS OF THE CONGREGATION OF OUR LADY OF LOURDES*
1877

The Sisters of St. Francis of the Congregation of Our Lady of Lourdes were founded in Rochester, Minnesota, in December, 1877, as the result of an episcopal decree, severing, from their Motherhouse in the diocese of Chicago, the Minnesota missions of the Sisters of St. Francis of Joliet, Illinois, and constituting the sisters who elected to remain at the former branch houses in the diocese of St. Paul, a distinct religious community.

Mother M. Alfred Moes, Superior of the Congregation at Joliet, Illinois, until 1876, was in Minnesota, where, upon the invitation of the Right Rev. Thomas L. Grace, D.D., Bishop of St. Paul, she had opened an academy in Owatonna and another in Rochester—dedicated on December 8, 1877—before the announcement, on December 23rd, of the decision of the Right Rev. Thomas Foley, D.D., Bishop of Chicago.

In July, 1878, Mother Alfred was appointed Mother General of the Congregation formed at Rochester by the twenty-five sisters who had remained at the Minnesota missions. Other institutions, hospital and charitable, as well as educational, were in time established by Mother Alfred, notable among them St. Mary's Hospital, opened in Rochester in 1889.

*From the Annals of the Sisters of St. Francis of Mary Immaculate, Joliet, Ill., and from the Official Catholic Year Book, 1928 (P. J. Kenedy and Sons, N. Y.).

In 1910, continuing the educational work of the Order, the sisters founded the College of St. Teresa at Winona, Minnesota, which city —upon the establishment of the diocese of Winona, in 1889—had become the residence of the ordinary of the diocese, of which the present incumbent is the Right Rev. Francis M. Kelly, D.D.

With the Congregation numbering approximately seven hundred and twenty-five sisters, a provincialate known as the Province of the Immaculate Conception has been established, the Provincial house and novitiate being located at Sylvania, Ohio, in the diocese of Toledo.

Members of the Congregation are engaged in educational, hospital and charitable work in institutions in the archdiocese of St. Paul and in the dioceses of Cleveland, Columbus, Covington, Denver, Detroit, Duluth, Los Angeles and San Diego, Omaha, Superior and Toledo, as well as Winona.

Motherhouse and Novitiate, Rochester, Minnesota. (Diocese of Winona.)

FRANCISCAN SISTERS*
ST. LOUIS, MISSOURI
1878

The Franciscan Sisters known as the Daughters of the Sacred Hearts of Jesus and Mary, maintaining their local Motherhouse at the convent connected with St. Anthony's Hospital in St. Louis, have carried on the works of their Order in the United States since 1878.

The Community, numbering approximately four hundred and fifty members, is active in hospital and charitable work in the arch-dioceses of Chicago, Dubuque, Milwaukee and St. Louis, and in the dioceses of Belleville, Denver and Green Bay.

Motherhouse and Novitiate, 3520 Chippewa Street, St. Louis, Mo. (Archdiocese of St. Louis.)

SISTERS OF ST. FRANCIS OF BAY SETTLEMENT†
1880

The Congregation of the Sisters of St. Francis of Bay Settlement was founded in 1880 in the state of Wisconsin, through the zeal and efforts of the Very Rev. Edward Daems, pastor of Holy Cross Church, near Green Bay, Wisconsin, and later vicar general of the diocese of Green Bay.

---

*From data supplied by the Franciscan Sisters, St. Louis, Mo., and from the Official Catholic Year Book, 1928.

†From data and material supplied by the Sisters of St. Francis, St. Francis Convent, Green Bay, Wis.

The young women who taught in the parochial schools, and gave instructions to the children and visited the sick in the several country mission under Father Daems, were established as a community of members of the Third Order of St. Francis. On the death of Father Daems the young community received a bequest from him of about one hundred acres of land, "to be used for the site of a convent home."

SISTER PAULINE LA PLANTE
Shortly before her death in 1926 at the age of 80

Sister Christine Rousseau as Superior, assisted by Sister Pauline La Plante, and Sister Mary Pius Doyle, at once formulated plans for the building of a first convent.

On March 14, 1881, the rules of the Community were approved by the Right Rev. F. X. Krautbauer, D.D., Bishop of Green Bay, and in 1886 the first mission school was begun at De Pere, Wisconsin. Among the charitable institutions conducted by the sisters is the McCormick Memorial Home for the Aged, in Green Bay, Wisconsin.

ST. FRANCIS CONVENT, TOWN OF SCOTT, GREEN BAY, WISCONSIN

In 1905 the Community was affiliated with the Franciscan Order in Rome.

SUMMARY

Sisters of St. Francis of Bay Settlement.

Founded in the United States in 1880.

Habit: The habit is black, with a scapular, white cincture and collar, and a black veil lined with white.

Approximate number in Community, 70.

Active in educational and charitable work in the diocese of Green Bay.

Motherhouse and Novitiate, St. Francis Convent, Town of Scott, Green Bay, Wisconsin. (Diocese of Green Bay.)

FRANCISCAN SISTERS OF BALTIMORE CITY*

1881

Among the many religious communities of women in the United States active today in the various fields of labor open to them, the Franciscan Sisters who came to Baltimore, Maryland, in 1881, from their Motherhouse at Mill Hill, London, England, are the only non-colored sisters in this country devoting themselves exclusively to work for the colored race.

CONVENT OF OUR LADY AND ST. FRANCIS, BALTIMORE, MARYLAND

The Congregation of Franciscan Sisters at St. Mary's Abbey, Mill Hill, London, was founded in London in 1868 by Mother Mary

*From data and material supplied by the Franciscan Sisters of Baltimore City, Baltimore, Md.

Francis, for the work of alleviating miseries caused by poverty and neglect, and for the nursing of the sick and helping in parish schools.

When England's distinguished prelate, Herbert Cardinal Vaughan, made a protracted stay in the United States as a young cleric, interested in seeing what apostolic missionary work was done for the colored race, he discussed the situation with the archbishop of Baltimore, the Most Rev. James Gibbons, later made cardinal priest.

The two future cardinals, agreeing on the need of sisterhoods in the vast field under discussion, the archbishop of Baltimore admitted that the religious communities in the country were already overburdened with work. Father Vaughan then volunteered to make a plea to the Mother Abbess at Mill Hill in behalf of this cause which Archbishop Gibbons had at heart.

Having long desired such an opportunity for missionary labor, the Franciscan Sisters in London, to whom Father Vaughan appealed, accepted the mission, and on December 5, 1881, four of their number set out from Mill Hill for the United States, where, welcomed to Baltimore by the archbishop, they at once established their convent.

A FRANCISCAN SISTER OF BALTIMORE CITY

A small house on St. Paul Street in Baltimore became the first St. Elizabeth's Home for Colored Children, and was the forerunner of the well-equipped institution of the same name, located now in the suburban district of Baltimore, where nearly two hundred colored orphan children were cared for by the Franciscan Sisters of Baltimore City, as the Community is familiarly termed.

A few years later a group of sisters from the now large Community in Baltimore went to Richmond, Virginia, where, working exclusively among the colored people, they conduct a high school and grammar school, and visit the sick in their own homes and in hospitals. They also hold evening classes in industrial work and give instructions to those who wish to enter the Church. Much the same activities are also being carried on by sisters from Baltimore in Norfolk, Virginia, and Wilmington, North Carolina.

In May, 1899, a residence on Maryland Avenue and Twenty-third Street, Baltimore, was given to the Community, and here a United States novitiate was then established. Previous to this time, aspirants who wished to become members of the Order had to go to the Motherhouse at Mill Hill, London.

An industrial school for colored girls is conducted at the novitiate on Maryland Avenue, and serves as part of the novitiate training for the novices.

Continuing in this country to devote themselves exclusively to labor for the colored race, the Franciscan Sisters of Baltimore City readily adapt themselves to any activities assigned them in this evangelical work.

SUMMARY

Franciscan Sisters of the Third Order Regular (Baltimore, Md.)

Founded in England in 1868.

Established in the United States in 1881.

Habit: The habit is of black serge, with a long scapular, and the white Franciscan cord. The headband and kerchief are of white linen and the veil is black.

Approximate number in Community in United States, 90.

Active in educational, charitable and social service work among colored people in the archdiocese of Baltimore and in the dioceses of Raleigh and Richmond.

U. S. *Novitiate,* Convent of Our Lady and St. Francis, 2226 Maryland Avenue, Baltimore, Maryland. (Archdiocese of Baltimore.)

SISTERS OF ST. FRANCIS OF THE MISSION OF THE IMMACULATE VIRGIN*

1882

The Sisters of St. Francis of the Mission of the Immaculate Virgin constitute the Congregation of Sisters of St. Francis of the Third Order Conventuals, whose Motherhouse has been established at New Hamburg, New York.

In the year 1900 the Community was incorporated under the title, Sisters of St. Francis of the Mission of the Immaculate Virgin, so named from their first mission, that founded in 1882 by the Rev. John C. Drumgoale, and known as the Mission of the Immaculate Virgin for the Protection of Homeless and Destitute Children in the City of New York. This, continuing under the direction of the sisters, is located at 381 La Fayette Street and Mount Loretto Avenue, Staten Island, New York.

In their labors, which now include educational and hospital work, as well as the care of charitable institutions, the sisters of the Com

---

*From *The Catholic Church in the United States of America* (Vol. II) (The Catholic Editing Company, N. Y.) and from the Official Catholic Directory, 1929, and the Official Catholic Year Book, 1928.

munity, of now fully two hundred and fifty members, are active not only in the archdiocese of New York, but also in the dioceses of Brooklyn and Newark.

> *Motherhouse and Novitiate,* Mt. St. Clare, New Hamburg, New York.   (Archdiocese of New York.)

SISTERS OF THE SORROWFUL MOTHER*
1889

The Congregation of the Sisters of the Sorrowful Mother, also known as Sisters of Charity, under the Rule of the Third Order of St. Francis Assisi, was founded in 1883, at Rome, by Mother Mary

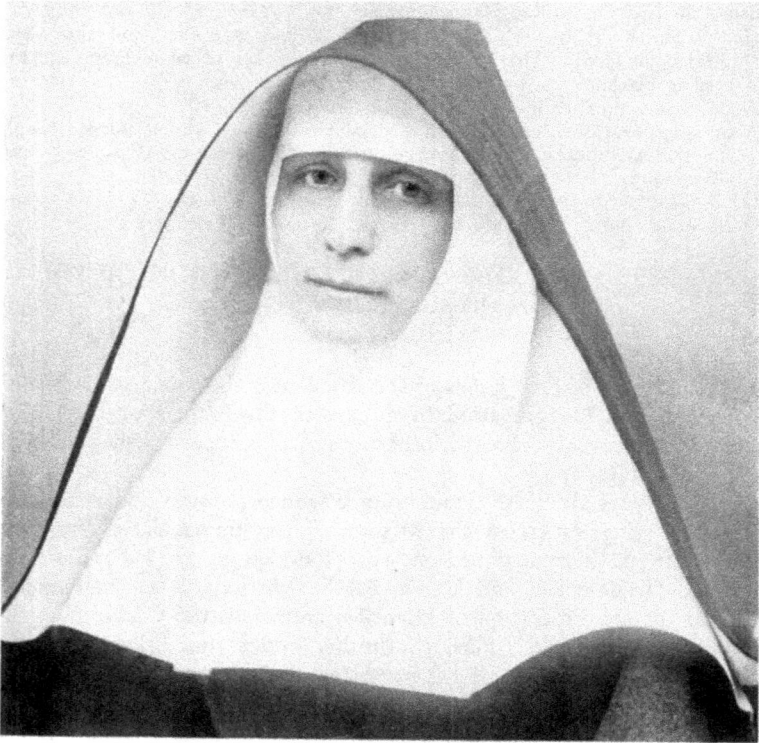

MOTHER MARY FRANCES STREITEL
Foundress in 1883 of the Sisters of the Sorrowful Mother

*From data and material supplied by the Sisters of the Sorrowful Mother, North Milwaukee, Wis.

Frances Streitel, for the greater honor and glory of God, self-sanctification and the salvation of souls, through the work of nursing and teaching.

CONVENT OF THE SORROWFUL MOTHER, NORTH MILWAUKEE, WISCONSIN

A few years after their establishment at Rome, two of the sisters were given papal permission to solicit alms in the United States. While they were in St. Louis for this purpose, ardent friends made successful efforts to have the sisters remain in the country and take charge of a small hospital in Wichita, Kansas. Negotiations to this effect were made, and in December, 1889, the Sisters of the Sorrowful Mother were received into the diocese by the Right Rev. John Joseph Hennessy, D.D., second bishop of Wichita, St. Francis' Hospital in that city being considered their first American foundation.

SISTERS OF THE SORROWFUL MOTHER

While retaining its affiliation with the General Motherhouse in Rome, on Via Aurelia, close to the Vatican, a United States Novitiate was established at St. Mary's Convent, Marshfield, Wisconsin, and later transferred to Milwaukee, where Mother Johanna, pioneer Superior, resides as Superior General of the United States Community.

The Sisters of the Sorrowful Mother, in addition to their parochial school work in various dioceses, conduct the St. Francis Health Resort in Denville, New Jersey, and have established and maintain many hospitals throughout the states. With those with whom they come in contact the sisters zealously strive to increase greater and special love for Our Lady of Sorrows and for their patron, St. Francis of Assisi.

SUMMARY

Sisters of the Sorrowful Mother.
Founded in Italy in 1883.
Papal Approbation of Rules, March 6, 1911, by Pope Pius X.
Established in the United States in 1889.
Habit: The habit is of grey wool, the Community being under the Rule of the Third Order of St. Francis Assisi, in which the original habit was grey.
Approximate number in Community in United States, 450.
Active in educational and hospital work in the archdioceses of Milwaukee and Santa Fé, and in the dioceses of Green Bay, La Crosse, Newark, Oklahoma, Superior, Wichita and Winona.
United States Novitiate, Convent of the Sorrowful Mother, North Milwaukee, Wisconsin.

LITTLE FRANCISCAN SISTERS OF MARY*
1889

Through the solicitude of the Rev. Joseph Brouillet in behalf of the orphans and aged, as well as in the interests of educational work, the Congregation of the Little Franciscan Sisters of Mary was founded in the year 1889, in Worcester, Massachusetts, with Mother Mary Joseph as foundress and first Superior.

The Rev. Ambrose Martial Fafard is looked upon as co-founder of the Congregation, and through his efforts its activities extended into Canada in 1891, when at Baie St. Paul, in the Province of Quebec, the sisters assumed charge of a home for the aged, and engaged in other benevolent work.

The Congregation in the United States, numbering approximately one hundred and ten sisters, and active in educational, hospital and charitable work in the dioceses of Portland and Springfield, is subject to the jurisdiction of the American Motherhouse and novitiate, at Baie St. Paul, P.Q., Charlevoix County, Canada.

In the United States the Community is under Mother Marie

*From data supplied by the Little Franciscan Sisters of Mary, Convent of St. Francis of Assisi, Worcester, Mass.

Vincent de Paul as Superior, assisted by Sisters Marie du Divin Coeur, Marie Leon, M. Precieux Sang, and M. François de Borgia, residing at the Convent of St. Francis of Assisi, Worcester, Massachusetts.

FRANCISCAN SISTERS

LITTLE FALLS, MINNESOTA*

1891

The Congregation of the Franciscan Sisters of the Order of St. Francis of the Immaculate Conception was founded at Rome, in the year 1866, by Mother Mary Ignatius Hayes, for missionary service.

St. Francis Convent, Little Falls, Minnesota

After some years of activity in missionary service in Italy, a series of disasters overtook the Community, bringing about a necessary re-adjustment and change for the Congregation.

Through the influence of the Franciscan Provincial, the Congregation came to the United States, where the sisters in 1891 established a foundation in the diocese of St. Cloud. The bishop, the Right Rev. Otto Zardetti, D.D., saw the Congregation well established in the diocese, and its Motherhouse opened in Little Falls, Minnesota, with Mother Mary Francis as first Superior. In 1894 Bishop Zardetti was transferred to Bucharest, Roumania, where he was raised to the dignity of archbishop.

*From data supplied by the Franciscan Sisters, St. Francis' Convent, Little Falls, Minn.

In addition to hospitals in Little Falls, Breckenridge, Moorhead and Perhan, Minnesota, one of the most important institutions in charge of the Congregation is the Marquette University Hospital in Milwaukee; here the sisters also conduct the training school for nurses maintained at the hospital.

The present Superior General of the Congregation is Mother Mary Teresa.

SUMMARY

Franciscan Sisters of the Order of St. Frances of the Immaculate Conception.

Founded in Italy in 1866.

Established in the United States in 1891.

Habit: The habit is plain brown, with a scapular, white cord with three knots, brown Franciscan rosary, black veil, white starched linen guimpe and band.

Approximate number in Community in United States, 150.

A FRANCISCAN SISTER OF THE IMMACULATE CONCEPTION

Active in educational, hospital and charitable work in the archdiocese of Milwaukee, and in the dioceses of Crookston and St. Cloud.

United States Motherhouse and Novitiate, St. Francis' Convent, Little Falls, Minnesota. (Diocese of St. Cloud.)

SISTERS OF ST. FRANCIS OF THE IMMACULATE CONCEPTION*

1891

The Congregation of the Sisters of St. Francis of the Immaculate Conception was founded at Peoria, Illinois, on the 2nd of February, 1891.

Upon the invitation of the Most Rev. John Lancaster Spalding, D.D., then bishop of the diocese of Peoria, Mother M. Pacifica Forrestal established this Community for the purpose of teaching and carrying on various charitable works, the most important of which is the care of the diocesan orphanage at Peoria.

Mother M. Pacifica, as foundress, continues Superior of the Congregation, which is under the direction of the ordinary of the diocese of Peoria.

*From data supplied by the Sisters of St. Francis, Immaculate Conception Convent, Peoria, Ill.

SUMMARY

Sisters of St. Francis of the Immaculate Conception.
Founded in the United States in 1891.
Habit: The habit is of black serge, with a black scapular, white cord, and a
large black rosary. The veil is black and the guimpe, coif and head-band
are white.
Approximate number in Community, 175.
Active in educational and charitable work in the archdiocese of St. Louis and
in the dioceses of Peoria and Springfield in Illinois.
Motherhouse and Novitiate, Immaculate Conception Convent, Hedding
Avenue, Peoria, Illinois. (Diocese of Peoria.)

SISTERS OF ST. FRANCIS OF PERPETUAL ADORATION*
1893

The Congregation of the Sisters of St. Francis of Perpetual
Adoration, established in Nevada, Missouri, in 1893, forms a diocesan
Community of the Order of Sisters of St. Francis, founded in 1424 at
Grimmenstein, Ct. Appenzell, Switzerland.

Through the personal efforts of the Right Rev. Ignatius Conrad,
O.S.B., of New Subiaco, Arkansas, five sisters from the Convent of
St. Ottilia at Grimmenstein came to the United States in 1893, and
at once repaired to the convent home prepared for them near Nevada,
Missouri, in the diocese of Kansas City.

ST. FRANCIS CONVENT, NEVADA, MISSOURI

The five sisters composing the new Community of Sisters of St.
Francis were Sister M. Bernardine Faeh, Sister M. Bonaventure
Rosenberg, Sister M. Xavier Blattez and Sister M. Basilia Kueng, with
Sister M. John Hau as Superior.

*From data supplied by the Sisters of St. Francis, Nevada, Mo.

Soon after their arrival on September 5, 1893, the Community opened a school in Nevada, thus beginning, with the approbation of the Right Rev. John J. Hogan, D.D., first bishop of the diocese of Kansas City, the active labors of the Congregation in the United States.

In November of the same year the Community was augmented by two more zealous religious from the Swiss Motherhouse, Sister M. Crescencia Grueninger and Sister M. Angela Baumgartner.

Two years after the establishment of the Congregation in the United States the sisters extended their work to the care of orphans and destitute children, in orphanages.

On September 25, 1915, fire demolished St. Francis' Convent and Orphanage and a period of severe struggle and hardship followed. By 1917, however, a new St. Francis' Convent has been erected on the tract of two hundred acres of land which the sisters have under cultivation, and from which are derived many of the supplies used in the convent and orphanage. Perpetual Adoration of the Blessed Sacrament is observed by the Community at the Motherhouse.

SUMMARY

Sisters of St. Francis of Perpetual Adoration.
Founded in Switzerland in 1424.
Papal Approbation of Rules in 1521, by Pope Leo X.
Established in the United States in 1893.
Habit: The habit is of dark brown, with a scapular and a cincture of white
    wool. A gold ring and black mantle are worn after religious profession.
Approximate number in Community in United States, 40.
Active in educational and charitable work in the diocese of Kansas City.
United States Motherhouse and Novitiate, St. Francis' Convent, Nevada,
    Missouri. (Diocese of Kansas City.)

FRANCISCAN SISTERS OF ST. KUNEGUNDA*
1894

The Polish Congregation of the Franciscan Sisters of St. Kune-gunda was founded in Chicago, Illinois, in the year 1894, during the archbishopric of the Most Rev. James E. Quigley, D.D.

The Community, of approximately three hundred and twenty members, is engaged in parochial school work and the conducting of homes for the aged, in the archdiocese of Chicago and the dioceses of Altoona, Belleville, Cleveland, Fort Wayne and Pittsburgh.

> *Motherhouse,* 2649 North Hamlin Avenue, Chicago, Illinois.
> *Novitiate,* Our Lady of Victory Convent, Lemont, Illinois.
> (Archdiocese of Chicago.)

*From the Official Catholic Year Book, 1928.

BERNARDINE SISTERS*
1901

The Bernardine Sisters of the Third Order of St. Francis, or Bernardine Sisters, form a Polish Community founded in 1901 in Reading, Pennsylvania, by Mother Veronica Grzedowska.

To respond to an appeal for parochial school teachers, two sisters from the convent of the Franciscan cloistered nuns in Zakliczyn, Poland, were granted a dispensation from their enclosure and sent to the United States where they were received into the archdiocese of Philadelphia by the Most Rev Patrick J. Ryan, D.D.

Mother Veronica served as first Superior of the new Community, which at once established a General Motherhouse and Novitiate in Reading.

MOTHER M. VERONICA GRZEDOWSKA

SACRED HEART CONVENT, READING, PENNSYLVANIA

*From data and material supplied by the Bernardine Sisters, Reading, Pa.

From there the Congregation is now governed by Mother M. Hedwig Leszczynska as Superior General, assisted by her Council, under the jurisdiction of the Archbishop of Philadelphia.

While the Community does not include any nursing or hospital work in its ordinary activities, the sisters responded with every helpfulness among the stricken during the influenza epidemic in 1918.

SUMMARY

Bernardine Sisters of the Third Order of St. Francis.

Founded in the United States in 1901.

Habit: The habit is of brown wool. A scapular and white woolen cincture with three knots are worn.

Approximate number in Community, 450.

Active in educational and charitable work in the archdiocese of Philadelphia, and in the dioceses of Altoona, Fall River, Hartford, Harrisburg, Pittsburgh, Providence, Scranton, Springfield and Trenton.

Motherhouse and Novitiate, Sacred Heart Convent, Reading, Pennsylvania. (Archdiocese of Philadelphia.)

SISTERS OF ST. JOSEPH OF THE ORDER OF ST. FRANCIS*
1901

MOTHER M. FELICIA

Forming the nucleus of the Congregation of the Sisters of St. Joseph of the Order of St. Francis, were several Polish speaking sisters from the Motherhouse of the School Sisters of St. Francis, in Milwaukee, Wisconsin.

In 1901, at the suggestion of clergymen of the Polish nationality, and with the approval of the Right Rev. Sebastian Messmer, D.D., ordinary of the diocese of Green Bay, before his appointment, in 1903, as Archbishop of Milwaukee, these sisters established a new community.

In an attractive pine grove in the northern part of the city,

*From data and material supplied by the Sisters of St. Joseph of the Order of St. Francis, Stevens Point, Wis., and Cleveland, Ohio.

a Motherhouse was erected at Stevens Point, Wisconsin, in the diocese of Green Bay.

Mother M. Felicia was chosen first Superior of the Community. She was succeeded in office by Mother M. Boleslaus, and after an interval of ten years was again elected Superior. Mother Felicia,

St. Joseph's Convent, Stevens Point, Wisconsin

St. Joseph's Convent, Garfield Heights, Cleveland, Ohio

now assisted by Sister M. Sylvestra, has been an indefatigable worker in this Congregation, composed especially of Polish speaking women.

MOTHER M. CLARE

In 1926, with the permission of the Right Rev. Paul P. Rhode, D.D., Bishop of Green Bay, and under the auspices of the Right Rev. Joseph Schrembs, D.D., Bishop of Cleveland, the Congregation established a Provincial house and novitiate in Cleveland, where for nineteen years the sisters had been teaching. On the completion of the building for the new Provincial house, St. Joseph's Convent on Granger Road, Garfield Heights, Cleveland, the two hundred members of the Community already laboring in the diocese of Cleveland were assigned to the new provincialate, under Mother Clare as Provincial Superior. With this development the Motherhouse at Stevens Point now forms the provincialate for all activities of the Congregation in cities west of Cleveland.

Schools have rapidly been established by the sisters, and the Community has witnessed a remarkable growth in the years since its foundation, during which time the work of the Congregation has been confined to the purpose for which it was originally founded, the education of youth in parochial, academic and boarding schools.

SUMMARY

Sisters of St. Joseph of the Order of St. Francis.
Founded in the United States in 1901.
Habit: The habit, veil and scapular are black; a white cincture is worn.
Approximate number in Community, 600.
Active in educational work in the archdioceses of Chicago and Milwaukee, and in the dioceses of Cleveland, Detroit, Fort Wayne, Green Bay, Hartford, La Crosse, Peoria and Superior.
Eastern Provincial house, St. Joseph's Convent, Granger Road, Garfield Heights, Cleveland, Ohio. (Diocese of Cleveland.)
Motherhouse and Western Provincial house, St. Joseph's Convent, Stevens Point, Wisconsin. (Diocese of Green Bay.)

POLISH FRANCISCAN SCHOOL SISTERS*

1901

The Congregation of the Polish Franciscan School Sisters was founded in St. Louis, Missouri, May 29, 1901, by Sister M. Ernestine,

SISTER M. ERNESTINE
Foundress in 1901 of the Polish Franciscan School Sisters

to foster religious vocations among Polish women, and to teach Polish children in parochial schools. Sister M. Solana served as first Superior.

---

*From data and material supplied by the Polish Franciscan School Sisters, Ferguson, Mo.

33

The rules of the Congregation have been approved by the Most Rev. John J. Kain, D.D., Archbishop of St. Louis, and, with its increasing number, the Community, under Mother M. Hilaria as present Superior, and Sister M. Ernestine as Novice Mistress, has extended its activities into other dioceses, as it carries on the work for which it was founded.

SUMMARY

Polish Franciscan School Sisters.
Founded in the United States in 1901.
Habit: The brown habit of the Franciscans is worn.
Approximate number in Community, 200.
Active in educational work in the archdioceses of Chicago, Cincinnati and
St. Louis, and in the dioceses of Belleville, Kansas City, Peoria, Sioux City and Wheeling.
Motherhouse, Convent of Our Lady of Perpetual Help, 3419 Gasconade Street, St. Louis, Missouri.
Novitiate, Villa St. Joseph, Ferguson, Missouri. (Archdiocese of St. Louis.)

FRANCISCAN MISSIONARIES OF MARY*
1904

On May 21, 1839, there was born at Nantes, in Brittany—the child of Christian parents, and the direct descendant of notable soldier-ancestry—Hélène de Chappotin, later, as Mother Mary of the Passion, the valiant foundress of generations of missionaries, in a new institute, that of the Franciscan Missionaries of Mary.

Initiated at first into a primarily contemplative religious life, Mother Mary of the Passion was early acquainted, through branch labor in India, with the immensity of the missionary apostolate, and the establishment of the new Community in 1877—with the approbation of Pope Pius IX—was the consequence of her call to consecrate herself to it unreservedly.

St. Brieuc, in Brittany—that land of vigorous faith—was the scene of the first foundation of the Institute, in its provision for missionary activities in India and elsewhere. The novitiate was soon established at Les Châtelets, a country estate near St. Brieuc.

Desiring to securely stabilize the young Institute, through affiliation with one of the great religious orders, Mother Mary of the Passion in 1882 obtained for its members, for all time, tertiary participation in the spirit, labors and privileges of the Franciscans.

Fittingly the first three houses were in India, where the plan of this missionary Community had germinated, St. Brieuc, in Catholic Brit-

---

*From data and material supplied by the Franciscan Missionaries of Mary, Procure for Foreign Missions, 363 Fruit Hill Ave., North Providence, R. I.

tany, which was to give so many religious to the Institute, and—through an establishment in 1882—in Rome, the center of Catholicism and the seat of truth.

MOTHER MARY OF THE PASSION (1839-1904)
Foundress of the Franciscan Missionaries of Mary

Through the house founded in Tai-Yuan, one of several foundations in China, the Institute was supernaturally blessed, and its labors sealed when the missionary life of a little band of its members was crowned with martyrdom.

In the chaos of the Boxer Rebellion, in 1900, in June, after the issuance of a civil edict summarily ordering apostasy from the

Christian faith, or death, seven Franciscan Missionaries of Mary— who had valiantly rejected proposals of flight in disguise, while there was yet time—with three bishops and Franciscan friars, after a form of trial were massacred by soldiers and populace.   The religious who thus gave up their lives were Mother Marie Hermine of Jesus, Superior, Mother Mary of Peace, Mother Mary Clare, Sister Mary of St. Nathalia, Sister Mary of St. Just, Sister Mary Adolphine and Sister Mary Amandine.

Hardly less glorious is the account of the work of the Institute among the lepers.   Since 1898, when for the first time this charity was added to their missionary activities, members of the Community have labored among these outcasts of humanity.

The religious—active in the United States since 1904—devote themselves in this country, in accordance with the purpose for which they were founded, to work of a missionary character, conducting workrooms, day nurseries, catechism classes and clubs, visiting hospitals and prisons, and assisting immigrants.

A feature of primary importance in the life of the Franciscan Missionary of Mary is the adoration of the Blessed Sacrament.   In all the houses of the Institute throughout the world, with the religious watching before It in turn, the Blessed Sacrament is exposed daily from morning until night.   This devotion binds the Institute together, and spiritually fortifies its members in their exhaustive active lives.

The government of the Institute of the Franciscan Missionaries of Mary is vested in a Superior General, who, together with her Council is elected at the General Chapter for twelve years.   The Order is divided into provinces, each similarly ruled by a Provincial Superior and her Council, subject to the Motherhouse, which is located in Rome, with the novitiate now at Grottaferrata, not far distant from it.

SUMMARY

Franciscan Missionaries of Mary.
Founded in India in 1877.
Established in the United States in 1904.
Papal Approbation of Rules, May 14, 1896, by Pope Leo XIII.
Habit: The entire habit, including the rosary and footwear, is white.   Outside the convent, a grey mantle and black veil are worn.
Approximate number in Community in United States, 200.
Active in missionary work in the archdioceses of New York and Boston, and in the dioceses of Brooklyn, Fall River and Providence.
United States Provincial house, 4 Bell Street, Providence, Rhode Island.
United States Novitiate, 399 Fruit Hill Avenue, North Providence, Rhode Island.   (Diocese of Providence.)

FRANCISCAN SISTERS OF THE ATONEMENT*
1909

Symbolical of the spirit and character of the Franciscan Sisters of the Atonement is the zealous motto associated with their missionary activities—*Ut Omnes Unum Sint*—"That all may be one."

The Sisters of the Atonement were founded December 15, 1898, at Graymoor, New York, through Mother Lurana Mary Francis, as a branch Congregation of the Anglican Society of the Atonement, inculcating especially the spirit of St. Francis Assisi. After ten years of spiritual struggle, and missionary labor in the interests of general Church Unity, under the sanction of the Sovereign Pontiff, Pope Pius X, the corporate reception of the Society of the Atonement into the Church, retaining its name and Institute, took place on October 30, 1909.

With its entrance into the faith every activity of the

MOTHER LURANA MARY FRANCIS
Foundress and Superior General of the Franciscan Sisters of the Atonement

*From data and material supplied by the Franciscan Sisters of the Atonement, Graymoor, Garrison, N. Y.

Society was intensified. As the missionary spirit had been an important factor in the organization of the Community, so was it still perceptible in its work.   The issuance of *The Lamp,* the organ of the Graymoor Institute, was continued with renewed zeal, and the Church Unity Octave, which originated with this magazine while it was still an Anglican publication, was endorsed and widely promoted. This Octave—whose object, the reunion of Christendom with the Holy See, the Society has made peculiarly its own—is now observed by millions of Catholics annually from January 18th, the feast of St. Peter's Chair at Rome, to January 25th, the feast of the Conversion of St. Paul.

The Franciscan Sisters of the Atonement were founded for the purpose of the furtherance of the reunion of all Christians, and the undertaking of work of a missionary character, especially catechetical teaching among the poor, non-Catholics and non-Christians, at home and in foreign missions.   In accordance with their Constitutions, they also provide opportunities for retreats, and instructions for those desiring to enter the Church.

In New York City—where members of the Community are in charge of the office records and service at the Catholic Medical Mission Board national headquarters—as well as in Philadelphia, the sisters have engaged in missionary work, laboring in immigrant sections, and conducting social settlements.   Crossing the continent, Sisters of the Atonement have established distant mission houses, in California, and from Texas, in the south, into northern Canada. Several houses of retreat are also maintained by the Community. In the interests of these their fields of activity, near and far, the Sisters of the Atonement edit a quarterly bulletin, *The Candle.*

The Society of the Atonement is comprised of three congregations, the Friars of the Atonement—in co-operation with whom the foundation of the sisters' Institute was made by Mother Lurana—the Sisters of the Atonement and the tertiaries in the world, all under the Rule of the Third Order of St. Francis, designated as Regular or Secular according to the observance of the religious or secular life.

Graymoor, beautifully situated in New York state, midway between Garrison and Peekskill, and sequestered from the outside world by the wooded highlands of the Hudson, although little more than an hour's ride from New York City—has become a missionary center whose influence is felt and recognized not only throughout America, but in every part of the missionary world.

Accommodating many of the pilgrims and visitors who wish either to make a retreat or to enjoy a few days' restful quiet, the Franciscan Sisters of the Atonement maintain a guest house, Our

Lady's Hostel, on the grounds at Graymoor, where their own Mother-house and novitiate are ideally located, and their widespread mission-ary labors centralized.

ST. FRANCIS CONVENT, GRAYMOOR, GARRISON, NEW YORK

SUMMARY

Franciscan Sisters of the Atonement.

Established in the United States in 1909.

Habit: The habit and scapular are gray brown, with a white cord and a rosary. A crucifix is worn below a white wimple falling in soft irregular folds. The veil is black and the forehead band white. Sandals are worn indoors.

Approximate number in Community, 115.

Active in missionary and social service work in the archdioceses of Baltimore, New York and Philadelphia, and in the dioceses of Amarillo, Galveston, Monterey-Fresno, Ogdensburg and Pittsburgh.

Motherhouse and Novitiate, St. Francis Convent, Graymoor, Garrison, New York.

SCHOOL SISTERS OF THE THIRD ORDER OF ST. FRANCIS*

1913

This Congregation, dating its foundation from the founding in Italy of the Franciscan Third Order, by St. Francis of Assisi, has for more than fifty years engaged exclusively in the work of teaching.

The Congregation, one of whose descendent communities was sent to the United States in 1913, had established, many years previously, a community in Maribor, Austria. This community in 1888 sent several of its members to Czechoslovakia, where, in Slatinany, a new foundation was made, under Mother Hyacinta Zahalka as Superior.

With the growth of the new community a number of schools were opened, prominent among them a normal school in Chrudim

---

*From data supplied by the School Sisters of the 3rd Order of St. Francis, Pittsburgh, Pa.

and a Women's College in Prague. The rules of this foundation, adapted to the conditions, were approved on February 2, 1900, by the

MOTHER M. XAVERIA FÜRGOTT

Right Rev. Edward Brynych, Bishop of Königgratz, Czecho-slovakia.

It was from the community in Prague that six sisters, with Mother M. Louise Kilb, O.S.F., as Superior, were sent to the United States in 1913. Arriving in New York on August 15th, they proceeded at once to Pennsylvania, where they were received into the diocese of Pittsburgh.

With the opening of the school year, soon after their arrival, these School Sisters of the Third Order of St. Francis opened two Slovak schools. One, St. Gabriel's, in Pittsburgh, became at once the site of the American Motherhouse and no-vitiate of the Community. The second school opened at this time was St. Clement's, in Tarentum, Pennsylvania.

MT. ASSISI ACADEMY, BELLEVUE, PITTSBURGH, PENNSYLVANIA

With increasing numbers in the Community, the sisters now con-duct additional Slovak schools in the diocese of Pittsburgh, and have also extended their work beyond that diocesan district to other Pennsylvania localities, as well as to New Jersey and Ohio.

In the year 1927, under the direction of Mother M. Xaveria Fürgott, General Superior of the Congregation, whose Motherhouse is now located in Brevnov, Czechoslovakia, a new United States Motherhouse was built in Pittsburgh, and in connection with it the sisters now maintain Mt. Assisi Academy for Slovak girls, conducting there both grade and high school classes, under the present superiorship of Mother M. Methodia Bradac.

SUMMARY

School Sisters of the Third Order of St. Francis.
Established in the United States in 1913.
Habit: The habit is of black serge, with a black cincture.
Approximate number in Community in United States, 100.
Active in educational work in the dioceses of Altoona, Cleveland, Erie, Newark and Pittsburgh.
Motherhouse and Novitiate, Mt. Assisi Academy, Bellevue Station, Pittsburgh, Pennsylvania. (Diocese of Pittsburgh.)

FRANCISCAN SISTERS OF MARY IMMACULATE AND ST. JOSEPH FOR THE DYING*

1917

The California Community of the Franciscan Sisters of Mary Immaculate and St. Joseph for the Dying marks its origin in the United States as the result of the efforts of the Very Rev. Hugo-linus Joseph Storff, at the time Provincial of the Franciscans in San Francisco, now Definitor General of the Order of Friars Minor in Rome.

Under the superiorship of Sister M. Ottilia, who has continued in that office, sisters from Rome in 1917 inaugurated the work of the Community in Cali-fornia. There, under rules approved in 1919 by the Right Rev. John J. Cant-well, D.D., Bishop of Los Angeles and

FRANCISCAN SISTERS OF MARY IMMACULATE AND ST. JO-SEPH FOR THE DYING

*From data and material supplied by the Franciscan Sisters of Mary Immaculate and St. Joseph for the Dying, Monterey, Calif.

San Diego, they have established a Motherhouse in Monterey, in the diocese of Monterey-Fresno, of which the Right Rev. John B. MacGinley, D.D., is the first and present bishop.

ST. JOSEPH'S CONVENT, MONTEREY, CALIFORNIA

Wearing the brown woolen habit of the Franciscan Order, the members of this Community, unique in its dedication, teach in parochial schools in the diocese, consecrating their lives, prayers and labors for the salvation of the dying.

Motherhouse and Novitiate, St. Joseph's Convent, Monterey, California. (Diocese of Monterey-Fresno.)

FRANCISCAN SISTERS OF PERPETUAL ADORATION*

1921

The Congregation of the Franciscan Sisters of Perpetual Adoration of the Most Blessed Sacrament was founded at Troyes, in France, in the year 1854, by Mother Mary Clare, a devout follower of St. Francis Assisi, thus to maintain the traditions of the Franciscan Order, which since its foundation, has ever been most fervent in the worship of the Divine Eucharist.

In 1871, through the activities of Mother Mary of the Holy Cross De Morawska, this branch of the Order was transplanted, and the Monastery of Lemberg, then founded, has since been looked upon as the Motherhouse of the Franciscan Sisters of Perpetual Adoration —although each foundation of the Order, according to the Consti-

*From data and material supplied by the Franciscan Sisters of Perpetual Adoration, 1453 East Boulevard, Cleveland, Ohio.

tutions, is independent, subject to its own bishop as the representative of the Sovereign Pontiff.

To the Right Rev. Joseph Schrembs, D.D., fifth bishop of Cleveland, is the United States indebted for the establishment in this country, in the city of Cleveland, of this Congregation.

Learning of the extreme poverty to which the disastrous World War had reduced the Franciscan Community of Perpetual Adoration, in Vienna, Bishop Schrembs, induced by his great devotion to the Most Blessed Sacrament and his ardent desire to establish the Perpetual Adoration in his diocese, welcomed two of the sisters to his episcopal city, and offered them as a temporary convent home, a residence owned by the diocese, located at 11025 Euclid Avenue, in Cleveland.

With kindly solicitude and foresight for their immediate need of

MOTHER MARY OF THE HOLY CROSS

PERPETUAL ADORATION CONVENT, CLEVELAND, OHIO

friends, Bishop Schrembs entrusted the two sisters to the special care of the Ladies' Catholic Benevolent Association in Cleveland.

With enthusiastic response, the benevolent women of Cleveland shared with Bishop Schrembs his welcome to the sisters as they saw to the furnishing of the new convent home and the equipment of the little chapel.

On Christmas night, 1921, with the holy sacrifice of the mass celebrated by the bishop, the little community, consisting of the two professed sisters from Austria, one American novice and two postu-lants, was established, with episcopal enclosure, and exposition of the Most Blessed Sacrament was solemnly inaugurated, marking the foundation of this Franciscan branch of Sisters of Perpetual Adoration in America.

At once the little chapel became a mecca for the devout, who shared from without the grille the adoration and prayers of these cloistered nuns in their Cleveland home. With the establishment of the People's Eucharistic League, and monthly public devotions, the friends as well as members of the Community increased.

In July, 1926, following the sale to Western Reserve University of the diocesan property which included the Euclid Avenue convent, the Franciscan Sisters of Perpetual Adoration removed to a new home in Cleveland, at 1453 East Boulevard.

SUMMARY

Franciscan Sisters of Perpetual Adoration of the Blessed Sacrament.
Founded in France in 1854.
Established in the United States in 1921.
Papal Approbation of Rules by Pope Pius X.
Habit: The habit and long scapular are brown; the head-dress is white, with a long black veil over a short white one. The emblem of a small mon-strance, the Franciscan cord, and white sandals are worn. The extern sisters wear gray habits, and shoes.
Approximate number in Community, 30.
Engaged in contemplative life in the diocese of Cleveland.
Convent and Novitiate, Perpetual Adoration Convent, 1453 East Boulevard, Cleveland, Ohio. (Diocese of Cleveland.)

MISSIONARY SISTERS OF THE IMMACULATE CONCEPTION
1922

In mid-year of 1922 there were introduced into the United States from their convents in Münster, Germany, and in the Amazon district

*From data and material supplied by the Missionary Sisters of the Immaculate Conception, St. Bonaventure, N. Y., and Paterson, N. J.

of Brazil, sisters of a community of noblest lineage, garbed in Our Lady's blue and white, and wearing on their breasts medals symbolical of the name of their congregation, Missionary Sisters of the Immaculate Conception.

Through the episcopal courtesy of the Right Rev. William Turner, D.D., the Congregation was welcomed to the diocese of Buffalo, where the sisters were received at St. Bonaventure, near Allegany, New York.

The founding of the Conceptionist Order, of which the Congregation of the Missionary Sisters of the Immaculate Conception is a branch, antedated by but a few years the discovery of America, and too was effected through the generosity of Queen Isabella, who heeded the Franciscan friar's plea in behalf of the cause of Columbus—erstwhile guest at the Franciscan Convent of La Rabida.

In the year 1484, Isabella, Queen of Spain, visited the convents of the kingdom, seeking spiritual solace and asking prayers from holy souls that Spain would soon be liberated from Moorish domination. At the Cistercian Convent in

BLESSED BEATRICE OF SILVA
(1424-1490)

Foundress of the Conceptionist Sisters

Toledo the nuns told her of a holy woman, who for forty years had dwelt with them as a humble servant, and whose face, covered always with a white veil, they had never seen. Upon the command of the queen the summoned servant lifted her veil, and Isabella gazing beheld none other than her cousin, Beatrice of Silva, noted from her earliest youth for her holiness and her beauty, whom her own mother, another Queen Isabella, had persecuted and driven from court.

Though Beatrice was then sixty years of age, the withdrawn veil revealed her face as fair and beautiful as when, forty years before, she had been hurried from the court and unjustly cast for three days, without food or drink, into a dungeon.

To her cousin the queen, Beatrice then told of an apparition

vouchsafed her in her solitude; that as she fervently prayed for the protection of her holy virginity, her cell was pervaded by an unearthly light, and before her eyes Mary herself appeared, clothed in a white habit and mantle of heavenly blue, with the Divine Child in her arms, and that assuring her of her freedom the Blessed Virgin had revealed that she was to found an order in honor of her

ST. JOSEPH'S NOVITIATE, PATERSON, NEW JERSEY

Immaculate Conception, whose members were to wear a habit and mantle similar to that in which she appeared.

Beatrice then told her cousin of being miraculously freed from the dungeon and directed by the Seraphic St. Francis and a companion friar with him, St. Anthony, to the Convent of St. Dominic at Toledo, where for forty years thereafter she had awaited the time for the fulfillment of her mission.

Recognizing the hand of God directing the life of His virgin servant, the queen gave Beatrice a mansion from her private possessions. Twelve ardent souls who had joined with her in the Palace de Galiana then formed with Beatrice the first community of Conceptionist Sisters. To the habit which they adopted, modeled on that shown to their foundress, the Conceptionist Sisters then added the hemp cord of St. Francis.

Down through the centuries the work of Beatrice—now Blessed Beatrice—has come, the Order, under Franciscan direction, having adopted modified rules of the Poor Clares, and its nuns living purely contemplative lives within the cloisters of their convents.

On July 7, 1910, through the initiative of the Right Rev. Amandus Bahlmann, Bishop of Argos—prelate of Santarem—the Holy See granted four Conceptionist Sisters of the monastery in Rio de Janeiro, dispensation from papal enclosure, with approval of their establishment of a convent at Santarem, in Brazil, the members of the community of which were to devote themselves to the instruction and education of youth, the nursing of the sick in hospitals and private homes, and the conducting of retreat houses for women.

Mother Mary Immaculate of Jesus, first Superior General of the new foundation, continues to serve in that office. From the Convent of the Immaculate Conception, at Santarem, now established as the General Motherhouse and novitiate of this branch of the Conceptionist Order, other foundations soon followed, especially at first in South America. In 1915, during the World War, a house for postulants was opened at Münster, in Westphalia, Germany. This, on December 8, 1918, was established as a second novitiate of the new Community.

On September 16, 1923, a little more than a year after the arrival of the little community at St. Bonaventure, New York,

A MISSIONARY SISTER OF THE IMMACULATE CONCEPTION

a United States novitiate was opened at Paterson, New Jersey. With it, as with the other novitiates of the Missionary Sisters of the Immaculate Conception, is combined a Chapel of Perpetual Adoration, where, clothed in the white habit and blue mantle as shown to Blessed Beatrice of Silva, the sisters spend their hours of prayer.

Among the initial works of the Community in the United States has been the establishment in Paterson of a home for convalescent children and a retreat house for girls and women.

During the jubilee year of 1929 the name of Missionary Poor Clares of the Immaculate Conception, as the members of this branch of the Conceptionist Order had until then been known, was changed by His Holiness, Pope Pius XI, to Missionary Sisters of the Immaculate Conception, in honor of the Immaculate Conception of the Mother of God, the special patroness of the Congregation.

SUMMARY

Missionary Sisters of the Immaculate Conception.
Founded in Brazil in 1910.
Established in the United States in 1922.

Papal Approbation of Rules in 1929 by Pope Pius XI.

Habit: The habit is white, with a sky-blue scapular and mantle, the white Franciscan cord, and seven-decade Franciscan rosary. A medal is worn bearing the image of the Immaculate Conception and the Blessed Sacrament surrounded by adoring angels.

Approximate number in Community in United States, 70.

Active in charitable work in the archdiocese of New York and the dioceses of Buffalo and Newark.

United States Novitiate, St. Joseph's Novitiate, Squirrelwood Road, Paterson, New Jersey. (Diocese of Newark.)

HOSPITAL SISTERS OF ST. FRANCIS*

PEORIA, ILLINOIS

The Sisters of St. Francis whose Motherhouse is established at St. Francis Hospital in Peoria, Illinois, constitute a Community of nearly four hundred sisters, who are active chiefly in hospital work in the archdiocese of Chicago and the dioceses of Davenport, Marquette and Peoria.

Motherhouse and Novitiate, St. Francis Hospital, 616 Glen Oak Avenue, Peoria, Illinois. (Diocese of Peoria.)

FRANCISCAN SISTERS OF THE IMMACULATE CONCEPTION*

ROCK ISLAND, ILLINOIS

In addition to the Franciscan Sisters of the Immaculate Conception, whose Motherhouse is maintained at Little Falls, Minnesota, a Community of approximately fifty sisters has established its headquarters at St. Anthony's Hospital in Rock Island, Illinois.

Motherhouse and Novitiate, St. Anthony's Hospital, Rock Island, Illinois. (Diocese of Peoria.)

MISSIONARY FRANCISCAN SISTERS OF THE IMMACULATE CONCEPTION*

Missionary Franciscan Sisters of the Immaculate Conception, whose Motherhouse is in Rome. Italy, have established their American headquarters at Tenafly, New Jersey. The Community in the United States consists of approximately three hundred and thirty sisters, who are active in educational, charitable and social service work in the archdioceses of Boston, Chicago, New York and Philadelphia, and in the dioceses of Brooklyn, Newark, Pittsburgh, Rockford, St. Cloud, Savannah and Syracuse.

*From the Official Catholic Year Book, 1928.

SCHOOL SISTERS OF ST. FRANCIS*

CONCEPTION, MISSOURI

The School Sisters of St. Francis in the diocese of St. Joseph form a Community of approximately forty-five sisters.

Motherhouse and Novitiate, St. Francis Convent, Conception, Missouri. (Diocese of St. Joseph.)

SISTERS OF ST. FRANCIS†

MARYVILLE, MISSOURI

The Community of Sisters of The Third Order of St. Francis whose Motherhouse and novitiate are maintained at St. Francis Hospital, Maryville, Missouri, is composed of nearly eighty sisters, who are engaged principally in hospital work in the dioceses of Lincoln, Oklahoma, and St. Joseph.

Motherhouse and Novitiate, St. Francis Hospital, 614 East First Street, Maryville, Missouri. (Diocese of St. Joseph.)

FRANCISCAN SISTERS†

ST. JOSEPH'S CONVENT, BUFFALO, NEW YORK

The more than three hundred and fifty sisters who constitute the Community known as the Franciscan Sisters, Minor Conventuals, with their Motherhouse at St. Joseph's Convent, Buffalo, New York, conduct schools in the archdioceses of Baltimore, Boston and Milwaukee, and in the dioceses of Buffalo, Detroit, Hartford, Springfield, Harrisburg and Trenton.

Motherhouse and Novitiate, St. Joseph's Convent, 179 Clark Street, Buffalo, New York. (Diocese of Buffalo.)

FRANCISCAN MINIMS SISTERS*

Franciscan Minims Sisters are teaching at the Sacred Heart School at Bisbee, Arizona, in the diocese of Tucson.

FRANCISCAN SISTERS OF CALAIS, FRANCE*

Franciscan Sisters of Calais, France, are in charge of St. Francis Sanitarium and training school for nurses, at Monroe, and Our Lady of the Lake Sanitarium at Baton Rouge, Louisiana.

---

*From the Official Catholic Directory, 1929.
†From the Official Catholic Year Book, 1928.

CHRONOLOGICAL TABLE*

Foundations in the United States of Third Order Franciscan Sisters

1849—St. Francis, Wisconsin.
1851—Oldenburg, Indiana.
1855—Philadelphia, Pennsylvania (Glen Riddle).
1858—Cincinnati, Ohio (Hartwell).
1859—Allegany, New York.
1860—Syracuse, New York.
1861—Buffalo, New York.
1865—Joliet, Illinois.
1865—Peekskill, New York.
1868—Clinton, Iowa.
1868—Pittsburgh, Pennsylvania.
1869—Manitowoc, Wisconsin.
1869—Tiffin, Ohio.
1871—La Crosse, Wisconsin.
1872—St. Louis, Missouri.
1874—Buffalo, New York (Stella Niagara).
1874—Detroit, Michigan.
1874—Milwaukee, Wisconsin.
1875—Dubuque, Iowa.
1875—La Fayette, Indiana.
1875—Springfield, Illinois.

1876—Joliet, Illinois.
1877—Rochester, Minnesota.
1878—St. Louis, Missouri.
1880—Green Bay, Wisconsin.
1881—Baltimore, Maryland.
1882—New York City.
1889—Milwaukee, Wisconsin.
1889—Worcester, Massachusetts.
1891—Little Falls, Minnesota.
1891—Peoria, Illinois.
1893—Nevada, Missouri.
1894—Chicago, Illinois.
1901—Reading, Pennsylvania.
1901—St. Louis, Missouri.
1901—Stevens Point, Wisconsin.
1904—Providence, Rhode Island.
1909—Garrison, New York (Graymoor).
1913—Pittsburgh, Pennsylvania.
1917—Monterey, California.
1921—Cleveland, Ohio.
1922—St. Bonaventure, New York.

GENERAL SUMMARY

Third Order Franciscan Sisters.

Papal Approbation of Rule in 1521 by Pope Leo X; approbation also as given to individual communities.

Established in the United States in 1849.

Habit: The typical Franciscan habit is brown, with a white cord with three knots, symbolical of the vows. Many communities of Third Order Franciscan Sisters, however, are distinguished as such in their garb only by the Franciscan cord and a special scapular.

Approximate number in communities in United States, 20,000.

Active in educational, hospital, charitable, missionary and social service work, and engaged in contemplative life, in the archdioceses of Baltimore, Boston, Chicago, Cincinnati, Dubuque, Milwaukee, New Orleans, New York, Philadelphia, Portland in Oregon, St. Louis, St. Paul, San Francisco and Santa Fé, and in the dioceses of Albany, Alexandria, Altoona, Amarillo,

*In addition to a small number of communities of Third Order Franciscan Sisters, other than those of the above listed foundations, who may be engaged in teaching, hospital or charitable work in the United States, as missions or new foundations in the course of development, there are also known foundations, whose dates were not supplied, in Rock Island, Ill., Maryville and Conception, Mo., Newton, Mass., Passaic, N. J., and Clarksburg, W. Va., and second foundations in Buffalo, N. Y., and Peoria, Ill.

Baker City, Belleville, Bismarck, Boise, Brooklyn, Buffalo, Burlington, Cheyenne, Cleveland, Columbus, Covington, Crookston, Davenport, Denver, Des Moines, Detroit, Duluth, El Paso, Erie, Fall River, Fort Wayne, Galveston, Grand Island, Grand Rapids, Great Falls, Green Bay, Harrisburg, Hartford, Helena, Indianapolis, Kansas City, La Crosse, Lead, Leavenworth, Lincoln, Los Angeles and San Diego, Louisville, Marquette, Mobile, Monterey-Fresno, Nashville, Newark, Ogdensburg, Oklahoma, Omaha, Peoria, Pittsburgh, Portland, Providence, Raleigh, Richmond, Rochester, Rockford, Sacramento, St. Cloud, St. Joseph, Savannah, Scranton, Seattle, Sioux City, Sioux Falls, Spokane, Springfield, Springfield in Illinois, Superior, Syracuse, Toledo, Trenton, Tucson, Wheeling, Wichita, Wilmington and Winona.

LADIES OF THE SACRED HEART OF MARY*

1851

AT the behest of the Right Rev. Amadeus Rappe, D.D., Bishop of Cleveland, a community of Ladies of the Sacred Heart of of Mary came from France, and in 1851 established at Cleveland, Ohio, St. Mary's Orphan Asylum for girls.

Participating according to need, and in proportion to their numbers, in charitable work in Cleveland during the following years, the Ladies of the Sacred Heart of Mary now conduct there St. Joseph's Orphanage for girls, and maintain Madonna Hall, a residence home for business women.

In addition to their institutions in Cleveland, members of the Congregation, attired in quiet secular garb, are active in educational, charitable and social service work in several cities in the United States.

*From the annals of the diocese of Cleveland, and from the Official Catholic Directory, 1929.

SISTERS OF CHARITY OF ST. AUGUSTINE*

1851

HE United States history of the Sisters of Charity of St. Augustine—descendent congregation of the Augustianian Sisters, founded in Arras, France, in 1223, and re-organized there in 1814, after having disbanded during the French Revolution—begins soon after the establishment of Ohio's second diocese, that of Cleveland.

Carrying out plans made by the Right Rev. Amadeus Rappe, D.D., first bishop of the new diocese, a group of Sisters of St. Augustine from Boulogne-sur-Mer, France, sailed from Havre on September 24, 1851, to go to Cleveland to care for the orphans and the sick. On this trip Mother Bernardine, Sister Francoise and two postulants, who composed the little community, were accompanied by the Very Rev. Louis de Goesbriand, Vicar General of the diocese of Cleveland, later first bishop of Burlington, who was returning at that time from a visit to France.

MOTHER ST. JOSEPH MUSELET

Upon their arrival in Cleveland, Ohio, the Sisters of St. Augustine became the guests of the Ursulines, who the previous year had come to the city from the same section of France. Remaining with the Ursulines until December 8th, the two postulants were clothed in the habit of the Sisters of St. Augustine, Mademoiselle Louise Brulois becoming Sister Mary Augustine, and Mademoiselle Cornelie Muselet, Sister Mary St. Joseph, after which they rejoined their community, which as Sisters of Charity of St. Augustine then established a convent home in the western section of Cleveland, at the time known as Ohio City.

True to their title of Sisters of Charity, and while awaiting the erection of the hospital which was to be the scene of their first

*From data and material supplied by the Sisters of Charity of St. Augustine, St. Augustine's Convent, Cleveland, Ohio.

labors in the United States, the sisters went about the city on rounds of charity, visiting the sick and assisting the needy.

On August 5, 1852, St. Joseph's Hospital, the first hospital in what is now the city of Cleveland, was opened, and Mother Bernardine, the Superior of the Community, admitted and registered its first patients.

Born in 1815 at Landrecies, France, Mother Bernardine had been received into the Congregation of the Sisters of St. Augustine in 1832. In time appointed Mistress of Novices, and chosen Superior of the American mission after she had been nearly four years Superior of l'Hôpital St. Louis, at Boulogne-sur-Mer, Mother Bernardine was eminently qualified for the responsibility of her work in Cleveland.

When Mother Bernardine saw the Sisters of Charity of St. Augustine thoroughly established, she returned to France, accompanied by Sister Francoise.

Mother Mary Ursula Bissonnette, a diocesan candidate—who had previously devoted herself to the service of the stricken during the cholera epidemic in 1849—and who had made her novitiate at the Ursuline Convent, later being received into the Augustinian Community, succeeded to the office of Superior.

With the establishment of St. Vincent's Orphanage in 1853 the Sisters of Charity of St. Augustine entered upon a phase of charitable work to which they have since given much attention. Mother St. Joseph Muselet, of the pioneer group from France, was placed in charge of the education and training of the orphan boys confided to the care of the Community, and continued in this position for many years.

Under the superiorship of Mother Mary Augustine, likewise of the Community from France, St. Joseph's Hospital was supplanted in Cleveland by Charity Hospital, which opened its doors October 10, 1865, to receive the sick and wounded soldiers returning from the Civil War. The nursing was done exclusively by members of the Community until 1898, when the first school of nursing was established at the hospital.

In the years which have followed, the Community, while confining its activities to the diocese of Cleveland, has become engaged in the environs of the episcopal city, and directs St. Thomas' Hospital in Akron, and Mercy and Little Flower Hospitals in Canton, in addition to Charity, St. John's and St. Ann's in Cleveland, each with its own training school for nurses.

Having also conducted orphanages in the diocese, since 1853, the Sisters of Charity of St. Augustine, with Sister Mary Carmelita as Superior, are now in charge of Parmadale, the Children's Village of St. Vincent de Paul, established in 1925 at Parma, near Cleveland.

St. Augustine's Convent, Lakewood, Cleveland, Ohio

Erected with wisdom and foresight through the efforts of the Right Rev. Joseph Schrembs, D.D., fifth bishop of Cleveland, this Children's Village, with its "cottage homes," is a monumental work— an extensive twentieth century development and outgrowth of the one-time orphan asylum.

With the progress of the Cleveland Community, teaching has been added to the activities of the sisters. In 1925 a new and spacious

St. Augustine's Academy was opened at the Motherhouse, which since 1888 has been maintained in Lakewood on the shores of Lake Erie, on the west side of Cleveland. Here reside Mother M. Brigid, Superior General of the Congregation, and her Council of administration, Sisters Alphonsine, Geraldine, Marcelline, Marguerite, Mechtildes and Patricia.

SUMMARY

Sisters of Charity of St. Augustine.
Founded in France, as Sisters of St. Augustine, in 1223.
Established in the United States in 1851.
Habit: The habit is gray, with a black domino and veil. A rosary is worn on a black cincture.
Approximate number in Community, 250.
Active in educational, hospital and charitable work in the diocese of Cleveland.
Motherhouse and Novitiate, St. Augustine's Convent, 14808 Lake Avenue, Lakewood, Cleveland, Ohio. (Diocese of Cleveland.)

SISTERS OF CHARITY OF LEAVENWORTH*

1851

THE Congregation of the Sisters of Charity of Leavenworth originated as a congregation at Nashville, Tennessee, in the year 1851.

Ten years previously Sisters of Charity of Nazareth had come from their Kentucky convent home to Tennessee, where in the city of Nashville, and under the auspices of the Right Rev. Richard P. Miles, O.P., D.D., they opened a boarding and day school and later a hospital and orphanage.

Through the Asiatic cholera siege which ravaged the country in 1848, and which was particularly malignant in Nashville, these daughters of Mother Catherine Spalding had devoted themselves night and day to the poor, who without nurses and adequate medical assistance battled the plague.

With the cessation of the disease, and a return to normalcy, Bishop Miles made known to the sisters of the Motherhouse at Nazareth, Kentucky, his desire to form them into a diocesan community. In answer to this proposal, Mother Catherine, coming at once to Nashville, left her daughters in Tennessee free to remain and form the nucleus of such a community as the bishop desired or to return to their convent home at Nazareth.

Of the Sisters of Charity of Nazareth in the diocese, six elected to remain. A Motherhouse was then secured for the new Community, of which Mother Xavier Ross was appointed Superior, and which was composed of Sister Vincent Kearney, Sister Joanna Bruner, Sister Ellen Davis, Sister Jane Francis Kennedy and Sister Baptista Kelly. In addition to these original members, the Community was early augmented by the reception of candidates who applied for admission to it.

Soon after his appointment by Bishop Miles as ecclesiastical superior of the Community, the Rev. Ivo Schacht, visiting Europe, procured for it from the Motherhouse of the Daughters of Charity in Paris, important and helpful books pertaining to the daily meditation, monthly retreat, and the formula of prayers of the Daughters of Charity, whose Rules of St. Vincent de Paul were being followed by the Nashville Sisters of Charity.

*From data and material supplied by the Sisters of Charity of Leavenworth, Leavenworth, Kan., and from *The History of the Sisters of Charity of Leavenworth, Kansas,* by a member of the Community.

In the immediately ensuing years, the sisters encountered such insurmountable local difficulties that at length a decision was made to extend their sphere of usefulness beyond the limits of Tennessee.

With this in view Mother Xavier visited St. Louis in 1858 during a conference of bishops then being held there. Meeting at this time the celebrated Jesuit missionary of the Indians, the Rev. Peter De Smet, also on a visit in St. Louis, Mother Xavier learned from him that the Jesuit bishop, the Right Rev. J. B. Miege, Vicar Apostolic of the Indian Territory East of the Rocky Mountains, who was in attendance at the bishops' council, was anxious to secure sisters for Leavenworth, Kansas, where he was maintaining his episcopal residence.

In an interview which she then had with Bishop Miege, Mother Xavier was urged to arrange for a transfer of the Community from Tennessee to Kansas. This she did

SISTER MARY MAGDALEN
A Sister of Charity of
Leavenworth

in the same year, following a visit which she prudently made to the new field before the Community decided on the change.

Schools and a novitiate were soon opened by the Community in Leavenworth, where the sisters had established their headquarters by the end of the year 1858. Before the close of the following year, complying with the bishop's wishes, plans were made for the opening of a boarding school, and in the spring of 1860 St. Mary's Academy, forerunner of St. Mary's College and Academy of today, was erected in Leavenworth. Soon after its opening the new institution was filled to capacity by pupils from nearly every city in Kansas, as well as from Missouri, Colorado, New Mexico, Wyoming and Utah.

At the end of the first month of the year 1861 the Territory of Kansas was admitted to the Union as a free state. Three months later the great Civil War began, and found Kansas divided in conflict between its Free State settlers, who established their headquarters at Lawrence and the new capital city, Topeka, and the Slave State supporters, headquartering at Leavenworth and Lecompton. Though the commandant at Fort Leavenworth assured the sisters that they should not be molested, this did not wholly allay their concern during the years of duress which followed. When wounded men of both sides were brought to Fort Leavenworth, the sisters volunteered their

St. Mary's Academy, Leavenworth, Kansas

services, which, however, were not accepted as they were not needed among the many volunteer nurses, though they were instrumental in doing much good, both in their schools and St. Vincent's Orphanage, opened in 1863, and St. John's Hospital, opened early in 1864.

Concluding the first decade of years of the Community in Kansas, the sisters received, through the thoughtfulness of Bishop Miege, the Apostolic Benediction of Pope Pius IX, and from the legislature of the state of Kansas their certificate of incorporation, under the title of St. Mary's Female Academy, conducted by the Sisters of Charity of St. Vincent of Paul, of Leavenworth.

The next year the Community, which had already established various missions in Kansas, received Bishop Miege's approval of its acceptance of a mission in Helena, Montana, which Father De Smet wished the Leavenworth sisters to undertake. St. Vincent's Academy and St. John's Hospital, opened in Helena in 1870, and still conducted there, together with a second orphanage and infants' home since established, bespeak the activities of the Community in the city. The sisters have further established St. Vincent's Hospital and its school for crippled children at Billings, St. James' Hospital in Butte, St. Ann's at Anaconda and St. Joseph's at Deer Lodge, where they also conduct an academy, in addition to their work in many parish and mission schools throughout the state.

Not restricting their labors to Kansas and Montana localities, but continuing in the region of the Rocky Mountains, from Montana into Colorado, Wyoming and to New Mexico, the Sisters of Charity of Leavenworth are now in charge of many well-equipped hospitals, orphanages, parochial schools and academies.

For nearly fifty years, Mother Xavier Ross, natively of Cincinnati, Ohio, who with her companion sisters left familiar and dear scenes in Kentucky and Tennessee for the vast new chosen territory, untiringly and courageously labored, as she shared with the members of the rapidly growing Community their trials and struggles and rewards in the many institutions and missions of their founding, which together with those of more recent establishment are outstanding works of the Sisters of Charity of Leavenworth, loyal followers of the apostle of charity, St. Vincent de Paul.

SUMMARY

Sisters of Charity of Leavenworth.
Founded in the United States in 1851.
Papal Approbation of Rules, December 31, 1922, by Pope Pius XI.
Habit: The habit, cape and apron are black. A black veil is worn over a white cap.
Approximate number in Community, 530.
Active in educational, hospital and charitable work in the archdiocese of Santa Fé and the dioceses of Cheyenne, Denver, Great Falls, Helena, Kansas City and Leavenworth.
Motherhouse and Novitiate, St. Mary's Academy, Leavenworth, Kansas. (Diocese of Leavenworth.)

SISTERS OF ST. BENEDICT*

$\mathcal{T}$HE Benedictine Sisterhood dates from the time of the great patriarch, St. Benedict (480-543), its foundress being his twin sister, St. Scholastica. The annals of history contain little definite information as to the rule followed by St. Scholastica and the pious companions who lived a community life with her in a monastery she established in the vicinity of the Abbey of Monte Cassino, not far distant from Rome, where St. Benedict and his followers dwelt.

Though the enduring Rule of St. Benedict was not then sufficiently formulated to have been the designated rule of these earliest nuns of the Order, St. Benedict, in his devotion to his sister, must have been the spiritual advisor and guide of those in the community presided over by her.

Before the end of the tenth century, the Rule of St. Benedict had been adopted by many communities of women, as well as men.

The motto of the Benedictine Order, *Ora et labora,* has come down through centuries, and today, as generations ago, the life of a true Benedictine is summed up in the same words—*Pray and labor.*

To various Benedictine communities, in their respective periods, belonged St. Hilda, St. Lioba, St. Thecla and St. Walburga, as well as St. Gertrude the Great, and her sister, St. Mechtilde. Among the numerous other Benedictine saints is the learned and holy Abbess, St. Hildegarde, known as the "Sibyl of the Rhine."

Surviving Europe's history-making epochs, suffering oppression, suppression and restoration, the Benedictine Order is today one of the world's oldest and foremost religious orders.

ST. MARY'S, PENNSYLVANIA

1852

To an ancient foundation of the Benedictine Nuns in Germany the United States owes its first community of followers of St. Scholastica.

In his solicitude for the Christian education of the youth of America, the land of his adoption, the Archabbot Boniface Wimmer, O.S.B., petitioned the Benedictine Nuns of his native country,

*From data and material supplied by the respective communities of the Sisters of St. Benedict in the United States, and from the Official Catholic Year Book, 1928.

Bavaria, to send sisters to assist in the pioneering educational work in America.

A small colony of nuns, under Mother Benedicta Riepp, O.S.B., arrived in the United States from Eichstadt, Germany, in 1852, and were received in the diocese of Pittsburgh.

ST. JOSEPH'S CONVENT, ST. MARY'S, PENNSYLVANIA

One of the attempts at Catholic colonization in Pennsylvania had been made at about this time by Mathias Benzinger and J. Eschbach of Baltimore, who purchased a large tract of land in Elk County, and founded there a town. This new town, St. Mary's, was chosen for the site of the first labors of these Benedictines, and the institution then established there is looked upon as the mother foundation of the now numerous ones since founded throughout the country by the Benedictine Nuns. Many foundations in different parts of the United States have been made from the mother foundation.

In the United States, as well as in the countries of the Old World, each Benedictine community, being diocesan, functions independently as a Motherhouse, and maintains its own novitiate, and thus pre-serves the family spirit characteristic of the Benedictine Order, as may be gleaned from the Holy Rule written by St. Benedict.

With their community numbering now nearly one hundred, the sisters of the mother foundation are continuing the work of the education of youth, by conducting academies and high schools, as well as grade schools, in the diocese of Erie, erected from the original diocese of Pittsburgh.

Motherhouse and Novitiate, St. Joseph's Convent, 303 Church Street, St. Mary's, Pennsylvania. (Diocese of Erie.)

ERIE, PENNSYLVANIA
1856

In June of 1856 the Benedictine foundation at St. Mary's, Penn-sylvania, made its first extension in the diocese by sending a colony of six sisters to the episcopal city of Erie, where they were received by the bishop, the Right Rev. Josue M. Young. Soon after the estab-lishment of the community at St. Benedict's, a Motherhouse was established there, and the insti-tution was recognized as an inde-pendent foundation with its own novitiate.

The community grew rapidly, and was soon able to establish other permanent foundations in dioceses of the country.

In the diocese of Erie, now under the episcopacy of the Right Rev. Mark Gannon, D.D., the sis-ters, forming a community of nearly one hundred members, continue their educational work, conducting

A Sister of St. Benedict

St. Benedict's Convent, Erie, Pennsylvania

as their foremost institution St. Benedict's Academy, at the Mother-house and novitiate.

Motherhouse and Novitiate, St. Benedict's Convent, 327-345 East Ninth Street, Erie, Pennsylvania. (Diocese of Erie.)

ST. JOSEPH, MINNESOTA

1857

The first extension of the Benedictine Sisters in the United States, beyond the diocese of the original foundation at St. Mary's, Pennsylvania, took place in the year 1857, when a foundation was made in St. Cloud, Minnesota.

Composing the community which left St. Mary's to do educational work in the northwest—included then in the vast diocese of St. Paul—were Mother Benedicta Riepp, Sisters Willibalda Scherbauer, Gertrude Capser, Gregoria Moser, Evangelista Kremeter, and three postulants, Prisca Mayer, Mary Walter and Josephine Lejal.

ST. BENEDICT'S CONVENT, ST. JOSEPH, MINNESOTA

In 1863 the community removed to St. Joseph, outside the city of St. Cloud, which in 1889, with the erection of the diocese of St. Cloud, became the site of the episcopacy, of which the Right Rev. Joseph F. Busch, D.D., is the present incumbent.

St. Benedict's College and Academy, established at the Mother-house in St. Joseph in 1880, was incorporated as an institution for the higher education of young women, March 23, 1887. In 1910 collegiate work was begun, and the college now ranks among the foremost Catholic colleges for women in the United States.

The community at St. Joseph, of which Mother M. Louisa Walz, O.S.B., is Superior, has the distinction of being not only the largest community of Benedictine Sisters in the United States, numbering more than a thousand members, but is reputed the largest in the world as well. The educational and charitable activities of the sisters, in their many institutions, have been extended beyond the diocese of St. Cloud, into the archdiocese of St. Paul and the dioceses of Bismarck, Crookston, Fargo, La Crosse, Seattle and Superior.

Motherhouse and Novitiate, St. Benedict's Convent, St. Joseph, Minnesota. (Diocese of St. Cloud.)

RIDGELY, MARYLAND
1857

Intimately associated with the history of the dioceses in Pennsylvania and the diocese of Wilmington is the foundation of Sisters of St. Benedict whose Motherhouse is in Ridgely, Maryland.

When the first band of Benedictine Nuns arrived in the United States, it was the Right Rev. Michael O'Connor, beloved bishop of Pittsburgh, who welcomed them to his diocese. Upon the erection of the see of Erie, Elk County—where the new community had established its foundation, at St. Mary's—was included in the counties comprising it.

In the readjustment following this division, and that the Benedictines might remain in his diocese, Bishop O'Connor invited the sisters at St. Mary's to make a new foundation there. Six sisters from the parent house were accordingly sent for the new mission, which was established in 1857 at Indiana, Pennsylvania, where the community engaged in the educational work necessary in the environment.

Little more than ten years later the diocese of Wilmington was erected, and in his zealous plans for the education of youth in the diocese, its second bishop, the Right Rev. Alfred A. Curtis, D.D., invited the Benedictine Nuns to establish a foundation there.

To comply with this, permission was obtained for the transfer of the community to Ridgely, Maryland, in the diocese of Wilmington, from where the sisters, now numbering about seventy-five, under the ecclesiastical jurisdiction of the Right Rev. E. J. Fitzmaurice, D.D., Bishop of Wilmington, extend their educational activities to academies and parochial schools in the archdiocese of Philadelphia, and the diocese of Newark. The Motherhouse and novitiate are located at St. Gertrude's Convent in Ridgely, where an academy and boarding school are conducted.

Motherhouse and Novitiate, St. Gertrude's Convent, Ridgely, Maryland. (Diocese of Wilmington.)

COVINGTON, KENTUCKY
1859

Sisters from St. Benedict's Convent, in Erie, Pennsylvania, composed the foundation community of Benedictines which zealously began its labor in Covington, Kentucky, in 1859, six years after the establishment of the diocese of Covington.

Pursuing successfully the educational work of the Order, the community increased in numbers, and in proportion opened missions throughout the diocese, to which it has confined its work.

In 1890 St. Walburg Academy, adjoining the convent, was erected, and in 1907 Villa Madonna Academy was established and opened as a boarding school. In 1921 Villa Madonna College was founded, and is maintained by the community, which now numbers approximately one hundred and sixty sisters.

VILLA MADONNA, LUDLOW, COVINGTON, KENTUCKY

Novitiate, Villa Madonna, Ludlow, Kentucky. *Motherhouse*, St. Walburg Convent, 116 East 12th Street, Covington, Kentucky. (Diocese of Covington.)

CHICAGO, ILLINOIS
1861

To the Benedictine foundation in Erie, Pennsylvania, and the fervor of one of the country's Benedictine bishops, the Right Rev.

Louis M. Fink, D.D., Chicago owes the inauguration there in 1861 of the work of the Sisters of St. Benedict.

At that time, and prior to his elevation to the see of Leavenworth, Bishop Fink was pastor of St. Joseph's Church in Chicago, to which parish the Benedictine Sisters from Erie were invited, to take charge of the school.

In the course of the years which then followed, and with its growth in numbers and the extension of its activities, the transfer of the community to still larger quarters than those originally obtained was necessitated. The Convent and Academy of St. Scholastica were therefore erected on an attractive site on Ridge Boulevard, in Rogers Park, and here since 1905 have been maintained the Mother-house and novitiate of the Benedictine Sisters of Chicago, now approximately one hundred and seventy in number, and active in educational work not only in the archdiocese of Chicago but also in the diocese of Denver.

> *Motherhouse and Novitiate,* Convent of St. Scholastica, 7430 Ridge Boulevard, Rogers Park, Chicago, Illinois. (Archdiocese of Chicago.)

ATCHISON, KANSAS
1863

Mt. St. Scholastica's Convent was founded in Atchison, Kansas, in 1863, within the first decade of years of the founding of the city,

MT. ST. SCHOLASTICA'S CONVENT, ATCHISON, KANSAS

and under the ecclesiastical auspices of the Right Rev. J. B. Miege, S.J., predecessor in the see of the Benedictine bishop, the Right Rev. Louis M. Fink, D.D., who had served as his assistant, and who in 1877 was appointed first bishop of Leavenworth, on the establishment of that diocese, covering then the state of Kansas.

With the growth of the city and the stabilizing of the various pioneer missions of the Church, the Benedictine Sisters of Mt. St. Scholastica's, who had come to Atchison from St. Benedict's at St. Joseph, Minnesota, kept apace in the extension of their activities in not only the diocese of Leavenworth, but also in the new dioceses later erected in Kansas, and in those surrounding the state.

The splendid modern institution now composing Mt. St. Scholastica's at Atchison is advantageously located on an eminence south of the city, and comprises a connected scheme of distinct buildings, chief in the group being the convent and novitiate, the college, academy and music hall.

The community, numbering approximately four hundred and twenty-five sisters, is active principally in educational work in the dioceses of Concordia, Davenport, Denver, Des Moines, Kansas City, Leavenworth, Lincoln, Omaha and St. Joseph.

Motherhouse and Novitiate, Mt. St. Scholastica's Convent, Atchison, Kansas. (Diocese of Leavenworth.)

FERDINAND, INDIANA

1867

The foundation of the Benedictine Nuns at Ferdinand, Indiana, was made in August, 1867, by sisters from St. Walburg Convent in Covington, Kentucky. The first Indiana home of the community was in a house vacated by the Sisters of Providence, who, prior to the arrival of the Benedictines, had been in charge of the school in Ferdinand.

With Sister Benedicta as first Superior, the little community of four sisters rapidly increased in numbers and as rapidly opened new missions in the state. During Sister Benedicta's administration, purchase was made, in 1872, of sixty-four acres of land adjoining the grounds of the small convent which had been built.

In 1883 work was begun on the splendid building for the permanent Motherhouse of the community. In addition to the Motherhouse, with its novitiate, and beautiful chapel, where the privilege of Perpetual Adoration has been obtained, the institution at Ferdinand includes also the Academy of the Immaculate Conception, which is conducted there by the sisters.

The community, which now numbers about two hundred and fifty members, confines its activity to educational work in the diocese

of Indianapolis, as a diocesan community, under the direct jurisdiction
of the ordinary of the diocese, the Right Rev. Joseph Chartrand, D.D.

Motherhouse and Novitiate, Convent of the Immaculate Conception, Ferdinand, Indiana. (Diocese of Indianapolis.)

ELIZABETH, NEW JERSEY

1868

The community of Benedictine Sisters of St. Walburg Motherhouse and novitiate in Elizabeth, New Jersey, was founded in 1868 by Sisters of St. Benedict from Newark, with Mother Walburga Hock serving as first Superior.

Mother Monica Dalton is the present Superior of the community, which, now numbering approximately one hundred and seventy-five

BENEDICTINE CONVENT OF ST. WALBURG, ELIZABETH, NEW JERSEY

sisters, conducts the Benedictine Academy, a day and boarding school for girls, connected with the Motherhouse, as well as the Bender Memorial Academy, in Elizabeth, and the Benedictine Academy in Paterson, New Jersey.

In addition to this academic work, and their work in parochial schools not only in the diocese of Newark but in the archdioceses of Baltimore and New York, where the community also labors, the sisters are engaged in charitable and hospital work, Our Lady of Victory Sanitarium and school of nursing, also known as Benedictine Hospital, in Kingston, New York, being among the foremost of their institutions.

In its activities in the archdiocese of Baltimore the community maintains a convent in Washington, D. C., as the residence of the sisters engaged in school work there and attending the Catholic University and Sisters' College. This Washington residence, now the Benedictine Convent, was formerly known as the Brooks mansion, from which the vicinity of Brookland was named, and is of further historical interest as the site of the inauguration, in 1911, of the Catholic Sisters' College, and where for two years the college classes were conducted.

Motherhouse and Novitiate, Benedictine Motherhouse of St. Walburg, 851 North Broad Street, Elizabeth, New Jersey. (Diocese of Newark.)

COVINGTON, LOUISIANA

1870

St. Scholastica's Convent, in Covington, Louisiana, is the home of the Benedictine community which was founded in 1870 at New Orleans, by Mother M. Alexia Lechner, Prioress of St. Walburg Convent, Covington, Kentucky. Mother M. Scholastica Hoeveller was first Superior of the new community.

In 1902 the foundation was transferred from New Orleans to the present site in Covington, Louisiana. An academy and boarding

St. Scholastica's Convent, Covington, Louisiana

school are conducted at St. Scholastica's Convent, the Motherhouse and novitiate of this Benedictine community, of which Mother M. Florentine Yokum is the present Superior, and which is active in educational work in the archdiocese of New Orleans.

Motherhouse and Novitiate, St. Scholastica's Convent, Covington, Louisiana. (Archdiocese of New Orleans.)

PITTSBURGH, PENNSYLVANIA
1870

That the Benedictine Nuns might continue to have a foundation in the diocese of Pittsburgh—into which they had been received on their arrival in the United States in 1852—a colony of nuns was sent to Pittsburgh in 1870 from the mother foundation at St. Mary's in Elk County, Pennsylvania, one of the counties included in the diocese of Erie on its separation from the diocese of Pittsburgh. Following the automatic transfer of the mother foundation to the new diocese, another foundation had been made in the Pittsburgh diocese in 1857, but this had later been transferred to the diocese of Wilmington.

With Mother M. Cyrilla as Prioress, the community, now numbering more than one hundred sisters, is active in educational work among nearly four thousand children in the parochial schools of the diocese of Pittsburgh.

Motherhouse and Novitiate, St. Mary's Convent, 4530 Perryville Road, N.S., Pittsburgh, Pennsylvania. (Diocese of Pittsburgh.)

BRISTOW, VIRGINIA
1870

In 1870, during the episcopacy of the Right Rev. John McGill, D.D., in the diocese of Richmond, the Benedictine mother foundation at St. Mary's, Pennsylvania, sent a colony of sisters to Virginia.

Establishing their convent as St. Edith's, in Bristow, the sisters at once engaged in educational work in the diocese, and in time beyond its confines.

In 1901, with the approbation of the bishop, the Right Rev. Augustus Van de Vyver, D.D., the community became an independent foundation, and the convent, known as St. Benedict's, its Motherhouse.

St. Gertrude's High School, in Richmond, affiliated with the Catholic University of America, is conducted by these Benedictine Sisters, who have also among their principal institutions a school for boys, Linton Hall, near Bristow. In 1928 Linton Hall Guest House, in Bristow, was opened by the sisters. The Right Rev. Andrew J. Brennan, D.D., Bishop of Richmond, officiated at the inaugural services of the women's retreat that marked its opening.

Connected with the convent the sisters conduct St. Anne's Char-itable Institute, for poor, friendless white girls. In addition to their

St. Benedict's Convent, Bristow, Virginia

activities in the diocese of Richmond, the near one hundred sisters of this community of Benedictines are active also in the diocese of Pittsburgh.

> *Motherhouse and Novitiate,* St. Benedict's Convent, Bristow, Virginia. (Diocese of Richmond.)

YANKTON, SOUTH DAKOTA

1874

From the picturesque convent, "Maria Rickenbach," on a peak of the Swiss Alps, came the community of Benedictine Nuns which in 1874 established its foundation in the United States, locating at first in Maryville, Missouri.

Soon after his appointment to the see of Sioux Falls, in 1880, the saintly Benedictine bishop, the Right Rev. Martin Marty, D.D., appealed to the Benedictine Nuns in Missouri for a foundation for his diocese. In compliance with this appeal, the foundation in Mary-ville was transferred to the new diocese in South Dakota.

The convent home of the community, with its privilege of con-tinuous adoration of the Blessed Sacrament, was then established at Yankton, and the sisters at once engaged in educational work and began the instruction of the children of the Sioux Indians, so dear to the heart of the Benedictine bishop. In addition to their edu-

cational work in the diocese of Sioux Falls, the sisters of this Bene-
dictine community have established and conduct Sacred Heart
Hospital in Yankton, and St. Mary's Hospital in Pierre, South
Dakota.

The community, of approximately two hundred and eighty sisters,
is engaged in educational work in the dioceses of Bismarck, Denver
and Omaha, as well as in the diocese of Sioux Falls.

Motherhouse and Novitiate, Benedictine Convent of the Sacred
Heart, Yankton, South Dakota.   (Diocese of Sioux Falls.)

NAUVOO, ILLINOIS
1875

St. Mary's Convent, in Nauvoo, Illinois, located on the grounds
where from 1839 to 1846 the costly Mormon Temple and Arsenal

St. Mary's Convent, Nauvoo, Illinois

stood, was established in 1875 by sisters from the Benedictine foundation in Chicago. Connected with the convent is an academy, and
"The Spalding Institute" for boys.

The community, numbering approximately a hundred members,
is active in educational work in the diocese of Peoria.

Motherhouse and Novitiate, St. Mary's Convent, Nauvoo, Illinois.
(Diocese of Peoria.)

SIOUX CITY, IOWA
1878

In the year 1878 a community of Sisters of St. Benedict was established at Elkton, South Dakota, and its headquarters were maintained there until transferred to the present site in Sioux City, Iowa.

Continuing under the superiorship of Mother M. Gertrude McDermott, Prioress, and under the ecclesiastical jurisdiction of the Right Rev. Edmund Heelan, D.D., bishop of the diocese of Sioux City, the community is engaged chiefly in charitable and hospital work in Sioux City. Extending their work into the diocese of Denver, the sisters in 1927 opened a hospital at Sterling, Colorado.

Motherhouse and Novitiate, St. Benedict's Convent, 45th and Douglas Streets, Sioux City, Iowa. (Diocese of Sioux City.)

FORT SMITH, ARKANSAS
1879

In 1879 the Benedictine Sisters of Immaculate Conception Convent, in Ferdinand, Indiana, sent a community of sisters to Arkansas, to open St. Scholastica's Academy, in Shoal Creek.

St. Scholastica's Convent, Benedictine Heights, Fort Smith, Arkansas

In 1888, the community of sisters of this southern state became independent, and Mother Meinrada Lex was chosen first Superior.

During the years which followed, the Benedictine Sisters engaged actively in charitable, educational and hospital work in the diocese of Little Rock, and with the growth of the community, extended their labors to the nearby dioceses of Dallas, Kansas City and St. Joseph.

In 1924, the Arkansas Motherhouse and novitiate of this Benedictine community of approximately one hundred and ninety sisters, of which Mother Perpetua Gerard is now Superior, were transferred from St. Scholastica's Convent, at Shoal Creek, to Fort Smith, at the site of St. Scholastica's Convent there, in connection with which an academy for girls is also conducted.

> *Motherhouse and Novitiate,* St. Scholastica's Convent, Benedictine Heights, Fort Smith, Arkansas. (Diocese of Little Rock.)

GUTHRIE, OKLAHOMA
1879

The community of the Benedictine Sisters of the Sacred Hearts, with their headquarters now at Guthrie, Oklahoma, was founded in the year 1879, by sisters from St. Mary's, Pittsburgh, Pennsylvania, who, under the direction of Mother M. Paula Riley, established their foundation in Creston, Iowa.

For a time the sisters engaged in educational work in Creston and other missions originally in the vast diocese of Dubuque, which upon its division were included in the diocese of Des Moines. In 1892 the entire community was transferred to Oklahoma, and the Motherhouse was established in Guthrie, at that time the ecclesiastical center of the state. Upon the erection of the diocese of Oklahoma in 1905, with the see in Oklahoma City, all educational work in the diocese became more stabilized and the activities of religious educators more noteworthy.

In 1916 St. Joseph Academy, which had been established at the convent Motherhouse in Guthrie, was chartered as a college, under the name of "Catholic College of Oklahoma for Women," and empowered to grant degrees by the Oklahoma State Board of Education, which in 1918 directed that it be listed as an accredited school. In that year also the college was affiliated with the Catholic University of America, and in 1919 it was accorded the same recognition by the University of Oklahoma.

St. Joseph's was the first convent in Oklahoma to open its doors to women retreatants. Since the opening retreat there, in June, 1917, attended by eighty women, appreciative of the initiative of the community sponsoring it, the retreat movement, then in its infancy, has

ST. JOSEPH'S CONVENT, GUTHRIE, OKLAHOMA

become widespread. To facilitate the attendance at the retreats, which have become an annual event at St. Joseph's, the sisters have provided for the care of the children of mothers who follow the spiritual exercises.

In 1922 the Benedictine Sisters of the Sacred Hearts, with a number of the Benedictine communities in the United States, united under one Constitution, and under the title of "The Congregation of St. Scholastica" received papal approval for seven years. The united communities are still independent in the management of their temporalities, each subject to episcopal jurisdiction and each maintaining its own novitiate. The benefits of the union in one congregation are purely spiritual. The Mother President of the Benedictine Sisters of the Congregation of St. Scholastica resides in the Motherhouse of the community to which she belongs by profession.

Prominent among the schools conducted in the diocese of Oklahoma, to which the Benedictine community in Guthrie confines its labors, is the Monte Casino High School for girls, which it has established in Tulsa.

Motherhouse and Novitiate, St. Joseph's Convent, Guthrie, Oklahoma. (Diocese of Oklahoma.)

CULLMAN, ALABAMA

1880

The foundation of the Benedictine Nuns in Alabama, laboring in the state from Covington, Kentucky, since 1880, was made in 1903, with their establishment of Sacred Heart Convent in Cullman, in the northern part of the state, north of the city of Birmingham.

SACRED HEART CONVENT, CULLMAN, ALABAMA

To the energy and zeal of the first Prioress, Mother M. Ottilia, is due the erection of this southern Motherhouse, in its healthful and scenic location in the state, the center of the educational activity of the community in the diocese of Mobile.

Motherhouse and Novitiate, Sacred Heart Convent, Cullman, Alabama. (Diocese of Mobile.)

MT. ANGEL, OREGON

1882

The Benedictine community of Convent Queen of Angels, at Mt. Angel, Oregon, was founded in 1882 by the Right Rev. Abbot Adelhelm Odermatt, O.S.B. Mother Mary Bernardine Wachter was the first Superior of the community.

A year after the establishment of the foundation, Perpetual Adoration of the Blessed Sacrament was begun, and has since been continued by the community.

Connected with the Motherhouse and maintained by the community are Mt. Angel Academy and Normal School, both standardized by the state of Oregon. In addition to their school work, which is confined in the United States to the archdiocese of Portland in Oregon, sisters from this community, of approximately one hundred and fifteen members, are in charge of an Indian school on the west coast of Vancouver Island, British Columbia.

Motherhouse and Novitiate, Convent Queen of Angels, Mt. Angel, Oregon. (Archdiocese of Portland in Oregon.)

STURGIS, SOUTH DAKOTA

1889

Upon the invitation of the bishop of Sioux Falls, the Right Rev. Martin Marty, O.S.B., D.D., the Benedictine Nuns of Melchthal, Switzerland, in 1889 sent a colony of sisters to the United States to establish a Benedictine Convent at Sturgis, South Dakota, then in the new diocese.

Mother Angela Arnet was Prioress of the community which began its work of education and religious instruction of the children

ST. MARTIN'S CONVENT, STURGIS, SOUTH DAKOTA

of the Black Hills. St. Martin's Academy, an accredited school of the state, for day and boarding pupils, has been established in con- nection with the Motherhouse, and is affiliated with the Catholic University of America.

In 1902, with the erection of the diocese of Lead, in the south- western section of the state, the community in Sturgis was auto- matically included in the new see, now under the episcopal juris- diction of the Right Rev. John J. Lawler, D.D. In addition to engaging in educational work the sisters direct St. Joseph's Hospital at Deadwood, Our Lady of Lourdes Hospital at Hot Springs, and St. John's Hospital at Rapid City, all in South Dakota.

Motherhouse and Novitiate, St. Martin's Convent, Sturgis, South Dakota. (Diocese of Lead.)

LAKE JOVITA, FLORIDA
1889

Holy Name Convent, the home of the Benedictine Nuns in the diocese of St. Augustine, was founded in Pasco County, Florida, in March, 1889, by Mother Dolorosa Scanlan, from the Benedictine foundation in Pittsburgh.

HOLY NAME CONVENT, LAKE JOVITA, FLORIDA

Holy Name Academy, a boarding and day school, established at the Motherhouse, is among the important institutions conducted by the community. St. Benedict's Preparatory Hall, a boarding school for little boys, is likewise maintained by the sisters at the academy. The activities of the community are centered in educational work in the diocese of St. Augustine.

Motherhouse and Novitiate, Holy Name Convent, Lake Jovita, Florida. (Diocese of St. Augustine.)

DULUTH, MINNESOTA
1892

In 1892, three years after the establishment of the Minnesota diocese of Duluth, and under the auspices of its first bishop, the Right Rev. James McGolrick, D.D., a Benedictine foundation was made in the city under the title of the Sacred Heart Institute. Directing the new foundation and its initial activity was Mother M. Scholastica Kerst.

In 1909 the academy which had been opened in Duluth was transferred to the Motherhouse, which is built on an eminence, where it commands a splendid view of Lake Superior and its picturesque harbor. Here also a college for women was established in 1911.

The Benedictine community of Duluth, with a membership now of approximately three hundred and twenty sisters, has not only extended its labors beyond its home diocese—now under the jurisdiction of the Right Rev. Thomas A. Welch, D.D.—but has also widened the scope of its work to include the maintenance and conducting of hospitals and charitable institutions, as well as schools and colleges, in the archdioceses of Baltimore, Chicago and St. Paul, and in the diocese of Duluth.

Motherhouse and Novitiate, Villa Sancta Scholastica, Kenwood Park, Duluth, Minnesota. (Diocese of Duluth.)

SACRED HEART, OKLAHOMA
1892

The foundation of Benedictine Sisters of Our Lady of Belloc, at Nazareth Convent, Sacred Heart, Oklahoma, was established in 1892 by a group of Benedictine Nuns from France, who had volunteered to devote their lives to the welfare of the first Catholic Indian Mission in Oklahoma.

This Indian Mission, dating from 1880, was established by the Benedictines, who that year located in Oklahoma at Sacred Heart Abbey, in Pottawattomi County.

The community, with Sister M. Philomena as Superior, carries on the work allotted to its ministrations in the diocese of Oklahoma.

United States Provincial house, Nazareth Convent, Sacred Heart, Oklahoma. (Diocese of Oklahoma.)

LISLE, ILLINOIS
1895

The community of Benedictine Sisters now located at Lisle, Illinois, was founded in 1895 by the Most Rev. Patrick A. Feehan, D.D., then archbishop of Chicago, and the Right Rev. Abbot Nepomucene Jaeger, O.S.B.

Sister M. Nepomucene Jaeger, O.S.B., of St. Mary's Convent, N.S., Pittsburgh, Pennsylvania, served as first Superior of the community.

The convent home in Chicago being too small to accommodate the increasing community, two hundred acres of land were purchased at Lisle, Illinois, not far distant, and the sisters in 1912 transferred to the first completed unit of the splendid building erected there for a Motherhouse and normal school.

The community, of approximately one hundred and fifty sisters, with its headquarters at Sacred Heart Convent, is active in educational and charitable work in the archdiocese of Chicago and the diocese of Superior.

> *Motherhouse and Novitiate,* Sacred Heart Convent, Lisle, Illinois. (Archdiocese of Chicago.)

COTTONWOOD, IDAHO

1908

The foundation of Sisters of St. Benedict whose Motherhouse and novitiate are maintained at St. Gertrude's Convent, Cottonwood,

ST. GERTRUDE'S CONVENT, COTTONWOOD, IDAHO

Idaho, was established in 1908.   Prior to that time a mission had been opened at Cottonwood, served by Sisters of St. Benedict from Colton, Washington, who were of the ancient monastery at Sarnen, in central Switzerland.

In addition to their activities at the Motherhouse, located at Cottonwood—four thousand feet above sea level, and with particularly favorable climatic conditions—the nearly one hundred and thirty sisters of this community teach at St. Joseph's parochial school at Cottonwood, and in various parish schools in the dioceses of Seattle and Spokane, as well as the diocese of Boise.

> *Motherhouse and Novitiate,* St. Gertrude's Convent, Cottonwood, Idaho.   (Diocese of Boise.)

GARRISON, NORTH DAKOTA
1916

In compliance with the request of the Right Rev. Vincent Wehrle, O.S.B., D.D., the learned and zealous bishop of Bismarck, the mother foundation of the Benedictine Nuns in the United States sent forth, in 1916, this latest of its many colonies for a new foundation.

Under Mother M. Pia Tegler, the little community from St. Joseph's Convent, St. Mary's, Pennsylvania, established the new foundation at Elbowoods, North Dakota, and at once took charge of

SACRED HEART CONVENT, GARRISON, NORTH DAKOTA

not only the Indian school there, but of other parish schools in the diocese of Bismarck.

On August 15, 1920, the convent was transferred to its present location in Garrison. Continuing under Mother M. Cecilia Bauer, Prioress, the community—whose work is principally of a missionary character, and in a section of the country not prolific in religious vocations—although yet small, has grown rapidly, and already been enabled to extend its work not only in the diocese of Bismarck but also into the diocese of Fargo, where the sisters are in charge of a number of parochial schools.

Motherhouse and Novitiate, Sacred Heart Convent, Garrison, North Dakota. (Diocese of Bismarck.)

36

CROOKSTON, MINNESOTA
1919

Ten years before the erection of the diocese of Crookston by the Holy See in 1910, Benedictine Sisters from their Motherhouse, Villa Sancta Scholastica, at Duluth, had been sent to Crookston, Minnesota, where in temporary quarters, known as Riverside Hospital, they cared for the sick who sought their ministrations. Upon the purchase of a suitable site in the city, St. Vincent's Hospital was then erected and opened in 1902 by the sisters. In that year also Mother M. Scholastica Kerst, Superior of the community at Duluth, sent sisters to open a school at Red Lake Falls, near Crookston.

When in the spring of 1910, the diocese of Duluth was divided, and that of Crookston erected, an impetus was given educational work within the limits of the territory, and the Benedictine Sisters from Duluth at once took charge of the new schools then opened, including the Cathedral High School.

In May, 1919, upon the request of the Right Rev. Timothy Corbett, D.D., first bishop of Crookston, the Most Rev. John T. McNicholas, O.P., D.D., present archbishop of Cincinnati, at that time bishop of Duluth, granted forty-two Benedictine Sisters of the Duluth community permission to devote themselves entirely to work in the diocese of Crookston. Mother Eustacia Beyenka was appointed Superior of the new community, which was a dependency of the Motherhouse in Duluth until July 22, 1922, when the Sovereign Pontiff, Pope Pius XI, approved its work and sanctioned it as an independent body.

Prior to this the community, which had temporarily maintained its headquarters at St. Vincent's Hospital in Crookston, had purchased the E. M. Walsh property, comprising a residence and a fifty-acre tract of thickly wooded land on the Red Lake River. This had become the residence of the sisters in December, 1920. Following the later purchase of additional adjoining land, Mt. St. Benedict Academy for resident and day pupils was erected at the Motherhouse site, forming the first unit of a general plan which is to be developed as the work of the institution progresses.

The solemn blessing of the spacious new building took place on Sunday, September 2, 1923, with Bishop Corbett officiating, and the Right Rev. Alcuin Deutsch, O.S.B., Abbot of St. John's Abbey, Collegeville, Minnesota, as speaker on the occasion.

Aside from the usual garden and orchard at the Motherhouse site, the Sisters of St. Benedict in Crookston have at Mount St. Benedict, as a unique addition, an apiary, and commercialize the industry of beekeeping. The honey is shipped to distant points, as well as served as beneficent food for the sisters, their patients and pupils,

MT. ST. BENEDICT CONVENT, CROOKSTON, MINNESOTA

and the surplus golden fragrant wax is made into pure beeswax candles, the production of which is the result of the community's own experiments in wax craft.

Continuing under the superiorship of Mother M. Eustacia, the nearly one hundred and seventy-five members of the community at Mt. St. Benedict, in addition to their hospital work, are now in charge of many schools throughout the diocese of Crookston, and have extended their school work into the diocese of Bismarck. Since the summer of 1924 the sisters have also engaged in conducting vacation classes in religion in districts where there are no Catholic schools.

> *Motherhouse and Novitiate,* Mt. St. Benedict Convent, Crooks-
> ton, Minnesota. (Diocese of Crookston.)

BENEDICTINE SISTERS OF PERPETUAL ADORATION*

1875

The establishment in the United States of the first Benedictine Convent of Perpetual Adoration of the Blessed Sacrament, at Con-ception, Clyde, Missouri, on December 6, 1875, was the result of a

*From data and material supplied by the Benedictine Sisters of Perpetual Adoration, Clyde, Mo.

Benedictine Abbot's personal appeal to the Benedictine Motherhouse in Switzerland. Visiting the Benedictine Convent, "Maria Rickenbach," in that country, the Right Rev. Abbot Frowin Conrad, O.S.B., of Conception Abbey, Conception, Missouri, petitioned the Congregation to send nuns to open a convent of their Order in his mission district in America.

To accede to this request five sisters, with Mother M. Anselma Felber, O.S.B., as Superior, left their convent home in the picturesque mountains of Switzerland to establish a convent of Eucharistic worship on the prairies of Missouri. For many years the sisters endured untold hardships, but never did they waver in their sublime intention, although perseverance in the Perpetual Adoration entailed many sacrifices for them, as pioneer members of the Community. They worked hard and often each kept several hours of adoration during the day, and again at night, but regardless of fatigue they rose to pay homage to the hidden God.

When the Adoration Chapel was struck by lightning, and the roof and walls were torn away, the two adorers, uninjured, continued kneeling in prayer. When a cyclone swept away part of the roof and caused much destruction there was no cessation of the Perpetual Adoration of the Blessed Sacrament.

The Convent of Perpetual Adoration, which had so humble a beginning, has been marvellously blessed. A numerous community now surrounds the Tabernacle in a beautiful chapel not wholly unworthy of the Lord of Hosts. Two or four sisters kneel constantly in the sanctuary, praying in a subdued tone of voice. These are called the "official" adorers, but each sister not appointed for an "official" hour, keeps an hour of adoration privately each day before the Most Blessed Sacrament exposed.

"How lovely are Thy Tabernacles, O Lord of Hosts," the adorers exclaim each morning as their day of prayer and labor begins. Outside the time of prayer, many and varied are the employments of the community. Like the Duke of Bohemia, St. Wenceslaus, who out of veneration for the Holy Eucharist, himself sowed the wheat, baked the altar breads, and brought them to the church, the Benedictine Sisters assigned to the host department realize their privilege in preparing altar breads. Twelve electric baking machines are operated by the sisters, and churches in Missouri and the surrounding states of Iowa, Kansas, Illinois, Nebraska, and even as far west as Washington and California, are supplied with altar breads from this convent, nearly 100,000 being the average number prepared weekly. One million altar breads were made and furnished by the sisters in

BENEDICTINE SISTERS OF PERPETUAL ADORATION, CLYDE, MISSOURI

this department for the International Eucharistic Congress in Chicago, in June, 1926.

Another department of activity conducted in this monastic institution is the printery, an establishment in which the sisters themselves produce the magazine "Tabernacle and Purgatory," monthly, in English and German. Publications on devotional subjects are also issued from the convent press, and, uniting labor and prayer, the

ST. SCHOLASTICA'S CONVENT, CLYDE, MISSOURI

sisters work zealously at these, sending them forth as messengers of truth and love of God to thousands of interested readers.

Consistent with the Benedictine Rule, permitting the Institute to adapt its members to any needed work, these Benedictine Sisters conduct at the Motherhouse, St. Joseph's Academy, a boarding school for girls.

In 1925, marking the Golden Jubilee year of the Benedictine Convent of Perpetual Adoration, at Clyde, Missouri, the Constitutions drawn up for all future Benedictine Convents of Perpetual Adoration in the United States, were, under His Holiness, Pope Pius XI, on the commendation of the Right Rev. Francis Gilfillan, D.D., Bishop of St. Joseph, approved by the Holy See under the new Code of Canon Law, on the feast of St. Scholastica, February 10, 1925.

Under the present administration of Mother M. Dolorosa Mergen, O.S.B., a foundation outside of Missouri has been made, fittingly, in Mundelein, Illinois, as a memorial of the twenty-eighth Eucharistic Congress, held in Chicago in 1926, with Mundelein one of the memorable sites of the occasion.

On June 7, 1928, the feast of Corpus Christi, that day having been especially chosen by His Eminence, George Cardinal Mundelein, the Benedictine Convent of Perpetual Adoration in Mundelein was opened, and in the temporary chapel of the convent His Eminence officiated at the impressive ceremonies inaugurating a new throne of grace and mercy, and another Benedictine Convent in the United States for the Perpetual Adoration of the Blessed Sacrament.

SUMMARY

Benedictine Sisters of Perpetual Adoration.
Established in the United States in 1875.
Papal Approbation of Rules, February 10, 1925, by His Holiness, Pope Pius XI.
Habit: The habit, veil, girdle and scapular are black, with a white linen collarium. An emblem showing a Sacred Host, with the Sacred Heart in the center, surrounded by rays of glory and a crown of thorns, is worn on the breast.
Approximate number in Community, 200.
Engaged in contemplative life and active in educational work in the arch-diocese of Chicago and the diocese of St. Joseph.
Motherhouse and Novitiate, St. Scholastica's Convent, Clyde, Missouri. (Diocese of St. Joseph.)

OLIVETAN BENEDICTINE SISTERS*

1893

The last quarter of the nineteenth century witnessed a slow but steady increase in the Catholic population of northeast Arkansas, and the opening of Catholic schools, at least in the larger centers of population, became imperative.

In view of this need the Right Rev. Edward Fitzgerald, D.D., Bishop of Little Rock, urged the Benedictine Sisters in Clyde and Maryville, Missouri, to send sisters to his diocese. Complying with the bishop's request, under the direction of the Right Rev. Msgr. J. E. Weibel, since returned to Switzerland, but at that time missionary in charge of the entire region of northeast Arkansas, a community of Sisters from the Benedictine Convent of Perpetual Adoration at Clyde, and sisters from Maryville, of the Benedictine community later

An Olivetan Benedictine Sister

*From data and material supplied by the Olivetan Benedictine Sisters, Holy Angels' Convent, Jonesboro, Ark.

transferred to Yankton, South Dakota, were established December 13, 1887, at Pocahontas, Arkansas, at the Convent of Our Lady of the Rock.

Mother M. Beatrice Renggle, O.S.B., of the original band of Benedictine Sisters who left Switzerland and established in Clyde, Missouri, in 1875, the Benedictine Convent of Perpetual Adoration, acted as Superior of the new foundation.

The sisters at once began their work of teaching, and established Catholic schools in northeast Arkansas.

In accordance with the desire of Bishop Fitzgerald, the sisters in 1893 were affiliated with the Congregation of Mt. Olive in Rome, and adopted the white habit of that Congregation, retaining, however, the vows and Rules of St. Benedict.

HOLY ANGELS' CONVENT, JONESBORO, ARKANSAS

With the obvious need of a hospital for this section of Arkansas, the Congregation, henceforth known as the Olivetan Benedictine Sisters, in 1906 erected and opened St. Bernard's Hospital in Jonesboro.

In 1898 the Motherhouse was moved from Pocahontas, and canonically established at Holy Angels' Convent in Jonesboro. The novitiate for the Congregation is continued at the site of the first foundation, the Convent of Our Lady of the Rock, at Pocahontas, Arkansas.

SUMMARY

Olivetan Benedictine Sisters.
Established in the United States in 1893.
Habit: The Benedictine habit, white instead of the traditional black, owing to affiliation with the Olivetan Benedictines at Rome, is worn.
Approximate number in Community, 130.
Active in educational and hospital work in the dioceses of Dallas and Little Rock.
Motherhouse, Holy Angels' Convent, Jonesboro, Arkansas.
Novitiate, Convent of Our Lady of the Rock, Pocahontas, Arkansas. (Diocese of Little Rock.)

FRENCH BENEDICTINE SISTERS*

1906

The Congregation of sisters known as the French Benedictines was founded in the year 1883, at Beloc, Basses, Pyrenees, France, by the French Benedictine Fathers of the Primitive Observance.

Oppressed by the laws of France, affecting religious congregations of women, the French Benedictine Sisters in 1906 accepted the invitation of the Most Rev. James H. Blenk, S.M., D.D., Archbishop of

ST. GERTRUDE'S CONVENT, RAMSAY, LOUISIANA

*From data and material supplied by the French Benedictine Sisters, St. Gertrude's Convent, Ramsay, La.

New Orleans, to establish the Congregation in the United States in that archdiocese. Through the influence of the Right Rev. Abbot Paul Schaeuble, O.S.B., of St. Joseph's Abbey at Ramsay Station, Louisiana, the industrial school there was assigned to the direction of the Community.

The Motherhouse of the Congregation was then established at Ramsay, with Mother Gertrude Berho as Prioress. Continuing in this position, Mother Gertrude is assisted by the other original officers, Mother Scholastica, Mother Mary and Mother Stanislaus.

SUMMARY

French Benedictine Sisters.
Founded in France in 1883.
Established in the United States in 1906.
Habit: The black habit of the Benedictines is worn.
Approximate number in Community, 40.
Active in educational work in the archdiocese of New Orleans.
Motherhouse and Novitiate, St. Gertrude's Convent, Ramsay, Louisiana.
(Archdiocese of New Orleans.)

MISSIONARY BENEDICTINE SISTERS*
1923

A MISSIONARY BENEDICTINE SISTER

The Congregation of Missionary Benedictine Sisters, more generally known as Benedictine Sisters, was founded in 1885 in Reichenbach, Germany, through the endeavors of the Rev. P. Andreas Amrhein, O.S.B.

The need for sisters for foreign missionary work gave an impetus to the establishment of this Congregation, which was founded chiefly for this purpose.

Upon the invitation of the Most Rev. Jeremiah J. Harty, D.D., Archbishop of Omaha, the Congregation sent a community of sisters to the United States.

With Mother M. Diemud Gerber as Prioress, in which capacity

*From data and material supplied by the Missionary Benedictine Sisters, St. Gertrude's Convent, Raeville, Neb.

she continues to serve the community, the sisters began their school work in the country in Raeville, Nebraska, July 31, 1923, and their hospital work in 1924, when they took charge of Sacred Heart Hospital at Lynch, Nebraska.

The community in the United States retains its affiliation with the General Motherhouse in Tutzing, Bavaria. The Motherhouse and novitiate for this country have been established at the site of its first mission, in Nebraska. From here, in 1927, two of the sisters of the community were transferred to the foreign mission of the Congregation, in Manila, Philippine Islands.

SUMMARY

Missionary Benedictine Sisters.
Founded in Germany in 1885.
Papal Approbation of Rules in 1924, by His Holiness, Pope Pius XI.
Established in the United States in 1923.
Habit: The habit and veil are black, with a white guimpe. In the tropics all white is worn.
Active in educational and hospital work in the U. S. in the diocese of Omaha.
United States Motherhouse and Novitiate, St. Gertrude's Convent, Raeville, Nebraska. (Diocese of Omaha.)

CHRONOLOGICAL TABLE

Foundations in the United States of the Benedictine Sisters*

1852—St. Mary's, Pennsylvania.
1856—Erie, Pennsylvania.
1857—Indiana, Pennsylvania (Ridgely, Md.).
1857—St. Joseph, Minnesota.
1859—Covington, Kentucky.
1861—Chicago, Illinois.
1863—Atchison, Kansas.
1867—Ferdinand, Indiana.
1868—Elizabeth, New Jersey.
1870—Bristow, Virginia.
1870—New Orleans, Louisiana (Covington, La.).
1870—Pittsburgh, Pennsylvania.
1874—Maryville, Missouri (Yankton, S. D.).
1875—Clyde, Missouri.
1875—Nauvoo, Illinois.
1878—Elkton, South Dakota (Sioux City, Iowa).

1879—Creston, Iowa (Guthrie, Okla.).
1879—Shoal Creek, Arkansas (Fort Smith, Ark.).
1880—Cullman, Alabama.
1882—Mt. Angel, Oregon.
1887—Pocahontas, Arkansas (Jonesboro, Ark.).
1889—Lake Jovita, Florida.
1889—Sturgis, South Dakota.
1892—Duluth, Minnesota.
1892—Sacred Heart, Oklahoma.
1895—Lisle, Illinois.
1906—Ramsay, Louisiana.
1908—Cottonwood, Idaho.
1916—Garrison, North Dakota.
1919—Crookston, Minnesota.
1923—Raeville, Nebraska.

*A foundation of Sisters of St. Benedict is also located at St. Vincent de Paul Home, 1119 South Alamo Street, San Antonio, Tex. (Archdiocese of San Antonio.)

GENERAL SUMMARY

Benedictine Sisters.
Founded in Italy in the time of St. Benedict (480-543).
Established in the United States in 1852.
Habit: The usual habit and scapular are of black serge, with a black veil; the coif and head band are of white linen. A rosary of large beads is suspended from a black cloth cincture, and a gold ring with the inscription I.H.S. is worn.
Approximate number in communities in United States, 4,500.
Active in educational, hospital and charitable work and engaged in contemplative life in the archdioceses of Baltimore, Chicago, New Orleans, New York, Portland in Oregon, St. Paul and San Antonio, and in the dioceses of Bismarck, Boise, Concordia, Covington, Crookston, Dallas, Davenport, Denver, Des Moines, Duluth, Erie, Fargo, Indianapolis, Kansas City, La Crosse, Lead, Leavenworth, Lincoln, Little Rock, Mobile, Newark, Oklahoma, Omaha, Peoria, Pittsburgh, Richmond, St. Augustine, St. Cloud, St. Joseph, Seattle, Sioux City, Sioux Falls, Spokane, Superior and Wilmington.

SISTERS OF THE INCARNATE WORD
AND BLESSED SACRAMENT*

1853

THE Order of the Incarnate Word and Blessed Sacrament, which was introduced into the United States in 1853, was founded at Roanne, France, in 1625, by Jeanne Chézard de Matel, natively of the city, and an illustrious and saintly woman, then in the twenty-ninth year of her age.

The first monastery of the Order, which in 1627 was transferred from Roanne to Lyons, was canonically founded in Avignon, France, in 1639, its nuns bound by solemn vows and subject to papal enclosure, and consecrated in their contemplative life to the Incarnate Word and special homage to the Blessed Sacrament, while devoting themselves to the education of girls.

After more than one hundred and fifty years of existence, the Religious of the Incarnate Word and Blessed Sacrament were, at the time of the French Revolution, dispensed from their solemn vows, thenceforth taking but simple perpetual vows, and being subject to episcopal enclosure only. The distinctive habit of the religious continues identical with that divinely revealed to the holy foundress three centuries ago.

In 1853, following a trip to Europe by the Lazarist missionary, the Right Rev. J. M. Odin, D.D., at the time bishop of Galveston, a small group of Sisters of the Incarnate Word and Blessed Sacrament, having volunteered to go to his aid in the New World, founded at Brownsville, Texas, the first convent of their Order in the United States.

With Mother St. Claire as Superior, the little community from France soon proved a potent help to the zealous bishop and the mission priests.

In 1866, sisters from the community in Brownsville were sent to Victoria, Texas, where a second foundation was made. In the course of the years since, other convents of the Order have likewise been established in and beyond Texas.

Each community of the Sisters of the Incarnate Word and Blessed Sacrament is independent, but all follow the same Rules and

*From data and material supplied by the Sisters of the Incarnate Word and Blessed Sacrament, Brownsville, Tex., and from the Official Catholic Directory, 1929.

Constitutions, and in accordance with these an annual report of receptions, deaths and matters of community importance, is sent to the mother foundation house at Lyons, France.

MOTHER JEANNE CHÉZARD DE MATEL (1596-1670)
Foundress of the Order of the Incarnate Word and Blessed Sacrament

The various foundations in the United States have established and maintain a number of mission and parochial schools, some of which are located in other than the dioceses of their headquarters. The Sisters of the Incarnate Word and Blessed Sacrament devote themselves in the United States chiefly to educational work, conducting academies at practically all their community centers in the country.

SUMMARY

Sisters of the Incarnate Word and Blessed Sacrament.

Founded in France in 1625.

Papal Approbation of Rules in 1633 by Pope Urban VIII.

Established in the United States in 1853.

Habit: The habit is of white serge, with a red cincture and a red scapular, on the front of which is embroidered a monogram, *I.H.S.*, and a heart surmounted by three nails, with the words *Amor Meus* in the center, the whole being surrounded by a crown of thorns. In choir a red cloak is worn; a gold ring is received at profession. The veil is black.

Approximate number in communities in United States, 400.

Active chiefly in educational work in the archdiocese of San Antonio and the dioceses of Belleville, Cleveland, Corpus Christi, Galveston and Pittsburgh.

United States Motherhouses and Novitiates:

Incarnate Word Convent, 714 St. Charles Street, Brownsville, Texas. (Diocese of Corpus Christi.)

Incarnate Word Academy, 715 Carancahua Street, Corpus Christi, Texas. (Diocese of Corpus Christi.)

Academy of the Incarnate Word, 609 Crawford Street, Houston, Texas. (Diocese of Galveston.)

Convent of the Incarnate Word and the Blessed Sacrament, Conception Road, San Antonio, Texas. (Archdiocese of San Antonio.)

Convent of St. Ludmila, Shiner, Texas. (Archdiocese of San Antonio.)

Nazareth Convent, Victoria, Texas. (Archdiocese of San Antonio.)

Incarnate Word Convent, 6618 Pearl Road, Cleveland, Ohio. (Diocese of Cleveland.)

SISTERS OF THE PRESENTATION OF THE BLESSED VIRGIN MARY*

FITTINGLY the only religious order of women introduced into the United States during the ecclesiastically memorable year 1854, was the Order of the Sisters of the Presentation of the Blessed Virgin Mary, a community of which arrived in San Francisco on December 1, 1854.

The name of the foundress of the Presentation Order, Nano Nagle, ever stirs those who know the story of the blithe girl, descendant on one side of the same family as the celebrated apostle of temperance, Father Theobald Mathew, and on the other side related to the famous orator and statesman, Edmund Burke.

Honoria Nagle was born in Ballygriffin, near Mallow County, Cork, Ireland, in the year 1728. Growing to girlhood, Nano, as she was called, was sent to France to complete her schooling under Catholic auspices, while staying with relatives in Paris. Her studies completed, Garret Nagle's daughter was introduced into a brilliant social circle of the court.

On an occasion during this period, Nano, returning with her friends from a ball which had lasted beyond daybreak, noted the opening of the doors of a church, and the entrance to it of a crowd of poor workmen and women who had been waiting on the steps. With a pang of conscience she said to herself: "They are doing the one thing necessary. What am I doing?"

Answering the question from the depths of her heart, Nano Nagle, in her twenty-second year, then "cast off the spirit of the world, and was inwardly clothed with the spirit of Jesus Christ." Returning soon afterward to her home by the Blackwater, Nano awaited the manifestation of God's will for her, peaceful in the certainty that she was asked to surrender her whole being in the service of the Sovereign Master.

Conditions in Ireland restraining her from consecrating herself at once to the instruction of Irish children who were being denied Catholic educational training, she went for a while to a convent in France. Convinced, however, that her mission lay in her own country, and on the advice of her directors, Nano returned to Ireland. There, bereft of her dearest family ties, she, of her own great means,

---

*From data and material supplied by the Sisters of the Presentation of the B.V.M., Presentation Convent, San Francisco, Calif., and from the Catholic Encyclopedia and the Official Catholic Year Book, 1928.

not only established two schools and conducted catechism classes, aided by some equally earnest companions, but she also established an asylum at Cork for aged and infirm women and for working women, whose perseverance in faith and virtue was a source of solicitude to her.

With a view to perpetuating her work, Miss Nagle was instrumental in the establishment in Cork of a foundation of Ursulines, the community for which was sent from the convent of the Order at Rue St. Jacques, Paris, being composed of young women whom she had sent from Ireland for their novitiate as Ursulines. The Ursuline Rule, however, provided only for educational work, and not except in necessity for the various works of charity intended for for the sisterhood Miss Nagle felt was needed.

The founding of the Presentation Order, in 1775, was Nano Nagle's response to this need, as she and three companions that year began their novitiate together, as Sisters of the Sacred Heart of Jesus. On June 29, 1776, the ardent foundress received the religious habit, and the name Sister St. John of God. For but eight years was Mother Mary of St. John of God spared to her Institute. Having spent herself for the poor she was taken from them in the fifty-fifth year of her age.

In 1791 the name of the Institute was changed from that of Sisters of the Sacred Heart of Jesus to Sisters of the Presentation. The rule which Nano Nagle and her companions had adopted, and which had been drawn up for them by the Curé of St. Sulpice, providing for annual vows and private renewal of them each year, remained in force until 1793, when the Sovereign Pontiff gave the formal approbation of the Church to the Rules of the Order of the Presentation.

From that year the Order began to spread. Its convents were asked for at Killarney, Dublin, Waterford, Lismore, Limerick and elsewhere in and beyond Ireland. The first foreign mission of the Order was established at St. John's, Newfoundland, in 1833, and from it alone have been made more than twelve other foundations of the Order.

SAN FRANCISCO, CALIFORNIA

1854

It was to the Presentation Convent at Midleton, Ireland, that the Rev. Hugh P. Gallagher appealed in 1854, in the name of the archbishop of San Francisco, the Most Rev. Joseph S. Ale many, O.P., D.D., for a colony of Presentation Nuns for California. So earnestly did Father Gallagher plead the need for religious to teach the many children, of all conditions and nationalities, brought to California during the mad rush for gold, that his request was granted.

SISTER M. A. BERCHMANS
A Presentation Nun, San Francisco, California

After an eventful journey across the Isthmus, the community from Midleton, composed of Mother Mary Xavier Daly, Mother Mary Augustine Keane, Sister Mary Clare Duggan and Sister Mary Ignatius Lanigan, under Mother Mary Joseph Cronin as Superior, made its foundation in San Francisco on December 1, 1854.

In the course of their labors in the ensuing years, the Presentation Sisters in California established convents of the Order not only in San Francisco but also in Berkeley and Sonoma. The earthquake of 1906 destroyed their buildings in the archiepiscopal city, but the sisters, with the courage of pioneers, soon built anew, and continue their educational work of now nearly

PRESENTATION CONVENT, SAN FRANCISCO, CALIFORNIA

four score years in California, conducting schools in San Francisco, Berkeley and Gilroy, as well as Los Angeles.

Motherhouse and Novitiate, Presentation Convent, 281 Masonic Avenue, San Francisco, California. (Archdiocese of San Francisco.)

NEW YORK CITY
1874

The introduction of the Presentation Order into New York City in 1874 was made through the Rev. A. J. Donnelly, pastor of St. Michael's Church, who, upon the completion of its school building, went to Dublin, Ireland, for the purpose of securing Sisters of the Presentation to take charge of the girls' division of the school.

Complying with Father Donnelly's request, a community composed of two sisters from the Presentation Convent in Dublin and two from a convent of the Order at Clondalkin, with seven postulants, arrived in New York in September of 1874, and entered on their long and successful work at St. Michael's School.

In addition to taking charge of St. Michael's Home for Destitute Children, at Mt. St. Michael, Green Ridge, Staten Island, and establishing other convents and schools in New York, Sisters of the Presentation of this community have established a foundation convent of the Order at Fitchburg, Massachusetts.

Motherhouse, Presentation Convent, Mt. St. Michael, Green Ridge, Staten Island, New York. (Archdiocese of New York.)
Novitiate, Presentation Convent, Mt. St. Joseph, Newburgh, New York. (Archdiocese of New York.)

DUBUQUE, IOWA
1875

From Ireland, the country of its beloved foundress, Nano Nagle, there came another community of Sisters of the Presentation to the United States. For neither the eastern nor western coast was the new foundation destined, but for Iowa, in the central section of the country.

The Presentation Convent in Dubuque is now the center of the activities of a community of more than two hundred sisters, who are engaged in educational work in Colorado, Nebraska and South Dakota, as well as in Iowa.

Motherhouse and Novitiate, Mt. Loretto, 1229 Mt. Loretto Avenue, Dubuque, Iowa. (Archdiocese of Dubuque.)

FARGO, NORTH DAKOTA
1880

In 1880, nine years before the erection of any diocese in North Dakota, the Sisters of the Presentation established a convent in the state at Fargo, where, under the jurisdiction of the vicar apostolic of Dakota, the Right Rev. Martin Marty, Benedictine bishop and missionary, they began their work of teaching and took charge of an orphanage and a school connected with it.

The community at Fargo is now engaged in conducting a number of parochial schools and academies throughout the diocese.

Motherhouse and Novitiate, Presentation Convent, North Broad-way, Fargo, North Dakota. (Diocese of Fargo.)

WATERVLIET, NEW YORK
1881

In 1881 Sisters of the Presentation further extended their activities in New York with the opening of St. Colman's Home at Watervliet.

In addition to the convent established at the home, an industrial school is conducted there in the interests of the more than two hundred orphan children under the care of the sisters.

Motherhouse and Novitiate, St. Colman's Convent, Watervliet, New York. (Diocese of Albany.)

ABERDEEN, SOUTH DAKOTA
1886

While South as well as North Dakota was included in the eccle-siastical territory of the vicariate apostolic of Dakota, Sisters of the Presentation, from the convent which had been established at Fargo, in 1886 sent a small community of their number to Aberdeen, South Dakota.

The sisters at once engaged in educational work there, and in addition took charge of St. Luke's Hospital at Aberdeen, in 1901, St. Joseph's at Mitchell in 1906, and McKennan Hospital at Sioux Falls in 1912, all in South Dakota, and in the diocese of Sioux Falls, which was erected in 1889.

From their Motherhouse at Aberdeen the sisters are active throughout the diocese, as well as in the diocese of Great Falls.

Motherhouse and Novitiate, Presentation Convent, Aberdeen, South Dakota. (Diocese of Sioux Falls.)

FITCHBURG, MASSACHUSETTS
1886

In 1886, upon the invitation of the Rev. P. J. Garrigan, later appointed bishop of Sioux City, sisters from the Presentation Convent in New York City were sent to take charge of St. Bernard's School at Fitchburg, Massachusetts.

With their convent established at St. Bernard's, the members of this community conduct other schools in the vicinity of Fitchburg, and mission schools also in Rhode Island.

Motherhouse and Novitiate, St. Bernard's Presentation Convent, Fitchburg, Massachusetts. (Diocese of Springfield.)

SUMMARY

Sisters of the Presentation of the Blessed Virgin Mary.
Founded in Ireland in 1775.
Papal Approbation of Rules, December 26, 1805, by Pope Pius VII.
Established in the United States in 1854.
Habit: The habit is of black serge, with a woolen veil, and linen guimpe and bandeau.
Approximate number in communities in United States, 950.
Active in educational, hospital and charitable work in the archdioceses of Dubuque, New York and San Francisco, and in the dioceses of Albany, Denver, Fargo, Great Falls, Lead, Los Angeles and San Diego, Omaha, Providence, Sioux City, Sioux Falls and Springfield.

DAUGHTERS OF THE CROSS*

1855

$\mathcal{OF}$OUNDED in 1640, at Paris, by Madame Marie l'Huillier de Villeneuve, who had been under the personal direction of St. Francis de Sales, before his holy death in 1622, the Daughters of the Cross follow in their religious life the Constitutions which St. Francis wrote for the first Visitandines.

In the United States there was erected, in 1853, the diocese of Natchitoches, comprising the northern part of the state of Louisiana, and the Right Rev. Augustus M. Martin was consecrated and appointed its first bishop. Soon after his consecration Bishop Martin went to France to secure priests for the diocese.

While visiting Brittany he became acquainted with the Community of the Daughters of the Cross, at Tréguier, and through this meeting, and upon his invitation, the Congregation of the Daughters of the Cross sent to the United States in 1855 a community of ten sisters, with Mother Mary Hyacinth as Superior.

The first foundation of the Congregation in this country was made in Louisiana, at Avoyelles Parish, in a country town among the planters. Mother Hyacinth had need of her strong physical constitution and extraordinary mental vigor in the arduous work of establishing the missions in the parishes of the diocese. After eight ocean trips in the interests of the schools in Louisiana, Mother Hyacinth returned to France to take charge of the novitiate there.

In 1868, during the trying period of Reconstruction, St. Vincent's was founded at Cocoville, near the city of Shreveport, Louisiana. The property at the time of its purchase was in a dilapidated condition, having been vacated when the owner left to participate in the Civil War, and the one-time beautiful estate was a wilderness. Enduring untold hardships, the sisters laboriously persevered in their efforts to restore the place to a habitable and inviting condition, and by September St. Vincent's was ready for its first pupils.

In 1869 the Motherhouse, which had been established at Cocoville, was transferred to St. Vincent's, at Shreveport.

St. Vincent's was just beginning to show its efficient organization, after the direful effects of the Civil War, when there occurred the yellow fever epidemic of 1873. The Daughters of the Cross dis-

---

*From data and material supplied by the Daughters of the Cross, St. Vincent's College, Shreveport, La.

continued their chosen work in the classroom, became nurses, and hastened to the bedsides of the sick and dying. Many of the sisters contracted the dread malady, and three of them succumbed to its ravages.

MOTHER MARY HYACINTH

By 1889 St. Vincent's was one of the most flourishing boarding schools of the south. With the growth of the school new buildings had been erected, and plans were being made in 1906 for the construction of the main building of Greater St. Vincent's when a disastrous fire wiped out the labor of many years.

From the ashes, phoenix-like, the new Greater St. Vincent's soon rose, and with the completion of the buildings the work of the teachers returned to normalcy.

On August 6, 1910, under the episcopacy of the Right Rev. Cornelius Van de Ven, D.D., the diocese of Natchitoches was transferred to Alexandria, comprising the same territory as included in the former diocese. The United States Community of the Daughters

ST. VINCENT'S, SHREVEPORT, LOUISIANA

of the Cross is diocesan, and subject to the jurisdiction of the ordinary of the diocese of Alexandria.

St. Vincent's College, affiliated with the Catholic University of America, and incorporated under the laws of the state of Louisiana, with full power to grant diplomas and confer degrees, is foremost among the institutions conducted in the United States by the Daughters of the Cross, and their monument in the educational world of today.

SUMMARY

Daughters of the Cross.
Founded in France in 1640.
Established in the United States in 1855.
Habit: The habit is of black serge, with a black veil, white cap and guimpe.
Approximate number in Community in United States, 90.
Active in educational work in the diocese of Alexandria.
United States Motherhouse and Novitiate, St. Vincent's, Shreveport, Louisiana.
    (Diocese of Alexandria.)

SISTERS OF OUR LADY OF CHARITY
OF THE REFUGE*†

1855

*C*ONTINUING in the United States the work of reclama-
tion and preservation of girls, according to the Rules and
Constitutions as given by their holy founder, St. John
Eudes, upon the establishment of the first house of the Order, the
Sisters of Our Lady of Charity of the Refuge, also known as Good
Shepherd Sisters, in 1855 made their first foundation in this country
at Buffalo, New York, under the auspices of the Right Rev. John
Timon, C.M., D.D., first bishop of Buffalo.

Following this foundation, the sisters were invited to extend their
work into other dioceses, each establishment becoming an independent
center, according to the rule ever followed by the Congregation. In
their institutions in the United States the sisters pursue the work of
the Order, so well developed in France by the saintly Mother
Euphrasia Pelletier, during her years as Superior of the Refuge at
Tours, before the establishment of the Generalate at the Good Shepherd Convent in Angers.

SUMMARY

Sisters of Our Lady of Charity of the Refuge.
Founded in France in 1641.
Papal Approbation of Rules in 1741, by Pope Benedict XIV.
Established in the United States in 1855.
Habit: The habit is white, with a white girdle and a black veil.
Approximate number in communities in United States, 300.
Active in social service work of reclamation and preservation of girls, in the
following monasteries, each an independent Motherhouse and novitiate:
Monastery of Our Lady of Charity of Refuge, Grimes and Montana
Streets, San Antonio, Texas. (Archdiocese of San Antonio.)
Monastery of Our Lady of Charity, 485 Best Street, Buffalo, New York.
(Diocese of Buffalo.)
Monastery of Our Lady of Charity, 3233 Main Street, Buffalo, New York.
(Diocese of Buffalo.)

---

*From Clarke's *Life of Reverend Mother Mary of St. Euphrasia Pelletier*
(Burns & Oates, London), and from the Official Catholic Directory, 1929
(P. J. Kenedy and Sons, New York).
†The history of the Sisters of Our Lady of Charity of the Refuge, and
the history of the Sisters of Our Lady of Charity of the Good Shepherd of
Angers are the same up to the time of the formation of the Generalate in
1835. (See page 280.)

Monastery of Our Lady of Charity, Fort Worth and Cockrell Hill Roads, Dallas, Texas.   (Diocese of Dallas.)

Monastery of Our Lady of Charity of Refuge, Green Bay, Wisconsin. (Diocese of Green Bay.)

Monastery of Our Lady of Charity, 1125 Malvern Avenue, Hot Springs, Arkansas.   (Diocese of Little Rock.)

Monastery of Our Lady of Charity, 1615 Lowrie Street, Troy Hill, N.S., Pittsburgh, Pennsylvania.   (Diocese of Pittsburgh.)

Eudes Institute, 1625 Lincoln Avenue, E.E., Pittsburgh, Pennsylvania. (Diocese of Pittsburgh.)

Monastery of Our Lady of Charity, Edington Lane, Wheeling, West Virginia.   (Diocese of Wheeling.)

THE GREY NUNS*

*A*MONG the names of twelve noted widow-foundresses of orders whose members are among the thousands of women devoting their lives in the cause of religion in the United States is that of Ven. Marie Marguerite d'Youville.

VEN. MARIE MARGUERITE D'YOUVILLE (1701-1771)
Foundress of the Grey Nuns

Marie Marguerite Dufrost de Lajemmerais was born at Varennes, near Montreal, Canada, on October 15, 1701, of distinguished parents,

*From the annals of the Grey Nuns.

her father an officer in the Royal Army, her mother the daughter of the governor of Three Rivers, Canada.

A part of her education was received under the guidance of the Ursulines at Quebec, and at the age of twenty-one she was married to Monsieur d'Youville. Eight years later she was left a widow, with three children, and though burdened with a heavy debt, which in her resourcefulness she at once prepared to take care of, Madame d'Youville became distinguished for her charity to the needy and her great piety.

With three equally charitable young women, Mademoiselle Louise Thaumur Lassource, Mademoiselle Demers and Mademoiselle Cusson, Madame d'Youville united on October 30, 1738, and the little group, living together under a provisional rule, practiced the spiritual and corporal works of mercy, even to receiving into their house a number of poor people to whom they ministered.

In 1747 the General Hospital at Montreal was entrusted to the care of Madame d'Youville and her associates, to whom, under the title of *Soeurs de la Charité de l'Hôpital Général,* was transferred on June 3, 1853, the rights and privileges which had been granted by letters patent to the original founders of the hospital in 1694. The distinctive grey garb adopted in 1755 by Mother d'Youville and those who constituted with her the Sisters of Charity of the General Hospital of Montreal early gave rise to the accepted appella-tion, "Grey Nuns."

For thirty-three years Mother d'Youville, who has been declared Venerable by the Church, valiantly carried on her works of charity, and in the nearly two centuries since, the Grey Nuns of Montreal and those of communities descendent from that of the mother foun-dation continue in her footsteps in the practice of the spiritual and corporal works of mercy.

TOLEDO, OHIO*

1855

The introduction of the Grey Nuns into the United States took place in the year 1855. At the instance of the vicar general of the diocese, the Very Rev. Augustine S. Campion, pastor of St. Francis de Sales' Church, in Toledo, Ohio, the Right Rev. Amadeus Rappe, D.D., Bishop of Cleveland, petitioned the Grey Nuns of

*From data supplied by the Sisters of Charity of the General Hospital of Montreal, 390 Guy Street, Montreal, Canada, and from *The Church in Northern Ohio,* by the Rev. George F. Houck.

Montreal for sisters to take charge of an orphan asylum which through arrangements made by Father Campion was opened that year in Toledo.

With charity befitting the daughters of Ven. Marie Marguerite d'Youville, a favorable response was made to Bishop Rappe's request, and the Grey Nuns of Montreal sent four sisters, who with Sister Fernand as Superior arrived in Toledo in October, 1855, and at once took charge of the orphanage, which as St. Vincent's continues under their direction.

In the seventy-five years since undertaking this their first mission in the United States, the Grey Nuns of Montreal have taken charge of many institutions in this country, and now send from their Canadian Motherhouse, to missions in the United States under its direct jurisdiction, nearly one hundred and eighty sisters, who are engaged in educational, hospital, charitable and social service work in the archdiocese of Boston and the dioceses of Fargo, Manchester, Springfield, Toledo and Trenton.

Motherhouse and Novitiate of the Sisters of Charity of the General Hospital of Montreal, 390 Guy Street, Montreal, Canada. (Archdiocese of Montreal.)

BUFFALO, NEW YORK*

1857

One of the early foundations made from the Motherhouse of the Grey Nuns at the General Hospital at Montreal was that made in Ottawa, Ontario, on February 20, 1845, by Mother Elizabeth Bruyère, at the instance of the Right Rev. Patrick Phelan, S.S., D.D., Bishop of Kingston.

It was to this already prospering Community of Ven. Marie Marguerite d'Youville's daughters, established as the Grey Nuns of the Cross, that an appeal was made by the Oblate Fathers in Buffalo, New York, for sisters to take charge of schools there and to visit the poor and sick of their parishes.

In October of 1857, with Sister St. Peter as Superior, the Grey Nuns of the Cross, having arrived in Buffalo from Ottawa, began the work of their Community in the United States. Holy Angels' parish became the site of the early educational activities of the Grey Nuns in Buffalo, and Holy Angels' Academy, opened by them, soon ranked among the prominent educational institutions in the diocese.

*From data supplied by the Grey Nuns of the Cross, Sussex and Water Streets, Ottawa, Ont., Canada.

Other academies and parochial schools, not only in New York, but also in Pennsylvania, New Jersey, Massachusetts and other localities, were likewise established by the Community, as was also a hospital at Plattsburg, and two hospitals and an orphanage at Ogdensburg, New York.

D'Youville College, in Buffalo, New York, incorporated in April, 1908, by special action of the New York State Legislature, and duly registered by the University of the State of New York, and invested with the power of conferring degrees, was opened by the Grey Nuns for the reception of its first students in September of that year.

Having generously sent of their number sisters who for many years were engaged in the United States on the missions of the Community, and who later formed the nucleus at Buffalo of the first United States foundation of Grey Nuns, the Grey Nuns of the Cross now have as their missions in this country St. Joseph's School at Lowell and Our Lady of Lourdes' School at Haverill, both in Massachusetts and in the archdiocese of Boston.   In addition to these missions the Grey Nuns of Ottawa are also now engaged in teaching at Holy Cross School at Ogdensburg, New York, in the diocese of Ogdensburg.

Motherhouse and Novitiate of the Grey Nuns of the Cross, Sussex and Water Streets, Ottawa, Ontario, Canada.   (Archdiocese of Ottawa.)

LEWISTON, MAINE*

1878

On May 8, 1840, Grey Nuns from the mother foundation at Montreal were sent, in response to an appeal from the parish curé there, to establish a foundation at St. Hyacinthe, in the Province of Quebec, Canada.

From the first the work of this Community of Grey Nuns has been the care of the aged, of invalids and of orphans and the visiting of the sick in their own homes, the poor and prisoners.   The establishment of hospitals and schools also early engaged the attention of the Sisters of Charity of the Hôtel-Dieu, as the members of the Community were known.

In 1878 sisters of the Community were sent to the United States, where their first mission was the conducting of a school at Lewiston,

*From data supplied by the Sisters of Charity of the Hôtel-Dieu de St. Hyacinthe, St. Hyacinthe, P.Q., Canada.

Maine. This school, however, was soon afterward used as a hospital, and is today the St. Mary's Hospital at Lewiston, in charge of the Grey Nuns from St. Hyacinthe. Following this first mission at Lewiston, the Community later took charge there of the Healy Asylum and the Hospice Marcotte.

In the meantime sisters were also sent from St. Hyacinthe's Hôtel-Dieu to New Hampshire, where they took charge of orphanages in Manchester and Rochester, and of St. Louis Hospital at Berlin, while at Woonsocket, Rhode Island, they have taken charge of the Hospice Saint-Antoine.

To carry on these activities in institutions in the dioceses of Manchester, Portland and Providence, nearly one hundred and eighty-five Grey Nuns are now missioned to the United States from St. Hyacinthe's, under the direct jurisdiction of the Motherhouse there.

Motherhouse and Novitiate of the Sisters of Charity of the Hôtel-Dieu de Saint-Hyacinthe, Hôtel-Dieu, St. Hyacinthe, P.Q., Canada.

FALL RIVER, MASSACHUSETTS*

1890

From a foundation in Canada, made by the Grey Nuns of the mother foundation at Montreal, and which in 1854 was recognized as an independent community of Grey Nuns, under the title Sisters of Charity of Quebec, sisters were missioned to Fall River, Massachusetts, in 1890.

The first United States mission of the Community, that of the care of the orphans at St. Joseph's Orphanage in Fall River, was later followed by the sisters being placed in charge of the Sacred Heart Home for the Aged, at New Bedford, Massachusetts, both missions being in the diocese of Fall River. In time the Grey Nuns of Quebec were also given charge of the French-American Orphanage and St. Joseph's Home for the Aged in Lowell, Massachusetts, in the archdiocese of Boston.

Nearly eighty Sisters of Charity of Quebec are now missioned to these Massachusetts institutions from their Motherhouse at Quebec.

Motherhouse and Novitiate of the Sisters of Charity of Quebec, 5 Rue St. Olivier, Quebec, Canada. . (Archdiocese of Quebec.)

*From data supplied by the Sisters of Charity of Quebec, 5 Rue St. Olivier, Quebec, Canada.

PHILADELPHIA, PENNSYLVANIA*

1922

In order to maintain and fructify in the United States the already flourishing educational and charitable institutions established as missions by the Grey Nuns of Ottawa, the Community of the Grey Nuns of the Sacred Heart was founded at Buffalo, on August 24, 1921, under the special patronage of His Eminence, Dennis Cardinal Dougherty, Archbishop of Philadelphia, former bishop of Buffalo.

MOTHER MARY AUGUSTINE

The headquarters of the new Community were maintained in Buffalo until the following year, 1922, when the Motherhouse and novitiate of the Congregation of the Grey Nuns of the Sacred Heart, the newest branch of the ancient Canadian Institute of Madame d'Youville's founding, were established in the archiepiscopal city of Philadelphia. Mother Mary Augustine, who served as first Superior General of the Grey Nuns of the Sacred Heart, died in November, 1922.

Under Mother Verecunda, present Superior General, the Congregation continues its activities in religious educational work at D'Youville College and Holy Angels' Academy in Buffalo, St. Mary's High School, Ogdensburg, New York; Immaculate Conception High School, Lowell, Massachusetts; and Melrose Academy, Melrose Park, Pennsylvania, as well as in parochial schools in Buffalo, Jackson Heights and Corona, Long Island; Carteret, New Jersey; and Mahanoy City and Melrose Park, Pennsylvania. Barton-Hepburn Hospital and St. John Hospital, Ogdensburg, New York; Champlain Valley Hospital, Plattsburg, New York, and the City Orphanage in

*From data and material supplied by the Grey Nuns of the Sacred Heart, Oak Lane, Philadelphia, Pa.

Ogdensburg are also under the direction of the Grey Nuns of the Sacred Heart, who, now more than two hundred in number, are

MOTHERHOUSE OF THE GREY NUNS OF THE SACRED HEART, OAK LANE, PENNSYLVANIA

active in educational, hospital and charitable work at these institutions in the archdioceses of Boston and Philadelphia and the dioceses of Brooklyn, Buffalo, Ogdensburg and Trenton.

Motherhouse and Novitiate of the Grey Nuns of the Sacred Heart, West Avenue, Oak Lane, Pennsylvania. (Archdiocese of Philadelphia.)

GENERAL SUMMARY

The Grey Nuns.

Founded in Canada in 1738.

Papal Approbation of Rules, July 30, 1880, by Pope Leo XIII, and as given the individual Communities.

Established in the United States in 1855.

Habit: The habit is French grey, with a black veil, cape and cincture. After profession a silver ring is worn, and a silver crucifix, adorned with fleur-de-lis, and suspended by a black cord, is worn on the breast.

Approximate number in the United States, 700.

Active in educational, hospital, charitable and social service work in the archdioceses of Boston and Philadelphia, and in the dioceses of Brooklyn, Buffalo, Fall River, Fargo, Manchester, Ogdensburg, Portland, Providence, Springfield, Toledo and Trenton.

DAUGHTERS OF CHARITY, SERVANTS OF THE POOR*

1856

THE Congregation of the Daughters of Charity, Servants of the Poor, many of whose members have labored in the United States, especially in the northwest, since 1856—sometimes referred to as the Sisters of Providence of Montreal, or Sisters of Charity of Providence—was founded in Montreal, Canada, March 25, 1843.

To the holy and learned bishop, the Right Rev. Ignace Bourget, to whom Montreal owes the establishment of many of its progressive institutions, is due the founding as a religious community of a group of pious and charitable women in Montreal—who, under the leadership of Madame Jean Baptiste Gamelin, had been for some time caring for a number of infirm and poor aged women, sheltered in Madame Gamelin's own home—and who formed the nucleus of the Daughters of Charity, Servants of the Poor.

With the establishment of the Congregation, which carries in its name the spirit and work of its noble foundress, its activities were planned to include the care of orphans and the sick and the instruction of youth.

Marie Emélie Eugénie Tavernier, having been left a widow and childless at the age of twenty-eight, had not hesitated to devote her life and the wealth which was hers upon the death of her husband, Monsieur Gamelin, to the poor, whom she took into her own home and cared for as a faithful servant. Upon her death, in 1851, Madame Gamelin left a Congregation well organized to carry on her work, as has been shown throughout the many years since.

Five years after the death of Mother Gamelin, sisters of her Community responded to the call of the Right Rev. A. M. A. Blanchet, formerly a canon of the Montreal Cathedral, who having been appointed bishop of the diocese of Nesqually, now the diocese of Seattle, asked their aid in the new see in the northwestern part of the United States. The little community of Sisters of Charity, Servants of the Poor, who, with Mother Joseph of the Sacred Heart

*From data and material supplied by the Daughters of Charity, Servants of the Poor, Providence Motherhouse, 1271 St. Catherine Street, East, Montreal, Canada.

as Superior, responded to Bishop Blanchet's appeal, arrived in the Territory of Washington and established their convent home at Van-couver, on December 8, 1856.

MOTHER GAMELIN
Died September 23, 1851
Foundress of the Daughters of Charity, Servants of the Poor

Engaging at once in the service of the poor, the sisters two years later opened at Vancouver, St. Joseph's Hospital, the pioneer hos-pital of the region. A short time afterward their educational work in the vicinity was sufficient to evoke the establishment of an academy, which was opened at Walla Walla for boarders and day pupils. St. Mary's Hospital also opened at Walla Walla, was another early institution of the sisters, as was the School of the Sacred Heart, which

MT. ST. VINCENT, SEATTLE, WASHINGTON

was conducted in two departments, one for white girls, and one for the Indian girls of the Colville tribe.

Six years after the introduction of the Congregation into the United States, the Motherhouse in Montreal, which had continued to send sisters to the missions in Washington, as well as those established in Oregon, sent a community to St. Ignatius, Montana, where at the request of the celebrated Jesuit missionary, the Rev. Peter De Smet, the first work of the sisters was the opening of a boarding school for Indian girls.

The journey which the sisters were obliged to make before reaching the scene of their future labors was one of the most eventful in the annals of religious orders of women in the United States. The first white women to cross the Coeur d'Alene Mountains, these intrepid religious traveled from Montreal to New York, then went by way of the Isthmus of Panama to San Francisco, and then to Vancouver, where they rested and prepared for the last lap of their long journey, which was made by horseback.

In 1873 a second group of sisters from the Motherhouse reached the Montana missions, and, establishing their headquarters at Missoula, they too were soon engaged in teaching the children and caring for the sick and poor. Each succeeding year then saw the Sisters of Charity, Servants of the Poor, establishing or maintaining institutions opened to meet the needs of the region. Hospitals, orphanages and homes for the aged, in addition to schools and academies, marked their progress in the west and northwest, not only in Montana, Washington and Oregon, but also in Idaho, and in later years in Alaska.

Contemporaneously with their establishment of convents and missions, and various institutions in the northwest of the United States, Mother Gamelin's Daughters of Charity, from Providence Motherhouse at Montreal, were likewise active in the east, worthily following her noble example in charitable practices.

To facilitate the work of the Congregation in its many hospitals, schools and benevolent institutions in the United States, a provincialate has been established with its Provincial house and novitiate at Mt. St. Vincent, Seattle, where Mother Vincent Ferrer is now Provincial Superior. A second northwestern United States provincialate of the Congregation has its headquarters at Sacred Heart Hospital, in Spokane, Washington, with Mother Gaudentia as the present Provincial Superior. Members of the Congregation who are engaged in school, hospital and orphanage work in New Hampshire, New Jersey and Vermont are under the direct jurisdiction of the General Motherhouse at Montreal.

The government of the Congregation is vested in the Superior General, the Provincial Superiors, appointed by her in the respective provinces, and the local Superiors appointed for the various houses. Mother Amarine is present Superior of the Congregation, residing at the General Motherhouse, Providence Convent, located at 1271 St.

MOTHER JOSEPH OF THE SACRED HEART

Catherine Street, East, Montreal, Canada, in the archdiocese of Montreal.

SACRED HEART HOSPITAL, SPOKANE, WASHINGTON

SUMMARY

Daughters of Charity, Servants of the Poor.
Founded in Canada in 1843.
Established in the United States in 1856.
Papal Approbation of Rules, September 12, 1900, by Pope Leo XIII.
Habit: The habit is of black serge, in honor of Our Lady of the Seven Dolors.
Approximate number in Community in the United States, 750.
Active in educational, hospital, charitable and social service work in the archdioceses of Portland in Oregon and San Francisco, and in the dioceses of Boise, Burlington, Great Falls, Helena, Manchester, Newark, Seattle and Spokane.
United States Provincial house (Province of St. Ignatius), Sacred Heart Hospital, Spokane, Washington. (Diocese of Spokane.)
United States Provincial house and Novitiate (Province of the Sacred Heart), Mt. St. Vincent, Seattle, Washington. (Diocese of Seattle.)

SISTERS OF ST. AGNES*

1858

THE Sisters of St. Agnes form a congregation founded at Barton, Washington County, Wisconsin, in 1858.

The Rev. Casper Rehrl, D.D., a zealous pioneer missionary, realizing the need of sisters for the education of youth,

MOTHER M. AGNES HAZOTTE

*From data and material supplied by the Sisters of St. Agnes, St. Agnes Convent, Fond du Lac, Wis.

567

founded this Community primarily for this purpose and established its Motherhouse in Barton.

On August 1, 1870, under Mother Mary Agnes Hazotte as Superior General, and the Very Rev. Francis Hass, O.M.Cap., spiritual director, and with the permission of the Right Rev. John Martin Henni, D.D., at that time bishop of what was then the diocese

St. Agnes Convent, Fond du Lac, Wisconsin

of Milwaukee, the Motherhouse of the Congregation was transferred to Fond du Lac, Wisconsin.

The Sisters of St. Agnes, in their now large number, continue to devote themselves, through their schools in the various dioceses in which they have opened missions, to the educational work for which they were founded. At Fond du Lac, in addition to St. Mary's Springs Academy, they have erected and conduct St. Agnes' Hospital and Training School for Nurses, and St. Anthony's Hospital in Hays, Kansas, in the diocese of Concordia, is under their direction.

In New York City the sisters of the Congregation of St. Agnes conduct *The Leo House,* a hospice for the laity, resident or transient, and also especially suitable for transient religious. Located as it is at 332 West 23rd Street, and convenient to steamship piers and railroads, this institution fills a unique place among the activities of religious orders of women in the United States.

SUMMARY

Sisters of St. Agnes.

Founded in the United States in 1858.

Papal Approbation of Rules, July 11, 1880, by Pope Leo XIII.

Habit: The habit is black, with a black veil lined with white, white wimple, and a circular collar.

Approximate number in Community, 740.

Active in educational, hospital and charitable work in the archdioceses of Chicago, Milwaukee and New York, and in the dioceses of Altoona, Concordia, Fort Wayne, Green Bay, Marquette, Pittsburgh, Superior and Toledo.

Motherhouse and Novitiate, St. Agnes Convent, 380 East Division Street, Fond du Lac, Wisconsin. (Archdiocese of Milwaukee.)

SISTERS OF THE HOLY NAMES OF JESUS AND MARY*

1859

THROUGH the zeal of one of North America's greatest pioneer missionary prelates, the Most Rev. Francis N. Blanchet, D.D., first archbishop of Oregon City—now the archdiocese of Portland in Oregon—the Congregation of the Sisters of the Holy Names of Jesus and Mary was introduced into the United States in the year 1859.

The Congregation of the Sisters of the Holy Names of Jesus and Mary was founded at Longueuil, opposite Montreal, in the Province of Quebec, Canada, on December 8, 1844. At this time the diocese of Montreal offered few facilities for religious education, and the Oblate Fathers on their missionary labors in the diocese, realizing the need of teaching religious, had made efforts to procure for Canada Sisters of the Holy Names of Jesus and Mary, a new sisterhood established at Marseilles, France, by Msgr. Charles Eugene de Mazenod, founder of their own Society, the Oblates of Mary Immaculate.

While awaiting the arrival of the hoped for community from France, the Oblates had organized at Beloeil, in the Province of Quebec, Canada's first parochial sodality of the Blessed Virgin Mary. Among the members of the new sodality it was expected there would be found candidates for the French community, which, however, finally relinquished the plan of the distant foundation.

Borrowing then from France, with modification for the new conditions, the rule and dress, as well as the title of the Sisters of the Holy Names of Jesus and Mary, an independent foundation was made, with the approval of the Right Rev. Ignace Bourget, first bishop of Montreal. Those forming the nucleus of this Canadian community were Miss Eulalie Durocher, the president of the sodality, who from early childhood had aspired to the religious life, Miss Henriette Céré and Miss Mélodie Dufresne.

After a period of probation which was spent at Longueuil, P.Q., the three aspirants, who had been under the ecclesiastical superiorship of the Rev. J. B. Honorat, Superior of the Oblates, were admitted to vows, December 8, 1844. This date, therefore marks the birth

*From data and material supplied from and through the Sisters of the Holy Names, Convent of the Holy Names, Montreal, P.Q., Canada.

of the Institute of the Sisters of the Holy Names of Jesus and Mary.

Miss Durocher, who is looked upon as foundress of the Congregation, and who imbued her sodalist associates with her fervor, became

MOTHER MARIE-ROSE DUROCHER
Foundress in 1844 of the Sisters of the Holy Names of Jesus and Mary

Mother Marie-Rose and first Superior, while Miss Céré and Miss Dufresne became respectively Sister M. Madeleine and Sister M. Agnes.

Five years later the young Community was bereft by death of Mother Marie-Rose, who, however, had so communicated her views and her spirit to her associates, that she continued to live in them, and they assiduously carried out her plans as outlined in manuscript notes she left for their guidance.

Initiated as they had been in the religious life by missionary priests, it was characteristic of the apostolic spirit of the Sisters of the Holy Names that they responded to Bishop Blanchet's appeal for sisters in 1859. Twelve of their number, with Mother Mary Veronica of the Crucifix as Superior, soon left Canada on the long, tedious voyage, by way of Panama, for Oregon, where on November 6, 1859, they inaugurated their activities in the United States with the opening of St. Mary's Academy at Portland, then a town of little more than two thousand inhabitants.

By an indult of the Holy See, dated April 9, 1871, a United States Novitiate of the Order was established at Oswego, Oregon, and in 1894, with the establishment of an Oregon Provincialate, the many houses which the sisters had opened, in the interval, in Washington as well as Oregon, were placed under a Provincial Superior residing at the convent at Marylhurst.

CONVENT OF THE HOLY NAMES, MARYLHURST, OSWEGO, OREGON

At Oswego, in addition to the normal school they maintain at Marylhurst, the Sisters of the Holy Names are in charge of the Christie Home for Orphan Girls.

The year 1893 marked for the Community the chartering of St. Mary's Academy and College at Portland, with power to confer degrees, and its students were made eligible to state diplomas. In 1907 academies of the Holy Names in Seattle and Spokane, Washington, were granted powers to establish normal departments and to issue State Normal certificates.

During this development of the institutions of the Congregation in the vicinity of its first United States mission, the Motherhouse in Canada had responded, in 1865, to an invitation from the Right Rev. John J. Conroy, Bishop of Albany, and established a convent and academy in Albany, New York.

Almost simultaneous with the invitation from Bishop Conroy, the Right Rev. Augustin Verot, D.D., Bishop of St. Augustine, applied to the Motherhouse for the opening of a convent and academy of the Order at Key West. These requests of the two bishops having been complied with, the convents and institutions opened in their dioceses were, in 1894, constituted a canonical provincialate of the Order, with its provincial head-quarters at Albany.

Scarcely had the sisters opened their convent at Key West, when, during the small-pox epidemic of 1870, they served as volunteer nurses in the pest house filled with victims of the disease. Later, during the Spanish-American War, the con-vent at Key West was offered to the United States for hospital pur-poses, and was accepted in the name of the Government by Admiral W. T. Sampson. After training as nurses, the Sisters of the Holy Names were rewarded in their new task by numerous conversions among the soldiers.

MOTHER M. VERONICA OF THE CRUCIFIX

In Key West and Tampa, Florida, the Sisters of the Holy Names, in addition to their academies and other schools in the diocese, have labored since 1865 among the colored.

In 1868, but three years after the establishment of its convents in the eastern and southern sections of the country, a second mission to the far west was undertaken by the Community in Canada. Sanc-tioned by the archbishop of San Francisco, the Most Rev. Joseph S. Alemany, O.P., D.D., this mission was opened at Oakland, Cali-fornia, where the sisters at once engaged in the work of teaching, to which the Congregation is chiefly devoted.

The convent then opened at Oakland was in 1894 made the seat of a California Provincialate of the Order. There the sisters also

CONVENT OF THE HOLY NAMES, ALBANY, NEW YORK

conduct Holy Name College, an institution fully accredited to the State University at Berkeley, and empowered by act of the California State Legislature to confer degrees.

The Constitutions of the Congregation of the Sisters of the Holy Names of Jesus and Mary, providing primarily for the sanctification

CONVENT OF THE HOLY NAMES, OAKLAND, CALIFORNIA

of its members, are so adapted to educational needs as to secure the development of the Catholic ideal, while complying with governmental regulations for public instruction. Studies are stimulated by a General Directress, who organizes conventions, secures professors for normal training, provides for annual examinations, and encourages personal initiative and original research.

Teaching comprises the life-work of the majority of the Sisters of the Holy Names, but for the candidates without aptitude for this work, who desire to embrace an apostolic life of quiet household labors, an auxiliary sisterhood is maintained.

The nearly nine hundred Sisters of the Holy Names now in the United States, engaged chiefly in educational work, remain subject, under Provincial Superiors, to the jurisdiction of the Motherhouse, located at 1430 Mount Royal Boulevard, Montreal, P.Q., Canada.

In the government of the Congregation, Mother Marie-Odilon, present Superior General, is assisted by the officers and the Provincial Superiors of the twelve provinces of the Order.

SUMMARY

Sisters of the Holy Names of Jesus and Mary.
Founded in Canada in 1844.
Established in the United States in 1859.
Papal Approbation of Rules, June 26, 1901, by Pope Leo XIII.
Habit: The habit and cape are of black serge; a black apron is also part of the garb. The veil, of nun's veiling, hangs eight inches below the elbow. The coif of linen has a plain border of linen gauze. A plain linen band covers the forehead, and a simple linen collar turns down a half inch over the neck band of the cape. An ebony cross, with a brass figure of Christ, and a border of brass, is suspended from the neck by a black woolen cord, and fastened by a loop on the left side of the cape, near the heart. A gold ring is worn on the ring finger of the right hand.
Approximate number in the United States, 900.
Active chiefly in educational work in the archdioceses of Baltimore, Chicago, Cincinnati, New York, Portland in Oregon, and San Francisco, and in the dioceses of Albany, Baker City, Brooklyn, Detroit, Duluth, Los Angeles and San Diego, St. Augustine, Seattle, Spokane and Syracuse.
United States Provincial house and Novitiate (Provincialate of Oregon), Convent of the Holy Names, Marylhurst, Oswego, Oregon. (Archdiocese of Portland in Oregon.)
United States Provincial house and Novitiate (Provincialate of California), Convent of the Holy Names, 2036 Webster Street, Oakland, California. (Archdiocese of San Francisco.)
United States Provincial house (Provincialate of New York), Convent of the Holy Names, 628 Madison Avenue, Albany, New York. (Diocese of Albany.)

SISTERS OF THE CONGRÉGATION DE NOTRE DAME*

1860

NEARLY two hundred years before the establishment of its first mission in the United States, in 1860, the Congrégation de Notre Dame had been founded in Montreal, Canada, by the intrepid French woman, Marguerite Bourgeoys, who by decree of the Sovereign Pontiff, Pope Pius IX, was in 1878 declared Venerable.

Closely associated in the early history of Canada, with the name of Mother Mary of the Incarnation and Madame de la Peltrie, who unfurled the banner of St. Angela Merici and the Ursulines in the New World, and with the name of another dauntless and holy French woman, Jeanne Mance, is that of Ven. Marguerite Bourgeoys.

Born in the city of Troyes, France, on April 17, 1620, of parents noted for their virtue and high character, Marguerite Bourgeoys, intensely pious and of an unusually happy disposition, which made her much sought after in society, early gave evidence of a predilection for the religious life. As she was seemingly not destined for any of the established religious orders, her confessor had received her, with two other devout young women, as aspirants to a new religious community he was engaged in forming, and which he planned would combine the active and the contemplative life.

The death of one candidate and the withdrawal of another brought an end to this plan of her zealous confessor, but Sister Bourgeoys had absorbed well the lessons in religious life given by Père Jandret, and was fortified by them when she was inspired to offer to go to Canada, and there open a school, especially for the instruction of Indian girls.

This she bravely did in 1653, and after five years spent in the education and religious instruction of the Indian girls in Montreal, or *Ville-Marie,* as the island was then called, Sister Bourgeoys returned to her native land in quest of co-laborers who would form with her a religious community for the work, which had outgrown her strength.

---

*From data and material supplied by the Sisters of the Congrégation de Notre Dame, Notre Dame Academy, 1338 Oregon Avenue, Chicago, Ill., and from *Lives of the Catholic Heroes and Heroines of America,* by John O'Kane Murray, and the Official Catholic Directory, 1929.

With four companions who were well fitted for the proposed work, she returned to Montreal, and the little community took possession of its first community home, a house which Governor De

VEN. MARGUERITE BOURGEOYS (1620-1700)
Foundress of the Congrégation de Notre Dame

Maisonneuve placed at their disposal. Appropriately for its natal place, *Ville-Marie,* the community became known as the Congré-gation de Notre Dame, devoted to the work of Catholic education in day and boarding schools. With its growth in numbers, and the development of schools in Canada, the Congregation established various missions and educational institutions of the highest standards throughout its provinces, all under the jurisdiction of the Mother-house, continuously maintained in Montreal.

In 1860, during the episcopacy in Chicago of the Right Rev. James Duggan, D.D., Sisters of the Congrégation de Notre Dame de Montreal, Canada, were sent to open a school at Bourbonnais, Illinois, where there was a large settlement of French Canadians. Notre Dame Academy, a boarding school still maintained by the sisters at Bourbonnais, in addition to their work in the parish school, was opened as the first activity of the Congregation in the United States. Academies and schools are now conducted by the Sisters of the Congrégation de Notre Dame, in Chicago and New York; Lew-iston, Maine; St. Alban, Vermont; Providence, Rhode Island; Water-bury, Connecticut; and many other cities in the country, all as missions from the Motherhouse. Notre Dame Academy and boarding school of the Immaculate Conception, conducted by the Congregation at Waterbury, Connecticut, was established in 1869, thus dating as one of the earliest of the United States missions of the Congregation.

On June 28, 1889, the Sovereign Pontiff, Pope Leo XIII, approved the Rules of the Congrégation de Notre Dame de Montreal, Canada.

Two hundred sisters of the Congregation, missioned to the United States from the Motherhouse at Montreal, are now engaged in edu-cational work in the archdioceses of Chicago and New York and in the dioceses of Burlington, Hartford, Portland and Providence.

Motherhouse and Novitiate, 1010 Sherbrooke Street, West, Montreal, P.Q., Canada. (Archdiocese of Montreal.)

RELIGIOUS OF THE HOLY CHILD JESUS*

1862

THE introduction of the Society of the Holy Child Jesus into the United States in 1862 was the realization of the long cherished hope of its foundress, Mother Cornelia Connelly, a native and former resident of Philadelphia, and was made possible by the generosity of an English duchess, the grand-daughter of Charles Carroll of Carrollton, Maryland.

Founded at Derby, England, in the summer of 1846, under the direction of the distinguished prelate, Nicholas Wiseman, then bishop, later cardinal, first archbishop of Westminster, the Society of the Holy Child Jesus was formed that its members might devote their lives to the education of girls.

Mother Connelly, formerly Cornelia Peacock, was the youngest of six children of a wealthy and distinguished Protestant family in Philadelphia. At the age of twenty-three she was married to the Rev. Pierce Connelly, an Episcopalian minister, five years her senior, a man who had received a university education, and who, possessed of ability and ambition, was apparently well fitted to make her happy.

Four years after their marriage, and while living in Natchez, Mississippi, where Mr. Connelly was appointed rector of Trinity Church, their residence being in the near vicinity of a Catholic convent, Mr. and Mrs. Connelly were impelled to study the religion of those whom they saw devoting their lives in its cause. Before long both became convinced of the truth of the Catholic faith, and in August, 1835, Pierce Connelly renounced his Anglican Orders.

Wishing to be received into the Church in Rome, Mr. Connelly removed with his family to New Orleans, Louisiana, in preparation for departure for Europe. Mrs. Connelly, however, desirous of the sacraments as soon as possible, was received into the Church soon after reaching New Orleans. A few months later, in Rome, where the American converts were hospitably welcomed, Mr. Connelly entered the Church. During their stay in the Eternal City Mr. and Mrs. Connelly were admitted to an audience with the Sovereign Pontiff, Pope Gregory XVI, who received them with paternal kindness.

---

*From data and material supplied by the Religious of the Holy Child Jesus, Sharon Hill, Pa., and Waukegan, Ill., and from *The Life of Cornelia Connelly, Foundress of the Society of the Holy Child Jesus*, by a member of the Society. (Longmans, Green & Co.)

After sojourning for a time in Europe Mr. and Mrs. Connelly and their three children then went to New Orleans, where Mr. Connelly became professor of English at the Jesuit College of St. Charles

MOTHER CORNELIA CONNELLY (1809-1879)
Foundress of the Society of the Holy Child Jesus

at Grand Coteau, Louisiana.   While in Rome Mrs. Connelly had become acquainted with the Religious of the Sacred Heart at the Trinità dei Monti, and was happy in renewed contact with members of the Society when she and her husband secured for their home at

Grand Coteau a cottage on the grounds of the Convent of the Sacred Heart.

Mrs. Connelly engaged in giving music lessons at the convent, and with her acquaintance with the religious, together with the guidance of her spiritual director, she made rapid strides in the spiritual life. At this time, as a wife and mother, and living in the world, she was making daily meditation and the examen of conscience, general and particular, twice daily according to the method of St. Ignatius. The results of her examination of conscience she recorded, marking how she had carried out the practice of the particular examen, the number of her daily faults, and their comparison week by week and month by month.

In these devotions Cornelia Connelly did not neglect the duties of her state in life, or her domestic responsibilities, but elevated them and accomplished them more faithfully. Strengthened by grace so

CONVENT OF THE HOLY CHILD JESUS, SHARON HILL, PENNSYLVANIA

drawn down, she was able to make unflinchingly the sacrifice of her domestic felicity when her husband told her of his desire to become a priest, and discussed with her the obvious conditions to be met for its fulfillment.

After many delays Mr. Connelly went to Rome and laid his petition before ecclesiastical authorities. More than a year later
Mrs. Connelly, who with her husband had previously made a vow
of chastity, was called to Rome from the convent at Grand Coteau.

Having satisfied the ecclesiastical authorities as to her consent
necessary before the desired dispensation could be granted to her
husband, Mrs. Connelly became a resident at the Convent of the
Sacred Heart in Rome, pending the time when her youngest child
should reach an age no longer requiring her particular care. After
a long interval, Mrs. Connelly, in an interview with the Holy Father,
Pope Gregory XVI, spoke of her desire to join the Carmelite Order,
and learned of his wish that she should interest herself instead in the
establishment of a needed educational religious order in England,
which might be extended from there to her native country.

Events of the Oxford Movement in England, from 1833 to 1845,
with its resultant reception into the Church of many noted converts,
were well known to the Sov-
ereign Pontiff, especially through
the representations of Bishop
Wiseman, under whom, following this interview at Rome,
Mrs. Connelly and a few companions were installed at Derby,
England, on October 13, 1846,
as the nucleus of the new community Bishop Wiseman asked
her to found.

MOTHER M. XAVIER NOBLE

After her years of contact
with the Religious of the Sacred
Heart, whose rule she had
studied and whose holy foundress, St. Madeleine Sophie, she
had known in Rome, Mother
Connelly—as she was known
from the beginning of her community life — was eminently
qualified for the proposed work.
She therefore at once inaugurated for herself and her com-
panions at Derby the practices of the religious life, according to the
rule she had written, at the desire of Bishop Wiseman, and with them
assumed the garb she planned as the postulant's habit.

On December 16, 1846, upon the conclusion of a retreat which the little community made, Bishop Wiseman conferred on its three members the habit which Mother Connelly had designed. The name of the new Society was of Mother Connelly's own choosing, and bears in its significant title her special devotion to the Holy Child Jesus.

Caring for nearly two hundred children in nearby parochial schools, Mother Connelly and her companion sisters soon accepted the additional charge of a crowded night-school and Sunday-school. At this time also individual instruction for the reception of the sacraments was given to factory girls at Derby in the Midlands.

The following announcement, which appeared in England in 1847, defining the scope of the work of the first boarding school, carries in it the keynote of the spirit and plan of the educational institutions of the Order now established in many countries. "St. Mary's Convent, Derby, of the Holy Child Jesus. The objects which are contemplated in this Convent are to give, upon the sound basis of the practice of all their religious duties, such a solid education to a large and increasing class of Girls as will best enable them to fill their office in Society, while at the same time, they will be thoroughly instructed in the details of domestic life, and in all such arts as are the most practically useful in the service of our Holy Mother the Church."

With the later transfer of the boarding school and convent from Derby to St. Leonard's-on-Sea, the Society of the Holy Child Jesus entered upon a period of growth and expansion, although the years were not without trials for the fervent convert and foundress— trials not pertaining exclusively to the development of the Society. Mother Connelly, however, fortified by an intense spirituality, and apparently oblivious of personal sufferings, bravely withstood the difficulties she was forced to encounter, as she laid well the founda- tion of the Community, which was early ranked among the prominent educational orders of the Church.

As an American, Mother Connelly long looked forward to the time when the work of the Society of the Holy Child Jesus should be extended to the United States. She entered upon definite plans toward this end when the Society received the offer of a gift of two thousand acres of land in Lycoming County and a hundred and fifty acres at Towanda in Bradford County, all in Pennsylvania, the donor of the gift being the widowed Duchess of Leeds, who had become a friend of Mother Connelly's, and who had sought admis- sion to the Society, but had not been encouraged as a suitable subject.

During a visit to Europe in 1862, on the occasion of the canoniza-tion of the Japanese Martyrs, which took place that year in Rome, the Right Rev. James F. Wood, D.D., Bishop of Philadelphia, and later its first archbishop, accompanied by the Right Rev. John McCloskey, D.D., then bishop of Albany—later archbishop and cardinal, called at St. Leonard's, where Bishop Wood gave his personal assurance to Mother Connelly of a welcome for her religious in his diocese and arranged that the community chosen to establish the new mission should travel to the United States under his protection.

Mother Mary Xavier Noble was then appointed Superior, with Mother Lucy Ignatia Newsham as her assistant, of the group, includ-ing also three professed sisters and a postulant, who arrived in New York from Liverpool on August 12, 1862, and reached Philadelphia the same day, remaining there until the 18th, when they proceeded

Entrance
HOLY CHILD CONVENT, WAUKEGAN, ILLINOIS

to Towanda, accompanied by the Rev. C. I. Carter, Vicar General of the diocese.

The "mansion" which they had been assured was on the estate at Towanda was found to have suffered from neglect on the part of the agents, and the grounds, equally uncared for, presented the newly arrived religious with the hardships that fell to the lot of the pioneer communities in the country, but undeterred they at once entered upon their work of education in the United States.

The following year a second group of sisters was sent from England, and with their arrival the Society began its work of teaching in Philadelphia. Shortly after this the convent at Towanda was reluctantly but wisely relinquished, and following an interval which Mother Mary Xavier and the community spent in Philadelphia, purchase was made of a Quaker Academy at Sharon Hill in Delaware County, about six miles from the city. Taking possession of the new site for its Motherhouse and novitiate, the community opened a school there in September, 1864. A little less than ten years later Mother Connelly, at the expressed desire of Father Carter, visited the community in the United States, remaining for five weeks at the convent at Sharon Hill, and at this time opened a new convent in West Philadelphia, which she named St. Leonard's House.

In the ensuing years the Religious of the Holy Child Jesus established educational institutions in nearby eastern states and in far and middle western States, among them being boarding schools at Summit, New Jersey; Suffern, New York; New York City; Cheyenne, Wyoming; Waukegan, Illinois; and Portland, Oregon.

Collegiate work was included in the curriculum of the Society in the United States in 1922, with the opening of Rosemont College in one of Philadelphia's beautiful suburbs. In the group of buildings at Rosemont the auditorium recalls in its name, Mayfield Hall, the historic English estate which the Duchess of Leeds purchased and presented to the Society for the site of its novitiate, which was transferred to it in 1863.

The government of the Society is vested in a Mother General and a General Council, residing at the Motherhouse in Rome, at 10 Via Boncompagni, and Provincial Superiors of the different provinces. As present Provincial Superior of the Eastern Province in the United States, Mother Mary Felix resides at Sharon Hill, Pennsylvania, while Mother Mary Hildegarde, at the Convent of the Holy Child, Waukegan, Illinois, is Provincial Superior of the Western Province.

SUMMARY

Religious of the Holy Child Jesus.
Founded in England in 1846.
Established in the United States in 1862.
Papal Approbation of Rules in 1893, by Pope Leo XIII.
Approximate number in Community in United States, 320.
Active in educational work; *Eastern Provincialate,* in the archdioceses of Boston, New York and Philadelphia and in the diocese of Newark; *Provincial house and United States Novitiate,* Convent of the Holy Child Jesus, Sharon Hill, Pennsylvania (Archdiocese of Philadelphia); *Western Provincialate,* in the archdioceses of Chicago and Portland in Oregon and in the diocese of Cheyenne; *Provincial house,* Convent of the Holy Child Jesus, 1201 North Sheridan Road, Waukegan, Illinois (Archdiocese of Chicago).

SISTERS OF ST. MARY OF NAMUR*

1863

HE Institute of the Sisters of St. Mary of Namur, devoted exclusively to the education of girls, was founded in Namur, Belgium, in 1819, by a Cistercian priest, the Rev. Nicholas Joseph Minsart, pastor of the Church of St. Loup in Namur, where the Motherhouse of the Order has been continued.

The establishment of the Institute in the United States in 1863 is due to the zeal of the renowned and beloved Jesuit missionary, Father De Smet, who, in 1861, while visiting his native land, requested the Sisters of St. Mary to send a community to America. Before the petition of the saintly missionary—who had returned to his chosen mission field in this country—could be complied with, civil strife in the United States had severed the north and south, and the Superior, Mother Claire, hesitated to send her sisters to a strange land at such a crucial time. Father De Smet, however, hastened to dissipate her fears, and urged the establishment of a foundation of the Order in the diocese of Buffalo, where the bishop, the Right Rev. John Timon, C.M., D.D., was desirous of a community of foreign nuns to conduct schools.

Accordingly, in August, 1863, on the completion of initial negotiations with Bishop Timon, five Sisters of St. Mary —of German, French, Belgian and Irish parentage—set sail for the United States, under the personal guidance of the noted missionary, the Rev. Father Smarius, S.J., who was on his way to Chicago. The religious who composed this community

MOTHER EMILIE

*From data and material supplied by the Sisters of St. Mary of Namur, St. Joseph's Academy, Lockport, New York.

of five, from the convent in Namur, were Mother Emilie, Superior, and later first Provincial of the American missions, Sisters Mary Claver, Mary of St. Joseph, Augustine and Paula.

The first United States mission house of the Congregation, which is active throughout Europe, was then opened in the diocese of Buffalo, at Lockport, New York. This house was later established as the first American Provincial Motherhouse of the Institute. The opening of schools by the community followed the completion of the newly erected convent.

The early American history of the Institute marks the first extension of its labors beyond the confines of the diocese of Buffalo—to the state of Texas.

Bishop Timon, formerly prefect apostolic of Texas, responded promptly and whole-heartedly to the request of the Right Rev. C. M. Dubuis, D.D., Bishop of Galveston, for sisters for his diocese, and Mother Emilie at once consented to send a community to the south.

MT. ST. MARY, BUFFALO, NEW YORK

Missions of the Institute were opened in Dallas, Denison, Fort Worth, Sherman, Waco and Wichita Falls—all then in the extensive Texas diocese of Galveston, but for the most part later included in the territory of the diocese of Dallas, on its establishment in 1890.

In 1886 Mother Emilie extended the work of the Institute into Canada. Sacred Heart Academy, opened at that time, at Vankleek Hill, Ontario, has since become the Provincial house and novitiate for the Institute in Canada, where missions are conducted in the diocese of Ottawa, and the vicariate apostolic of Northern Ontario.

Retaining affiliations with the Motherhouse at Namur, Belgium, subject to the General Superior and her Council, residing there, the Institute of the Sisters of St. Mary of Namur in America now comprises three provincialates, with the Provincial houses located in Buffalo, New York; Fort Worth, Texas; and Vankleek Hill, Ontario.

Under the efficient administration of Mother Veronica, Provincial Superior for the Eastern Provincialate, Mt. St. Mary was erected in

OUR LADY OF VICTORY CONVENT, FORT WORTH, TEXAS

Buffalo, and upon its completion in 1928, transfer was made to it of the Eastern Provincialate offices and novitiate, previously maintained at St. Joseph's Academy at Lockport.

In addition to its many educational institutions in the United States, in the interest of the university work of the sisters, the Institute of the Sisters of St. Mary of Namur maintains a House of Studies, noted as the first permanent building of the Sisters' College of the Catholic University of America, Washington, D. C.

SUMMARY

Sisters of St. Mary of Namur.
Founded in Belgium in 1819.
Established in the United States in 1863.
Papal Approbation of Rules, June 6, 1914, by Pope Pius X.
Habit: The habit is of black serge, with a black apron. The head-dress, coif, guimpe and bandeau, are of white linen. At the right side of the belt a large rosary, with a brass crucifix and a medal of the Blessed Virgin, is worn.
Approximate number in Community in United States, 500.

Active in educational work; *Eastern Provincialate*, in the archdiocese of Boston and in the dioceses of Buffalo and Syracuse; *Provincial house and Novitiate*, Mt. St. Mary, Delaware Avenue, Hertel Station, Buffalo, New York (Diocese of Buffalo); *Southwestern Provincialate*, in the dioceses of Dallas, Galveston and Monterey-Fresno; *Provincial house and Novitiate*, Our Lady of Victory Academy, 3410 South Hempill Street, Fort Worth, Texas (Diocese of Dallas).

SISTERS OF THE HOLY HUMILITY OF MARY*

1864

*T*HE Community of the Sisters of the Holy Humility of Mary was founded in the diocese of Nancy, at Dommartin-sous-Amance, France, in the year 1855, by the Rev. John Joseph Begel, pastor of the two villages, Laitre and Dommartin, noted for his charity to the destitute, and his love of little children, particularly the poor and neglected.

It was from Father Begel's earnest longing to help his fellowmen that the Institute, which now has its home near Youngstown, Ohio, known as Villa Maria, developed and grew. Father Begel, to obtain teachers for the children of the two parishes, Laitre and Dommartin, applied to various communities and lay persons.

Three pious women offered their services gratuitously, and Mademoiselle Antoinette Potier, a wealthy lady of Dommartin, volunteered not only her assistance but her home, as well as the means to defray the necessary expenses of a school and the teachers. The following year she and her companions asked Father Begel to give them a rule of life whereby they could serve God more perfectly and unreservedly, thus furthering his project for the establishment of a religious community. Upon its presentation, Bishop Menjeau, of Nancy, approved the rule, and on August 29, 1858, bestowed upon the Order the title of Sisters of the Holy Humility of Mary, blessed their home, and promised to assist them. Mademoiselle Antoinette Potier was chosen Superior of the little group, and was known as Mother M. Magdalen.

The Community was founded especially for the education of youth, in town and country districts, while the secondary objective was the performance of any charitable works, possible without detriment to the sisters' principal vocation, teaching.

The training of orphans, hospital work and the care of altars in the parishes where the sisters teach has accompanied the Community's educational efforts.

Obstacles to the progress of the Congregation in France came from the unfriendly attitude of the government toward religious

*From data and material supplied by the Sisters of the Holy Humility of Mary, Villa Maria Convent, Lowellville, Ohio, and from the Catholic Universe-Bulletin, Cleveland, Ohio, and the Official Catholic Year Book, 1928.

orders. In the fall of 1863 the Rev. Louis Hoffer, who was visiting in France from the United States, learned of the new Community, and applied for sisters to teach in his parochial school at Louisville, Ohio, in the diocese of Cleveland.

The Right Rev. Amadeus Rappe, D.D., Bishop of Cleveland, knowing the situation in France, invited the entire Community to come to America to make its home in his diocese in the western world. Father Begel assenting to this change, the sisters were preparing to leave their native land when their foundress, Mother Magdalen, died March 7, 1864. The sisters, accompanied by Father Begel, later set sail from Havre, May 30, 1864, and arrived in America on June 18th.

The troubles following the Civil War delayed the execution of the plans of the bishop of Cleveland, and he assigned to the Congregation, temporarily, a two hundred and fifty-acre tract of land near New Bedford, Pennsylvania, which the Right Rev. Michael O'Connor, D.D., Bishop of Pittsburgh, had in 1859 transferred to the

VILLA MARIA CONVENT, NEAR LOWELLVILLE, OHIO

jurisdiction of Bishop Rappe of Cleveland. An orphan asylum for boys, which had been established there in charge of the Sisters of Charity of St. Augustine, had been removed to Cleveland for better accommodations.

The difficulties with which the new Community struggled for

so long gradually lessened. Under the leadership of Mother Mary Anna Tabouret, whom the sisters love and revere as their American foundress, it was impossible for the Community not to prosper. In 1869 the convent was enlarged, and in 1878 another addition was erected.

In 1870, on the request of the Right Rev. John J. Hogan, D.D., Bishop of St. Joseph, sisters of the Community were sent to Chilli-cothe, Missouri, for school work in the vicinity.

In 1875 two of the sisters from this western mission severed con-nections with the Motherhouse, establishing the present Congregation at Ottumwa, Iowa. They retained the same title, although the blue habit was changed to black, and a cross worn in place of the medal of the Blessed Virgin. This Community, with a membership now of nearly two hundred, is engaged mainly in educational work in the archdiocese of Dubuque, and in the dioceses of Davenport and Des Moines.

Prior to the death of Father Begel, on January 23, 1884, after a long illness, the Very Rev. Msgr. John Klute directed the Com-munity until July 2, 1881, when the Right Rev. Richard Gilmour, successor to Bishop Rappe in the see of Cleveland, appointed the Rev. Nicholas Franche, nephew of Father Begel, to succeed him in the direction of the Community. As the Right Rev. Msgr. Franche he continues as the chaplain at Villa Maria, the Motherhouse in Lowellville.

With undaunted spirit Mother Anna, though an invalid, governed the Community during twenty years of trials and difficulties, until she resigned the superiorship in 1883, when the Community held its first election, presided over by Bishop Gilmour. Mother Mary Odile, who succeeded as Superior, held office for six years, and in the summer of 1889 Mother M. Patrick, the first American Superior, was elected to the office of Superior General, in which position she continues, with her residence at Villa Maria.

In August, 1924, a normal school at Villa Maria received state recognition, but was closed in June, 1928, in order to affiliate with the Central Catholic Normal School opened at Cleveland, Ohio, under the auspices of the Right Rev. Joseph Schrembs, D.D., Bishop of Cleveland.

Our Lady of Lourdes Academy, in Cleveland, and Mount Marie Boarding School and Academy, in Canton, are prominent educational institutions of the Congregation, which also directs St. Joseph's Hospital, in Lorain, and St. Elizabeth's Hospital, in Youngstown, Ohio.

An Orthopœdic School is conducted by the Sisters of the Holy Humility of Mary at the Rosemary Home for Crippled Children, located at Euclid Village, in the near vicinity of Cleveland. Owing its existence, since 1922, to the generosity of Mr. C. A. Grasselli, and requiring only suffering childhood for admission to its charities, this institution, officially known as the Johanna Grasselli Home for Crippled Children, contrives to provide for the many individual needs of its little charges, and veritable transforma- tions of soul and body frequently com- pensate for the labors of the Community in the "Rosemary."

In 1929 the Sisters of the Holy Hu- mility of Mary, also known as the "Blue Nuns," acquired the Coulby residence, in the center of a seventy-two acre beauti- fully landscaped and wooded estate in Wickliffe, Ohio, near Cleveland, and here the Motherhouse of the Community is later to be located.

A Sister of the Holy Humility of Mary, Villa Maria, Lo- wellville, Ohio

SUMMARY

Sisters of the Holy Humility of Mary.
Founded in France in 1855.
Established in the United States in 1864.
Habit: (Ohio Community) The habit is of blue flannel, with a pleated skirt and waist. A black veil is worn over a white under veil, and a large silver medal of the Blessed Virgin, suspended on a blue woolen tape, hangs over the guimpe, which is white and rounded. A silver band ring is worn on the third finger of the left hand.
Approximate number in Community (Ohio), 370.
Active in educational, hospital and charitable work in the diocese of Cleveland.
Motherhouse and Novitiate, Villa Maria, Lowellville, Ohio. (Diocese of Cleveland.)
Approximate number in Community (Iowa), 200.
Active in educational, hospital and charitable work in the archdiocese of Dubuque, and the dioceses of Davenport and Des Moines.
Motherhouse and Novitiate, St. Joseph's Convent, Villa Maria, Grand View Avenue, Ottumwa, Iowa. (Diocese of Davenport.)

40

SISTERS OF CHARITY OF THE INCARNATE WORD*

1866

GALVESTON, TEXAS

HE Congregation of the Sisters of Charity of the Incarnate Word has the distinction of having been founded in France definitely for labor in the United States. Its establishment in 1866 was due to the zeal of the Right Rev. C. M. Dubuis, D.D., second bishop of Galveston, who while visiting France, his native country, applied to Mother Angelique, Superior of the Sisters of the Incarnate Word and Blessed Sacrament, at the monastery in Lyons, to train for service in his distant mission field candidates who should be sent to her.

To this request Mother Angelique acceded, and immediately admitted into the monastery three subjects who were to form the nucleus of the new congregation, needed to take charge of hospitals and orphanages and engage in other works of mercy in the extensive Texas diocese.

Shortly after having received the religious habit, the first Sisters of Charity of the Incarnate Word, as they were known, embarked for their field of labor, imbued with the fervor of the holy foundress of the Order of the Incarnate Word and Blessed Sacrament, Mother Jeanne Chézard de Matel, and with their title—given them by Mother Angelique—at once indicating their motives and the spirit actuating them.

Though the civil strife between North and South had ceased, Mother M. Blandine Mathlin and her companion sisters of the new Congregation found, on their arrival in the United States, late in 1866, the horrors of the war everywhere visible. Scarcely had they then become established at Galveston, Texas, where they were gladly welcomed by Bishop Dubuis, when they began labor among the plague-stricken of yellow fever.

Other recruits for the Community, trained at the monastery at Lyons, soon joined their sisters in Galveston, whose Superior had become a victim of the dread disease, her death, however, increasing

---

*From data and material supplied by the Sisters of Charity of the Incarnate Word, Incarnate Word Convent, Galveston, Texas, and from the Official Catholic Directory, 1929.

rather than dampening the ardor of the Sisters of Charity of the Incarnate Word in their works of mercy.

In addition to having early sent a community of sisters to San Antonio, Texas, the Sisters of Charity of the Incarnate Word of the United States foundation house in Galveston have established and maintain well-equipped hospitals with training schools for nurses, not only in Galveston and Houston—now the site of their Mother-house and novitiate, and the residence of the present Mother General, Mother M. Placidus Mulcahy—but also in Beaumont, Temple, and Texarkana, Texas; Shreveport and Lake Charles, Louisiana; and Long Beach, California. Orphanages are also conducted by the Community in nearly all these cities or in cities nearby.

For the benefit of candidates in Ireland desiring admittance to the Community, the sisters maintain a Receiving House in County Clare, Ireland.

SUMMARY

Sisters of Charity of the Incarnate Word (Houston, Texas).
Founded in France in 1866.
Established in the United States in 1866.
Papal Approbation of Rules in 1912, by Pope Pius X.
Habit: The habit is of black serge, with a long scapular on the front of which is embroidered in red silk a crown of thorns encircling the monogram of the Holy Name, I.H.S., and underneath it a heart surmounted by three nails, enclosing the motto, *Amor Meus.* The guimpe and bandeau are of white linen. A silver crucifix and gold ring are worn.
Approximate number in Community, 335.
Active in hospital and charitable work in the dioceses of Alexandria, Galveston, Lafayette, Little Rock and Los Angeles and San Diego.
Motherhouse and Novitiate, Villa de Matel, Lawndale Avenue, Houston, Texas. (Diocese of Galveston.)

SAN ANTONIO, TEXAS*
1869

In the year 1869, in compliance with the wish of the Right Rev. C. M. Dubuis, D.D., Bishop of Galveston, the territory of which then included the entire state of Texas, a second foundation of the Sisters of Charity of the Incarnate Word was made in the Lone Star State.

With Mother M. Madeleine Chollet as Superior, a small community of sisters from the convent which had been established three

*From data and material supplied by the Sisters of Charity of the Incarnate Word, Alamo Heights, San Antonio, Tex.

years previously in Galveston, took formal possession, on October 21, 1869, of the new convent prepared for them, replacing the one they were to have occupied on their arrival in the spring, but which had been destroyed by fire. In the interval, the community had been hospitably made welcome at the Ursuline Convent.

Retaining, throughout the vicissitudes and struggles of their pioneer days, the primitive spirit of the Congregation, and keeping unchanged the religious habit conferred on the first members at the Monastery of the Incarnate Word and Blessed Sacrament at Lyons, France, the Sisters of Charity of the Incarnate Word, whose Motherhouse is at San Antonio, Texas, while devoted especially to the cause of education, are extensively engaged also in hospital and orphanage work, particularly in the southwestern part of the country.

A SISTER OF CHARITY OF THE INCARNATE WORD, SAN ANTONIO, TEXAS

With their first residence in San Antonio serving as their convent and as a hospital, which was called Santa Rosa Infirmary, the sisters entered immediately on their duties of caring for the sick. With the city's growth, increasing demands called for a larger building, and this in time was erected on West Houston Street, replacing the original structure of Santa Rosa Infirmary, to which had been added many but always inadequate extensions.

In 1872 the Community was called upon to provide a home for orphan children. This was temporarily maintained at the hospital, the institution being transferred, in 1874, to a new and suitable building opened as St. Joseph's Orphanage, which has been continued, as one of many such charitable establishments now under the direction of the sisters.

The year 1874 brought to the state of Texas an ecclesiastical division of the diocese of Galveston and the erection of that of San Antonio. Upon his advent to the new see, its first bishop, the Right Rev. A. D. Pellicer, D.D., urged the Sisters of Charity of the Incarnate Word to engage in school work, and San Fernando parochial school was accordingly opened at the orphanage. With the establishment of this school, in March, 1875, the sisters inaugurated

CONVENT OF THE INCARNATE WORD, ALAMO HEIGHTS, SAN ANTONIO, TEXAS

their work in the vast educational field, where the institutions under their charge are today, as are their many hospitals, among the foremost in the country.

Little more than ten years had passed when, with the pressing need for sisters, to fill the many demands on the Community, Mother St. Pierre Cinquin, who had succeeded as Superior, acting upon episcopal advice, made a journey to Europe, where she secured a number of desirable candidates for the Community. Similar journeys were later made, each occasioning the reception of a number of French, German and Irish aspirants, eager to devote their lives to the service of the Incarnate Word.

To meet the needs of the Community for a larger Motherhouse and novitiate, a tract of land comprising two hundred and eighty-three acres, at the head of the San Antonio River, on River Avenue, in Alamo Heights, three and a half miles from the city of San Antonio, was purchased in 1897. A spacious and beautiful residence on the property was used as the novitiate, which was transferred to it in June, 1897. Upon the completion of the Motherhouse, novitiate and academy building in 1900, this residence was left for the use of the chaplain.

To develop educational work, a systematic preparation of the sisters for the work of teaching was early given attention at the Motherhouse, and a summer normal school was established. When the Catholic University of America, at Washington, D. C., opened its doors for the higher education of women, the Sisters of Charity of the Incarnate Word, of San Antonio, were among the first to attend it and receive degrees.

A worthy result of the earnest efforts of the Community is Incarnate Word College at San Antonio. Comprising this institution, empowered to grant degrees, is a group of schools, including the college of arts and sciences, the college and preparatory school of music, the school of art, the academy, the school of home economics, and a model grade school in conjunction with the department of education in the college of arts and sciences.

The Community has established a Generalate, with its seat at San Antonio, and maintains Provincial houses and novitiates, including a provincialate in Mexico.

In County Galway, Ireland, the sisters conduct a House of Studies for the training of candidates who desire to enter the Community.

SUMMARY

Sisters of Charity of the Incarnate Word (San Antonio, Texas).
Founded in France in 1866.
Community established in 1869.
Papal Approbation of Rules in 1910 by Pope Pius X.
Habit: See Habit description on page 595.
Approximate number in Community, 850.
Active in educational, hospital and charitable work in the United States;
    Provincialate of San Antonio, in the archdiocese of San Antonio and the
    dioceses of Corpus Christi, Dallas and Amarillo; *Provincial house* and
    Novitiate, Incarnate Word Convent, Alamo Heights, San Antonio, Texas
    (Archdiocese of San Antonio); *Provincialate of St. Louis,* in the arch-
    dioceses of Baltimore, Chicago and St. Louis, and in the dioceses of
    Dallas, Kansas City, Oklahoma and St. Joseph; *Provincial house and
    Novitiate,* Incarnate Word Convent, Our Lady's Mount, Wellston Station,
    Normandy, Missouri (Archdiocese of St. Louis); *Provincialate of New
    Orleans,* in the archdioceses of New Orleans and San Antonio, and in
    the dioceses of Amarillo, Dallas and El Paso; *Provincial house* (pro tem),
    St. Joseph's Infirmary, Fort Worth, Texas (Diocese of Dallas).
General Motherhouse, Convent of the Incarnate Word, Alamo Heights, San
    Antonio, Texas. (Archdiocese of San Antonio.)

SISTERS OF DIVINE PROVIDENCE*

HE Congregation of the Sisters of Divine Providence was founded in Lorraine in the year 1762 by Ven. John Martin Moye, a learned and zealous priest of the diocese of Metz. From among the many devout young women who had placed themselves under his spiritual direction, Father Moye chose those who formed this Congregation, whose mission, it was intended, should be the establishment and conducting of schools for children, especially in rural districts, the care of the sick and the practice of other works of mercy.

Suffering suppression during the period of the French Revolution, the Congregation was afterwards re-established, and from its Mother-house at St. Jean de Bassel, in the diocese of Metz, Lorraine, many missions and foundations have been established, among them two in the United States.

TEXAS

1866

During a visit which he made to Europe in the interest of his diocese, that of Galveston, which included in its territory at the time the entire state of Texas, the Right Rev. C. M. Dubuis, D.D., appealed to the Sisters of Divine Providence at their Motherhouse at St. Jean de Bassel, Lorraine, asking the aid of sisters in his vast field of labor.

A small community was then sent in compliance with Bishop Dubuis' request, and under his direction established a convent at Austin, Texas, in 1866. Two years later this was transferred to Castroville, where, as a missionary priest, Bishop Dubuis had early erected a church.

A SISTER OF DIVINE PROVIDENCE, SAN ANTONIO, TEXAS

*From data and material supplied by the Sisters of Divine Providence, Convent of Our Lady of the Lake, San Antonio, Texas, and from the Catholic Encyclopedia.

Engaging in needed school work, the sisters were soon joined by applicants for membership in the community.

Following arrangements made with the Motherhouse in Europe for the establishment of the community in Texas as an independent foundation, Mother St. Andrew Feltin was chosen its first Superior in 1884.

With its subsequent growth in numbers, and the need of further facilities than Castroville afforded, the Motherhouse and novitiate were in 1895 transferred to San Antonio, which since the arrival of the Sisters of Divine Providence in Texas had become the seat of a new diocese—though it has now been, since 1926, an archiepiscopal city.

The year following the transfer of the Motherhouse from Castro-ville to San Antonio, Our Lady of the Lake College was founded. The first building erected at its present location was designed to serve as a novitiate and boarding school. As the Congregation grew and the number of students increased, so also were buildings, equip-ment, courses and the scope of the work developed, until the Mother-house and college institution now comprises nearly a dozen buildings, including Moye Hall and a beautiful Gothic church.

Offering its first college courses in 1912, Our Lady of the Lake College has since been recognized and accredited by the leading educational standardizing bodies of the country.

SUMMARY

Sisters of Divine Providence (Texas).
Founded in Lorraine in 1762.
Established in the United States in 1866.
Papal Approbation of Rules, December 12, 1912, by Pope Pius X.
Habit: The habit and cape are of black serge, with a round white guimpe
   A white cornette and a black veil are worn.
Approximate number in Community, 600.
Active chiefly in educational work in the archdioceses of Baltimore, San
   Antonio and Santa Fé, and in the dioceses of Alexandria, Amarillo,
   Corpus Christi, Dallas, Galveston, Lafayette, Little Rock, Los Angeles and
   San Diego, and Oklahoma.
Motherhouse and Novitiate, Our Lady of the Lake Convent, San Antonio,
   Texas. (Archdiocese of San Antonio.)

KENTUCKY*

1889

In response to an invitation personally extended by the Right Rev. Camillus P. Maes, D.D., Bishop of Covington, on the occasion

---

*From the Catholic Encyclopedia and the Official Catholic Directory, 1929.

of a visit he made at the Motherhouse of the Sisters of Divine Providence at St. Jean de Bassel, Lorraine, three sisters of the Congregation were sent from the Motherhouse to Covington, Kentucky, where they arrived in August, 1889.

The community became established in one of the historical mansions of northern Kentucky, which, as St. Martin's Convent, served for many years as the headquarters for the province, from whence the sisters went forth to the many missions confided to them.

In 1908, St. Anne's Convent, erected on an estate secured for the purpose at Melbourne, Kentucky, became the site of a new Provincial house for the Sisters of Divine Providence of Kentucky, now approximately four hundred in number, and engaged in educational, charitable and social service work in the archdioceses of Baltimore, Cincinnati and New York, and in the dioceses of Columbus, Covington, Providence, Toledo and Wheeling.

United States Provincial house and Novitiate, St. Anne's Convent, Melbourne, Kentucky. (Diocese of Covington.)

LITTLE SISTERS OF THE POOR*

1868

𝒪𝒻 EW religious congregations carry in their title the message of their mission and their work as do the Little Sisters of the Poor, founded in France, in the year 1839.

Simple as is the life of those in this hospitaller Congregation, now entering upon the last decade of a hundred years in the service of the aged poor, the mere mention of their name, or suggestion of the presence of one of their number, brings at once a feeling of awe and reverence.

St. Servan, in Brittany, was the scene of the first ministrations of the Little Sisters of the Poor. Jeanne Jugan, a devout and humble young woman, who was born at Cancale, in the village of Petites-Croix, near St. Servan, October 28, 1792, serving in a hospital, became acquainted with a pious and charitable woman who bequeathed to her her worldly possessions, and continued her work of nursing, with Françoise Aubert, an aged retired servant, sharing her home, and uniting with her in good works.

In the same town lived Marie Jamet and Virginie Tredaniel. Marie, as a child, had been taken on frequent visits to the hospital, where she was manifestly happy in roaming the wards. As she grew up she habitually visited sick neighbors, read to them, watched by their bedside, and for the needy ones obtained assistance from the rich.

To Virginie Tredaniel sorrows came in early life. Bereft of family and home, she was entrusted by her guardian to the care of Jeanne Jugan and Françoise Aubert, and soon there began that community life destined to become permanent.

In January, 1838, a new curate, appointed to St. Servan, arrived there. From the very beginning of the ministry of the Abbé Le Pailleur, it was evident that the poor children, the sick and the abandoned appealed to him especially. Anxious for definite charitable work, and perceiving the virtues of these four earnest women, who had been brought together, he revised the rule of life which two of the four had drawn up, and for two years, 1838-1840, directed them in the observance of it.

---

*From data and material supplied by the Little Sisters of the Poor, St. Pern, France, and from supplied bibliography: *History of the Little Sisters of the Poor*, by Rev. A. Leroy (R. & T. Washbourne, London), and *La Congrégation des Petites Soeurs des Pauvres* (Librairie Letouzey et Ané, Paris).

Early in the winter of 1839 Jeanne Jugan learned of a poor old woman, blind and infirm, who had just lost her sister, her only support. Touched by her sad fate, Jeanne took the old woman to her own house, and to feed her first pensioner worked later each night. Soon afterward, a feeble and infirm old servant, in sorrowful plight, sought the good Jeanne, and the pious girl likewise received her into her home.

Two months later, a young woman who was ill asked to be admitted to Jeanne's home, now become almost a hospice for the aged poor, that she might die there and leave her earnings and few belongings with them. Jeanne and Françoise received her, and under their careful nursing Madeleine Bourges recovered, and wishing to consecrate her life to the service of others, and to assist these good women in their work, remained with them.

Removing to larger quarters, in the late December of 1841, these companions in charity soon housed twelve poor old women, at a loss, however, as to how to feed them. "I will go out and beg for them," Jeanne said. "It will be easier for me to beg than for these poor unfortunate women, broken down by age and infirmities." This was a decisive plan, and the beginning of the collecting of alms which was to become an essential part of the work of the evolving hospitaller Congregation.

And Sister Jeanne, as the befriended ones called her, went forth with her basket, which was soon very well known. Françoise attended to the housekeeping; Virginie and Madeleine contributed their earnings, and prolonged their hours of labor far into the night, while Marie, still with her parents, yet wishing to do her part, bought and sold vegetables for the benefit of the poor.

As others sought admission, and larger quarters were required, they were encouraged by a generous woman's assistance, to purchase an old convent which was for sale. In May, 1842, the association, which had become partly organized, and religious in character, chose Jeanne Jugan as Superior of the Servants of the Poor, the title then adopted. The care of the aged poor, of both sexes, was included in their plan of work.

A uniform dress, and religious symbols were gradually adopted by those forming the little foundation, which now included Marie Jamet. On December 8, 1842, religious vows of chastity and obedience were made for one year by the little community at St. Servan.

As the number of their guests, of both sexes, increased, the hospitallers ingeniously planned their work, that indolence might not be encouraged in their midst. Great care was necessarily exercised in the expenditures for fire and light, and the sisters saw to the food provision of the poor before partaking, however frugally, of any food themselves.

On February 7, 1844, the Servants of the Poor pronounced the simple vows of poverty and hospitality, as they had already made those of chastity and obedience.   Though knowing the vows were temporary and tentative, they were pledged to the service of God and the poor, and were encouraged as a Community by the admit‐tance of a first postulant. At this time they took amongst themselves names as religious, Marie Jamet, chosen Superior that Jeanne Jugan might be freer for outside work, becoming Marie Augustine de la Compassion; Jeanne, Marie de la Croix; Virginie Tredaniel, Marie Thérèse de Jésus; and Madeleine Bourges, Marie Joseph. Regarding themselves as religious hospitallers, they then changed their title of "Servants of the Poor," to "Sisters of the Poor," which they had indeed become.

In 1845 Jeanne Jugan was awarded by the French Academy the first Montyon prize of virtue, of 3,000 francs. The celebrated Dupin, appointed for the oration for the occasion, in concluding his speech said: "There remains a problem which no doubt presents itself to the mind of each one of you. How it is possible that Jeanne could provide the expense of such a house? How can I explain it? Provi‐dence is great.   Jeanne is indefatigable, Jeanne is eloquent; Jeanne has prayer, Jeanne has tears, Jeanne has toil, Jeanne has her basket which she ever brings back full. Saintly woman! The Academy places in that basket the sum of which it can dispose at discretion; it decrees you an award of 3,000 francs."   And Jeanne used her 3,000 francs to finish building a new house for her poor.

In 1846, with the opening of a small hospice at Rennes, the exten‐sion of the work of the Little Sisters of the Poor began.

The year 1852 brought the episcopal decree of approbation, by the bishop of Rennes, to the hospitaller Congregation, and that year also marked the opening of houses in Germany and Belgium. Upon the request of the Empress Eugénie the Little Sisters began their third hospice in Paris, adding to the achievements of this epochal period in the history of the Congregation.

On July 9, 1854, the sisters saw their Community raised to the dignity of a religious Congregation approved by the Holy See. In the thirty‐six houses, hearts were overwhelmed with joy, and the old people understood that the Church, in adopting the hospitaller work, became their mother in a special manner. Two years later, on January 9th, responding to an appeal from the Superior General,

Napoleon issued an Imperial Order authorizing legally the institution of the Little Sisters of the Poor, and giving it a right to civil life.

To procure this recognition, necessary for the protection of the Congregation, a statement of the assets and debits of the Motherhouse was asked. The civil administration questioned the account, as the assets of the Little Sisters presented no income to serve for the food and maintenance of the sisters. Explanations followed that there was no income to present, that the sisters in every establishment—in number in proportion to the number of old people, were nourished, like their charges, from the collections and leavings, and that their clothing also came from donations, a benefactor often providing material and sometimes garments. It was further—and satisfactorily—explained that the sisters in the novitiate did not share in the charity, their maintenance there being supplied from the dowries brought by the candidates, and that house expenses were lessened by the employment of the healthy in the homes, according to their respective crafts. In the debits of the Little Sisters, it was detailed, there could be no mention of daily expenses, as they were provided for, day by day, by means of alms and collections. The issuance of the Imperial Decree showed the final satisfaction of the administration.

A necessary outcome of the rapid growth of the Congregation was the choice of a place for a permanent Motherhouse and novitiate. A lucrative estate, "La Tour," in the parish of St. Pern, was procured, and on April 1, 1856, the Little Sisters of the Poor took possession of this property, between Rennes and Dinan, where now, as La Tour St. Joseph, St. Pern, Ille-et-Vilaine, France, the General Motherhouse and novitiate of the Congregation are maintained, though novitiates are also conducted at central houses of the Congregation, in the various countries of Europe, Asia, Africa, and in North and South America.

The Congregation of the Little Sisters of the Poor began its labor in America with the advent of a colony of "Little Sisters" to the United States, in 1868. The Right Rev. John Loughlin, D.D., Bishop of Brooklyn, welcomed the seven sisters on their arrival from France, and became the first benefactor of their work by encouraging the immediate erection of their home in his diocese and in the episcopal city.

In their new home, which comprised three rented houses in Brooklyn, the Little Sisters of the Poor received their first pensioner on September 20, 1868, and then, as Jeanne Jugan had done in St. Servan, the Little Sisters, with Mother Marie de la Conception as temporary Superior, began their work in the United States, as basket in hand, they went forth to secure provisions for the needs of the first, and the other pensioners soon admitted to the home.

MOTHER MARIE DE LA CROIX (JEANNE JUGAN)
Foundress in 1839 of the Little Sisters of the Poor,
and Mother Marie de la Conception

As previously arranged at the Motherhouse for the introduction of the work into the United States, a second colony of sisters from La Tour St. Joseph was sent out, with Cincinnati as its destination. Mrs. Sarah Peter, a distinguished and charitable resident of that city, had interested the archbishop, the Most Rev. John B. Purcell, D.D., in the work of the Congregation, and among the last activities of the aged woman in behalf of the establishment in Cincinnati of many of the pioneer communities of religious orders of women, was the use of her influence and her material encouragement for the success of the work of the Little Sisters of the Poor, who arrived in Cincinnati on October 14th. Their first home in that city was near the Cathedral, in a building formerly used as a school.

Before the close of 1868, the Motherhouse in Brittany sent its third colony to the United States. New Orleans was the chosen site for the opening of a southern house. On their arrival there, it was not the greatness and beauty of the city, nor the immense river, nor the tropical flowers which appealed to the Little Sisters, but the name on the house awaiting them: "Home of St. Joseph."

The charitable women of New Orleans had previously undertaken work there for widows and old people, however the results were not satisfactory, and the institution was entrusted to the Little Sisters of the Poor, that they might transform it into a home for the aged poor, and maintain it according to their own system. The Home of St. Joseph, special patron of the Congregation, became a true home, and a gratification to the people and to the Most Rev. J. M. Odin, D.D., who had welcomed the sisters to his archdiocese. In appreciation of the coming of the Little Sisters, the city not only paved, at its own expense, the street which gave access to the establishment transferred to the sisters, but also made a generous donation for the necessary repairs and improvements of the house.

In April of the following year, while a committee was arranging for the purchase of property for them, a group of Little Sisters, sent from the Motherhouse in France, opened a home in a rented house on Calvert Street in Baltimore.

The next month St. Louis received the fifth American colony; in August Philadelphia welcomed the sisters, and one month later Louisville, too, welcomed a group of the hospitallers. Within a year seven houses were established in the United States, and to labor in each a sufficient number of able sisters, of various nationalities, had come from France.

The work attracted the sympathies of all classes and all races, and the homes were filling with old people, without distinction as to creed or nationality. The year 1870 saw the continuance of the work of the opening of homes. Boston, interested by the clergy and stirred by the press, over the work of the Congregation, furnished an establishment for a home. Almost at the same time the Little Sisters opened a home for the aged poor in Cleveland, Ohio, where the Right Rev. Amadeus Rappe, D.D., who had given for their use a house which would only accommodate a few besides the sisters, when it was found necessary to purchase property, resigning his episcopal see that year, gave the sisters four thousand dollars toward their purpose.

A house, opened in September in New York City, completed the number of new establishments for 1870. Two years later, homes had been opened in Washington, Albany and Pittsburgh, totalling thirteen of the present fifty-two in the United States. Vocations had come, along with the foundations, and comprehension of the great work being done by the sisters was evidenced by the ever ready generosity of the people, who had learned to welcome the opportunity of true charity occasioned by the Little Sister on her errand of providing for those sharing the shelter of the home in which she labored among the aged and infirm, with heavenly patience and kindness.

U. S. NOVITIATE OF THE LITTLE SISTERS OF THE POOR,
QUEENS, LONG ISLAND, NEW YORK

According to the Constitutions, the houses of the Little Sisters of the Poor are not allowed endowments, fixed incomes or regular allowances from the civil administration, but must depend entirely on the charities of the faithful and the alms collected by the sisters. Generous offers have at times been made the sisters, but acceptance of anything which might violate the spirit and the essence of the hospitaller Congregation was sacrificed as the lesser sacrifice in their ultimate interests in behalf of God's poor for whom they labor.

With the Little Sisters of the Poor, devoting themselves in the closest manner, by the vow of hospitality, to the service of the aged and ailing poor, old age begins at sixty; from this age upward the needy are admitted to their homes, and there are inmates of eighty and ninety years, and occasionally centenarians. In the homes, nearly all similar in architecture as in construction, the sections for the men and for the women have their separate sitting rooms, yards, dormitories and dining rooms, and for both a side in the chapel is designated.

The Little Sisters give themselves up to the work of hospitality. With them there are no servants, no paid employees. They wait on the inmates and share among themselves the work of the house.

No distinction exists among them; all are equally the Little Sisters of the Poor, alike in title, alike in rights, alike in duties.

Each house is directed by a Superior called the Good Mother, helped by a Sister Assistant and by a Sister Counsel. A number of houses constitute a province, presided over by a Good Mother Provincial, aided by her Council. The houses and the provinces are in turn dependent upon the Motherhouse, which has as its head a Superior General and six Assistants, elected by the Chapter, which is held every six years.

The probation of the postulants in the Congregation begins, ordinarily, in the nearest local house. Here they acquaint themselves with the various duties of hospitality, and make a trial of the Little Sisters' mode of life. If they are contented, and suited to the life they are then received into the novitiate, where by degrees they receive both religious and professional training.

Trials, innumerable, unrecorded, unheralded, must ever have been the lot of the Little Sisters in their work courageously done, when as strangers they entered strange lands, and amidst strange people proceeded to the building and personal maintenance of their homes for the destitute aged poor.

The history of their work—throughout the world—and of their pensioners, replete with anecdotes and accounts of Providential help in times of dire want and perplexity, is a mystery supreme which can be fathomed only by those who know the great faith and trust of the Little Sisters of the Poor, and the power, at the Divine Throne, of their unfailing patron, St. Joseph.

SUMMARY

Little Sisters of the Poor.
Founded in France in 1839.
Established in the United States in 1868.
Papal Approbation of Rules, March 1, 1879, by Pope Leo XIII.
Habit: The habit is of black serge, held in at the waist by a woolen cord. A black merino kerchief crossed over the chest, and a white neckerchief are worn, as well a white bonnet, fastened under the chin, and a headband on the forehead.
Approximate number in Community in United States, 1075.
Active in the conducting and maintenance of homes for the aged poor in the archdioceses of Baltimore, Boston, Chicago, Cincinnati, Milwaukee, New Orleans, New York, Philadelphia, St. Louis, St. Paul and San Francisco, and in the dioceses of Albany, Brooklyn, Cleveland, Denver, Detroit, Grand Rapids, Hartford, Indianapolis, Kansas City, Louisville, Mobile, Los Angeles and San Diego, Nashville, Newark, Pittsburgh, Providence, Richmond, Savannah and Wilmington.

United States Provincial houses, Eastern Provincialate, Bushwick and De Kalb Avenues, Brooklyn, New York (Diocese of Brooklyn); *Western Provincialate,* North Fullerton and Sheffield Avenues, Chicago, Illinois (Archdiocese of Chicago); *Southern Provincialate,* Preston and Valley Streets, Baltimore, Maryland (Archdiocese of Baltimore).

United States Novitiate, Queens, Long Island, New York. (Diocese of Brooklyn.)

POOR HANDMAIDS OF JESUS CHRIST*

1868

THE Congregation of the "Ancilla Domini" Sisters, the Poor Handmaids of Jesus Christ, as they are more generally known, owes its foundation to the zealous charity of Catherine Kasper, of Dernbach, Germany.

Born of humble parentage and living a life of utter simplicity, Catherine longed from the depths of her heart to relieve the sufferings and hardships of the needy. With neither wealth nor influence hers, but with good will and charity, her strong heart knew no obstacles to the accomplishment of good. As she grew older, in addition to helping her family, she visited the sick and afflicted, nursing, or giving any needed aid in cooking, housework, or care of children.

Several young women, attracted by her loving charity, soon joined her in her work of nursing and caring for the sick, and Catherine, desiring to devote her life formally to the honor of God and the service of the poor and sick, appealed to the bishop of Limburg for advice as to the fulfillment of her aim.

Seeing the efforts of the little band of charity workers, the bishop sanctioned for the devout young leader and her companions, community life, and continued united devotion to the care of the sick and poor. In 1851 a little house, which had been built for them by the kind people of Dernbach, was blessed by the bishop, and the habit and veil intended to distinguish the five young women as Poor Handmaids of Jesus Christ, was bestowed on them.

The brave Superior, Mother Mary, as she was called, and her earnest co-workers, fast multiplying in number, never faltered in their purpose—the furtherance of God's honor through devotion to His sick and poor. When the urgent necessity of caring for and instructing orphans was borne in upon Mother Mary, she took upon herself and her community the responsibility of their upbringing, and since 1854 this work has been among the duties and tasks of the Poor Handmaids of Jesus Christ, as the Congregation has spread to Holland, England and the United States.

Upon the invitation of the Right Rev. John Luers, D.D., of the diocese of Fort Wayne, and through the efforts of the Rev. Edward Koenig, pastor of St. Paul's Church, Fort Wayne, Indiana, the first

*From data and material supplied by the Poor Handmaids of Jesus Christ, Convent Ancilla Domini, Retreat St. Amalia, Donaldson, Ind.

representatives of the Congregation came to the United States on August 30, 1868.

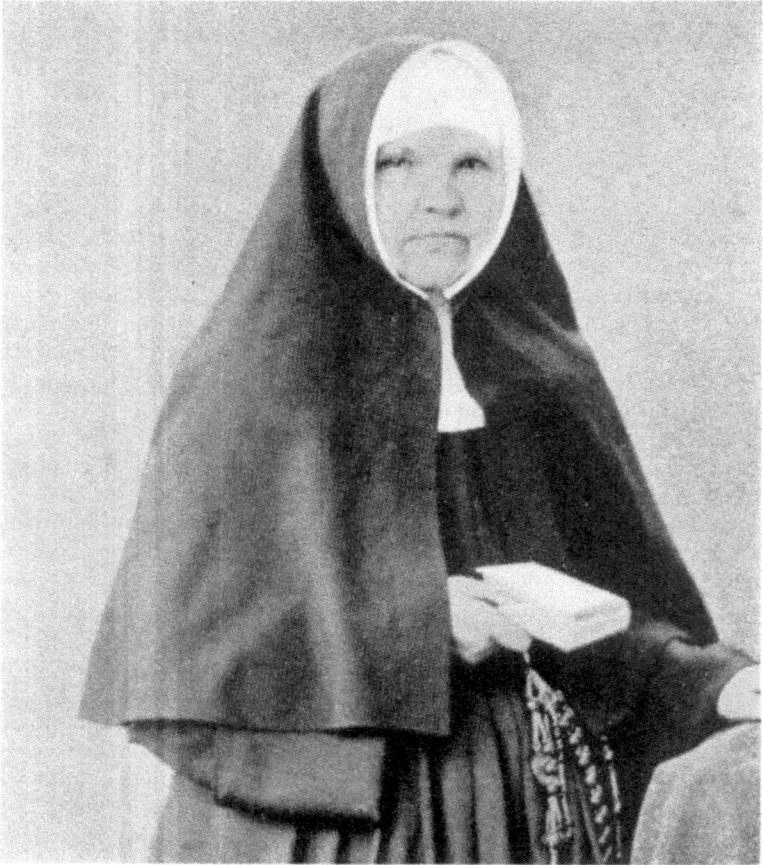

MOTHER MARY CATHERINE KASPER
Foundress in 1851 of the Poor Handmaids of Jesus Christ

The first mission entrusted to them was in the little village, Hesse Cassel, Indiana. The activities of the Poor Handmaids were gradually extended from here beyond Indiana, and throughout the country they devoted themselves to their ordained work, augmented by teaching.

Associated with the many large and prominent hospitals which the sisters have established and conduct, standard training schools for nurses are maintained. Most recent among the new institutions of the Congregation is St. Catherine's Hospital in East Chicago, Indiana. The new hospital, which is now owned by the sisters, was built under the joint auspices of the Ancilla Domini Sisters, under the direction of Mother Tabitha, the Provincial Superior, and the Manufacturers' Association of East Chicago. The Right Rev. John F. Noll, D.D., Bishop of Fort Wayne, presided at the formal opening of the hospital.

MOTHER MARY FIRMATA
Superior General in 1925 of the Poor Handmaids of Jesus Christ

The largest orphanage conducted by the Community is the Angel Guardian Orphanage of Chicago, noted as the first institution of its kind to have adopted the cottage system

CONVENT ANCILLA DOMINI, DONALDSON, INDIANA

in order to bring the atmosphere of home to its homeless charges.

In addition to their other work, the Ancilla Domini Sisters conduct catechism classes in Gary, Indiana, where the pupils in the public schools are allowed to attend class periods of instruction in their respective religious beliefs.

In 1922 the new Motherhouse of the Poor Handmaids of Jesus Christ at Donaldson, Indiana, was completed and occupied. In addition to the novitiate and normal school, there is conducted there an accredited high school open to girls who are too young to enter the Community, but who aspire to this end, and therefore wish to complete their secular education with the Poor Handmaids of Jesus Christ.

SUMMARY

Poor Handmaids of Jesus Christ.
Legal Title: The Ancilla Domini Sisters.
Founded in Germany in 1851.
Papal Approbation of Rules in 1890, by Pope Leo XIII.
Established in the United States in 1868.
Habit: The habit is black, with a black veil covering a white cap, on a starched linen band encircling the face. A white linen collar and forehead band are worn.
Approximate number in Community in United States, 650.
Active in educational, hospital and charitable work in the archdioceses of Chicago and St. Paul, and in the dioceses of Belleville, Fort Wayne, Springfield in Illinois, and Superior.
United States Motherhouse and Novitiate, Convent Ancilla Domini, Retreat St. Amalia, Donaldson, Indiana.

SISTERS OF ST. ANN*

1870

THE Congregation of the Sisters of St. Ann, which began its work in the United States in 1870, was founded in 1848 at Vaudreuil, Quebec, by Marie-Esther Blondin, a native of Terrebonne, in the Province of Quebec.

From her earliest years Mademoiselle Blondin, the third child in a family of twelve, showed a marked inclination to the religious life, and when she asked her parents to allow her the advantages of a convent education with the Sisters of the Congréga- tion de Notre Dame at their school which had been established at Ter- rebonne in 1826, they generously made sacri- fices to do so.

In time Mademoiselle Blondin was admitted to the novitiate of the Con- grégation de Notre Dame, and given the name *Soeur Sainte- Christine.* However, ill- health forced her for a time to relinquish her aspirations to become a religious.

Recovering her health, and having been con- vinced that she was called to devote her life to the education of chil-

MOTHER MARY ANNE (1809-1890)
Foundress of the Sisters of St. Ann

dren in a new institute, Mademoiselle Blondin was allowed, by the Right Rev. Ignace Bourget, Bishop of Montreal, to begin community

*From data and material supplied by the Sisters of St. Ann, Lachine, P.Q., Canada.

life with four companions, who with her, as Sisters of St. Ann, took their vows in the parish church of Vaudreuil on September 8, 1850.

Eight years later, the Community, which has since received papal approbation, had increased sufficiently to cross the continent and open schools and hospitals in Victoria, British Columbia.

Extending beyond the many Canada dioceses where they estab-lished mission houses, sisters of the Congregation began their work in the United States in 1870, when they took charge of schools in New York state.

ST. ANN'S CONVENT, MARLBORO, MASSACHUSETTS

Following their initial work in the country, the sisters, from their Motherhouse, which is maintained at Lachine, Canada, in the archdiocese of Montreal, were sent into New England, where they engaged in parochial school work in parishes largely composed of French-Canadians. Among the many schools conducted by the Sisters of St. Ann in the United States is St. Ann's Academy at Marlboro, Massachusetts, where the Congregation has established a Provincial house for its more than three hundred members active in educational work in this country in the archdiocese of Boston and the dioceses of Albany, Providence and Springfield.

United States Provincial house, St. Ann's Academy, Marlboro, Massachusetts. (Archdiocese of Boston.)

SISTERS OF THE IMMACULATE HEART*

1871

RANKING as the pioneer teaching order in southern California is the Californian Institute of the Sisters of the Immaculate Heart.

Founded on July 2, 1848, in Olot, Spain, by the Rev. Joaquin Masmitja, for the special work of the education of young women, the Community made its first foundation in the United States at Gilroy, California, in 1871, with Mother Raymunda Cremadell as Superior.

The introduction of the Congregation to the United States was in response to an invitation extended by the Right Rev. Thaddeus Amat, C.M., D.D., of Los Angeles, California.

Continuing the special work for which the Institute was founded, Immaculate Heart College was established in 1906 in Hollywood, at the site of the Motherhouse which had been erected there. Mother Mary Genevieve is Superior General of the Congregation.

SUMMARY

Sisters of the Immaculate Heart.
Founded in Spain in 1848.
Papal Approbation of Rules in 1907, by Pope Pius X.
Established in the United States in 1871.
Habit: The habit is blue, with a black scapular, white coif and black veil.
Approximate number in Community in United States, 160.
Active in educational work in the dioceses of Los Angeles and San Diego, and Monterey-Fresno.
United States Motherhouse and Novitiate, 5515 Franklin Avenue, Hollywood, California. (Diocese of Los Angeles and San Diego.)

*From data supplied by the Sisters of the Immaculate Heart, Immaculate Heart College, Hollywood, Calif.

SISTERS OF THE HOLY FAMILY*

1872

THE Society of the Sisters of the Holy Family, which engages in catechetical and social service work in California, was founded in San Francisco in 1872 by Miss Elizabeth Armer, who had been devoting herself to catechism teaching, the organizing of sodalities and sewing classes, and caring for the children of working women.

The Very Rev. J. J. Prendergast directed the formation by Miss Armer of this group of women, who as religious would perpetuate her work, which at that time was considered charitable, though in the daily caring for the children of working women, Sister Mary Dolores, as Miss Armer was known, laid well the foundation of the more modernly-designated day-nursery work, a work which affords the religious an opportunity of contact not only with the child but also with the tired mother, who cannot but respond to her zealous efforts.

Maintaining their headquarters at San Francisco, the Sisters of the Holy Family, now numbering approximately a hundred and seventy-five, are active in catechetical and social service work in the archdiocese of San Francisco and in the dioceses of Los Angeles and San Diego and Monterey-Fresno.

Motherhouse and Novitiate, Hayes and Fillmore Streets, San Francisco, California. (Archdiocese of San Francisco.)

---

*From data supplied by the Sisters of the Holy Family, San Francisco, Calif., and from the Catholic Encyclopedia and the Official Catholic Year Book, 1928.

SISTERS OF THE MOST HOLY SACRAMENT*

1872

THE Congregation of the Sisters of Perpetual Adoration of the Blessed Sacrament, or properly, Sisters of the Most Holy Sacrament, was founded by Blessed Mechtilde de Baar, at Paris in 1654.

The Thirty Years War was then ravaging all Europe, and the pious queen of France, Anne of Austria, touched at the widespread misery, addressed herself to a saintly priest of St. Sulpice, the Rev. M. Picoté, begging him to make a vow, in her name, of whatever he judged would appease the wrath of God, and remove the scourge from her country.

After fervent prayer, Father Picoté came to the conclusion that nothing would more glorify God and draw down His mercy than the foundation of an Order of women who would, day and night, render Him homage of adoration, praise, thanksgiving and needed reparation in the most Holy Sacrament of the Altar.

Blessed Mother Mechtilde was entrusted by the queen, who aided her in the work, with the foundation of the first convents of the Order, and on the 25th of March, 1654, the Perpetual Adoration of the Blessed Sacrament—since extended throughout Europe, in many convents of the Community—was begun.

In 1851, the Rev. Aloysius Faller, wishing to propagate devotion to the Blessed Sacrament, asked and obtained sisters of this Order from a convent at Rosenheim, Alsace, for Bellemagny, Htl. Alsace, Ht. Rhin, and from here the Superior General and United States foundress, Mother M. Augustine, was sent in 1872, with three other sisters, to establish the Community in America.

Primarily the Order is devoted to the Perpetual Adoration of the Blessed Sacrament, and day and night two or more sisters succeed each other every hour before the tabernacle. In the Motherhouse, or in a community where the sisters are numerous enough to keep the adoration by fours, they may, with the permission of the ordinary of the diocese, have the perpetual solemn exposition of the Blessed Sacrament. During their hours of adoration, besides offering reparation for sacrilege, the sisters pray for all mankind, particularly for the exaltation of the Church, for the sovereign pontiff and the clergy,

---

*From data and material supplied by the Sisters of the Most Holy Sacrament, 2321 Marais Street, New Orleans, La.

and for the conversion of sinners and infidels, as well as for their benefactors and for the poor souls in purgatory.

The secondary object of the Congregation is the education of children in academies and parochial schools, and the care of orphans. The sisters also devote time to the making of vestments and all kinds of Church articles.

In 1872 the Most Rev. N. J. Perche, Archbishop of New Orleans, first established these sisters in the parish of the Annunciation at New Orleans, where they assumed charge of the parochial school. In 1879 they also opened St. Agnes' Academy for boarders and day scholars. The chapel adjoining the Motherhouse and novitiate was erected in 1894, and the following year the school building next to the convent was completed.

The convent at Pascagoula, Mississippi, in the diocese of Natchez, to which an academy and parochial school are attached, was founded in October, 1882. Situated near the sea coast, this institution serves as a summer resort—ideal because of the fresh sea breezes, the strengthening sea baths, and the tang of the pine woods, for the sisters and the children who pass their vacations there.

In 1890 a convent was founded in Gretna, Louisiana, a suburb of New Orleans. Here the sisters conduct a boarding school for little boys from six to twelve years of age, and teach in parochial schools.

At Breaux-Bridge, Louisiana, in 1891, a convent was established, on the banks of the Bayou Tèche, and another foundation was made in New Orleans, in 1899, on St. Maurice's Avenue, in the garden district of the city. In 1900 a convent was established in Crowley, Louisiana, followed by the opening of an academy and parochial schools.

Further extending, in the south, the Perpetual Adoration of the Blessed Sacrament, in the old historic city of Pensacola, Florida, opposite St. Rosa's Island, where the first mass on American soil is said to have been celebrated, a convent of the Order was established in 1907, and, as supplementary to practically all its foundations, an academy is maintained, and the sisters teach in parish schools.

SUMMARY

Sisters of the Most Holy Sacrament.
Founded in France in 1654.
Established in the United States in 1872.
Approximate number in Community in United States, 200.
Engaged in contemplative life and active in educational work in the archdiocese of New Orleans and in the dioceses of Lafayette, Mobile and Natchez.
Motherhouse and Novitiate, Perpetual Adoration Convent, 2321 Marais Street, New Orleans, Louisiana. (Archdiocese of New Orleans.)

SISTERS OF PROVIDENCE (HOLYOKE, MASSACHUSETTS)*

1873

THE Sisters of Providence with their Motherhouse at Holyoke, Massachusetts, forming a diocesan Congregation under the direct jurisdiction of the bishop of Springfield, were founded as such in the year 1892, with the Right Rev. Thomas D. Beaven, second bishop of Springfield, as ecclesiastical superior.

The work of the Community had been inaugurated in Massachusetts in 1873, when Sisters of Charity of Providence were sent from Providence Motherhouse at Kingston, Ontario, to open a mission in Holyoke. Coming to the diocese at the instance of the Right Rev. Patrick T. O'Reilly, D.D., its first bishop, they began the charitable work of caring for orphans, and soon afterward of ministering to the sick in hospitals opened at Holyoke and Worcester, and in time at Springfield, Pittsfield, and other cities of the diocese.

Following their establishment as an independent Congregation, and under the efficient planning of Bishop Beaven, Brightside, the Motherhouse center of the Sisters of Providence was developed at Holyoke, and there was erected there Holy Family Institute, a home for boys, Bethlehem Infant Asylum and Beaven-Kelly Home for

SISTER MARY MONICA
A Sister of Providence

aged men. Homes for aged women, homes for girls, and day nurseries are now also conducted in the diocese by the Sisters of Providence, who, in addition to directing these institutions, as well as hospitals, training schools for nurses, and a sanitarium, Greylock Rest, at Adams, Massachusetts, engage in parochial school work.

*From data supplied by the Sisters of Providence, Holyoke, Mass., and from the Catholic Encyclopedia and the Official Catholic Directory.

The provisions of the Rule of the Sisters of Providence of the diocese of Springfield permit them to undertake any work which the bishop of the diocese may see fit to entrust to them.

SUMMARY

Sisters of Providence (Holyoke, Massachusetts).
Established in the United States in 1873.
Approximate number in Community, 400.
Active in educational, hospital, charitable and social service work in the diocese of Springfield.
Motherhouse, Convent of Our Lady of Victory, Brightside, Holyoke, Massachusetts. (Diocese of Springfield.)
Novitiate, Westfield, Massachusetts. (Diocese of Springfield.)

SISTERS OF CHRISTIAN CHARITY*

1873

THE Congregation of the Sisters of Christian Charity, Daughters of the Blessed Virgin Mary of the Immaculate Conception, was founded in 1849 at Paderborn, Westphalia, Germany, by Pauline von Mallinckrodt, a daughter of the renowned statesman, Detmar von Mallinckrodt, and Bernardine von Hartmann.

MOTHER PAULINE VON MALLINCKRODT (1817-1881)
Foundress of the Sisters of Christian Charity

Pauline was born June 3, 1817, at Minden in Westphalia, the eldest of four children who were all given an excellent religious and liberal education. Sacrificing the splendors of a brilliant career which

*From data and material supplied by the Sisters of Christian Charity, Maria Immaculata Convent, Wilmette, Ill.

her high social rank offered, she resolved to become a religious, and to devote herself to the Christian education of youth.

Complying with the requests of her ecclesiastical superiors, Pauline, with three associates, laid the foundation of a new Order, which adopted the significant title, "Sisters of Christian Charity"; the additional name, "Daughters of the Blessed Virgin Mary of the Immaculate Conception" was later conferred on the Sisterhood by the Sovereign Pontiff, Pius IX.

The sisters, favored by both civil and ecclesiastical authorities, were laboring fruitfully until the year 1871, when the so-called *Kulturkampf* broke out, with its host of attending evils. When the

MARIA IMMACULATA CONVENT, WILMETTE, ILLINOIS

"May Laws" of 1871 compelled all the Catholic teaching orders to abandon their activities, the Sisters of Christian Charity were also confronted with the alternative of renouncing either their calling or their habit. The far-sighted foundress did not lose courage, but with the intrepid spirit and zeal of an apostle and missionary, directed her ambition beyond the seas in quest of a new field of labor.

The Church in the United States was at the time greatly in need of religious teachers, and here the exiled Community received a welcome, on its arrival in 1873. In response to the request of the Rev. Father Bogaerts, rector of St. Henry's Church in New Orleans, a convent and parochial school were established in that city.

The Right Rev. William O'Hara, D.D., first bishop of Scranton, interested in the establishment of the Order in his diocese, invited the Sisters of Christian Charity to found a Provincial house there. He expressed the desire of placing all the German parochial schools of his diocese in charge of the sisters, and soon afterward arrangements were made for the opening of a parochial school and St. Ann's Academy in Wilkes-Barre.

A high eminence in the eastern part of Wilkes-Barre, then known as Park Hill, was chosen as the most suitable site for the erection

MALLINCKRODT CONVENT, MENDHAM, NEW JERSEY

of the Provincial house, and all preliminary arrangements for the construction of the building having been completed, Mother Pauline and a companion sister who had come to the United States returned to Europe.

Mother Mathilde, who was appointed Provincial Superior in the United States, and who was well fitted for the leadership of the Community in the New World, may be looked upon, because of her association with Mother Pauline, as the co-foundress of the Congregation.

In 1878 the newly erected Mallinckrodt Convent in Wilkes-Barre, became the general American Provincial Motherhouse and novitiate of the Community. For more central location this was transferred, in 1916, to Maria Immaculata Convent, in Wilmette, Illinois, in the archdiocese of Chicago, and was so maintained there until its recognition as the official western Provincial Motherhouse and novitiate, with the establishment of a corresponding eastern house in Mendham, New Jersey, in the diocese of Newark.

A normal and training school for the young sisters at the Motherhouse, now known as Mallinckrodt College, which was incorporated in Wilmette in 1918 for the higher education of women, is now recognized by several state departments of education as a junior college.

The establishments of the Congregation of the Sisters of Christian Charity, Daughters of the Blessed Virgin Mary of the Immaculate Conception, are all affiliated with the original Motherhouse at Paderborn, and are visited at regular intervals by both the Mother Provincial and the Mother General. The close union existing in the Order, despite its widespread activities, preserves and transmits in the Community the spirit of the first foundation, in all its vigor and purity.

SUMMARY

Sisters of Christian Charity, Daughters of the Blessed Virgin Mary of the Immaculate Conception.

Founded in Germany in 1849.

Established in the United States in 1873.

Papal Approbation of Rules, February 4, 1888, by Pope Leo XIII.

Approximate number in Community in United States, 920.

Active in educational and charitable work, *Eastern Provincialate*, in the archdioceses of Baltimore, New York and Philadelphia, and in the dioceses of Brooklyn, Harrisburg, Newark and Scranton; *Motherhouse and Novitiate*, Mallinckrodt Convent, Mendham, New Jersey (Diocese of Newark); *Western Provincialate*, in the archdioceses of Chicago, Cincinnati, New Orleans, St. Louis and St. Paul, and in the dioceses of Belleville, Detroit and Sioux City; *Motherhouse and Novitiate*, Maria Immaculata Convent, Wilmette, Illinois (Archdiocese of Chicago).

SISTERS OF THE PRÉSENTATION DE MARIE*

1873

THE Congregation of the Présentation de Marie was founded by the Ven. Marie Rivier in 1796, at Bourg, St. Andéol, Ardèche, France, the intention of the holy foundress being that the Congregation should devote itself principally to the education of youth.

In 1853 a foundation was made in Canada, in Marieville, in the Province of Quebec, and here the sisters engaged in educational work for girls. Later this community established its Provincial Motherhouse at St. Hyacinthe, in the Province of Quebec, and from this Convent of the *Présentation de Marie* sisters of the Congregation first came to the United States in 1873, beginning their mission activities in Glens Falls, New York.

The habit of the sisters is black with a white coif, black silk head-dress, and a silver cross on a neck cord.

MOTHER M. ST. DAVID, OF THE SISTERS
OF THE PRÉSENTATION DE MARIE

The activities of the more than five hundred Sisters of the Presentation, now in the United States, include educational work in the dioceses of Burlington, Manchester, Portland, Providence and Springfield.

*From data and material supplied by the Sisters of the Présentation de Marie, St. Hyacinthe, P.Q., Canada.

SISTERS OF THE IMMACULATE CONCEPTION*

1873

THE Congregation of the Sisters of the Immaculate Conception was founded in the year 1873 at Labadieville, Louisiana, by the Rev. Cyprian Venissat. Father Cyprian was impelled to thus provide religious teachers for the children of families still suffering impoverishment, the aftermath of the Civil War.

Though continuing their school work in Labadieville, the sisters have established their Motherhouse and novitiate in New Orleans, and are engaged in parochial school work there, and in missions in the archdiocese and in the diocese of Lafayette. There are approximately forty-five sisters in the Community.

Motherhouse and Novitiate, Convent of the Immaculate Conception, 3037 Dauphine Street, New Orleans, Louisiana. (Archdiocese of New Orleans.)

*From the Catholic Encyclopedia and the Official Catholic Year Book, 1928.

SISTERS OF CHARITY OF OUR LADY, MOTHER OF MERCY*

1873

HE Congregation known as the Sisters of Charity of Our Lady, Mother of Mercy, was founded in Holland in 1832, by the Rev. John Zwijsen, before his consecration as bishop, aided by Mary M. Leijsen, for the purpose of engaging in all works of charity, and especially in the work of the education of children in parish schools.

In 1853 Bishop Zwijsen, the founder of the Congregation, was made Archbishop of Utrecht and Primate of Holland, being the first to fill this position in nearly three hundred years. The Congregation of his own establishing immediately supplied the great need in the diocese for the education of girls in Catholic institutions. Fresh impetus was given the religious Community, and with it began the extension of its labors to other countries.

On October 4, 1873, in response to the invitation of the Right Rev. F. P. MacFarland, D.D., Bishop of Hartford, a community of the Sisters of Charity of Our Lady, Mother of Mercy, came to the United States. The sisters, under Mother M. Carola as Superior, established their Motherhouse in Baltic, in eastern Connecticut, and at once assumed charge of the nearby parochial schools.

In later years, Holy Family Academy, a boarding school for young ladies, was opened at Baltic, and the educational standards of this school have been recognized by the Connecticut State Board of Education and by the Board of Regents of New York.

A SISTER OF CHARITY OF OUR LADY, MOTHER OF MERCY

The General Motherhouse of the Congregation is at Tilburg, in the diocese of Bois-le-duc, Holland, Mother M. Christine being Superior General. The government of the Community in the United States

*From data supplied by the Sisters of Charity of Our Lady, Mother of Mercy, Convent of the Holy Family, Baltic, Conn.

is under Mother M. Francis as Superior, assisted by Sister M. Evangelista and Sister M. Lucice, all residing at the local Motherhouse.

Consistent with a special vow taken by the Congregation, the sisters perform any charitable work suitable for religious women.

In 1897, upon the request of the Right Rev. Bishop Wulfing, the General Motherhouse sent a community of sisters to take charge of the leper colony at Parimaribo, South America. Here the sisters care for hundreds of these unfortunates, lessening their miseries and sufferings by physical and religious ministrations. Everything is done to alleviate the sad condition of the victims of this malady. Those well enough to be around are given some useful and interesting occupation; the children are taught various trades, and the sisters are frequently consoled by the resignation in suffering and the edifying deaths of their leper patients.

SUMMARY

Sisters of Charity of Our Lady, Mother of Mercy.
Founded in Holland in 1832.
Papal Approbation of Rules, December 18, 1843, by Pope Gregory XVI.
Established in the United States in 1873.
Habit: The habit is of black serge, with a black veil and scapular, and a white coif and guimpe. A silver cross is worn on the breast.
Approximate number in Community in United States, 120.
Active in educational, hospital and charitable work in the diocese of Hartford.
United States Motherhouse and Novitiate, Convent of the Holy Family, Baltic, Connecticut. (Diocese of Hartford.)

SISTERS OF NOTRE DAME*

HE Congregation of the Sisters of Notre Dame, with Provincial houses in the United States in the cities of Cleveland and Toledo, Ohio, and Covington, Kentucky, owes its origin to the Rev. Theodore Elting, a zealous priest of Coesfeld, Germany.

To three Sisters of Notre Dame from Amersfoert, Holland, who had received their religious training and the rule of Blessed Julie Billiart at the fountain source of the Order in Namur, Father Elting confided the conventual training of Hildagonda Wollbring and Lisette Kuehling, two devout young women of Coesfeld. On October 1, 1850, the religious habit was conferred on these two candidates, who as Sister Aloysia and Sister Ignatia became the first members of the new Community, whose chief activity was to be the education and instruction of the young.

The number of novices and sisters rapidly increasing, a normal school for the education of teachers was opened. In a short time pastors of different parishes in Westphalia and Rhenish-Prussia applied for sisters to teach the children of their schools. As the official examinations passed by the religious proved them competent to teach, the Prussian government readily consented to their appointment, but with the proviso that they should be independent of foreign authority. The severance of all relationship with the community at Amersfoert, Holland, followed this ruling, and the Sisters of Notre Dame then in 1855 established the convent at Coesfeld as the Motherhouse of the Congregation, which continued to follow the rule of Blessed Julie Billiart.

CLEVELAND, OHIO
1874

With the breaking out of the *Kulturkampf* in Germany in 1871, the Sisters of Notre Dame were among the first to suffer the necessity of seeking new fields for their religious labors.

At the invitation of the Right Rev. Richard Gilmour, D.D., Bishop of Cleveland, upon the suggestion of the Rev. Father Westerholt, pastor of St. Peter's Church in that episcopal city, the Congregation made there its initial foundation in the United States.

Mother M. Chrysostom Heck, who in 1872, upon the death of

---

*From data and material supplied by the Sisters of Notre Dame, Notre Dame Provincial Convents, Cleveland, Ohio; Toledo, Ohio; and Covington, Ky.

Mother M. Anna, the first Superior General, had been elected her successor, accompanied the first party of sisters to the United States, and with them arrived in Cleveland, Ohio, in July, 1874. The Congregation's first educational work in the country began two months later, when the sisters then took charge of St. Peter's and other parochial schools in Cleveland.

For a time after the arrival in Cleveland of this first band of exiled nuns, the sisters made their United States headquarters at Covington, Kentucky, to which they had been invited by the bishop, the Right Rev. Augustus M. Toebbe, D.D.

By October, 1877, nearly two hundred sisters of the Community were engaged in educational work in the country of their adoption. At this time Mother M. Chrysostom let the contract for the erection in Cleveland of a structure on Superior Avenue and Seventeenth Street. This when completed became the General Motherhouse of the Congregation, and the residence of the Superior General, which was then transferred to it from Covington.

MOTHER MARY CECILIA ROMEN

In 1878 Notre Dame Academy was established, and soon took its place among the prominent educational institutions of Cleveland. In 1883 a boarding school for girls was opened in Woodland Hills. Encroachments in the environment, however, later necessitated the relinquishment of this as a boarding school, but the site was retained for an orphanage until 1929, when it was purchased by the Benedictine Fathers for a new high school location.

In 1886 the Prussian government allowed the return of the exiled sisters. Mother Chrysostom, desiring to re-open an institution in Germany, returned there with three sisters in May, 1887. They were joyfully received at their own convent in Vechta, Oldenburg, where about twenty-five sisters had been permitted to remain in charge of a boarding school.

A site in the picturesque village of Muelhausen, in Rhenish-Prussia, was at once chosen by Mother Chrysostom for a new Mother-house. Here the General Motherhouse of the Congregation of the Sisters of Notre Dame was established, and has been continued as the seat of administration, the foundation in Cleveland ranking now as senior provincialate in the United States.

Upon the death of Mother Chrysostom, in 1895, she was succeeded in office by her First Assistant, Mother M. Cecilia Romen, who, prior to her election as Assistant Superior General, had spent more than ten years in the United States, where she was well known and greatly beloved.

With the rapid increase of the Community in Cleveland and the growth of its schools, the need for new and larger buildings was apparent. Under Sister Mary Louise as Provincial Superior, property was therefore secured at Ansel Road and Superior Avenue, overlooking Rockefeller Park and East Boulevard. Commodious buildings, planned and equipped for convent and school, were erected,

NOTRE DAME CONVENT, CLEVELAND, OHIO

and on January 5, 1915, the Provincial Motherhouse, and the grade and academic high schools were transferred to the new location. This change permitted the expansion of the higher educational work of the Community.

With this transfer completed, the building on Superior Avenue and East Seventeenth Street, which had been enlarged in 1896, was utilized as a hospice for Catholic young women. In 1928, following renovation of the interior, the former Motherhouse was re-opened as a hospice for resident and transient women, and is known as the Catholic Young Women's Hall, conducted by the Sisters of Notre Dame.

In September, 1922, Notre Dame College, empowered to confer degrees, was founded in Cleveland by Mother Cecilia, Superior General of the Congregation, the Right Rev. Joseph Schrembs, D.D., Bishop of Cleveland, having given the movement his cordial approval. Temporary buildings on Ansel Road were occupied for the college, which was conducted in connection with the teacher training school, which had been established for some time.

September, 1928, in the administration of Mother Mary Evarista Harks as Provincial Superior of the Cleveland Community, marked the opening of the first building unit of the new Notre Dame College, in the University Heights section of Cleveland. On November 25th, following its opening for classes, formal dedication of the new building took place. On this auspicious occasion Bishop Schrembs was cele-brant of the mass, after which the "Ecce Sacerdos Magnus" and a special arrangement of the "Veni Creator" and other hymns were sung by the sisters' choir.

Simultaneous with this event was the visit of Mother M. Antoine, Superior General of the Congregation, succeeding Mother M. Cecilia, whose death occurred at the General Motherhouse in Muelhausen, Germany, on March 8, 1925. Mother Antoine's timely visit was part of the itinerary of the visitation which, as Superior General, she made to all the foundations of the Congregation, going from Southern to Central Europe, and from South America to North, where, in the United States, her visit extended from the east to the far Pacific Coast.

COVINGTON, KENTUCKY
1875

Soon after the arrival in Cleveland of the Sisters of Notre Dame from their Motherhouse in Coesfeld, Germany, the Bishop of Cov-ington, the Right Rev. Augustus M. Toebbe, D.D.—whose sister, Sister Mary Modesta, was of their number, and who later became the first Provincial Superior of the Order in America—invited the Congregation to establish a foundation in Covington.

Accepting Bishop Toebbe's invitation, the Sisters of Notre Dame maintained their United States headquarters in Covington until 1879, when, upon completion of the erection of a convent building, Cleve-land was made the central point of their activities, although they continued their school work in Covington.

NOTRE DAME CONVENT, ST. JOSEPH HEIGHTS, COVINGTON, KENTUCKY

In 1924, under the episcopacy of the Right Rev. Francis W. Howard, D.D., who the year previous had succeeded to the see of Covington, Covington was made a second provincial center for the Congregation in the United States. On September 12th, two years later, Bishop Howard presided at the ceremony of the laying of the cornerstone of the new provincial convent and academy erected at St. Joseph Heights, Dixie Highway, Covington. The formal opening of the building, in 1927, marked a new epoch in the annals of the Sisters of Notre Dame in the diocese of Covington, now under the provincial superiorship of Sister M. Angela.

TOLEDO, OHIO

1877

Upon the transfer from Germany to the United States, between the years 1874 and 1884, of nearly two hundred members of the

Congregation of the Sisters of Notre Dame, missions were at once provided for many of the sisters in schools not only in Cleveland, Ohio, and its near vicinity, as well as in Kentucky, but also in that part of Ohio which since 1910 has been included in the district of

NOTRE DAME NOVITIATE, TOLEDO, OHIO

the diocese of Toledo, Delphos, Ohio, having received the sisters in 1876, and Toledo in 1877.

From that period the Sisters of Notre Dame continuously increased their work in the schools in Toledo and its environs, as parochial school after parochial school was placed under their charge. The year 1904 saw the opening of the present academy at 1111 West Bancroft Street, which is today one of the foremost educational institutions in the city of Toledo, and which, in 1925, was one of seven secondary schools in the diocese under the direction of the Community.

In August, 1924, with the approbation of the Right Rev. Samuel A. Stritch, D.D., Bishop of Toledo, a third provincialate of the Congregation of the Sisters of Notre Dame in the United States was established in the diocese of Toledo, with Toledo as its center. A candidates' preparatory school was at once opened there, and is now established in the recently erected and spacious novitiate building, which was auspiciously dedicated on December 8, 1925, one of the units of a group of new buildings belonging to the Congregation, and advantageously located at Monroe Street and Secor Road in Toledo.

SUMMARY

Sisters of Notre Dame.

Founded in Germany in 1850.

Established in the United States in 1874.

Papal Approbation of Rules in 1900, by Pope Leo XIII.

Habit: The habit and veil are black. A silver cross is worn on the breast and a large rosary is worn at the side.

Approximate number in Community in United States, 950.

Active in educational and charitable work;

Provincialate of Cleveland, in the dioceses of Cleveland, Los Angeles and San Diego, and Superior; *Provincial house and Novitiate,* Notre Dame Convent, 1325 Ansel Road, Cleveland, Ohio. (Diocese of Cleveland.)

Provincialate of Covington, in the diocese of Covington; *Provincial house and Novitiate,* Notre Dame Convent, St. Joseph Heights, Dixie Highway, Covington, Kentucky. (Diocese of Covington.)

Provincialate of Toledo, in the diocese of Toledo; *Provincial house,* Notre Dame Convent, 1111 West Bancroft Street, Toledo, Ohio; *Novitiate,* Notre Dame Convent, Monroe Street and Secor Road, Toledo, Ohio. (Diocese of Toledo.)

THE POOR CLARES*

1875

$\mathcal{S}$OON after St. Francis of Assisi, early in the thirteenth century, with a few followers had begun his evangelical life, and laid the foundation of the Order of Friars Minor,

ST. CLARE OF ASSISI (1194-1253)
Co-Foundress of the Order of Poor Clares

*From data and material supplied by the Poor Clares, Cleveland, Ohio, and Omaha, Neb.

his example drew many to leave the world, espouse poverty and follow Christ.

First among the women to aspire to this life of perfection was St. Clare, a noble maiden of Assisi. On the night of Palm Sunday, 1212, St. Francis clothed her in his habit of penance, and assigned to her the little convent of San Damiano, near Assisi.

Here St. Clare was soon joined by others who wished to imitate her austere and contemplative manner of life. Thus the first members of the now large Second Order of St. Francis, the Poor Clares, began their community life and fervently observed the exercises of extreme poverty, nocturnal Office and rigorous fast and abstinence prescribed by their Rule, and the enclosure to which they pledged themselves in a special vow.

The newly founded Order soon spread from Italy to France and other European countries, and, animated by the remembrance of their holy foundress and St. Francis, the nuns were long inspired to strict observance of the Rule, and to high sanctity.

In the course of the years, however, the first fervor abated. Relaxations prevailed, and displaced the austerity and religious discipline originally intended to distinguish the Poor Clares. Many things proclaimed the need of a reform in the Community.

POOR CLARE MONASTERY OF THE BLESSED SACRAMENT, CLEVELAND, OHIO

At about this time God raised up another saint destined to be a new light in the Order of St. Clare, and to restore it to much of its primitive fervor.

Born in 1380, in Picardy, France, St. Colette, who was reared in an atmosphere of prayer and penance, had sought in vain for a community in which the Rule of St. Clare was faithfully observed,

MOTHER MARY MAGDALEN
BENTIVOGLIO (1834-1905)

and had become a recluse, when she was divinely bidden to reform the Order of her predilection.

To insure in her foundations the perfect observance of the first Rule of St. Clare, St. Colette then wrote explanations and developments of it, known as the Constitutions of St. Colette, and hence, to the present day, in the Poor Clare monasteries tracing their origin to communities of her reform, the sisters are designated as Poor Clare-Colettines, and this single distinction between these followers of the Colettine reformed Rule, and the Poor Clares regular, or Franciscan Poor Clares, is still made in the houses of the Order.

Under the zeal of the two "Mothers" of the Community, St. Clare and St. Colette, various foundations of the Poor Clares had been made and stabilized throughout Europe.

About the year 1792 a group of Poor Clares, oppressed by the Revolution in France, came to the United States, and took up their abode at Georgetown, D. C., where they opened a school for their support. Unable, however, to establish a permanent institution, upon the death of the Abbess, her successor sold the property, and with her companions returned to their European convent.

The permanent establishment of the Poor Clares in this country is due to the courage and perseverance of two noble ladies of Rome, sisters by blood as well as in religion, Sister Maria Madalena Bentivoglio, and Sister Maria Costanza Bentivoglio.

In 1875, in obedience to His Holiness, Pope Pius IX, and the Superior General of the Franciscan Order, these two sisters left the Monastery of San Lorenzo-in-Panisperna, in Rome, to come to the United States.

Their history, from the time of their arrival in New York, October 11, 1875, is one of sufferings, trials and disappointments. The American Provincial of the Franciscan Fathers, to whom the sisters had been especially recommended, arranged for them to go to Cleveland, Ohio, from New Orleans—whither they had gone while awaiting a diocesan location for their first American foundation.

Some months after their establishment in Cleveland—in compliance with the request of the Franciscan Provincial, plans were

MONASTERY OF ST. CLARE, OMAHA, NEBRASKA

made for the reception of a band of Poor Clare-Colettines, from the community at Dusseldorf, Germany, in view of the fusion of the two communities, and the conformance of the Italian Poor Clares to the customs and Rule of the Poor Clare-Colettines.

In 1877, therefore, at the invitation of the Right Rev. Richard Gilmour, D.D., Bishop of Cleveland, and through the Franciscan Provincial, the Rev. Gregory Janknecht, O.F.M., five Poor Clare-Colettines came to the United States from Dusseldorf, and were established at the Poor Clare monastery in Cleveland. Mother Veronica Von Elmendorf was then appointed Abbess.

To preserve singleness of rule in the community, the Italian Poor Clares attempted to conform to the more generally observed Consti-

43

tutions of St. Colette, but the trying climate and unaccustomed mode of life, led to the acceptance, in 1878, of an invitation for a separate foundation of these Franciscan Poor Clares, distinct from the Poor Clare-Colettines. Through the generosity of Mr. John A. Creighton, of Omaha, Nebraska, and his zealous wife, the sisters were enabled to found, in that city a monastery of their Order, according to the observance of the Rule of St. Clare.

With the growth of the communities both in Omaha and Cleveland—where, in 1928, through the Right Rev. Joseph Schrembs, Bishop of Cleveland, Perpetual Adoration was solemnly inaugurated in the chapel of the monastery—other foundations of the Poor Clares in the United States have been made, each independent, with its own Abbess, and its novitiate, and their contemplative life of prayer and sacrifice, in the true monastic spirit of the holy foundress of the Order, has drawn down, wherever they have been established, special blessings and graces.

SUMMARY

The Poor Clares.
Founded in Italy in 1212.
Papal Approbation of Rules, August 9, 1253, by Pope Innocent IV.
Established in the United States in 1875.
Habit: The habit is of coarse grey frieze, or natural wool, made in tunic form, and held in at the waist by a linen cord with four knots, symbolical of the four vows, poverty, chastity, obedience and enclosure. The wool of the habit recalls the Lamb of God. Its coarseness and sombre hue typify poverty and penance, and its thickness denotes charity. The sisters wear sandals of cloth.
Approximate number in communities in United States, 400.
Engaged in contemplative life in the following monasteries in the United States, each with its own novitiate:
Franciscan Poor Clares

> Monastery of St. Clare, 38 Bennett Street, Boston, Massachusetts. (Archdiocese of Boston.)
> St. Clare's Monastery of the Blessed Sacrament, 720 Henry Clay Avenue, New Orleans, Louisiana. (Archdiocese of New Orleans.)
> Monastery of the Poor Clares, 328 Haven Avenue (West 181st Street), New York, New York. (Archdiocese of New York.)
> Monastery of St. Clare, Southeast corner Girard and Corinthian Avenues, Philadelphia, Pennsylvania. (Archdiocese of Philadelphia.)
> Monastery of St. Clare, Kentucky Avenue, Evansville, Indiana. (Diocese of Indianapolis.)
> Monastery of St. Clare, 29th and Hamilton Streets, Omaha, Nebraska. (Diocese of Omaha.)
> Convent of St. Clare, Hawthorne and Princeton Streets, Spokane, Washington. (Diocese of Spokane.)
> Monastery of the Poor Clares, Bordentown, New Jersey. (Diocese of Trenton.)

Poor Clare-Colettines

Monastery of the Poor Clares, 53rd and Laflin Streets, Chicago, Illinois. (Archdiocese of Chicago.)

St. Joseph's Monastery of the Poor Clares, 1505 34th Avenue, Fruitvale Station, Oakland, California. (Archdiocese of San Francisco.)

Monastery of the Blessed Sacrament, 3501 Rocky River Drive, Cleveland, Ohio. (Diocese of Cleveland.)

Monastery of the Poor Clares, 215 Los Olivos Street, Santa Barbara, California. (Diocese of Los Angeles and San Diego.)

Corpus Christi Monastery, 2107 South Main Street, Rockford, Illinois. (Diocese of Rockford.)

St. Clare's Monastery, Sauk Rapids, Minnesota. (Diocese of St. Cloud.)

SISTERS OF DIVINE PROVIDENCE
(PITTSBURGH, PENNSYLVANIA)*

1876

THE Sisters of Divine Providence whose Provincial Mother-house is established at Allison Park, near Pittsburgh, Pennsylvania, are a branch of the Congregation of Sisters of Divine Providence founded in 1851, at Mayence, Germany, by the Right Rev. W. E. von Ketteler, bishop of the diocese.

Deploring the lack of educational facilities for the children of his diocese, and realizing the misery of the sick and the distress of the poor there, Bishop von Ketteler conceived the project of founding a religious order of women whose chief purpose would be the education of youth and the nursing of the sick.

Amelia de la Roche, a fervent and distinguished convert whom he had received into the Church, and who had expressed her desire

PROVIDENCE HEIGHTS CONVENT, ALLISON PARK, PENNSYLVANIA

to consecrate her life in the service of God's poor, possessed, he was convinced, the qualifications essential for the one who should lead the community he had in view. With this in mind Bishop von Ketteler arranged that she should be received at the Convent of Divine Providence at Ribauville, Alsace, where she accordingly made

*From data and material supplied by the Sisters of Divine Providence, Allison Park, Pa.

her novitiate, and at the end of the canonical year pronounced her vows.

Upon her return to Mayence, Amelia de la Roche, as Mother Marie de la Roche, was appointed Superior of the Community which was formed on September 29, 1851, with the admission to it of four gifted young women, for whose guidance Bishop Ketteler drew up a rule and Constitutions founded on those of St. Vincent de Paul. Knowing that careful preparation is a pre-requisite for any profession, and doubly so for the religious teacher, whose life-work is the education of the young, the bishop at once appointed able priests of his diocesan seminary to train the members of the new Community in the practices of the religious life and the duties incumbent on them as religious teachers.

For nearly a quarter of a century the Sisters of Divine Providence had worked zealously in the field of education and in the alleviation of the misery of the poor and the sick in hospitals and homes, when through the enforcement of the "May Laws," in 1871, they were compelled to abandon the scenes of their various activities. For the preservation of the Community, its founder, Bishop von Ketteler, advised its transfer across the Atlantic in acceptance of an invitation to the diocese of Cleveland, extended to the sisters by the Very Rev. E. J. Vaatman.

On June 6, 1876, the Sisters of Divine Providence left Germany to continue in the United States their work in the cause of Christian education and their works of mercy. Upon their arrival in New York they proceeded at once to Dungannon, Ohio, a small town in the diocese of Cleveland, where, however, they remained but a short time. At the request of the Rev. A. Hune, pastor of Sts. Peter and Paul Church, East Liberty, Pennsylvania, they went to Pennsylvania, where they were received into the diocese of Pittsburgh, and in October of the same year the foundation of their first Provincial house was laid in the episcopal city, with Mother Francis Borgia as first Provincial Superior in America.

A Sister of Divine Providence (Pittsburgh, Pa.)

Her love of prayer and religious observance, joined to remarkable energy and business ability, made Mother Francis an able leader for

the Community in America, which from the outset increased rapidly in membership, and which until 1915 confined its activities to parochial school teaching and boarding school work.

The sisters conduct Divine Providence Academy at Larimer Avenue, East Liberty, and Mt. Immaculata Alpha School at Lincoln Avenue, Pittsburgh, the latter a grade boarding school, opened in 1926 at Mt. Immaculata, upon the transfer of the Motherhouse and novitiate from that site to their present advantageous location at Allison Park, about twelve miles from Pittsburgh.

In 1915 the sisters extended the sphere of their activities in the country when St. John's Hospital, on the Northside, Pittsburgh, which had been previously directed by seculars and later by deacon-esses, was placed under their care. The hospital work of the Com-munity has since been extended to Granite City, Illinois, where the sisters are in charge of St. Elizabeth's Hospital.

To foster religious vocations, the Sisters of Divine Providence have established, as have many other congregations in the country, an Aspirant School for young girls not yet of canonical age for admission to the Community, but who wish to be trained in religious and secular subjects, while continuing their secondary school work, with this in view.

SUMMARY

Sisters of Divine Providence (Pittsburgh, Pennsylvania).
Founded in Germany in 1851.
Established in the United States in 1876.
Approximate number in Community, 500.
Active in educational, hospital and charitable work in the dioceses of Altoona,
    Columbus, Pittsburgh, Springfield in Illinois, and Wheeling.
Provincial Motherhouse and Novitiate, Providence Heights Convent, Allison
    Park, Pennsylvania. (Diocese of Pittsburgh.)

RELIGIOUS OF THE SACRED HEART OF MARY*

1877

THE Congregation of the Sacred Heart of Mary, which was introduced into the United States in 1877, was founded in France, at Béziers in the diocese of Montpelier, on February 24, 1849, by the Very Rev. Pierre Gailhac, a saintly and zealous priest, and by Madame Apollonie Pelissier Cure, a wealthy and devout widow.

In his ardent desire to save souls, Father Gailhac conceived the idea of his pre-eminent work, the foundation of the Congregation of the Religious of the Sacred Heart of Mary, an institute devoted to the education of young girls. The Sovereign Pontiffs, Pius IX and Leo XIII, in turn encouraged, blessed and approved his zealous project.

Upon the death of her husband, Madame Cure, in religion Mother St. John, sustained by her faith and piety, heard the call of God to a more perfect life. After the many trials to which her spiritual director wisely subjected her, she was finally allowed, with the authorization of her bishop, to give herself and her holdings to the service of God, and on February 24, 1849, Madame Cure, at the age of forty, in company with two chosen companions, formed the Congregation of the Sacred Heart of Mary.

The large fortune of the holy foundress was then used to establish three orphanages and a boarding school, and for twenty years Mother St. John directed the Congregation, which rapidly increased in numbers. She encouraged her spiritual daughters by her good example, and inculcated in them a love of the interior life, and a desire for religious perfection. As a result, too, of her pious efforts, the spirit of the Institute of the Religious of the Sacred Heart of Mary, is primarily a spirit of faith, and, in their semi-cloistered life, the religious strive by prayer, by the practice of virtue and by application to study, to adapt themselves to the various employments of the Institute, while keeping in mind their beautiful motto, "All for Jesus through Mary."

On one of his visits to Rome, the venerable founder of the Congregation became acquainted with the estimable American convert, Mrs. Sarah Peter of Cincinnati, who urged him to send a community

*From data and material supplied by the Religious of the Sacred Heart of Mary, Marymount College, Tarrytown-on-Hudson, N. Y.

of the Religious of the Sacred Heart of Mary to take charge of a school in that city. Accordingly, on February 14, 1877, a little band of six, destined for the first foundation of the Institute in the New World, left the Motherhouse in Béziers, France.

MOTHER ST. JOHN PELISSIER CURE (1809-1869)
Co-Foundress of the Institute of the Religious of the
Sacred Heart of Mary

On February 17th, having heard mass in the Church of Notre Dame at Havre, the religious embarked on the steamer "St. Laurent," and reached New York on February 28th. Learning that Mrs. Peter, who was to have welcomed them at their Ohio destination, had died in the meantime, the little group of French nuns, pending a decision regarding the continuance of their journey to Cincinnati, went to Sag Harbor, Long Island, with interested friends whom they had met en route. Here they received a warm welcome from the Rev. T. Heffernan, who requested that they remain in Sag Harbor, as he was anxious for nuns to take charge of a school and to give religious instruction to the young people of his parish.

In view of the unexpected death of the kind benefactress through whom the Cincinnati mission was to have been established, the Motherhouse at Béziers sanctioned the acceptance of the mission at Sag Harbor. On March 11, 1877, the Right Rev. John Loughlin, D.D., Bishop of Brooklyn, who had welcomed the nuns to his diocese, dedicated their new convent home to St. Joseph.

On the feast of the Sacred Heart of Mary, August 29, 1877, the first two pupils entered the boarding school opened by the community in Sag Harbor. The first American postulant entered the Order October 20, 1878. During the next few years considerable property was acquired at Sag Harbor, and the building was improved and enlarged so as to provide classrooms and dormitories for resident students.

Marymount, in New York, at Tarrytown on the Hudson, formerly known as the Reynard Estate, now the site of the United States Motherhouse and novitiate of the Religious of the Sacred Heart of Mary, was made possible in 1907, by Mr. James Butler of New York, who presented it in memory of his wife, as his initial gift to the Institute.

Mr. Butler, noted for his many philanthropic and charitable bequests, and upon whom the Holy Father has conferred the decorations of the Order of St. Gregory, has enriched Marymount with subsequent additions of property, on which the several buildings which now comprise the institution have been erected. On May 30, 1923, the Butler-Memorial Chapel—an architectural masterpiece—was dedicated by the archbishop of New York, the Most Rev. Patrick J. Hayes, D.D., later created cardinal-priest of the Church.

At Marymount School and College, where the advantages are many and varied, the religious aim to give their pupils an education—moral, physical and intellectual—in keeping with the spirit of the holy founders of the Institute. For the benefit of students who wish to go abroad for study, a Paris branch of the college has been established, with arrangements which provide for full credit for the courses followed.

In addition to their educational work at the Motherhouse, the religious have recently opened, in New York City, Marymount Academy, occupying the former Burden mansion on Fifth Avenue at 84th Street, purchased and given to the Congregation by Mr. Butler.

Extending their work beyond the archiepiscopal city and Brooklyn, the Religious of the Sacred Heart of Mary, active at Marymount on the eastern coast of the country, have now established on the western coast, in Los Angeles, California, another Marymount school for girls.

MARYMOUNT, TARRYTOWN-ON-HUDSON, NEW YORK

The Congregation, which is represented through Europe and in the two Americas, is governed by a Superior General who resides at the Motherhouse, maintained at Béziers, Hérault, France. Its houses have been established in accordance with the regulations laid down by Canon Law and apostolic constitutions, and each is governed by a local Superior and two Councilors, appointed by the Superior General and her Council for a term of three years, with only one re-election in the same house.

In August, 1926, Mother Mary Joseph was elected Superior General of the Congregation, and is the first religious other than a French woman chosen for this office. Prior to this, Mother Joseph served as Mother Vicar of the North American Vicariate of the Order, and was president of Marymount College.

SUMMARY

Religious of the Sacred Heart of Mary.
Founded in France in 1849.
Established in the United States in 1877.
Papal Approbation of Rules, July 10, 1880, by Pope Leo XIII.
Habit: The habit, as worn by the foundress, is navy blue, with a long train. The veil is black and the coif white.
Approximate number in Community in United States, 250.
Active in educational work in the archdiocese of New York and in the dioceses of Brooklyn and Los Angeles and San Diego.
United States Motherhouse and Novitiate, Marymount, Tarrytown-on-Hudson, New York. (Archdiocese of New York.)

RELIGIOUS OF JESUS AND MARY*

1877

$\mathcal{OF}$ ROM the annals of the Congregation of the Religious of Jesus and Mary, one learns that the Congregation was founded in Lyons, France, in 1818, by Claudine Thévenet. In the pages of "Cameos" from its history, one discerns that the Congregation originated during the days of "The Terror," as historians are wont to call the harrowing period of the French Revolution, and that to the brave, forgiving heart of Marie Claudine Thévenet, the world owes the Religious of Jesus and Mary.

Breathless and agonized, her white lips murmuring over and over again: "My God, forgive the murderers, they know not what they do," Claudine Thévenet stood in the crowd in the city of Lyons, witness to a horrible massacre, and the cruel murder of her two beloved brothers, having for remembrance the sublime words of her brother's whispered farewell to her: "Forgive them, Cladie, as we do!"

The courage that could uphold a girl of nineteen through such a scene, the noble heart that at such a moment of torture could forgive the executioners, were strengthened and ennobled in the years of the maturing of the fine character of Claudine Thévenet, whose prayer, through her suffering, was that God would make known to her her life-work.

Again, after a lapse of twenty years, a scene in Lyons. France is at peace with all the world, but steadfast Christians, true to the faith through all vicissitudes, realize the dangers of the time and the need for zealous religious effort. It is the 31st of July, of the year 1816, on the feast of St. Ignatius Loyola, that a group of pious women are in the little chapel of St. Bruno, in the old Carthusian monastery. Religion has been restored in France, but there is still danger for such societies as the little group represents, as it meets for the first solemn reception of members into the Association of the Sacred Heart of Jesus, by the founder and director, the Abbé Coindre.

Each associate has there solemnly promised to cast all the merits and works of her life into the spiritual treasury of the association, as common property, to observe its rules and regulations, and to labor

---

*From data and material supplied by the Religious of Jesus and Mary, Provincial Motherhouse, Sillery, P.Q., Canada, and from *The Congregation of Jesus and Mary, Cameos from Its History* (Burns & Oates, London).

courageously, all her life, for her own perfection and sanctification.
The gabled roof echoed back the renewal of their baptismal vows,
and their consecration to the Sacred Hearts of Jesus and Mary.

MOTHER MARY ST. IGNATIUS
Foundress in 1818 of the Congregation of the Religious of Jesus and Mary

They were not nuns, these women, but souls burning with love
of God, anxious to help their neighbor and convinced that to do so
fruitfully they must first strive to perfect themselves. The president of this association of devout women was Marie Claudine
Thévenet.

Five years later in France, another scene, but away from Lyons, in the little town of Monistrol, in the diocese of Le Puy. With ecclesiastical authority, the venerable Père Coindre conferred on the same company of women the religious habit, and allowed Claudine Thévenet, as Mother St. Ignatius, and her companions, to make their vows of religion which bound them to live in poverty, chastity and obedience until death.

"To train souls for heaven, by a truly Christian education" was the aim of the new institute in its convent home at Fourvière. Its first work, an orphanage where poor and abandoned children were cared for, and taught the lucrative trade of silk-weaving, for their future support, was soon followed by the opening of a boarding school for children. Wherever the Congregation spread, thereafter, schools for the rich and poor stood side by side sharing equally the zeal and affection of Claudine Thévenet's followers.

Toward the end of 1841, to the little convent at Fourvière, just four years after the death of the noble-hearted foundress, came a call for religious workers, from far-off India. In reply to the appeal of the bishop of Agra, the answer was, "Behold the handmaids of the Lord." In January, 1842, six sisters left their convent home at Fourvière and went across the wintry seas, through the storms of the Arabian desert to waiting Agra. The annals of their history tell of events in India, in the tragic year of 1857, in the days of "the Mutiny," when Claudine Thévenet's daughters lived anew, with her courage, through experiences which fall to the lot of few religious, but the works of the holy foundress have survived, and today her Congregation, with its Motherhouse in the Eternal City, has convents and institutions throughout Europe, in India and in North, South and Central America.

MOTHER M. CYRILLA, OF THE RELIGIOUS
OF JESUS AND MARY

The first North American foundation was made in

1855, at Levis, Quebec, when Mother St. Cyprian and seven sisters from their convent in Lyons, France, responded to the request of the archbishop of Quebec for sisters for the education of French-Canadian young girls.

In 1877, through the efforts of the Rev. Father Bédard, pastor of the Church of Notre Dame de Lourdes, in Fall River, Massachusetts, the Congregation of the Religious of Jesus and Mary made—with Mother St. Francis Xavier as Superior, its first foundation in the United States. Its first work was in behalf of the education of the French-Canadian immigrants in Fall River. Other missions for this purpose were later undertaken throughout New England.

Extending its work into New York City, the Congregation opened a home known as Our Lady of Peace Residence, an establishment which provides a centrally located hospice for business girls or women, strangers or alone in the city. In this spacious and well-equipped and arranged home they are shielded, protected by the sisters, and enjoy the privilege of access to a house chapel. During the day, sisters from this residence-home, on West 14th Street, go through New York's busy streets to the heart of "Little Italy," where they instruct and assist in the schools for the children of Italian immigrants, as they carry on the work of their holy foundress.

SUMMARY

Religious of Jesus and Mary.
Founded in France in 1818.
Established in the United States in 1877.
Papal Approbation of Rules in 1847, by Pope Pius IX.
Habit: The habit and veil are black; the fluted cap is white. A silver cross, tasseled cord and a rosary are worn.
Approximate number in Community in United States, 250.
Active in educational and charitable work in the archdiocese of New York, and in the dioceses of Fall River, Manchester and Providence.
United States Novitiate, Convent of Jesus and Mary, Highland Mills, New York. (Archdiocese of New York.)

DOMINICAN NUNS*

1880

IN the year 1880, on the 24th of June, four Dominican Nuns left the Monastery of the Most Blessed Sacrament, at Oullins, near Lyons, France, for America, to found a monastery of their Order at Newark, New Jersey.

Reaching Newark on the 6th of July, the nuns remained with the Sisters of Charity at Seton Hall College, until the temporary house secured for them at Newark was ready for occupancy. On July 29th, the feast of St. Martha, when the Blessed Sacrament was placed in their little chapel, the four nuns, with one postulant as a lay sister, were enclosed, and began the exercise of their regular religious observances, with Mother Mary of Jesus as Superior.

Bound by rule to the Perpetual Adoration of the Blessed Sacrament, and to such austerities as rising at midnight for the Matins of the Divine Office, perpetual abstinence, long fasts, the use of board beds, strict enclosure, and the endurance of cold, in a land of comfort the life of these cloistered Dominican Sisters of the Second Order seemed to defy even the most sanguine hopes. However, the community grew and prospered, and within two years after its coming to this country land was secured for a permanent settlement, and the erection of a monastery proper.

In April, 1884, the community moved to its new home in Newark, the Monastery of St. Dominic, which was built upon the plan of the pristine monasteries of the Old World, having its arched cloister, traditional well, a vault as a resting place for the departed, and double grilles, separating from the outer world those consecrated to God's special service.

At the end of nine years the monastery was filled to capacity, and the Most Rev. Michael Augustine Corrigan, D.D., who, previously, as bishop of Newark, had welcomed the nuns there, claimed for New York, his archiepiscopal city, a foundation of the Order.

The erection of the New York establishment was begun May 26, 1889. Seven nuns came from the Newark monastery and settled in a temporary house at Hunts Point, on the east side of New York, above the Harlem River. Upon completion of the building, known

---

*From data and material supplied by the Dominican Nuns, Corpus Christi Monastery, Hunts Point, Bronx, New York City, and St. Dominic's Monastery, Newark, N. J.

as Corpus Christi Monastery, the nuns, with Mother Mary of Jesus as Prioress, at once entered it and resumed the life of the cloister. Here Mother Mary of Jesus died, on May 4, 1924, at the age of eighty-five.

Rapid again was the expansion of contemplative life on this new soil. When in the fall of 1890 the nuns took possession of this

MONASTERY OF ST. DOMINIC, NEWARK, NEW JERSEY

monastery, they numbered twenty-one, and as time went on they were joined by many others, to devote themselves to God through the chanting of the Divine Office, adoration, prayer, penance and sacrifice.

In the spring of 1906 the Monastery of St. Dominic at Newark sent out a group of nuns to establish a foundation at Detroit, Michigan. The making of this foundation—significant because it marked the inauguration of the Perpetual Adoration of the Blessed Sacrament in the diocese of Detroit—was directed by Mother Mary Emmanuel, one of the original community from France, who had succeeded Mother Mary of Jesus as Prioress of the Newark community in 1889.

Virginia Noel, as Mother Mary Emmanuel was known in the world, was born in New York City, December 20, 1850. Educated by private governesses, and later in the convents of France, she became a religious of the Second Order of St. Dominic at the monastery at Oullins in 1875. In Albany, New York, at the Monastery of the Immaculate Conception, which she had herself founded, on November 21, 1915, Mother Mary Emmanuel died on November 28, 1928.

The parent-house at Newark—from which have come, directly or indirectly, all the foundations of the cloistered Dominican Sisters

44

of the Second Order in the United States—retains the primal spirit and rule of the Order, owing its origin to the Monastery of the Blessed Sacrament, at Oullins, France, which is directly descendent from the monastery founded by St. Dominic himself at Prouille, in 1206.

St. Dominic, fired with zeal for the salvation of souls, gathered together a chosen company called to an apostolate of prayer and penance for the sinning world, and especially for the conversion of heretics and infidels. To these followers he communicated his own aspirations, and ordained for them a mode of life which has been handed down to us in all the purity of its first saintly inspirations.

In the monasteries of the Dominican Sisters of the Second Order in the United States, papal enclosure is observed, together with the labors as well as the rules of the old monastic life of centuries ago. The nuns assiduously cultivate the art of illumination, working too on parchment, as did the religious of the Middle Ages. To this art work they unite the making of the finest ecclesiastical embroideries in gold and silk. It may be said truly that their toil is of love, as are their lives, offered to Jesus in the holy Sacrament of the Altar.

SUMMARY

Dominican Nuns (Cloistered Dominican Sisters of the Second Order).
Founded in France in 1206.
Papal Approbation of Rules in 1216, by Pope Honorius III.
Established in the United States in 1880.
Habit: The habit, symbolizing purity and austerity, is a white tunic, with a scapular reaching almost to the ground, a black cope, and a black veil.
Approximate number in communities in United States, 230.
Engaged in contemplative life in the following monasteries, each with its own novitiate:

> Monastery of the Holy Name, 1960 Madison Road, Cincinnati, Ohio. (Archdiocese of Cincinnati.)
> Corpus Christi Monastery, Lafayette and Baretto Streets, Hunts Point, Bronx, New York City. (Archdiocese of New York.)
> Corpus Christi Monastery, Oak Grove Avenue, Menlo Park, California. (Archdiocese of San Francisco.)
> Monastery of the Immaculate Conception, 115 Washington Avenue, Albany, New York. (Diocese of Albany.)
> Monastery of the Blessed Sacrament, Oakland Avenue and Boston Boulevard, Detroit, Michigan. (Diocese of Detroit.)
> Monastery of the Angels, 728 West 28th Street, Los Angeles, California. (Diocese of Los Angeles and San Diego.)
> Monastery of St. Dominic, 13th Avenue between 9th and 10th Streets, Newark, New Jersey. (Diocese of Newark.)

SISTERS OF BON SECOURS*

1881

THE Congregation of Bon Secours was founded in Paris, France, January 24, 1824, by the Most Rev. H. L. de Quelen, Archbishop of Paris, for the care of the sick and needy in their own homes.

The coming of the Bon Secours to this country in 1881 was due to His Eminence, James Cardinal Gibbons. Leading physicians of Baltimore, realizing the necessity of trained nurses for the care of the sick and poor in their own homes, requested Archbishop Gibbons, before his elevation to the cardinalate, to secure religious for this purpose.

In response to the physicians' appeal, an invitation was sent to the Sisters of Bon Secours in France. At that time the United States was considered a foreign missionary country, and when the Order complied, as it did at once, to fill this need, the sisters came as laborers to a foreign mission.

Arriving in the United States, the Community was established in Baltimore, Maryland, on May 24, 1881, with Mother Ferdinand as first Superior.

During the years which followed the Community expanded its work to meet the various modern developments in the care of the sick in their own homes, and in hospitals, clinics, convalescent homes, day nurseries, orphanages, a home for crippled children, district visiting, nursing and other institutions.

During the World War, as during the Franco-Prussian and the Commune, the Bon Secours did active service in *les Ambulances,* first aid, and work in temporary military hospitals in France, and at the United States naval base in Queenstown, Ireland.

Though not in the United States at the time of the Civil War, two Bon Secours Sisters from Baltimore, nursed during his last illness one of its great leaders, the hero of the famous ride, General Sheridan. As his nurses they accompanied the veteran general from Washington, on the war boat, "Swatara," to Nonquitte, on the New England coast, where he died in 1888.

These Sisters of Bon Secours in the United States—now under Mother Urban as Superior General—have established a Motherhouse and novitiate in Baltimore. The Community in this country main-

*From data supplied by the Sisters of Bon Secours, Baltimore, Md.

tains its connection with the General Motherhouse at 20 Rue Notre Dame des Champs, Paris, France.

SUMMARY

Sisters of Bon Secours.

Founded in France in 1824.

Papal Approbation of Rules in 1864, by Pope Pius IX.

Established in the United States in 1881.

Habit: The habit of black serge, with a black veil, white fichu, white fluted cap, and white cuffs to off-set the sombre black near the sick, is similar to the dress of the ancient Briton peasants.

Approximate number in Community in United States, 100.

Active in hospital, nursing and charitable work in the archdioceses of Baltimore and Philadelphia and in the diocese of Detroit.

United States Motherhouse and Novitiate, Convent of Bon Secours, 2000 West Baltimore Street, Baltimore, Maryland. (Archdiocese of Baltimore.)

SISTERS OF BON SECOURS (NEW YORK)*

1882

THE Sisters of Bon Secours, or, as they are often called, the Bon Secours, who began labor in the United States in 1882, were founded in the year 1840 at Arcis-sur-Aube, France, by the Rev. Paul Sébastien Millet, for the special work of nursing the sick in their own homes, regardless of creed or nationality, wealth or poverty.

On February 15, 1882, through the mediation of Mrs. Ward, one of New York's zealous Catholic women, two Bon Secours, Sister Madeleine de Pazzi and Sister Ambroise, left France and came to the United States. Pending a suitable location, the newly arrived nurses were kindly received by the Sisters of Charity, at the Foundling Asylum at 68th Street and Third Avenue.

A small house was soon procured at 146 East 22nd Street, and from there the Bon Secours began their work of nursing in New York City. After two years they removed to 152 East 66th Street. Five years more passed and the little community had been so augmented that another change was necessitated, and on July 19, 1889, possession was taken of the present home at 1195 Lexington Avenue.

With Sister Winefride as Superior, and still under the gentle influence of the now venerable Sister Ambroise, who has been spared to see her loved community one of the most active in the city, the sisters, who derive their support from voluntary contributions, devote themselves exclusively to the work of nursing, for which the Congregation was founded.

SISTER AMBROISE, AT THE AGE OF 82

The General Motherhouse, with which the United States community is affiliated, is in Troyes, Aube, France. From there the

*From data supplied by the Bon Secours, 1195 Lexington Avenue, New York, N. Y.

Bon Secours aided in nursing the sick and wounded in France and Italy during the World War, and there are kept the records of the brave sisters who were awarded national decorations for their helpful war services.

SUMMARY

Sisters of Bon Secours (New York).
Founded in France in 1840.
Papal Approbation of Rules by Pope Pius IX.
Established in the United States in 1882.
Active in nursing work in the archdiocese of New York.
United States Motherhouse, Convent of the Bon Secours, 1195 Lexington Avenue, New York, New York. (Archdiocese of New York.)

SISTERS OF ST. JOSEPH OF PEACE*

1884

THE Congregation of the Sisters of St. Joseph of Peace, which began its activities in this country in November of the year of its founding, 1884, was instituted at Nottingham, England, by the Right Rev. Edward G. Bagshawe, then bishop of Nottingham, later appointed a titular archbishop.

The special object in the formation of the Congregation was to provide a community of sisters who should devote themselves to the domestic and industrial training of girls, particularly of the working class, with a view of promoting peace and happiness in families, in union with and in imitation of the Holy Family of Nazareth. From the first, as was the intention of Bishop Bagshawe, the sisters engaged also in educational work, the instruction of converts, visiting the sick poor, and caring for orphans, the blind, and the sick in hospitals.

The Right Rev. W. M. Wigger, D.D., Bishop of Newark, who became deeply interested in the work of the new Institute in England, and who was convinced of the good resulting from a community of such religious devoted to the protection and training of girls, extended the Sisters of St. Joseph of Peace an invitation to establish a foundation in his diocese.

A SISTER OF ST. JOSEPH OF PEACE

Mother M. Evangelista, who became the first Superior of the American foundation, came with a companion to the United States in November, 1884, and in accordance with the wish of Bishop Wigger located in St. Peter's parish in Jersey City, and soon afterward assumed charge of the orphans at St. Joseph's Home. In the spring of 1885 Mother M. Ignatius and a companion came from Nottingham, and also entered on the work for girls.

*From data and material supplied by the Sisters of St. Joseph of Peace, St. Joseph's Convent, Jersey City, N. J.

A site was secured on the Palisades overlooking the Hudson River, at Englewood, New Jersey, and here a novitiate was established, and a large building was erected for a vacation home for girls.

ST. JOSEPH'S HOME, JERSEY CITY, NEW JERSEY

The care of the blind was then undertaken as one of the first activities of the Community, and at St. Joseph's Home for the Blind at Jersey City a high standard of perfection has been reached in the use of the Braille system. At this institution the adult blind are employed in various branches of industry. In the interest of the orphans and the blind under their charge there is edited at the Motherhouse "The Orphans' Messenger and Advocate of the Blind."

In the east, in addition to now conducting at Jersey City, together with their other institutions there, St. Mary's Residence for Business Girls, and Loretto Hall at Newark, the Congregation is in charge of The Marie Claire, St. Joseph's Villa, at Hohokus, New

Jersey. This establishment, a spacious rest house for women, was opened in 1925, having been donated to the sisters by the Hon. Thomas J. Maloney and Mrs. Marie Claire Maloney, dis-

St. Michael's Villa, Englewood, New Jersey

tinguished Catholic philanthropists whose home is maintained nearby at Saddle River, New Jersey.

In 1890, extending its labors from the Atlantic to the Pacific coast, the Community established St. Joseph's Hospital at Bellingham, Washington, where the Western Provincial house and novitiate are also now located. In Seattle, Washington, the sisters carry on their work for girls by conducting St. Teresa's Club, another residence for business girls.

In 1896, Mother Teresa Moran, who now serves as first assistant to Mother M. Agatha, Superior General of the Congregation, extended the work of the Congregation to Canada by opening Mater Misericordiæ Hospital at Rossland, B. C., and on March 12, 1923, the Congregation inaugurated its missionary activities in Alaska.

Most recent in the hospital work of the Sisters of St. Joseph of Peace was the opening, on October 4, 1925, at Teaneck, New Jersey, of Holy Name Hospital, one of the outstanding works of the adminis- tration of Mother M. Agatha. Located on the site of the famous Phelps Manor, in Bergen County, New Jersey, and surrounded by large lawns and small groves of rare European trees, Holy Name Hospital—within one year rated as an A-1 hospital by the American College of Surgeons—the first hospital opened in the east by the Sisters of St. Joseph of Peace, is a worthy monument of their now more than two score years of religious endeavor in the United States.

ST. JOSEPH'S HOSPITAL, BELLINGHAM, WASHINGTON

SUMMARY

Sisters of St. Joseph of Peace.
Founded in England in 1884.
Established in the United States in 1884.
Papal Approbation of Rules, June 24, 1929, by His Holiness, Pope Pius XI.
Habit: The habit is of black serge with a scapular of the same color and material, and a linen head-dress. A silver crucifix is worn.
Approximate number in Community, 300.
Active in educational, hospital, charitable and social service work in the United States in the archdiocese of Philadelphia and in the dioceses of Newark, Seattle and Trenton.

Eastern Provincial house and Novitiate, St. Michael's Villa, Englewood, New Jersey. (Diocese of Newark.)

Western Provincial house and Novitiate, St. Joseph's Hospital, Bellingham, Washington. (Diocese of Seattle.)

General Motherhouse, St. Joseph's Convent, Jersey City, New Jersey. (Diocese of Newark.)

SISTERS OF THE HOLY FAMILY OF NAZARETH*

1885

THE history of the Congregation of the Holy Family of Nazareth is inseparably linked with the life-story of its holy foundress, Mother Frances Siedliska, a woman of noble qualities and rare virtues, of a distinguished and wealthy Polish family, whose plans and efforts were from the beginning auspiciously blessed by the Sovereign Pontiff, when she sought guidance and help in Rome.

Frances Siedliska was born November 12, 1842, at Roszkowa Wola, the ancestral home of her family. From her early childhood she was inclined toward the religious life, and was later encouraged to consecrate herself to it, by her spiritual director, Father Leander Lendzian, a Capuchin priest. In encouraging his devout penitent to carry out her definite desire to be a religious, in which, for a time, she met with strenuous opposition from her family, Father Leander did so as a matter of duty toward her, for a Capuchin brother had confided to him an account of a vision on the subject, vouchsafed him after the death of a Franciscan Tertiary, revealing that Frances Siedliska—entirely unknown to the brother—was called to the religious life, and referring to the particular work for which she was destined.

After his penitent's recovery from a serious illness, and when she had been given paternal permission to devote herself to God, Father Leander, in his direction of her soul, gradually made known to her the nature of the vision which had been disclosed to him.

On July 2, 1873, Frances was allowed to take the vows of poverty, chastity and obedience, and was advised by Father Leander to take charge of the already existing little band of Franciscan Tertiaries— one of whose number had appeared, after her death, in the vision to the Capuchin brother.

In September, 1873, accompanied by one of the tertiaries, Mother Frances visited Rome, where she was permitted to submit her plans and desires to the Sovereign Pontiff, Pope Pius IX, who, imparting the apostolic benediction, encouraged her to persevere in her undertaking.

*From data and material supplied by the Sisters of the Holy Family of Nazareth, St. Stanislaus' School, Cleveland, Ohio.

Soon after this, Frances and her band of tertiary companions went to Lourdes, where they spent some time in humble and fervent prayer, seeking light in the choice of an appropriate and favorable

MOTHER FRANCES SIEDLISKA (1842-1902)
Foundress of the Congregation of the Holy Family of Nazareth

place for the establishment of the new community, the plans of which had now taken definite shape in the mind of the fore-ordained foundress.

Rome was decided on as the site of the home of the community, and early in 1875 headquarters were established there.   On January

16, 1884, the community transferred to a home at Via Machiavelli 18, purchased by Mother Siedliska for a permanent Motherhouse of the Order, and the residence of the Superior General and her Council.

HOLY FAMILY CONVENT, DES PLAINES, ILLINOIS

The Rules of the Congregation of the Holy Family of Nazareth—as, in accordance with the special devotion of the holy foundress, the new community was known—included the observance of the contemplative and active life, and were instituted according to the Rule of St. Augustine, which serves for many communities as the basis of their religious life.

The zeal of Mother Siedliska soon drew many candidates to the Congregation. Desirous of beginning active labors in her native land, she was, in 1881, given diocesan permission to establish a community of her sisters at Cracow, the metropolis and heart of the devastated kingdom of Poland. There the sisters began active missionary work by teaching catechism to children, preparing them for the sacraments, and conducting retreats for young women.

Soon the field of labor broadened, and other missions were rapidly opened in Poland. Requests for sisters came, meanwhile, not only from within, but from without the country, including one from the United States, urging that sisters be sent to Chicago, to take charge of an orphanage and a school founded chiefly for Polish immigrants.

Although fully comprehending the difficulties connected with the establishment of the distant mission, Mother Siedliska, upon the advice of ecclesiastical authorities, consented not only to undertake it, but to accompany in person the community of eleven sisters chosen for labor in America, under Mother Raphael as Provincial Superior.

Previous to their departure for the United States, on June 17, 1885, the eleven sisters, with their foundress, were given an audience

HOLY FAMILY CONVENT, TORRESDALE, PENNSYLVANIA

with the Sovereign Pontiff, Pope Leo XIII, who bestowed his apostolic benediction on them, in view of their future work in the new mission field.

MOTHER LAURETTA LUBOWIDZKA

Having landed at New York, July 4, 1885, Mother Siedliska and her companions from Rome left immediately for Chicago, where a small convent awaited them in St. Joseph's parish. Here the sisters opened the first of the many schools which they now conduct in the city, in addition to their orphanage, day-nursery and hospital work. The principal hospital of the community is that of St. Mary of Nazareth, opened, originally, in 1892. A corps of sixty sisters is retained at this hospital—newly erected and enlarged in 1902—in connection with which a training school for nurses has been established.

After installing the Congregation in Chicago, Mother Siedliska returned to the Motherhouse in Rome, but visited the United States again in 1889 and in 1896. In the meantime houses were opened in various European cities, including Paris and London.

With the rapid growth of the Congregation in the United States, provincialates have been established to facilitate the government of

MT. NAZARETH, BELLEVUE, PITTSBURGH, PENNSYLVANIA

the Community, which has extended its activities into many cities throughout the country.

In 1908 the novitiate, which had early been established in Chicago, was transferred to a new and spacious institution erected in Des-Plaines, Illinois, under the auspices of the Most Rev. James E. Quigley, D.D., then archbishop of Chicago, who had presented eighty acres of land there for this foundation.

The Congregation has been under Mother Lauretta Lubowidzka as Mother General, since the death, on November 21, 1902, of the holy foundress—the cause of whose beatification was introduced less than twenty years later, with the Right Rev. Msgr. John Bressan as its Postulator.

The Congregation of the Holy Family of Nazareth has at present as its Cardinal-Protector in Rome His Eminence, William Cardinal Van Rossum.

SUMMARY

Sisters of the Holy Family of Nazareth.

Founded in Italy in 1875.

Established in the United States in 1885.

Papal Approbation of Rules (Revised in conformance with the New Code of Canon Law), June 4, 1925, by His Holiness, Pope Pius XI.

Habit: The habit is black, with a cream white cordian-pleated round collar of woolen silk, a black veil over a white-edged black cap, a silver reliquary cross, fringe-finished sash, and a rosary.

Approximate number in Community in United States, 1300.

Active in educational, hospital and charitable work

Province of the Sacred Heart of Jesus, in the archdioceses of Chicago and Santa Fé, and in the diocese of Fort Wayne; *Provincial house and Novitiate,* Des Plaines, Illinois. (Archdiocese of Chicago.)

Province of St. Joseph, in the dioceses of Altoona, Cleveland, Columbus, Detroit, Erie and Pittsburgh; *Provincial house and Novitiate,* Mt. Nazareth, Bellevue Station, Pittsburgh, Pennsylvania. (Diocese of Pittsburgh.)

Province of the Immaculate Conception of the Blessed Virgin, in the archdioceses of Baltimore, Boston and Philadelphia, and in the dioceses of Brooklyn, Hartford, Newark, Springfield and Syracuse; *Provincial house and Novitiate,* Grant and Frankford Avenues, Torresdale, Pennsylvania. (Archdiocese of Philadelphia.)

SISTERS OF THE DIVINE COMPASSION*

HE Congregation of the Sisters of the Divine Compassion, whose activities have so far been confined to the archdiocese of New York, was founded in New York City in 1886 by the distinguished convert-prelate, the Very. Rev. Thomas S. Preston.

Msgr. Preston, a native of Hartford, Connecticut, was early drawn to the service of God and a life of celibacy and entered the ministry in his twenty-second year. Leader of the High Church Party during his student life at the Episcopal Seminary, he was gradually convinced of the validity of the Catholic position, and three years after beginning his life as an Episcopal minister he resigned his charge at St. Luke's Church in New York City and was received into the one true fold of the Apostolic Church, and admitted to the seminary in New York in preparation of his ordination to the priesthood.

For more than forty years Msgr. Preston held a prominent place in the archdiocese of New York, serving in the office of Chancellor and Vicar General, and in time being made Domestic Prelate and Prothonotary Apostolic. Gifted in directing others spiritually, he guided many to the religious life, among whom was Mary Dannat Starr, who became the foundress-Superior of the Sisters of the Divine Compassion.

Mary Dannat Starr was born in New York City, April 27, 1838, of Protestant parents, and was the eldest of six children. Developing keen religious sensibilities, she started on a path of religious enquiry, and finally presented herself to Msgr. Preston, then parish priest of St. Ann's Church on the east side of New York, from whom she received instructions preparatory to her reception into the Church on April 11, 1868.

Devoting her life thereafter to works of charity, and realizing the solicitude of Msgr. Preston for his people, whom he sought to aid temporally as well as spiritually, in the daily visitations of his ministry, the fervent convert's socialized solution of the problem was the opening of a sewing school where the children of the district could be brought together, and be taught habits of thrift as well as instructed in the truths of religion.

*From data and material supplied by the Sisters of the Divine Compassion, Our Lady of Good Counsel College, White Plains, N. Y.

Conscious that in time, in order to perpetuate it, it would be necessary to appeal to some religious community trained and prepared to
take up such a work as had developed under the efficient leadership

MOTHER MARY VERONICA (1838-1904)
Foundress of the Sisters of the Divine Compassion

of Mary Dannat Starr, aided by a number of devout women who
co-operated with her—and who for some years had been under his
direction as an association—Msgr. Preston was inspired to propose
that the members of the little society seal and sanctify their labors
with the enduring character of the religious state.

On May 28, 1886, the Most Rev. Michael Augustine Corrigan, D.D., Archbishop of New York, gave his blessing and solemn approbation to the Rules and Constitutions, which, with the Divine Compassion as their keynote and inspiration, Msgr. Preston had drawn up for the new sisterhood, known as Sisters of the Divine Compassion.

The first Superior of the Community then formed was Mary Dannat Starr—henceforth known as Mother Mary Veronica—who felt that in yielding to the suggestion of her spiritual director to become a religious she was but binding herself to the task to which she had so long devoted herself, and who was prevailed upon to submit to the evident designs of Providence and assume the leadership of the new religious Institute.

Until 1890 the Sisters of the Divine Compassion maintained their headquarters at 136 Second Avenue, New York City, when following the purchase of desirable property, consisting of twelve acres of well cultivated land, and a fine spacious country residence at White Plains, New York, removal was made to it, and, as the Convent of Our Lady of Good Counsel, it was made the site of their Motherhouse and novitiate.

In 1915, deviating from but not abandoning their club and settlement work, the Sisters of the Divine Compassion established an academy at the Motherhouse, and as soon as their numbers permitted undertook the conducting of parochial schools. In September, 1923, upon the completion of a commodious new building erected at the Motherhouse site, the College of Our Lady of Good Counsel was opened for the higher Catholic education of young women.

Motherhouse and Novitiate, Convent of Our Lady of Good Counsel, White Plains, New York. (Archdiocese of New York.)

SISTERS OF ST. MARY*

1886

THE Congregation of St. Mary, a diocesan Community, of distinct United States origin, was founded in the little town of Sublimity, Oregon, in the year 1886, by the Most Rev. William H. Gross, C.SS.R., Archbishop of Oregon City, now known as the archdiocese of Portland in Oregon.

Oregon at the time was an undeveloped, sparsely populated region, yet there was evident need for religious teachers in the many missions of the archdiocese. To fill this need, Archbishop Gross formed the Congregation of St. Mary for the special work of teaching. Mother M. Seraphim was chosen first Superior, and she zealously labored to stabilize the foundation for educational work in the vast archdiocese.

In January, 1891, the first mission house of the Community was opened at Verboorts, Oregon. Two months later the sisters took charge of the diocesan orphanage at St. Mary's, near Beaverton.

In 1894 the novitiate was transferred from Sublimity to St. Mary's. Connected with their Motherhouse, St. Mary's Convent, also now located there, within easy reach of Portland, the sisters conduct St. Mary's Institute.

MOTHER M. SERAPHIM

The Community is consecrated to the Blessed Virgin, and in its spiritual exercises especially devoted to the Most Precious Blood. Mother M. Juliana, aided by four Councilors, at present governs the Congregation, which is under the jurisdiction of the Most Rev. Edward D. Howard, D.D., Archbishop of Portland in Oregon.

*From data and material supplied by the Sisters of St. Mary, St. Mary's Convent, Beaverton, Ore.

SUMMARY

Sisters of St. Mary.

Founded in the United States in 1886.

Habit: The habit is of black serge, with a full length scapular, black veil, while coif and linen collar.

Approximate number in Community, 150.

Active in educational and charitable work in the archdiocese of Portland in Oregon.

Motherhouse and Novitiate, St. Mary's Convent, Beaverton, Oregon. (Archdiocese of Portland in Oregon.)

SISTERS OF MISERICORDE*

1887

THE Congregation of the Sisters of Misericorde, whose primary work is the protection and assistance of unfortunate women and girls, and the care of the sick, was founded in Canada by the Right Rev. Ignace Bourget, Bishop of Montreal, and Madame Rosalie Jetté, January 16, 1848.

Having fruitfully exercised her ardent zeal for works of charity during her brief married life, Madame Jetté, upon the death of her husband, devoted herself still more whole-heartedly to the relief of the misfortunes of her fellow creatures.

When, soon afterward, at the prevalence of much sin and suffering, a plan for the reclamation of unmarried mothers and their little ones, took shape in the mind of Bishop Bourget, and he chose Madame Jetté—on her consent to his proposal, as the person most fitted to execute this project, the work of the Misericorde, was on May 1, 1845, definitely begun.

Housed first in a humble dwelling known as the hospice, Madame Jetté soon witnessed the expansion of her beloved work, and in more extensive property on Wolfe Street, in 1848 the little Community was established on a firm basis, and the characteristic name, Sisters of Misericorde, conferred on Madame Jetté and her companions.

During its six pioneer years the Community had harbored four hundred and thirty-six penitents, and had secured the baptism and saved the lives of more than three hundred infants. Its work, however was not to be confined to reclamation.

The charity of Madame Jetté—in religion Mère Marie de la Nativité, soon found expression in the establishment in the United States of hospitals of the Congregation, for general care of the sick.

Through the instrumentality of the Rev. John McQuirk, a maternity hospital to which a general hospital was later added, established in New York City in 1887, with Sister St. Stanislaus as Superior, was the first United States foundation of the Community.

For the relief especially of abandoned children, a group of sisters, through the Right Rev. Sebastian G. Messmer, D.D., Bishop of Green Bay, and later Archbishop of Milwaukee, in 1900 founded in Green

*From data and material supplied by the Sisters of Misericorde, Convent of Misericorde, 470 Dorchester Street, East, Montreal, P.Q., Canada.

Bay a hospital, since enlarged and adequately meeting modern demands.

In Oak Park, Illinois, a suburb of Chicago, the need for a Catholic general hospital and the endeavors of Dr. John Wesley Tope, a non-

MOTHER MARY OF THE NATIVITY
Foundress in 1848 of the Congregation of the Sisters of Misericorde

Catholic, with ecclesiastical authorities, led to the opportune establishment there, in 1907, of a hospital, well located and amply equipped.

Again the solicitous efforts of Archbishop Messmer resulted in

a foundation of the Sisters of Misericorde, and the former beautiful episcopal residence in Milwaukee became their property in 1908, and was remodeled for hospital use.

In 1914 the Huber Memorial Hospital, so called after the non-Catholic physician whose legacy endowed it, was founded in Pana, Illinois.

All the institutions of the Sisters of Misericorde in the United States are at present general hospitals, subject to the Motherhouse at 470 Dorchester Street, East, in Montreal.

With Sister Marie Immaculate Conception as present United States Superior, assisted by Sister St. Clare d'Assise, and Sister St. Philippe de Neri, the Congregation, mindful of its ordained devotion to Our Lady of Mercy, and the motivating spirit of Misericorde, continues its modern extensive charitable work, in which it so well exemplifies and fulfills the purposes of its foundation.

SUMMARY

Sisters of Misericorde.
Founded in Canada in 1848.
Papal Approbation of Rules, March 21, 1905, by Pope Pius X.
Established in the United States in 1887.
Approximate number in Community in United States, 100.
Active in hospital and charitable work in the archdioceses of Chicago, Milwaukee and New York, and in the dioceses of Green Bay and Springfield in Illinois.

MISSIONARY SISTERS OF THE SACRED HEART*

1889

THE Institute of the Missionary Sisters of the Sacred Heart was founded at Codogno, Italy, on November 14, 1880, by Mother Francesca Xaveria Cabrini. The name of the Order clearly indicates its nature and wide scope and purpose, the extension of the reign of the Sacred Heart in all souls and over all places.

Mother Frances Xavier Cabrini was born in St. Angelo Lodigiano, Italy, on July 15, 1850. She was baptized Mary Frances, on the same day—the Jesuit feast of the "Forty Martyrs." The youngest of many children, and always frail, she was the special care of her eldest sister. Her parents and entire family were people of faith and unblemished morals. When Frances was seven years of age, the reading in the home circle of the Annals of the Propagation of the Faith stirred in her child heart the desire of going to China, and missionary work was ever afterward the constant object of her thoughts.

In her twentieth year she was bereft, within a few months of one another, of both her father and mother. Completing a normal course, Frances, obtained her teacher's diploma, and at the request of the pastor of St. Angelo she taught there for two years, although most desirous of becoming a religious. Again she sacrificed the pursuance of her longing when, in 1874, on the recommendation of the bishop of Lodi, she assumed the direction of an educational institution established by the pastor of Codogno. The companions she gathered about her during the years which followed formed with her the nucleus of the religious congregation which she founded on November 14, 1880, and of which, a month later, the bishop of Lodi signified his approval, under the title of Missionary Sisters of the Sacred Heart.

Though engaged, with her Community, in normal and day school work in Milan and at Borghetto Lodigiano, Mother Cabrini went to Rome in September of 1887, to secure the approbation of her Congregation, to open a house, and to obtain permission from the Sovereign Pontiff to go to the foreign missions.

*From data and material supplied by the Missionary Sisters of the Sacred Heart, Sacred Heart Villa, New York, N. Y.

In 1889 the Most Rev. Michael Augustine Corrigan, D.D., Arch-bishop of New York, invited Mother Cabrini to found an orphanage and an Italian school in New York City.

MOTHER FRANCES XAVIER CABRINI (1850-1917)
Foundress of the Institute of the Missionary Sisters of the Sacred Heart

Encouraged to accept this invitation, by the Holy Father, Pope Leo XIII, who pointed out to her that her mission field lay in the west, instead of the east, Mother Cabrini, accompanied by six sisters, left Codogno for Paris on March 19th, and sailed from Havre for New York, arriving there on the 31st of the same month. On April

2nd an orphanage was opened in New York City for the children of Italian immigrants, the first funds for the foundation of this work being furnished by the Count and Countess Luigi Palma di Cesnola.

The Missionary Sisters of the Sacred Heart had begun their labors in the United States, and before Mother Cabrini returned to Italy, the last of July, a free school in the lower section of the city had also been opened by the sisters.

The following April, Mother Cabrini returned to New York, and purchased from the Jesuit Fathers the beautiful Villa Manresa, located at West Park on the Hudson. To this new location the Sacred Heart Orphanage was transferred and a United States novitiate was established there for the Congregation.

In 1892 Mother Cabrini was again in New York, after having visited in Central America, and in New Orleans, where she promised to found a house. On September 15th of the same year Columbus Hospital of New York was opened in a rented house, inaugurating the hospital work of the Congregation in the United States.

From houses she was establishing in Europe, and in South and Central America, Mother Cabrini crossed the seas to the United States twenty-four times. Traveling from New Orleans to New York, New York to Chicago and Seattle, and through California to Denver, as well as journeying to Philadelphia and Scranton, and through Brooklyn and into New Jersey, the indefatigable foundress spent herself in her Master's work, as she laid well the many splendid United States foundations of the Institute, whose Motherhouse is maintained in Rome. Mother Cabrini imbued her followers with the true spirit of the Congregation and its devotion to the Sacred Heart of Jesus in the sacrament of His love, and—though exposition of the Blessed Sacrament is observed every Friday in the houses of the Institute, and more frequently whenever possible—the privilege of Perpetual Adoration of the Blessed Sacrament, in a central house of the Congregation, as ardently desired by the holy foundress, is anticipated by the Missionary Sisters of the Sacred Heart.

SUMMARY

Missionary Sisters of the Sacred Heart.
Founded in Italy in 1880.
Established in the United States in 1889.
Papal Approbation of Rules, July 12, 1907, by Pope Pius X.
Habit: The habit is black, with a black silk veil, a black cap and bow, and a cape and cincture. A silver cross is suspended from the neck, and a gold ring, bearing a crucifix, is worn on the right hand.
Approximate number in Community in United States, 550.

Active in educational, hospital and charitable work in the archdioceses of
   Chicago, New Orleans, New York and Philadelphia, and in the dioceses
   of Brooklyn, Denver, Los Angeles and San Diego, Newark, Scranton
   and Seattle.

United States Provincial house and Novitiate, Sacred Heart Villa, 701 Fort
   Washington Avenue at 190th Street, New York, New York. (Archdiocese of New York.)

SERVANTS OF THE HOLY HEART OF MARY*

1889

HE Congregation of the Servants of the Holy Heart of Mary was founded in Paris in 1860, by the Rev. Francis J. B. Delaplace, of the Congregation of the Holy Ghost. Forming the first community of the Congregation were Miss Jeanne Marie Moisan and the young women actively engaged in the girls' orphanage which had been established by the Association of the Holy Family, under the direction of Father Delaplace.

Animated with the desire of consecrating their work to God, under a rule and special religious exercises, the earnest band of workers was elevated to a religious community. Candidates were not wanting in the development of the Institute, which in a few years spread to other dioceses in France, where the sisters devoted themselves to the education of the poor and the care of the sick.

In 1889 the Congregation sent sisters to the United States. With Mother Mathild as Superior, the little community's first charge was the infirmary and linen room of St. Viator College, Bourbonnais, Illinois. Two years later, following arrangements made by the Rev. A. Granger, of Kankakee, Illinois, four sisters of the community at St. Viator College went to Kankakee to open the Emergency Hospital, now known as St. Mary's, one of the most progressive of the institutions conducted by the Congregation. A training school for nurses has been

MOTHER MATHILD

*From data and material supplied by the Servants of the Holy Heart of Mary, Holy Family Convent, Beaverville, Ill.

established at this hospital, as well as at Mercy Hospital in Champaign County, Illinois, between the two cities, Urbana and Champaign, which is now in charge of the Servants of the Holy Heart of Mary.

Participation by the Community in school activities in the United States began in 1895, when the sisters opened a boarding school, Holy Family Academy, at Beaverville, Illinois. The sisters later took charge of parochial schools in Chicago and nearby localities. Boarding schools have since been opened at Manteno and Momence, Illinois, and the Community also conducts two villas, one at Momence for little girls from two to six years of age, and one at Beaverville for little boys of the same age.

Two years after the establishment of the academy and a convent in connection with it at Beaverville, Illinois, a novitiate was canonically erected there, while the foundation house of the Institute, at 41 Rue Lhomond, Paris, continues to be the Motherhouse of the Congregation in the United States.

SUMMARY

Servants of the Holy Heart of Mary.
Founded in France in 1860.
Papal Approbation of Rules, May 13, 1913, by Pope Pius X.
Established in the United States in 1889.
Habit: The habit is of black serge, with a black veil and white wimple. A blue girdle encircles the waist and hangs from the left side. The medal of the Institute, on the rosary, represents on one side the Holy Heart of Mary, with the inscription: *Tuus sum ego salvus me fac* (I am thine, save me); and on the other side, the Holy Family, with the inscription: *Et erat subditus illis* (And He was subject to them). An ebony cross with a silver corpus hangs from a blue neck cord, and a silver ring is worn on the ring finger of the left hand.
Approximate number in Community in United States, 120.
Active in educational, hospital and charitable work in the archdiocese of Chicago and in the diocese of Peoria.
United States Provincial house and Novitiate, Holy Family Convent, Beaverville, Illinois. (Diocese of Peoria.)

MISSION HELPERS, SERVANTS OF THE SACRED HEART*

1890

HE work of the Institute of Mission Helpers, Servants of the Sacred Heart, was inaugurated in Baltimore in 1890, when a few devoted women—whom missionary zeal had united for some time—with the approbation and encouragement of His Eminence, James Cardinal Gibbons, began their community life at 416 West Biddle Street, Baltimore, with Mother M. Demetrias as Superior.

As one of the first religious orders to recognize and fill the need for Catholic welfare work, the Mission Helpers for years labored practically alone in the extensive field of religious social service, in which several other communities—still all too inade-quate for the needed work of reclamation, are now engaged.

At first devoting themselves exclusively to work among the colored people, under the direc-tion of the Josephite Fathers, the Mission Helpers, perceiving the evident need of religious instruc-tion for white children, and spiritual assistance for many inmates of institutions, broad-ened the scope of their mis-sionary activities to include catechism classes at the convent and in rural districts, and general institutional social service work.

MOTHER M. DEMETRIAS

Aiding pastors as parish visitors, the Mission Helpers, particularly in large or congested districts, sought out negligent Catholics, inducing them to return to the sacraments, and exerting other influences for good.

*From data and material supplied by the Mission Helpers, Servants of the Sacred Heart, Towson, Md.

687

In 1897 Cardinal Gibbons, realizing the needs of Catholic deaf mutes, confided to the Community the care of these children of silence, and the sisters opened in Baltimore St. Xavier's Home for the Deaf, the only institution of its kind in the province.

In response to the invitation of the Right Rev. James A. McFaul, D.D., Bishop of Trenton, the Mission Helpers in 1898 extended their apostolate beyond Maryland, with the opening in Trenton of St. James' Day Nursery and Kindergarten, and from this center have since conducted their catechetical and missionary work in Trenton and its environs.

SACRED HEART CONVENT, TOWSON, MARYLAND

Porto Rico became the scene of missionary activities of the Community in 1902, when, at the request of the Right Rev. James H. Blenk, S.M., then bishop of Porto Rico, the Mission Helpers introduced their twofold catechetical and visitation work.

The year 1905 brought the Community to New York City and West New Brighton, Staten Island, where its work is especially fruitful, and in 1921, at the invitation of the Most Rev. J. F. Regis Canevin, D.D., then bishop of Pittsburgh, the Mission Helpers made a foundation in that city, and now conduct there St. Anne's Day Nursery, and the Raphael Home, a temporary shelter for poor children.

Under Mother M. Lambert as Superior General, the Motherhouse and novitiate of the Institute have been established on Joppa Road, near Charles Street Avenue, in Towson, Maryland.

SUMMARY

Mission Helpers, Servants of the Sacred Heart.
Founded in the United States in 1890.
Habit: The habit and cincture are black; the long thin veil is pinned to a plain white starched cap, square-shaped over the face. The collar is round, coming down over the breast, and a plain silver crucifix hangs just below it.
Approximate number in Community, 160.
Active in social service work in the archdioceses of Baltimore and New York and in the dioceses of Pittsburgh and Trenton.
Motherhouse and Novitiate, Sacred Heart Convent, Joppa Road, Towson, Maryland. (Archdiocese of Baltimore.)

SISTERS ADORERS OF THE PRECIOUS BLOOD*

1890

THE Institute of the Sisters Adorers of the Precious Blood was founded at St. Hyacinthe, P.Q., Canada, on September 14, 1861, by Miss Aurelie Caouette, who was remarkable for her lively faith and love of prayer, and who became in religion Mother Catherine-Aurelie of the Precious Blood. This saintly religious had, in the execution of her great work, the hearty approval and personal co-operation of the Right Rev. Joseph La Rocque, Bishop of St. Hyacinthe, and the Very Rev. J. S. Raymond, Superior of the seminary and vicar general of the diocese.

The essential object of the Congregation, which was established only after many and severe trials, is to especially honor the Precious Blood of Our Lord, and to make reparation for those who, forgetting the price of their souls, fail in gratitude to Him Who shed His adorable blood for us.

A SISTER ADORER OF THE PRECIOUS BLOOD

Within their cloister these contemplative nuns spend their lives in penance, prayer, and sacrifices, offered to God for the salvation of souls. At midnight they rise and spend an hour before the Blessed Sacrament, atoning for the sins of the day just passed, and soliciting blessings for the day then dawning. At the very hour when God is most offended these religious offer earnest supplications to Heaven for sinners, and take upon themselves the punishment due to others, chastising their own bodies that God may spare and convert those whose hearts are turned from Him.

*From data and material supplied by the Sisters Adorers of the Precious Blood, Monastery of the Precious Blood, Portland, Ore., and from the Official Catholic Directory, 1929.

Each monastery of the Institute of the Sisters Adorers of the Precious Blood is independent, and, subject to the local ordinaries, is ruled according to the same form of government as the foundation house. Each monastery has its own novitiate and receives its own subjects, who may be choir, lay, or tourière sisters.

Except for the required hours of recreation, time not spent in prayer in the monasteries of the Order the sisters give to work. They make all kinds of Church vestments and articles of piety, and, in the variety of the occupations, mould and paint statues and crucifixes. All work is performed in silence and in a spirit of penance, and the household duties are shared by all the sisters in common.

The Congregation was established in the United States in 1890, under the patronage of the Right Rev. John Loughlin, D. D., then bishop of Brooklyn, in whose episcopal city the first of its monasteries in this country was founded. Following the introduction of the Institute into the United States, monasteries were established in Portland, Oregon, and Manchester, New Hampshire. At the latter foundation the religious accommodate women retreatants.

SUMMARY

Sisters Adorers of the Precious Blood.

Founded in Canada in 1861.

Papal Approbation of Rule, October 20, 1896, by Pope Leo XIII.

Established in the United States in 1890.

Habit: The habit of the choir sisters is of white serge, with a long red scapular, in honor of the Immaculate Conception and the Precious Blood. A small red cross is sewn upon the black veil, and a cincture of red cloth with a pendant upon which the instruments of the Passion are painted in white, is worn. The guimpe and band are of white linen. A silver ring is worn on the ring finger of the right hand, and a silver reliquary cross is worn on the breast, engraven with the three mottoes symbolical of their vocation: *Precieux Sang, Marie Immaculee,* and *Jesus Hostie.* The habit of the lay sisters and the tourière sisters is black.

Approximate number in communities in United States, 100.

Engaged in contemplative life in the following monasteries, each with its own novitiate:

> Monastery of the Precious Blood, 220 East 76th Street, Portland, Oregon. (Archdiocese of Portland in Oregon.)
>
> Monastery of the Sisters Adorers of the Precious Blood, Fort Hamilton Parkway and 54th Street, Brooklyn, New York. (Diocese of Brooklyn.)
>
> Monastery of the Precious Blood, 555 Union Street, Manchester, New Hampshire. (Diocese of Manchester.)

SISTERS OF THE BLESSED SACRAMENT FOR INDIANS AND COLORED PEOPLE*

1891

$\mathcal{CE}$ENTURIES ago the Indians received the heritage of the faith, rich and enlivened by the blood of the pioneer martyr missionaries, but apathy and neglect to foster this early fertility had palpably weakened Catholicity among the race, when, to devote itself exclusively to the needed Christian training of the Indians, and the negroes as well, the Congregation of the Sisters of the Blessed Sacrament for Indians and Colored People was founded in Philadelphia, in 1891, by Miss Katharine Drexel.

The daughter of Francis A. Drexel, one of Philadelphia's leading financiers and philanthropists, Miss Drexel, though born to a life of ease and wealth, yearned to devote herself entirely to the service of God, whom she felt was calling her in a special way to the religious life, but seemed unable to decide on entrance into any then-existent order.

Confident of Miss Drexel's zeal and benevolence, the Right Rev. Martin Marty, D.D., appointed to the vicariate apostolic of Dakota in 1880, and later bishop of Sioux Falls and St. Cloud, appealed to her in behalf of the Christian education of the Indians in his extensive see. Government appropriations, instituted under the administration of President Grant, in the interest of the Indians, for their schooling under religious auspices, would partially support the undertaking. Schools, principally, were required, to make possible Catholic training. The bishop met a ready response in Miss Drexel's generosity. Without delay she financed the erection and equipment of Catholic mission schools for Indian children; two of these were established in South Dakota, and three others, in Minnesota, New Mexico and Wyoming, respectively.

Later Miss Drexel, traveling in the west and southwest, personally visited these establishments brought about by her charity, and witnessed the missionary work being carried on in them by members of different religious communities. Little did she dream, however, that she herself, with a devoted sisterhood, would soon be actually

---

*From data and material supplied by the Sisters of the Blessed Sacrament for Indians and Colored People, St. Elizabeth's, Cornwells Heights, Pa.

laboring amidst the same missionary scenes, and, moreover, conse-crated exclusively to work among the Indian and colored races.

In January, 1887, Miss Drexel and her sister, while abroad, were received in private audience by Pope Leo XIII. Miss Katharine, in

MOTHER M. KATHARINE DREXEL
Foundress and Superior General of the Congregation of the Sisters of the Blessed Sacrament for Indians and Colored People

speaking to the Holy Father, dwelt on the great need of laborers among the Indians, and in the simplicity of her soul begged him to send some missionaries to work among them. With the smile for which he was remarkable, lighting up that singularly clear eye, by which he seemed to pierce the future, and with a voice, the tones of which touched the innermost depths of Miss Drexel's soul, he replied: "Why not become a missionary yourself, my child?"

Coming at the moment when she was struggling with the prompt-ings of grace, this seemed, as undoubtedly it was, the voice of God Himself.

In obedience to the counsel of her spiritual director, the Right Rev. James O'Connor, D.D., Bishop of Omaha, formerly pastor of St. Dominic's Church, Holmesburg, Pennsylvania, near which the family had established a summer home, Miss Drexel, on May 6, 1889, entered the novitiate of the Sisters of Mercy in Pittsburgh, there to prepare and fit herself for the work of the formation of a new society for missionary work among Indians and Negroes.

Under the helpful guidance of the daughters of the saintly Mother McAuley, at their Motherhouse in Pittsburgh, and beholding the exemplification of the exterior charities of the active apostolate, as well as the characteristic spirit of the interior life, Sister Mary Katharine, as Miss Drexel was then called, and companions who had joined her, began their separate community life, under the auspices of the Sisters of Mercy, and pledged themselves, in a special vow, to labor solely for the Indian and colored races. The Most Rev. Patrick J. Ryan, D.D., Archbishop of Philadelphia, who succeeded Bishop O'Connor in the direction of the young Society, appointed Mother Katharine first Superior of the new Community, which then numbered thirteen members.

With the purchase of a site for the Motherhouse, near Phila-delphia, arrangements were made for a temporary novitiate at St. Michael's, Torresdale, the old homestead of the Drexel family, and in May, 1891, the Sisters of the Blessed Sacrament left for their new home.

In 1892, on the feast of St. Francis Xavier, one of the special patrons of the Community, the sisters were formally transferred from the temporary novitiate at Torresdale to St. Elizabeth's Convent, Cornwells Heights, Bucks County, Pennsylvania, where the Motherhouse had been established, and soon afterward began, locally and in distant missions, the work that has become associated with them.

In June, 1894, the sisters opened St. Catherine's Boarding School for Pueblo Indians, at Santa Fé, New Mexico, and from here have since conducted catechism classes, caring for and visiting their Indian charges.

A boarding and industrial school was opened at Rock Castle, Virginia, in 1899, primarily to educate colored girls for competent and Christian teaching in southern schools.

St. Michael's Boarding School for Navajo Indians was established in 1903 in Arizona, and an academy for the higher education of colored girls was later opened in Nashville, Tennessee. In 1925 the Community further extended its activities, now widespread

Courtyard View
CONVENT OF THE BLESSED SACRAMENT, ST. ELIZABETH'S,
CORNWELLS HEIGHTS, PENNSYLVANIA

throughout the country, with the foundation of Xavier College for colored girls, in New Orleans.

With only zeal and charity to limit their activities in their chosen field, all kinds of educational, catechetical and settlement work, the care of orphans and the sick, and the visiting of prisoners, are within the scope of the Sisters of the Blessed Sacrament for Indians and Colored People, as their varied works today testify.

Since the discontinuance, in 1900, of all Government appropriations for so-called sectarian mission schools, most of the existing Catholic schools have been almost entirely supported by the Bureau of Catholic Indian Missions, in Washington, D. C. With the interests of the Bureau, as the official agency established in the capital for the transaction of the affairs of the Catholic Indian missions with the United States Indian Office, Mother M. Katharine has generously allied herself, and contributes to it annually. Through her instru-mentality, also, and helping to supply, in part, the deficit in the resources for the missions on the final withdrawal of Government tuition for the Indian pupils of the mission schools, the Society for the Preservation of the Faith among Indian Children, or Preservation Society, was founded. This association collects from its members a yearly fee of one dollar.

In Washington the Sisters of the Blessed Sacrament for Indians and Colored People assist in the office management and editing of *The Indian Sentinel,* issued quarterly by the Bureau of Catholic Indian Missions, of which the Right Rev. Msgr. William Hughes is the present director. The convent of the sisters in Washington is known as Tekakwitha House, after the noble Mohawk Indian maiden, Kateri Tekakwitha.

The question is often asked why this Congregation has been called Sisters of the Blessed Sacrament. The answer is found in the Constitutions of the Institute, according to which the Blessed Sacra-ment is to be the inspiration of its members, and their binding tie in their missionary labors among both the Indian and colored races.

During the archbishopric of the Most Rev. Edmond F. Prender-gast, D.D., in the archdiocesan see of Philadelphia, the privilege of daily exposition of the Blessed Sacrament in the chapel of the Motherhouse was granted to Mother M. Katharine for the Con-gregation.

Furthering their three-fold apostolate, the Sisters of the Blessed Sacrament for Indians and Colored People, at their Motherhouse in Cornwells Heights, Pennsylvania, edit monthly *Mission Fields at Home,* in advancement of their work.

As the Institute is a missionary Congregation, the government is general as well as central, and Mother M. Katharine Drexel, who has continued as Superior General, has, to aid her in the administra-tion of the Community, four Councilors-General, three of whom are respectively, Assistant-General, Treasurer-General and Secretary-General, and a proportionate number of subordinate officers, according to the needs of the Congregation.

SUMMARY

Sisters of the Blessed Sacrament for Indians and Colored People.
Founded in the United States in 1891.
Papal Approbation of Rules, May 25, 1913, by Pope Pius X.
Habit: The habit and scapular are of black woolen material. An ebony crucifix is worn on the breast. A black woolen veiling is worn over an underveil of starched muslin; the forehead band is of starched linen. The guimpe is of white starched muslin, descending in front a little below the top of the scapular. Around the waist the sisters wear a white cord with three knots, and with a rosary attached to the left side. A church cloak of white serge is worn at all ceremonies, on feast days of the Congregation, and during adoration of the Blessed Sacrament. After final profession a silver ring is worn on the third finger of the left hand.
Approximate number in Community, 320.
Active in educational, charitable and social service work among Indians and Negroes in the archdioceses of Baltimore, Boston, Chicago, Cincinnati, New Orleans, New York, Philadelphia, St. Louis and Santa Fé, and in the dioceses of Brooklyn, Cleveland, Columbus, Galveston, Lafayette, Mobile, Nashville, Natchez, Omaha, Richmond, Savannah, Sioux Falls and Tucson.
Motherhouse and Novitiate, Convent of the Blessed Sacrament, St. Elizabeth's, Cornwells Heights, Pennsylvania. (Archdiocese of Philadelphia.)

LITTLE SISTERS OF THE ASSUMPTION*

1891

THE founding of the Congregation of the Little Sisters of the Assumption, in Paris, France, in 1865, was the inspired work of the holy Assumptionist priest, the Rev. Etienne Pernet, who beheld as in a vision the plan of such a community, its scope and details.

Keeping the project in mind, Père Etienne but awaited the time for its development. Meanwhile he directed the charitable endeavors of three young women who had sought him, asking for some sick persons to look after. To these three, Mlle. Marie Maire and two companions, he directed Mlle. Antoinette Fage, a fervent and devout woman, forty years of age, and a native of Paris, earning her livelihood as a dressmaker, who had placed herself under his spiritual guidance, and whom he realized was the chosen one for the development of the institute he had in view, for which he drew up the rules.

Accepting the suggestion of her director as the voice of Providence, Mlle. Fage joined the little band, and in July, 1865, the small community became established at 233 Rue St. Dominique. Not long afterward, Mlle. Fage found herself at the head of a community of eight, and named Superior, becoming Mère Marie de Jésus, while Marie Maire became Soeur Marie de la Croix.

During the following summer, cholera ravaged the poorest quarters of Paris, and the little community responded heroically with its services to those in need. In that year, also, Mother Mary of Jesus, as foundress, was allowed to make her first vows. On the feast of the Assumption, 1867, she renewed them, and at that time a decision was made that the members of the Congregation should be known as the Little Sisters of the Assumption.

War between France and Prussia breaking out shortly after the Little Sisters of the Assumption had become domiciled, and Father Pernet, their zealous founder, becoming a military chaplain, a religious garb for the Community was not decided upon until July 2, 1875. The Institute was then formally erected by the cardinal archbishop of Paris, who conferred on the sisters the religious habit and received their first canonical vows.

---

*From data and material supplied by the Little Sisters of the Assumption, 1624 Poplar Street, Philadelphia, Pa.

Within the next two decades of years the "nursing sisters of the sick poor," as the Little Sisters of the Assumption are described, from the nature of their work, had several houses in Paris, and establishments as well in other cities of France, and in England and Ireland.

MOTHER MARY OF JESUS (1824-1883)
Foundress of the Little Sisters of the Assumption

The sisters nurse the sick poor in their own homes, irrespective of creed or nationality, and without remuneration. They also assist in the house and help the family, exerting a beneficent influence and effecting much good.

In 1891 members of the Community came to the United States, and were received into the archdiocese of New York by its gracious archbishop, the Most Rev. Michael Augustine Corrigan, D.D.

Two years after inaugurating their charitable work in the city of New York, the Little Sisters of the Assumption were visited by their venerable founder, Father Pernet, who, accompanying four Little Sisters sent from France to join the New York foundation, spent a few weeks there. After this visit, Father Pernet, opportunely in Rome, interested himself in the first decree of the papal approbation of the Congregation, which was granted in 1897.

The Community now has two houses in New York City, one at 246 East Fifteenth Street, where postulants are received, before making their novitiate at the General Motherhouse in Paris, and another at 340 Convent Avenue. From a third convent in Philadelphia, the Little Sisters of the Assumption, as in New York, go forth on their merciful work of nursing the sick poor in their own homes.

United States Foundation house, 246 East 15th Street, New York, New York. (Archdiocese of New York.)

INSTITUTE OF THE BLESSED VIRGIN MARY*

1892

THE Institute of the Blessed Virgin Mary, whose members in several branches of the Order are known as "Ladies of Loretto," was founded by Mary Ward, a noble English lady, born in Yorkshire in 1585.

Though connected by blood with most of the great Catholic families of Yorkshire, Mary Ward, in 1606, entered a convent of Poor Clares at St. Omer, in Flanders, as a lay sister. Finding that her religious vocation was not for the contemplative life, she resolved to devote herself, as a religious, to active work, especially that of the education of girls.

With some devoted companions, she established an entirely new institute—the first of its kind in the history of religious orders of women. At this period there was no organization of women following the rule of religious life, not bound to enclosure, and it had been clearly manifested to Mary Ward that her special vocation was to draw souls to God by the education of youth, a calling to which the cloistered life, as it was then observed, presented many difficulties. Therefore it became the object of her life and labors to form an institute whose members should devote themselves to this great work, and she took the Rule of St. Ignatius as a guide for their way of living, adapting it to a community of women, without in any way claiming affiliation with the Society founded by this illustrious saint.

In an enterprise so unprecedented, she had, as might have been expected, peculiar difficulties to encounter, and those of a nature calculated to discourage a heart less brave and less firmly established in God. So great was the opposition in England to this break with the past—the establishment of an uncloistered community of women, that the new Institute was finally suppressed in that country, following the issuance, in 1631, of a Bull of Pope Urban VIII.

With his papal permission, however, Mother Ward and those of her community who had remained with her, transferred their activities to Munich, where they were graciously received by the

---

*From data and material supplied by the Institute of the Blessed Virgin Mary, Loretto Abbey, Motherhouse and Novitiate, 403 Wellington Street, West, Toronto, Canada.

Elector of Bavaria, Maximilian I. Shortly after this, Mother Ward opened a convent of the Order in Rome. Her work was not destroyed, but reconstituted to meet papal approval. In 1639, with letters from Pope Urban VIII, Mother Ward returned to England and was received there by Queen Henrietta Marie. Three years later Mother Ward died in the convent which she had established at Heworth, near York.

In just tribute to Mother Ward and in loyal memory of the third centenary of the holy foundress, Cardinal Bourne, that great Churchman in the see of Westminster, said, "The very existence of modern educational and charitable congregations was made possible by the supernatural foresight, the heroic perseverance and the terrible disappointments and sufferings of Mary Ward. She waged the battle, to the point of defeat, of which they are reaping the victory. To no one, after their own special founders, do they owe greater gratitude than to Mary Ward."

In 1686 the community at Heworth transferred to the site of the present convent, Micklegate Bar, York, the oldest existing convent in England. It was to this convent-school, as a pupil, that John Ball of Dublin sent his nine year old daughter, Frances. Remaining there until the death of her father, in 1808, Frances then spent some years at home with her mother. In 1818, under the spiritual direction of Archbishop Murray of Dublin, Frances returned to York and entered the novitiate of the Institute of the Blessed Virgin Mary. In 1822, having completed her novitiate, she was sent, at the request of Archbishop Murray, with companion sisters, to establish the Institute in Ireland. The new foundation was made at Rathfarnham, a short distance from Dublin, and was called Loretto Abbey, hence the local appellation, "Loretto Nuns," which prevails in Ireland and America.

Mother Frances Ball, who died in 1861, was a woman of great piety and great administrative ability. She devoted her energies to the establishment of schools, and the development of the Institute.

The different foundations in America owe their origin to the zeal of the Right Rev. Dr. Power, Bishop of Toronto, and the co-operation extended to him by Mother Frances, who, on August 5, 1847, sent sisters to Toronto, and established its first Catholic educational institution for girls. On the death of Mother Ignatia Hutchinson, the Superior of the pioneer band of "Loretto Nuns," Mother Teresa Dease, also from Rathfarnham, was chosen her successor. During Mother Teresa's administration, the Institute of the Blessed Virgin Mary was introduced into the United States.

In 1892, through the efforts of the Rev. Bernard Murray, the indefatigable pastor of St. Bernard's Church in Englewood, in Chicago, Loretto Nuns, with Mother M. Christina as Superior, were sent from the Motherhouse in Toronto to open in that parish, in Chicago, their first United States school.

The Institute has since extended its activities to other schools in Chicago, and to schools in the diocese of Marquette. Loretto Academy, 6541 Stewart Avenue, Chicago, conducted in connection with St. Bernard's School, is the mother institute of the Order in the United States, governed by superiors appointed from the General Motherhouse in Toronto, and under its jurisdiction.

MOTHER TERESA DEASE

While adapting itself to the needs of the country, and fitting its members to meet the demands made by modern standards of education, the Institute preserves the ideals of its holy foundress, in the formation of a high type of Christian womanhood.

In their establishment, in Toronto, in 1911, of Loretto Abbey College—affiliated to the University of Toronto, through St. Michael's Federated College, and in their being the first religious outside of the United States to act as hostesses—as they graciously did through Mother M. Alberta, and the sisters and alumnae of Loretto Academy, Niagara Falls, Ontario, in August, 1928—to the Eighth Biennial Convention of the International Federation of Catholic Alumnae, the members of the Institute but further carried out the ideals of the saintly woman, called from the quiet and contemplation of the cloister to the gaze and criticism of the public, in the contacts necessary in the implanting of Christian education, in the highest degree, for Catholic womanhood throughout the centuries.

SUMMARY

Institute of the Blessed Virgin Mary.
Founded in Bavaria in 1609.

Papal Approbation of Rules, February 15, 1877, by Pope Pius IX.
Established in the United States in 1892.
Approximate number in Community in United States, 85.
Active in educational work in the archdiocese of Chicago and the diocese of
    Marquette.
Loretto Branch Novitiate, 6541 Stewart Avenue, Chicago, Illinois.   (Arch-
    diocese of Chicago.)

HELPERS OF THE HOLY SOULS*

1892

THE Society of the Helpers of the Holy Souls, especially devoted to the relief of the Church suffering, through meritorious active works of charity, was founded in Paris, January 19, 1856, by Mlle. Eugénie Marie Smet of Lille, France.

Throughout her childhood, love for the souls in Purgatory distinguished the foundress of this Society, and led her, when she realized the lack of a religious community primarily for their aid, to appeal for and receive approbation of her project for the formation of such an order.

Fittingly was the holy foundress known in religion as Mother Mary of Providence. Under her guidance as first Superior of the Society of the Helpers of the Holy Souls, and her extraordinary trust in the Providence of God, foundations were made beyond France, and the charitable activities of the sisters were extended to the principal countries of Europe, and also China, where owing to circumstances, the sisters have included teaching in their work.

Thus to the contemplative life the sisters join the active, drawing from the former the strength to practice the spiritual and corporal works of mercy among the living for the solace of the dead.

On May 29, 1892, through the efforts of Miss Adele LeBrun, and others whom she had interested in the cause of their coming, seven members of the Society of the Helpers of the Holy Souls, with Mother Mary of St. Bernard as Superior, came to the United States and were installed in the house prepared for them in New York, at 25 Seventh Avenue.

Soon the poor of the neighborhood learned to appreciate the blessing which had been sent them, and went to the convent with all their troubles and sorrows of soul and body, knowing they would never be turned away comfortless.

In 1894, the house on Seventh Avenue proving inadequate to their growing needs, the Helpers established their central foundation in the United States at 112-118 E. 86th Street.

In their social service work among the sick-poor in their own homes or in hospitals, and in settlement houses, where they provide for the religious instruction of neglected children, and the spiritual

*From data and material supplied by the Helpers of the Holy Souls, 114 East 86th Street, New York City.

and temporal welfare of the unfortunate, the Helpers of the Holy Souls—typically described as "soul-thirsty," find many opportunities

MOTHER MARY OF PROVIDENCE (1825-1871)
Foundress of the Society of the Helpers of the Holy Souls

for unseen good works that bring refreshment to the souls in Purgatory.

The sisters, who labor gratuitously among the poor and sick, and derive their own support from voluntary outside offerings, in addition to the ordinary vows of religion, bind themselves, by the Heroic Act of Charity, to resign in favor of the dead all the satisfactions which they would otherwise gain for themselves, or which might be applied to them by others, during their lives or after death.

Soon after the foundation of the Society, an association of honorary members was formed, to accommodate those desirous of sharing in the good works of the Helpers, without formally severing themselves from the duties of ordinary life.

CONVENT OF OUR LADY OF PROVIDENCE, CHAPPAQUA, NEW YORK

Later, to satisfy the wish of a group of women who longed to imitate still more closely than was intended for the honorary members, the religious observances and charities of the sisters, the organization of the "Lady Associates" was originated. The obligations of this group are more extensive than those of the honorary members. They make a formal consecration, attend mass at stated times in the convent chapel, work for the poor and daily recite the Vespers for the Dead, uniting their prayers and labors in behalf of the souls in Purgatory to the zeal of the religious.

There are many orders doing deeds of mercy, and many engaged in the great work of the Christian education of children, but none other so combines in its mission—as does the Society of the Helpers of the Holy Souls, the two-fold object of aiding and uplifting Christ's needy ones on earth, while at the same time, by the merits of its prayers and good works, freeing suffering souls from Purgatory, where His justice demands that they should be detained until they are "whiter than snow," and rendered worthy to enjoy the Beatific Vision.

SUMMARY

Helpers of the Holy Souls.

Founded in France in 1856.

Papal Approbation of Rules, June 25, 1878, by Pope Leo XIII.

Established in the United States in 1892.

Habit: The habit is all black, simple and plain, and subject to slight change according to the times and climate.

Approximate number in Community in United States, 100.

Active in social service work in the archdioceses of Chicago, New York, St. Louis and San Francisco.

United States Novitiate, Convent of Our Lady of Providence, St. Elmo's Hill, Chappaqua, New York.   (Archdiocese of New York.)

RELIGIOUS OF OUR LADY OF THE RETREAT IN THE CENACLE*

1892

*A*T La Louvesc, France, famed as the shrine of St. John Francis Regis, the Society of Our Lady of the Retreat in the Cenacle was founded in 1826, originating, in the Providence of God, directly through the peculiar needs of this little town, a mecca of French pilgrims.

Inspired to erect a needed hostel, where the women pilgrims could profitably pass the time of their pilgrimages in suitable devotions, while receiving religious instruction, the Rev. Jean Pierre Etienne Terme, with the co-operation of Marie Victoire Couderc, known in religion as Mother Thérèse Couderc, laid the foundation of the Society of the Cenacle and its distinctive work. To further the object of the pilgrimages, Father Terme required the guests to make a novena, or to participate in the religious exercises at the convent hospice for at least three days.

The plan of the Institute was approved by the Bishop of Viviers, Msgr. Bonnell, and under the guidance of Mother Thérèse Couderc, its foundress, as Superior, the first members of the Community began their work with the opening of the first of their now many "Cenacles" for the giving of retreats, in La Louvesc, on the summit of the mountains where St. Francis Regis died.

The title of "Religious of Our Lady of the Cenacle," appropriately linking the character of the Institute with that of the model retreat, the upper room and Cenacle of Jerusalem—where the apostles "were persevering with one mind in prayer with the women and Mary, the Mother of Jesus," was early bestowed on the members of the new Society.

Lyons, in 1845, harbored the second Cenacle of the Society, and houses were later opened in Paray-le-Monial, and other cities throughout France, Italy, England, Germany, Holland, Switzerland and Belgium, where the European Motherhouse and novitiate were established, in Brussels, at 126 rue Hôtel des monnaies, now under Mother Marie Majoux, former Superior of the Cenacle of New York, as Superior General.

In 1892 members of the Society first came to the United States,

*From data and material supplied by the Religious of Our Lady of the Cenacle, Cenacle of St. Regis, 628 West 140th Street, New York, N. Y.

and were received in New York City by the Most Rev. Michael Augustine Corrigan, D.D., Archbishop of New York.

With Mother de Grimaldi as first Superior of the American Community, the religious pursued their chosen work, the conducting

MOTHER THÉRÈSE COUDERC
Foundress in 1826 of the Society of Our Lady of the Retreat in the Cenacle

of retreats, and the teaching of Christian Doctrine, to which the choir sisters especially devote themselves, in accordance with a promise appended to the vows. The labors of the religious in New York, at the Cenacle of St. Regis, overlooking the Hudson River, have been amply rewarded, and a recent estimate shows that in the course of five years thirty-five thousand retreatants, resident at different times at this Cenacle, and directly under its religious influence, have found in it spiritual rest and refreshment.

In 1906 the first United States Cenacle outside of New York was established in Newport, Rhode Island, at 21 Battery Street, where it commands a beautiful outlook on Narragansett Bay.

CENACLE NOVITIATE, LAKE RONKONKOMA, LONG ISLAND, NEW YORK

The Boston Cenacle was opened in 1910, in response to the invitation of His Eminence, William Cardinal O'Connell, who has since that time supported and encouraged the apostolic activities of the religious.

In Chicago, in 1920, in answer to an invitation from His Eminence, George Cardinal Mundelein, D.D., then Archbishop of Chicago, a Cenacle was opened at 513 Fullerton Parkway, and rapidly became an important spiritual factor in the city.

The novitiate and retreat house established in May, 1922, on the wooded estate and at the former summer home, the gift to the Society of Miss Maude Adams, non-Catholic actress, are located near Lake Ronkonkoma, Long Island, New York.

The Society, which is governed by a Superior General, is in this country now under the direction of the United States Vicar Provincial, Mother Teresa de La Chapelle, residing at the United States Provincial house and novitiate at Lake Ronkonkoma.

The outcome of the labors of the Religious of Our Lady of the Cenacle depends particularly on silence, prayer and recollection, and through the recitation of the Divine Office according to the Roman

Breviary, and the daily exposition of the Blessed Sacrament, the religious obtain blessings on their active apostolic labors—catechetical instruction and the training of cathechists.   In addition to this religious teaching, the Cenacles established in the United States now offer to women of every rank, the opportunity—conveniently suited to leisure from home or business—of complete seclusion, while obtaining a right spiritual perspective of daily life in the restfulness and calm of a retreat.

SUMMARY

Religious of Our Lady of the Retreat in the Cenacle.
Founded in France in 1826.
Papal Approbation of Rules by Pope Pius IX.
Established in the United States in 1892.
Habit: The habit, adapted from the French peasant costume of the period of the foundation of the Society, is of black, with a white fluted bonnet and black veil, silver cross, French wedding ring of gold, and purple cape. This color had become associated with St. Francis Regis.
Approximate number in Community in United States, 220.
Engaged in catechetical work and the conducting of retreats in Cenacles in the archdioceses of Boston, Chicago and New York, and in the dioceses of Brooklyn and Providence.
United States Provincial house and Novitiate, The Cenacle, Lake Ronkonkoma, Long Island, New York.   (Diocese of Brooklyn.)

THE LITTLE COMPANY OF MARY*

1893

PECIFICALLY for the work of nursing the sick and praying for the dying, the Little Company of Mary was founded at Nottingham, England, in 1877, by Mary Potter, distinguished for her spiritual writings, who though designated as the Mother Foundress of the Congregation, during her life was known to all who loved her—whether sisters or seculars, as simply "Mother."

With its General Motherhouse maintained in Rome, and the affairs of the Congregation under a Cardinal-Protector, foundations of the Community have been made throughout Europe, and in Australia, New Zealand, South Africa and North and South America.

Upon the Invitation of the Most Rev. Patrick A. Feehan, D.D., first archbishop of Chicago, and at the request of Mr. C. A. Mair, benefactor and life-long friend of the Little Company of Mary, the Order came to Chicago, Illinois, in 1893.

Chicago was chosen as the site of the first foundation in the United States in deference to the dying wish of Mr. Mair's wife, whom the sisters had nursed during a mortal illness in Rome.

Established in a small house located on the site of the present Motherhouse in Chicago, where the Congregation has continued its American activities, the sisters, with Mother M. Veronica as first United States Superior, began their charitable labors in this country by attendance of the sick in their own homes, and daily "watches" before the Blessed Sacrament for the dying.

MOTHER M. PATRICK

*From data supplied by the Little Company of Mary, 4130 Indiana Avenue, Chicago, Ill.

In September, 1928, His Eminence, George Cardinal Munde-lein, D.D., gave his approbation to the plan of the sisters for the erection of what will be one of Chicago's largest hospitals. The new hospital, of nine stories, with a capacity of six hundred beds, is to be located in Evergreen Park, on the south side of the city.

Prior to the election of Mother M. Stanislaus, the present United States Superior, Mother M. Patrick, becoming known and loved throughout the archdiocese, for many years served the American Community in that office.

SUMMARY

The Little Company of Mary.
Founded in England in 1877.
Papal Approbation of Rules, April 24, 1893, by Pope Leo XIII.
Established in the United States in 1893.
Habit: The habit is of black serge, with a scapular and a black veil faced
   with blue. For nursing, a habit of white, with a blue linen veil, is worn.
Active in hospital and nursing work in the archdiocese of Chicago.
United States Motherhouse and Novitiate, Convent of the Little Company of
   Mary, 4130 Indiana Avenue, Chicago, Illinois. (Archdiocese of Chicago.)

MANTELLATE SISTERS, SERVANTS OF MARY*

HE historic name, "Mantellate Sisters," has long denoted the followers of St. Juliana Falconieri in the tertiary branch of the privileged Order of Servants of Mary, whose inspired foundation took place in the thirteenth century.

The Order of Servants of Mary, or Servites, especially set apart for the propagation of devotion to the sorrows of Mary, was founded in the year 1233 by seven holy Florentine patricians. Having renounced their riches and withdrawn from their families, the pious founders, members of a confraternity of the Blessed Virgin, were living a community life of prayer and penance, when they were miraculously bidden by Mary herself to retire from the world even further, and establish the Order of her Servants, under the Rule of St. Augustine.

Some years later, the Second Order of Servites, made up of cloistered nuns, was instituted.

It was through the influence of her uncle, St. Alexis Falconieri, one of the seven holy founders, who trained her in Christian practices from her earliest youth, that St. Juliana, who was born in Florence in 1270, resolved to dedicate her life to God. From St. Philip Benizi, illustrious in the Order of Servants of Mary, who had written a rule for the Third Order, she received the tertiary habit in 1285, thus becoming the foundress of the entire Third Order of Servites.

In 1304 the Servite Order received definite papal approbation.

After her mother's death, Juliana and several companions began community life, and in 1305 established the first convent of the Sisters of the Third Order of Servites, or Mantellate Sisters, Servants of Mary.

Wearing the black garb ordained for the Servite Order, in remembrance of the sorrows of Mary, the Mantellate Sisters, so designated because of their long mantle and the short-sleeved habit they adopted to facilitate work, devoted themselves to prayer and mortification, the care of the sick, and other charities.

For thirty-five years, during which her sanctity attracted many novices to the Mantellate, and until the end of her life, Juliana directed her Community, and was remarkable for her many virtues, her great devotion to the Blessed Sacrament and to the dolors of Mary.

*From the Catholic Encyclopedia and *Our Lady of Sorrows Messenger*, published by the Servite Fathers, Chicago, Ill.

After her holy death, on June 12, 1341, the impress of the Sacred Host, which she had been unable to receive in Holy Communion, but which had been laid on a corporal on her breast, was

ST. JULIANA FALCONIERI (1270-1341)
Foundress of the Mantellate Sisters, Servants of Mary

found stamped on St. Juliana's heart. In memory of this extraordinary occurrence, her spiritual daughters have since worn a representation of the Sacred Host on their habits.

Perpetuating in their work the spirit of their venerated foundress, the Mantellate Sisters, Servants of Mary, have extended their varied activities beyond Italy, and into France, England, and other European countries.

OMAHA, NEBRASKA*

1893

The community of sisters of the Order of Servants of Mary, whose United States Provincial Motherhouse is maintained at Omaha, Nebraska, came to this country from England in 1893, during the superior generalship of Mother M. Philomena Morel. Mother Mary Gertrude Gui-naw, who at an early age had consecrated her life to the service of God in this historic Order, was sent with five com-panion sisters to take charge of a school at Mt. Vernon, Indi-ana, in response to an appeal for teachers for his school made by the Rev. F. B. Luebbermann, pastor of St. Matthew's Church.

Through the persevering energy of Mother Gertrude, this foundation of the daughters of St. Juliana, of the Congrega-tion in England, was stabilized

MOTHER M. ALOYSIA

in the United States. Its novitiate, established for a time at Enfield, Illinois, and later at Cherokee, Iowa, was transferred to Omaha, Nebraska, in 1921, upon the invitation of the Right Rev. J. J. Harty, D.D., Bishop of Omaha.

During the construction of Our Lady of Sorrows Convent, Mother Gertrude established the headquarters of the community in the old Chinese Mission House on Bedfard Avenue, while Mt. St. Mary's Convent, where a junior college for girls was established in 1929, was maintained as an academy.

Mt. St. Mary's at Cherokee, Iowa, and the splendid new institu-tion at Omaha, now the site of the United States headquarters of the community, and the residence of Mother M. Aloysia, present Superior Vicaress, stand as lasting monuments to the memory of Mother Ger-

---

*From data and material supplied by the Servants of Mary, Convent of Our Lady of Sorrows, Omaha, Neb.

trude, the zealous English Mantellate Sister who for more than thirty years was the mainstay of the community, and whose death occurred at St. Mary's Priory, in London, on May 29, 1929.

CONVENT OF OUR LADY OF SORROWS, OMAHA, NEBRASKA

SUMMARY

Mantellate Sisters, Servants of Mary.

Founded in Italy about 1285.

Established in the United States (London Congregation) in 1893.

Papal Approbation of Rules (London Congregation), July 28, 1924, by Pope Pius XI.

Habit: The Servite habit, black in honor of the sorrows of Mary, is worn, with a black veil lined with white, a close-fitting pleated white wimple, and a long black scapular. The image of a Host is worn on the scapular over the heart, in remembrance of the miracle wrought at the death of St. Juliana. On occasions a black mantle is worn.

Approximate number in community in United States (London Congregation), 140.

Active in educational work in the dioceses of Belleville, Denver, Ogdensburg, Omaha and Sioux City.

United States Provincial house and Novitiate, Convent of Our Lady of Sorrows, 74th and Military Streets, Omaha, Nebraska. (Diocese of Omaha.)

LADYSMITH, WISCONSIN*

1912

The Congregation of Servants of Mary which was established at Ladysmith, Wisconsin, in 1912, has its affiliation as Servite Sisters through its founding by Mantellate Sisters from Pistoia, Italy.

---

*From data and material supplied by the Servants of Mary, Convent of Our Lady of Sorrows, Ladysmith, Wis.

Under the episcopal patronage of the zealous bishop, the Right Rev. J. M. Koudelka, D.D., who succeeded to the see of Superior the year following their establishment, the Servite Sisters of Ladysmith were encouraged in their foundation, and entered upon an era of progress as religious teachers, and worthy daughters of St. Juliana, whose rule they follow.

With the establishment of St. Mary's Hospital at Ladysmith in 1918 the Sisters inaugurated their work in hospitals and the conducting of training schools for nurses.

Under the present administration of Mother M. Alphonse, Superior General of the Congregation, its educational labors have recently been extended beyond Wisconsin into West Virginia.

A SERVANT OF MARY, LADYSMITH, WISCONSIN

CONVENT OF OUR LADY OF SORROWS, LADYSMITH, WISCONSIN

SUMMARY

Mantellate Sisters, Servants of Mary.

Founded in Italy about 1285.

Established in the United States (Ladysmith Congregation) in 1912.

Habit: The Servite habit, black in honor of the sorrows of Mary, is worn, with a black veil lined with white, a close-fitting white wimple, and a long black scapular. The image of a Host is worn under the scapular, in remembrance of the miracle wrought at the death of St. Juliana. The rosary of the Seven Dolors is suspended from a leather cincture.

Active in educational and hospital work in the dioceses of Superior and Wheeling.

Motherhouse and Novitiate (Ladysmith Congregation), Convent of Our Lady of Sorrows, Ladysmith, Wisconsin. (Diocese of Superior.)

BLUE ISLAND, ILLINOIS*

1916

From their Motherhouse in the ancient Italian city of Pistoia, at the foot of the Apennines, in the valley of the Ombrone, Mantellate Sisters, Servants of Mary, of the Congregation founded there in 1861, in 1916 responded to an appeal of the Servite Fathers in Chicago, Illinois, and provided a small community of sisters to engage in educational and charitable work in the city and its vicinity.

In 1926 the Mantellate Sisters who formed the community established in Chicago in 1916, and who are dependent on the Motherhouse of the Congregation at Pistoia, Italy, where Mother William is the present Superior General, established their United States Motherhouse and novitiate at Blue Island, Illinois.

Mother Louise, the Superior of the first group of sisters sent to this country from Pistoia, directs the community at Blue Island, which is engaged in educational work, and maintains a boarding school for motherless children in connection with the convent.

Continuing their mission work in Chicago, the Mantellate Sisters

MOTHER LOUISE

*From data and material supplied by the Servants of Mary, Mother of Sorrows Institute, Blue Island, Ill.

from Blue Island conduct there a nursery, kindergarten, home for working girls, and Sunday school classes.

MOTHER OF SORROWS INSTITUTE, BLUE ISLAND, ILLINOIS

SUMMARY

Mantellate Sisters, Servants of Mary.

Founded in Italy about 1285.

Established in the United States (Pistoia, Italy, Congregation) in 1916.

Papal Approbation of Rules (Pistoia, Italy, Congregation) by Pope Pius X in 1913.

Habit: The Servite habit, black in honor of the sorrows of Mary, is worn, with a black veil lined with white, a close-fitting white wimple, and a long black scapular. The image of a Host is worn under the scapular, in remembrance of the miracle wrought at the death of St. Juliana. The rosary of the Seven Dolors is suspended from a leather cincture.

Active in educational, charitable and social service work in the archdiocese of Chicago.

United States Motherhouse and Novitiate, Mother of Sorrows Institute, 13811 South Western Avenue, Blue Island, Illinois. (Archdiocese of Chicago.)

48

RELIGIOUS HOSPITALLERS OF ST. JOSEPH*

1894

*WW*HILE Canada was yet a wilderness, a pious layman, Jerome le Royer de la Dauversière, a gentleman of Anjou, France, was inspired to establish a colony in that distant land, in honor of the Blessed Virgin.

A Providential incident in Paris brought him into contact with the Abbé John James Olier, afterward known as the illustrious founder of the Seminary of St. Sulpice. Together they originated in 1636, the Company of Montreal "for the conversion of the savages and the maintenance of the Catholic religion in Canada."

For four years Monsieur Dauversière, assisted by Abbé Olier and some zealous associates, labored with plans to build on the island of Montreal a town to be called *Ville-Marie*. The plan included the establishment there of three religious communities—one of secular priests to direct the colonists and convert the Indians, one of nuns to nurse the sick, and one of nuns to teach the faith to the children.

The Company of Montreal purchased the island and prepared to carry out its carefully made plans. While Monsieur Dauversière applied himself to the task of forming a community of hospital nuns, Ven. Marguerite Bourgeoys of Troyes was inspired to co-operate in this venture, and prepared to provide the nuns needed for teachers in the new colony. This she did by founding the Congrégation de Notre Dame in *Ville-Marie*, on the island of Montreal.

To Jeanne Mance, born in 1606, in Nogent-le-Roi, France, Montreal owes its first hospital. On the death of her parents, Mademoiselle Mance, an accomplished woman of great spirituality, felt impelled to devote herself to Christ's service in the distant Canadian missions. Visiting Paris, she learned of the Montreal Company, and there, under inspiring circumstances, she met Monsieur Dauversière, from whom she learned anew of the great work to be done in *Ville-Marie*.

In the spring of 1642 Mademoiselle Mance arrived in Montreal, where she shared with joy the hardships, dangers, and untold privations which marked the beginning of the new town. Her house

---

*From data and material supplied by the Religious Hospitallers of St. Joseph, Fanny Allen Hospital, Winooski, Vt., and from *Lives of the Catholic Heroes and Heroines of America*, by John O'Kane Murray, and from the Official Catholic Year Book, 1928.

became the hospital, and there for nearly seventeen years she attended to the sick and wounded, her only early assistants being four or five charitable women whom she had brought from France.

Physically disabled from an accident, this pioneer heroine of Montreal returned to France in 1658, to seek help in the work now beyond her strength. The time had come for the advent to *Ville-Marie* of the hospital nuns, as included in the original plans for the colony.

Co-operating with Monsieur Dauversière, in LaFlèche in 1636, in his efforts to have a community of nuns to care for the sick in France and in the New World, was Marie de la Ferre, a member of a distinguished family of Anjou. As first Superior of the Congregation of religious women then assembled, Mother de la Ferre is called the foundress of the Institute of the Religious Hospitallers of St. Joseph, established in 1636 and soon after approved by the bishop of Angers.

A group of these nuns accompanied Mademoiselle Mance on her return to Montreal in 1659, and in her hospital-home the Religious Hospitallers began their work in the New World, and there in the city where saintly Jeanne Mance, nearly three hundred years ago, labored and died, they continue to carry on the charitable work for which they were founded.

From their historic Hôtel-Dieu in Montreal came the first Religious Hospitallers to the United States. Through the efforts of the Right Rev. John S. Michaud, D.D., coadjutor and successor of Bishop De Goesbriand, first Bishop of Burlington, and through the munificence of Mr. and Mrs. Michael Kelly of Colchester, Vermont, the Religious Hospitallers of St. Joseph, in 1894, established their first hospital in the United States—named for the first woman of United States birth to enter the Order, and because of family interests in the locality.

Fanny Allen Hospital was established October 15, 1894, in Winooski Park, a suburb of the city of Burlington, Vermont. The hospital is located on a brow of the highland overlooking the Winooski River, and in sight of the Green mountains. Mother Bonneau served as first Superior of the new institution, and was followed in office by Mother Renaud; in 1906 Mother Rose Rooney was elected Superior.

Fanny Allen, daughter of Ethan and Frances Allen, was born in Sunderland, Vermont, November 13, 1784. She went to Burlington with her parents in 1787 when General Allen established his family on a farm, part of which is now Ethan Allen Park. Ethan Allen was one of the members of the Onion River Land Company, and was consequently one of the proprietors of the Winooski Valley. The land on which stand the Fanny Allen Hospital and Fort Ethan Allen, was included in the original grant.

SISTER FANNY ALLEN
(1784-1819)

In 1805 Fanny Allen asked and obtained permission from her parents to go to a Montreal convent to complete her education. There she sought instruction in Catholic doctrine, and was received into the Church. On September 29, 1808, she entered the novitiate of the Religious Hospitallers of St. Joseph, at the Hôtel-Dieu in Montreal. Her example, her piety and her prayers contributed to the conversion of many to the Catholic faith. Sister Allen died September 10, 1819, and her remains lie under the chapel of the Hôtel-Dieu in Montreal.

In 1904 the Religious Hospitallers were received in Chicago, where, continuing under the superiorship of Mother Cecilia Murray, foundress-Superior in Chicago, they are in charge of St. Bernard's Hôtel-Dieu. The novitiate for Chicago has been established at Mt. St. Joseph, Palos Park, Cook County, Illinois.

In 1917 a foundation was established in Polson, Montana, in the diocese of Helena, when the Hospitallers opened a Hôtel-Dieu there.

On the seventieth anniversary of the consecration of the Right Rev. Louis De Goesbriand, D.D., construction was begun of the Bishop De Goesbriand Hospital in Burlington. This was dedicated as a memorial to him by the Right Rev. Joseph J. Rice, D.D., successor to the see. On September 11, 1924, Bishop Rice presided at the opening of the hospital, now a branch of the Fanny Allen Hospital.

In 1927 a foundation of the Hospitallers was made in the archdiocese of Milwaukee, when St. Joseph's Hospital was established in Hartford, Wisconsin. Each foundation of the Religious Hospitallers of St. Joseph has its own officers, council and novitiate, and is under the jurisdiction of the ordinary of the diocese.

SUMMARY

Religious Hospitallers of St. Joseph.

Founded in France in 1636.

Papal Approbation of Constitutions, May 12, 1865, by Pope Pius IX.

Established in the United States in 1894.

Approximate number in communities in United States, 100.

Active in hospital work in the following institutions, each with its own novitiate:

St. Bernard's Hôtel-Dieu, 6337 Harvard Avenue, Chicago, Illinois. *Novitiate,* Mt. St. Joseph, Palos Park, Illinois. (Archdiocese of Chicago.)

St. Joseph's Hospital, Hartford, Wisconsin. (Archdiocese of Milwaukee.)

Fanny Allen Hospital, Winooski, Vermont. (Diocese of Burlington.)

Bishop De Goesbriand Hospital, Pearl and South Prospect Streets, Burlington, Vermont. (Diocese of Burlington.)

Hôtel-Dieu, Polson, Montana, (Diocese of Helena.)

SISTERS OF THE DIVINE SAVIOUR*

1894

THE Sisters of the Divine Saviour form a Congregation founded at Rome, on December 8, 1888, by the Very Rev. Francis of the Cross Jordan, founder of the Salvatorian Fathers.

In establishing this Congregation for women, Father Jordan's objective was the procuring of sisters for assistance in schools, hospitals and foreign missions.

In 1895 the Most Rev. F. X. Katzer, D.D., Archbishop of Milwaukee, while visiting in Rome, invited the Congregation to his archdiocese. Accordingly a community, with Sister M. Raphaela as Superior, was sent within the year, and soon after its establishment in Milwaukee in 1894, began its work in the United States by engaging in home nursing.

With the growth of the Community in the United States, the sisters extended their labors into other dioceses, and zealously undertook school, hospital and charitable work, as the diocesan needs required.

Under the jurisdiction of the General Motherhouse in Rome, a Provincial house and American novitiate have been established in Milwaukee, on the site of the first United States home of the Community. The Provincial Superior, Sister Seraphine, resides at this institution.

SUMMARY

Sisters of the Divine Saviour.
Founded in Italy in 1888.
Papal Approbation of Rules in 1911, by Pope Pius X.
Established in the United States in 1894.
Approximate number in Community in United States, 230.
Active in educational, hospital and charitable work in the archdiocese of
    Milwaukee, and in the dioceses of Green Bay, La Crosse and Superior.
United States Provincial house and Novitiate, St. Mary's Convent, 3506
    Center Street, Milwaukee, Wisconsin. (Archdiocese of Milwaukee.)

*From data supplied by the Sisters of the Divine Saviour, St. Mary's Convent, Milwaukee, Wis.

FAITHFUL COMPANIONS OF JESUS*

1896

BORN of the intense desire of a noble woman in pursuit of evangelical perfection, and longing to be, like the women at the foot of the Cross and at the tomb, a faithful companion of Jesus, the Congregation of the Faithful Companions of Jesus was founded at Amiens, France, in the year 1820, by Madame de Bon-nault, Viscountess de Bonnault d'Houet.

Marie Madeleine de Bengy, afterwards Madame de Bonnault d'Houet, was born on the 21st of September, 1781, at Chateauroux, France. The child of an ancient and illustrious family, consecrated, on the day of her birth, to the Blessed Virgin, the little girl early gave proof of quick and ready intelligence; the stories of Holy Scripture especially delighted her, and she was never weary of looking at the pictures in a large folio volume of the Bible.

Educated during the period of the French Revolution, Victoire, as she was called by her family, developed into womanhood. In 1804, docile to the will of her parents, she married the Viscount de Bonnault, but the union of the young couple was of short duration, for in less than a year M. de Bonnault died after a severe illness.

From the time of her husband's death, and after Madame d'Houet had again taken her place in her social sphere, the action of Divine Grace began to manifest itself in a marvelous way in her life. Detached, step by step, and almost unconsciously to herself, from the world which she really loved, she increased her almsgiving and good works.

In her charity Madame d'Houet, on one occasion, disguised herself as a peasant and acted as nurse in one of the hospitals at Issoudun, when a number of Spanish prisoners crowded the wards, stricken and dying with typhus fever. After some weeks of such devotedness she herself contracted the fever, and, her condition becoming serious, she was given the Last Sacraments.

Recovering from this illness, she continued more than ever zealous in good works, seeing, in the light of faith, our Lord Jesus Christ, in the poor whom she served.

In 1814, having met the Rev. Joseph Varin in Amiens, she placed herself under his spiritual direction. Convinced that she was called

---

*From data and material supplied by the Faithful Companions of Jesus, Fitchburg, Mass.

to the religious life, yet not impelled toward any of the orders suggested to her, Madame d'Houet became a prey to a spiritual anguish
which lasted for several years.

MOTHER DE BONNAULT D'HOUET (1781-1858)
Foundress of the Congregation of the Faithful Companions of Jesus

It was during a retreat she made at Amiens, in Holy Week of
1820, that Madame d'Houet was inspired to found a new institute,
the Society of the Faithful Companions of Jesus.

The outlines of the new Society took form with striking clarity
in the mind of the pious foundress, for Madame d'Houet plainly

discerned the end to be attained by her followers, the imitation and service of Christ in a new and distinctive character—the personal reproduction, as far as possible, of the lives of the holy women who followed the Saviour and ministered to Him. From the inspired writings of the Evangelists Madame d'Houet drew the plan of the Society of the Faithful Companions of Jesus, and from the same source the name which the Congregation bears.

Delays and discouragements marked the foundation years, and the profound humility of the ardent foundress, as evidenced by her years of struggle and her efforts to accept the dictates of spiritual advisors, was the virtue which inspired her to persevere in her great work. Madame d'Houet looked upon herself as the least among her religious. In later years, at the close of community exercises, she often caused a Hail Mary to be said for the person who needed it most in the Society. "I really believe that Hail Mary was for me," she would say, "for I need it more than anyone else."

The young Congregation soon began to spread. While free schools for the poorer classes were opened in connection with the house at Amiens, Madame d'Houet made other foundations in France, including the establishment of boarding schools for girls.

In 1825 the foundation of Ste. Anne d'Auray was begun. This house, close to the historical shrine erected by Catholic Brittany to honor St. Anne, was not only the site of a boarding school, but also, after the war of 1870, of the novitiate of the Society. One of Madame d'Houet's most important foundations was that in Paris, where the General Motherhouse of the Society is now maintained.

As the beloved foundress advanced in years her piety and virtue shone with greater brightness. In 1854 she was an invalid, suffering acutely until her holy death, on Easter Monday, April 5, 1858.

Immediately after Madame d'Houet's death persons felt more drawn to solicit her intercession than to pray for her, and many experienced the happy effects of their confidence in her aid. The cause of the beatification and canonization of their foundress was later introduced by the Faithful Companions of Jesus.

Having extended its activities beyond France, in Europe, the Society made a foundation in Prince Albert, Canada, in 1883, followed by one in the United States.

For a short time after the arrival of the Faithful Companions in this country they were in Fond du Lac, Wisconsin, but on the invitation of the Right Rev. Thomas D. Beaven, Bishop of Springfield, the Society in 1896 made a foundation in Fitchburg, Massachusetts, which as the mother foundation in the United States has been designated the site of the local novitiate for the Faithful Companions of Jesus.

Upon the invitation of the Right Rev. William A. Hickey, D.D., Bishop of Providence, the Society in 1922 made in that episcopal city another New England foundation, known as Blessed Sacrament Convent.

SUMMARY

Faithful Companions of Jesus.
Founded in France in 1820.
Papal Approbation of Rules in 1922, by Pope Benedict XV.
Established in the United States in 1896.
Habit: The habit, shawl, cap and veil are black. Since 1925 a white bandeau, and a white collar inside the border of the cap, have been worn.
Active in educational work in the dioceses of Providence and Springfield.
United States Novitiate, St. Joseph's Convent of the Faithful Companions of Jesus, Fitchburg, Mass. (Diocese of Springfield.)

RELIGIOUS OF PERPETUAL ADORATION*

1900

THE Congregation of the Religious of Perpetual Adoration, which was introduced into the United States in 1900, in Washington, D. C., was founded at Brussels, Belgium, in 1857.

Mademoiselle Anna de Meeus, for many years active in an association which was organized in Brussels in 1848, whose members practiced the adoration of the Blessed Sacrament and provided for poor churches, was the foundress of this Congregation—wholly devoted to the propagation of the knowledge, love and adoration of the Blessed Sacrament.

The Constitutions of the Congregation of the Religious of Perpetual Adoration were definitely approved by Pope Pius IX in March, 1872.

United States Foundation house, 1419 V Street, N.W., Washington, D. C. (Archdiocese of Baltimore.)

*From the Catholic Encyclopedia and the Official Catholic Directory, 1929.

731

SISTERS OF THE RESURRECTION*

1900

ORIGINATING at Rome in 1891, through the efforts of the Rev. Celine Borzecka, of the Congregation of the Resurrection, the Congregation of the Sisters of the Resurrection undertook as its essential work the instruction of children, and the maintenance of orphanages, sanitariums and homes for girls.

Complying with the request of the Very Rev. Francis Gordon, C.R., of the archdiocese of Chicago, for sisters to conduct Polish parochial schools, and under the guidance and direction of Sister Anna Strzelecka, the present United States Superior, the Community was first established in this country in 1900 in Chicago, where, in addition to its parochial school work, Resurrection Academy is now conducted at the novitiate.

SUMMARY

Sisters of the Resurrection.

Founded in Italy in 1891.

Papal Approbation of Rules, July 17, 1923, by His Holiness, Pope Pius XI.

Established in the United States in 1900.

Habit: The habit is of pleated black serge, with a black woolen cincture, and a black veil, white cap, guimpe and wimple. A silver cross is worn on the breast.

Approximate number in Community in United States, 300.

Active in educational, charitable and social service work in the archdioceses of Chicago and New York, and in the dioceses of Albany, Fargo and Omaha.

United States Novitiate, 7432 Talcott Avenue, Norwood Park, Chicago, Illinois. (Archdiocese of Chicago.)

*From data supplied by the Sisters of the Resurrection, 7432 Talcott Avenue, Chicago, Ill.

MISSIONARY SISTERS, SERVANTS OF THE HOLY GHOST*

1901

THE Congregation of Missionary Sisters, Servants of the Holy Ghost, a community of which was missioned to the United States in 1901, with Techny, Illinois, as the scene of its labors, was founded at Steyl, Holland, in 1890, by the Rev. Arnold Janssen, who in 1875 had established the Society of the Divine Word.

Realizing the need of an auxiliary sisterhood to assist the members of the Society of the Divine Word in their difficult apostolate in the foreign missions, the zealous founder, Father Janssen, designed the Community of Missionary Sisters, Servants of the Holy Ghost, to labor as coworkers in the missionary activities of the Society.

On the feast of the Holy Name of Jesus, January 17, 1892, twelve young women, who, knowing of Father Janssen's project, had offered themselves for the apostolic work and prepared themselves for community life by spending some months with the sisters then in charge of the Mission Seminary at Steyl, Holland, were given the habit planned for the new community. Eighteen months later they made their religious profession, becoming the first Missionary Sisters, Servants of the Holy Ghost.

MOTHER M. COLUMBA
Superior General of the Missionary Sisters, Servants of the Holy Ghost

The new institution developed rapidly, and through a normal educational course outlined by the founder the sisters were trained for their missionary labors. In 1896 the Congregation, whose Mother-

*From data and material supplied by the Missionary Sisters, Servants of the Holy Ghost, Techny, Ill., and from the Official Catholic Directory.

house, Sacred Heart Convent, had been established at Steyl, Holland, was divided, and an allied Community, the Sisters, Servants of the Holy Ghost of Perpetual Adoration, was erected.

The Missionary Sisters, Servants of the Holy Ghost, beginning their labors in the United States at Techny, Illinois, in 1901, early aroused interest in the foreign mission activities of the Congregation, while they labored in caring for the aged at St. Ann's Home, and later through their educational work in the country, which was inaugurated with the opening of Holy Ghost Academy in connection with their convent at Techny. American candidates soon applying for admission to the Community, Holy Ghost Convent at Techny was made the seat of the United States Province of the Congregation, and there, in its easily accessible location—nine miles north of the city limits of Chicago—a novitiate has been established.

HOLY GHOST CONVENT, TECHNY, ILLINOIS

During its first decade of years in this country the Congregation began to send its members into the various mission districts of the Society of the Divine Word, and today the Missionary Sisters, Servants of the Holy Ghost, are engaged in apostolic work in the Philippines, New Guinea and China. In the United States they conduct many parochial schools for colored children, especially in Mississippi and Arkansas, three of the Mississippi schools alone—one each at Greenville, Jackson and Vicksburg—numbering an enrollment of more than twelve hundred colored children. In these localities the sisters also visit the sick among the colored people, and accomplish much as religious missionaries.

In view of the necessity of a practical knowledge of pharmacy and nursing, without which those at a foreign mission station are greatly handicapped, three hospitals are maintained in the United States by the Missionary Sisters, Servants of the Holy Ghost—St. Mary's, at Watertown, Wisconsin, and St. Theresa's, at Waukegan, Illinois, with training schools for nurses, and St. Joseph's, at New Hampton, Iowa. These well-equipped institutions provide opportunities for the training of the missionary sisters who are adapted for this work.

The primary aim of the Congregation of the Missionary Sisters, Servants of the Holy Ghost, is to work for the propagation of the faith, especially for the conversion of pagan peoples. To this end, it maintains novitiates in Germany, Austria, Argentina and Brazil, in addition to that at the Motherhouse in Holland, and that in the United States. In their work as auxiliary religious workers in the districts in which they labor, the Missionary Sisters, Servants of the Holy Ghost, do all in their power to help the natives both in body and soul, and teach them, besides the rudiments of civilized life, the way to save their souls and to gain heaven.

SUMMARY

Missionary Sisters, Servants of the Holy Ghost.

Founded in Holland in 1890.

Established in the United States in 1901.

Habit: The habit, scapular and mantle are dark blue, in honor of the humility of Our Lady, with a white cincture symbolizing her purity. A crucifix is worn around the neck on a red ribbon, and is surmounted by a medal of the Holy Ghost, bearing the inscription in Latin, "Come, Holy Ghost." A ring bearing the emblem of the Holy Ghost as a dove is also worn.

Approximate number in Community in United States, 300.

Active in foreign missionary work, and in educational, hospital, charitable and social service work in the United States in the archdioceses of Baltimore, Chicago, Dubuque, Milwaukee and St. Louis, and in the dioceses of Erie, Little Rock and Natchez.

United States Provincial house and Novitiate, Holy Ghost Convent, Techny, Illinois. (Archdiocese of Chicago.)

SISTERS, SERVANTS OF THE HOLY GHOST OF PERPETUAL ADORATION*

1915

HAT the Rev. Arnold Janssen, founder of the Society of the Divine Word and of the Congregation of the Missionary Sisters, Servants of the Holy Ghost, was a man of prayer as well as a man of action is shown by his establishment of still another enduring religious foundation. Convinced of the blessings ever wrought through prayer, he founded, on December 8, 1896, from amongst those assembled at their Motherhouse in Holland in preparation for an active missionary life, a congregation of sisters to lead a contemplative life. The members of the new community were to engage in the Perpetual Adoration of the Blessed Sacrament, for the propagation of the faith and the salvation of souls, and especially for the success of the apostolic labors of the Society.

A little less than twenty years after their founding, as Sisters, Servants of the Holy Ghost of Perpetual Adoration, and six years after the death of the zealous priest who had instituted a trinity of congregations, a group of ten of the religious arrived in this country from their cloister home in the Netherlands, to establish a first United States foundation in Philadelphia, Pennsylvania.

CONVENT OF DIVINE LOVE, PHILADELPHIA, PENNSYLVANIA

*From data and material supplied by the Sisters, Servants of the Holy Ghost of Perpetual Adoration, Convent of Divine Love, Philadelphia, Pa.

736

Desirous of establishing Perpetual Adoration in his archdiocese, and of having there a contemplative religious community devoted to it, to draw God's special blessing upon the archdiocese, and in particular upon its clergy, the Most Rev. E. F. Prendergast, D.D., Archbishop of Philadelphia, had extended the invitation which brought the Sisters, Servants of the Holy Ghost of Perpetual Adoration, through the European war-zone and over seas strewn with mines, to his archiepiscopal city, in May, 1915.

The Convent and Chapel of Divine Love having been prepared for the sisters in the City of Brotherly Love through the generosity of Archbishop Prendergast's friend, Mr. C. A. Lane, Perpetual Adoration was inaugurated on June 3rd, the feast of Corpus Christi, when the Blessed Sacrament, in the beautiful monstrance which had been presented for the purpose by the Drexel-Morrell family, was placed on solemn exposition by the archbishop. Daily and hourly since then, the faithful, rich and poor, and from all walks of life, have found their way to and frequented this Eucharistic shrine in the great metropolis.

A "SISTER OF DIVINE LOVE"

With Christ-like compassionate hearts, the Sisters of Divine Love, as the members of the Community are familiarly known, whose all-important apostolate is the salvation of the world, take upon themselves the needs, cares and intentions recommended to their supplications. Several times in the course of the hours of adoration, interruption is made by the recitation of liturgical prayers, and the Divine Office is chanted in union with thousands of priests and religious throughout the world. During the periods of the day allotted to work, the sisters occupy themselves in manual labor, in the making of Church vestments, fine needlework, painting and literary pursuits.

By 1918 a novitiate had been established at the Convent of Divine Love in Philadelphia, and in 1923 members of the cloistered community there united with five sisters from the Motherhouse in Steyl to found a Convent of Perpetual Adoration in the diocese of Lipa in the Philippine Islands. Five years later the Sisters, Servants

49

of the Holy Ghost of Perpetual Adoration opened a second Sacramental shrine in the United States. Located on Warne and Zealand Avenues, in North St. Louis, Missouri, on an incline opposite O'Fallon Park, and overlooking the Mississippi, Mount Grace Convent of Perpetual Adoration was auspiciously dedicated on the feast of Corpus Christi, 1928, under the patronage of the Most Rev. John J. Glennon, D.D., Archbishop of St. Louis.

SUMMARY

Sisters, Servants of the Holy Ghost of Perpetual Adoration.
Founded in Holland in 1896.
Established in the United States in 1915.
Habit: The habit, symbolizing the love of the Holy Ghost, is rose-colored; the veil, scapular and cloak are white. The silver emblem of a dove, the symbol of the Holy Ghost, is worn on the breast above a crucifix, and engraved on the ring that is worn.
Approximate number in Community in United States, 60.
Engaged in contemplative life in convents in the archdioceses of Philadelphia and St. Louis.
United States Provincial house and Novitiate, Convent of Divine Love, 2212 Green Street, Philadelphia, Pennsylvania. (Archdiocese of Philadelphia.)

SISTERS OF ST. URSULA OF THE BLESSED VIRGIN*

1902

HE founding of the Society of St. Ursula of the Blessed Virgin constituted the life work of Ven. Anne de Xainctonge, born at Dijon, France, November 21, 1567, the daughter of Jean de Xainctonge and Lady Marguerite Collard.

At an early age Anne showed her apostolic spirit as she taught catechism to the servants of the house, and to children of her own age whom she assembled for the purpose. Her teaching, remarkable for its clearness and precision, was indicative of the special educational work for which she was destined.

With an ardent zeal for the religious life, Anne renounced the social career before her and prepared herself for her chosen work, undeterred by the opposition to her plans—the result of existent prejudices against teaching and nursing as avocations for women.

After a long struggle, spiritual, temporal and physical, the saintly woman and two companions established their community home at Dôle, France, on June 16, 1606, thus founding the Society of St. Ursula of the Blessed Virgin, an uncloistered Community of women uniting the contemplative with the active life.

With a particular devotion to her Guardian Angel, Mother Anne, in the pursuit of her religious life, became known for her great sanctity and holiness. Soon after her death on June 8, 1621, following two years of illness, the documents necessary for her beatification were gathered, but the unceasing wars of the

MOTHER HÉLÈNE MARIE

*From data and material supplied by the Sisters of St. Ursula of the Blessed Virgin, Convent of Mt. Ave Maria, Phoenicia, N. Y.

739

times and the intervention of the French Revolution frustrated the pious undertaking, until, when her cause was again taken under consideration, Anne de Xainctonge, on November 25, 1900, was declared Venerable by Pope Leo XIII.

Although foundations of the Society were made in many European cities, it was not until 1901, during the persecution of the Belgian orders in France, that the Society was established in the United States.

Invited by and welcomed to New York City by its archbishop, the Most Rev. Michael Augustine Corrigan, D.D., sisters of the Society of St. Ursula of the Blessed Virgin were received by the Right Rev. Msgr. Joseph H. McMahon, in the newly established parish of Our Lady of Lourdes, of which he continues rector. Upon their arrival in New York, November 9, 1901, the sisters were first hospitably housed at the Cenacle, where they remained until the opening of their own new convent home in New York, January 6, 1902, in the parish of Our Lady of Lourdes.

Having developed its work to include other parishes of the archdiocese of New York, the Society recently extended its activities beyond the city, in its establishment of the Convent and Academy of St. Ursula, at 26 Grove Street, Kingston, New York.

The United States Community, under Mother Marie Marguerite as Superior, and Mother Hélène Marie as Mistress of Novices, continues to retain its connections with the Motherhouse, which has been transferred from France to Haverloo-les-Bruges, Belgium.

SUMMARY

Sisters of St. Ursula of the Blessed Virgin.
Founded in France in 1606.
Papal Approbation of Rules in 1898, by Pope Leo XIII.
Established in the United States in 1902.
Habit: The habit is black, with a small white pleated guimpe; the first habit was that of a Spanish widow in the 16th century.
Active in educational work in the archdiocese of New York.
United States Novitiate, Convent of Our Lady of Lourdes, 463 West 142nd Street, New York City. (Archdiocese of New York.)

VINCENTIAN SISTERS OF CHARITY*

1902

THE Congregation of Vincentian Sisters of Charity was founded in Vienna, Austria, in the year 1835 by Carolina Augusta, daughter of Franz I, Emperor of Austria. Mother Xaveria Strasser was first Superior of the Congregation then founded for the special purpose of teaching poor children and the care of the sick.

The Congregation extended its mission work to the United States in 1902, when sisters from Satu-Mare, Austria, Hungary, began, under the superiorship of Mother M. Emerentiana Handlovits, their community labors in Braddock, Pennsylvania, where St. Michael's parochial school was placed under their charge. Continuing its activities in the diocese of Pittsburgh, the Community, under Mother M. Emerentiana as Superior, has established a United States Motherhouse at Perrysville. In addition to their work in parochial schools throughout the diocese, the sisters conduct a Home for Incurables, at the Motherhouse site.

In 1928 the Right Rev. Joseph Schrembs, D.D., Bishop of Cleveland, invited the Vincentian Sisters of Charity to the diocese to engage in parochial school work in Cleveland

MOTHER M. EMERENTIANA HANDLOVITS

and its environs. Particular interest was taken in this invitation to the Community as formal announcement of it was made at the triennial convention of the First Catholic Ladies' Slovak Union during its session in Harrisburg, Pennsylvania, in September, 1928.

*From data and material supplied by the Vincentian Sisters of Charity, Perrysville, Pa., and Bedford, Ohio.

The new establishment in the diocese of Cleveland was made possible by the gift to Bishop Schrembs, for the purpose, of the former

VILLA SAN BERNARDO, BEDFORD, OHIO

suburban home of the Schatzinger family of Cleveland. This property, consisting of a residence and sixteen acres of ground, at Bedford, Ohio, was auspiciously dedicated as Villa San Bernardo, and is a Provincial house and second United States novitiate of the Vincentian Sisters of Charity, with Sister M. Berchmans Fialko serving as first Superior.

SUMMARY

Vincentian Sisters of Charity.

Founded in Austria in 1835.

Papal Approbation of Rules in 1835 by Pope Gregory XVI.

Established in the United States in 1902.

Habit: The habit is black, with a black veil over a white head-dress.

Approximate number in Community in United States, 280.

Active in educational and charitable work in the dioceses of Cleveland and Pittsburgh.

United States Provincial house and Novitiate, Villa San Bernardo, 1160 Twinsburg Road, Bedford, Ohio. (Diocese of Cleveland.)

United States Motherhouse and Novitiate, St. Vincent Hill, Perrysville, Pennsylvania. (Diocese of Pittsburgh.)

DAUGHTERS OF THE HOLY GHOST*

1902

THE Congregation of the Daughters of the Holy Ghost, designated because of their white habit as the "White Sisters," was founded in Brittany, France, in the year 1706, during the reign of Louis XIV.

Co-operating in the work of founding a community of religious women to care for the sick and needy, and to teach the children, particularly those of the poor, were the two who are looked upon as founders of the Congregation, Rénee Burel and Marie Balavenne.

After nearly two centuries, having survived the horrors of the revolution in France, the Congregation was harassed by the "law of 1901," forbidding those wearing religious garb to teach in France. Rather than secularize themselves the sisters left France and came to the United States in 1902.

Upon the invitation of the Right Rev. Michael Tierney, D.D., sixth bishop of Hartford, the Congregation made its first foundation in that episcopal city. A Provincial house was at once established there, with Mother Marie Alvarez as first Superior. In 1917 the seat of

MOTHER ST. GEORGE, OF THE DAUGH-TERS OF THE HOLY GHOST

the United States Provincialate was transferred to Putnam, Connecticut. The General Motherhouse of the Congregation has again been established in France, and there, at St. Brieuc, Côtes-du-Nord, Mother Marie Similien serves as Superior General of the Congregation. Mother Sainte Amélie is the present Provincial Superior in the United States.

*From data supplied by the Daughters of the Holy Ghost, Putnam, Conn.

In addition to teaching and conducting day nurseries, the sisters have opened boarding homes for girls. At St. Elizabeth's Home, in Hartford, nearly one hundred self-supporting girls are housed, under the religious influence of the sisters, who from this home also visit and care for the sick poor. In Newport, Rhode Island, "The Stella Maris," a home for convalescents, has been established and is conducted by the Congregation.

SUMMARY

Daughters of the Holy Ghost.
Founded in France in 1706.
Established in the United States, December 8, 1902.
Habit: The habit is white; for the street a black mantle is added.
Approximate number in Community in United States, 200.
Active in educational and social service work in the dioceses of Burlington, Fall River, Hartford, Ogdensburg, Providence and Springfield.
United States Provincial house and Novitiate, 31 Church Street, Putnam, Connecticut. (Diocese of Hartford.)

MISSIONARY ZELATRICES, SISTERS OF THE SACRED HEART*

1902

@HE Congregation of the Missionary Zelatrices, Sisters of the Sacred Heart, was founded in Italy in 1894 by the Right Rev. J. B. Scalabrini, Bishop of Piacenza, who a few years previously had founded the Congregation of Missionaries of St. Charles Borromeo, whose aim was the preservation of the Catholic faith among Italian emigrants.

Founded, likewise, primarily for the assistance of emigrated Italians in foreign lands, the Missionary Zelatrices, Sisters of the Sacred Heart, under Mother Domenica Geminiani as Superior, were intro-duced into the United States in June, 1902, their first work, as planned by Bishop Scalabrini, being with the children of the Sacred Heart parish, North Square, Boston.

The Congregation, which has now extended its activities in this country to New York, Missouri and Pennsylvania, remains subject to its General Motherhouse, Via Germano Sommeiler, 38, Rome, Italy, with a United States Provincial house at New Haven, Connecticut, under Sister Celestine Rigo as present Provincial Mother.

SISTER CELESTINE RIGO

SUMMARY

Missionary Zelatrices, Sisters of the Sacred Heart.
Founded in Italy in 1894.
Established in the United States in 1902.
Habit: The habit is black, with a black veil over a white hood, a short mantle, and a crucifix on the breast. A black sash ends on the right side, and a large rosary is worn on the left.

*From data and material supplied by the Missionary Zelatrices, Sisters of the Sacred Heart, New Haven, Conn.

Active in educational and social service work in the United States in the
archdioceses of New York and St. Louis, and in the dioceses of Hartford
and Pittsburgh.

United States Provincial house and Novitiate, Sacred Heart Convent, 295
Greene Street, New Haven, Connecticut. (Diocese of Hartford.)

SISTERS OF STE. CHRÉTIENNE*

1903

*F*OUNDED in France in 1807, the Sisters of Ste. Chrétienne,
retaining their affiliation with the Motherhouse in Metz,
France, began their activities in the United States in 1903.
Salem, Massachusetts was the site of their first labors in this country,
and there, at Ste. Chrétienne Academy, has been established Loring
Villa, the United States Provincial house of the Order.

The sisters are engaged in teaching in the archdiocese of Boston
and in the dioceses of Albany, Portland and Providence. The novitiate for the United States and Canada is located at Giffard, Province
of Quebec, Canada.

United States Provincial house, Loring Villa, Salem, Massachusetts. (Archdiocese of Boston.)

*From data supplied by the Sisters of Ste. Chrétienne, Loring Villa,
Salem, Mass.

DAUGHTERS OF JESUS*

1903

*S*HORTLY before the days of the terrors of the French Revolution, the Congregation of the *Filles de Jésus* was founded in Brittany, France, in the diocese of Vannes by the Rev. Pierre Noury and Mademoiselle Perrine Samson. The co-founder had little more than drawn up the rules of the Congregation, and secured for it the land on which its Motherhouse was to have been established, when he was forced into exile, and his work was left to another, who encouraged Mademoiselle Samson to open the first country school.

Having experienced various vicissitudes occasioned by the times, the Congregation in 1860 formally established its Motherhouse at the present site, known as *Kermaria*, Village of Mary.

Under the superiorship of Mother Blandina, the *Filles de Jésus*, at the instance of the Right Rev. Msgr. Legal de St. Albert, established their Order in Canada in 1902. There they were received into the diocese of Three Rivers by the Right Rev. Francis X. Cloutier, D.D., who gave them the former episcopal residence in which to open an American novitiate.

MOTHER ST. ELIZABETH

The following year, through the efforts of the Rev. James M. Vermaat, a zealous pastor in Montana, whose knowledge of their Community and rule had made him a firm friend of the Order, the Right Rev. John B. Brondel, of Helena, invited the Congregation to extend its activities to his vast diocese, which at that time included in its territory the entire state

*From data and material supplied by the *Filles de Jésus*, Trois-Rivières, P.Q., Canada.

747

of Montana. Mother St. Elizabeth, now Superior General of the Congregation, was at that time Provincial Superior at Three Rivers, and it was through her arrangements in complying with the request of Bishop Brondel, that in 1903 four sisters from the community in Three Rivers established a school and a hospital at Lewistown, Montana, included the next year in the district of the new diocese of Great Falls.

Here, at St. Joseph's Hospital, of which Mother Mary Anthony is Superior, twenty-four sisters from the Provincial house at Three Rivers, Canada, faithfully continue their initial work in the United States.

United States Foundation House, St. Joseph's Hospital, Lewistown, Montana. (Diocese of Great Falls.)

DAUGHTERS OF WISDOM*

1903

THE history of the Congregation of the Daughters of Wisdom, which established its first mission in the United States in 1903, begins three centuries before that year, with its founding at Poitiers, France, by Blessed Louis de Montfort.

From their Provincial house near Ottawa, Canada, the Daughters of Wisdom, whose Motherhouse is located at St. Laurent-sur-Sevre, Vendée, France, are missioned to the United States, where they engage in educational and hospital work in Maine and New York.

Outstanding among the institutions maintained by the sisters in this country is St. Charles Hospital and Home at Port Jefferson, Long Island, New York, where blind, crippled and defective children are cared for. In connection with this hospital and home the sisters conduct, for the benefit of the children, requiring prolonged hospitalization, a school which is a source of pride and gratification to the many benefactors of the institution, who co-operate generously in this charitable work of the Daughters of Wisdom.

*From the Catholic Encyclopedia, the Official Catholic Directory, 1929, and current news.

SISTERS OF ST. ZITA*

1903

THE Sisters of Reparation of the Congregation of Mary, intimately known in their home surroundings in New York City as the Sisters of St. Zita, were founded in that city in 1903.

The foundress of the Institute, Miss Ellen O'Keefe, who became in religion Mother Mary Zita, was born in County Limerick, Ireland, and emigrated to this country in 1864. As a nurse, Miss O'Keefe, moved with pity for the unfortunate women with whom she came in contact at the City Hospital, Blackwell's Island—women whose previous records often prevented their securing employment—determined to found a home where they could find shelter, and be given opportunity for industrial work.

With her personal savings she began such a home in 1890, and was soon joined in her charitable project by two friends, Mary Finnegan and Katherine Dunne, who formed with her, in 1913, with archiepiscopal approbation, the first community of Sisters of St. Zita, whose object is the care of friendless women. Any friendless woman, regardless of creed or nationality, is welcomed at the houses of the sisters, and may stay for life or go when she pleases.

In the spacious building of St. Zita's Home, which for many years has been established at 143 West 14th Street, in New York City, the Community labors with and supervises the work of more than two hundred women, engaged, as a source of income for the home, in institutional and ecclesiastical laundry work, and the replenishing of Church supplies on the ocean liners. The generosity of friends also aids in the support of the establishment.

With the completion of a new building on West 15th Street, extending through from the same location on 14th Street, a night refuge has been re-opened by the Sisters of St. Zita, now under the superiorship of Mother M. Francis, succeeding in office Mother M. Magdalen, the direct successor of the foundress, Mother Mary Zita.

Aiding Mother M. Francis in carrying on the work of the Institute, an auxiliary has been organized, composed of prominent Catholic women who co-operate generously with one of New York's smaller

---

*From data and material supplied by the Sisters of St. Zita, St. Zita's Home, 143 West 14th Street, New York, N. Y.

religious communities in the maintenance of what is recognized as one of the city's greatest charities.

MOTHER MARY ZITA O'KEEFE
Foundress in 1903 of the Sisters of St. Zita

Motherhouse and Novitiate, St. Zita's Home, 143 West 14th Street, New York, New York.   (Archdiocese of New York.)

SISTERS OF ST. MARY OF THE PRESENTATION*

1903

THE Congregation of Sisters of St. Mary of the Presentation, founded at Broons, Côtes-du-Nord, France, by Louise LeMarchand, was introduced into the United States through a Eudist missionary, travel-bent in the western states.

Father Fournier, the energetic pastor of St. Benedict's Church, in Wild Rice, North Dakota, told the visiting Eudist of the need there of religious teachers, and of his desire for a parochial school. Upon the suggestion of the visitor, and with the episcopal approbation of the Right Rev. John J. Shanley, D.D., Bishop of Fargo, the Presentation Sisters were invited to the diocese to open a school in Wild Rice.

Accordingly in 1903, Mother St. Cesaire and companion sisters of the Congregation from France reached the western site, and at once began in the United States their designate work of teaching.

Retaining filial relations with the Motherhouse in France, the Community has grown and extended its labors beyond the diocese of Fargo, and added to the scope of its work principally by the establishment of St. Margaret's Hospital and Training School for Nurses, in Spring Valley, Illinois, in the diocese of Peoria.

SUMMARY

Sisters of St. Mary of the Presentation.
Founded in France.
Established in the United States in 1903.
Habit: The habit is of black serge, simple and plain in its make, as a symbol of humility and death to the world.
Approximate number in Community in United States, 150.
Active in educational, hospital and social service work in the archdioceses of Baltimore, New Orleans, Portland in Oregon, and San Antonio, and in the dioceses of Fargo, Fort Wayne and Peoria.
United States Provincial house, St. Aloysius' Convent, Oakwood, North Dakota. (Diocese of Fargo.)

*From data supplied by the Sisters of St. Mary of the Presentation, St. Margaret's Hospital, Spring Valley, Ill.

SISTERS OF THE SACRED HEART OF JESUS*

1903

*T*HE Congregation of the Sisters of the Sacred Heart of Jesus · was founded by Angelique le Sourd at St. Jacut, Brittany, France, in 1816, especially for the free education of poor children and the care of the sick.

With religious persecution in France, sisters of this Community left for Canada in 1902, and established a foundation at Ottawa, Ontario.

In 1903, when women wearing the garb of religious were forbidden to teach in France, another band of sisters of the Community

SISTERS OF THE SACRED HEART OF JESUS

left for America, aiming to make a foundation in the United States. Upon an invitation to assist the Oblates of Mary Immaculate in their missionary work in the southwest, a decision was made to make San Antonio, Texas, the site of a new provincialate, and there, under

*From data and material supplied by the Sisters of the Sacred Heart, 2000 McCullough Avenue, San Antonio, Tex.

Mother Marie Bernard as Superior, the community began its work of care of the sick, and the education of children.

The community in the United States, maintaining its connection with the General Motherhouse at St. Jacut, Morbihan, Brittany, France, is under the jurisdiction of the local provincialate, of which Mother St. Firmin is the present Provincial Superior.

SUMMARY

Sisters of the Sacred Heart of Jesus.

Founded in France in 1816.

Established in the United States in 1903.

Habit: The habit is black, with a black veil over a white cornette. A silver crucifix is worn around the neck, and a black cord with three knots is worn as a cincture.

Active in the United States in educational and charitable work in the arch-diocese of San Antonio and the diocese of Corpus Christi.

United States Provincial house and Novitiate, Convent of the Sisters of the Sacred Heart, 2000 McCullough Avenue, San Antonio, Texas. (Arch-diocese of San Antonio.)

RELIGIOUS OF CHRISTIAN EDUCATION*

1904

THE Congregation of the Religious of Christian Education, introduced into the United States in 1904, was founded in Echauffour, in the Province of Normandy, France, in 1817. Its founder, M. l'Abbé Louis M. Lafosse, a native of Montreuil, in the same French province, who had suffered for his faith during the French Revolution, was appointed to the parish in Echauffour in 1805.

Desirous of establishing in his parish a school in which a high educational standard would be combined with thorough moral training, l'Abbé Lafosse assembled a group of able teachers, who, drawn towards the religious life, formed under his guidance the Congregation of Christian Education, and, as its first members, pronounced religious vows in his parish church on November 21, 1817.

A RELIGIOUS OF CHRISTIAN EDUCATION

In the ensuing years the Congregation opened houses in many parts of France, and later in England and Belgium, where, at Tournai, its General Motherhouse is now located.

In 1904, the Congregation, which had been signally honored by the French Government for the high standard of its educational institutions, opened a house in the United States, located at Huntington, West Virginia, prior to a permanent foundation at Boston, which resulted in the establishment of Marycliff Academy at Arlington Heights, Massachusetts.

In 1907 a second group of religious was sent from the Motherhouse, and under the efficient leadership of Mother Deplanck, opened on January 6, 1908, a day and boarding school in Asheville, North Carolina, in the diocese of Raleigh, of which the Right Rev. William J. Hafey, D.D., is now bishop.

*From data and material supplied by the Religious of Christian Education, St. Genevieve-of-the-Pines, Asheville, N. C.

In 1915 the College of St. Genevieve-of-the-Pines, established at the academy which the Religious of Christian Education had developed at Asheville, was recognized and empowered with the right to confer degrees.

Situated among the picturesque Blue Ridge Mountains in western North Carolina, its grounds adjoining the famous Vanderbilt estate, St. Genevieve's, occupying the center of an extensive campus, provides for its students country quiet and freedom within convenient distance from the city.

In addition to the usual college curriculum, and a conservatory of music maintained at St. Genevieve-of-the-Pines, this French educational Congregation conducts there St. Genevieve's Lycee, a French school, the two year course in which leads to a Professor's Diploma for French, stamped with the official seal of *L'Alliance Française*, Paris, France, which the school issues through the New York branch of the Institute.

SUMMARY

Religious of Christian Education.
Founded in France in 1817.
Papal Approbation of Rules, May 8, 1921, by Pope Benedict XV.
Established in the United States in 1904.
Habit: The habit is black, with a white coif and a black veil.
Active in educational work in the United States in the archdiocese of Boston and the diocese of Raleigh.

SISTERS OF ST. JOHN THE BAPTIST*

1906

HE Congregation of the Sisters of St. John the Baptist came into existence in the little town of Angri, Salerno, Italy, in the year 1878. The object of the two founders, Canon Alfonso M. Fusco and Sister M. Crocefissa Caputo, was to work for God's greater glory by striving for personal sanctity and laboring for the Christian education of orphans.

Trials and hardships marked the way to the success of their efforts. Having drawn up a rule of life, the saintly founders laid their plans before the ordinary of the diocese, Bishop Ammirante, who, greatly impressed with the zeal and holiness of these new apostles, approved and blessed their undertaking, giving them full permission to work in his diocese. In a short time a house was procured and converted into an orphanage, and not long afterward, when the care of some destitute children was entrusted to them, Sister Crocefissa Caputo and her companions, forming the nucleus of the new Congregation, began in organized form its characteristic work.

Under the patronage of St. John the Baptist, the Congregation developed and increased in numbers and efficiency. So rapid was the progress it made, so imbued with fervor and charity were its members, that the sphere of its influence was widened, and soon there arose in various cities of Italy new houses, and the labors of the Congregation extended from orphanages to nurseries, laboratories, catechetical centers, and finally to educational work in schools and colleges.

When the sisters realized that adequate care of their charges necessitated teaching, plans were at once made in preparation for the work.

According to Italian law, all teachers are obliged to pass the Regents' examinations. A house of the Congregation was therefore opened in Naples, where the sisters could attend the normal schools and prepare themselves for the classroom.

During the pontificate of Pope Leo XIII, the Baptistines established a house in Rome. In 1919 the Motherhouse of the Congregation was transferred to the Eternal City, and here also is the general novitiate of the order.

On the occasion of the great destruction wrought by the Reggio

*From data and material supplied by the Baptistine Sisters, 12 Amity Place, Newark, N. J.

and Messina earthquake, and later by another devastating earthquake, in southern Italy, the Baptistines received hundreds of unfortunate

SISTER M. CROCEFISSA CAPUTO
Co-Foundress in 1878 of the Baptistine Sisters

children, maimed, crippled, and suffering from painful injuries. When war broke out in Europe in 1914, and Italy called her men to arms, the sisters sheltered and cared for the bereft children, and at the request of the Vicar of Rome they also assisted in the nursing of the wounded in the military hospitals. Again as nurses, when the ravages of Spanish influenza brought mourning and desolation over

Italy, the Baptistines, departing from their ordained work, ventured where others feared to go.

But the Sisters of St. John the Baptist did not long confine their labors within the borders of their own country. Mother Bernardina D'Auria and a few zealous sisters who accompanied her were the first Baptistines to cross the ocean for the purpose of opening a house of their Congregation in America. Strange surroundings, new customs and a difficult language were but a few of the difficulties they had to encounter in adjusting themselves to their new environment.

In 1906, with the approval of the Right Rev. John J. O'Connor, Bishop of Newark, Mother Bernardina obtained permission from the Apostolic Delegate, the Most Rev. Diomede Falconio, to open a house of the Congregation in the parish of St. Lucy, in Newark, New Jersey. Subsequently the first work of the sisters in the United States was that of teaching in St. Lucy's school, in the parish where the Rev. Giuseppe Perotti continues as pastor.

In 1911 Sister Artemisia Cirillo, Mother General of the Order, came from Rome to visit the Newark community. Seeing its progress, and realizing the vastness of the field, she saw the necessity of sending more sisters from Italy to labor in the new mission.

In order to promote the spiritual and material welfare of the community, Sister Cirillo, having made three visitations to the United States, and therefore cognizant of the needs of the community in this country, petitioned His Eminence, Patrick Cardinal Hayes, to appoint an ecclesiastical superior for the Baptistines in America. On the recommendation of this petition by Cardinal Basilio Pompili, the Cardinal-Protector of the Congregation in Rome, Cardinal Hayes assigned the Very Rev. Msgr. Giuseppe Silipigni for the office of ecclesiastical superior of the Baptistine Sisters in America.

SUMMARY

Sisters of St. John the Baptist.

Founded in Italy in 1878.

Papal Approbation of Rules, June 24 (Feast of St. John the Baptist), 1917, by Pope Benedict XV.

Established in the United States in 1906.

Active in educational and charitable work in the archdiocese of New York and in the diocese of Newark.

United States Novitiate, St. John's Villa, Cleveland Place, Arrochar Park, Staten Island, New York. (Archdiocese of New York.)

SISTERS OF CHARITY OF ST. LOUIS*

1906

*T*O the blood of the martyrs of the Revolution, France, at the beginning of the nineteenth century, owes the Congregation of the Sisters of Charity of St. Louis, founded by the bereaved saintly widow of one of the first noble victims of *La Guillotine*.

Marie Louise Elizabeth de Lamoignon, born in Paris on the 3rd of October, 1763, sprang from one of the most illustrious of the administrative families of France. Her maternal grandmother, an able virtuous woman, undertook the education of Louise. Her direction was tender, enlightened and practical, neglecting no means of assisting the harmonious expansion of an unusually gifted nature. Under the tutelage of experienced teachers, Louise became as accomplished as she was naturally pious. Peacefully, piously, studiously, passed the childhood of a life which the Revolution was to fill with tragedy.

At the bidding of her parents Louise accepted the husband chosen for her, the young Count Edouard Mathieu Molé, and their marriage took place in 1780. The deaths of two of their five children brought the deepest sorrows of their early happy wedded years.

After the ruthless events in France in the autumn of 1789, Count Molé, like so many of his rank, migrated, with his little family, to England. When the decrees were promulgated in 1792, under which emigration was treated as a crime against the State, the property of the emigrants being confiscated, M. Molé and his family quietly returned to Paris.

The Terror brooded over stricken France. The prisons of Paris were crowded. The Count, like most of the aristocracy, was arrested and flung into prison. Through the devotion of a servant he made his escape and returned to his family. Again, however, he was arrested and imprisoned, and this time he quitted his dungeon only to mount the scaffold, on the 20th of April, 1794, in the thirty-fourth year of his age.

Madame Molé had not yet drained her cup of sorrow. Though an invalid from the shock of her husband's death, she was arrested a few weeks later by Robespierre's minions, and carried to the dreaded Conciergerie. Not till seven months after the death of Robespierre

---

*From data and material supplied by the Sisters of Charity of St. Louis, Sallaz Academy, Redford, N. Y.

on the scaffold, was Madame Molé set at liberty, and allowed to return with her family to her estate at Méry.

MOTHER ST. LOUIS MOLÉ (1763-1825)
Foundress of the Congregation of the Sisters of Charity of St. Louis

Here she found, even in the midst of devastation, that calm necessary to the rehabilitation of her troubled spirit and broken health. She accepted the will of God with love and adoration, and no complaining word passed her lips, but sentiments only of sweetness and submission.

Other family losses by death served more and more to detach the soul of Madame Molé from the world; she was not insensible to sorrow but superior to it. As soon as opportunity permitted she made known to her confessor, the Abbé de Pancemont, Curé of St. Sulpice, that on her husband's death she had taken a vow to conse-crate her life to God.

Having at length recovered her lawful properties, Madame Molé arranged for the future of her two children, then left Paris for Vannes, early in 1803, accompanied by her devoted mother and some pious friends who shared her religious aspirations.

Inspired by her spiritual director, who had been appointed to the bishopric of Vannes, Madame Molé, seeing that the task of the Church in France was now the formation of character in the younger generation, determined to found a congregation to undertake the education of girls.

Acquiring at Vannes an ancient convent, the building was speedily repaired and made habitable by Madame Molé, and her companions, who then inaugurated that life of penitence and charity which has served as an example for all her spiritual daughters.

Under the direction of the bishop of Vannes she planned the basis of the Congregation of the Sisters of Charity of St. Louis, and herself bore from the outset the name of Mother St. Louis.

From the time of the establishment of her Congregation, Mother St. Louis received into her house orphaned girls of the town of Vannes and its vicinity. For their support and training she estab-lished workrooms for weaving, lace-making and needlework, the direc-tion of which she shared with her companions. Inspired by a motive of perfect sacrifice, and sustained by sentiments of worthy pride, she desired that their work from the first should be self-supporting. It was her ambition and unvarying principle to maintain, by the doweries and labors of her daughters, the children for whose welfare she had undertaken to provide, and such today is the rule of the Sisters of St. Louis wherever Providence has given their mission scope.

In the opening of a boarding school, as well as a day school and free school, Mother St. Louis met a pressing need. In 1805 the board-ing school, as the Institute of St. Louis, was legally recognized as an establishment of education.

Some months prior to this recognition by the State, Mother St. Louis had taken advantage of the presence in Paris of Pope Pius VII, on the occasion of the imperial coronation of Napoleon, and in an audience with the Holy Father had obtained for her Order his per-sonal blessing and approval. Official pontifical recognition of her Constitutions was not then asked, as Mother St. Louis, with wise humility, preferred to submit her work to the test of time.

In 1807 the town of Auray was the site of the first of the widened activities of the Congregation. The new foundation had its orphanage and schools. Later it became, under the Abbé Deshayes, a center for retreats. This work, inaugurated in 1818, was from the beginning so successful that frequently the house proper did not suffice to accommodate the retreatants, and the sisters gave their cells to their guests.

Following soon after a royal ordinance, by Louis XVIII, in 1825, recognizing her Institute, Mother St. Louis died on March 4, 1825, leaving to the many foundations of her Order the memory of her great sanctity.

MOTHER MARY RAYMOND

The Sisters of St. Louis, like other congregations, suffered persecution under the laws enacted in France against religious orders, but remained in the country to protest them, and in 1907 the Government of the Republic bestowed on the Congregation the status of official recognition.

In 1903 His Eminence, Cardinal Bégin, Archbishop of Quebec, welcomed the daughters of Madame Molé on their first landing on Canadian soil.

Through the efforts of the Superior General, Mother Mary of Jesus, the Congregation of the Sisters of Charity of St. Louis began its work in the United States in 1906.

Upon the initiative of the Rev. Father Guenard, of Turton, South Dakota, the "French Sisters" were invited to his parish, in the diocese of Sioux Falls, and its bishop, the Right Rev. Thomas O'Gorman, D.D., wrote in French a personal letter to Mother Mary Raymond, Superior of the pioneering community, bidding the sisters from Brittany a warm welcome to his diocese, and assuring them of his blessing on, and interest in all their undertakings.

Continuing under the jurisdiction of the Motherhouse, founded at Vannes more than one hundred and twenty-five years ago, the foundations in the United States are under the direction of the American Provincialate, with headquarters at Bienville, Quebec. An English house of studies is maintained by the Congregation at its Academy of Our Lady of Victory, at Plattsburg, New York, in the diocese of Ogdensburg.

United States Foundation house, Little Flower Home, Turton, South Dakota. (Diocese of Sioux Falls.)

SISTERS OF THE INFANT JESUS*

1906

*D*EVOTED exclusively to the work of nursing the sick poor in their own homes, the Sisters of the Infant Jesus are typically described in the United States as the Nursing Sisters of the Sick Poor.

The Order was founded in 1835 at Neufchatel, France, by the Rev. Joseph Roussil, for the education of the poor and the care of

the sick in the country. Father Roussil was assisted in his zeal-ous work by a Miss Ruel, who later as Mother M. De Gon-zaga, served as first Superior of the new Congregation.

Aiming to extend its labors to the United States, the Con-gregation in France sent Mother Marie Antoinette, accompanied by Sister Stanislaus and Sister Emma, to this country, in view of the establishment of the Order in the west.

Arriving in New York on October 21, 1905, they were received as guests by the Little Sisters of the Poor, in Brooklyn.

Learning of the sisters' work, and of their zealous plans, the Right Rev. Charles E. McDon-nell, D.D., Bishop of Brooklyn,

MOTHER MARIE ANTOINETTE

invited them to remain there, assuring them that by so doing they would fill a long felt want in his diocese.

Amicable arrangements with the Motherhouse in France were fi-nally completed, and, as a diocesan Community in Brooklyn, the Sisters of the Infant Jesus, with a formal ceremony of blessing, opened their first convent in the United States at 266 Clinton Street, Brooklyn.

Regardless of race, color or creed, these sisters continue their

*From data and material supplied by the Sisters of the Infant Jesus, 439 Henry Street, Brooklyn, N. Y.

special work of nursing the sick poor. An auxiliary of women, who, though living in the world, are intensely interested in their labors, assists them, acting as an outpost to the mission, and soliciting sub' scriptions of money and clothing, while the sisters are the agents in the distribution of these necessary temporalities.

CONVENT OF THE INFANT JESUS, BROOKLYN, NEW YORK

To meet the needs of the increasing Community in Brooklyn, the convent Motherhouse and novitiate were later established at 439 Henry Street. Mother Mary Agnes has succeeded to the office of Superior, and in the government of the Congregation, subject to the bishop of Brooklyn, is assisted by the Councilor-Sisters, Mothers M. Emma and M. Pierre, and Sisters M. Germaine, M. Claire, M. Xavier and M. Etienne.

Further filling the needs of the Sisters of the Infant Jesus, a branch house has been established at the Convent of St. Francis de Sales, 181 Academy Street, Long Island City, Long Island.

SUMMARY

Sisters of the Infant Jesus.

Founded in France in 1835.

Established in the United States in 1906.

Habit: The habit is black, with a black cape that fastens in the back and does not pass the waist line. A black cincture and stiffly starched bonnet and guimpe are worn; the wimple and bandeau are unstarched.

Active in nursing and hospital work in the diocese of Brooklyn.

Motherhouse and Novitiate, Convent of the Infant Jesus, 439 Henry Street, Brooklyn, New York. (Diocese of Brooklyn.)

LADY MISSIONARIES OF ST. MARY*

1906

*I*N 1887, two years before the territory of Washington was admitted to the Union as a state, St. Mary's Mission, at Omak, was established for the Catholic Indians and scattered Catholic settlers of the region.

During the years which followed, only when the mission priest came did the faithful have aught to stir the ofttimes smoldering embers of their faith, until, in 1906, Madame Lucy Lalonde became the first Catechist Missionary, and gathering about her the children of the settlement, through her works of mercy enkindled in them the fire of faith.

A few zealous women, with Madame Lalonde, consecrated themselves to the apostolic work at hand, while others became benefactors and assisted in the inauguration of the work of the Lady Missionaries—who, year after year, have courageously and perseveringly continued bravely through their struggles, always seeing ahead the crown with the cross.

Though the little community is small

A LADY MISSIONARY OF ST. MARY

in numbers, and the years have marked slow growth for it, these earnest missionaries, with vows of poverty, chastity and obedience, have fervently consecrated themselves to missionary work, under the authority of a Directress and of the missionary whom they assist by teaching, caring for the sick and poor, and the performance of any charitable work for their ultimate end, the saving of souls.

Years of experience at this mission, in the diocese of Spokane, have proved the need of the community, and the worth, in it, of teachers, including those for music lessons and kindergarten classes, and good practical women; cooks, dressmakers, nurses and housekeepers; all provided they have the ardor of religion and the spirit of charity and self-sacrifice.

Motherhouse, St. Mary's Mission Convent, Mission, Omak, Washington. (Diocese of Spokane.)

*From data and material supplied by the Lady Missionaries of St. Mary, St. Mary's Mission and Convent, Omak, Wash.

LITHUANIAN SISTERS OF ST. CASIMIR*

1907

HE Congregation of the Lithuanian Sisters of St. Casimir, more generally known as Sisters of St. Casimir, was founded in the United States in 1907 distinctly for educational work among the Lithuanians, who were at that time particularly numerous among the many immigrants settling in the anthracite coal region of Pennsylvania.

When Casimir Kaupas of Gudelle, Lithuania, offered to devote herself to the cause of the Catholic education of Lithuanian children, she was advised by her brother, a leading cleric in the country, to fit herself for that work by entering a novitiate, and there pursuing help-ful studies, as well as practicing the religious life. This was arranged for with the Sisters of the Holy Cross, in Ingenbohl, Switzerland, where she was later joined by two other candidates for the same missionary work.

After two years of preparation the three were advised to com-plete their novitiate in the United States, the intended field of their future religious labors.

Interested by one of his diocesan clergy, the Rev. A. Staniuky-nas, D.D., of Holy Cross Church, Mt. Carmel, Pennsylvania, in the project of the founding of a community of Lithuanian sisters for work among their compatriots, the Right Rev. John W. Shana-han, D.D., Bishop of Harrisburg, asked Mother M. Cyril, Superior General of the Scranton Congregation of the Sisters, Servants of the Immaculate Heart of Mary, to receive the three zealous Lithuanian novices into their novitiate at Scranton for special training. Shortly after receiving a favorable reply to this request, and the arrival from Europe of the aspirants who were to form the nucleus of this new sisterhood for the country, the Sisters of the Immaculate Heart of Mary began their training.

Upon the satisfactory completion of their novitiate, the three foundation members, on August 29, 1907, received the habit planned for the new community, and the following day they were admitted to profession, the ceremony taking place in the convent chapel at Mt. St. Mary Seminary. The Right Rev. Michael Hoban, D.D.,

---

*From data supplied by the Sisters of St. Casimir, St. Casimir's Convent, Chicago, Ill., and from referred bibliography: *The Sisters of the I.H.M.* (P. J. Kenedy & Sons).

Bishop of Scranton, present in the sanctuary with Bishop Shanahan and numerous members of the clergy, preached, as did Bishop Shana-han, on the auspicious occasion of the founding of this Congregation, named in honor of the sainted King Casimir of Poland. At this time, Miss Casimir Kaupas was given the name of Sister Maria, while her two companions, Miss Judith Dvaranauikas and Miss Antoinette Unguraitis, were named respectively Sister Maria Immacu-lata and Sister Maria Concepta.

On October 7, 1907, the Sisters of St. Casimir opened their first mission, this being in Holy Cross parish at Mt. Carmel, Pennsyl-vania. Postulants for the new Community continued for a time to be received for religious training at Mt. St. Mary's in Scranton.

In the interests of the large Lithuanian population in Chicago, its archbishop, the Most Rev. James E. Quigley, D.D., invited the Sis-ters of St. Casimir to transfer their headquarters to that metropolis, to a desirable site near Marquette Park, which he chose for the pur-pose. Upon completion of the necessary permissions, secured from Rome by Bishop Shanahan, this transfer was made in January, 1911.

On August 24, 1913, the Community held its first election, and Sister Maria Kaupas, the foundress, was elected first Mother General of the Congregation of the Sisters of St. Casimir, which until this time had enjoyed the privilege of having as Superiors experienced leaders chosen from the Scranton Community of the Sisters, Servants of the Immaculate Heart of Mary.

Continuing under the superiorship of the zealous foundress, the Lithuanian Sisters of St. Casimir, from their centralized location, are now in charge of a number of missions through the archdiocese, and in addition accept opportunities of extending their work as the growth of the Congregation permits.

SUMMARY

Lithuanian Sisters of St. Casimir.
Founded in the United States in 1907.
Habit: The habit is of black serge, with a scapular and a blue cincture. The barbette and guimpe are of linen and the veil is black.
Approximate number in Community, 300.
Active in educational work in the archdioceses of Baltimore, Chicago and Philadelphia, and in the dioceses of Fort Wayne, Harrisburg, Scranton and Springfield.
Motherhouse and Novitiate, St. Casimir's Convent, 2601 West Marquette Road, Chicago, Illinois. (Archdiocese of Chicago.)

SISTERS OF OUR LADY OF CHRISTIAN DOCTRINE*

1908

THE Congregation of the Sisters of Our Lady of Christian Doctrine was founded in New York City, September 1, 1908, under the direction of His Eminence, John Cardinal Farley, Archbishop of New York.

The establishment of the Congregation was the result of the zealous efforts of the present Superior General, Mother Marianne of Jesus, who, as Miss Marion Frances Gurney, undertook settlement work as an Anglican. A native by birth of New Orleans, Louisiana, and the daughter of Colonel Asa Lord Gurney and Adeline Van Winkle, Miss Gurney, upon the completion of her education and later graduation from Wellesley College, Wellesley, Massachusetts, pursued her studies abroad, especially in France at the Sorbonne and College de France. Following her conversion in 1898, and her reception into the Catholic Church, Miss Gurney was instrumental in the organization of the Confraternity of Christian Doctrine and Normal Training School for Catechists in the archdiocese of New York, in 1902.

The Community of the Sisters of Our Lady of Christian Doctrine was founded and developed by Miss Gurney in order that she and her associates, as consecrated religious, might carry on activities to which they were already devoting themselves in the world. The work outlined for the new Community included social service, catechetical instruction, the direction of sodalities, social settlements and spiritual retreats, as well as the Americanization of immigrants and the preservation of their faith and the faith of their children.

During the World War, with its universal demands on religious, the Sisters of Our Lady of Christian Doctrine were among the foremost in New York war activities. From their settlement center, known as Madonna House, they organized the Columbus Volunteers of New York—a military training corps to prepare youths for the physical and moral dangers of war service—and, through the depot battalion of the volunteers, supplied hot coffee and sandwiches to night and day reliefs of naval and police guards on neighboring bridges and

*From data and material supplied by the Sisters of Our Lady of Christian Doctrine, Marydell, Nyack, N. Y.

the New York waterfront throughout the bitter winter of 1917-1918. They instituted a center of relief for needy families of service men, organized district headquarters for the Red Cross and Knights of

MOTHER MARIANNE OF JESUS
Foundress and Superior General of the Sisters of Our Lady of
Christian Doctrine

Columbus Drives, formed a Battalion of Prayer among wives, mothers and sisters of service men, and organized Welcome Home receptions for returning soldiers of the Madonna House district. The sisters also established and continued an annual Memorial Mass for soldiers of the district who died in service, co-operated in the erection of a Memorial Tablet at the Battery, holding a yearly procession of all the societies of Madonna House to this monument on Memorial Day, and for ten years maintained a home for convalescent and incurable ex-service men.

Located at 171-173-175 Cherry Street, the Institute of Our Lady of Christian Doctrine includes the sisters' convent, and Madonna House, with Madonna Day Nursery, which, in the very heart of the most densely populated, and therefore the poorest section of lower East Side New York, is the center of the activities of the Sisters of Our Lady of Christian Doctrine. No cherries grow there, but the

MARYDELL, NYACK, NEW YORK

neighborhood—a veritable orchard of children—has need of the day nursery, nursery clinic, baby room, and roof playground which Madonna House provides. In addition to Madonna House, the sisters at the Institute of Christian Doctrine conduct classes for the training of catechists and the instruction of converts, as well as in liturgy, Church history, English, citizenship, drama, music, crafts and home nursing. Boy and Girl Scout programs are also carried out at the Madonna House center, and many other progressive movements are taken up by the sisters, whose work is fruitfully rewarded by numerous marriages validated, and children and adults baptized and prepared for their first Holy Communion and for the sacrament of Confirmation. Other happy returns are theirs when they see business women, working boys and business men take advantage of the "days of recollection" arranged and conducted for them in turn at Madonna House.

In addition to conducting a vacation house at Peekskill, New York, the Sisters of Christian Doctrine have established at the site of their Motherhouse and novitiate—Marydell, Nyack-on-Hudson, New York—Camp Marydell, also known as Save-a-Life Farm. Here children suffering from anemia, malnutrition, and the other evils of poverty and overcrowding in a great city, children in iron braces and children of weak hearts, are given place—often through the generous aid of those wishing to be "summer mother" or "summer daddy" to the little ones in need of fresh air, farm products and health benefits, together with supervised recreation, which Marydell offers, under the direction and vigilance of the Sisters of Our Lady of Christian Doctrine.

SUMMARY

Sisters of Our Lady of Christian Doctrine.

Founded in the United States in 1908.

Habit: The habit is of black serge, with blue undersleeves, white coif and wimple and a black veil.

Active in catechetical and social service work in the archdiocese of New York.

Motherhouse and Novitiate, Marydell, Nyack, New York. (Archdiocese of New York.)

RELIGIOUS OF MARY REPARATRIX*

1908

ON December 8, 1854—the same day that the proclamation of the dogma of the Immaculate Conception stirred all Christendom—quietly and unheralded, yet also to the glory of the Mother of God, and miraculously prompted by an appeal from her, a new religious order was called into existence—the Society of Mary Reparatrix.

Baroness d'Hooghvorst, Emilie d'Oultremont, to whom the distinctive work and character of this Society was shown in a vision, was born in Belgium, in the Province of Liege, on October 11, 1818, at the Château of Wegimont, the residence of her father, Count Emile d'Oultremont.

Inheriting a lively faith, solid piety and great charity toward the poor, she was distinguished as a child by particular devotion to the Blessed Sacrament, and a tender love of the Mother of God.

In her nineteenth year she was married to Baron d'Hooghvorst. Left a widow at the age of twenty-seven, she consecrated herself to God by a vow of chastity. God's love then claimed her unreservedly, and at length the apostolate of reparation to which she was called, and the community of which she was to be the foundress, were revealed to her.

On May 1, 1857—less than three years after Mary Immaculate had deigned to manifest to Baroness d'Hooghvorst her desire to see herself replaced here on earth by souls who would bear her name, and consecrate themselves to special and fervent love, respect and reparation to Jesus in the Blessed Sacrament, in substitution for her—the work of the Society of Mary Reparatrix was begun, when its first house was opened at Strasburg, France.

After spending some months in the quiet of a Visitation Convent, that she might be thoroughly grounded in the science of religious life, Baroness d'Hooghvorst and eleven candidates to the new Community received the habit—in Mary's colors, blue and white, as shown to the holy foundress—with the bishop of Strasburg officiating at the ceremony.

So rapidly did the Community grow, that before the end of 1858

*From data and material supplied by the Religious of Mary Reparatrix, Convent of Mary Reparatrix, 14 East 29th Street, New York, N. Y., and from the Catholic News of New York (July 14, 1928).

a foundation had been made in Paris, marking the first extension of the Society, which now has houses throughout Europe, in foreign missions and in America.

MOTHER MARY OF JESUS (1818-1878)
Foundress of the Society of Mary Reparatrix

Through one of New York's most distinguished Catholic laywomen, the Countess Anne Leary, the Religious of the Society of Mary Reparatrix, from the Motherhouse in Rome, established a convent in New York City in 1908.

Shortly after the death, in 1909, of the Rev. Thomas J. Ducey, pastor of St. Leo's Church, on East 28th Street, between Fifth and Madison Avenues, the Most Rev. John Farley, D.D., Archbishop of New York, offered this church to the Religious of Mary Reparatrix for the transferred center of their work in New York City, and the zealous labor then inaugurated there has been continued now for more than twenty years.

In this well-known edifice, with its priceless paintings and beautiful furnishings, the Blessed Sacrament is daily exposed, from mass, at seven o'clock in the morning, until Benediction, at about five o'clock in the evening. During this time two religious are in constant adoration. In observance of the cloister, an iron grille nine feet high separates the nuns from the lay adorers in the church, devout men and women, who from morning until night visit this shrine of love and reparation in the heart of New York's fashionable business and hotel district.

There are two degrees in the Society, that of choir religious and coadjutrix sisters. To the former is especially entrusted the adoration of the Blessed Sacrament—exposed each Thursday night, as well as daily—and the chanting three times a day of the Office of the Sacred Heart, or that of the Immaculate Conception. The coadjutrix sisters combine with their hours of prayer, manual labor, and they as well as the choir religious may be sent on foreign missions.

The choir religious do not confine themselves entirely to contemplative exercises, but engage in charitable works inseparable from a

MOUNT MARY CONVENT OF MARY REPARATRIX, DETROIT, MICHIGAN

consistent life of reparation. Retreat houses, attached to most of the houses of the Society, where public and private retreats are given, prove a fruitful apostolate. The religious also conduct catechetical classes for converts and children of all ages, and direct clubs, sodalities and circulating libraries, according to the need.

Without rigorous canonical cloister, enclosure is observed in the houses of the Community, but visitors are freely admitted to the parlors and the sections reserved for retreatants.

The Society, until lately known in this country by the French title of *Marie Reparatrice,* is directly subject to the Holy See, and is divided into provincialates, each ruled by a Provincial Superior, under the Superior General who resides at the Motherhouse in Rome, at 9 Via dei Lucchesi.

In accordance with the spirit and intent of the Society—which attract it to metropolitan centers, as especially suited for its work of reparation—the second United States Convent of Mary Reparatrix was established in Detroit, Michigan.

In the fall of 1928, ten religious were sent to that city, from the community in New York, of which Mother Mary of Blessed John Fisher is Superior, and on October 11th established a temporary con-vent at 69 Burlingame Avenue, which was auspiciously opened under the patronage of the Right Rev. Michael J. Gallagher, D.D., Bishop of Detroit.

The Detroit convent, now permanently located, serves as the American novitiate for the Society of Mary Reparatrix, and here the religious pursue the work of the Institute as followed in New York, and in their notable and frequented houses of reparation and retreat throughout the world.

SUMMARY

Religious of Mary Reparatrix.

Founded in France in 1857.

Papal Approbation of Rules in 1883, by Pope Leo XIII.

Established in the United States in 1908.

Habit: The habit and foot-wear are white; the veil and scapular are light blue. A white rosary is suspended from the side, and on the breast a copper heart is worn, on one side of which are engraved in Latin the words, *I have come to cast fire on the earth and what will I but that it be enkindled,* and on the reverse side, representing the transpierced heart of Our Lady, *My Beloved to me and I to Him who feedeth among the lilies.* A ring, on which is engraved *Ancilla Jesu et Mariae,* is received at profession. In choir an additional white cloak and long white veil are worn.

Engaged in contemplative life, in a spirit of reparation, and active in cate-chetical work and the conducting of retreats in convents in the arch-diocese of New York and the diocese of Detroit.

United States Novitiate, Mount Mary Convent of Mary Reparatrix, 17330 Quincy Avenue, Detroit, Michigan. (Diocese of Detroit.)

SISTERS OF THE SACRED HEARTS AND PERPETUAL ADORATION*

1908

O atone for the outrages offered to the Sacred Hearts of Jesus and Mary, the Congregation of the Sisters of the Sacred Hearts of Jesus and Mary, and of Perpetual Adoration of the Blessed Sacrament—more simply known as *Dames de Picpus,* was founded at Poitiers, France, in 1794, by the Rev. Marie Joseph Coudrin, and Mother Henriette Aymer de la Chevalerie.

In the year 1827, priests of this same Congregation in France began missionary work in the Hawaiian Islands. On their application to the Motherhouse of this Congregation, in France, at 35 Rue Picpus, Paris, a band of nuns was sent in 1842 from France to assist the missionaries in the islands, but the ship bearing the little group was sunk at sea, and with it perished these first sisters of the Community en route to the islands.

In 1859 the Motherhouse sent out a second colony of nuns, and after a trying voyage of eight months the sisters landed, and established their Community in Honolulu, with Mother Maria Josepha as first Superior.

Through the Perpetual Adoration of the Blessed Sacrament, the Congregation continues to carry on the holy purpose of its foundation, in combining with contemplative life the active work of the instruction of youth, as exemplified in the United States in the diocese

A "DAME DE PICPUS"

of Fall River, where, while in charge of other schools in the diocese, the sisters conduct an academy for girls in connection with the convent which they have established at Fairhaven, Massachusetts.

*From data and material supplied by the *Dames de Picpus,* Sacred Hearts' Academy, Fairhaven, Mass.

SUMMARY

Sisters of the Sacred Hearts of Jesus and Mary, and of Perpetual Adoration of the Blessed Sacrament.

Founded in France in 1794.

Papal Approbation of Rules in 1817 by Pope Pius VII.

Established in the United States in 1908.

Habit: The habit, cape and scapular are all white; the image of the Sacred Heart is embroidered on the scapular. A white veil is worn over a white muslin cap, and a red mantle is worn for adoration as a symbol of reparation.

Active in educational work in the United States in the diocese of Fall River.

United States Foundation Mission house, Convent of the Sacred Hearts, Fairhaven, Mass. (Diocese of Fall River.)

MISSION WORKERS OF THE SACRED HEART*

1908

THE Congregation of sisters known in the United States as Mission Workers of the Sacred Heart was founded at Hiltrup, near Muenster, Germany, in the year 1899, through the efforts of the Rev. Hubert Linckens, of the Missionary Fathers of the Sacred Heart, a Society to which the Sovereign Pontiff, Pope Leo XIII, assigned missionary labor on the South Sea Islands.

MOTHER ELECTA

After some years of preparation for the work of the missions, the first band of the sisters, known in Germany as *Missions Schwestern vom Heiligsten Herzen Jesu*, left for that mission field on the islands of the Pacific Ocean.

The names of five of these sisters are the names of five martyrs, who on August 13, 1904, fell the victims of the fury of frenzied natives. That "The blood of the martyrs is the seed of the Church" was proved again when many natives requested religious instruction and Baptism, following the execution of these sisters, the process of whose beatification has recently been introduced.

While continuing in the mission field, when a new branch of activity was opened to the Congregation in Germany, and an opportunity was extended to the sisters to engage in school work in the United States, in the archdiocese of Philadelphia, the missionary Congregation eagerly accepted it as also their work—preordained by Divine Providence.

*From data and material supplied by the Mission Workers of the Sacred Heart, St. Michael's Convent, Bernharts, Pa.

ST. MICHAEL'S CONVENT, BERNHARTS, PENNSYLVANIA

With Mother Electa as Superior of the first mission band to the United States in 1908, the sisters at once began their labor in parochial schools in the archdiocese of Philadelphia. A little later they were invited to take charge of a sanitarium which had been established at Reading, Pennsylvania, for the care of sick and invalid religious. On the abandonment of the plan to continue this institution, arrangements were made by the Congregation whereby the property was purchased for the site of the American Motherhouse and novitiate at Bernharts, near Reading, for the now large Community in the United States, of which Mother Stephania is the present Superior.

Extending their labors in this country beyond the classrooms, to the care of the poor, the sick, the homeless and the aged, in homes, orphanages and hospitals, the Mission Workers of the Sacred Heart are now also in charge of St. Joseph's Health Resort, Sulphur Lick Springs, at Wedron, Illinois, near Ottawa.

A MISSION
WORKER OF THE
SACRED HEART

SUMMARY

Mission Workers of the Sacred Heart.
Founded in Germany in 1899.
Established in the United States in 1908.
Habit: The habit is of black serge, with a black scapular and cord, and a
black veil.   The head-dress is of white linen.   A small silver cross, bearing
the motto *Ametur ubique terrarum Cor Jesu Sacratissimum* (May the
Sacred Heart of Jesus be everywhere loved) is worn on the breast.
Approximate number in Community in United States, 230.
Active in educational, hospital and charitable work in the archdioceses of
Cincinnati, New York and Philadelphia, and in the dioceses of Columbus,
Peoria, Rockford and Wheeling.
United States Motherhouse and Novitiate, St. Michael's Convent, Bernharts,
Pennsylvania.   (Archdiocese of Philadelphia.)

DAUGHTERS OF THE EUCHARIST*

1909

*W*ITH the approval of His Eminence, James Cardinal Gibbons, the Society of the Daughters of the Eucharist was established in Baltimore, October 14, 1909. Founded by Katharine A. Dietz, for the self-sanctification of its members and the sanctification of souls by the performance of spiritual and corporal works of mercy, those forming the Society, well experienced in the practical field of social service work, carry on, particularly as parish visitors, the missionary labors for which they united.

With the first headquarters of the Society in Baltimore, at 521 N. Charles Street, pastors of the various parishes availed themselves of its aid, calling upon the Daughters of the Eucharist to perform services in helping to solve the ever present problems of the needy and unfortunate.

The reconstruction of the family forms a primary work and study for the Society, and with this in view its work is based on religious and sociological principles. The members of the Society in turn act as instructors for those ignorant of the truths of faith, or neglectful of their religious duties. They also act as counselors to those confused or misled by various harmful agencies who haunt the homes of the poor under the guise of social service. In every phase of spiritual and corporal charity the Daughter of the Eucharist renders aid.

In December, 1911, remaining in Baltimore, the Society transferred its headquarters to 1133 N. Gilmor Street, and in this house settlement work was begun. A chapel was erected under ecclesiastical authority, with permission for the reservation of the Blessed Sacrament. The Daughters of the Eucharist, who live a community life, and make the profession of the three vows of religion, wear no distinctive garb. This enables them to meet certain needs in their work which might possibly not be coped with by persons wearing a religious habit.

In 1915 the adjacent house, 1135 N. Gilmor Street, was purchased, and a day nursery and kindergarten established. In the course of their work, many cases were found where children were without proper care, through either the separation or death of parents, in consequence of which the little ones were given a home at the nursery.

---

*From data and material supplied by the Daughters of the Eucharist, 1133-1135 North Gilmor Street, Baltimore, Md.

The house soon became over-crowded, and in the spring of 1919 a commodious country home, with seven acres of ground, on Maiden Choice Road, near Catonsville, was purchased. A large group build-

MOTHER KATHARINE A. DIETZ
Foundress and Superior of the Daughters of the Eucharist

ing was erected, and all modern features installed for the country "Boarding Home School" then established, and since permanently maintained throughout the year.

The government of the Society, with the Motherhouse in Catonsville, is vested in Mother Katharine A. Dietz, Superior, Mother

Alice M. Russell, Treasurer, and Mother Eva Marie Kuhl, Secretary. The latest code of Canon Law is observed in the Society, whose members are active in social service and charitable work in the archdiocese of Baltimore.

Motherhouse and Novitiate, Convent of the Daughters of the Eucharist, Catonsville, Maryland. (Archdiocese of Baltimore.)

SISTERS OF STS. CYRIL AND METHODIUS*

1909

A COMMUNITY originated to fill an evident need of religious laborers especially in the different Slovak parishes in north-eastern Pennsylvania—where, particularly in the populous diocese of Scranton, the Slovak immigrants were numerous, the Sisters of Sts. Cyril and Methodius were founded in 1909.

Advantages in their favor were the industry, willingness to work, and ready ability of the immigrants to learn the language of the land of their adoption, circumstances counterbalanced by their lack of education, resulting from political oppression in their native land, and their poverty in the new country, which last, however, was rapidly being dispelled by the steady employment which America's great industries offered.

What could not be accomplished for these pioneers themselves would be done for their children—children born in this country, and therefore as true Americans as any others of whatsoever foreign ancestry, and who were to be numbered among the citizens of the United States. How could they be trained and educated for America? This the first leaders of the Slovaks in the country asked themselves.

The children could be taught in the public schools, but at that time their parents found scant sympathy in their new surroundings. They understood little and were misunderstood. A means must be devised—a teaching body that would serve as a mediator, comprehending both sides thoroughly. This teaching body proved to be the Sisters of Sts. Cyril and Methodius, whose first members were the young daughters of these Slovak parents, many of them possessing talents that, for development, needed only opportunity.

Through arrangements made with the Sisters, Servants of the Immaculate Heart of Mary, at Mt. St. Mary's, Scranton, by the Rev. Matthew Jankola, at the time pastor of St. Joseph's Church, Hazelton, Pennsylvania, the Superior General, Mother M. Cyril, consented to undertake the training for the religious life of the candidates for the new sisterhood.

*From data and material supplied by the Sisters of Sts. Cyril and Methodius, Villa Sacred Heart, Danville, Pa.

On the 11th of September, 1909, since commemorated as the foun-dation date of the Congregation, the Right Rev. Michael J. Hoban, D. D., Bishop of Scranton, received the vows of the three sisters who had then completed their novitiate at Mt. St. Mary's, and on the occasion of this cere-mony in the chapel there the habit of the new Community was con-ferred on eleven Slovak postulants.

For some time thereafter, until 1912, a Motherhouse and novitiate of the Sisters of Sts. Cyril and Methodius were maintained at Pittston, with Sister M. Loyola, of the Sisters of the Immaculate Heart of Mary, of Scranton, as Superior and Mistress of Novices. During this time, near Harrisburg, sisters of the new Community began their active charitable work at the Jed-nota Home, for orphaned Slovak children.

Following an election, at which Mother Mary Mihalik was chosen first Superior of the Sisters of Sts. Cyril and Methodius, an opportune

SISTER MARIE PHILOMENE
A Sister of Sts. Cyril and Methodius

offer of suitable accommodations for a Motherhouse and novitiate near the Jednota Home led to the formal establishment of their head-quarters there, in the diocese of Harrisburg.

Villa Sacred Heart, the present site of the Motherhouse, of which the Community took formal possession in the year 1919, was secured through the efforts of the Rev. T. F. X. Dougherty, rector of St. Joseph's Church in Danville, Pennsylvania, and with the help of other friends. An old residence home located on the outskirts of Danville, with its stately trees, its parkway with inviting benches of artistically wrought iron, and its marble statues representing the four seasons, Villa Sacred Heart provides a fitting home for the Congregation.

Under the auspices of the Right Rev. Philip R. McDevitt, D.D., present bishop of Harrisburg, a summer school for all the sisters of the Community was opened at Villa Sacred Heart. In 1922 there was established, and has since been continued there, Villa Sacred Heart Academy, the first Slovak high school for girls in America.

52

In proportion to its increase in numbers, the Community has extended its labors even beyond its native state, and, as true imitators

VILLA SACRED HEART, DANVILLE, PENNSYLVANIA

of St. Cyril and St. Methodius in their apostolic labors in behalf of those of the Slavic race, the Sisters of Sts. Cyril and Methodius faithfully carry out the purpose for which they were founded.

SUMMARY

Sisters of Sts. Cyril and Methodius.
Founded in the United States in 1909.
Papal Approbation of Rules by Pope Pius X.
Habit: The habit and scapular are of black serge. A barbette of white linen, white linen forehead band and guimpe are worn, with a black veil over an underveil of white muslin.
Approximate number in Community, 215.
Active in educational and charitable work in the archdioceses of New York and Philadelphia, and in the dioceses of Buffalo, Fort Wayne, Harrisburg, Hartford, Pittsburgh, Scranton and Syracuse.
Motherhouse and Novitiate, Villa Sacred Heart, Danville, Pennsylvania. (Diocese of Harrisburg.)

VENERINI SISTERS*

1909

HE Institute Venerini perpetuates in its name the memory of the foundress of the Congregation of Venerini Sisters, the Servant of God, Rosa Venerini.

Rosa Venerini was born at Viterbo, in Italy, on February 9, 1656. Responding to the Christian education zealously given her by her pious parents, she early in life determined to become a nun.

At Viterbo, on August 29, 1685, she opened her first free school for young girls. The advantages which resulted from the combination

VENERINI SISTERS

of the secular and religious education of the children were soon recognized, and Rosa Venerini was asked to found other schools and place them under the direction of the teachers who had previously been under her instruction.

On November 28, 1909, the Institute Venerini made its first foundation in the United States.

Through His Eminence, William Cardinal O'Connell, Archbishop of Boston, Venerini Sisters, with Mother Keller as Superior, came from Rome and made their first United States foundation in Lawrence, Massachusetts, their initial work being as assistants in the

*From data and material supplied by the Venerini Sisters, Venerini Convent, North Adams, Mass.

787

religious education of the Italian children of the Holy Rosary parish, in Lawrence.

The Community in the United States is under the Provincial Superiorship of Sister M. Augusta, and subject to the direct jurisdiction of the General Motherhouse in Rome, with Sister Marianna Piccinetti as Superior General. His Eminence, William Cardinal Van Rossum, C.SS.R., in Rome, is the Cardinal-Protector of the Institute Venerini.

SUMMARY

Institute Venerini (Venerini Sisters).
Founded in Italy in 1685.
Papal Approbation of Rules, December 2, 1836, by Pope Gregory XVI.
Established in the United States in 1909.
Habit: The habit is black with a white collar.
Active in educational and charitable work in the archdiocese of Boston, and the dioceses of Providence and Springfield.
United States Motherhouse and Novitiate, Venerini Convent, 74 Marshall Street, North Adams, Massachusetts. (Diocese of Springfield.)

DAUGHTERS OF THE MOST HOLY CROSS AND PASSION*

1910

HE Passionist Sisterhood, or Daughters of the Cross and Passion, as their holy founder, St. Paul of the Cross, called them
was founded at Tarquinia, Italy, May 3, 1771.

Having completed the foundation of the Order of Passionist
Fathers, whose life-work and vocation was to save the world by
reviving among men the remembrance of the sufferings and death of
our Lord and Saviour Jesus Christ, St. Paul's penitential zeal urged
him to establish an order for women, who, like the Passionist Fathers,
should devote themselves to the divine work of the salvation of souls
through devotion to Christ's passion, but, unlike them, should accomplish this not by preaching, or active
works, but by the practices of the
contemplative life—by prayer and
penance.

While the Passionist Fathers are
engaged in the preaching of the
sufferings of Jesus Christ, on missions and retreats, these nuns are
in contemplation at the foot of the
Cross with Mary, the sorrowful
Mother, interceding and imploring
the Divine assistance upon the missionaries, indirectly yet most effec-
tually spreading the remembrance
of Christ's passion, and co-operating in the salvation of souls.

Zealous for the success of his
plans, the ardent founder submitted
to the Holy Father, Clement XIV,
the rules he had drawn up for the
Passionist Nuns. On September 3,
1770—uniquely, before the later

MOTHER MARY OF JESUS
CRUCIFIED (1713-1787)
Co-Foundress of the Passionist
Nuns

foundation of the Community, on May 3, 1771—-papal approbation
was given the rules of the Order.

*From data and material supplied by the Passionist Nuns, Convent of
Our Lady of Sorrows, Carrick, Pa.

The establishment of the Passionist Nuns in America, nearly a century and a half later, was the realization of years of thought, prayers and efforts of the Passionist Fathers, and to the Very Rev. Joseph Stanislaus, Provincial of the Passionists, and his council, is due this foundation.

Acceding to their request, the Right Rev. J. F. Regis Canevin, D.D., Bishop of Pittsburgh, granted permission for the establishment of a monastery of the Passionist Nuns, with words of assurance that a diocesan community of contemplative religious had been long in his thoughts.

Before the five nuns chosen for the new foundation left Corneto for the United States in 1910, they were granted a private audience with Pope Pius X, and obtained his blessing for themselves, their work and their benefactors in the new country.

On their arrival in the United States, after spending a week in Hoboken, New Jersey, where a warm welcome was extended them by the Passionist Fathers and the Catholic people, the five nuns went to Pittsburgh, in which diocese their monastery was to be established. Their enclosure, and the observance of their Rule, which through the influence of Bishop Canevin, they were permitted to follow just as it had been brought from their Italian home, began on July 10, 1910, with Mother Mary Hyacinth of the Sacred Heart, serving as first Superior.

The Passionist Nuns are strictly cloistered, and their rule of life austere. Besides observing many days of fast and abstinence, they devote much time daily to prayer and to the chanting of the Divine Office, by the choir religious. At midnight an hour and a half is spent before the tabernacle, pleading for mercy upon sinners. In addition to the usual three vows of religion, these nuns take a fourth, to promote devotion to the passion of Jesus Christ, and a fifth, to observe perpetual enclosure.

Periodically throughout the year, retreats are held at their monasteries. Women in the world who desire to devote some days to spiritual devotions are then accommodated in the enclosure, and Passionist Fathers conduct the exercises for those thus assembled.

SUMMARY

Daughters of the Most Holy Cross and Passion.
Founded in Italy in 1771.
Papal Approbation of Rules, September 3, 1770, by Pope Clement XIV.
Established in the United States in 1910.
Habit: The habit, similar to that of the Passionist Fathers, is of rough black,

with a cloak; a white heart surmounted by a cross and bearing the inscription *Jesu Christi Passio*—the insignia of Christ's passion—is worn on the breast. Around the waist is a leathern belt to which a rosary is attached. The sisters do not wear shoes or stockings, but sandals only.

Approximate number in communities in United States, 50.

Engaged in contemplative life in the following monasteries, each with its own novitiate:

Convent of Our Lady of Sorrows, 2715 Churchview Avenue, Mt. Oliver Station, Pittsburgh, Pennsylvania. (Diocese of Pittsburgh.)

St. Gabriel's Convent, 1560 Monroe Avenue, Scranton, Pennsylvania. (Diocese of Scranton.)

RELIGIOUS TEACHERS FILIPPINI*

1910

$\mathcal{T}$HE Pontifical Institute of Religious Teachers Filippini, *Maestre Pie Filippini*, founded in Rome, Italy, by Blessed Lucia Filippini, for the special work of education, civil and religious, dates its history from 1692. The first Motherhouse was established in Rome by the holy foundress, and is located at Arco de Ginnasi 20.

In 1910, in response to the invitation of the Right Rev. Thomas J. Walsh, D.D., then bishop of Trenton, prior to his transfer to the see of Newark, Sister Rosa Leoni, Superior General of the *Maestre Pie Filippini*, sent a group of sisters from the Motherhouse in Rome, with Sister Concetta as Superior, to establish a foundation of their Pontifical Institute in the United States, where they were welcomed at Trenton by Bishop Walsh.

Soon engaging in parochial school work in Trenton and other New Jersey localities, the sisters accepted the numerous missions offered to them in proportion to their number, augmented by other members of the Institute sent from Rome. The Religious Teachers Filippini have also taken charge of schools at Baltimore, Maryland, and in New York City.

On May 22, 1921, Villa Victoria, a Trenton estate of more than fifty acres, located on Sanhican Drive, with a frontage on the Delaware River, was formally dedicated as the United States Motherhouse, normal school and novitiate of the American Province of St. Lucy of the Pontifical Institute of Religious Teachers Filippini, of which Sister Teresa Saccucci was appointed Provincial Superior.

Villa Victoria, as was the intention in its founding by Bishop Walsh, and as encouraged by the Right Rev. John J. McMahon, D.D., his successor as bishop of Trenton, receives and forms, fashions and educates—spiritually, mentally and morally—the candidates sent to it, that after their training they may be qualified to teach, as Italian-American sisters, the Italian-American parochial school children. For the fulfillment of this office, each candidate at Villa Victoria perfects herself in both the English and Italian languages.

For the benefit of candidates for the Religious Teachers Filippini in the United States, a high school was established at Villa Victoria

---

From data and material supplied by the Religious Teachers Filippini, Villa Victoria, Trenton, N. J.

792

in September, 1924, under the direction of the Franciscan Sisters from their Motherhouse at Glen Riddle, Pennsylvania, and the Sisters of

BLESSED LUCIA FILIPPINI (1672-1732)
Foundress of the Religious Teachers Filippini

Mercy from North Plainfield, New Jersey. Later, also for Italian-American girls wishing to prepare themselves for lives of service as Religious Teachers, who had not yet completed their grade school studies, a grammar school was added at Villa Victoria.

In addition to completing the normal studies at Villa Victoria, Trenton, New Jersey, many of the Religious Teachers Filippini have continued their educational work under the Sisters of Mercy at Georgian Court College, Lakewood, New Jersey.

SUMMARY

Religious Teachers Filippini *(Maestre Pie Filippini)*.
Founded in Italy in 1692.
Papal Approbation of Rules in 1704 by Pope Clement XI.
Established in the United States in 1910.
Approximate number in Community in United States, 140.
Active in educational work in the archdioceses of Baltimore and New York, and in the dioceses of Newark and Trenton.
United States Provincial house and Novitiate, Villa Victoria, Trenton, New Jersey. (Diocese of Trenton.)

BOHEMIAN SCHOOL SISTERS DE NOTRE DAME*

1910

*A*PPRECIATING the wisdom and foresight of St. Peter Fourier in his establishment of a religious congregation of women for the special work of education, the Rev. Gabriel Schneider, a humble and zealous priest in Bohemia, selected four young women of his parish sodality and placed them in training for this work at the Motherhouse of the School Sisters of Notre Dame, in Munich, Bavaria.

A few years later, after conferences with his bishop, the Right Rev. John Valerian Jirsik, and upon the advice of the archbishop of Munich, Father Schneider arranged for the return of these four young women, and the religious profession of the two who had completed their novitiate.

This ceremony of profession took place in the parish church in Hirschau, Bohemia, August 15th, 1853. Also on this occasion six postulants received the habit of this new Community of the School Sisters de Notre Dame.

Such was the beginning of the Bohemian branch of the Congregation established by St. Peter Fourier.

In 1854 a permanent Motherhouse was established in Horaždovic, Czechoslovakia, with the Congregation observing from the first the Rule of St. Augustine.

With the needs of the time and its increasing number, this Bohemian Congregation extended its activities to include every phase of educational work, and established missions in Bohemia, Moravia and Slovakia, where the sisters conduct public and parochial, grade, high, normal and vocational schools, as well as academies, day nurseries, kindergartens, orphanages and institutions for deaf-mutes.

With all their available sisters occupied in these European enterprises among the Bohemians, the Congregation could not grant the request for sisters for the United States, when in 1909 the Right Rev. Thomas Bonacum, D.D., Bishop of Lincoln, made a personal appeal to obtain sisters for the Bohemian parishes of his diocese. Shortly after his return from Europe, Bishop Bonacum died.

*From data and material supplied by the Bohemian School Sisters de Notre Dame, Convent de Notre Dame, Omaha, Neb.

In 1910 the Very Rev. C. A. Bleha, pastor of St. John of Nepo-
muk parish in St. Louis, the successor of Monsignor Joseph Hessoun—
the renowned founder of the first Bohemian Catholic parish in the
United States—during a visit at the Motherhouse in Horaždovic,

MOTHER M. GUALBERTA

again asked for sisters to come
and work among the Bohemians
in America. His errand was
successful, and sisters were
promised for the United States.

On May 10, 1910, five sisters, with Mother M. Gualberta
as Commissary, arrived in this
country, and were received into
the archdiocese of St. Louis by
His Grace, the Most Rev. J. J.
Glennon, D.D. While awaiting
the completion of the building
of the Hessoun Orphanage at
Fenton, Missouri—their first
mission — the newly arrived
community accepted the hospitality of the School Sisters of
Notre Dame in St. Louis.

In 1911 another band of
sisters came from Bohemia, and
the teaching in the Bohemian
Catholic school in Dodge,
Nebraska, was confided to them by the Rev. John St. Brož, Bohemian
poet and historian.

The first religious reception of candidates into the Order in
America took place in the temporary Motherhouse at Fenton, Missouri, on January 14, 1913.

Openings of other Bohemian schools and orphanages followed,
and the labors of the sisters were extended beyond the states of Missouri and Nebraska, and into Iowa.

With the establishment of these missions and the growth of the
Community, the need of a permanent central Motherhouse in America
was felt, and with the approbation of the Most Rev. J. J. Harty, D.D.,
Bishop of Omaha, the Congregation bought, in 1920, a farm of ten
acres, known as the "Seven Oaks Farm," situated in the northern
part of Omaha, then known as Florence.

In 1925 a spacious modern building—constituting at present only one-third of the proposed Motherhouse—was erected there, and is known as the Notre Dame Academy, a boarding and high school for young ladies. The solemn dedication of the academy took place on August 15, 1926, and in the following September it was opened to students.

SUMMARY

Bohemian School Sisters de Notre Dame.
Founded in Bohemia in 1853.
Papal Approbation of Rules, April 15, 1909, by Pope Pius X.
Established in the United States in 1910.
Habit: The habit is black, with a black mantle, woolen belt, white wimple and band.
Approximate number in Community in United States, 75.
Active in educational and charitable work among Bohemians in the arch-diocese of Dubuque, and in the dioceses of Lincoln and Omaha.
United States Provincial Motherhouse and Novitiate, Convent de Notre Dame, 3505 State Street, Omaha, Nebraska. (Diocese of Omaha.)

SISTERS OF ST. TERESA OF JESUS*

1910

THE Society of St. Teresa of Jesus, whose members are familiarly known as Teresian Sisters, was founded in Tarragona, Spain, June 23, 1876, by the Rev. Enrique De Osso, a prelate zealously interested in the Christian education of girls.

In 1910 the Teresian Sisters sent their first representatives to the United States. With Mother Dolores Aparicio as Superior, a mission was opened at San Antonio, Texas. The following year the sisters opened a parochial school mission at Uvalde, Texas, and in 1915 a foundation was made at New Orleans.

The Society in the United States, with Mother Dolores continuing as Superior, while affiliated with the Motherhouse in Barcelona, Spain, is under the direct jurisdiction of the provincialate at Havana, Cuba, of which Mother Dolores Escoda is present Provincial Superior.

SUMMARY

Sisters of St. Teresa of Jesus.
Founded in Spain in 1876.
Papal Approbation of Rules, December 15, 1908, by Pope Pius IX.
Established in the United States in 1910.
Habit: The habit is brown, with a double cape reaching to the waist, a white collar, and a black cap and veil.
Active in the United States in educational work in the archdioceses of New Orleans and San Antonio.
United States Novitiate, St. Teresa's Convent, 4018 South Presa Street, San Antonio, Texas. (Archdiocese of San Antonio.)

*From data supplied by the Teresian Sisters, St. Teresa's Academy, San Antonio, Tex.

SISTERS OF ST. BASIL THE GREAT*

1911

FOX CHASE, PENNSYLVANIA

*L*ABORING among the Ukrainian Greek Catholic people in the United States are members of the Order of Sisters of St. Basil the Great, which originated about the fourth century, when founded by St. Macrina, under the spiritual direction of her brother, St. Basil the Great.

Since that period the care of the sick and the education of children has been carried on as the special purpose of the Sisters of St. Basil, whose Congregation, allied with the Order of the Basilian Fathers, was blessed and approved by successive pontiffs of the early centuries.

In 1911 three Basilian Sisters, with Mother M. Helen as Superior, left their ancient community home in Lemberg, Galicia, and came to the United States to make a foundation of their Order in Philadelphia. This was in accordance with plans of the Right Rev. S. S. Ortynsky, D.D., first bishop of the Ukrainian Catholic diocese in the United States, who had perceived the need of sisters of the Greek Rite to open schools and orphanages, and enkindle and preserve the faith in those of the Ukrainian Greek Catholic diocese in this country.

MOTHER M. JOSAPHAT

In 1926 the community transferred its Motherhouse from Philadelphia to the present site in Fox Chase, Pennsylvania, where Mother M. Josaphat is Superior.

The community in the United States is under the episcopal juris-

*From data and material supplied by the Sisters of St. Basil the Great, Fox Chase, Pa.

diction of Bishop Ortynsky's successor, the Right Rev. Constantine Bohachewsky, D.D., with his episcopal residence at 815 North Franklin Street, Philadelphia, Pennsylvania.

SUMMARY

Sisters of St. Basil the Great.
Founded in Asia Minor about the Fourth Century, A.D.
Established in the United States for the Ukrainian Greek Catholics in 1911.
Habit: The habit and veil are black, with a black scapular and girdle, and with white wimple. A rosary is worn.
Active in educational and charitable work among Ukrainian Greek Catholics in Philadelphia and Fox Chase, Jenkintown, Pennsylvania; Chesapeake City, Maryland; Chicago, Illinois; and Cleveland, Ohio.
United States Motherhouse and Novitiate, St. Joseph's Convent, Fox Chase, Jenkintown, Pennsylvania. (Ukrainian Greek Catholic Diocese.)

FACTORYVILLE, PENNSYLVANIA*
1921

MOTHER MACRINA

The community of Basilian Sisters whose Motherhouse has been established at Factoryville, Pennsylvania, was founded in 1921 by Mother Macrina, for eight years successor in office of Mother M. Helen, first Superior in America of the Sisters of St. Basil.

To accede to the repeated requests of the Carpatho Rusins, who with the Ukrainians comprise the body of the Ruthenian Greek Catholics of the United States, Mother Macrina, with two sisters, formed a Basilian community to labor exclusively among the Carpatho Rusins of the Pittsburgh Ruthenian Greek Diocese, whose bishop at present is the Right Rev. Basil Takach, D.D.

For a short time Cleveland, Ohio, was made the headquar-

*From data and material supplied by the Sisters of St. Basil the Great, Factoryville, Pa.

ters of the new community, the sisters being engaged there in the care of an orphanage, now located, as St. Nicholas' Orphanage, at Elmhurst, Pennsylvania.

St. Nicholas' Orphanage, continuing under the direction of the Basilian Sisters, is maintained by the Greek Catholic Union, a benevolent society of the Carpatho Rusins, with a membership of more than two hundred and fifty thousand. In 1923 the orphanage became the temporary location of the Motherhouse, in connection with which a novitiate was then opened.

St. Basil's Convent, Factoryville, Pennsylvania

Following the acquisition, in 1927, of a large tract of land at Factoryville, Pennsylvania, on the Lackawanna Trail, transfer was made to it of the Motherhouse and novitiate, occupying a residence there pending the erection of suitable buildings not only for Motherhouse and novitiate purposes, but also for an academy.

SUMMARY

Sisters of St. Basil the Great.

Founded in Asia Minor about the Fourth Century, A.D.

Established in the United States for the Carpatho Rusins in 1921.

Habit: The habit is black, with a black scapular, girdle and *kaptur,* or veil, and white *kapka*—wimple. Three folds at the bottom of the habit, sleeves and *kapka* denote the three vows of poverty, chastity and obedience. A rosary is worn.

Active in educational and charitable work among the Carpatho Rusins in Scranton, Elmhurst, Factoryville and Wilkes-Barre, Pennsylvania, and in Trenton, New Jersey.

United States Motherhouse and Novitiate, St. Basil's Convent, Factoryville, Pennsylvania. (Diocese of Pittsburgh, Greek Rite.)

SISTERS OF ST. DOROTHY*

1911

ON August 15, 1928, there was held in the Vatican in Rome a ceremony honoring and advancing the cause of Blessed Paola Frassinetti—an event of joy to a little community of Sisters of St. Dorothy who had been laboring in the United States since 1911.

BLESSED PAOLA FRASSINETTI (1809-1882)
Foundress of the Sisters of St. Dorothy

*From data and material supplied by the Sisters of St. Dorothy, St. Patrick's Academy, Richmond, Staten Island, N. Y., and from the N.C.W.C. Bulletin, September, 1925.

Blessed Paola Frassinetti, the foundress of the Institute of Sisters of St. Dorothy, was born at Genoa, Italy, March 3, 1809. At the age of twenty-five, with the aid of an elder brother who had become a priest, as had her three other brothers, she founded the Community which at the time of her saintly death in 1882 had spread throughout Italy, and into Portugal and Brazil. A little more than ten years later, the Dorotheans, as the members of the Institute are also known, had extended their work to England, Belgium, Spain, Switzerland, Malta, and to the United States.

Following their introduction to New York City in 1911, under the auspices of the Most Rev. John Farley, D.D., Archbishop of New York, before his elevation to the cardinalate, the Sisters of St. Dorothy labored in educational and social service work there, as well as in Providence, Rhode Island. In 1919 the Dorotheans established a convent at Richmond, Staten Island, New York, which is now a Provincial house of the Institute.

In 1925 a hostel, a combination of convent, school, and home, entrusted to the care of the Sisters of St. Dorothy, was opened in Providence, Rhode Island, through the efforts of the Right Rev. W. A. Hickey, D.D., Bishop of Providence, and the Rev. Antonio P. Rebello, pastor of the Church of Our Lady of the Rosary.

The Providence Diocesan Council of Catholic Women has its headquarters at the hostel for its Immigration Committee, for the care of immigrants, who land in Providence in large numbers.

The ground floor of the hostel has a spacious rest and waiting room, where incoming immigrants may stay until the arrival of their families or friends, and dormitories have been installed for the benefit of those who are obliged to remain overnight. A cafeteria is also conducted there.

The National Council of Catholic Women, with its representatives at the office in the waiting room, assists the Sisters of St. Dorothy in caring for the strangers coming into a strange land.

SUMMARY

Sisters of St. Dorothy.

Founded in Italy in 1834.

Papal Approbation of Rules, August 23, 1889, by Pope Leo XIII.

Established in the United States in 1911.

Active in educational and social service work in the archdioceses of New York and Philadelphia, and in the dioceses of Detroit and Providence.

United States Provincial house and Novitiate, 256 Center Street, Richmond, Staten Island, New York. (Archdiocese of New York.)

SISTERS OF THE HOLY GHOST*

1911

*O*N 1911 there was received into the diocese of Pittsburgh a small group of Sisters of the Holy Ghost from Petrograd, Russia, members of a Congregation founded in Rome in 1890.

Mother Josephine Finatowitz, foundress of the Sisters of the Holy Ghost, a Russian by birth, and a member of the schismatic Russian Church, at the early age of eight wished to be received into the Church of Rome, but not until her thirteenth year was she allowed to do so. Some years later she went to Rome, where she was admitted to a Carmelite Convent.

When ill health prevented her from continuing under the Carmelite Rule, wishing to return to Russia to engage in missionary work there, and joined by two companions, she founded in Rome, in 1890, the Congregation of the Sisters of the Holy Ghost. Under ecclesiastical authority, Mother Josephine and her companions went to Russia four year later to labor there.

MOTHER JOSEPHINE
FINATOWITZ

Foundress and Superior of
the Sisters of the Holy Ghost

As religious missionaries in Russia the sisters endured persecution and hardships, while Mother Josephine more than once was obliged to appear in court, and made to suffer many indignities.

When the community of Sisters of the Holy Ghost in Pittsburgh severed its Russian ties, Mother Josephine came to the United States in 1913, accompanied by Sister Anthony, a native of Petrograd, and a member of the original Russian community, who had left Pittsburgh to bring her Superior from Europe.

Separating later from the community whose Motherhouse is now located at West View, Pittsburgh, Pennsylvania, Mother Josephine and Sister Anthony, after an interval, went to Cleveland, Ohio,

*From data and material supplied by the Sisters of the Holy Ghost, 12219 Corlett Avenue, Cleveland, Ohio.

devoting themselves there to the care of children in a small orphanage.

Under the episcopal jurisdiction of the Right Rev. Joseph Schrembs, D.D., a novitiate was canonically erected in Cleveland for the Congregation, and the rapidly increasing little community gathering under the superiorship of the venerable foundress was placed under the training of an efficient novice mistress from the Congregation of Sisters of St. Joseph of the Order of St. Francis in Cleveland, in preparation for activity in educational and charitable work in the diocese.

Motherhouse and Novitiate, Holy Ghost Convent, 12219 Corlett Avenue, Cleveland, Ohio. (Diocese of Cleveland.)

SACRAMENTINE NUNS*

1911

THE Congregation of the Sisters of the Blessed Sacrament, a convent of which was established at Yonkers, New York, in March, 1911, under the auspices of His Eminence, John Cardinal Farley, Archbishop of New York, was founded in Marseilles, France, in 1639, by Père Antoine, of the Dominican Order. Not until twenty years later, however, were the religious forming the Congregation established as the Sisters of the Blessed Sacrament. Completing the century and surviving the French Revolution, although among the victims were members of the Congregation, the Community then founded houses through France, and in England and Belgium.

In connection with the convent in Yonkers, New York, the Sacramentine Nuns, as the Sisters of the Blessed Sacrament are known, conduct the Academy of the Blessed Sacrament, a boarding and day school for girls, and devote themselves to the Perpetual Adoration of Our Lord in the Holy Eucharist.

United States Motherhouse and Novitiate, Monastery of the Blessed Sacrament, 23 Park Avenue, Yonkers, New York. (Archdiocese of New York.)

*From the Catholic Encyclopedia and the Official Catholic Directory, 1929.

SISTERS OF MERCY OF THE HOLY CROSS*

1912

HE Congregation of Sisters of Mercy of the Holy Cross was founded in Canton Schwyz, Switzerland, in 1852, by the zealous Franciscan priest, the Rev. Theodosius Florentini, in co-operation with the pious woman who as Mother M. Theresia Scherer devoted her life in the cause for which the Congregation was founded, teaching, nursing and other works of charity.

In 1912, sisters of the Community, with Sister M. Lauda Werner as Superior, were sent from their Motherhouse at Ingenbohl, Brunnen,

HOLY CROSS CONVENT, MERRILL, WISCONSIN

on Switzerland's beautiful Lake Lucerne, to distant Wisconsin in the United States, where, locating at Merrill, in the north central section of the state, they began the activities of their Congregation in this country by engaging in parochial school work.

*From data and material supplied by the Sisters of Mercy of the Holy Cross, Holy Cross Hospital, Merrill, Wis.

In 1923 a novitiate was established at the Holy Cross Convent in Merrill, which had been made possible by the generosity of its citizens, who three years later contributed largely toward the erection of Holy Cross Hospital for the city of Merrill, and Lincoln County, Wisconsin. This institution the Sisters of Mercy of the Holy Cross, under the present superiorship of Sister Mericia Baumhauer, are successfully conducting, as their initial hospital work in the United States, in addition to laboring now in Illinois, Missouri and North Dakota, as well as in Wisconsin.

SUMMARY

Sisters of Mercy of the Holy Cross.
Founded in Switzerland in 1852.
Papal Approbation of Rules in 1894 by Pope Leo XIII.
Established in the United States in 1912.
Habit: The habit and cape are black, with a small white collar. A black veil is worn over white headwear.
Active in the United States in educational, hospital and charitable work in the archdiocese of St. Louis, and in the dioceses of Belleville, Bismarck and Superior.
United States Novitiate, Holy Cross Novitiate, Park and Riverside Avenues, Merrill, Wisconsin. (Diocese of Superior.)

RELIGIOUS OF NOTRE DAME DE SION*

1912

THE Congregation of Notre Dame de Sion, a community of which was established in the United States, in Kansas City, Missouri, in 1912, was founded in Paris in 1843, by the Abbé Theodore Ratisbonne and his brother Marie Alphonse, of a rich and benevolent Israelite family of Alsace.

Rebellious and embittered over the conversion of his brother Theodore, who had embraced the Catholic religion in 1827, and had become a priest, Alphonse Ratisbonne, while visiting in Rome in 1842, and, on an occasion tarrying in the Church of *St. André della fratte,* while a friend transacted a business matter at the rectory nearby, was vouchsafed a vision of the Blessed Virgin, as she is represented on what is familiarly known as the Miraculous Medal. Alphonse had, some time previously, as a favor to a friend, accepted and worn—though defiantly—one of these medals. Receiving the gift of faith, at the time of the apparition, Alphonse asked for Baptism, and the name of Marie, and like his brother became a priest.

At this time, in France, many among the Jewish people were inclining toward Catholicism, and when the Abbé Theodore Ratisbonne, on the suggestion of his brother, Marie Alphonse, opened in Paris, in 1843, a house for the reception of Jewish children, to be educated, with their parents' consent, as Christians, there was no lack of candidates for admission.

To preside over this catechumenate, Abbé Ratisbonne chose two of his spiritual daughters at Strasburg, Madame Sophie Stouhlen and Mademoiselle Louise Catherine Weywada. The former, a childless widow fifty-four years of age, belonged to a fervent Catholic family which filled important positions in the magistracy and army, the latter, the eldest in a family of twenty-four children, had been brought up in this patriarchal home with the simplicity and rectitude of the ages of faith, and, like Madame Stouhlen, Mademoiselle Weywada had acquired, by the exercise of filial and fraternal devotedness, the aptitudes Abbé Ratisbonne knew necessary for the life of abnegation required of those on whom devolves the duty of educating souls.

Consecrating the work to the Blessed Mother, to designate it Abbé Ratisbonne added to the words *Notre Dame* the Biblical name

*From data and material supplied by the Religious of Notre Dame de Sion, 3823 Locust Street, Kansas City, Mo.

Sion, so often repeated in the psalms, as exactly characteristic of this work, which, as a lay apostolate, ended in 1847.

In the community life followed by Madame Stouhlen, Made-moiselle Weywada and the companions who, one by one, had joined them, the religious spirit had developed instinctively, and at their

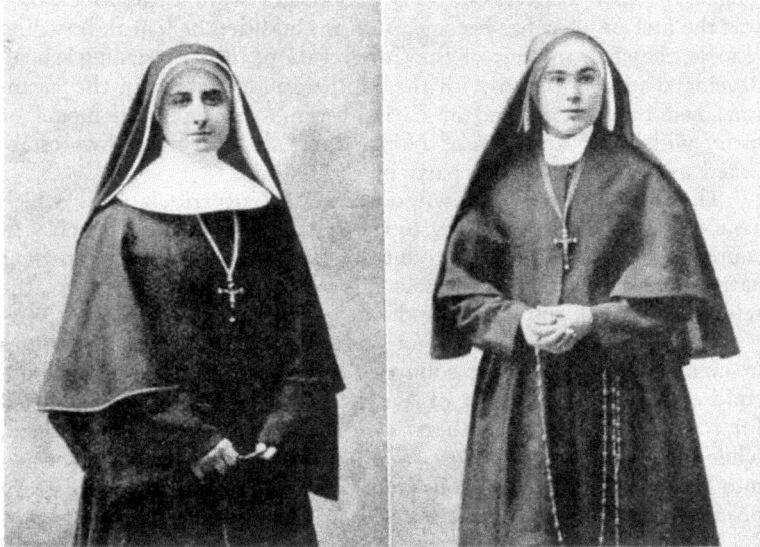

CHOIR NUN AND LAY SISTER
Congregation of Notre Dame de Sion

request the founder of the work of Notre Dame de Sion gave them a series of conferences to initiate them into the religious life.

Passing in review the different institutes of the Church, he showed them how each one reproduces one of Our Saviour's divine virtues and possesses a physiognomy which distinguishes it from all others. He admonished them to "imitate the compassionate love of Jesus for the children of Israel and His zeal to attract and convert them," and to keep always before them the fact that "Jesus sprang from this people; the Blessed Virgin was a daughter of this people; the apostles who spread the Gospel were Jews, and the adhesion of the Jews to the Christian faith will be, according to the prophecies, the signal of the most glorious triumph of the Church."

On September 8, 1848, Madame Stouhlen and her companions made their vows, and Madame Stouhlen was later the first of the

Congregation of Notre Dame de Sion to pronounce perpetual vows.

In 1847, for contacts, and in the hope of later conversions, the community had taken charge of a school in a manufacturing district of Than, for the children of the men, Alsatian Jews, whose employer longed for their conversion. The day-school work then undertaken was the first of what has become, with the addition of that in boarding schools, the chief interest of the Congregation, for its boarding school, developed in connection with the Motherhouse—which in the meantime had been established in Paris—became the type and model of many which the Religious of Notre Dame de Sion have since established and maintain in all parts of the world.

The Institute was not without the seal of tribulations, which assures solidity and perpetuity to the instruments of the Church. In countries plague-stricken, in countries desolated by war, and in their native country, disturbed by laws of oppression and suppression, the religious labored and persevered.

During the World War, Sion, which possessed important houses in many of the belligerent countries, received into the Motherhouse children from the suburbs of Paris, whose fathers were mobilized for service, and whose mothers were ill or unable to care for them, while other houses of the Congregation were temporarily transformed into hospitals, and the religious were personally active in nearly every phase of war-relief work.

With the consequent dispersion of many of the Old World communities during this period, religious were sent to this country, and located, for a time, in Louisville, Kentucky. On their removal to Kansas City, Missouri, on October 22, 1912, the Congregation of Notre Dame de Sion was formally established in the United States, with Mother Marie Théotime de Sion as Superior.

In the academy, a day and boarding school, known as the French Institution of Notre Dame de Sion, which was soon opened by the religious, the boarding school system, as perfected in the European houses of the Congregation, is carried out. All required English branches are taught—from kindergarten to college—but French is the language of the house and is compulsory for the students at all times except during English classes.

The religious here, as elsewhere, are semi-cloistered, and adhere to the original purpose of the Institute, providing for the care of converted Jewesses, and the instruction of catechumens. In connection with the convent in Kansas City, branches of the Archconfraternity of Prayer for the Conversion of the Jews, and the Archfraternity of Christian Mothers—both established by the Congregation —are maintained.

The Community in the United States, of which Mother Marie Irene de Sion is now Superior, though under the local jurisdiction of the Right Rev. Thomas F. Lillis, D.D., Bishop of Kansas City, retains its affiliations with the General Motherhouse in Paris, at 61 Rue Notre Dame des Champs, and the prayers and works of this community, in union with those of the entire Congregation, are especially offered for the conversion of the Jews.

SUMMARY

Religious of Notre Dame de Sion.

Founded in France in 1843.

Papal Approbation of Rules, December 14, 1874, by Pope Pius IX.

Established in the United States in 1912.

Habit: The veil is black, and the habit is of black woolen material, of straight form, with narrow sleeves, over which the choir-sisters wear a pair of wide sleeves in the chapel and parlour. A stiff white guimpe is worn over a round cape which is of the same material as the habit, and extends a little below the waist. The religious wear a cross of ebony, to which is attached the figure of Christ, in silver. The medal on their rosary of olive-stones bears, on one side, the effigy of Notre Dame de Sion, and, in relief, the words *Congrégation de Notre Dame de Sion,* and on the other side the crest of the Congregation, with the words, *In Sion firmata sum.*

Active in educational and catechetical work in the diocese of Kansas City.

United States foundation mission house, French Institution of Notre Dame de Sion, 3823 Locust Street, Kansas City, Missouri. (Diocese of Kansas City.)

PALLOTTINE MISSIONARY SISTERS*

1912

*T*HE Pallottine Missionary Sisters, or Pallottine Sisters, as they are familiarly known, compose a congregation founded in Rome in 1843 by Ven. Vincenzo Pallotti, founder of the Pious Society of the Missions, for which he was desirous of the auxiliary aid of a sisterhood.

In 1912, in response to a request from the Rev. Nicholas Hengers, of the Pious Society of the Missions, laboring in the United States, and in need of teachers for his parish school in Richwood, West Virginia, Sister M. Frances and three companions came to his assistance from the Motherhouse of their Congregation of Pallottine Sisters at Limburg, Germany.

Engaging for some years thereafter exclusively in parochial school work in West Virginia, the Pallottine Sisters have also extended their activities to the care of the sick, now conducting hospitals at Buckingham, Richwood and Huntington, West Virginia, in connection with which last institution the American Motherhouse and novitiate of the Community are now maintained.

A PALLOTTINE MISSIONARY
SISTER

SUMMARY

Pallottine Missionary Sisters.
Founded in Italy in 1843.
Established in the United States in 1912.
Habit: The habit, veil and scapular are black, with white wimple.
Approximate number in Community in United States, 100.
Active in educational and hospital work in the dioceses of Columbus, Omaha and Wheeling.
United States Motherhouse and Novitiate, St. Mary's Convent, Huntington, West Virginia. (Diocese of Wheeling.)

*From data and material supplied by the Pallottine Missionary Sisters, Sacred Heart Convent, Richwood, W. Va.

DAUGHTERS OF DIVINE CHARITY*

1913

TO Austria does the United States owe the Congregation of the Daughters of Divine Charity, participating in Catholic welfare work and teaching in this country.

The Congregation of the Daughters of Divine Charity was founded at Vienna in 1868, by Mother Franciska Lechner, formerly a Bavarian school teacher, for the special work of the Christian education of children, the care of homeless girls—especially the working girls of large cities, and the religious instruction of Hungarian children in the public schools.

Through the fervor of Bishop Arpal Varady, of Gyor, Hungary, the sisters in their convent in Budapest, newly aroused to zeal for the salvation of souls, asked and were granted permission by their Superior to seek new fields of activity in the United States. Mother Valeria, Provincial Superior, and Mother Kostka, Mistress of Novices, both of Budapest, were the pioneers from the Austrian Congregation of the Daughters of Divine Charity to arrive in New York City in 1913.

A DAUGHTER OF DIVINE CHARITY

Encountering but overcoming many difficulties, and joined, soon after, by other sisters from Austria, the Community opened a home for girls and thus began its labors in the United States. Parochial school work and religious instruction classes have since been undertaken by the sisters, who have extended their labors into several dioceses.

In 1919 during the influenza epidemic, the sisters actively assisted in the nursing, at Perth Amboy, New Jersey.

The Provincial house and novitiate, established at Arrochar, Staten Island, New York, is the residence of Sister M. Blanda Domin-

*From data supplied by the Daughters of Divine Charity, St. Joseph's Hill Academy, Arrochar, Staten Island, N. Y.

kovich, Superior of the Community in the United States, and her assistants, Sisters M. Hyacinth, M. Narcissa, M. Margaret and M. Melinda.

The Community continues affiliated with the General Motherhouse at Vienna, in Austria, the Superior General of the Order in 1928 being Mother Kostka, of the pioneer band of 1913.

SUMMARY

Daughters of Divine Charity.
Founded in Austria in 1868.
Papal Approbation of Rules in 1891, by Pope Leo XIII.
Established in the United States in 1913.
Active in educational, charitable and social service work in the archdiocese of New York, and in the dioceses of Fort Wayne, Hartford, Toledo and Trenton.
United States Provincial house and Novitiate, St. Joseph's Hill Convent, 205 Major Avenue, Arrochar, Staten Island, New York. (Archdiocese of New York.)

SISTERS, SERVANTS OF MARY*

1914

$\mathfrak{T}$HE Congregation of Sisters, Servants of Mary, Trained Nurses of the Sick, was founded in Madrid, Spain, in the year 1851. Its foundress, Mother Soledad Torres Acosta, was but twenty-five years of age, when, with six companions, she consecrated herself to the work of nursing the sick in their own homes, giving gratuitously and voluntarily all the services that illness called for and charity required. For those of the sick in need of material assistance the seven fervent women provided of their own means.

Combining with this work the primary purpose of the Congregation, self-sanctification, by the observance of the simple vows of religion and the Rules of the Institute, the sisters have recourse to the Blessed Mother of God, invoking her as the patroness and protectress of the Community under the title of *Health of the Sick*.

The Sisters, Servants of Mary, Trained Nurses of the Sick, minister to all classes, regardless of creed, sex or nationality, and for all provide the services they require, according to physicians' orders, excluding whatever does not conform to religious decorum. That they may scientifically fulfill their duties the Congregation instructs its members as trained nurses, in all necessary branches.

MOTHER SOLEDAD TORRES ACOSTA

Foundress in 1851 of the Sisters, Servants of Mary

Before sending a sister out on duty the Superior secures details in regard to the patient and the exact location and environment of his home. Whenever a sister goes to an unknown house on her first call she is accompanied by another sister.

To relieve the nursing sisters of all home responsibility, that they may devote their entire time to the care of the sick, the Congrega-

*From data and material supplied by the Sisters, Servants of Mary, 800 North 18th Street, Kansas City, Kan.

tion is made up also of lay sisters, who while otherwise participating in the duties and privileges of the Community, are exempt from the work of nursing.

SISTERS, SERVANTS OF MARY, KANSAS CITY, KANSAS

Members of the Congregation, under the superiorship of Mother Anastasia Borostiaga, came to the United States in 1914, and at the time came with American troops from Vera Cruz, Mexico, to the port of Galveston, whence they proceeded to New Orleans, where a first United States foundation was made. From their convent in the city at 1205 Esplanade Avenue the Sisters, Servants of Mary have since carried on the work for which their Congregation was founded.

In the course of the recent civil disturbances in Mexico, nearly all of the twenty-two houses of the Order which had been established there by sisters from the Motherhouse in Spain, were transferred from the country.

Following the initial foundation in New Orleans, a community of the Order was received in Kansas City, Kansas, and established a convent there which has become the United States Motherhouse and novitiate of the Order, where Mother Arrenia Goldaracena is now Superior.

CONVENT OF THE SISTERS, SERVANTS OF MARY, KANSAS CITY, KANSAS

In New York City, to meet a need, the sisters have opened the *Casa Maria* at 251 West 14th Street, a Spanish settlement and boarding home for girls.

On February 4, 1928, the sisters opened a house at 2400 South Grammercy Place, in Los Angeles, California, where also they now devote themselves to the special work for which the Community was founded.

The Congregation maintains its General Motherhouse at Plaza de Chamberi, 13, Madrid, Spain, and with its many establishments in Europe, North and South America, Porto Rico and Cuba, has four novitiates, two in Spain, and one each in Buenos Aires and Argentina, as well as in the United States.

SUMMARY

Sisters, Servants of Mary, Trained Nurses of the Sick.
Founded in Spain in 1851.
Papal Approbation of Rules in 1898, by Pope Leo XIII.
Established in the United States in 1914.
Active in nursing and social service work in the archdioceses of New Orleans and New York, and in the dioceses of Leavenworth and Los Angeles and San Diego.
United States Motherhouse and Novitiate, Convent of the Sisters, Servants of Mary, 800 North 18th Street, Kansas City, Kansas. (Diocese of Leavenworth.)

54

HANDMAIDS OF THE MOST PURE HEART OF MARY*

1917

THE Congregation of the Handmaids of the Most Pure Heart of Mary was founded in 1917, in Savannah, Georgia, through the zealous efforts of the Rev. Ignatius Lis-sner, S.M.A., in behalf of the colored people of Catholic faith.

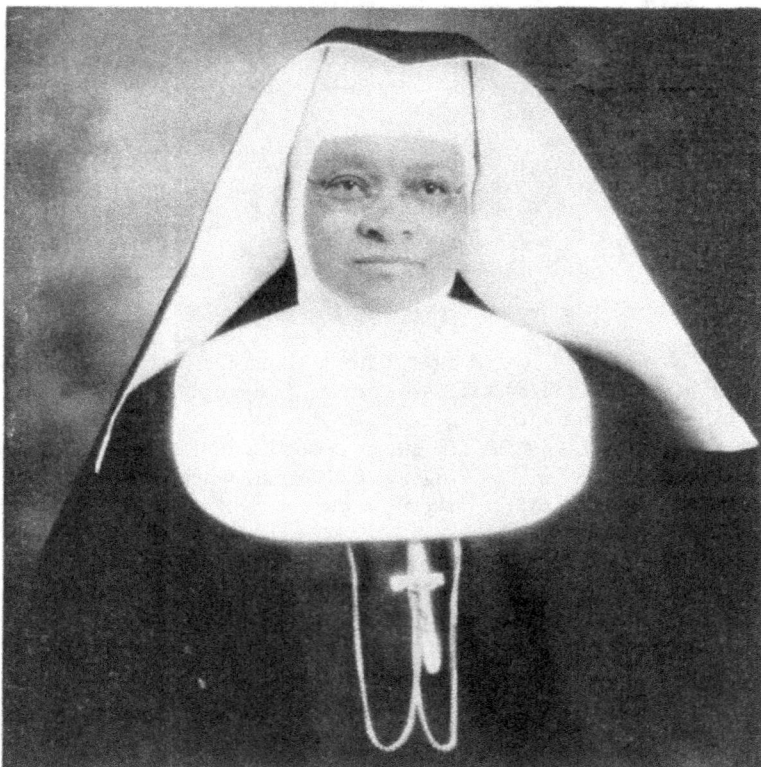

MOTHER M. THEODORE WILLIAMS
Foundress and Superior of the Congregation of the Handmaids of the Most Pure Heart of Mary

*From data and material supplied by the Handmaids of the Most Pure Heart of Mary, 8 East 131st Street, New York City.

With the assent of the Right Rev. Benjamin J. Keiley, D.D., Bishop of Savannah, the activities of the Congregation—soon after its founding—were transferred to New York. With the approbation of His Eminence, John Cardinal Farley, and under the continued guidance of Father Lissner, the Congregation established its Mother-house in New York City.

Mother M. Theodore Williams, foundress and first Superior, remains Superior of the Congregation. Carrying out the ideals and plans of the zealous founder, the sisters devote themselves to missionary work by propagating the Catholic faith among the colored people. Membership in the Community is limited to devout Catholic women of the colored race.

A day nursery, known as St. Benedict's Nursery, 27-29 West 132nd Street, in the neighborhood of the Motherhouse, has been opened by the sisters, and eighty-five colored children are under their care in this institution. At the Motherhouse, on East 131st Street, rooms have been fitted up to serve for club purposes for the young colored women who wish to avail themselves there of club privileges, and adult and children's religious instruction classes are also conducted.

Settlement work of every description is within the scope of the Constitutions of the Congregation, as with its growth in numbers it accepts every opportunity for the pursuance of its missionary labors among the colored people.

Motherhouse and Novitiate, St. Mary's Convent, 8 East 131st Street, New York, New York. (Archdiocese of New York.)

MISSIONARY CATECHISTS OF OUR BLESSED LADY OF VICTORY*

1918

*W*ITH an appeal to the Child of Mary in the world, and to all Catholic young women, to remember the duty each owes toward those of the faith who are famine-stricken in soul, the Rev. J. J. Sigstein, of the archdiocese of Chicago, on September 8, 1918, founded the Society of Missionary Catechists of Our Blessed Lady of Victory of Santa Fé, New Mexico.

Realizing, during a previous stay in the southwest, that the inherited Catholic faith of countless numbers, of Spanish or Mexican

VICTORY TRAINING INSTITUTE, VICTORY-NOLL, HUNTINGTON, INDIANA

descent, was being undermined, owing to the dearth of priests and religious workers, Father Sigstein zealously planned the Society for apostolic labor in the vast region of the border states, to combat this leakage in the Church.

With the sponsorship in the archdiocese of Santa Fé of its archbishop, the Most Rev. Albert T. Daeger, O.F.M., D.D., the foundation of the new Community was laid. The Right Rev. John F. Noll, D.D., Bishop of Fort Wayne, interested in the Mexican situation, aided

*From data and material supplied from Victory Training Institute, Huntington, Ind., and from *Our Sunday Visitor.*

in the establishment at Huntington, Indiana, in his diocese, of Victory Training Institute, where the Missionary Catechists are fitted for their future work as religious teachers, trained nurses, and social service workers.

The Missionary Catechists, who retain their family names, with but the prefix of "Catechist" in place of "Sister," are religious in the full sense of the word, living in community and taking the customary vows of religion.

Shortly after her entrance at Victory Training Institute, Victory-Noll, each candidate is consecrated to the service and love of Jesus through Mary. At the time of her consecration she receives a Mary-blue uniform and white veil. Later, if accepted, she receives the uniform and blue veil of a Probationer Catechist, and during a following period is trained to the religious life, pursues studies necessary to prepare her for her work, and is given lessons in the Spanish language.

As a Junior Catechist a candidate to the Society is usually then sent to Gary or Indiana Harbor, Indiana, the heart of the Calumet steel district, and after a year of labor among the Spanish-speaking people there she goes to the missions in the southwest.

In accordance with the aim in the establishment of the Society, the Missionary Catechists of Our Blessed Lady of Victory devote themselves, in their field of labor, to the religious instruction and Christian training of poor and neglected children, and visit and assist the needy, even in the most sparsely settled southwestern mission districts. The Catechists also engage in tabernacle work, caring for altars, baking altar breads, training servers, and sometimes leading in public devotions during the absence of the mission priest.

CATECHIST IDA KELLER
Of the Missionary Catechists
of Our Blessed Lady
of Victory

The members of the Society accept no remuneration for their services, depending on Catholic generosity for the sponsorship and support of their work in the extensive mission fields at home.

In October, 1926, a second training school of the Society was

opened at Las Vegas, New Mexico, in the archdiocese of Santa Fé, under the auspices of Archbishop Daeger, the honorary president of the Society.   Victory-Mount, as this new institution is named, serves for the reception of native Spanish-speaking subjects, who study there before completing their training at Victory-Noll, preparatory to returning to the southwest to become a potent influence as native missionaries among their own people.

SUMMARY

Missionary Catechists of Our Blessed Lady of Victory of Santa Fé, New Mexico.

Founded in the United States in 1918.

Habit: A navy blue uniform garb, with white collar and cuffs, and a navy blue veil, is worn.   After profession a silver medal of Our Lady of Victory is worn about the neck on a silver chain.

Active in catechetical, missionary and social service work in the archdioceses of Chicago and Santa Fé, and in the dioceses of Amarillo, Fort Wayne and Monterey-Fresno.

Motherhouse and Novitiate, Victory Training Institute, Victory-Noll, Huntington, Indiana.   (Diocese of Fort Wayne.)

MISSIONARY CANONESSES OF
ST. AUGUSTINE*

1919

THE Congregation of the Missionary Canonesses of St. Augustine was founded in August, 1897, by Mother Marie Louise De Meester, of Roulers, Belgium, chiefly to aid foreign missions through teaching, and the undertaking of any charitable labors.

The establishment of the Community was the outgrowth of the missionary zeal of Mother De Meester as a member of the teaching religious order of the Canonesses of St. Augustine.

Upon application to the bishop of Bruges, Mother Louise and a companion were granted permission to devote themselves wholly to the apostolic activities with which they had cooperated so fervently.

Quilon, in British India, was the scene of the first establishment of the Missionary Canonesses. Augmented by European postulants, the young Congregation spread rapidly in different parts of India, conducting several orphan homes, catechumen and industrial schools, dispensaries and hospitals. In the meantime native auxiliary sisters had been accepted who, under the direction of the European sisters, were trained to the religious life, proving of valuable aid in the work. With the exception of these sisters, who have continued to share in the labors and merits of the missionary life of the Community, the Congregation is composed entirely of choir nuns.

In 1910, at the expressed wish of the Sovereign Pontiff, Pope Pius X, Mother M. Louise extended the work of the sisters to the Philippine Islands, where they now have charge of many schools, in addition to conducting a college in Manila.

In response to an appeal from the Right Rev. Msgr. Joseph F. Stillemans, in behalf of the Belgian immigrants in New York City, St. John Berchmans' Convent—the first establishment of the Missionary Canonesses of St. Augustine in the United States, and the last foundation personally supervised by Mother M. Louise, was opened. Members of the Community, under Mother Marie Adrienne as Superior, arrived in New York on September 3, 1919, to work

*From data and material supplied by the Missionary Canonesses of St. Augustine, St. John Berchmans' Convent, New York, N. Y., and from "The Lacemakers of Belgium," by Agnes Roberts Martin in Good Counsel, June, 1927.

for the benefit of their compatriots in connection with the Belgian
Bureau, and visiting and nursing of the sick poor, as well as cate-

MOTHER MARIE LOUISE DE MEESTER (1856-1928)
Foundress of the Congregation of the Missionary Canonesses of St. Augustine

chism teaching for public school children, were soon added to their
duties.

At the Sesqui-Centennial Exhibition in Philadelphia, in 1926,
side by side with commercial wares, the white-robed Missionary
Canonesses displayed their rare and delicate lace handiwork. Subsequent to the Exhibition, *The Lacemakers of Belgium,* as they came

to be called, "remained to share with Philadelphia the beauty and the fruits of their widely-shuttled zeal," and from the convent of St. Clare of Montefalco, then established, and solemnly dedicated by His Eminence, Dennis Cardinal Dougherty, the Missionary Canon-esses of St. Augustine have since engaged in charitable work in Philadelphia, co-operating especially in the labors of the Augustinian Fathers. Here, as through a third United States establishment, in the diocese of Natchez, they carry on the missionary work to which the Congregation devotes itself now not only in Belgium, India and the Philippines, but also in Africa, China and the West Indies.

The Community in the United States retains its affiliations with the General Motherhouse in Louvain, Belgium, while the seat of the American government of the Community is maintained in New York City, Mother Marie Suzanne serving as Provincial Superior in 1928.

SUMMARY

Missionary Canonesses of St. Augustine.
Founded in Belgium in 1897.
Established in the United States in 1919.
Papal Approbation of Rules, October 1, 1926, by His Holiness, Pope Pius XI.
Habit: The habit, with the scapular, is of cream white serge, with a black veil. Outside the convent a full length black cape is worn, and for chapel services a long black cape with a train. The footwear is black.
Active in missionary work in the archdioceses of New York and Philadelphia, and the diocese of Natchez.
United States Provincial Motherhouse and Novitiate, Convent of St. John Berchmans, 437 West 47th Street, New York, New York. (Archdiocese of New York.)

DAUGHTERS OF OUR LADY OF MERCY*

1919

IN the year 1837, sanctioned by the bishop of Savona, the Right Rev. Agostina De Mari, the Congregation known as Daughters of Our Lady of Mercy was founded at Savona, Italy, by Mother Mary Joseph Rosullo for the special work of the education of children and the care of the poor and sick in hospitals.

From the Motherhouse in Savona the Congregation extended its work to South America, where missions have been established in Brazil, Chile and Uruguay, while in Argentina two provinces with novitiates have also been established. In Buenos Aires and Rosario, normal schools are also conducted. In addition to educational work in South America, the Daughters of Our Lady of Mercy are engaged in orphanage and hospital work there as in Italy.

Introduced into North America in 1919 by a small community composed of two sisters from the Motherhouse in Italy and three from Argentina, the Congregation of the Daughters of Our Lady of Mercy that year began its activities in the United States when a mission band, with Sister Mary Josephine Fortune as Superior, was received into the diocese of Springfield. There the sisters took charge of Sunday School classes, established a kindergarten and formed sewing classes in St. Ann's Mission Church in West Springfield, Massachusetts.

MOTHER M. JOSEPHINE FORTUNE

Augmented by other sisters sent from Europe to the new American missions, the Daughters of Our Lady of Mercy, having extended their mission work to Pennsylvania, opened at Hazleton, in 1922, in the diocese of Scranton, a novitiate in connection with their convent

*From data and material supplied by the Daughters of Our Lady of Mercy, Mater Misericordiæ Convent, York, Pa.

home. In 1927 this was transferred to the diocese of Harrisburg, where, with the approval of the bishop, the Right Rev. Philip R. McDevitt, D.D., it was located in Steelton, Pennsylvania, until the purchase in June, 1929, by the Congregation, of property in York,

MATER MISERICORDIÆ CONVENT, YORK, PENNSYLVANIA

to which final transfer of the novitiate was made, the convent there being also established as a Provincial house. Mother Mary Josephine continues as Superior of the Community in the United States.

SUMMARY

Daughters of Our Lady of Mercy.
Founded in Italy in 1837.
Papal Approbation of Rules in 1904 by Pope Pius X.
Established in the United States in 1919.
Active chiefly in educational and charitable work in the dioceses of Harris-
   burg, Hartford, Scranton and Springfield.
United States Provincial house and Novitiate, Mater Misericordiæ Convent,
   1141 East Market Street, York, Pennsylvania. (Diocese of Harrisburg.)

PARISH VISITORS OF MARY IMMACULATE*

1920

    THE Community of sisters, Parish Visitors of Mary Immaculate, laboring in the wide field of Catholic social service, and devoted to the active reclamation of souls, through missionary home-visiting and charitable endeavors, was founded in New York City by Julia Teresa Tallon, in religion Mother Teresa, August 15, 1920, with the approval and under the patronage of His Eminence, Patrick Cardinal Hayes, Archbishop of New York.

For some years prior to the canonical establishment of this Community, which is composed of home missionaries, trained catechists and professional social workers, the foundress and her zealous associates had devoted themselves as a group to the service of the poor and neglected, through the visitation of families, and subsequent religious instruction. Contemplation blessed and supernaturally motivated these early activities of the future religious. They assembled frequently for mutual edification, and in their lives of united recollection and apostolic labor laid an enduring foundation for the distinctive social service work soon to be definitely identified with the Parish Visitors.

Almost immediately after the inauguration of community life, with ecclesiastical sanction, at 328 West 71st Street, New York City, different pastors applied to Mother Teresa for the aid of the Parish Visitors. By the end of 1921 eight city parishes had members of the new Community engaging in local family visitation and taking a complete parish census, while giving right counsel and winning hardened hearts, or consoling stricken or embittered humanity.

It requires a year for the Parish Visitor's complete missionary visitation of the average New York parish, but the work is rich in spiritual results, and though many families move frequently, their temporary residence often affords them their only utilized opportunity for religious help and instruction. In their work the Parish Visitors accept nothing from the families they visit, nor from those they assist, responsibility for their services being assumed by the parish in which they labor.

The first home of the Community, known as St. Joseph's Con-

---

*From data and material supplied by the Parish Visitors of Mary Immaculate, Marycrest Novitiate, Monroe, N. Y.

vent, was soon recognized as its Motherhouse, while the novitiate was established at Marycrest, Monroe, New York.

MOTHER M. TERESA TALLON
Foundress and Superior of the Congregation of the Parish Visitors of
Mary Immaculate

In addition to their missionary labors from the Motherhouse, the sisters there edit and publish monthly "The Parish Visitor," a periodical describing and explaining their work, and aiding in its advancement.

The Parish Visitors co-operate with the St. Vincent de Paul Society, and other charitable agencies, and their work admirably supplements the appeal of the city pastor.

In the footsteps of the Good Shepherd, and under the special patronage of Mary Immaculate, the Visitor tactfully reaches and often

MARYCREST NOVITIATE, MONROE, NEW YORK

almost miraculously rights distress and waywardness unyielding to ordinary religious endeavor. In the course of her visitations she brings stray Catholics to Church and Church societies, assists immigrants, directs the young to wholesome recreation, and spreads helpful literature, sometimes visiting the court and other institutions in behalf of families.

The reconstruction and rehabilitation of the home is the acknowledged primary object of the Community, and to this end scientific methods of social service have been adopted, yet to the additional exercise of charity, and to the reanimation and renewal of their zeal in the convent, after the labors of the day, may be attributed the final successful completion of the work of the Parish Visitors.

SUMMARY

Parish Visitors of Mary Immaculate.

Founded in the United States, August 15, 1920.

Habit: The habit is of simple black serge, with a white lawn collar. Hats are used for street wear, while veils are worn in the convent. A silver medallion of the Immaculate Conception, and a rosary are worn.

Active in social service work in the archdiocese of New York.

Motherhouse, St. Joseph's Convent of the Sacred Heart, 328 West 71st Street, New York, New York.

Novitiate, Marycrest Novitiate, Monroe, New York. (Archdiocese of New York.)

SISTERS OF THE MOST HOLY TRINITY*

1920

HE Congregation of the Sisters of the Most Holy Trinity, whose activities in the United States began in 1920, was founded in Rome in the year 1198, following the approbation by the Sovereign Pontiff, Pope Innocent III, of the plans of Felix of Valois and John of Matha to found a religious order of men for the merciful work of the redemption of captives. From this foundation the Trinitarians, spreading through Europe, developed into one of the historic and prominent orders of the Church.

Continuing throughout the centuries, through divisions, through revolutions and wars, ever sharing the merciful work of the Trinitarian Fathers, have been the white-robed Sisters of the Most Holy Trinity, now among the religious orders of women in the United States, and thereby forming another historic link between the Old World and the new.

In the interests of the many Italian children of St. Anne's parish school in Bristol, Pennsylvania, His Eminence, Dennis Cardinal Dougherty, invited the Trinitarian Sisters to the arch-

MOTHER TERESA OF JESUS

diocese of Philadelphia. In 1920 Mother Teresa of Jesus, former Superior General of the Congregation, accompanied by two companion sisters, came from the Motherhouse in Rome to begin the missionary labors of the Order in the United States, and at once took charge of the designated school, attended by nearly five hundred children.

*From data and material supplied by the Sisters of the Most Holy Trinity, Holy Trinity Convent, Cleveland, Ohio.

Other sisters having arrived to augment the number already in Bristol, in addition to candidates whom she had been authorized to receive, Mother Teresa, in 1927, accepted the invitation of the Right Rev. Joseph Schrembs, D.D., Bishop of Cleveland, to take charge of the parochial school work in St. Rocco's parish in his episcopal city.

In 1929, following its authorization, a United States novitiate of the Order was formally opened in Cleveland, where, under the continued superiorship of Mother Teresa, it is maintained at the convent of the Trinitarian Sisters, the address of whose Motherhouse is Via Madonna del Riposo, Ne 3, Roma 45.

SUMMARY

Sisters of the Most Holy Trinity.

Founded in Italy in 1198.

Papal Approbation of Rule in 1198, by Pope Innocent III.

Established in the United States in 1920.

Habit: The habit is of heavy white cloth, with a white scapular. The veil of black "nuns' veiling" is lined with white of the same material. The plaited coif and bandeau are of white linen. An emblem of the cross, on the upper part of the scapular, is made by a bar of red crossed by a bar of blue. From the leather cincture is suspended a rosary and a brass medal, bearing on one side an emblem of the Holy Trinity, and on the other, imprints of St. Felix and St. John of Matha. The white of the habit signifies the purity of the Blessed Trinity, the blue, the Passion, and the red the love of the Holy Ghost.

Active in educational work in the archdiocese of Philadelphia and the diocese of Cleveland.

United States Novitiate, Holy Trinity Convent, St. Rocco's Place, 3205 Fulton Road, Cleveland, Ohio. (Diocese of Cleveland.)

SOCIAL MISSION SISTERS*

1922

THE Social Mission Society, introduced into this country in 1922, with the arrival in Cleveland, Ohio, of two of its representatives, was founded in Budapest, Hungary, in 1908.

To Edith Farkas, of Budapest, the Society owes its founding, when inspired with zeal by the Right Rev. Ottohar Prohaszka, the great rejuvenator of faith in modern Hungary, she organized a group of religious social workers as a society. With the founding of the Social Mission Society, a preparatory school was established where candidates for membership were trained for the religious life and social service, studying Sociology, Law, Economy, Moral Education and Hygiene.

From the fountain source of the now nation-wide organization, its members have gone forth to devote themselves exclusively to the spiritual welfare of souls, and to give themselves untiringly to social service work.

Familiar with their activities in Europe, the Right Rev. Joseph Schrembs, D.D., Bishop of Cleveland, invited sisters of the Society to inaugurate their work in his episcopal city. Responding to this invitation, Sister Hildegarde as Superior, accompanied by Sister Judith, arrived in Cleveland, Ohio, from Budapest, on October 4, 1922.

In a house secured for them in St. Margaret's parish, the congregation of which is chiefly of Hungarian extraction, the Social Mission Sisters began their labors in the United States. Establishing their con-

SISTER HILDEGARDE

*From data and material supplied by the Social Mission Sisters, 2438 Mapleside Avenue, Cleveland, Ohio.

833

55

convent home in the upper section of the house at 2927 East 116th Street, they opened the lower section as the Social Mission Settlement.

Making a survey of the district assigned them by Bishop Schrembs, the sisters realized and met the need of catechism classes, not only for the many Catholic children attending public schools, and without religious instruction, but also for adults who needed preparation for the reception of the sacraments. As a further result of the survey the sisters were soon instrumental in having a number of marriages validated.

SOCIAL MISSION CONVENT, CLEVELAND, OHIO

Through recreational clubs established at the Social Mission Settlement, and carried on under the supervision of a trained staff of volunteer workers, the sisters were enabled to conduct the settlement activities along approved lines, and those best fitting the needs of the district.

The work of the Social Mission Sisters in Cleveland, as home missionary activity, is supported by the Society for the Propagation of the Faith, and aided by the Mission Sisters' Guild, organized on June 1, 1923. An advisory board of twelve members assists the sisters in professional and financial matters, while members of the staff carry out the Settlement House programs, and plan for the more than one hundred volunteers, mainly Catholic public school teachers, who give an afternoon weekly to the work. Young men from the Major Seminary in Cleveland have charge of the boys' classes in catechism, and also assist in the general programs. Lay apostles from various sections of the city assist in the "follow up" work of the Community, whose district now extends to the territory of seven parishes.

In 1925 a suitable residence, secured for the sisters by Bishop Schrembs, was established as the Motherhouse and novitiate of the Community, under Sister Hildegarde as Superior, while the former convent quarters in the Settlement House were made use of for the extension of the work there.

SUMMARY

Social Mission Sisters.

Founded in Hungary in 1908.

Established in the United States in 1922.

Habit: The garb, adapted to the sisters' special vocation, is a tailored black dress, and a black hat, suited to the prevalent style. A gold ring, bearing the letters *I.H.S.,* is worn.

Active in social service work in the diocese of Cleveland.

Motherhouse and Novitiate, Social Mission Convent, 2438 Mapleside Avenue, Cleveland, Ohio. (Diocese of Cleveland.)

SISTERS OF THE POOR CHILD JESUS*

1924

THE Congregation of Sisters of the Poor Child Jesus, which was introduced into the United States in 1924, was founded in 1844 at Aachen, or as the city is generally known, Aix-la-Chapelle, Germany.

Clara Fey, who became in religion Mother Clara Fey, one of four school companions who formed its first community, is looked upon as the foundress of the Congregation, whose first work was the support of poor, orphan and destitute children.

Surviving the civic disturbances of the epochal era which followed its founding, and becoming in time one of the large religious congregations of Europe, the Sisters of the Poor Child Jesus established houses in Germany, Holland, Luxemburg, France and England.

From their Motherhouse at Simpelveld, Holland, sisters of the Congregation came to this country in 1924, and were received into the diocese of Wheeling by the Right Rev. John J. Swint, D.D. With Sister M. Theotima as present Superior, the sisters, whose garb is black, with a white scapular, are engaged in conducting schools in Parkersburg, Bliefield and Benwood, West Virginia.

United States Motherhouse and Novitiate, St. Raphael's Convent, 516 13th Street, Parkersburg, West Virginia. (Diocese of Wheeling.)

*From the annals of the diocese of Wheeling, the Catholic Encyclopedia and the Official Catholic Directory, 1929.

SISTERS OF THE PIOUS UNION OF OUR LADY OF GOOD COUNSEL*

1924

*H*AVING the distinction of being the first, and, at this time, the only religious body of women in the United States devoting itself exclusively to work for the hard-of-hearing and for the deaf, this community was established on September 8, 1924, at the St. Rita School for the Deaf, Cincinnati, Ohio.

Upon the advice of the Most Rev. Henry Moeller, D.D., then Archbishop of Cincinnati, and through the efforts of the Very Rev. Msgr. Henry J. Waldhaus, Chaplain, an organization was effected

SISTERS OF THE PIOUS UNION OF OUR LADY OF GOOD COUNSEL

at the St. Rita School, whereby the young women assisting the Sisters of Charity of Cincinnati, in charge at the Institute, in their work for the deaf, united in an association known as the Pious Union of Our Lady of Good Counsel.

As hearing is not essential for all laboring in the work among the deaf, and since the hard-of-hearing and the totally deaf can perform many of the duties in an institution for the deaf, membership in the new association was opened not only to the hearing, but to

*From data and material supplied by the Sisters of the Pious Union of Our Lady of Good Counsel, St. Rita Convent, Lockland, Cincinnati, Ohio.

young women hard-of-hearing or totally deaf, thus affording such the opportunity of devoting themselves to the service of God in the religious life.

In the interests of the St. Rita School for the Deaf, "The Silent Advocate," a publication explaining and furthering its work, is issued by the Institute.

St. Rita School for the Deaf, Lockland, Cincinnati, Ohio

From the first the association, under the patronage of St. Rita, an Augustinian nun, followed religious exercises according to the Rule of St. Augustine, and the members, on joining, took yearly the simple vows of religion. Eighteen months after its organization, the Pious Union had as many members. Sister Mary Rose, of the Community of Sisters of Charity of Cincinnati, has continued to serve as Mistress of Novices, over the young Community, for the canonical erection of which the Most Rev. John T. McNicholas, O.P., successor to the archbishopric of Cincinnati, has petitioned Rome.

Motherhouse and Novitiate, St. Rita School for the Deaf, Lockland, Cincinnati, Ohio. (Archdiocese of Cincinnati.)

POOR SISTERS OF NAZARETH*

1924

ENGAGED in the care of nearly one hundred orphan children at Nazareth House, Old Mission, San Diego, California, is a small community of the Poor Sisters of Nazareth, who in 1924 came to California from their Motherhouse, Nazareth House, Hammersmith Road, London, England.

The Poor Sisters of Nazareth, founded in London in 1851, are in charge of a number of girls' and boys' orphanages in the British Isles and in Australia.

In 1926 an interesting innovation was undertaken by these Nazareth Sisters, when twenty-five orphan girls from six Nazareth House convents in England, Scotland and Wales were taken to Nazareth Houses in Australia by three members of the Congregation. England being over-populated with women, the orphan girls' prospects not encouraging, and Australia in need of women, this plan of a change in environment for these young girls, volunteers, without a surviving parent or close relative, was developed.

The new emigration project was the result of a world tour made by the Mother General of the Sisters of Nazareth, who hope to provide for the future of their charges by sending such a party out every year.

United States Foundation house, Nazareth House, Old Mission, San Diego, California. (Diocese of Los Angeles and San Diego.)

*From data supplied by the Poor Sisters of Nazareth, San Diego, Calif., and from the N.C.W.C. News Service.

CATHOLIC MEDICAL MISSIONARIES*

1925

HE Society of Catholic Medical Missionaries was founded in September, 1925, with the approbation of the Most Rev. Michael J. Curley, D.D., Archbishop of Baltimore, for the purpose of providing the foreign mission fields with professional women medical workers, banded together in a religious community under the authority of the Church.

The seed for a society of this nature was sown more than two decades ago by Dr. Agnes McLaren, a convert Scotchwoman. Investigating for herself the conditions and needs in India, Dr. McLaren, after visiting government and Protestant mission hospitals, and conferring with several bishops, realized that often the woman doctor or nurse was the only missionary who could reach and aid the isolated, suffering and needy women of the harem and the zenana, and that medical work among them offered an opportunity of exerting the winning influence of the charity of Christ.

Unable to comply, because workers were not available, with petitions of several members of the hierarchy in India, for the foundation of a Catholic hospital for women and children, Dr. McLaren laid before the Sovereign Pontiff, Pius X, her desires and plans, and obtained his blessing for her medical mission labors. To assure continuity and stability of the work, she endeavored to lead religious communities to allow young nuns to study medicine, in order to supply the missions with women doctors. Unsuccessful in this, she communicated her project to young lay women, appealing, this time, not in vain.

Miss Anna Dengel, a native of the Austrian Tyrol, took her medical degree in the University of Cork, Ireland, and after practical experience in England, went to India to take charge of the hospital founded by Dr. McLaren in the Punjab. After four years of work there, Dr. Dengel became convinced of the great field for spiritual and corporal works of mercy awaiting Catholic women among their sisters of the east, who are debarred from contact with the outside world—even medical aid, as we understand it. Dr. Dengel also realized that her sphere was only an infinitesimal part of a wide field in India and elsewhere. To develop the work, to train missionaries

*From data and material supplied by the Catholic Medical Missionaries, Catholic Medical Mission House, Brookland, Washington, D. C.

along spiritual and professional lines for this difficult and responsible apostolate, to provide the necessary means, to facilitate stability and perseverance, a definite organization was required.

First Four Members of the Society of Catholic Medical Missionaries
Left to right, Dr. Joanna Lyons; Dr. Anna Dengel, Foundress and Superior of the Society; Sister Mary Laetitia, R.N.; and Sister Agnes Marie, R.N.

This was established in the United States, when, in the autumn of 1925, the Society of Catholic Medical Missionaries—as an independent society under the spiritual auspices of the Holy Cross Fathers of the Foreign Mission Seminary in Brookland, Washington, D. C., was formed, with their Provincial Superior, the Very Rev. Michael Mathis, C.S.C., as spiritual director.

In the spring of 1925, while in the United States on a missionary propaganda tour, Dr. Dengel, in conference with Father Mathis, made plans for the Society. The Constitutions were drawn up, and after being adapted to Canon Law by the Rev. Francis McBride, C.S.C., were presented to Archbishop Curley, who, on

June 12, 1925, as archbishop of Baltimore, gave his approbation to the founding of a house of the Society of Catholic Medical Missionaries in Washington, D. C.

In September, 1925, Dr. Joanna Lyons, Miss Evelyn Flieger, R.N., and Miss Marie Ulbrick, R.N., joined Dr. Dengel, facing a life of service and self-sacrifice as Medical Missionaries, and as pioneer members of a community entering a new and unexploited field for a religious society of women.

In the little chapel of the temporary home which they had established in Brookland, Washington, D. C., the garb of the new Society was conferred on its first four members, on the First Friday of March, 1926, by the Right Rev. Msgr. C. F. Thomas, Prot. Ap., the delegate for religious orders of women in the archdiocese of Baltimore.

At an impressive ceremony presided over by the Right Rev. Thomas J. Shahan, S.T.D., and at the conclusion of an eight-day retreat given by the Rev. Francis Walsh, O.S.B., Dr. Anna Dengel, Dr. Joanna Lyons, Sister Mary Laetitia Flieger and Sister Agnes Marie Ulbrick, on September 23, 1926, received their missionary crosses, solemnly promised to keep the evangelical counsels of poverty, chastity and obedience according to the Constitutions, and took an oath to remain in the Society for three years, to go without delay to any region or place to which they might be sent by the Superior of the Society, and to do the work assigned to them.

According to the Constitutions of the Society of Catholic Medical Missionaries, the members live in community, in the spirit of the evangelical counsels. After one year of probation, which is devoted to spiritual and missionary training, the candidates make the promises as made by the first four members. The Solemn Promise and Oath are renewed after three years for another period of three years, after which they are taken for life.

There are medical and non-medical members in the Society. The medical members must be graduates of a recognized school of medicine, dentistry, nursing or pharmacy, or they must have completed a course for technicians. The Society also admits candidates who possess no medical qualifications, either with a view of training them in some branch of the profession, or for the non-medical work of the Society, such as secretarial and social service work, journalism, housekeeping, and other activities necessary in the Community.

The first field of labor of the Catholic Medical Missionaries was in northern India, where in Rawalpindi, through the generosity of His Eminence, Dennis Cardinal Dougherty, His Eminence, Patrick

Cardinal Hayes, and benefactors throughout the United States, it was possible to erect the Holy Family Hospital. Formally blessed on December 14, 1927, by the Most Rev. Edward A. Mooney, the

CATHOLIC MEDICAL MISSION HOUSE, BROOKLAND, WASHINGTON, D. C.

Apostolic Delegate to India, this hospital was opened to receive patients on February 2, 1928, with Dr. Joanna Lyons, Sister Agnes Marie Ulbrick, R.N., and Sister Mary Laetitia Flieger, R.N., serving on its staff. Dr. Lyons had left for India immediately after the ceremony in September, 1926, and in the interval had been active there.

The scope of the medical work includes the provision and equip-ment of mission hospitals and dispensaries, medical schools, training schools for native nurses, infant welfare centers, plague camps, leper asylums and traveling dispensaries, which bring medical aid from village to village, also obstetrical work and visitation of the sick in their homes, which are of primary importance in mission countries.

The health of millions is undermined by malaria, hookworm, kalazaar, sleeping sickness, leprosy, tuberculosis and other malignant diseases, and the Medical Missionary, in this sphere of influence, where deeds rather than words are eloquent, through her charitable ministrations, wins the love and confidence of the people, and is enabled to dispel prejudice and superstition, and prepare them for the reception of the truth.

On March 12, 1929, final arrangements were completed by the Society for the purchase of a site for a Catholic Medical Mission House. Six and a quarter acres of land, with one large house and three small bungalows, overlooking the Sisters' College in Brookland, Washington, D. C., were secured, and Dr. Dengel and the Community soon afterward removed to the new location.

The Society publishes *The Medical Missionary,* a monthly bulletin in the interest of medical missions and the women of the Orient. Dr. Anna Dengel, foundress and Superior of the Society, is editor of the publication.

Appropriately has the Society of Catholic Medical Missionaries placed itself, as its distinctive seal indicates, under the patronage of the Blessed Virgin, under the title of "Cause of Our Joy," since its hopes and labors all focus on making true joy available to as many as possible, by bringing Christianity to them.

SUMMARY

Catholic Medical Missionaries.
Founded in the United States in 1925.
Habit: The members of the Society wear a grey uniform garb and black hat. A crucifix on a red cord is also worn. In the mission field they wear white for hospital work.
Active in foreign missionary work through medical services.
Motherhouse and Novitiate, Catholic Medical Mission House, Brookland, Washington, D. C. (Archdiocese of Baltimore.)

COMPANY OF MARY*

1926

SISTERS of the Company of Mary, a Congregation founded in Bordeaux, France, in 1607, by Blessed Jeanne de Leston-nac, came to the United States from Mexico in 1926, and were received into the diocese of Tucson, by its bishop, the Right Rev. Daniel J. Gercke, D.D.

Retaining affiliation with their General Motherhouse in Rome, Italy, the members of the Community in the United States, engaging in conducting kindergartens, catechism classes and mission schools in Los Angeles and Fresno, California, and in Tucson, Arizona, are under the jurisdiction of a Motherhouse in Vadado, Havana, Cuba.

SUMMARY

Company of Mary.
Founded in France in 1607.
Papal Approbation of Rules in 1609, by Pope Paul V.
Established in the United States in 1926.
Habit: The habit is of black serge, with white and black cloth around the head. A knitted cincture of black wool is worn.
Active in the United States in educational and missionary work in the dioceses of Los Angeles and San Diego, Monterey-Fresno and Tucson.
United States Novitiate, 1047 Tenth Street, Douglas, Arizona. (Diocese of Tucson.)

*From data supplied by the Company of Mary, Douglas, Ariz.

PASSIONIST SISTERS*

1927

O the initiative of the Right Rev. William A. Hickey, D.D., Bishop of Providence, is due the introduction into the United States in 1927 of the Sisters of the Most Holy Cross and Passion, generally known as Passionist Sisters. In that year Mother M. Gonzaga, accompanied by Sisters Dionysius, Louis and Pius, left their Motherhouse at Bolton, England, to establish in Providence, Rhode Island, the first United States mission of their Congregation.

The Congregation of the Sisters of the Most Holy Cross and Passion was founded in Manchester, England, in 1850, by the Rev. Gaudentius Rossi, an influential pioneer Passionist in England, who later became active in the Passionists' mission fields in America.

The foundation of this active order of Passionist Sisters was occasioned by the shortage of housing facilities and the consequent plight of working girls in the great industrial centers of England in the middle of the nineteenth century. To harbor and help such girls, Father Rossi called into existence this sisterhood, which, confronted for a time by great opposition to its proposed work, early gained prominence, in the interval, by engaging in educational work, and which opened in 1864, at Bolton, England, a first home for working girls.

On June 21, 1887, the Sovereign Pontiff, Pope Leo XIII, gave final approbation to the Rules of the Congregation, whose activities have so recently been inaugurated in the United States.

United States Foundation house, Assumption Convent, 530 Dexter Street, Providence, Rhode Island. (Diocese of Providence.)

*From the Catholic Encyclopedia, the Official Catholic Directory, 1929, and from *The Cross*, published by the Passionists, Mount Argus, Dublin.

MISSIONARY SISTERS OF OUR LADY OF AFRICA*

1929

THROUGH the distinguished French scholar and dignitary, Charles-Martial-Allemand Lavigerie, who became archbishop of Algiers, Africa, on March 27, 1867, the Missionary Sisters of Our Lady of Africa were founded in France in 1869, to supplement the apostolic labors of the Society of the White Fathers, whose aim is exclusively missionary, and exclusively for Africa.

The White Sisters, as the Missionary Sisters of Our Lady of of Africa are familiarly known, devote themselves by every work of mercy and charity to the African natives, both pagan and Moslem. They conduct schools, dispensaries, leper asylums, hospitals and work-rooms, where women and girls weave carpets or learn plain sewing. Even to the oases of the Sahara they have pursued their missionary work, feverently laboring and praying for the conversion of the Arabs and Mozabites who inhabit the Arabian Sands.

In 1894 the sisters penetrated into Central Africa, where they have formed a congregation of three hundred native nuns, who now assist them in teaching catechism, caring for the sick, and other works of mercy.

Promoting their field of missionary labor, hitherto little known here, and to reveal the need for many generous souls, willing to sacrifice all to labor for the evangelization of the Dark Continent, the Missionary Sisters of Our Lady of Africa have made in the United States the most recent of their establishments.

A MISSIONARY SISTER OF OUR LADY OF AFRICA

Through the kindness of the Right Rev. John J. McMahon, D.D., Bishop of Trenton, this foundation was made in his diocese, almost on the eve of Christmas, 1929, in Metuchen, New Jersey, upon the

*From data and material supplied by the Missionary Sisters of Our Lady of Africa, Metuchen, N. J.

opening there of a convent of the Congregation by a community of sisters from Africa, with Mother M. Sabine as Superior.

The Missionary Sisters of Our Lady of Africa are governed by a Superior General and her assistants at the Motherhouse, St. Charles, Birmandreis, Algiers, North Africa. From this institution the nearly one thousand members of the Congregation—drawn from France, Belgium, Holland, Germany, Canada and even the United States— imbued with apostolic zeal, based on love of the interior life, and a spirit of obedience, labor at more than a hundred missionary posts, located for the most part in British East and Central Africa.

SUMMARY

Missionary Sisters of Our Lady of Africa.
Founded in France in 1869.
Papal Approbation of Rules, December 14, 1909, by Pope Pius X.
Established in the United States in 1929.
Habit: The habit, scapular, veil and wimple are white. A silver crucifix, attached to a red silk cord, is worn on the breast, and a black and white rosary is suspended from the belt.
Active in missionary work in Africa.
United States Foundation House, Convent of the White Sisters, 6 Plainfield Avenue, Metuchen, New Jersey. (Diocese of Trenton.)

SISTERS OF THE ASSUMPTION*

THE Congregation of the Sisters of the Assumption, which is represented in the United States by a community engaged in conducting the Academy of the Assumption in Philadelphia, Pennsylvania, was founded in France in 1839.

The foundress of the Congregation, Eugénie Milleret de Bron, in religion Mère Marie-Eugénie de Jésus, was directed in her great work by the Abbé Combalst, who had been inspired to establish the Institute during a pilgrimage to the shrine of Ste. Anne d'Auray.

The aim of the sisters in their work of the education of girls is to combine fruitfully a thorough secular education with a solid moral and religious training.

United States Foundation house, Convent of the Assumption, Ravenhill, West Schoolhouse Lane, Germantown, Pennsylvania. (Archdiocese of Philadelphia.)

SISTERS AUXILIARY OF THE APOSTOLATE†

Forming a Community founded in Canada less than thirty years ago by the Rev. Francis Olszeweski, the Sisters Auxiliary of the Apostolate, now in charge of parochial schools in West Virginia, constitute a diocesan Community under the jurisdiction of the Right Rev. John J. Swint, D.D., Bishop of Wheeling.

United States Foundation house, 142 Maple Avenue, Monongah, West Virginia.

SISTERS OF THE ASSUMPTION OF THE B.V.M.‡

The Congregation of the Sisters of the Assumption of the Blessed Virgin Mary, whose Motherhouse is in the episcopal city of Nicolet, Province of Quebec, Canada, is represented in this country by approximately two hundred of its members, who are engaged in parochial school work in the archdiocese of Boston and in the dioceses of Albany, Burlington, Hartford, Manchester, Providence and Springfield.

*From the Catholic Encyclopedia and the Official Catholic Directory, 1929.
†From the annals of the diocese of Wheeling.
‡From the Official Catholic Year Book, 1928.

CAPUCHIN SISTERS OF THE CHILD JESUS*

Small communities of the Capuchin Sisters of the Child Jesus, properly associated with the Third Order Franciscan Sisters, are active in the United States in educational, charitable and social service work in the dioceses of Newark and Wheeling.

PALLOTTINE SISTERS OF CHARITY†

Pallottine Sisters of Charity from their Motherhouse in Rome are engaged in educational, charitable and social service work in this country in the archdioceses of Baltimore and New York, and the dioceses of Newark and Providence.

DAUGHTERS OF THE DIVINE REDEEMER‡

The Congregation of the Daughters of the Divine Redeemer, founded at Oedenburg, Hungary, in 1863, is represented in the United States by a community of about sixty sisters, engaged in educational and charitable work in Pittsburgh and nearby dioceses.

United States Motherhouse and Novitiate, St. Joseph's Convent, Elizabeth, Pennsylvania.   (Diocese of Pittsburgh.)

SISTERS OF THE HOLY CROSS AND OF THE SEVEN DOLORS§

The Congregation of the Sisters of the Holy Cross and of the Seven Dolors, whose Motherhouse is maintained at St. Laurent, Canada, in the archdiocese of Montreal, and which has a United States Provincial house at Nashua, New Hampshire, was founded at St. Laurent in 1847.

The first community of this now large Congregation, which engages in educational and charitable work in Canada and the nearby border section of the United States, was formed by a group of Sisters of the Holy Cross from the Motherhouse at Le Mans, France, and Sisters of the Holy Cross from the pioneer United States foundation of the Order, at Bertrand, Michigan.

---

*From the Official Catholic Directory, 1929.
†From the Official Catholic Year Book, 1928.
‡From the Catholic Encyclopedia and the Official Catholic Directory, 1929.
§From the annals of the Sisters of the Holy Cross, and the Official Catholic Directory, 1929.

Nearly three hundred Sisters of the Holy Cross and of the Seven Dolors are now active in this country, chiefly in educational work, in the dioceses of Burlington, Fall River, Hartford, Manchester, Ogdensburg and Springfield.

United States Provincial house, 71 Chestnut Street, Nashua, New Hampshire. (Diocese of Manchester.)

SISTERS MARIANITES OF THE HOLY CROSS*

Among the United States foundations of the Sisters of the Holy Cross of Le Mans, France, is that of the Sisters Marianites of the Holy Cross, which was established in New Orleans, Louisiana, in 1849, when four sisters were sent from the Motherhouse in France to conduct an orphan asylum in that city.

Extending their work to other activities according to the need, and their growth in numbers, sisters of the community in New Orleans were sent to New York in 1854, where, together with Sisters of the Holy Cross from Bertrand, Michigan, and St. Laurent, Canada, a foundation was established.

In addition to their educational and charitable work now in the archdioceses of New Orleans and New York, and in the diocese of Natchez, the Sisters Marianites of the Holy Cross conduct the French Hospital at 450 West 34th Street, in New York City.

United States Novitiate, 222 Main Street, Tottenville, Staten Island, New York. (Archdiocese of New York.)

United States Provincial house and Novitiate, North Rampart and Congress Streets, New Orleans, Louisiana. (Archdiocese of New Orleans.)

SERVANTS OF THE HOLY GHOST AND MARY IMMACULATE†

The Congregation of the Servants of the Holy Ghost and Mary Immaculate, whose Motherhouse is located in San Antonio, Texas, is composed of approximately a hundred and twenty sisters, active in the archdioceses of New Orleans and San Antonio, and in the dioceses of Amarillo, Dallas, Lafayette, Mobile, Natchez, Oklahoma, St. Joseph and Wichita.

Motherhouse and Novitiate, Grand View Heights, East End, San Antonio, Texas. (Archdiocese of San Antonio.)

*From the annals of the Sisters of the Holy Cross, and the Official Catholic Directory, 1929.

†From the Official Catholic Directory, 1929.

RELIGIOUS OF THE HOLY UNION OF THE SACRED HEARTS*

The Religious of the Holy Union of the Sacred Hearts, whose United States Provincial house is in Fall River, Massachusetts, are active in the country in the archdioceses of Baltimore and Boston, and in the dioceses of Brooklyn, Fall River and Providence.

United States Provincial house, 466 Prospect Street, Fall River, Massachusetts. (Diocese of Fall River.)

SISTERS SERVANTS OF THE IMMACULATE HEART OF MARY†

The Sisters Servants of the Immaculate Heart of Mary, who are active in the United States in the archdiocese of Boston and the diocese of Portland, are of the Congregation of Sisters Servants of the Immaculate Heart of Mary founded at Quebec in 1859 for the special work of the reclamation of girls and the education and care of children. The Motherhouse of the Congregation is at 74 Rue Lachevrotière, Quebec, Canada.

United States Provincial house, 69 Adams Street, Biddleford, Maine. (Diocese of Portland.)

SISTERS OF ST. JOAN OF ARC*

The Congregation of Sisters of St. Joan of Arc, members of which are active in the United States in the dioceses of Albany, Hartford, Manchester, Portland, Providence and Springfield, main-tains its Motherhouse and novitiate at Bergerville, Canada, in the Province of Quebec.

SISTERS OF ST. JOSEPH‡

Sisters of St. Joseph from St. Trudpert, Baden, Germany, have recently been introduced into the diocese of Cleveland. At Louis-ville, Ohio, in the diocese, they conduct St. Joseph's Hospice, for the non-dependent aged, while in Cleveland they are occupied with the domestic work at the Seminary of Our Lady of the Lake.

*From the Official Catholic Directory, 1929.
†From the New Catholic Dictionary (The Universal Knowledge Founda-tion, New York) and the Official Catholic Directory, 1929.
‡From the annals of the diocese of Cleveland.

SISTERS OF THE THIRD ORDER REGULAR OF MARY*

Honoring, in the name of their convent, recently established in the United States, Blessed Pierre Chanel, proto-martyr of Oceanica, and zealous French missionary of the Society of Mary, the Sisters of the Third Order Regular of Mary, in Boston, Massachusetts, signify their relationship with the Order of the Marist Fathers, as the Society of Mary is frequently called.

The Sisters of the Third Order Regular of Mary, whose purpose it is to assist in the foreign missionary labors of the Marists, maintain their convent in Boston as a Procure of the Congregation.

United States Foundation house, Convent of Blessed Chanel, 13 Isabella Street, Boston, Massachusetts. (Archdiocese of Boston.)

MISSIONARY SISTERS OF THE DIVINE CHILD†

The Community of the Missionary Sisters of the Divine Child was established in Buffalo, New York, on August 12, 1927, by the Right Rev. William Turner, D.D., Bishop of Buffalo, for the purpose of missionary work, especially among children.

Motherhouse, 473 Niagara Street, Buffalo, New York. (Diocese of Buffalo.)

POOR SISTERS OF JESUS CRUCIFIED AND THE SORROWFUL MOTHER‡

The Congregation of Jesus Crucified and the Sorrowful Mother was founded in the United States for educational and charitable work, as well as social service, among the Lithuanians of the diocese of Scranton.

Motherhouse and Novitiate, St. Mary's Villa, Elmhurst, Pennsylvania. (Diocese of Scranton.)

LITTLE SISTERS OF THE HOLY FAMILY§

The Little Sisters of the Holy Family form a congregation which was founded at Memramcook, New Brunswick, April 19, 1880, by the Rev. Camille Lefebvre and Mother Marie Léonie.

*From the Catholic Encyclopedia and the Official Catholic Directory, 1929.
†From the annals of the diocese of Buffalo.
‡From the Official Catholic Directory, 1929.
§From data supplied by the Little Sisters of the Holy Family, Convent of the Little Sisters of the Holy Family, Sherbrooke, P.Q., Canada, and from the Official Catholic Year Book, 1928.

Carrying out the intentions of their zealous founders, that the work of the Congregation should be in the service of God's ordained ministers, more than one hundred of the Little Sisters of the Holy Family, whose Motherhoue is now maintained at Sherbrooke, P.Q., Canada, are engaged in the United States in domestic work in seminaries, colleges and episcopal residences in the archdioceses of Baltimore, Boston, Philadelphia and San Francisco, and in the dioceses of Buffalo and Manchester.

DAUGHTERS OF ST. MARY OF PROVIDENCE*

The Congregation known as the Daughters of St. Mary of Providence, founded in Italy in 1872 by the Rev. Louis Guanella, has been represented in the United States since 1913.

In that year Mother Rose Bertolini, accompanied by five sisters of the Congregation, from Como, Italy, inaugurated their work in this country in Chicago, Illinois, where their activities are now centered in St. Mary of Providence Institute, for retarded and subnormal girls.

Sister Mary Del-Co' is Superior of the Community in the United States, which remains subject to the jurisdiction of the Motherhouse at Como, Lora, Italy, under Mother Rose Colombo as present Superior General of the Congregation.

The sisters wear a black woolen habit, with a short cape, a white collar just visible, and a cap of black tibet. A crucifix of white metal, containing a relic, is worn suspended from the neck.

Members of the Congregation are engaged in educational, hospital, charitable and social service work in the archdioceses of Chicago and Milwaukee, and the diocese of Sioux Falls.

> *United States Foundation house,* St. Mary of Providence Institute, 4242 N. Austin Avenue, Chicago, Illinois. (Archdiocese of Chicago.)

SISTERS OF OUR LADY OF THE HOLY ROSARY†

Sisters of Our Lady of the Holy Rosary, from their Motherhouse in the episcopal city of Rimouski, in the Province of Quebec, Canada, engage in parochial school work in the United States in the diocese of Portland, where their present activities are centered in Frenchville, Maine.

*From data supplied by the Daughters of St. Mary of Providence, St. Mary of Providence Institute, Chicago, Ill.
†From the Official Catholic Year Book, 1928.

SALESIAN SISTERS*

Small communities of the Salesian Sisters of Bd. Don Bosco are engaged in charitable and social service work in New Jersey.

Foundation house, 41 Ward Street, Paterson, New Jersey. (Diocese of Newark.)

SISTERS OF THE SOCIAL SERVICE*

The Sisters of the Social Service, whose title stands for the specific purpose of their Community, are active in the diocese of Los Angeles and San Diego, maintaining their headquarters at 707 West Second Street, Los Angeles, California.

*From the Official Catholic Directory, 1929.

SUPPLEMENT

With the courteous permission of the P. J. Kenedy and Sons, New York, publishers of the Official Catholic Directory, the following lists have been especially compiled from the 1930 issue of the Official Catholic Directory. The classifications used have been chosen for practical use and information.

UNITED STATES MOTHERHOUSES, PROVINCIAL HOUSES, NOVITIATES, OF RELIGIOUS ORDERS OF WOMEN

Names of convents and addresses given refer to and include Motherhouses and novitiates. Use of the word "Provincial house" ordinarily refers to a novitiate also. The specific mention "Motherhouse" indicates a novitiate at a separate location.

Special abbreviations used: *Cong.*, Congregation; *Inst.*, Institute; *M. H.*, Motherhouse; *Prov. H.*, Provincial house; *Reg.*, Regular; *R. U.*, Roman Union.

ALABAMA

CULLMAN—Srs. of St. Benedict, Sacred Heart Convent.
HOLY TRINITY—Missionary Servants of the Most Blessed Trinity, Holy Trinity Cenacle.
MOBILE—Srs. of Mercy, Novitiate, 853 St. Francis St.
——Visitation Nuns, Visitation Convent, Spring Hill Ave.

ARIZONA

DOUGLAS—Company of Mary, Convent, 1054 Tenth St.
NOGALES—Franciscan Minims, Franciscan Minims' Novitiate.
TUCSON—Carmelite Nuns, Monastery of the Blessed Sacrament, 846 N. 12th Ave.
——Srs. of the I. H. M., Holy Cross Convent, 7th Ave. & 22nd St.

ARKANSAS

FORT SMITH—Srs. of St. Benedict, St. Scholastica's Convent, Benedictine Hts.
HOT SPRINGS—Srs. of Our Lady of Charity of the Refuge, Monastery of Our Lady of Charity, 1125 Malvern Ave.
JONESBORO—Olivetan-Benedictine Srs., M. H., Holy Angels' Convent, 224 E. Mathews Ave.
POCAHONTAS—Olivetan-Benedictine Srs., Novitiate, Convent of Our Lady of the Rock.

CALIFORNIA

ALHAMBRA—Carmelite Nuns, Carmel of St. Teresa, 215 E. Alhambra Rd.
BAKERSFIELD—Carmelite Nuns, Monastery of Our Lady & St. Therese, Carmel-by-the-Sea.
BELMONT—Srs. of Notre Dame de Namur, Prov. Novitiate, Convent of Notre Dame.
BURLINGAME—Srs. of Mercy, Convent of Our Lady of Mercy (For the United Houses).
HOLLYWOOD—Srs. of the I. H. M., Immaculate Heart Convent, 5515 Franklin Ave.

Los Angeles—Carmelite Nuns, Carmelite Convent, 622 W. 18th St.
——Dominican Nuns, 2nd Order, Monastery of the Angels, 728 W. 28th St.
——Srs. of St. Joseph of Carondelet, Mt. St. Mary's, Prov. H., 3300 W. Slauson Ave.
——Srs. of the Social Service, 707 W. Second St.
Menlo Park—Dominican Nuns, 2nd Order, Corpus Christi Monastery, Oak Grove Ave.
Mission San José—Srs. of St. Dominic (California Cong. of the Queen of the Holy Rosary), Queen of the Holy Rosary Dominican Convent.
Monterey—Franciscan Srs. of Mary Immaculate and St. Joseph for the Dying, St. Joseph's Convent.
Oakland—Srs. of the Holy Names, Prov. H., 2036 Webster St.
——Srs. of Mercy, Novitiate, 1840 34th Ave.
——Poor Clares (Colettines), St. Joseph's Monastery, 1505 34th Ave.
Orange—Srs. of St. Joseph of Orange, Nazareth Convent, 380 S. Batavia St.
Sacramento—Srs. of Mercy, St. Joseph's Convent, 9th & G Sts.
San Diego—Carmelite Nuns, Carmelite Monastery of the Trinity, 3803 Georgia St.
San Francisco—Srs. of the Holy Family, Convent of the Holy Family, Hayes & Fillmore Sts.
——Srs. of the Presentation of the B. V. M., Presentation Convent, 281 Masonic Ave.
San Gabriel—*Adoratrices Perpetuas de Sta. Maria de Guadalupe.*
San Rafael—Srs. of St. Dominic (Cong. of the Holy Name), Dominican Convent, Grand Ave.
Santa Barbara—Poor Clares (Colettines), Monastery of the Poor Clares, 215 Los Olivos St.
Santa Clara—Carmelite Nuns, Carmelite Monastery of the Infant Jesus, 1000 Lincoln St.
Santa Rosa—Ursuline Nuns in California, Ursuline Convent, 10th & B Sts.

COLORADO

Denver—Srs. of Mercy, Novitiate of Our Lady of Mercy, 1661 Milwaukee St.

CONNECTICUT

Baltic—Srs. of Charity of Our Lady, Mother of Mercy, Convent of the Holy Family.
Hartford—Srs. of Mercy, M. H., St. Joseph's Convent, 160 Farmington Ave.
——Srs. of Mercy, St. Augustine's Novitiate & Normal School, 481 S. Quaker Lane.
——Srs. of St. Joseph (Chambéry), Prov. H., Convent of Mary Immaculate, 27 Park Rd.
New Haven—Missionary Zelatrices, Srs. of the Sacred Heart, Prov. H., 295 Greene St.
Putnam—Daughters of the Holy Ghost, Prov. Convent, 31 Church St.

DELAWARE

Wilmington—Visitation Nuns, Monastery of the Visitation, Gilpin & Bayard Aves.

DISTRICT OF COLUMBIA

WASHINGTON—Catholic Medical Missionaries, Catholic Medical Mission House, Bunker Hill Rd., Brookland.
——Religious of Perpetual Adoration, Perpetual Adoration Convent, 1419 V St., N. W.
——Visitation Nuns, Georgetown Visitation Convent, 1500 35th St., N. W.

FLORIDA

LAKE JOVITA—Srs. of St. Benedict, Holy Name Convent.
ST. AUGUSTINE—Srs. of St. Joseph, St. Joseph's Convent.

GEORGIA

AUGUSTA—Srs. of St. Joseph of Carondelet, Prov. H., St. Joseph's Convent, 2542 Belleview St.

IDAHO

COTTONWOOD—Srs. of St. Benedict, St. Gertrude's Convent.

ILLINOIS

ALTON—Ursuline Nuns (R. U.), Branch Novitiate, Convent of the Holy Family, 211 Danforth St.
AURORA—Srs. of Mercy, M. H., Mercy Convent, 185 N. Lake St.
——Srs. of Mercy, Novitiate, Mercy Convent, Lincoln Highway.
BEAVERVILLE—Servants of the Holy Heart of Mary, U. S. Novitiate, Holy Family Convent.
BLUE ISLAND—Mantellate Srs., Servants of Mary, Novitiate, Mother of Sorrows Inst., 138th St. & Western Ave.
CHICAGO—Felician Srs., O. S. F., Prov. H., 3800 Peterson Ave., Rogers Park.
——Franciscan Srs. of St. Kunegunda, M. H., Franciscan Convent, 2649 N. Hamlin Ave.
——Helpers of the Holy Souls, Prov. H., 1300 S. St. Louis Ave.
——Institute of the B. V. M., Loretto Branch Novitiate, 6541 Stewart Ave.
——Little Company of Mary, Convent of the Little Company of Mary, 4130 Indiana Ave.
——Little Srs. of the Poor, Prov. Convent, N. Fullerton & Sheffield Aves.
——Poor Clares (Colettines), Monastery of the Poor Clares, 53rd & Laflin Sts.
——Religious Hospitallers of St. Joseph, M. H., St. Bernard's Hotel Dieu, 6337 Harvard Ave.
——Religious of the Sacred Heart, Vicariate house, Convent of the Sacred Heart, 6250 Sheridan Rd.
——Srs. of Mercy, Prov. H., St. Xavier's Convent, 4900 Cottage Grove Ave.
——Srs. of Mercy, St. Patrick's Convent, Park & Oakley Aves., West Side.
——Srs. of the Resurrection, Novitiate, 5959 Talcott Ave., Norwood Park.
——Srs. of St. Benedict, St. Scholastica's Convent, Rogers Park, 7430 Ridge Ave.
——Srs. of St. Casimir, St. Casimir's Convent, 2601 W. Marquette Rd.
DECATUR—Ursuline Nuns, Ursuline Convent of St. Theresa, N. Water St.

DES PLAINES—Srs. of the Holy Family of Nazareth, Prov. Convent of the Sacred Heart.

JOLIET—Srs. of the 3rd Order of St. Francis of Mary Immaculate, St. Francis' Convent, 220 Plainfield Ave.

——Franciscan Srs. of the Sacred Heart, St. Joseph's Hospital, 426 N. Broadway.

LA GRANGE—Srs. of St. Joseph, Our Lady of Bethlehem Academy, Ogden & Peck Aves.

LEMONT—Srs. of the 3rd Order of St. Francis (Slovenian), Franciscan Prov. H.

——Franciscan Srs. of St. Kunegunda, Novitiate, Our Lady of Victory Convent.

LISLE—Srs. of St. Benedict (Czech.), Benedictine Convent of the Sacred Heart.

NAUVOO—Srs. of St. Benedict, St. Mary's Convent.

PALOS PARK—Religious Hospitallers of St. Joseph, Novitiate, Mt. St. Joseph.

PEORIA—Srs. of St. Francis of the Immaculate Conception, Convent, Hedding Ave.

——Hospital Srs. of the 3rd O. S. F., St. Francis Hospital, 616 Glen Oak Ave.

ROCKFORD—Poor Clares (Colettines), Corpus Christi Monastery, S. Main St.

ROCK ISLAND—Visitation Nuns, Villa de Chantal Convent, 2000 Sixteenth Ave.

RUMA—Srs. Adorers of the Most Precious Blood, Precious Blood Inst., Red Bud.

SPRINGFIELD—Srs. of St. Dominic, Convent of Our Lady of the Sacred Heart, W. Monroe St. & Lincoln Ave.

——Hospital Srs. of St. Francis, St. John's Hospital, 8th & Mason Sts.

TECHNY—Missionary Srs., Servants of the Holy Ghost, Prov. H., Holy Ghost Convent.

WAUKEGAN—Religious of the Holy Child Jesus, Prov. H., 1201 N. Sheridan Rd.

WILMETTE—Srs. of Christian Charity, Prov. H., Maria Immaculata Convent, Ridge Rd. at Walnut Ave.

INDIANA

DONALDSON—Poor Handmaids of Jesus Christ, Convent Ancilla Domini, Retreat St. Amalia.

EVANSVILLE—Poor Clares (Franciscan), Monastery of St. Clare, Kentucky Ave.

FERDINAND—Srs. of St. Benedict, Convent of the Immaculate Conception.

HUNTINGTON—Missionary Catechists of O. B. L. V., Victory Training Inst.

LA FAYETTE—Poor Srs. of St. Francis Seraph of the Perpetual Adoration, St. Francis Convent, Hartford & 14th Sts.

NEW ALBANY—Carmelite Nuns, Carmelite Monastery, 411 E. 9th St.

NOTRE DAME—Srs. of the Holy Cross, St. Mary's Convent.

OLDENBURG—Srs. of the 3rd Order Reg. of St. Francis, Convent of the Immaculate Conception.

ST. MARY-OF-THE-WOODS—Srs. of Providence, Providence Convent, St. Mary-of-the-Woods.

TIPTON—Srs. of St. Joseph, St. Joseph's Convent.

IOWA

BETTENDORF—Carmelite Nuns, Regina Coeli Monastery.
CEDAR RAPIDS—Srs. of Mercy, Mt. Mercy Convent of the Sacred Heart, Elmhurst Drive.
CLINTON—Srs. of the 3rd O. S. F. of the Immaculate Conception, Mt. St. Clare Convent, Fairview Ave.
COUNCIL BLUFFS—Srs. of Mercy, Mt. Loretto Novitiate, 1201 E. Broadway.
DUBUQUE—Srs. of Charity of the B. V. M., St. Joseph's Convent, Mt. Carmel.
——Srs. of the 3rd O. S. F. of the Holy Family, St. Francis Convent, Mt. St. Francis.
——Srs. of Mercy, Prov. Novitiate, Mt. St. Agnes, Asbury Rd.
——Srs. of the Presentation of the B. V. M., Mt. Loretto, 1229 Mt. Loretto Ave.
——Visitation Nuns, Visitation Convent, De Sales Hts., Alta Vista St. & Julien Ave.
OTTUMWA—Srs. of the Holy Humility of Mary, St. Joseph's Convent, Villa Maria, Grand View Ave.
SIOUX CITY—Srs. of St. Benedict, M. H., St. Vincent's Hospital, 624 Jones St.
——Srs. of St. Benedict, Novitiate, St. Benedict's Convent, 45th & Douglas Sts.

KANSAS

ATCHISON—Srs. of St. Benedict, Mt. St. Scholastica's Convent.
CONCORDIA—Srs. of St. Joseph, Nazareth Convent.
FORT SCOTT—Srs. of Mercy, Mercy Convent.
GREAT BEND—Srs. of St. Dominic, Immaculate Conception Convent, 1715 Polk St.
KANSAS CITY—Srs., Servants of Mary, Convent of the Srs., Servants of Mary, 800 N. 18th St.
LEAVENWORTH—Srs. of Charity of Leavenworth, St. Mary's Convent.
PAOLA—Ursuline Nuns, Ursuline Convent.
WICHITA—Srs. of St. Joseph, Mt. St. Mary's Convent.

KENTUCKY

COVINGTON—Srs. of Notre Dame, Prov. H., St. Joseph Heights, Dixie Highway.
——Srs. of St. Benedict, M. H., St. Walburg's Convent, 116 E. 12th St.
GEORGETOWN—Visitation Nuns, Visitation Convent, Cardome.
LOUISVILLE—Ursuline Nuns, Convent of the Immaculate Conception, 3115 Lexington Rd.
LUDLOW—Srs. of St. Benedict, Novitiate, Villa Madonna.
MELBOURNE—Srs. of Divine Providence, Prov. H., St. Anne Convent.
NAZARETH—Srs. of Charity of Nazareth, Nazareth Motherhouse.
NERINX—Srs. of Loretto at the Foot of the Cross, Loretto Motherhouse.
ST. CATHARINE—Srs. of St. Dominic, St. Catherine of Sienna Convent.
ST. JOSEPH—Ursuline Nuns, Mt. St. Joseph Convent.

LOUISIANA

COVINGTON—Srs. of St. Benedict, St. Scholastica's Convent.
NEW ORLEANS—Carmelite Nuns, Monastery of St. Joseph & St. Teresa, 1236 N. Rampart St.

——Poor Clares (Franciscan), St. Clare's Monastery of the Blessed Sacra-
ment, 720 Henry Clay Ave.
——Srs. of the Cong. of Our Lady of Mt. Carmel, Mt. Carmel Convent,
Adams Ave. & Robert E. Lee Blvd., Lakeview.
——Srs. Marianites of the Holy Cross, Prov. H., Rampart & Congress Sts.
——Srs. of the Holy Family (Colored) Holy Family Convent, 717 Orleans St.
——Srs. of the Immaculate Conception, Convent of the Immaculate Con-
ception, 3037 Dauphine St.
——Srs. of Mercy, Convent of Our Lady of Mercy, 1017 St. Andrew St.
——Srs. of the Most Holy Sacrament, Perpetual Adoration Convent, 2321
Marais St.
——Srs. of St. Dominic, Dominican Convent, 7214 St. Charles Ave.
——Srs. of St. Joseph, Prov. H., St. Joseph's Convent, 2116 Ursuline Ave.
RAMSAY—French Benedictine Srs., St. Gertrude's Convent.
SHREVEPORT—Daughters of the Cross, St. Vincent's Convent.

MAINE

BIDDLEFORD—Srs. Servants of the I. H. M., Prov. H., 69 Adams St.
PORTLAND—Srs. of Mercy, St. Joseph's Convent of Mercy, 605 Stevens
Ave.
SOUTH BERWICK—Srs. of St. Joseph, Novitiate of Srs. of St. Joseph.
WATERVILLE—Ursuline Nuns, Mt. Merici Convent, Western Ave.

MARYLAND

BALTIMORE—Carmelite Nuns, Carmelite Monastery, Caroline & Biddle Sts.
——Daughters of the Eucharist, 1133-1135 N. Gilmor St.
——Franciscan Srs. for Colored Missions, Convent and Novitiate of Our
Lady and St. Francis, 2226 Maryland Ave.
——Srs. of the Good Shepherd, Prov. H., 25 S. Mount St.
——Little Srs. of the Poor, Prov. H., Preston & Valley Sts.
——Oblate Srs. of Providence (Colored), St. Frances Convent, E. Chase St. &
Forrest Place.
——School Srs. of Notre Dame, Prov. H., Aisquith St. & Ashland Ave.
——Srs. of Bon Secours, Bon Secours Convent, 2000 W. Baltimore St.
——Visitation Nuns, Visitation Convent, Roland Park, Roland Ave. & Belle-
more Rd.
BETHESDA—Visitation Nuns, Monastery of the Visitation of Holy Mary.
CATONSVILLE—Dominican Srs. of the Perpetual Rosary, Monastery, College
Rd.
——Visitation Nuns, Mt. de Sales Convent of the Visitation.
EMMITSBURG—Daughters of Charity of St. Vincent de Paul, Prov. H., St.
Joseph's Convent.
FREDERICK—Visitation Nuns, Convent of the Visitation.
GOVANS—Srs. of Mercy, Mercy Villa, General M. H. for the Srs. of Mercy
of the Union in the U. S. A.
MT. WASHINGTON—Srs. of Mercy, Prov. Novitiate, Mt. St. Agnes Convent.
RIDGELY—Srs. of St. Benedict, St. Gertrude's Convent.
TOWSON—Mission Helpers, Servants of the Sacred Heart, Sacred Heart Con-
vent, West Joppa Rd.

MASSACHUSETTS

BOSTON—Carmelite Nuns, Carmelite Monastery, 61 Mt. Pleasant Ave., Rox-
bury.
——Poor Clares (Franciscan), Monastery of St. Clare, 38 Bennett St.
——Srs. of St. Joseph, M. H., Mt. St. Joseph Convent, 617 Cambridge St.,
Brighton.
FALL RIVER—Dominican Srs., Convent of St. Catherine of Sienna.
——Dominican Srs. of the Presentation of the B. V. M., Prov. H., St. Ann's
Hospital.
——Srs. of Mercy, Mt. St. Mary's Convent.
——Religious of the Holy Union of the Sacred Hearts, Prov. H., 466 Pros-
pect St.
——Srs. of St. Joseph, Prov. H., St. Teresa's Convent, 2501 S. Main St.
FITCHBURG—Faithful Companions of Jesus, St. Joseph's Convent, Columbus
St.
——Srs. of the Presentation, St. Bernard's Convent.
FRAMINGHAM—Srs. of St. Joseph, Novitiate, Bethany House, Bethany Rd.
HOLYOKE—Srs. of Providence, M. H., Convent of Our Lady of Victory,
Brightside.
MARLBORO—Srs. of St. Ann, Prov. H., St. Ann's Convent, Broad St.
NORTH ADAMS—Venerini Srs., Prov. Convent, 74 Marshall St.
SALEM—Srs. of Ste. Chrétienne, Prov. H., Loring Villa, 262 Loring Ave.
SPRINGFIELD—Srs. of St. Joseph, St. Joseph's Convent, 62 Elliot St.
——Dominican Srs. of the Perpetual Rosary, Monastery, 1430 Riverdale St.,
West.
WALTHAM—Srs. of Notre Dame de Namur, Prov. H., 62 Newton St.
WESTFIELD—Srs. of Providence, Novitiate.
WORCESTER—Srs. of Mercy, St. Gabriel's Convent of Mercy, 46 High St.

MICHIGAN

ADRIAN—Srs. of St. Dominic, St. Joseph's Convent.
DETROIT—Carmelite Nuns, Monastery of St. Therese of the Child Jesus, 1534
Webb Ave.
——Dominican Nuns, 2nd Order, Monastery of the Blessed Sacrament, Oak-
land Ave. & Boston Blvd.
——Felician Srs., O. S. F., Prov. H., 4232 St. Aubin Ave.
——Religious of Mary Reparatrix, U. S. Novitiate, Mount Mary, 17330
Quincy Ave.
GRAND RAPIDS—Carmelite Nuns, Carmelite Monastery of Our Lady of Guada-
lupe, 1256 Walker Ave., N. W.
——Srs. of St. Dominic, Sacred Heart Convent, Marywood, Fulton St., East.
——Srs. of Mercy, Novitiate, Mt. Mercy Convent, 1425 Bridge St., N. W.
Monroe—Srs., Servants of the I. H. M., St. Mary's Convent, Elm Ave.
NAZARETH—Srs. of St. Joseph of the Diocese of Detroit, Nazareth Convent.
ST. IGNACE—Ursuline Nuns, Ursuline Academy of Our Lady of the Straits.

MINNESOTA

CROOKSTON—Srs. of St. Benedict, Mt. St. Benedict Convent.
——Srs. of St. Joseph, Novitiate, St. Joseph's Convent.

57

DULUTH—Srs. of St. Benedict, Villa Sancta Scholastica.

——Corpus Christi Carmelites, U. S. Novitiate, Corpus Christi House.

LITTLE FALLS—Franciscan Srs. of the Immaculate Conception, St. Francis Convent.

MANKATO—School Srs. of Notre Dame, Prov. H., Convent of Our Lady of Good Counsel.

ROCHESTER—Srs. of St. Francis of the Cong. of Our Lady of Lourdes, St. Mary's Convent.

ST. JOSEPH—Srs. of St. Benedict, St. Benedict's Convent.

ST. PAUL—Sisters of the Good Shepherd, Prov. H., Milton & Blair Sts.

——Srs. of St. Joseph of Carondelet, Prov. H., Fairview Ave. & Randolph St.

——Visitation Nuns, Convent of the Visitation, Grotto St. & Fairmount Ave.

SAUK RAPIDS—Poor Clares (Colettines), St. Clare's Monastery.

MISSOURI

CLAYTON—Carmelite Nuns, Carmel of St. Joseph.

CLYDE—Benedictine Srs. of Perpetual Adoration, St. Scholastica's Convent.

CONCEPTION—School Srs. of St. Francis, St. Francis' Convent.

FERGUSON—Polish Franciscan School Srs., Novitiate, Villa St. Joseph.

KIRKWOOD—Ursuline Nuns, Ursuline Convent, St. Angela Park, 800 E. Monroe St.

MARYVILLE—Srs. of the 3rd Order of St. Francis, St. Francis' Hospital.

NEVADA—Srs. of St. Francis of Perpetual Adoration, St. Francis Convent.

NORMANDY—Daughters of Charity of St. Vincent de Paul, Prov. H., Marillac Seminary.

O'FALLON—Srs. of the Most Precious Blood, St. Mary's Institute.

ST. LOUIS—Franciscan Srs., Daughters of the Sacred Hearts, St. Anthony's Hospital, 3520 Chippewa St.

——Sisters of the Good Shepherd, Prov. H., 3801 Gravois Ave.

——Polish Franciscan School Srs., M. H., Convent of Our Lady of Perpetual Help, 3419 Gasconade Ave.

——Religious of the Sacred Heart, Vicariate house, Maryville, Convent of the Sacred Heart, 2900 Meramec St.

——Srs. of Charity of the Incarnate Word, Prov. H., Incarnate Word Convent, Our Lady's Mount, Wellston Sta.

——Srs. of St. Joseph of Carondelet, St. Joseph's Academy, 6400 Minnesota Ave.

——Srs. of St. Joseph of Carondelet, Prov. H., Convent of Our Lady of Good Counsel, 1849 Cass Ave.

——Srs. of St. Mary of the 3rd Order of St. Francis, M. H., St. Mary's Infirmary, 1536 Papin St.

——Srs. of St. Mary of the 3rd Order of St. Francis, Novitiate, St. Mary's Hospital, 6420 Clayton Rd.

——Visitation Nuns, Convent of the Visitation, 5448 Cabanne Ave.

ST. LOUIS, SOUTH—School Srs. of Notre Dame, Prov. H., Sancta Maria in Ripa, Ripa Ave.

SPRINGFIELD—Visitation Nuns, St. de Chantal Convent of the Visitation, Elfindale.

WEBSTER GROVES—Srs. of Mercy, Prov. H., St. Joseph's Convent of Mercy.

MONTANA

GREAT FALLS—Srs. of the Humility of Mary, Sacred Heart Convent.
——Ursuline Nuns (R. U.), Mt. St. Angela, M. H. of Ursulines in Eastern Montana.
POLSON—Religious Hospitallers of St. Joseph, Hotel Dieu Hospital.
ST. IGNATIUS'—Ursuline Nuns (R. U.), Prov. H. for Northwest, Villa Ursula.

NEBRASKA

OMAHA—Poor Clares (Franciscan), Monastery of St. Clare, 29th & Hamilton Sts.
——Srs. of Mercy, Prov. H., Convent of Mercy, 1424 Castellar St.
——School Srs. de Notre Dame, Prov. H., 3505 State St.
——Mantellate Srs., Servants of Mary, Prov. H., Convent of Our Lady of Sorrows, 74th & Military Sts.
RAEVILLE—Missionary Benedictine Srs., St. Gertrude's Convent.
YORK—Ursuline Sisters, Nazareth Convent.

NEW HAMPSHIRE

MANCHESTER—Srs. Adorers of the Precious Blood, Monastery, 555 Union St.
——Srs. of Mercy, Mt. St. Mary's Convent.
NASHUA—Srs. of the Holy Cross and of the Seven Dolors, Prov. H., 71 Chestnut St.

NEW JERSEY

BORDENTOWN—Poor Clares (Franciscan), Franciscan Monastery of the Poor Clares.
CALDWELL—Srs. of St. Dominic, Mt. St. Dominic.
CAMDEN—Dominican Srs. of the Perpetual Rosary, Monastery, 1500 Haddon Ave.
CONVENT STATION—Srs. of Charity of St. Vincent de Paul, St. Elizabeth's Convent.
ELIZABETH—Srs. of St. Benedict, Benedictine Convent, 851 N. Broad St.
ENGLEWOOD—Srs. of St. Joseph of Peace, Prov. H., St. Michael's Villa.
JERSEY CITY—Srs. of St. Joseph of Peace, M. H., St. Joseph's Home, 81 York St.
LODI—Felician Srs., O. S. F., Prov. H., S. Main St.
MENDHAM—Srs. of Christian Charity, Prov. H., Mallinckrodt Convent.
MORRISTOWN—Carmelite Nuns, Monastery of the Most Blessed Virgin Mary of Mt. Carmel, 189 Madison Ave.
NEWARK—Dominican Nuns, 2nd Order, Monastery of St. Dominic, 13th Ave. & E. 9th St.
——Baptistine Srs., M. H., St. John the Baptist Convent, 1012 Amity Place.
NORTH PLAINFIELD—Srs. of Mercy, Mt. St. Mary's Convent.
PASSAIC—Capuchin Srs. of the Child Jesus, Mt. Carmel Convent, 52 Park Place.
PATERSON—Missionary Srs. of the Immaculate Conception, Novitiate, Convent of the Immaculate Conception, Squirrelwood Rd.

SUMMIT—Dominican Srs. of Perpetual Adoration and the Perpetual Rosary, Monastery, 63 New England Ave.
TRENTON—Religious Teachers Filippini, Prov. H., Villa Victoria.
UNION CITY—Dominican Srs. of the Perpetual Rosary, Monastery, 14th & West Sts.

NEW YORK

ALBANY—Dominican Srs. (Cong. of St. Catharine de Ricci), 886 Madison Ave.
——Dominican Nuns, 2nd Order, Monastery of the Immaculate Conception, New Scotland Ave.
——Religious of the Sacred Heart, Vicariate house and U. S. Novitiate, Convent of the Sacred Heart, Kenwood.
——Srs. of the Holy Names, Prov. Convent, 628 Madison Ave.
——Srs. of Mercy, Convent of Mercy, 634 New Scotland Ave.
ALLEGANY—Srs. of the 3rd O. S. F., St. Elizabeth's Convent.
AMITYVILLE—Srs. of St. Dominic (Brooklyn), Novitiate House.
BEACON—Ursuline Nuns (R. U.), Ursuline Novitiate, Hiddenbrook.
BLAUVELT—Srs. of St. Dominic, St. Dominic's Convent.
BRENTWOOD, L. I.—Srs. of St. Joseph (Brooklyn), St. Joseph's Convent.
BROOKLYN—Carmelite Nuns, Monastery of Our Lady of Mt. Carmel, 745 St. John's Place.
——Dominican Srs., M. H., Holy Cross Convent, 157 Graham Ave.
——Dominican Srs., Novitiate, Amityville, Long Island.
——Little Srs. of the Poor, Prov. H., Bushwick & De Kalb Aves.
——Little Srs. of the Poor, U. S. Novitiate, Queens, Long Island.
——Sisters of the Infant Jesus, Convent of the Infant Jesus, 439 Henry St.
——Srs. Adorers of the Precious Blood, Monastery, Ft. Hamilton Pky. & 54th St.
——Srs. of Mercy, M. H., St. Francis Convent, 273 Willoughby Ave.
——Visitation Nuns, Visitation Convent, Ridge Blvd. & 89th St.
BUFFALO—Carmelite Nuns, Carmelite Monastery, 75 Carmel Rd.
——Dominican Srs. of the Perpetual Rosary, Monastery, 335 Doat St.
——Franciscan Srs., Minor Conventuals, St. Joseph's Convent, 179 Clark St.
——Srs. of Our Lady of Charity of the Refuge, Monastery, 485 Best St.
——Srs. of St. Joseph, Convent of Mt. St. Joseph, 2064 Main St.
——Srs. of Mercy, Mt. Mercy Convent of Our Lady of Mercy, 1475 Abbott Rd.
——Srs. of St. Mary of Namur, Prov. H., Mt. St. Mary, Delaware Ave., Hertel Sta.
——Missionary Srs. of the Divine Child, 473 Niagara St.
BUFFALO, EAST—Felician Srs., O. S. F., Prov. H., Cheektowaga, William & Kennedy Sts.
CHAPPAQUA—Helpers of the Holy Souls, Novitiate of Our Lady of Providence, St. Elmo's Hill.
GARRISON—Franciscan Srs. of the Atonement, St. Francis Convent, Graymoor.
HAMBURG—Franciscan Srs. of St. Joseph, Immaculate Conception Convent, South Park & Soule Rd.
HAWTHORNE—Servants of Relief for Incurable Cancer (Dominican Cong. of St. Rose of Lima), Rosary Hill Home.
HIGHLAND MILLS—Religious of Jesus and Mary, U. S. Novitiate, Convent of Religious of Jesus and Mary.

LAKE RONKONKOMA—Religious of the Cenacle, U. S. Novitiate.

MONROE—Parish Visitors of Mary Immaculate, Marycrest Novitiate.

NEWBURGH—Srs. of St. Dominic (Cong. of the Most Holy Rosary), Mt. St. Mary-on-the-Hudson.

——Srs. of the Presentation of the B. V. M., Novitiate, Mt. St. Joseph.

NEW HAMBURG—Srs. of St. Francis of the Mission of the Immaculate Virgin, Mt. St. Clare Convent.

NYACK—Srs. of Our Lady of Christian Doctrine, Marydell.

NEW YORK CITY—Baptistine Srs., Novitiate, St. John's Villa, Cleveland Place, Arrochar Park, S. I.

——Carmelite Nuns, Carmelite Convent, 300 Gun Hill Rd., Bronx.

——Daughters of Divine Charity, Prov. H., St. Joseph's Hill, 205 Major Ave., Arrochar, S. I.

——Dominican Nuns, 2nd Order, Corpus Christi Monastery, LaFayette and Baretto Sts., Hunts Point, Bronx.

——Dominican Srs. of the Sick Poor, Convent of the Immaculate Conception, 140 W. 61st St.

——Handmaids of the Most Pure Heart of Mary (Colored), St. Mary's Convent, 8 E. 131st St.

——Helpers of the Holy Souls, Vicariate Convent, 112-118 E. 86th St.

——Srs. Marianites of the Holy Cross, Novitiate, 222 Main St., Tottenville, S. I.

——Missionary Canonesses of St. Augustine, St. John Berchmans' Convent, 437 W. 47th St.

——Missionary Srs. of the Sacred Heart, Novitiate, Sacred Heart Villa, 701 Fort Washington Ave.

——Parish Visitors of Mary Immaculate, M. H., St. Joseph's Convent of the Sacred Heart, 328 W. 71st St.

——Poor Clares (Franciscan), Monastery, 328 Haven Ave. near 180th St.

——Religious of the Cenacle, Prov. H., Cenacle of St. Regis, 628 W. 140th St.

——Srs. of Bon Secours, Convent of Bon Secours, 1195 Lexington Ave.

——Srs. of Charity, Mt. St. Vincent-on-Hudson.

——Srs. of St. Dorothy, Convent, 256 Center St., Richmond, S. I.

——Srs. of the Presentation, Mt. St. Michael, Green Ridge, S. I.

——Ursuline Nuns (R. U.), Prov. H., Mt. St. Ursula Convent, 200th St. & Marion Ave., Bedford Park.

——Visitation Nuns, Monastery, 256th St. & Arlington Ave., Riverdale-on-Hudson.

OSSINING—Foreign Mission Srs. of St. Dominic, Maryknoll Convent.

PEEKSKILL—Franciscan Missionary Srs. of the Sacred Heart, St. Joseph's Convent, Mt. St. Francis.

——Srs. of the Good Shepherd, Prov. Convent, Mt. Florence.

PLATTSBURG—Srs. of Mercy, Loretto Novitiate.

ROCHESTER—Carmelite Nuns, Carmelite Convent.

——Srs. of Mercy, Mercy Convent, St. John Park, Charlotte Sta.

——Srs. of St. Joseph, Nazareth Convent, Brighton Sta., Pittsford.

ST. BONAVENTURE—Missionary Srs. of the Immaculate Conception, Mother-house.

SCHENECTADY—Carmelite Nuns, St. Teresa's Monastery, 1138 Duane St.

SPARKILL—Dominican Srs., Dominican Convent of Our Lady of the Rosary.

STELLA NIAGARA—Srs. of St. Francis of Penance and Christian Charity, Seminary of Our Lady of the Sacred Heart.
SYOSSET—Srs. of Mercy (Brooklyn), Convent of Mercy Novitiate.
SYRACUSE—Dominican Srs. of the Perpetual Rosary, Monastery, 802 Court St.
——Srs. of the 3rd O. S. F., Minor Conventuals, St. Anthony's Convent, 1024 Court St.
TARRYTOWN—Religious of the Sacred Heart of Mary, Convent of the Sacred Heart of Mary, Marymount.
TROY—Srs. of St. Joseph of Carondelet, Prov. H., St. Joseph's Seminary.
WATERTOWN—Srs. of St. Joseph, St. Joseph's Convent, 362 Main St.
WATERVLIET—Srs. of the Presentation of the B. V. M., St. Colman's Convent.
WHITE PLAINS—Srs. of the Divine Compassion, Convent of Our Lady of Good Counsel, 52 N. Broadway.
WILLIAMSVILLE—Srs. of the 3rd O. S. F., St. Mary of the Angels Convent of Perpetual Adoration, Mill St.
YONKERS—Srs. of the Blessed Sacrament, Convent of the Blessed Sacrament, 23 Park Ave.

NORTH CAROLINA

BELMONT—Srs. of Mercy, Sacred Heart Convent.

NORTH DAKOTA

FARGO—Srs. of the Presentation of the B. V. M., Sacred Heart Convent.
GARRISON—Srs. of St. Benedict, Sacred Heart Convent.
HANKINSON—Srs. of St. Francis, Franciscan Convent.
KENMARE—Ursuline Nuns, Ursuline Convent.
OAKWOOD—Srs. of St. Mary of the Presentation, Prov. H., St. Aloysius' Convent.

OHIO

AKRON—Srs. of St. Dominic, Convent of Our Lady of the Elms, 1230 W. Market St.
BEDFORD—Vincentian Srs. of Charity, Prov. H., Villa San Bernardo.
CALDWELL—Ursuline Nuns, Ursuline Convent.
CINCINNATI—Dominican Nuns, 2nd Order, Monastery of the Holy Name, 1960 Madison Rd.
——Srs. of the Good Shepherd, Prov. H., Our Lady of the Woods, Elmwood Place, Carthage.
——Srs. of Mercy, Prov. H., Convent of the Divine Will, 1409 Freeman Ave.
——Srs. of Notre Dame de Namur, Prov. H., Notre Dame Convent, 111 Grandin Rd., East Walnut Hills.
——Srs. of the Pious Union of Our Lady of Good Counsel, St. Rita School for the Deaf, Lockland.
——Srs. of St. Joseph, Novitiate, St. Joseph's Convent, 6532 Beechmont Ave.
——Ursuline Nuns, St. Ursula Convent, 1339 E. McMillan St., Walnut Hills.
CLEVELAND—Carmelite Nuns, Carmel of the Holy Family, 11127 St. Clair Ave.
——Franciscan Srs. of Perpetual Adoration, 1453 East Blvd.

——Poor Clares (Colettines), Monastery, 3501 Rocky River Drive.
——Srs. of Charity of St. Augustine, St. Augustine's Convent, 14808 Lake Ave., Lakewood.
——Srs. of the Incarnate Word and the Blessed Sacrament, 6618 Pearl Rd.
——Srs. of the Holy Ghost, 12219 Corlett Ave.
——Srs. of the Most Holy Trinity, Holy Trinity Convent, St. Rocco's Place, 3205 Fulton Rd.
——Srs. of Notre Dame, Prov. H., Notre Dame Convent, 1325 Ansel Rd.
——Srs. of St. Joseph, St. Joseph's Convent, 3430 Rocky River Drive.
——Srs. of St. Joseph of the Order of St. Francis, Prov. H., Turney & Granger Rds.
——Social Missions Srs., 2438 Mapleside Ave.
——Ursuline Srs., Ursuline Convent, E. 55th St. & Scovill Ave.
COLUMBUS, EAST—Srs. of St. Dominic, St. Mary of the Springs Convent.
DAYTON—Srs. of the Precious Blood, Convent of Our Lady of the Precious Blood, Salem Hts.
FREMONT—Srs. of Mercy, Convent of Our Lady of the Pines.
HARTWELL—Srs. of the Poor of St. Francis, Prov. H., St. Clara's Convent.
LOWELLVILLE—Srs. of the Holy Humility of Mary, Villa Maria Convent.
MT. ST. JOSEPH—Srs. of Charity of Cincinnati, Convent of Mt. St. Joseph-on-the-Ohio.
ST. MARTIN—Ursuline Nuns, Ursuline Convent of the Immaculate Heart of Mary, Brown Co.
SYLVANIA—Srs. of St. Francis of the Cong. of Our Lady of Lourdes, Prov. Convent.
TIFFIN—Srs. of the 3rd O. S. F., St. Francis' Convent, Walnut & Melmore Sts.
TOLEDO—Srs. of Notre Dame, Prov. H., 1111 W. Bancroft St.
——Srs. of Notre Dame, Novitiate, Notre Dame Convent, Monroe St. & Secor Rd.
——Ursuline Nuns, Ursuline Convent of the Sacred Heart, 2413 Collingwood Ave.
——Visitation Nuns, Monastery of the Visitation, 1745 Parkside Blvd.
YOUNGSTOWN—Ursuline Nuns, Ursuline Convent, 217 W. Raven St.

OKLAHOMA

GUTHRIE—Srs. of St. Benedict, Cong. of St. Scholastica, St. Joseph's Convent.
OKLAHOMA CITY—Carmelite Srs. of St. Teresa of the Child Jesus, Carmel of the Little Flower, 520 W. Wheeler St.
SACRED HEART—Benedictine Srs. of Our Lady of Belloc, Prov. H., Nazareth Convent.

OREGON

BEAVERTON—Srs. of St. Mary, St. Mary's Convent.
MT. ANGEL—Benedictine Srs., Queen of Angels Convent.
OSWEGO—Srs. of the Holy Names, Novitiate, Marylhurst.
PARK PLACE—Sisters of Mercy, Novitiate.
PENDLETON—Srs. of the 3rd O.S.F., Prov. H., St. Francis Novitiate.
PORTLAND—Srs. Adorers of the Precious Blood, Monastery, 220 E. 76th St.
——Srs. of the Holy Names, Prov. H., St. Mary's Convent, 5th & Market Sts.

PENNSYLVANIA

ALTOONA—Carmelite Nuns, Monastery, 5519 Sixth Ave., Roselawn.

BADEN—Srs. of St. Joseph, Mt. Gallitzin Convent.

CAMP HILL—Dominican Srs. of the Perpetual Rosary, Dominican Monastery, Enola.

COLUMBIA—Srs. Adorers of the Most Precious Blood, St. Joseph's Convent, Gethsemane.

CORNWELLS HTS.—Srs. of the Blessed Sacrament for Indians and Colored People, Convent of the Blessed Sacrament, St. Elizabeth's.

CRESSON—Sisters of Mercy, Prov. Nov., Convent of Mercy.

DALLAS—Srs. of Mercy, Prov. H., Villa St. Teresa Convent.

DANVILLE—Srs. of Sts. Cyril and Methodius, Sacred Heart Villa.

ELMHURST—Poor Srs. of Jesus Crucified and the Sorrowful Mother (Lithuanian), St. Mary's Villa.

ERIE—Srs. of St. Benedict, St. Benedict's Convent, 327-345 E. 9th St.

——Srs. of St. Joseph, Villa Maria Convent, W. 8th St.

——Srs. of Mercy, M. H., Mercyhurst Convent, Glenwood Hills.

FACTORYVILLE—Srs. of St. Basil the Great (for the Carpatho-Rusin Catholics), St. Basil's Convent.

FOX CHASE—Srs. of St. Basil the Great (for the Ukrainian Greek Catholics), St. Joseph's Convent.

GERMANTOWN—Srs. of the Good Shepherd, Prov. Convent, Chew & Penn Sts.

GLEN RIDDLE—Srs. of the 3rd O. S. F., Convent of Our Lady of Angels, La Verna Hts.

GREENSBURG—Srs. of Charity, St. Joseph's Convent, Seton Hill.

McKEESPORT—Felician Srs., O. S. F., Prov. H., Convent of Our Lady of the Sacred Heart.

——Daughters of the Divine Redeemer, St. Joseph's Convent, Elizabeth.

MERION—Srs. of Mercy, Mater Misericordiae Convent.

PERRYSVILLE—Vincentian Srs. of Charity, Convent, St. Vincent's Hill.

PHILADELPHIA—Carmelite Nuns, Monastery, 66th Ave. & York Rd., Oak Lane.

——Grey Nuns of the Sacred Heart, Convent, Melrose Pk., Oak Lane.

——Poor Clares (Franciscan), Monastery, Girard & Corinthian Aves.

——Srs. of St. Francis, Prov. H., 1604 W. Allegheny Ave.

——Srs. of St. Joseph, Mt. St. Joseph, Chestnut Hill.

——Srs., Servants of the Holy Ghost of Perpetual Adoration, Convent of Divine Love, 2212 Green St.

PITTSBURGH—Benedictine Srs., 4530 Perrysville Rd., Bellevue Branch, N. S.

——Passionist Nuns, Our Lady of Sorrows Convent, 2715 Churchview Ave., Mt. Oliver Sta.

——School Srs. of the 3rd O. S. F., Mt. Assisi Convent, 934 Forest Ave., Bellevue Sta.

——Srs. of Divine Providence, Mt. Immaculate M. H., Allison Pk., Three Degree Rd.

——Srs. of the Holy Family of Nazareth, Prov. H., Mt. Nazareth, Bellevue Sta.

——Srs. of the Holy Ghost, 5246 Clarwin Ave., West View, Bellevue Branch.

——Srs. of Mercy, Mt. Mercy, St. Mary's Convent of Mercy, 3333 Fifth Ave., Oakland Sta.

——Srs. of Our Lady of Charity of the Refuge, Monastery, 1615 Lowrie St., Troy Hill, N. S.

——Srs. of Our Lady of Charity of the Refuge, Eudes Inst., 1625 Lincoln Ave., E. E.

——Srs. of St. Francis (Lithuanian), Mt. Providence, Castle Shannon, South Hills Sta.

——Srs. of the 3rd Order of St. Francis, Mt. Alvernia, Evergreen Ave., Millvale Sta.

——Ursuline Nuns, Ursuline Convent, 201 S. Winebiddle Ave.

READING—Bernardine Srs. of the 3rd Order of St. Francis, Sacred Heart Convent.

——Mission Workers of the Sacred Heart, St. Michael's Convent, Bernharts.

SCRANTON—Passionist Nuns, St. Gabriel's Convent, 1560 Monroe Ave.

——Srs., Servants of the I. H. M., Mt. St. Mary of the Immaculate Conception, Marywood.

ST. MARY'S—Srs. of St. Benedict, St. Joseph's Convent, 303 Church St., Elk County.

SHARON HILL—Religious of the Holy Child Jesus, Convent of the Holy Child Jesus.

TITUSVILLE—Srs. of Mercy (Erie) Novitiate, St. Joseph's Convent.

TORRESDALE—Srs. of the Holy Family of Nazareth, Prov. H., 9701 Frankford Ave.

WEST CHESTER—Srs., Servants of the I. H. M., Novitiate, Villa Maria.

YORK—Daughters of Our Lady of Mercy, Mater Misericordiae Convent.

RHODE ISLAND

CUMBERLAND—Srs. of Mercy, Novitiate, Mt. St. Rita Mercy Convent, Grants Mills.

PROVIDENCE—Srs. of Mercy, Prov. H., St. Francis Xavier Convent, 60 Broad St.

——Srs. of the Passion and Cross, Assumption Convent, 530 Dexter St.

PROVIDENCE, NORTH—Franciscan Missionaries of Mary, Novitiate, 399 Fruit Hill Ave.

SOUTH CAROLINA

CHARLESTON—Srs. of Our Lady of Mercy, Convent of Our Lady of Mercy, Legare & Queen Sts.

COLUMBIA—Ursuline Nuns, Convent of the Immaculate Conception, 1505 Assembly St.

SOUTH DAKOTA

ABERDEEN—Srs. of the Presentation of the B. V. M., Presentation Convent.

STURGIS—Benedictine Srs., St. Martin's Convent.

YANKTON—Benedictine Srs., Convent of the Sacred Heart, Mt. Marty.

TENNESSEE

NASHVILLE—Dominican Srs., St. Cecilia's Convent, Eighth Ave., N. & Clay St.

TEXAS

BROWNSVILLE—Srs. of the Incarnate Word and the Blessed Sacrament, Convent, 714 St. Charles St.

CORPUS CHRISTI—Srs. of the Incarnate Word and the Blessed Sacrament, Incarnate Word Convent, 715 Carancahua St.

DALLAS—Carmelite Nuns, Carmelite Convent, 2003 Wichita St.

——Srs. of Our Lady of Charity of the Refuge, Monastery, Mt. St. Michael.

EL PASO—Servants of the Sacred Heart and of the Poor, Novitiate, 237 Tobin Place.

——Srs. of Perpetual Adoration, Monastery, 1401 Magoffin Ave.

FORT WORTH—Srs. of Charity of the Incarnate Word, Prov. H., pro tem, St. Joseph's Infirmary.

——Srs. of St. Mary of Namur, Prov. H., Convent of Our Lady of Victory, 3410 S. Hemphill St.

HOUSTON—Srs. of St. Dominic, Sacred Heart Convent, Almeda Rd.

——Srs. of Charity of the Incarnate Word, Villa de Matel, Lawndale Ave.

——Srs. of the Incarnate Word and the Blessed Sacrament, Incarnate Word Convent, 609 Crawford St.

LAREDO—Ursuline Nuns, Ursuline Convent.

SAN ANTONIO—Benedictine Srs., St. Joseph's Convent, Las Gallinas.

——Srs. of Charity of the Incarnate Word, Incarnate Word Convent, Alamo Hts.

——Srs. of Divine Providence, Convent of Our Lady of the Lake.

——Servants of the Holy Ghost and Mary Immaculate, Grand View Hts., 300 Yucca St.

——Srs. of the Incarnate Word and the Blessed Sacrament, Convent, Conception Rd.

——Srs. of Our Lady of Charity of the Refuge, Monastery, 1900 Montana St.

——Srs. of the Sacred Heart of Jesus, Prov. H., 2000 McCullough Ave.

——Srs. of St. Teresa of Jesus, Prov. Convent, 4018 S. Presa St.

SHINER—Srs. of the Incarnate Word and the Blessed Sacrament, Incarnate Word Convent.

TEXARKANA—Ursuline Nuns (R. U.), Prov. H., 518 W. 3rd St.

VICTORIA—Srs. of the Incarnate Word and the Blessed Sacrament, Nazareth Convent.

UTAH

SALT LAKE CITY—Srs. of Perpetual Adoration, Convent, 529 W. Fourth St.

VERMONT

BURLINGTON—Srs. of Mercy, Mt. St. Mary's Convent, Mansfield Ave.

RUTLAND—Srs. of St. Joseph, Mt. St. Joseph's Convent.

WINOOSKI—Religious Hospitallers of St. Joseph, Fanny Allen Hospital, Winooski Park.

VIRGINIA

BRISTOW—Srs. of St. Benedict, St. Benedict's Convent.

RICHMOND—Visitation Nuns, Monte Maria, 2209 E. Grace St.

WYTHEVILLE—Visitation Nuns, Villa Maria, Convent of the Visitiation.

WASHINGTON

BELLINGHAM—Srs. of St. Joseph of Peace, Prov. H., St. Joseph's Hospital.
EVERETT—Dominican Srs. (Cong. of the Holy Cross), St. Dominic's Convent, 2715 Everett Ave.
MUKILTEO—Ursuline Nuns (R. U.), Novitiate, Ursuline Convent.
OMAK—Lady Missionaries of St. Mary, St. Mary's Convent.
SEATTLE—Carmelite Nuns, Monastery, 1808 18th Ave.
——Daughters of Charity, Servants of the Poor, Prov. H., Mt. St. Vincent, 4831 35th Ave., S. W.
SPOKANE—Poor Clares (Franciscan), Monastery, Hawthorne & Princeton Sts.
——Daughters of Charity, Servants of the Poor, Prov. H., Sacred Heart Hospital.
TACOMA—Srs. of St. Dominic, Dominican Convent, Marymount.
TACOMA, SOUTH—Visitation Nuns, Visitation Convent, Visitation Villa.

WEST VIRGINIA

CLARKSBURG—Capuchin Srs., Sacred Heart Convent, 535 Hornor Ave.
FAIRMONT—Srs. of St. Joseph, Villa St. Joseph Convent.
HUNTINGTON—Pallottine Missionary Srs., St. Mary's Convent.
MONONGAH—Srs. Auxiliary of the Apostolate, 142 Maple Ave.
PARKERSBURG—Srs. of the Poor Child Jesus, St. Raphael's Convent, 516 13th St.
——Visitation Nuns, Visitation Convent, De Sales Hts.
WHEELING—Carmelite Nuns, Monastery of St. Teresa and St. John of the Cross, Pleasant Valley.
——Srs. of Our Lady of Charity of the Refuge, Monastery of Our Lady of Charity, Edgington Lane.
——Visitation Nuns, Mt. de Chantal Convent of the Visitation.

WISCONSIN

FOND DU LAC—Srs. of St. Agnes, St. Agnes' Convent, 380 E. Division St.
GREEN BAY—Srs. of Our Lady of Charity of the Refuge, Monastery of Our Lady of Charity, Webster & Polier Aves.
——Srs. of St. Francis of Bay Settlement, St. Francis' Convent.
HARTFORD—Religious Hospitallers of St. Joseph, St. Joseph's Hospital.
KENOSHA—Srs. of St. Dominic, Cong. of St. Catherine of Sienna, St. Catherine of Sienna Novitiate, North Milwaukee Ave.
LA CROSSE—Dominican Srs. of the Perpetual Rosary, Dominican Monastery.
——Srs. of the 3rd Order of St. Francis of the Perpetual Adoration, St. Rose Convent, 709 S. 9th St.
LADYSMITH—Mantellate Srs., Servants of Mary, Convent of Our Lady of Sorrows.
MANITOWOC—Franciscan Srs. of Christian Charity, Holy Family Convent, Alverno.
MERRILL—Srs. of Mercy of the Holy Cross, Novitiate of the Holy Cross, Riverside Ave.
MILWAUKEE—Dominican Srs. of the Perpetual Rosary, Monastery, 68th St. & Mt. Vernon Ave.

——Srs. of Mercy, Our Lady of Mercy Convent, 666 24th St.

——Srs. of the Divine Saviour, Prov. H., St. Mary's Convent, 3506 Center St.

——School Srs. of Notre Dame, Convent of the School Srs. of Notre Dame, 676 Milwaukee St.

——School Srs. of St. Francis, St. Joseph's Convent, Layton Blvd. & Greenfield Ave.

MILWAUKEE, NORTH—Srs. of the Sorrowful Mother, Convent of Our Lady of Sorrows.

RACINE—Srs. of St. Dominic, Convent of St. Catherine of Sienna, 1209 Park Ave.

RICE LAKE—Srs. of the 3rd Order of St. Francis, St. Joseph's Hospital.

ST. FRANCIS—Srs. of the 3rd Order of St. Francis of Assisi (Srs. of Penance and Charity), St. Francis' Convent.

SINSINAWA—Srs. of St. Dominic, St. Clara Convent.

STEVENS POINT—Srs. of St. Joseph of the Order of St. Francis, St. Joseph's Convent.

SUPERIOR—Srs. of St. Joseph, St. Joseph's Convent, 1412 E. 2nd St.

WAUWATOSA—Carmelite Srs. of the Divine Heart of Jesus, Convent, 168 Kavanaugh Ave.

COLLEGES IN THE UNITED STATES CONDUCTED BY RELIGIOUS ORDERS OF WOMEN

Figures in parentheses after names and addresses in the following lists refer to the page in this book giving an account of the community conducting the respective college, hospital or hospice, even though the sketch may contain no mention of the particular institution.

CALIFORNIA

BELMONT—College of Notre Dame (264).
HOLLYWOOD—College of the Immaculate Heart, 5515 Franklin Ave. (617).
LOS ANGELES—Mt. St. Mary's College, 3300 W. Slauson Ave. (214).
MENLO PARK—College of the Sacred Heart (115).
OAKLAND—College of the Holy Names, 2036 Webster St. (570).
SAN FRANCISCO—Notre Dame College, Dolores & 16th Sts. (264).
——San Francisco College for Women* (115).
SAN RAFAEL—Dominican College, Grand Ave. (139).
SANTA ROSA—Ursuline College, 10th & B Sts. (1).

COLORADO

DENVER—Loretto Heights College, Loretto P. O. (101).

CONNECTICUT

NEW HAVEN—Albertus Magnus College (133).

DISTRICT OF COLUMBIA

WASHINGTON—Georgetown Visitation Convent (Junior College), 1500 35th St., N. W. (52).
——Immaculata Seminary (Junior College) 4300 Wisconsin Ave., N. W. (255).
——Trinity College, Michigan Ave. (262).

ILLINOIS

CHICAGO—St. Xavier's College for Women, 4928 Cottage Grove Ave. (297).
JOLIET—Assisi Junior College for Young Women, 303 Taylor St. (431).
RIVER FOREST—Rosary College (136).
SPRINGFIELD—St. Joseph's Ursuline Sisters Springfield Junior College (1).

INDIANA

NOTRE DAME—St. Mary's College (272).
ST. MARY-OF-THE-WOODS—St. Mary-of-the-Woods College (255).

* Opening in September, 1930.

IOWA

CEDAR RAPIDS—Mt. Mercy Junior College of the Sacred Heart, Elmhurst Drive (351).
CHEROKEE—Mt. St. Mary's Junior College (717).
CLINTON—Mt. St. Clare College, Fairview Ave. (437).
DAVENPORT—Immaculate Conception Junior College, 801 Main St. (185).
DUBUQUE—Clarke College, Seminary & Locust Sts. (185).
OTTUMWA—St. Joseph's Junior College, Villa Maria, Grand View Ave (592).

KANSAS

ATCHISON—Mt. St. Scholastica's College (514).
LEAVENWORTH—St. Mary's College (504).
PAOLA—Ursuline Sisters' College (1).
SALINA—Marymount College (235).

KENTUCKY

COVINGTON—Villa Madonna College, Ludlow P. O. (513).
LOUISVILLE—Nazareth College, 851 S. Fourth Ave. (109).
——Sacred Heart Junior College, 3111 Lexington Rd. (20).
NAZARETH—Nazareth Junior College (109).
ST. JOSEPH—Mt. St. Joseph Junior College (24).

LOUISIANA

GRAND COTEAU—Normal College of the Sacred Heart (115).
NEW ORLEANS—St. Mary's Dominican College, 7214 St. Charles Ave. (142).
——Xavier College (Colored) 5116 Magazine St. (692).
——Ursuline College, 2635 State St. (7).
SHREVEPORT—St. Vincent's College (550).

MAINE

PORTLAND—St. Joseph's College for Women, 605 Stevens Ave. (326).

MARYLAND

BALTIMORE—College of Notre Dame of Maryland, Charles Street Ave. (404).
——St Catherine's Normal Institute, 954 Harlem Ave. (272).
EMMITSBURG—St. Joseph's College (75).

MASSACHUSETTS

BOSTON—Emmanuel College of Notre Dame, 400 The Fenway (267).
CHICOPEE—College of Our Lady of the Elms (234).
WESTON—Regis College, Wellesley St. (233).

MICHIGAN

ADRIAN—St. Joseph College (154).
DETROIT—Marygrove College, Six Mile Rd. & Wyoming Ave. (386).
GRAND RAPIDS—Sacred Heart College, Marywood, Fulton St., E. (152).
——Mt. Mercy College, 1425 Bridge St., N. W. (343).
NAZARETH—Nazareth College (242).

MINNESOTA

DULUTH—College of St. Scholastica (526).
ST. JOSEPH—St. Benedict's College (511).
ST. PAUL—College of St. Catherine, Cleveland Ave. & Randolph St. (210).
WINONA—College of St. Teresa (464).

MISSOURI

ARCADIA—Arcadia Ursuline College (13).
KANSAS CITY—St. Teresa Junior College, 56th & Main Sts. (235).
ST. LOUIS—Fontbonne College, Wydown & Big Bend Blvds. (209).
——Maryville, College of the Sacred Heart, 2900 Meramec St. (115).
——Sancta Maria in Ripa Junior College, Ripa Ave., S. (405).
WEBSTER GROVES—Webster College, Lockwood & Plymouth Aves. (101).

NEBRASKA

OMAHA—College of St. Mary, 1424 Castellar St. (324).
——Duchesne College of the Sacred Heart, 36th & Burt Sts. (115).
YORK—St. Ursula's Junior College (35).

NEW JERSEY

CONVENT STATION—College of St. Elizabeth (94).
LAKEWOOD—Georgian Court College (342).

NEW MEXICO

SANTA FÉ—St. Francis Summer College (460).

NEW YORK

ALBANY—College of St. Rose, 979 Madison Ave. (212).
BROOKLYN—St. Joseph's College, 245-253 Clinton Ave. (225).
BUFFALO—D'Youville College, Porter & Prospect Aves. (560).
NEW ROCHELLE—College of New Rochelle, 29 Castle Place (29).
NEW YORK CITY—College of Mt. St. Vincent-on-Hudson (80).
——Manhattanville, College of the Sacred Heart, Convent Ave. & W. 133rd St. (115).
ROCHESTER—Nazareth College, 402 Augustine St. (228).
TARRYTOWN—Marymount College (647).
WHITE PLAINS—Good Counsel College, 52-58 Broadway (673).

NORTH CAROLINA

ASHEVILLE—St. Genevieve-of-the-Pines (754).

OHIO

CINCINNATI—Clifton, College of the Sacred Heart, 525 LaFayette Ave. (115).
CLEVELAND—Notre Dame College, College Rd., South Euclid (631).
——Ursuline College, 2234 Overlook Rd. (15).
COLUMBUS, EAST—College of St. Mary's of the Springs (130).
MT. ST. JOSEPH—College of Mt. St. Joseph-on-the-Ohio (86).
TOLEDO—Mary Manse College, 2425 Collingwood Ave. (17)

OKLAHOMA

GUTHRIE—Catholic College (522).
OKLAHOMA CITY—Mt. St. Mary's College, Capitol Hill (358).

OREGON

BAKER—St. Francis' College (418).
PORTLAND—St. Mary's College, 5th & Market Sts. (570).

PENNSYLVANIA

DALLAS—Misericordia College (346).
ERIE—Mercyhurst College, Mercyhurst Blvd. (335).
——Villa Maria, W. 8th St. (226).
GREENSBURG—Seton Hill College (98).
IMMACULATA—Immaculata College (391).
PHILADELPHIA—Mt. St. Joseph College, Chestnut Hill (216).
PITTSBURGH—Mt. Mercy College for Girls, 3333 Fifth Ave. (289).
ROSEMONT—Rosemont College of the Holy Child Jesus (579).
SCRANTON—Marywood College, Mt. St. Mary's (393).

TENNESSEE

MEMPHIS—St. Agnes' College, 697 Vance Ave. (129).

TEXAS

EL PASO—Loretto College, Austin Terrace (101).
FORT WORTH—College of Our Lady of Victory (586).
SAN ANTONIO—Incarnate Word College, N. Broadway (596).
——Our Lady of the Lake College (599).

UTAH

SALT LAKE CITY—College of St. Mary-of-the-Wasatch (272).

VERMONT

BURLINGTON—Trinity College of Burlington, Mansfield Ave. (337).

WASHINGTON

SEATTLE—Forest Ridge, Junior College of the Sacred Heart (115).

WISCONSIN

MADISON—Edgewood College of the Sacred Heart, 1000 Edgewood Ave.
(136).
MILWAUKEE—Mount Mary College, 90th & Burleigh Sts. (407).

HOSPITALS, INFIRMARIES, SANITARIUMS, SANATORIA, IN THE UNITED STATES CONDUCTED BY RELIGIOUS ORDERS OF WOMEN

The following names and addresses refer to hospitals, unless otherwise specified.

ALABAMA

BIRMINGHAM—St. Vincent's, 27th St. (79).
GADSDEN—Holy Name of Jesus (Missionary Servants of the Most Blessed Trinity).
MOBILE—Providence Infirmary (79).
——Alabama Maternity Hospital and Infant Home (79).
——City (79).
MONTGOMERY—St. Margaret's, Adams & Ripley Sts. (79).

ARIZONA

NOGALES—St. Joseph's (306).
PHOENIX—St. Joseph's, 4th & Polk Sts. (306).
PRESCOTT—Mercy (306).
TUCSON—St. Mary's Hospital and Sanatorium (204).

ARKANSAS

ELDORADO—Warner-Brown, 460 W. Oak St. (301).
FORT SMITH—St. Edward's Mercy (301).
HOT SPRINGS—St. Joseph's Infirmary (301).
JONESBORO—St. Bernard's (535).
LITTLE ROCK—St. Vincent's Infirmary, 10th & High Sts. (109).
MORRILTON—St. Anthony's (521).
TEXARKANA—Michael Meagher Memorial, 5th & Walnut Sts. (594).

CALIFORNIA

ARCATA—Trinity (246).
BAKERSFIELD—Mercy, Truxton Ave. & C St. (306).
BURBANK—Mother Cabrini Preventorium (681).
EUREKA—St. Joseph's (246).
FRESNO—St. Agnes (272).
HANFORD—Sacred Heart, 1025 Douty St. (159).
LONG BEACH—St. Mary's Long Beach (594).
LOS ANGELES—Queen of Angels', 2301 Bellevue Ave. (463).
——St. Vincent's, 2131 Ocean Beach Ave. (79).
MODESTO—St. Mary's, 17th & H Sts. (306).
OXNARD—St. John's (306).
OAKLAND—Providence, 30th & Webster Sts. (562).

ORANGE—St. Joseph's, 380 S. Batavia St. (246).
RED BLUFF—St. Elizabeth's (285).
SACRAMENTO—Mater Misericordiae, 40th & J Sts. (313).
SAN DIEGO—Mercy, Hillcrest Drive (306).
SAN FRANCISCO—St. Mary's, 2200 Hayes St. (306).
——St. Elizabeth's Infant Hospital, Van Ness Ave. & Filbert St. (79).
——St. Joseph's, Park Hill & Buena Vista Aves. (681).
——Mary's Help Hospital, 145 Guerrero St. (79).
SAN JOSÉ—O'Connor Sanitarium, Race & San Carlos Sts. (79).
SANTA BARBARA—St. Francis', E. Micheltorena St. (463).
STOCKTON—St. Joseph's, N. California St. (139).

COLORADO

COLORADO SPRINGS—St. Francis (460).
——Glockner Sanitarium and Hospital (86).
DEL NORTE—St. Joseph's Sanitarium (237).
DENVER—St. Anthony's, W. 16th Ave. & Quitman St. (460).
——St. Joseph's, 18th Ave. & Humboldt St. (504).
——The Mercy, 1619 Milwaukee St. (352).
DURANGO—Mercy (352).
GRAND JUNCTION—St. Mary's (504).
LEADVILLE—St. Vincent's (504).
PUEBLO—St. Mary's Hospital and Sanitarium (86).
STERLING—St. Benedict's (521).
TRINIDAD—Mt. San Raphael (86).

CONNECTICUT

BRIDGEPORT—St. Vincent's (79).
HARTFORD—St. Agnes', Steele Rd. (304).
——St. Francis', 370 Collins St. (236).
NEW HAVEN—Hospital of St. Raphael, 1442 Chapel St. (94).
WATERBURY—St. Mary's, 56 Franklin St. (236).
WILLIMANTIC—St. Joseph's, 88 Jackson St. (629).

DELAWARE

WILMINGTON—St. Francis', Clayton & 8th Sts. (418).

DISTRICT OF COLUMBIA

WASHINGTON—Georgetown University Hospital, 35th & N Sts., N. W.
    (418).
——Providence, D & E Sts., S. E. (79).
——St. Ann's Maternity, 2300 K St., N. W. (79).

FLORIDA

JACKSONVILLE—St. Vincent's (79).
MIAMI BEACH—Allison (425).
PENSACOLA—Pensacola (79).

GEORGIA

ATLANTA—St. Joseph's Infirmary, 294 Courtland St. (363).
SAVANNAH—St. Joseph's, Taylor & Habersham Sts. (363).

IDAHO

BOISE—St. Alphonsus', 412 State St. (272).
LEWISTON—St. Joseph's, 415 Sixth St. (204).
NAMPA—Mercy (368).
POCATELLO—St. Anthony's Mercy Hospital (368).
WALLACE—Providence, Canyon Ave. (562).
WENDELL—St. Valentine's (528).

ILLINOIS

ALTON—St. Anthony Infirmary and Sanitarium, 2120 Central Ave. (409).
——St. Joseph's, 5th St. & Central Ave. (79).
AURORA—St. Charles', N. 4th & Spring Sts. (463).
——St. Joseph's, 35 West Park Ave. (367).
——Mercyville Sanitarium, Lincoln Highway (367).
AVISTON—Sacred Heart (611).
BELLEVILLE—St. Elizabeth's, 328 W. Lincoln St. (458).
BELVIDERE—St. Joseph's (235).
BLOOMINGTON—St. Joseph's (496).
BLUE ISLAND—St. Francis, Gregory & York Sts. (444).
BREESE—St. Joseph's (272).
CAIRO—St. Mary's Infirmary (272).
CENTRALIA—St. Mary's, 207 N. Elm St. (611).
CHICAGO—St. Anne's, 4900 Thomas St. (611).
——St. Anthony de Padua, 2875 W. 19th St. at Marshall Blvd. (681).
——St. Bernard's Hotel Dieu, 6337 Harvard Ave. (722).
——Mother Cabrini Memorial, 1200 Gilpin Place (681).
——Columbus, 2548 Lake View Ave. (681).
——St. Elizabeth's, 1433 N. Claremont Ave. (611).
——St. Joseph's, 2100 Burling St. (79).
——Lewis Memorial Maternity, 3000 S. Michigan Ave.
——Little Company of Mary Hospital, 95th St. & California Ave. (713).
——St. Mary of Nazareth, 1120 N. Leavitt St. (667).
——Mercy, 2537 Prairie Ave. (296).
——Misericordia Hospital and Maternity Home, 2916 W. 47th St. (296).
——Municipal Isolation, 34th St. & Hamlin Ave. (611).
——John B. Murphy, 620 Belmont Ave. (296).
——Sheridan Park, 620 Belmont Ave. (296).
——St. Vincent's Maternity, 721 N. La Salle St. (79).
CHICAGO HEIGHTS—St. James', 1423 Chicago Rd. (460).
DANVILLE—St. Elizabeth's, 601 Green St. (463).
DECATUR—St. Mary's, 220 S. Webster St. (458).
DEKALB—St. Mary's (367).
EAST ST. LOUIS—St. Mary's, 810 Missouri Ave. (611).
EFFINGHAM—St. Anthony's, 812 W. Railroad Ave. (458).

ELGIN—St. Joseph's (463).
EVANSTON—St. Francis', 355 Ridge Ave. (460).
FREEPORT—St. Francis' (463).
GALESBURG—St. Mary's, Tompkins & Cherry Sts. (496).
GRANITE CITY—St. Elizabeth's, 21st & Iowa Sts. (644).
HIGHLAND—St. Joseph's (458).
JACKSONVILLE—Our Saviour's, 446 State St. (272).
JOLIET—St. Joseph's, 426 N. Broadway (463).
KANKAKEE—St. Mary's, 485 W. Merchant St. (685).
KEWANEE—St. Francis' (496).
LA SALLE—St. Mary's (463).
LINCOLN—St. Clara's (496).
LITCHFIELD—St. Francis', 706 S. State St. (458).
MACOMB—St. Francis' (496).
MURPHYSBORO—St. Andrew's, 6th & Mulberry Sts. (465).
OAK PARK—Oak Park, 525 Wisconsin Ave. (678).
PANA—Huber Memorial (678).
PEORIA—St. Francis', 616 Glen Oak Ave. (496).
PONTIAC—St. James' (496).
QUINCY—St. Mary's, 1420 Broadway (421).
RED BUD—St. Clement's (383).
ROCKFORD—St. Anthony's (436).
ROCK ISLAND—St. Anthony's (496).
SPRINGFIELD—St. John's, 8th & Mason Sts. (458).
——St. John's Sanitarium (458).
SPRING VALLEY—St. Margaret's (751).
STREATOR—St. Mary's, 615 S. Bloomington St. (496).
TAYLORVILLE—St. Vincent's, 423 S. Walnut St. (383).
URBANA—Mercy, Park Ave. & Wright St. (685).
WAUKEGAN—St. Theresa's, W. Washington St. (733).
WEDRON—St. Joseph's Health Resort, Sulphur Lick Springs (778).

INDIANA

ANDERSON—St. John's, Jackson & 20th Sts. (272).
BEECH GROVE—St. Francis' (460).
EAST CHICAGO—St. Catherine's, 4321 Fir St. (611).
ELWOOD—Mercy (239).
EVANSVILLE—St. Mary's, 1113 First Ave. (79).
FORT WAYNE—St. Joseph's, Main St. & Broadway (611).
GARRETT—Sacred Heart, 220 Ijam St. (463).
GARY—St. Mary's Mercy, 540 Tyler St. (611).
HAMMOND—Mt. Mercy Sanitarium, 1628 Ridge Rd. (285).
——St. Margaret's, 30 Clinton St. (460).
INDIANAPOLIS—St. Vincent's Infirmary, Fall Creek Blvd. (79).
KOKOMO—Good Samaritan, 509 E. Vaile Ave. (239).
LA FAYETTE—St. Elizabeth's, Hartford & 14th Sts. (460).
LAPORTE—Holy Family, 205 E St. (611).
LOGANSPORT—St. Joseph's, 26th & North Sts. (460).
MICHIGAN CITY—St. Anthony's, Wabash & Ann Sts. (460).
MISHAWAKA—St. Joseph's, 4th & Spring Sts. (611).

NEW ALBANY—St. Edward's (460).
ROME CITY—Kneipp Sanitarium (376).
SOUTH BEND—St. Joseph's, Madison St. & Notre Dame Ave. (272).
TERRE HAUTE—St. Anthony's, 1000 S. 6th St. (460).

IOWA

ANAMOSA—Mercy (351).
BURLINGTON—St. Francis' (496).
——Mercy (437).
CARROLL—St. Anthony's (413).
CEDAR RAPIDS—Mercy, 9th St. & 6th Ave. (351).
CENTERVILLE—St. Joseph's Mercy (361).
CLINTON—St. Joseph's Mercy (331).
COUNCIL BLUFFS—St. Bernard's (361).
——Mercy (361).
CRESCO—St. Joseph's Mercy (348).
DAVENPORT—Mercy, 2316 Marquette St. (331).
——St. Elizabeth's Sanitarium for Women (331).
——St. John's Sanitarium for Men (331).
DES MOINES—Mercy, 4th & Ascension Sts. (361).
DUBUQUE—St. Joseph's Mercy, James St. & Peabody Ave. (348).
——St. Joseph's Sanitarium (348).
FORT DODGE—St. Joseph's Mercy (348).
FORT MADISON—Sacred Heart (496).
GRINNELL—St. Francis' (437).
IOWA CITY—Mercy, 505 Bloomington St. (345).
——St. Joseph's Sanitarium (345).
KEOKUK—St. Joseph's, 14th & Exchange Sts. (496).
LEMARS—Sacred Heart (457).
MARSHALLTOWN—St. Thomas' Mercy (285).
MASON CITY—St. Joseph's Mercy, 84 Beaumont Drive (348).
NEW HAMPTON—St. Joseph's (733).
OELWEIN—Mercy (351).
OTTUMWA—St. Joseph's, 1600 N. Ash Ave. (592).
SIOUX CITY—St. Joseph's Mercy, 21st & Court Sts. (351).
——St. Vincent's, 624 Jones St. (521).
WATERLOO—St. Francis', 1407 Independence Ave. (465).
WAVERLY—St. Joseph's Mercy, 312 S. Orange St. (348).
WEBSTER CITY—St. Joseph's Mercy, Des Moines & Ohio Sts. (348).

KANSAS

CONCORDIA—St. Joseph's (235).
DODGE CITY—St. Anthony's, 1800 Central Ave. (237).
EMPORIA—St. Mary's, 122 Exchange St. (460).
FORT SCOTT—Mercy, 816 Burke St. (362).
GREAT BEND—St. Rose's, 3304 Broadway Ave. (157).
HAYS—St. Anthony's (567).
HUTCHINSON—St. Elizabeth's, 20th & Monroe Sts. (362).
INDEPENDENCE—Mercy, 816 Myrtle St. (362).

IOLA—St. John's (237).
KANSAS CITY—Providence, 18th & Tauromee Aves. (504).
——St. Margaret's, 8th & Vermont Aves. (421).
LEAVENWORTH—St. John's (504).
PARSONS—Mercy, E. Chess Ave. (362).
PITTSBURG—Mt. Carmel (237).
SABETHA—St. Anthony's Murdock Memorial (235).
SALINA—St. John's (235).
TOPEKA—St. Francis', 6th St. & Morris Ave. (504).
WICHITA—St. Francis', 928 N. Emporia Ave. (470).
——Wichita, 1102 W. Douglas (237).
WINFIELD—St. Mary's (237).

KENTUCKY

COVINGTON—St. Elizabeth's, 21st & Eastern Ave. (421).
LEXINGTON—St. Joseph's (109).
LOUISVILLE—St. Agnes' Sanitarium, 2016 Newburg Rd. (109).
——St. Anthony's, St. Anthony Place (460).
——St. Joseph's Infirmary, 735 Eastern Parkway (109).
——St. Mary and St. Elizabeth's, 1367 S. 12th St. (109).

LOUISIANA

BATON ROUGE—Our Lady of the Lake Sanitarium (497).
CARVILLE—National Leprosarium (79).
LAKE CHARLES—St. Patrick's Sanitarium, 8 Ryan St. (594).
MONROE—St. Francis' Sanitarium (497).
NEW ORLEANS—Charity, Tulane Ave. (79).
——Hotel Dieu, 2004 Tulane Ave. (79).
——Mercy, Leonce Soniat Memorial, 1321 Annunciation St. (332).
——St. Joseph's Maternity (79).
SHREVEPORT—Schumpert Memorial Sanitarium, Margaret Place (594).

MAINE

EAGLE LAKE—Northern Maine General (472).
HOULTON—Madigan Memorial (326).
LEWISTON—St. Mary's General, 318 Sabbatus St. (558).
PORTLAND—The Queen's, 218 State St. (326).
WATERVILLE—Sisters' Hospital (79).

MARYLAND

BALTIMORE—St. Agnes', Caton & Wilkens Aves. (79).
——Bon Secours, 2003 W. Fayette St. (659).
——Mercy, N. Calvert, Saratoga & Courtland Sts. (309).
——Mt. Hope, Retreat for the Insane and Sick (79).
——St. Joseph's, Caroline & Oliver Sts. (418).
CUMBERLAND—The Alleghany, 215 Decatur St. (79).

MASSACHUSETTS

ADAMS—Greylock Rest Sanitarium (621).
BOSTON—Carney, Old Harbor St., South Boston (79).
——St. Elizabeth's, 736 Cambridge St., Brighton (418).
CAMBRIDGE—Holy Ghost (for incurables), 1575 Cambridge St. (555).
FALL RIVER—St. Ann's (169).
HOLYOKE—Providence, 679 Dwight St. (621).
LAWRENCE—Protectory of Mary Immaculate (555).
LOWELL—St. John's, 14 Bartlett St. (79).
MONTAGUE CITY—Farren Memorial (621).
PITTSFIELD—St. Luke's, 185 East St. (621).
SPRINGFIELD—Mercy, 233 Carew St. (621).
——St. Mary's (Maternity) (621).
WORCESTER—St. Vincent's, 73 Vernon St. (621).

MICHIGAN

ANN ARBOR—St. Joseph's Mercy, 326 N. Ingalls St. (348).
BATTLE CREEK—Leila Y. Post Montgomery, North Ave. & Emmett St. (348).
BAY CITY—Mercy, 16th & Franklin Sts. (343).
CADILLAC—Mercy, Oak & Hobart Sts. (343).
DEARBORN—St. Joseph's Retreat (for mental and nervous cases) (79).
DETROIT—Providence, 2500 West Grand Blvd. (79).
——St. Joseph's Mercy, 2200 East Grand Blvd. (348).
——St. Mary's, 1420 St. Antoine St. (79).
DOWAGIAC—Lee Sanitarium (348).
ESCANABA—St. Francis' (496).
FLINT—St. Joseph's, 720 Ann Arbor St. (241).
GRAND RAPIDS—St. Mary's, Cherry & Lafayette Sts. (343).
GRAYLING—Mercy (343).
HAMTRAMCK—Hamtramck Municipal, 9850 Falcon St. (464).
HANCOCK—St. Joseph's (204).
JACKSON—Mercy, 530 Lansing Ave. (371).
KALAMAZOO—Borgess, 328 Portage St. (241).
——New Borgess, Gull Rd. (241).
LANSING—St. Lawrence, 1210 W. Saginaw St. (371).
MANISTEE—Mercy Hospital and Sanitarium (Mineral Baths), 13th & Vine Sts. (343).
MARQUETTE—St. Mary's (496).
MENOMINEE—St. Joseph's (496).
MONROE—Mercy (241).
MT. CLEMENS—St. Joseph's, 20 Parkview Ave. (86).
——St. Joseph's Sanitarium (Sulphur Springs), 215 North Ave. (86).
MUSKEGON—Mercy, 1521 Jefferson St. (343).
PONTIAC—St. Joseph Mercy (348).
SAGINAW—St. Mary's, 830 S. Jefferson Ave. (79).

MINNESOTA

BRAINERD—St. Joseph's, 523 N. Third St. (526).
BRECKENRIDGE—St. Francis' (473).

CROOKSTON—St. Vincent's (530).
DULUTH—St. Mary's, 5th Ave. E. & 3rd St. (526).
LITTLE FALLS—St. Gabriel's (473).
MANKATO—St. Joseph's and City (470).
MINNEAPOLIS—St. Mary's, 2500 Sixth St. (204).
MOORHEAD—St. Ansgar's (473).
NEW ULM—Loretto (611).
PERHAM—St. James' (473).
ROCHESTER—St. Mary's (464).
ST. CLOUD—St. Joseph's Sanatorium (511).
——St. Cloud (511).
ST. PAUL—St. Joseph's, Exchange & 9th Sts. (204).
WABASHA—St. Elizabeth's (470).

MISSOURI

BOONVILLE—St. Joseph's, E. Morgan St. (521).
CAPE GIRARDEAU—St. Francis', Good Hope & Pacific Sts. (465).
HANNIBAL—St. Elizabeth's, Broadway & Virginia St. (497).
JEFFERSON CITY—St. Mary's, 505 Bolivar St. (443).
JOPLIN—St. John's, 22nd St. & Connor Ave. (363).
KANSAS CITY—St. Joseph's, Linwood Blvd. & Prospect Ave. (235).
——St. Mary's, 2800 Main St. (443).
——St. Vincent's Maternity, 23rd St. & College Ave. (79).
MARYVILLE—St. Francis', 614 E. First St. (497).
NORMANDY—Mother of Good Counsel (for Incurables, and Convalescents'
    Sanitarium) (421).
ST. CHARLES—St. Joseph's, 218 S. Clay St. (443).
ST. JOSEPH—St. Joseph's, 923 Powell St. (79).
ST. LOUIS—St. Ann's Maternity, 5301 Page Blvd. (79).
——St. Anthony's, 3520 Chippewa St. (465).
——De Paul, Kingsway & Spalding Ave. (79).
——St. John's, 307 S. Euclid Ave. (311).
——St. Louis Mullanphy, 3225 Montgomery St. (79).
——St. Mary's Infirmary, 1536 Papin St. (443).
——St. Mary's, 6420 Clayton Rd. (443).
——Mt. St. Rose Sanatorium, 9101 S. Broadway (443).
——St. Vincent's Sanitarium (for nervous and mental cases) (79).
SEDALIA—St. Mary's, Broadway & Ohio Sts. (596).
SPRINGFIELD—St. John's, Main & Nicholas Sts. (363).
WASHINGTON—St. Francis' (458).

MONTANA

ANACONDA—St. Ann's (504).
BILLINGS—St. Vincent's (504).
——St. Vincent's Orthopedic (504).
BUTTE—St. James, S. Idaho Ave. & W. Silver St. (504).
CONRAD—St. Mary's (128).
DEER LODGE—St. Joseph's (504).

FORT BENTON—St. Clare's (562).
GREAT FALLS—Columbus (562).
——St. Elizabeth's Maternity (562).
HAVRE—Sacred Heart (454).
HELENA—St. John's (504).
KALISPELL—Kalispell General, 723 Fifth Ave. (351).
LEWISTOWN—St. Joseph's (747).
MILES CITY—Presentation Nuns (548).
MISSOULA—St. Patrick's (562).
POLSON—Hotel Dieu (722).
ST. IGNATIUS—Holy Family (562).

NEBRASKA

ALLIANCE—St. Joseph's (454).
COLUMBUS—St. Mary's (460).
GRAND ISLAND—St. Francis' (460).
KEARNEY—Good Samaritan (460).
LINCOLN—St. Elizabeth's (460).
LYNCH—Sacred Heart (519).
McCOOK—St. Catherine of Sienna (129).
NEBRASKA CITY—St. Mary's (497).
OMAHA—St. Catherine's, 811 Forest Ave. (324).
——St. Joseph's Creighton Memorial, 10th & Castellar Sts. (460).
WEST POINT—St. Joseph's (440).

NEVADA

RENO—St. Mary's, W. 6th St. (139).

NEW HAMPSHIRE

BERLIN—St. Louis' (558).
MANCHESTER—Our Lady of Lourdes (555).
——Our Lady of Perpetual Help (Maternity), 292 Concord St. (318).
——Sacred Heart (318).
NASHUA—St. Joseph's (555).

NEW JERSEY

DENVILLE—St. Francis' Health Resort (470).
ELIZABETH—St. Elizabeth's, 204 S. Broad St. (94).
HOBOKEN—St. Mary's, 4th St. & Willow Ave. (421).
JERSEY CITY—St. Francis, 25 East Hamilton Place (421).
MONTCLAIR—St. Vincent's (Infants'), 45 Elm St. (94).
MORRISTOWN—All Saints', Mt. Kemble Ave. (94).
NEW BRUNSWICK—St. Peter's General (555).
NEWARK—St. James', Elm St. (469).
——St. Michael's, High St. & Central Ave. (421).
ORANGE—St. Mary's, 135 South Centre St. (469).

PASSAIC—St. Mary's, 211 Pennington Ave. (94).
PATERSON—St. Joseph's, 703 Main St. (94).
RIDGEWOOD—Divine Providence (for incurables), (94).
TEANECK—Holy Name (663).
TRENTON—St. Joseph's, Hamilton Ave. & Chambers St. (418).

NEW MEXICO

ALBUQUERQUE—St. Joseph's Hospital and Sanatorium (86).
CARLSBAD—St. Francis' (375).
CLAYTON—St. Joseph of Nazareth (667).
DEMING—Holy Cross Sanatorium, Mahoney Park (272).
GALLUP—St. Mary's (460).
LAS VEGAS—St. Anthony's Hospital and Sanitarium (86).
ROSWELL—St. Mary's (470).
SANTA FÉ—St. Vincent's Sanitarium and Hospital (86).

NEW YORK

ALBANY—St. Peter's, 879 Broadway (322).
——Maternity, 30 N. Main Ave. (80).
AMSTERDAM—St. Mary's, 427 Guy Park Ave. (204).
AUBURN—Mercy (427).
BATAVIA—St. Jerome's General, 16 Bank St. (319).
BINGHAMPTON—Lourdes, 169 Riverside Drive (79).
BROOKLYN—Holy Family, 151-155 Dean St. (80).
——St. Catherine's, 133 Bushwick Ave. (140).
——St. Cecilia's Maternity, 484 Humboldt St. (140).
——St. Charles' Reception Hospital (Crippled Children), 277 Hicks St. (748).
——St. Mary's, 1298 St. Mark's Ave. (80).
——St. Peter's, Henry St. (421).
BUFFALO—Buffalo Hospital of the Sisters of Charity, 1833 Main St. (79).
——Emergency General, Pine & Eagle Sts (79).
——Mercy General, Abbott Rd. & Choate Ave. (319).
——Providence Retreat, 2157 Main St. (79).
——St. Mary's Maternity, 126 Edward St. (79).
COLD SPRING—Loretto Convalescent Home for Women (432).
ELMIRA—St. Joseph's, 555 E. Market St. (227).
FAR ROCKAWAY, L. I.—St. Joseph's, 327 Broadway (225).
GABRIELS—Sanatorium Gabriels-in-the-Adirondacks (for incipient consumption), (329).
HARRISON—St. Vincent's Retreat (for mental and nervous diseases of women), North St. (80).
HAWTHORNE—Rosary Hill Home (Cancer Hospital), (165).
HEMPSTEAD, L. I.—Mercy, Oceanside Ave. (763).
HORNELL—St. James' Mercy (313).
JAMAICA, L. I.—Mary Immaculate, 89th Ave. & 153rd St. (140).
KINGSTON—Our Lady of Victory, Mary's Avenue (516).
LACKAWANNA—Our Lady of Victory (Women's and Children's), Ridge Rd. (220).

Long Island City—St. John's, 12th St. & Jackson Ave. (225).
Nanuet—St. Agatha Preventorium (for children), (80).
New York City—Columbus (General), 226 E. 20th St. (681).
——Columbus (Extension), 457 W. 163rd St. (681).
——French, 450 W. 34th St. (851).
——House of Calvary (incurables), Featherbed Lane & McComb's Dam Rd., Bronx (162).
——Misericordia (General and Maternity), 523-539 E. 86th St. (678).
——New York Foundling, 175 E. 68th St. (80).
——St. Ann's Maternity, 130 E. 69th St. (80).
——St. Elizabeth of Hungary (for women), Ft. Washington Ave. & 190th St. (409).
——St. Francis' (General), Brook Ave. & E. 142nd St., Bronx (421).
——St. Francis' (for incurables), 605-617 E. 5th St. (421).
——St. John's (Infants'), 175 E. 68th St. (80).
——St. Joseph's (for consumptives), Brook Ave. & E. 143rd St., Bronx (421).
——St. Rose's Free Home for Incurable Cancer, 71 Jackson St. (165).
——St. Vincent's Hospital of the City of New York, 11th & 12th Sts. & 7th Ave. (80).
——St. Vincent's Hospital of the Borough of Richmond (General and Maternity), Bard & Castleton Aves., W. New Brighton, Staten Island, N. Y. (80).
——Seton (Tuberculosis Hospital for Men), Spuyten Duyvil Parkway (80).
——Seton Nazareth Branch (Tuberculosis Hospital for Women and Children), Spuyten Duyvil Parkway (80).
Niagara Falls—Mt. St. Mary's, Ferry Ave. & 6th St. (409).
Ogdensburg—A. Barton Hepburn (560).
——St. John of God (City Quarantine), (560).
Plattsburg—Champlain Valley (560).
Port Jefferson, L. I.—Brooklyn Hospital for Crippled Children (748).
Port Jervis—St. Francis', 160 E. Main St. (409).
Poughkeepsie—St. Francis', Hill Crest Park (409).
Rochester—St. Mary's 909 W. Main St. (79).
St. Joseph's—St. Joseph's Sanatorium (128).
Saranac Lake—St. Mary's of the Lake (339).
Spring Valley—St. Elizabeth's (Convalescents' Hospital), (80).
Suffern—Good Samaritan (80).
Syracuse—St. Joseph's, 301 Prospect Ave. (427).
——St. Mary's (Maternity), 1601 Court St. (79).
Troy—St. Joseph's (Maternity), 4th & Jackson Sts. (204).
——Troy (79).
Tupper Lake—Mercy General (339).
Utica—St. Elizabeth's, 2209 Genesee St. (427).
Watertown—Mercy, 218 Stone St. (339).
White Plains—St. Agnes' (General and for Crippled Children), North St. (409).
Woodhaven, L. I.—St. Anthony's, Woodhaven Blvd. & Fulton St. (421).
Yonkers—St. Joseph's, 127 S. Broadway (80).

NORTH CAROLINA

ASHEVILLE—St. Joseph's Sanatorium, 428 Biltmore Ave. (285).
CHARLOTTE—Mercy (285).
GREENSBORO—St. Leo's (79).

NORTH DAKOTA

BISMARCK—St. Alexius (529).
BOTTINEAU—St. Andrew's (751).
DEVILS LAKE—Mercy (357).
DICKINSON—St. Joseph's (806).
FARGO—St. John's (204).
GRAND FORKS—St. Michael's (204).
JAMESTOWN—Holy Trinity (204).
MINOT—St. Joseph's (454).
VALLEY CITY—Mercy (357).
WILLISTON—Mercy (357).

OHIO

AKRON—St. Thomas', 444 N. Main St. (500).
CANTON—Mercy, 731 Market Ave. (500).
——Little Flower (for children), (500).
CINCINNATI—Good Samaritan, Clifton & Dixmyth Aves. (86).
——St. Francis' (for incurables), Queen City Ave. (421).
——St. Mary's, Linn & Betts Sts. (421).
——St. Joseph's Maternity, Tennessee Ave. & Reading Rd. (86).
CLEVELAND—St. Alexis', 5163 Broadway (460).
——St. Ann's Maternity, 3409 Woodland Ave. (500).
——St. John's, 7911 Detroit Ave. (500).
——St. Vincent's Charity, E. 22nd St. & Central Ave. (500).
COLUMBUS—Mt. Carmel, State & Davis Sts. (272).
——St. Ann's Maternity, 1555 Bryden Rd. (454).
——St. Anthony's, Hawthorne & Taylor Aves. (421).
——St. Francis', State & 6th Sts. (421).
DAYTON—St. Elizabeth's, 135 Hopeland Ave. (421).
HAMILTON—Mercy, 116 Dayton St. (315).
KENTON—San Antonio, North & Wayne Aves. (86).
LIMA—St. Rita's, High & Baxter Sts. (369).
LORAIN—St. Joseph's, Broadway & 20th Sts. (590).
MT. VERNON—Mercy (Hinde-Ball), (109).
PORTSMOUTH—Mercy, 1248 Kinney's Lane (464).
SANDUSKY—Providence, 1912 Hayes Ave. (464).
TIFFIN—Mercy (369).
TOLEDO—Mercy, 2219 Madison Ave. (369).
——St. Vincent's, 2213 Cherry St. (555).
WARREN—St. Joseph's Riverside (590).
YOUNGSTOWN—St. Elizabeth's, 1026 Belmont Ave. (590).
ZANESVILLE—Good Samaritan, Ashland & Laurel Aves. (440).

OKLAHOMA

MCALESTER—St. Mary's Infirmary, 7th & Creek Sts. (596).
OKLAHOMA CITY—St. Anthony's, 601 W. 9th St. (497).
PONCA CITY—Ponca City (237).
TULSA—St. John's, 1923 S. Utica St. (470).

OREGON

ASTORIA—St. Mary's (562).
BAKER—St. Elizabeth's (418).
BEND—St. Charles' (240).
MEDFORD—Sacred Heart, Medford Heights (562).
NORTH BEND—Mercy (366).
ONTARIO—Holy Rosary (159).
PENDLETON—St. Anthony's (418).
PORTLAND—St. Vincent's, 25th & Hoyt Sts. (562).
ROSEBURG—Mercy (366).

PENNSYLVANIA

ALLENTOWN—Sacred Heart, 6th & Turner Sts. (681).
BEAVER FALLS—Providence, 3rd Ave. & 9th St. (98).
CARBONDALE—St. Joseph's (394).
DARBY—St. Francis' (for convalescent women and girls), (659).
DUBOIS—Dubois, S. Main St. (335).
ERIE—St. Vincent's, 24th & Sassafras Sts. (226).
JOHNSTOWN—Mercy, 1020 Franklin St. (350).
LANCASTER—St. Joseph's (418).
NEW CASTLE—New Castle, S. Mercer & Phillips Sts. (439).
PERRYSVILLE—Incurables (741).
PHILADELPHIA—Columbus, 1307 S. Broad St. (681).
——Misericordia, 54th St. & Cedar Ave. (321).
——St. Agnes', 1900 S. Broad St. (418).
——St. Joseph's, Girard Ave. (79).
——St. Mary's, 1567 Palmer St. (418).
——St. Vincent's (for women and children), 70th St. & Woodland Ave. (79).
PITTSBURGH—Mercy, Pride & Locust Sts. (289).
——Pittsburgh, Frankstown Ave. & Washington Blvd. (98).
——Roselia Maternity, Cliff & Manilla Sts. (98).
——St. Francis', 45th St., Arsenal Station (439).
——St. John's (General), 3339 McClure Ave., N. S. (644).
——St. Joseph's, 2117 Carson St. (239).
POTTSVILLE—Good Samaritan (681).
READING—St. Joseph's, 12th & Walnut Sts. (418).
SCRANTON—Mercy, 746 Jefferson Ave. (345).
——St. Joseph's (Children's and Maternity), 2010 Adams Ave. (394).
——St. Mary's Keller Memorial, 916 Hickory St. (409).
WILKES-BARRE—Mercy, 196 Hanover St. (345).

RHODE ISLAND

HILLSGROVE—St. Francis' (Tuberculosis), (418).
PROVIDENCE—St. Joseph's, Broad & Peace Sts. (418).

SOUTH CAROLINA

CHARLESTON—St. Francis Xavier Infirmary, 264 Calhoun St. (183).

SOUTH DAKOTA

ABERDEEN—St. Luke's (548).
DEADWOOD—St. Joseph's (525).
HOT SPRINGS—Our Lady of Lourdes (525).
MILBANK—St. Bernard's Providence (854).
MITCHELL—St. Joseph's (548).
PIERRE—St. Mary's (519).
RAPID CITY—St. John's (525).
SIOUX FALLS—McKennan (548).
YANKTON—Sacred Heart (519).

TENNESSEE

KNOXVILLE—St. Mary's (328).
——Villa Marie (for convalescents), Central Ave. (328).
MEMPHIS—St. Joseph's, Jackson Ave. (460).
NASHVILLE—St. Thomas' Hospital and Sanitarium, 20th Ave. & Hayes St. (79).

TEXAS

AMARILLO—St. Anthony's (596).
AUSTIN—Seton Infirmary, 26th & Rio Grande Sts. (79).
BEAUMONT—Hotel Dieu (594).
BOERNE—St. Mary's Sanatorium (596).
BROWNSVILLE—Mercy (364).
CORPUS CHRISTI—Spohn Sanitarium, Third St. (596).
DALHART—Loretto (667).
DALLAS—St. Paul's (79).
EL PASO—Hotel Dieu, 1014 Stanton St. (79).
——St. Joseph's Sanatorium, 1901 Grandview Ave. (235).
FORT WORTH—St. Joseph's Infirmary (596).
GALVESTON—St. Mary's Infirmary (594).
HALLETTSVILLE—Renger (541).
HOUSTON—St. Joseph's Infirmary, 1910 Crawford St. (594).
LAREDO—Mercy (364).
MARSHALL—Texas-Pacific (596).
PARIS—St. Joseph's Infirmary (596).
PORT ARTHUR—Gates Memorial (594).
SAN ANGELO—St. John's Sanitarium (596).

Supplement   895

SAN ANTONIO—Santa Rosa Infirmary, 745 W. Houston St. (596).
SHERMAN—St. Vincent's Sanitarium (79).
SLAYTON—Mercy (365).
TEMPLE—Santa Fé (594).
WACO—Providence Sanitarium (79).

UTAH

SALT LAKE CITY—Holy Cross, 1045 E. First St. (272).

VERMONT

BURLINGTON—Bishop De Goesbriand, Pearl & S. Prospect Sts. (722).
ST. JOHNSBURY—St. Johnsbury (562).
WINOOSKI—Fanny Allen, Winooski Park (722).

VIRGINIA

NORFOLK—St. Vincent's Hospital and Sanitarium, Wood & Church Sts. (79).

WEST VIRGINIA

BUCKHANNON—St. Joseph's, 94 W. Main St. (812).
CHARLESTON—St. Francis', 333 Laidley St. (219).
CLARKSBURG—St. Mary's, 464 Washington Ave. (219).
HUNTINGTON—St. Mary's, First Ave. & 29th St. (812).
PARKERSBURG—St. Joseph's, Fifth & Avery Sts. (219).
RICHWOOD—Sacred Heart, 4 Maple St. (812).
WHEELING—Wheeling, 109 Main St. (219).

WASHINGTON

ABERDEEN—St. Joseph's, G & Fifth Sts. (162).
BELLINGHAM—St. Joseph's (663).
CHEHALIS—St. Helen's (162).
CHEWELAH—St. Joseph's (162).
COLFAX—St. Ignatius' (562).
EVERETT—Providence (562).
OLYMPIA—St. Peter's, 420 Mills St. (562).
PASCO—Our Lady of Lourdes', Fourth & Park Sts. (204).
PORT TOWNSEND—St. John's (562).
SEATTLE—Columbus, 1019 Madison St. (681).
——Providence, 17th Ave. & E. Jefferson St. (562).
SPOKANE—Sacred Heart, 8th & Brown Aves. (562).
TACOMA—St. Joseph's (418).
VANCOUVER—St. Joseph's (562).
WALLA WALLA—St. Mary's (562).
WENATCHEE—St. Anthony's (663).
YAKIMA—St. Elizabeth's (562).

WISCONSIN

APPLETON—St. Elizabeth's, 1506 S. Oneida St. (465).
ASHLAND—St. Joseph's (611).
BARABOO—St. Mary's Ringling Memorial (443).
CHIPPEWA FALLS—St. Joseph's, Pearl & Spruce Sts. (458).
COLUMBUS—St. Mary's (726).
DODGEVILLE—St. Joseph's (473).
EAU CLAIRE—Sacred Heart of Jesus, Dewey St. (458).
FOND DU LAC—St. Agnes', 390 E. Division St. (567).
GREEN BAY—St. Mary's, 403-411 S. Webster Ave. (678).
——St. Vincent's, 840 S. Webster Ave. (458).
HARTFORD—St. Joseph's (722).
JANESVILLE—Palmer Memorial Mercy, 566 N. Washington St. (336).
KENOSHA—St. Catherine's Memorial (159).
LA CROSSE—St. Francis', 1020 Market St. (413).
LADYSMITH—St. Mary's (719).
MADISON—St. Mary's, 720 S. Brooks St. (443).
MANITOWOC—Holy Family, Western Ave. & 24th St. (440).
MARSHFIELD—St. Joseph's (470).
MERRILL—Holy Cross, Park & Riverside Aves. (806).
MILWAUKEE—Marquette University, 200 Ninth St. (473).
——Misericordia, 2224 Juneau Ave. (678).
——Sacred Heart Sanitarium, 575 Layton Blvd. (450).
——St. Mary's Hill Sanitarium, 545 27th Ave. (450).
——St. Mary's, North Ave. at Lake Drive (79).
——St. Joseph's, Reservoir Ave. & Fourth St. (465).
——St. Vincent's Maternity, 483 Greenfield Ave. (678).
OSHKOSH—Mercy, 185 Hazel St. (470).
——St. Mary's, Boyd St. (470).
PORTAGE—St. Saviour's (726).
RACINE—St. Mary's, 1526 Grand Ave. (465).
RHINELANDER—St. Mary's (470).
RICE LAKE—St. Joseph's (409).
SHEBOYGAN—St. Nicholas', 1430 N. Ninth St. (458).
SPARTA—St. Mary's, Main & K Sts. (413).
STEVENS POINT—St. Michael's, 313 N. Fremont St. (470).
SUPERIOR—Good Samaritan, 1926 Iowa Ave. (223).
——St. Francis' (460).
——St. Mary's, Clough & Broadway (611).
TOMAHAWK—Sacred Heart (470).
WATERTOWN—St. Mary's, 1301 Main St. (733).
WAUSAU—St. Mary's, Maple Hill (726).

HOSPICES AND BOARDING HOMES IN THE UNITED STATES CONDUCTED BY RELIGIOUS ORDERS OF WOMEN

ARKANSAS

HOT SPRINGS—St. John's Hospice, 591 W. Grand Ave. (536).

CALIFORNIA

SAN FRANCISCO—St. Francis Home for Working Girls, Central Ave. & Waller St. (409).

COLORADO

DENVER—St. Rose's Home, 952 Tenth St. For Girls and Business Women (409).

CONNECTICUT

HARTFORD—St. Elizabeth's Home, 118 Main St. For Self-Supporting Girls (743).
NEW HAVEN—St. Joseph's, 311 Greene St. Home for Working Girls (743).

DISTRICT OF COLUMBIA

WASHINGTON—St. Catherine's Home for Self-Supporting Girls, 101 North Carolina Ave., S. E. (285).

ILLINOIS

CHICAGO—The Cenacle, 513 Fullerton Parkway. House for Retreatants (709).
——Guardian Angel Home for Girls, 4600 Gross Ave. (476).
——House of Providence, 1121 Orleans St. For Women with or without Employment (409).
——Mercy Girls' Business Club, 2834 S. Wabash Ave. (296).
——Our Lady of Perpetual Help, 1444 W. Division St. (667).
——Resurrection Home for Girls, 1849 N. Hermitage Ave. (732).
PEORIA—St. Mark's Hall for Young Women, Bradley Ave. & Underhill St. (496).
QUINCY—St. Joseph's Home for Working Girls, 1315 N. 8th St. (421).
SPRINGFIELD—The Rita Club for Business Women, 7th & Cass Sts. (474).

IOWA

COUNCIL BLUFFS—St. Mary's Home, 225 Harmony St. For Nurses and Working Women (361).
DAVENPORT—St. Mary's Home, 1334 W. 8th St. For Working Girls (331).

DES MOINES—St. Catherine's Hall, 17th St. & Grand Ave. For Working
Women (361).
DUBUQUE—Mary of the Angels Home, 605 Bluff St. For Women and
Girls (457).
——Our Lady of Lourdes Home, 75 W. 17th St. For Employed Women
(457).

KENTUCKY

LOUISVILLE—Visitation Home, 957 Fourth Ave. For Working Girls (334).
——Sacred Heart Home, 218 E. College St. (334).
NEWPORT—Mt. St. Martin Young Women's Institute (601).

MARYLAND

BALTIMORE—Kirkleigh Villa, Roland Park. Guest House for Women (79).
——Catholic Ladies' Home, 616 Park Ave. (599).

MASSACHUSETTS

ADAMS—Greylock Rest (621).
BOSTON—St. Helena's House, 89 Union Park St. For Working Girls (555).
——St. Clement's House for Women, 61 W. Brookline St. (233).
——The Cenacle, 196 Lake St., Brighton. House for Retreatants (709).
FALL RIVER—St. Francis Guild, 182 Whipple St. Home for Working Girls
(483).
FRAMINGHAM—Archbishop Williams' Memorial, Bethany Rd. Rest House
for Women (233).
LOWELL—St. Joseph's Home, 213 Pawtucket St. (555).
——St. Patrick's Home, 15 Cross St. For Working Girls (425).
LYNN—St. Theresa's House for Working Girls, 32 City Hall Square (109).
NEWBURYPORT—St. Theresa's Home for Working Girls, 52 Lime St. (852).
SPRINGFIELD—St. Luke's Home for Working Girls, 85 Spring St. (621).
WORCESTER—St. Joseph's Home for Working Girls, 52 High St. (325).

MICHIGAN

DETROIT—Mount Mary, 17330 Quincy Ave. House for Retreatants (709).
SAGINAW—The Thomas and Marie "Merrill Home" for Working Girls, 1209
S. Michigan Ave. (151).

MISSOURI

KANSAS CITY—St. Catherine's Home for Catholic Working Girls, 11th St. &
Forest Ave. (363).
ST. LOUIS—Sisters of Mercy Home for Business Girls and Women, 2228
Locust St. (311).
——St. Mary's House for Women Retreatants, University City (443).

MONTANA

GREAT FALLS—St. Mary's Home for Working Girls.

NEBRASKA

OMAHA—Home for Young Women, 1908 Davenport St. (324).
——St. Rita's Home, 18th & Cass Sts. (324).

NEW HAMPSHIRE

HOOKSETT—Mt. St. Mary's Rest House for Women (318).
MANCHESTER—House of St. Martha (318).

NEW JERSEY

ATLANTIC CITY—Rita Mercy Hall, 210 Grammercy Place. Guest House for Ladies (285).
BLOOMFIELD—Sacred Heart Young Women's Catholic Association—Home for Girls (94).
CALDWELL—Villa of the Sacred Heart. Rest House for Ladies (146).
HOHOKUS—The Marie Claire, St. Joseph's Villa. Rest House for Ladies (663).
JERSEY CITY—St. Mary's Residence for Business Girls, Grand & Washington Sts. (663).
NEWARK—Loretto Hall. Residence for Business Girls, 175 Broadway (663).
PATERSON—St. Francis' Home for Working Girls, 25 Jackson St. (94).
POINT PLEASANT—St. Joseph's-by-the-Sea. Vacation House for Business Women, and Convalescents' Home (162).
RIDGEWOOD—Mt. St. Andrew Villa. Rest House (94).

NEW YORK

ALBANY—Dominican Home for Women, 886 Madison Ave. (162).
BUFFALO—*Casa Misericordia,* 303 North St. Home for Working Girls (319).
——St. Felix Home for Polish Working Girls, 792 Fillmore Ave. (448).
——St. Martha's Home for Women and Working Girls, 765 Washington St. (409).
——St. Mary's Home for Working Girls, 125 Edward St. (220).
CATSKILL—Villa St. Joseph, Prospect Ave. (409).
COLD SPRING—Loretto Rest and Convalescent Home (432).
GARRISON—Our Lady's Hostel. Graymoor Pilgrim House (485).
LAKE RONKONKOMA—The Cenacle. For Retreatants ('709).
MAMARONECK—St. John's Convalescent Home (80).
OSSINING—Bethany House, Maryknoll. Rest House for Women (173).
NEW YORK CITY—Assisium Institute, 13 W. 128th St. Boarding Home for Students and Business Girls (432).
——Belgian Bureau—House of the Holy Family, 431 W. 47th St. For Immigrant Girls and Women from Holland and Belgium (823).
——*Casa Maria,* 251 W. 14th St. Boarding Home for Spanish Girls (815).
——Catholic Center for the Blind, 221 E. 79th St. Boarding Home for Blind Working Girls (162).
——Cenacle of St. Regis, 628 W. 140th St. House for Retreatants (709).
——Convent of Jesus and Mary, 3135 Kingsbridge Ave. Ladies' Residence (652).

——Devin Clare Residence, 415 W. 120th St. Residence for Self-Supporting Girls (293).
——Jeanne d'Arc Home, 253 W. 24th St. Boarding Home for French Girls (601).
——The Leo House, 332 W. 23rd St. (567).
——Our Lady's Institute, 4691 Park Ave. Boarding Home for Business Girls (673).
——Our Lady of Peace Home, 225 W. 14th St. Residence for Self-Supporting Ladies and Girls (652).
——Regina Angelorum Working Girls Home, 112-118 E. 106th St. (293).
——St. Dominic's Guild for Business Girls & Residence for Retreatants, 203-207 E. 71st St. (162).
——St. Elizabeth's House. Home for Working Girls (German), 421 E. 148th St. (508).
——St. Elizabeth's Residence Home for Business Girls, 415 W. 51st St. (409).
——St. Joseph's Home, 425 W. 44th St. Home for Polish Girls and Women.
——St. Joseph's Residence for Business Girls, 47 E. 81st St. (293).
——St. Joseph's Patronage for Working Girls, 523 W. 142nd St. (448).
——St. Margaret's Residence for Self-Supporting Young Girls, 213 Alexander Ave. (432).
——St. Mary's Home, 231 E. 72nd St. Boarding Home for Working Girls (813).
——St. Raphael's, 332 W. 23rd St. For German and other Immigrants (567).
——St. Zita's Home, 143 W. 14th St. Free Home for Friendless Women in the City of New York (749).
——Susan Devin Residence, 2916 Grand Concourse. Residence for Self-Supporting Women (293).
NIAGARA FALLS—*Casa Maria,* Guest House for Ladies, 237 Fourth St. (319).
SARATOGA—Our Lady Star of the Sea, Home for Convalescents and Retreatants, 36 White St. (162).
SPRING VALLEY—St. Elizabeth's Convalescent Home (293).
TROY—Seton Home for Working Girls, 548 River St. (80).
TUCKAHOE—St. Eleanora's Home. For Convalescents (80).

OHIO

CAREY—Pilgrims' Hospice (442).
CINCINNATI—The Fontbonne, 425 E. Fifth St. For Business Women and Girls (223).
——Mt. Carmel Home, 1413 Freeman Ave. For Working Girls and Women (316).
CLEVELAND—Catholic Young Women's Hall, 1736 Superior Ave. (631).
——Madonna Hall, 1906 E. 82nd St. For Business Women and Girls (499).
COLUMBUS—St. Rita's Retreat, 1415 Broad St. For Working Girls (454).
DAYTON—Loretto Guild Home, 217 N. Ludlow St. For Business Women (162).
FRANK—Pilgrim House (375).
LOUISVILLE—St. Joseph's Hospice. Boarding Home for the Aged (852).
NORMAN—Newman Hall, 707 W. Boyd St. (599).

OREGON

PORTLAND—The Jeanne d'Arc. For Girls Employed and Out of Employment (366).

PENNSYLVANIA

ALLENTOWN—Sacred Heart Home. For Non-Dependent Aged Women (778).

ALTOONA—*Casa Regina*, Sodality House (393).

ERIE—Our Lady of Peace House, 244 E. 10th St. For Self-Supporting Girls and Women (335).

FENELTON—Our Lady of the Woods Convalescent Home (439).

HARRISBURG—Mercy Home. Boarding Home for Working Girls (285).

MANTZVILLE—St. Michael's Home. Boarding Home for the Aged (418).

NORRISTOWN—St. Joseph's Boarding Home for Aged Women (280).

PHILADELPHIA—Dominican House of Retreats and Catholic Guild, 1812-1814 Green St. (162).

——Maryville House, Chew St. & Church Lane, Boarding Home for the Aged (280).

——St. Ann's Widows' Home, 212-214 Franklin St. (216).

——St. John's Alliance House, 336 S. 13th St. For Working Girls and Business Women (216).

——St. Joseph's House for Working Girls, 2114 N. Hancock St. (409).

——St. Mary's House, 1624-30 N. Broad St. For Business Women and Girls (285).

——St. Regis House for Business Women, 822-824 Pine St. (285).

PITTSBURGH—St. Ann's Temporary Home for Women, 28 Fernando St. (687).

——St. Mary's Home for Working Girls, 13 Tunnel St. (289).

SCRANTON—St. Joseph's Shelter, 317 Linden St. Temporary Home for Friendless Women (393).

RHODE ISLAND

NEWPORT—The Cenacle, Battery St. House for Retreatants (709).

——Stella Maris Home for Convalescents, 91 Washington St. (743).

PROVIDENCE—Institute of the Sisters of St. Dorothy, 457 Benefit St. (802).

——St. Maria's Home for Working Girls, 125 Governor St. (409).

——St. Margaret's Home for Working Girls, 211 Friendship St. (409).

TEXAS

AUSTIN—Newman Hall. Catholic Home for Young Women. 21st & Guadalupe Sts. (155).

KINGSVILLE—Misericordia Hall. Home for Students (285).

VERMONT

BURLINGTON—St. Joseph's Villa, Colchester Ave. (337).

VIRGINIA

BRISTOW—Linton Hall Guest House (518).

WASHINGTON

SEATTLE—St. Teresa's Club, 906 Terry Ave.   Residence for Business Girls
(663).

WISCONSIN

MILWAUKEE—Calaroga, 431 Galena St.   Boarding Home for Young Ladies
(128).

——St. Catherine's Home, 1131 Michigan St.   Boarding Home for Young
Ladies (359).

——St. Clara's Home for Working Girls, 705 National Ave. (359).

GLOSSARY

With Some Special Explanations

From the Catholic Encyclopedia and authentically supplied material

ABBESS—Superior of a monastic community of twelve or more nuns. Associated with the Benedictines and Poor Clares.

ACTIVE—Applied to communities which do active work—educational, hospital, etc., and are not cloistered.

ARCHIEPISCOPACY—Administration of an archbishop.

ARCHIEPISCOPAL—Referring to an archbishop.

BANDEAU—See *Habit.*

BARBETTE—See *Habit.*

BURSAR—One who fills the office of treasurer in a religious community.

CANONESSES—Congregations of women, similar to Canons, professing the common life, and observing a modified religious rule, often that of St. Augustine.

CANON LAW—Assembled statutes and rulings enacted by the highest Church authorities with regard to ecclesiastical affairs.

CARDINAL PROTECTOR—Cardinal entrusted with the interests of a given religious community, and appointed the representative of its causes.

CHOIR—Coming together of religious in the chapel for the recitation of the Office.

CHOIR NUN—See *Sister.*

COADJUTRIX SISTER—See *Sister.*

CINCTURE—See *Habit.*

CLOISTER—Enclosed part of convent, also known as enclosure, of a contemplative or cloistered order.

CLOISTERED—Properly applied only to contemplative orders which observe a strict cloister, beyond which the cloistered nuns do not go, and to which adult visitors are not admitted, except in cases of necessity.

CLOTHING—Ceremony, called also investiture, at which the religious habit is conferred on the candidate who has completed her postulancy.

COIF—See *Habit.*

COLLARIUM—See *Habit.*

COMMUNITY—Properly limited, meaning the group of religious persons of the same sex in a particular convent. Broadly used to signify a religious order, congregation, etc.*

CONGREGATION—Properly a religious community with all the essentials of religious life, the three perpetual vows and ecclesiastical approbation, but without the solemn vows which characterize an order. In a wider sense an institute which has not perpetual vows is called a congregation.

CONTEMPLATIVE—Applied to cloistered communities whose members devote themselves to a life of contemplation, or prayer and penance. The life of the contemplative nun is a definite calling and not inactive. In addition to spiritual exercises, the guidance of souls through helpful counsels, the

*In this work the word *community* carries a limited meaning, and *Community* a broad meaning.

903

making of the finest ecclesiastical vestments, altar linens and articles of devotion, the preparation of altar breads and the chaining of rosaries, as well as various manual labors, occupy the time of cloistered religious, and are fittingly done in the spirit of the contemplative life.

CONVENT—Fixed dwelling of a religious community.

CONVENTUALS—Designation, since 1517, of that branch of the Franciscan Order, which observes the Rule with certain lawfully accorded dispen-sations with regard to poverty. The name has not been restricted to the Franciscans, but similarly signifies a distinction in the observance of the rule in other orders.

CORNETTE—See *Habit.*

DEPOSITARY—Trustee or guardian in a religious community.

DEPUTATRIX—Lay person employed by a community for small shopping and commissions which would otherwise occupy the time of the religious.

DIOCESAN—Applied to a community subject to the jurisdiction of the bishop of the diocese in which its Motherhouse is located, though it may not necessarily confine its activities to that diocese.

DISCALCED—Without shoes, as distinguished from Calced. Associated with the Carmelites.

DOWRY—In a religious sense, the sum of money or property that a candidate brings into the community in which she desires to be professed, as an endowment if she remains in the convent. Where there is no stipulated amount for the dowry it is ordinarily regulated by the circumstances of the applicant and the type of work of the order. Sometimes it may be advisedly dispensed with.

ENCLOSURE—See *Cloister.*

EPISCOPACY—Term of administration of a bishop.

EPISCOPAL—Referring to a bishop.

EPISCOPATE—See *Episcopacy.*

EXTERN—See *Sister.*

FOUNDATION—Properly an independent house or administrative center of a religious community.

GENERALATE—National or international form of government of a religious order, by which its houses are grouped (a) in provincialates in a country, each with its own Provincial house and provincial government, and under a central Motherhouse; (b) under a General Motherhouse, geographically in various national provinces—again divided into provincialates or vicariates, each with its own Provincial house or Vicariate house and provincial or vicariate superiors, and with a provincial, or recognizing a central, novitiate.

GRILLE—Lattice marking entrance to the enclosure of cloistered communities. Beyond it adult visitors, except when absolutely necessary, do not pass, and the cloistered religious do not go outside it without ecclesiastical dispensation.

HABIT—Distinctive garb of a religious community, its form and color often symbolizing the spirit and object of the order. Ordinarily sisters wear a veil, over a cap or coif. Otherwise a large head-dress—termed a cornette—may be worn, or simply a cap or coif. The forehead piece worn with a veil, and which is usually black or white, is also called a bandeau. The wimple is a covering of linen or other material, laid in folds for the neck, chin and sides of the face; a guimpe, also of

linen or other material, is sometimes worn about and below the neck.
A head covering extending about the neck and sides of the face, and
under the chin, may be termed a barbette. A large collar is sometimes
designated as a collarium. The cincture is a girdle or cord worn about
the waist, three knots on the cord signifying the three religious vows,
poverty, chastity and obedience. With most religious habits large
rosaries are worn, as well as, often, the special emblem or insignia of
the community. To facilitate their work some communities have adopted,
in place of an obvious habit, an appropriate uniform garb, or modest
secular dress. Postulants in a community ordinarily wear quiet dress,
or a simple religious garb, while novices, usually distinguished by a white
veil, in general wear the characteristic habit of the community, but without
any insignia of profession. Slight differences sometimes mark the habit
of choir nuns and lay sisters of the same community.*

INSTITUTE—Religious community with perpetual vows, approved by episcopal
authority, and closely resembling a congregation; also an approved community in which the vows are not perpetual, but renewed annually or
at stated times.

INVESTITURE—See *Clothing.*

LAY SISTER—See *Sister.*

MISSION—Site of activities of a community from a foundation house or the
Motherhouse.

MISSION HOUSE—Sub or branch house or institution where members of a community labor from a foundation house or their Motherhouse.

MONASTERY—Religious house in which the monastic life, aiming at withdrawal
from the world and worldly ideals, through self-abnegation, is observed.

MOTHERHOUSE—Recognized headquarters of a religious community and seat of
its executive power.

NOVICE—Religious aspirant who has received the habit, and who is being
trained for her future work, and formed to the religious life according
to the rule of the community.

NOVITIATE—Department of a convent, or the separate institution of a religious
community in which the novices, under the direction of the Mistress of
Novices, pass a definite period of training and preparation for the duties
of the community life prior to their profession.

NUN—See *Sister.*

OBLATES—Men or women, not professed religious, who have offered themselves to God in the religious life, or who, although remaining laymen,
unite in certain labors and exercises of a religious order, and share in
its spiritual benefits.

OFFICE—Certain liturgical prayers recited by religious at fixed hours of the
day or night.

ORDER—Institute fully approved by the Holy See, having solemn vows of
religious life, and under pontifical jurisdiction.

PAPAL APPROBATION OF RULES†—Pontifical approval of the rules or constitutions of a religious community, either by a preliminary decree of commendation—praise, or confirmation, or finally, and in full.

*Habit descriptions in this work refer to the garb of the professed religious, and in com-
munities in which there are choir nuns and lay sisters, unless otherwise specified, apply to
the choir nuns.
†In this book it has been the intention to quote the final or latest approbation.

PERPETUAL ADORATION—Properly, uninterrupted adoration of the Blessed Sacrament exposed day and night.

POSTULANT—Aspirant to the religious life who has been accepted on probation and who is asking the habit. The vocation of the postulant is tested during a period of six months or more. During this time she leads the life of the religious, seeing it in all its phases, and her aptitude for it is generally determined before her entrance into the novitiate and the community proper.

PRIORESS—Superior of a monastic community of twelve or more nuns. Associated with the Carmelites and the Dominicans.

PROCURE—House usually of a primarily missionary religious community, established apart from its chief field or fields of labor in order to make known and promote its distant work.

PROCURATRIX—One in charge of the business affairs of a religious community.

PROFESSION—Ceremony at which the religious aspirant who has completed her novitiate consecrates herself to the religious life in a particular order, either by simple vows, perpetually, after several years of temporary vows, or by solemn vows after simple perpetual vows have been tentatively taken.

PROVINCE—Properly an ecclesiastical division of territory according to dioceses, each province centering from an archdiocese, and with the archiepiscopal city as its seat. Also used as a grouping of the houses of a religious community, usually according to location.

PROVINCIALATE—Grouping, also sometimes termed a province or vicariate, of certain houses of a religious community, usually according to location, each provincialate or vicariate having a central provincial or vicariate house, and provincial or vicariate superiors.

PROVINCIAL HOUSE—See *Provincialate.*

REGULAR—See *Third Order.*

RELIGIOUS—See *Sister.*

RELIGIOUS LIFE—Mode of life, irrevocable in its nature, of those who profess to aim at Christian perfection by the three perpetual vows of poverty, chastity and obedience.

RULE—Principles drawn up for the guidance of a religious community.

SECOND ORDER—A religious order of women connected by origin and rule with a monastic religious order of men. A second order has the same spirit and labors for the same ends as its first order, although following a necessarily modified rule, and not engaging in active labors due to its solemn vows, imposing enclosure.

SECULARIZATION—A temporary or permanent laying off of the religious habit, and return to the world. Civil oppression has sometimes necessitated this for various communities.

SEMI-CLOISTERED—Applied to the members of communities whose cloister is not defined by a grille, but who have free access to the convent parlors and premises, although they do not leave the community grounds except for necessary travel, or other legitimate reasons.

SISTER—One who consecrates herself to God in the religious life. Properly a sister takes simple vows, and a nun solemn vows. Choir nuns are so called, in some communities, because they recite the Office in common in choir. In the same communities in which they are recognized, in preference to many dispensations from this obligation of saying the Office, those who can not readily fulfill this duty, nor do the distinctive work of the institute, voluntarily enter as lay sisters or coadjutrix sisters.* They co-operate in the work of the community by manual labor, and at the same time share in its spirit and spiritual privileges. Members of semi-cloistered orders are sometimes called religious, as well as nuns. Externs enter cloistered orders for the purpose of intermediary work outside the grille, attending to the daily concerns of the community. In some cloistered or semi-cloistered communities a tourière acts as portress, her duties much resembling an extern's.

SOCIETY—Properly the voluntary association of a number of persons who pledge themselves to work together for a definite end. Hence sometimes fittingly applied to religious communities, chiefly certain congregations bound by perpetual vows, and often semi-cloistered.

SUPERIOR—One at the head of a religious community or institution.

TERTIARY—See *Third Order.*

THIRD ORDER—Body of followers, known as tertiaries, of a third rule drawn up for those who early grouped themselves about the standard of a first or second order, desiring to pattern themselves according to its ideals and principles. Third orders were originally established for the benefit of secular persons, however many of these later formed approved religious communities—ordinarily congregations with simple vows, all wearing in general the characteristic habit of the order, and known as the third order regular, distinguished from the third order secular. Not all religious orders have third orders attached to them, but those which recognize an order of nuns as their second order—such as the Carmelites, Dominicans and Franciscans—have tertiaries as well. Communities of the same third order regular are organized as separate congregations, and are distinguished from each other by an individual title. Foundations of first and second orders are the ordinary centers for secular tertiaries.

TOURIÈRE—See *Sister.*

VICARIATE—See *Provincialate.*

VICARIATE HOUSE—See *Provincialate.*

VISITATRIX—Religious officially entrusted with the visitation of the houses, or a group of houses, of a religious community.

VOCATION, RELIGIOUS—A call to serve God in the religious life. A firm will to enter religion, for good motives, such as self-sanctification and the greater glory of God, is the ordinary mark of a vocation. Inner conviction, or the voice of conscience suggesting the religious state, either with or without any sensible attraction to it, may also be the indication of a religious vocation. While a vocation usually carries with it the idea of a particular order, the religious aspirant should be guided, in any doubt, by her native inclinations and aptitudes. In general the qualifications for admission to any religious community are the same. The applicant should be a practical Catholic, of unblemished moral character, sound in mind and body, and, unless in exceptional cases, between the ages of sixteen and thirty, and free from home obligations. Widows are not excluded from all religious orders. On application to or interview with the Reverend Mother Superior of the community, an application blank may be obtained, with details as to the credentials further required for acceptance.

---

*Many orders are composed of choir nuns and lay sisters, and the distinction may exist in some communities whose histories in this book contain no reference to it.

Vows—Means of observing the evangelical counsels, in the religious life. The usual three religious vows, poverty, chastity and obedience, are taken because, implying renunciation of material goods, the world and self-will, they are the logical fulfillment of the counsels of perfection. The vow of stability, or perseverance in the community, is also sometimes taken. Any other additional vow usually pertains directly to the work of the community. Final vows are either simple and perpetual, or solemn. The profession of simple perpetual vows is usually preceded by several years of temporary vows, and a solemn profession can be made only after a simple profession. Solemn vows, which are taken only in communities which observe enclosure, denote a more absolute self-surrender and entail greater obligations than simple vows, but also carry with them greater spiritual privileges. Solemn vows, and simple vows in congregations whose rule has received papal sanction, must be dispensed from by the Holy See, while vows taken in religious communities with but episcopal approbation may be dispensed from by episcopal authority.